Long Have I Loved You

A Theologian Reflects on His Church

Walter J. Burghardt, S.J.

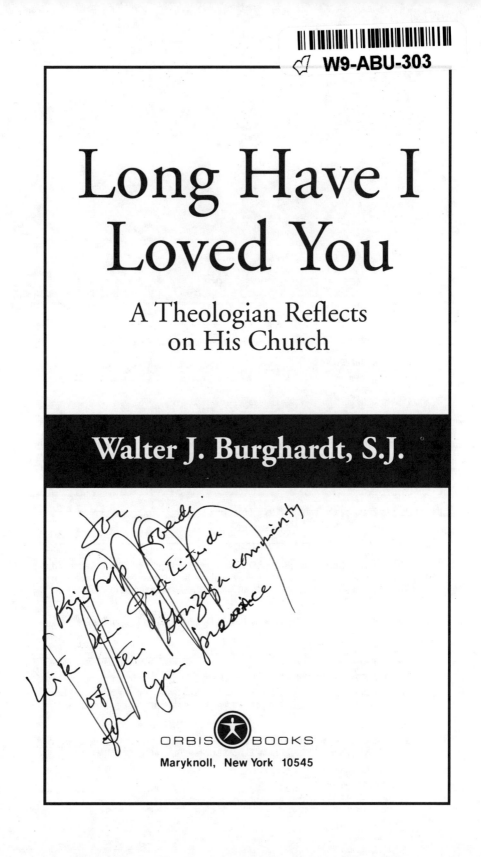

ORBIS BOOKS

Maryknoll, New York 10545

Second Printing, July 2000

The Catholic Foreign Mission Society of America (Maryknoll) recruits and trains people for overseas missionary service. Through Orbis Books, Maryknoll aims to foster the international dialogue that is essential to mission. The books published, however, reflect the opinions of their authors and are not meant to represent the official position of the society. To obtain more information about Maryknoll and Orbis Books, please visit our website at www.maryknoll.org.

Published in 2000 by Orbis Books, P.O. Box 308, Maryknoll, New York 10545-0308 U.S.A.

Manufactured in the United States of America

Library of Congress Cataloging-in-Publication Data

Burghardt, Walter J.
    Long have I loved you : a theologian reflects on his church / Walter J. Burghardt.
        p.   cm.
    Includes index.
    ISBN 1-57075-296-6 (paper)
    1. Burghardt, Walter J. 2. Jesuits – United States – Biography.   I. Title
  BX4705.B89423 A3 2000
  282'.73'0904 – dc21
                                                                    99-040097

Contents

Preface   v

1. *From Demosthenes to Damascene:*
   Classics and Patristics   1

2. *From Seminary to University:*
   Theology Yesterday and Today   23

3. *From Luther to Paul VI:*
   Isolation and Ecumenism   66

4. *From Prior Testament Prophet to New Testament*
   Preacher:The Art and Craft of Preaching   106

5. *From Cain to Antichrist:*
   Social Injustice and the Just Word   148

6. *From Manresa to El Salvador:*
   Jesuit Spirituality   180

7. *From Genesis to Bonhoeffer:*
   Free Like God   209

8. *From Jesus Christ to Vatican II:*
   Ordained Priesthood   234

9. *From the Samaritan Woman to the Catholic Tomorrow:*
   Apostolate of the Laity   265

10. *From Eve to Mary to …?:*
    Women in the Church   289

11. *From the Apostle Paul to John Paul II:*
    Crisis in the Church   328

12. *From Hippocrates to Kevorkian:*
    Catholicism and the Medical Profession   357

13. *From Life to Life:*
    On Turning Eighty-Five   383

14. *Epilogue:*
    Grateful Memories   401

Notes   433

Appendix:
Publications of Walter J. Burghardt, S.J.   485

Index of Personal Names   504

Preface

An autobiography this is not. I do indeed enter into the story, but the story is not so much about me as it is about realities and events, movements and changes, crises and quandaries, theology and spirituality, church and world. It is a reflection on much of a century. One man's reflection, yes, but enfleshed by hundreds of other minds, faces, voices, hearts. Here an explanation is in order.

Once again, fellow Jesuit John Gallen is partially responsible for a book of mine. Back in 1978, when he was directing the liturgy program at the University of Notre Dame, John asked me to deliver the keynote address at the Seventh Annual Conference of the university's Center for Pastoral Liturgy. The conference theme was provocative: "Human Journeys, Liturgical Journeys." Its overarching thesis? The liturgy ritualizes, symbolizes, sacramentalizes what goes on in the rest of our lives. To liturgical prayer we bring our daily experience. It was my task to illustrate the human journey, leaving to liturgiologists the more difficult burden of revealing how human journeys become liturgical journeys, how the memorializing of Jesus' passion, death, and resurrection connects your story and mine with the story of the Suffering Servant.

Encouraged by Robert Heyer, then of the Paulist Press, now with Sheed and Ward, I expanded the original paper into a modest paperback, *Seasons That Laugh or Weep: Musings on the Human Journey* (Paulist, 1983). Not a scholarly tome. I simply enriched my profoundly personal memories with the experiences of others, especially as these emerge from literature, from biography, from the fine arts. Why? To stimulate others to remember, perhaps persuade some man or woman whose winter is discontent to start living. Nothing I have ever written has elicited such widespread, favorable, grateful reactions.

Several years ago John Gallen broached a related idea, a fresh kind of autobiography. Not the usual chronological type, from my first mewl to my latest homiletic eructation. The story has a certain chronology, but the years do not move on rigidly, inflexibly, unbendingly. They return time and again, because the chapters focus on movements that often run parallel or intersect. The chapters are shaped around areas of thinking and living that have engaged my attention through most of this century, areas that were and are and will be of concern to countless others. I look back into a living past, I stare into my present, I peer into the future.

I cannot claim historical or theological objectivity. My biases will inevitably seep through. But they will be recognizable. Rarely will I argue a bias; such argumentation is discoverable in numerous articles and books of mine.

So then, not a scholarly tome. I write with broad strokes. I am painting a set of pictures in which I have been an active character, not usually featured but very intimately involved. I write from the inside out. My hope? Simply that my experiences may illuminate significant areas of human, religious, and Christian developments. Their retelling may play a small but not insignificant role in what I understand tradition to be: the best of the past, infused with the insights of the present, with a view to a more human, more Christian future.

Finally, many a reader will surely discover in the title of these memoirs a play on St. Augustine's confession to God, "Late have I loved you."

ONE

From Demosthenes to Damascene

Classics and Patristics

It all began in secondary school, Jesuit-run St. Francis Xavier High School, a semimilitary academy on the west side of 16th Street in downtown New York. In my day, 1927–31, three years of Greek, four of English, and four of Latin introduced us teenagers to the liberal arts. We trudged parasang after parasang with Zenophon, donned female costumes to re-present Ophelia to Hamlet, echoed Julius Caesar's "Veni, vidi, vici" ("I came, I saw, I conquered"), were drugged and/or exhilarated as prosecutor Cicero caustically hammered at a Roman conspirator, "How long, O Catiline, will you abuse our patience?"

Poetry and Rhetoric

It was, however, the Jesuit juniorate (equivalently the first two years of college) three miles above Poughkeepsie, New York, that honed my humanistic future. At St. Andrew-on-Hudson (now owned by a CIA, the Culinary Institute of America) a year of poetry and a year of rhetoric captivated me beyond redemption. Words became my lifeblood, the air I breathed, democratic Athens and its Acropolis my intellectual city.

Still alive in me is Demosthenes thundering in his *Philippics* to unbelieving Athenians against the threat of Philip II of Macedon. I reveled in his struggle to overcome a harsh voice, weak lungs, an awkward manner. I raced with him as he climbed steep hills reciting speeches, shouted with him as he drowned out the roar of ocean waves with pebbles in his mouth.

There was the peerless trio of Greek tragedians expanding my imagination, at times in ways offensive to my limited experience. In his *Oresteia* majestic Aeschylus molded the myth of mother-murdering Orestes, traced the development of justice in a terrifying tale that moves from murder to revenge to remorse to divine mercy.

1

Master of character and pre-Hitchcock suspense, Sophocles entranced and troubled me with the tragedy of Oedipus unwittingly killing his father and marrying his mother. Euripides, ever the realist, critic of conventional morality, insightful portrayer of women, shocked me with an oft-repeated *Medea,* the mother who killed her children in revenge upon their father. It was Aristotle, I believe, who said that Sophocles portrayed men and women as they should be, Euripides as they are. Greek tragedy was lightened by comedy (from a Greek word meaning "merrymaking"), specifically by Aristophanes, at once obscene and touchingly lyrical. I laughed to his mocking irony, even croaked to the music of his frogs, "Brekekekex, ko-ax, ko-ax."

There was, of course, epic Homer, who may have been an illiterate bard, may or may not have been blind, may never have existed. But authorship was hardly our youthful concern. The *Iliad* that has fascinated three millennia captured many of us eager Jesuits with its musical expression of war's heroism and tragedy, the fateful quarrel between Achilles and Agamemnon, brave Hector dragged around Troy's walls behind Achilles' chariot. And we reveled in the *Odyssey* that details Odysseus' adventures as he tries to return home after fighting for Greece against Troy, an itinerary that symbolizes life's journey and the search for self-fulfilment.

Regrettably, too little of the supposedly premier woman poet Sappho survived to let us appreciate Plato's "tenth Muse." Too little time remained to appreciate Pindar, unparalleled in ancient Greece for lyric poetry, for the odes he invented.

On the Roman side, the artists who delighted me were Vergil and Horace. We young Jesuits were pious enough, biased enough, to lean toward the thesis that in Vergil's fourth pastoral *Eclogue* the miraculous child about to inaugurate a new age was none other than the Christ child. But for the most part, from the *Aeneid*'s opening, "Arms and the man I sing," it was Vergil's mastery of language that moved me, not his message that Rome's mission under Augustus was to bring peace and justice to the world. Horace was sheer delight. I even wrote Latin odes in imitation of his "Carpe diem" ("Live today!"), his "Nunc est bibendum" ("It's cocktail time"), hardly in a position to take the exhortations with utmost seriousness.

In English literature Shakespeare mesmerized me. Even before Laurence Olivier and Kenneth Branagh brought the monarch to celluloid life, I roamed the camp with Henry V at night, musing on the burdens of kings: "What infinite heart's ease / Must kings neglect, that private men enjoy!" With Romeo I chastely forsook my very name for Juliet: "Call me but love, and I'll be new baptiz'd." I shared Hamlet's "native hue of resolution . . . sicklied o'er with the pale cast of thought." Even before Buchenwald and Auschwitz, I could feel Shylock's ageless cry of the Jew, "If you prick us, do we not bleed?"

But there was so much more than the Bard. There was Robert Herrick urging us to "Gather ye rosebuds while ye may"; Thomas Gray's "curfew toll[ing] the knell of parting day"; Christina Georgina Rossetti asking, "Does the road wind uphill all the way?"; Swinburne's "hounds of spring on winter's traces"; Tennyson commanding the bugle to "set the wild echoes flying"; Robert Burns' delightful "John Anderson, my jo, John"; Richard Crashaw's hymn to "the Admirable Saint Teresa"; William Blake's "Tiger, tiger, burning bright / In the forests of the night"; Coleridge's "ancient Mariner" holding the Wedding-Guest "with his glittering eye"; Edgar Allan Poe mourning "the wind [that] came out of the cloud one night / Chilling and killing my Annabel Lee"; Elizabeth Barrett Browning pleading,

> If thou must love me, let it be for naught
>   Except for love's sake only. . . .
> Love me for love's sake, that evermore
>   Thou mayst love on, through love's eternity.

With Francis Thompson I fled the Hound of Heaven's "majestic speed, deliberate instancy." I resonated with Gerard Manley Hopkins comparing the Blessed Virgin to the air we breathe:

> If I have understood,
> She holds high motherhood
> Towards all our ghostly good
> And plays in grace her part
> About man's beating heart,
> Laying, like air's fine flood,
> The deathdance in his blood;
> Yet no part but what will
> Be Christ our Saviour still.[1]

With Cyrano in his last hour, I watched the Venetian-red leaves fall to the ground:

> Yes — they know how to die. A little way
> From the branch to the earth, a little fear
> Of mingling with the common dust — and yet
> They go down gracefully — a fall that seems
> Like flying.[2]

With Carl Sandburg, I experienced Chicago as the "hog butcher of the world"; went "down to the seas again" with John Masefield; sang an ode to Shelley's west wind, "thou breath of Autumn's being"; looked with Keats into Chapman's Homer; heard the revolutionary rustling of Whitman's *Leaves of Grass*. And for some strange reason, I cannot forget a young Jesuit seriously reciting the opening of Shelley's "To a Skylark" in inimitable Brooklynese: "Hail to thee, blithe spirit! / There never wuz a boid like you."

We Jesuit "juniors" memorized poetry standing at table (the whole of "The Hound of Heaven," for example), waiting for the large community at St. Andrew-on-Hudson to assemble and say grace before meals — the texts in the interior of the birettas we held piously in our hands (we ate with our "hats" on!). Was it an awareness of idleness as the devil's workshop? I think not. We simply took advantage of any and every opportunity to fill our minds, our souls, with the power, the beauty, the rawness, the seduction of syllables, to enter the kingdom of the imagination. I have never ceased to be grateful for the insistence on memory — memorizing and declaiming large sections of poetry. Thus were we shaped, fashioned, put in tune with the awesomeness of God's creation, with the breadth of human creativity.

The Lure of Patristics

The "classic" experience has never left me. It has transformed me, molded my yearning for the true, the beautiful, and the good. Paradoxically, I "left" the classics (but only in the background) the day in 1933 when my professor of rhetoric, Jesuit Philip X. Walsh, handed me seven letters written in Greek around the year 110 A.D. by the third bishop of Antioch, Ignatius, as he was hustled in chains from Syria to Rome to be clawed by wild beasts in the Colosseum. The letters have been termed the most beautiful pearls of ancient Christian literature. What gripped Ignatius was a passionate love for his crucified Lord, a love so overpowering that it breaks through grammar; language is inadequate, and his ideas tumble headlong one upon another. I was particularly taken by a passage in his letter to the Christians of Rome. He longs to see them, to embrace them; but he is afraid — afraid, he says, of their love; their love may destroy him. Their influence with civil authority may save him, and he does not want that. And so he writes one of the most moving passages in early Christian literature.

I am writing to all the churches and state emphatically to all that I die willingly for God, provided you do not interfere. I beg you, do not show me unseasonable kindness. Suffer me to be the food of wild beasts, which are the means of my making my way to God. God's wheat I am, and by the teeth of wild beasts I am to be ground that I may prove Christ's pure bread. Better still, coax the wild beasts to become my tomb and to leave no part of my person behind: once I have fallen asleep, I do not wish to be a burden to anyone. Then only shall I be a genuine disciple of Jesus Christ when the world will not see even my body. Petition Christ on my behalf that through these instruments I may prove God's sacrifice. Not like Peter and Paul do I issue any orders to you. They were apostles, I am a convict; they were free, I am until this moment a slave. But once I have suffered, I shall become a freedman of Jesus Christ, and, united with him, I shall rise a free man. Just now I learn, being in chains, to desire nothing.

All the way from Syria to Rome I am fighting wild beasts, on land and sea, by day and night, chained as I am to ten leopards, that is, a detachment of soldiers, who prove themselves the more malevolent for kindnesses shown them. Yet in the school of this abuse I am more and more trained in discipleship, "although I am not therefore justified" [1 Cor 4:4]. Oh, may the beasts prepared for me be my joy! And I pray that they may be found to be ready for me. I will even coax them to make short work of me, not as has happened to some whom they were too timid to touch. And should they be unwilling to attack me who am willing, I will myself compel them. Pardon me — I know very well where my advantage lies. At last I am well on the way to being a disciple. May nothing "seen or unseen" [Col 1:16] fascinate me, so that I may happily make my way to Jesus Christ! Fire, cross, struggles with wild beasts, wrenching of bones, mangling of limbs, crunching of the whole body, cruel tortures inflicted by the devil — let them come upon me, provided only I make my way to Jesus Christ.[3]

This gift from Philip Walsh corresponded to a gift three years before, when on my entrance into the Jesuit novitiate the master of novices, Leo M. Weber, put into my hands a little book called *The Spiritual Exercises of St. Ignatius* (more on this later). These two books, each by an Ignatius, proved to be the springboard for, respectively, my intellectual and spiritual journeys.

At this point, an important observation — a realization that struck me only several decades later.[4] For many a critic, Ignatius of Antioch is a fanatic. Over 40 years ago a prolific author wrote of him: This "strange saint, wandering slowly toward Rome, left his mark on Christianity. All the wilder elements descend from him, from the terrible look in his eyes."[5] From this point of view, Ignatius is Christianity at its worst, sanctity at its most repugnant. This lust for martyrdom is a neurotic thing. This thirst for fire and cross and wild beasts is unnatural. It is a weakling's flight from reality. Death is his love — not life. Here I had to face the other Ignatius — the founder of my Jesuit order speaking to one of his first companions, James Laínez:

> *Ignatius:* Tell me, Master Laínez, what do you think you would do, were God our Lord to say: "If you want to die soon, I will release you from the prison of this body and give you eternal glory. If you prefer to stay alive, I give you no assurance as to what will become of you...." If our Lord told you this, and you thought that by remaining for some time in this life you could render some outstanding service to His Divine Majesty, which would you choose?
>
> *Laínez:* I must confess, Father, I would choose to go soon to enjoy God and to assure my salvation and to avoid the perils in so important a matter.
>
> *Ignatius:* I certainly would not. If I thought that by remaining in this life I could render some signal service to our Lord, I would beg Him to leave me here until I had done it; and I would not think twice of the peril to me or the assurance of my salvation.[6]

But to read Ignatius of Antioch is to recognize that, for him, martyrdom is not a selfish episode, that the Church knows no martyrs who have loved only God and not their sisters and brothers. "My love for you," he wrote to a Christian community on his way to death, "overflows all bounds."[7] In the Colosseum, as on Calvary, "the good shepherd lays down his life *for his sheep*" (Jn 10:11) — not merely in their stead, to save them from a similar fate, but for their sanctification, so that grace, a little more of God's life, may thrill through the Christian body. "The blood of Christians is seed"[8] indeed: It produces other Christians, and it produces better Christians.

It is perilous to contrast Ignatius of Antioch with Ignatius of Loyola for one basic reason: The Spanish Ignatius had a remarkable devotion to the Syrian. In honor of the martyr, he changed his name from Iñigo to Ignatius. The first of his maxims was a phrase from the first Ignatius: "My Love has been crucified."[9] He made the motto of his Jesuit order the first three letters of the name of Jesus in Greek (IHS) because he had read in *The Golden Legend* that when the Romans tore out the heart of the martyred Ignatius, they found those letters graven on his heart in gold. The words of our Lord remain true: Greater love there cannot be, for God or man or woman, than the love which lays down life itself in witness of love.

Three years of philosophical studies followed (1934–37) at the Jesuit scholasticate Woodstock College, 18 miles northwest of Baltimore. It was a rigid triennium, structured in Scholastic fashion from minor logic and epistemology, through ontology and cosmology and psychology, to ethics and natural theology. I genuinely enjoyed it, delighted in it, but (a later realization) in some measure for the wrong reasons: the structure, the clarity, the certainty — these appealed to, testified to, my youthfulness, my immaturity. We needed special permission to read our adversaries; they were sufficiently summarized by the teacher. I can still feel the ice that covered the classroom as a perhaps imprudent question elicited the cold answer, "Mr. Rogers, have you been *reading* something?" Only two Jesuit professors (in ethics and rational psychology) allowed us to think for ourselves, insisted that we do so, suggested *different* ways of looking at the same reality, the same problem — displeasing to many of us, especially as we prepared for oral examinations in Latin.

I was uniquely fortunate. For all practical purposes, I was already destined by my religious superiors for specialization in patristics. In consequence, I could touch, if ever so lightly, the movement from Aristotle and Plato to the Christian Greek apologists of the second century, to thinkers like Gregory of Nyssa and Augustine. I could revel in historians of philosophy such as Bréhier and Romeyer, Copleston and Gilson and Ueberweg, even wrestled with the fundamental problem, Can there be a Christian philosophy?

Philosophy was followed by a year of teaching at Regis High School in New York City. After seven hidden years of prayer and study, we scholastics descended on "the world" with a vengeance. I still find it difficult to realize that, far from resenting my schedule, I relished it: 25 hours of class a week (Latin, Greek, and English), school librarian, moderator of the Homeric Academy, coach of the junior varsity and (undefeated!) freshman basketball teams.

Theology

Original plans for my serious involvement in patristics called for my Jesuit theological years to be spent in Belgium under the direction of a first-rate patristics scholar, Joseph de Ghellinck, whose three-volume *Patristique et moyen âge* (Paris 1946–49) was to prove a remarkable resource when I began to teach at Woodstock. De Ghellinck looked forward with keen anticipation to directing a patrologist-to-be from our patristic wasteland. Unfortunately, in 1938 the war clouds were already gathering over Europe, and from the experience of World War I it was clear that the name Burghardt would hardly sit well with the Belgian people. And so I came to rural Woodstock in Maryland, common house of theology for the New York and Maryland Provinces of the Society of Jesus.

For all its isolation along the banks of the not so tawny Patapsco, Woodstock proved a memorable four years (1938–42). I fell in love with theology. Why? Primarily, I believe, because I experienced theology not simply as an academic discipline required for ordination, but as the Church's ceaseless effort to understand what God has said to us and is saying now. True, Catholic theological method in my undergraduate days did not stress the search, the quest — save for a deeper understanding of what was already known and accepted. Scripture and theology still operated in the shadow, the aftermath, of the Modernist controversy. I shall dwell on this in greater detail in chapter 2; here I want to stress the importance of one remarkable Jesuit for my development in patristics in those undergraduate days of theology. I mean John Courtney Murray, quite new to Woodstock, not yet the Murray who would liberate the Catholic Church and its theology from a devastatingly narrow tradition on religious liberty.

Highly pertinent for me, Murray was unique among Woodstock's (and surely most other seminary) professors in the stress he placed on the Fathers of the Church. His presentation of the Trinity over a whole year moved through four "modes" (*modi* — the lectures were largely in Latin): the scriptural, the patristic, the doctrinal, and the dogmatic. And so he moved majestically from Exodus 3:14 to the Cappadocian Fathers to Aquinas to the church councils.

To grasp Murray's insight into the significance of the Church Fathers, you must move to 1948 when he introduced to readers of *Theological Studies* the new series of French translations entitled Sources chrétiennes. In three incisive paragraphs he presented two profound reasons for seeking a more vital possession of the patristic heritage through more extensive and profound study of entire texts.

First, such a study admirably serves to bridge the gap that has been created, in the opinion of many, between theology and spirituality. The Fathers of the Church are not only teachers of Christian doctrine but masters of the spiritual life; not only do their works give guidance to the mind in its search for the truth of God, but they also afford inspiration to the whole soul in its search for God Himself. In this respect, patristic study offers a valuable completion of, and possibly a necessary corrective to, the more rigidly intellectualist mentality created by the student's immersion in Scholastic thought.

Secondly, the works of the Fathers present Christian thought in an earlier stage of its formation — a formation certainly not uninfluenced by the intellectual and spiritual problems of the ages in which the Fathers wrote, and by the currents of philosophic thought and human aspiration which were abroad in those ages. In these works, therefore, the student may see theology, as it were, at work at the fundamental task of its own development, its vital assimilation of all that is true in human thought, its sensitive response to the problems and needs of the Christian soul, as these are created by man's inescapable necessity of living his Christian faith in the context of a particular age. The Fathers were witnesses to the Church's traditional faith, and its doctors; but their witness was not uttered, and their doctrine was not formed, *in vacuo*. They spoke as living men, to living men, whose souls were stirred by man's permanent restlessness, his desire for God, but whose thinking and living were conditioned by the temporal exigencies of a passing epoch that was simply a stage in the march of our total humanity towards the *vir perfectus*. Consequently, the Fathers not only give us their witness itself; they also are models for our own manner of witnessing.

From this standpoint, therefore, their high value is that they introduce us to two problems that are indeed extremely delicate but that must be faced quite honestly — the problem of the development of Christian thought through its historical past, and the problem of the address we are to make to our own intellectual and spiritual world. Admittedly, there are immense possibilities of intellectual agony opened to one who would wrestle with the problem of the "relativities" inherent, certainly in theologies, and even in a sense in the statement of faith itself. However, these agonies must be undergone, if theology is to be perennially alive, and if faith is to be "the power of God unto salvation" for those who believe in every age, against the seductions of rival faiths. And the Fathers are our earliest models of this type of intellectual courage.[10]

Catholic University

It was with the Murray vision as controlling inspiration that in 1943 I moved with high enthusiasm to the Catholic University of America, expressly to do doctoral work in patristics.[11] The attraction was Johannes Quasten, and Quasten alone. Sworn enemy of the fast degree, he was a demanding teacher. Under him you learned, like him, to be intolerant only of superficiality and to eschew the glittering generality. Not dynamic in the usual sense, quite undramatic, he was at his best with a small interested group — best of all one-on-one in the master-apprentice relationship.

The pedagogical charism of this exile from Adolf Hitler's Germany was his ability to fire the few with a fresh vision of the past. You began to believe and to live what Adolf Harnack had said to him: "You will achieve as much as you are willing to sacrifice for." In his presence the early Eucharist, for example, came alive — in the second-century apologist Justin's *thysia logikē* (not simply "reasonable" sacrifice but sacrifice of the Logos and our own inner logos), in the 22–line epitaph of Abercius, in the *Apostolic Tradition* of Hippolytus, through the mystagogical catecheses (Eastertide homilies) of Cyril of Jerusalem to the newly baptized. Quasten made ancient texts come alive as no other had ever done for me. And without fail, the life was sparked not by exhortation but by evidence — especially the omnipresent Quasten collection of ancient Eucharistic and liturgical texts *Monumenta eucharistica et liturgica vetustissima* (Bonn 1935–37).

But Quasten the teacher was fashioned by Quasten the scholar. In this area three facets of his work have influenced me through almost half a century. There was the Quasten of the series Studies in Christian Antiquity. Here again was an entrancing vision. The context of SCA was the confrontation between Christianity and the culture in which it developed once it overleaped the bounds of its birthplace. For Quasten had pledged himself to carry on the pioneering work of Franz Josef Dölger, to develop in America a circle of scholars permeated with the same mentality and equipped with tested tools of research, theologians with a feeling for theology and philologists deeply rooted in theology. Quasten's fundamental assumption was that early Christianity cannot be intelligently understood without a thorough knowledge of classical culture. He leaned to W. Halliday's strong affirmation, "no one who is devoid of any sympathetic understanding of pagan thought and literature can have anything of essential value to tell us about the contemporary Christians."[12] And so, a half century ago, we took advantage, *as theologians,* of the research of Catholic scholars like Odo Casel and Josef Jungmann, Germain Morin and Giovanni Mercati, and of scholars with divergent beliefs who, in the tradition of Festugière and Cumont, of Halliday and Bonner and Nock, emphasized the pagan milieu of early Christianity rather than the encounter as such.[13]

What Quasten communicated to me and, I believe, to a (tragically small) segment of the American Catholic community was a sense of history, an awareness of cultural contexts, a realization that Christianity is inescapably involved in the ebb and flow of time, that affirmations and doctrines, words and syllables cannot be interpreted in isolation from their original milieu. Moreover, under Quasten's influence we became aware of a missionary concern that has grown ever more neuralgic: the attitude of the Church to a foreign culture. In those days Bishop Paul Yu-Pin was pointing out that, although the seventeenth century saw close to 300,000 Catholics in China, Christianity "could not succeed," because the Church, in striking at ancestor "worship" and reverence for Confucius, was, in the eyes of the people, the cultural invader of China.[14] If the nations that do not know Christ are to accept him in their corporate fulness, accommodation to culture without compromise of creed is a missiological necessity: "the Church must prove that she can engraft the supernatural upon a naturally good tree and can be a profitable foster mother of any genuine culture, no matter what its origin."[15] The problem is as old as Peter (Acts 10–11), but the principles were already incarnate in the practice of the infant Church.[16]

Then there was the Quasten of the multivolume *Patrology* (1950 ff.), the expert in patristics, archeology, and early liturgy who set before an appreciative international readership the richness of our patristic past (authors, ideas, bibliographies), well-worn knowledge, and fresh discoveries. We who had sat under him at the Catholic University of America were not surprised, only delighted, to discover in these volumes all that was so admirable in the professor: simplicity, thoroughness, order, insight. He was never content with sheer compilation. He controlled his materials — ancient texts and contemporary research — with a practiced ease. Unlike other manualists, he wrote to be read, not merely consulted; rarely has a scholar worn his learning so lightly.

Before Quasten came to Washington, patristics was a field a seminary professor could handle on the side (like being house librarian), while concentrating on some primary subject like dogma or Scripture. By his productive, at times exciting, scholarship Quasten made it clear that patristic study is not a luxury, that contemporary Christian doctrine can only suffer if it is divorced from early Christian monuments.

Then there is the Quasten of the series Ancient Christian Writers. It was fascinating to share with him the joys and frustrations of presenting the Fathers of the Church in translation to an English-speaking world increasingly impatient with the past. For a quarter century I worked with him at resolving editorial problems. I mean, first, the problem of content: patrology without pain but not without notes; for the copious ACW annotations are at once the justification for the translation and the guide to its meaning. I mean, second, the problem of translator and translation: how combine fidelity with limpidity, accuracy with intelligibility. I mean, third, the problem of readership: how educate the broadly educated and still serve the scholar.

Finally, Quasten was, almost from the beginning, a friend. Many times, as student and coeditor, I enjoyed his apartment in CU's Caldwell Hall, surrounded by one of the most precious of private early-Christian libraries (perhaps 11,000 volumes), exchanging ideas and the latest in literature. I savored his dinner dialogue, his cognac conversation, as he ranged from Münster to Tripoli, from the Good Shepherd in art through ecclesiastical politics to warm concern for my mother's illness. The patrologist's passion for perfection allowed only a blessed handful to experience the warmth and humanity that gave him life, the priest who helped form community not only by liturgical research but also by personal and communal worship, the heart that hid beneath the shy academic exterior, the loneliness that shadows so much of a scholar's existence, the love that must find its expression on the printed page.

Is it any wonder that when I preached for Quasten's golden jubilee as a priest on February 27, 1976, my homily (moving out from Wisdom 6:12–17, Ephesians 1:2–12, and Luke 2:41–52) was an effort to recapture — for the hundreds who packed the crypt of the Shrine of the Immaculate Conception — a man who lived with wisdom, a multifaceted man who wed entrancingly the past and the present, the old world and the new, the scholar and the priest?[17]

Werner Jaeger

With Quasten I must link another, related but quite different, influence on my patristics-cum-classics existence: Werner Jaeger. To grasp my meaning, you must go back to a book of memoirs in which octogenarian classicist Wilamowitz-Moellendorff recalled a gesture of generosity destined to seed a harvest far beyond his prevision:

> The restriction [of the Berlin Corpus] to the pre-Nicene Fathers was warranted from a practical standpoint, but it excluded precisely the greatest Christian writers of the fourth century. For that reason I assigned the sum of money which had been presented to me for my sixtieth birthday [1908] to the publication of Gregory of Nyssa, and my colleague and friend Norden assumed the direction thereof. . . . [18]

The gesture was not impromptu; with it Wilamowitz proposed to pave the way for the philology of the twentieth century. It was his conviction that the barriers separating sacred and "profane" philology, dividing the history of the Church and of the Empire, were a serious hindrance to truth itself and should be destroyed. His favorite Christian authors were the Cappadocians Gregory of Nazianzus and Gregory of Nyssa. In 1911 he asked Werner Jaeger to edit Gregory of Nyssa's treatise *Against Eunomius,* leader of the radical wing of Arianism. From this initiative resulted Jaeger's promise never to cease working on the first critical text of all Gregory's works, the admirable *Gregorii Nysseni opera,* which Jaeger directed from his Institute of Classical Studies at Harvard University.[19]

It was my privilege to spend several days with Professor Jaeger at Harvard early in 1950. It was sheer delight to visit his rooms in the Widener Library, to examine the hundreds upon hundreds of manuscripts collected from distant shores, to see how carefully they were described (in his own hand), sorted, and filed, to hear him outline his plan to trace the influence of Gregory in the history of ideas through special monographs. It was particularly delightful to watch him in action — no haste, no waste, like a restful Buddha. As with Quasten, so with Jaeger, the classics and early Christian literature formed a continuum. The relationships these scholars lived and taught were a priceless legacy to me.

Teaching Patristics

Teaching patristics was a ceaseless wedding of joy and exasperation. Joy in introducing young Jesuits at Woodstock College (1946–74) to an area of theological literature completely unknown to them. Joy in seeing eyes light up as they came face to face with the Fathers, instead of just reading *about* them. Joy in their surprise, or delight, or even awe as Ignatius of Antioch, near a martyr's end, revealed for the first time a church structure of bishops, presbyters, and deacons. Bishop Polycarp of Smyrna caught their fancy when he replied to a proconsul in the arena urging him to revile Christ: "For six and eighty years I have been serving him, and he has done no wrong to me; how, then, dare I blaspheme my King who has saved me!"[20] Many were moved by the Greek apologists of the second century, courageous men like Justin Martyr and Athenagoras of Athens, the first Christian writers to address themselves in writing to the outside world: to a state that regarded the profession of Christianity as a capital crime, to the educated who despised Christians for their superstition and fanaticism, to the general populace that gave credence to rumors of cannibalism and sexual immorality.

Rather than run through a list of names strange and familiar from Clement of Rome to John of Damascus, let me focus on my favorite early writer and preacher, the scholar whom I delighted most to introduce to young minds. I mean third-century Origen, impressively learned, fascinatingly Christian, a sign of contradiction from his day to our day. Misunderstood and vilified for centuries, he was just then enjoying rehabilitation from scholars like Henri de Lubac. At a time when Christians were suspect for their separatism, their refusal to conform, their grudging citizenship in this world, their exasperating indifference to Roman interests, and a widespread contempt for the philosophy, poetry, and science of pagan antiquity, Origen transformed the catechetical school of cosmopolitan, cultured, sophisticated Alexandria into the first Catholic "university." For his "average" students, there was the general education of the freeborn Greek youth. What lay behind this? John Courtney Murray once phrased it with remarkable lucidity:

> Origen's purpose was the civilization of intelligence in order that it might be able to receive a fuller understanding of the doctrines that simply catechetical instruction by the Church had already made known to it.
>
> Christian faith can of course be received into an intelligence altogether rude; on the other hand, it does not necessarily

spring up in a cultivated intelligence. It is a gift of God. But what is given is truth, and the gift is made to a human intelligence. Therefore it makes on intelligence the demand that the truth, thus given, should be understood, insofar as intelligence can encompass its understanding. In this process of understanding a civilized intelligence is "of no small help." The civilization of intelligence is a humanistic and scientific process; the understanding of Christian faith is a religious and supernatural one. The processes are distinct, but they ought to be related; for they go on within the same one mind and soul. It was therefore the essential function of Origen's school to relate them, under the primacy of the process in which faith, a higher gift than intelligence, involves the Christian. Origen wanted his students to grow into an intelligent Christianity; but to this end it was necessary that intelligence itself should grow in them. And there could be no other means of growth than the acquisition of the intellectual skills, the assimilation of the body of knowledge, and the initiation into the traditions of civility, that made the society around them civilized.[21]

So much for Origen's average student. But there was a higher level in Origen's university, reserved for an intellectual elite. Here Origen came to grips with the problem of the day. Here church and museum met, Origen's newborn university and the age-old University of Alexandria. Here four steps characterized Origen's method: (1) Recognition of the rights of reason, awareness of the thrilling fact that the Word did not become flesh to destroy what was human but to perfect it. (2) Acquisition of knowledge, a sweepingly broad knowledge, the sheer materials for the students' contemplation, for their ultimate vision of the real. Listen to one of Origen's later pupils, Gregory of Neocaesarea:

Nothing was forbidden us, nothing hidden from us, nothing inaccessible to us. We were to learn all manner of doctrine — barbarian or Greek, mystical or political, divine or human. We went into and examined with entire freedom all sorts of ideas, in order to satisfy ourselves and enjoy to the full these goods of the mind. When an ancient thought was true, it belonged to us and was at our disposition with all its marvelous possibilities of delightful contemplation.[22]

(3) The indispensable task that is Christian criticism, the intelligent confrontation of the old with the new, the effort to link the

highest flights of naked reason with God's self-revelation, to communicate Clement of Alexandria's vision that "there is one river of truth, but many streams fall into it on this side and that." (4) A quality which suffused all the rest, what Gregory called "piety." Not some sort of emotional attachment to God divorced from the task of the university and the functioning of intelligence. Rather, a love of truth wherever it may be found — within Hellenism or heresy, in the mind of humans as well as in the mind of God — and a profound yearning to include all the scattered fragments of discovered truth under what Gregory called "the Holy Word, the loveliest thing there is."[23]

This "piety" Origen possessed to a high degree; this he imparted to those who sat around him. Once again Gregory is our star witness:

> Like some spark falling in the midst of my soul there was kindled and there blazed forth a love . . . both for the Holy Word, the loveliest thing there is, and for this man, His friend and His prophet. Struck deep by this love, I came to neglect all that should have been of interest to me: affairs, studies, even the law I so loved, home and kin. . . . One thing alone was dear . . . to me: philosophy and its teacher, this divine man — "and the soul of Jonathan was knit with David" (1 Sam 18:1).[24]

Joy indeed, but a certain amount of exasperation as well. Perhaps frustration is a more accurate term. Frustration because the patristic experience played so small a role in the theological education of seminarians. Frustration because the increasing decline of Latin and Greek in Jesuit high schools and colleges allowed only a handful of Jesuit scholastics each year to appreciate the rhetoric of an Augustine, a Chrysostom, a Leo the Great. Frustration because only a small minority could profit from the rich research on the Fathers; I mean specifically the secondary literature in French and German, Spanish and Italian.

Henri de Lubac

Several devotees of patristics played powerful roles in my professorial years at Woodstock. One was Henri de Lubac (1896–1991), a French Jesuit who suffered much from misunderstanding by less gifted men in the late '40s (he wrote me once to protest, gently but firmly, my own and others' use of the expression *la nouvelle théologie* — "the new theology" — in connection with his work).

Stimulated by Maurice Blondel, Joseph Maréchal, and Pierre Rousselot, he absorbed from them the courage to read out of Aquinas "the paradox of the spiritual creature that is ordained beyond itself by the innermost reality of its nature to a goal that is unreachable for it and that can only be given as a gift of grace."[25] After Pius XII's encyclical *Humani generis* (August 12, 1950), he was forbidden to teach and was expelled from Lyons; his books were banned, removed from Jesuit libraries. Yet he was never questioned, had not a single discussion with the papal curia or Jesuit authorities about the principal issues, was never informed of the precise accusations. He began to be rehabilitated in 1960 when John XXIII appointed him and Yves Congar as consultants to the Theological Commission that would prepare doctrinal schemata for Vatican II, and found his final "official" approval in 1983 when John Paul II named him a cardinal. How did he influence me? In three directions.

There was, first, de Lubac's conviction that a "return to the Fathers" was indispensable for the rejuvenation of Catholic theology. Joseph Komonchak has put it with admirable terseness and lucidity. De Lubac, he asserts,

> was never entirely convinced of the success or legitimacy of the great Thomistic attempt to "baptize" Aristotle in the thirteenth century. He contrasted the inclusiveness of the church fathers, "those masters of ontological symbolism," to the "dialectical antitheses" of the "Christian rationalists of the Middle Ages." In this judgment on the medieval, and even the Thomist, effort, there was a great contrast between de Lubac and scholars like Congar, Chenu, Rahner, and Lonergan. For de Lubac, if much had been gained by the rise of scholasticism, much had also been lost.[26]

There was, second, de Lubac's breath-taking inductive study of Origen's exegesis, an unparalleled examination of the "father of allegorism," based on the totality of the Alexandrian's extant exegetical work. He conducted his research in the midst of the search for "the spiritual sense of Scripture" earlier in this century — an area of high (and low) disagreement.[27] That search was, even for its warmest protagonists, but one aspect, if ever so fundamental, of a wider, a total reorientation of Christian life. The skeletal body was constructed with rare felicity by Jean Daniélou in an illuminating article on the symbolism of the baptismal rites.

The Christian faith has but one object: the mystery of Christ dead and risen. But this one only mystery subsists under different modes. It is prefigured in the Old Testament; it is realized historically in the life of Christ on earth; it is contained by way of mystery in the sacraments; it is lived mystically in souls; it is accomplished socially in the Church; it is consummated eschatologically in the kingdom of heaven. Thus the Christian has at his disposal, for the expression of that single reality, several registers, a symbolism of several dimensions. All Christian culture consists in grasping the bonds of union that exist between the Bible and liturgy, between the gospel and eschatology, between the mystical life and the liturgy. The application of this method to Scripture is called spiritual exegesis. Applied to the liturgy, it is called mystagogy; this latter consists in reading in the rites the mystery of Christ and contemplating beneath the symbols the invisible reality. Its great masters have been a Cyril of Jerusalem or an Ambrose in antiquity; nearer our own time, a Cabasilas or an Olier.... [28]

Although de Lubac was unable to persuade historical-critical exegetes of the broad validity of spiritual exegesis precisely as exegesis,[29] he did enable many like myself to read early Christian literature with deeper insight, even to profit more richly from Scripture.

There was, third, de Lubac's love for the Church. It was expressed, most touchingly for me, in a meditation on the Church at a post-Vatican II conference hosted by the University of Notre Dame in 1966. There this priest/scholar who had endured so much from his Church spoke of the Church as the mother who gave him Life. And he spoke with incomparable feeling of the Church as paradox:

I am told that she is holy, yet I see her full of sinners. I am told that her mission is to tear man away from his earthy cares, to remind him of his eternal vocation, yet I see her constantly preoccupied with the things of the earth and of time, as if she wished us to live here forever. I am assured that she is universal, as open as divine intelligence and charity, and yet I notice very often that her members, through some sort of necessity, huddle together timidly in small groups — as human beings do everywhere. She is hailed as immutable, alone stable and above the whirlpools of history, and then, suddenly, under our very eyes, she upsets many of the faithful by the suddenness of her renewals.[30]

More generally, my intellectual life was stimulated by a large number of patristic scholars across the world. Many of them I met at Oxford, on the occasion of several of the quadrennial International Conferences on Patristic Studies (more on this in the chapter on things ecumenical). I mean scholars like Kurt Aland, of the Church Fathers Commission within the German Academy of Sciences, editors of the Berlin Corpus of the early patristic authors; Père F. Graffin, S.J., editor of Patrologia orientalis, editions and translations of the early Christian literature of the Orient; Claude Mondésert, S.J., editor of the prolific series Sources chrétiennes, patristic critical editions, French translations, and commentaries; Mlle. A. M. la Bonnardière, editor of the acclaimed Biblia Augustiniana, inventory of Augustine's citations from Scripture; Ludwig Bieler, editor of Scriptores latini Hiberniae, which provides reliable texts and translations for the sources of the study of the Latin culture of medieval Ireland; M. l'abbé Marcel Richard, head of the Greek section of the prestigious L'Institut de recherche et d'histoire des textes, an institute founded to study the written transmission of human thought by drawing up complete and methodical inventories of manuscripts scattered throughout the world. During the 1955 Oxford Conference (see the chapter on ecumenism), I lived in the shadow and light of established scholars like Aland and Daniélou, Molland and Mohrmann and Marrou, Quispel and Capelle, Bouyer and Boyer and Botte, Grillmeier and R. M. Grant, Sagnard and Schmaus and Beryl Smalley, de Riedmatten and Rousseau, Florovsky, Jouassard, Metzger, Hanson, and Ortiz de Urbina.

Patristics Tomorrow

As I leave patristic research, I am intrigued by the question, What does the future hold for this rich area of investigation? Experts in the field have ventured various predictions. In December 1989 Notre Dame's Charles Kannengiesser looked back over a half century of patristics and offered a provocative piece of prognostication.[31]

In Kannengiesser's experience, the broader impulse that propelled patristics after 1948 was a spiritual and humanistic revival in Europe responding creatively to the destructive madness of World War II. It was a Christian response, linking separated believers with unbelievers in a scholarly effort to reappropriate the riches of late antiquity. The prewar biblical and liturgical revivals had prepared the postwar Catholic renaissance across Western Europe, climaxing at Vatican II. Together with the collapse of institutional and scholastic traditions within Catholicism, patristics moved from a defensive, intrachurch theological discipline into a secular enterprise. We can now bid good-bye to the spectacular developments in European patristics in the second half of the twentieth century.

What lies ahead? Study of Christian identity outside the boundaries of a Eurocentered classical Christianity. For that Christianity left an unfortunate legacy after the Enlightenment: an exegesis of Scripture generating a hierarchical and popular fundamentalism. Urgently needed, in Kannengiesser's view, is a structural reformation of Christian doctrines that holds together Scripture and faith, divine incarnation and church, letter and spirit in the observance of Christian practices — and this as a preliminary to a renewed spiritual exegesis of the Bible. Not a return to the allegories of a thousand years ago. Spirituality after Auschwitz and the nuclear terror, on a planet exposed to fatal forms of pollution, imposes a fresh Bible reading that confronts today's atheistic and materialistic convictions, engages the pluricultural encounter in any large city with Eastern gnostic ways of life. Christian identity calls for a new cultural consensus, alien to the familiar comforts of Eurocentered ideologies. The "Fathers" of past patristics will be recognized as the privileged witnesses of a cultural and religious tradition that needs to affirm itself in a world no longer linked with their world. "As the only sources that allow us to understand what really happens to Christianity when it adjusts to a new cultural cosmos, the message of the 'Fathers' will become meaningful in new ways."[32]

Provocative indeed. Not all researchers will agree with Kannengiesser. Still, the prognosis cannot be dismissed out of hand. Moreover, this fresh attempt to understand the significance of the Fathers is particularly striking if we take seriously a startling thesis proclaimed by Karl Rahner more than a decade ago. He claimed that the Second Vatican Council was, in a rudimentary form, *the Church's first official self-actualization as a world church,* and this break or transition has only one genuine parallel in church history, i.e., when the Church changed from a church of the Jews to a church of the Gentiles.[33] He "tried to make clear . . . that the coming-to-be of a world Church precisely as such does not mean just a quantitative increase in the previous Church, but rather contains a theological break in Church history that still lacks conceptual clarity and can scarcely be compared with anything except the transition from Jewish to Gentile Christianity."[34]

A similar but not identical approach has been advanced by Elizabeth A. Clark, a creative, influential force in the effort to recover Christian history as women's history.[35] "What is the present state and probable future of historical theology? The question can be succinctly answered: less theology, more history."[36] Clark correlates the shift from a theological to an historical emphasis in patristics with two phenomena affecting all contemporary scholarship on Christianity: (1) Domination of Christian studies by neo-orthodox theology has subsided. (2) Patristics has transferred from the seminary to the university. In this setting "patristics is no longer a discipline devoted primarily to the investigation of dogmatic developments in and for themselves; rather, it finds its new home amidst studies of the late ancient world, commanding attention as one among many cultural phenomena of late antiquity."[37]

Among a number of specific factors influential in this shift, Clark mentions the widespread growth of women's studies and the contemporary tendency to debunk the orthodox Fathers, "a manifest sympathy with the supposed heretics."[38] She argues that we will not appreciate the richness within patristics "unless we give equal voice to those who lost out in the evolution of mainstream Christianity, and unless we note with some care the methods by which those now called saints of the church won the day."[39]

Patristic scholar David G. Hunter believes that Clark's judgment may be premature. Aware of current attempts to place Christian doctrine within its political, social, and economic contexts, he insists that this development ought to lead to a renewal of theological understanding, should result in "a truly historical theology."[40] My own experience leads me to share Hunter's reservations.

Without denying the shifts in approach that have taken place, the new discoveries, and the eye-opening insights of women researchers, I fear that the sympathy for the underdog "heretics" and "the new secular environment in which patristic studies now flourish"[41] may undermine the very objectivity Clark legitimately treasures. I submit that if we are still talking about "historical theology," the substantive is still "theology." This suggests strongly that specialized historians in the field cannot neglect what theology is all about, complex and complicated as that question obviously is.

A splendid example is the most recent contribution to patristic theology by the Sterling Professor of History at Yale University, Jaroslav Pelikan, *Christianity and Classical Culture: The Metamorphosis of Natural Theology in the Encounter with Hellenism.*[42] In these Gifford Lectures for 1992–93, Pelikan plumbs the work of the so-called Cappadocian Fathers: Basil the Great, his brother Gregory of Nyssa, and their friend Gregory of Nazianzus — to whom he adds Macrina, sister of the first two and a genuine theologian in her own right. He submits that their influence on Byzantine Christianity rivals that of Augustine in the West. Besides their significance within the fascinating intrachurch Trinitarian struggles of the fourth century, they brought Christian theology into rich contact with the literature and philosophy of Greek culture and, in so doing, modified the face of both. This is not a museum-like antiquarianism. Without such research we would not understand the Orthodox theology of our own times, nor would we be in a position to grasp the actual ways in which Christianity and Hellenism influenced each other.[43]

In the last analysis, I agree that theologians dare not neglect the social sciences, the insights of women, the ideas of those who "lost out," and the "hermeneutics of suspicion." I submit, however, that it would be tragic for historical theology if the new approaches gave us narrow specialists unprepared to comprehend the language, the philosophy, the Christian culture — in short, the theology — of the men and women who saw themselves primarily as interpreters of God's Word.

TWO

From Seminary to University
Theology Yesterday and Today

My organized theological life began in a seminary, the Woodstock described in chapter 1, in the fall of 1938. Much as I relished those four years, it was only much later that I realized the context within which Catholic theology operated in the first half of the twentieth century. To clarify this, I must journey back briefly into theology's history.[1]

Theology's Classical Paradigm

Before the twelfth century, theology was exposition of Scripture. But Scripture was interpreted by appeal to the established tradition of ecclesiastical authorities: Augustine, Boethius, Damascene, and similar acknowledged representatives of the faith. A theologian had authority not on the ground of his own interpretations but only if his insights were consistent with those of his predecessors and the received doctrinal tradition.

This classical notion of authority held sway as theology developed toward an academic enterprise in the twelfth and thirteenth centuries. In the High Middle Ages the apex of theological achievement meant blending the individual theological voice into the harmonious chorus of past authorities. The early sixteenth century introduced a nuance here: The tradition of authorities was ultimately expressed in the reigning Roman pontiff as the most authentic interpreter of revelation in Scripture and tradition.

Here Rome and the Reformers shared a common presupposition. Both assumed that theology is responsible to an objective authority: for Rome, Scripture traditionally expounded; for the Reformers, Scripture alone. For both, truth was to be found not in individual or collective acts of theologizing but in the theologian's *representative* fidelity to divine revelation.

Despite that presupposition shared with Rome, the Reformers did

23

contribute to a different understanding of the theologian's vocation. "The virtual transformation of late-medieval European society by the personal efforts, criticism, and courage of the great Reformers — Luther, Zwingli, and Calvin — did much to cultivate the modern identification of authority and autonomy, and its assumption that truth is established through the genius of individual creativity."[2]

Still, this notion of individual authority did not reach full maturity until the eighteenth and nineteenth centuries, in the Enlightenment and Romanticism. An Enlightenment that reverenced autonomy disdained the heteronomous truth claims of Christian Scripture and tradition, and made for a paradigm-shift in conceptions of the theologian's task. In the face of Enlightenment rationalism, the Christian churches had to defend the integrity of their theological vision. Where did they find their most valuable resource? In the growing movement called Romanticism.

Of deep concern to the Romantic movement was the problem, how to reconcile truth and history. Truth, the Romantics claimed, was discoverable not in some objective metaphysical referent but only in its historical development. In this light, theologians could argue that rationalism, with its static model of truth, could not appreciate the depth or dynamism of divine revelation, now conceived as a process. "Since this development was primarily accessible through and in experience, the role of individual creativity in theological reflection was remarkably enhanced. The theologian was no longer seen as mimetically *representing* an objective revelation but as imaginatively *constructing* the immediate, though historical, experience of salvation."[3]

This fresh conception of theological responsibility took shape in the first theologies of tradition, the first theories of doctrinal development, formulated early in the nineteenth century — on the Protestant side by Friedrich Schleiermacher, on the Catholic side by Johann Sebastian Drey. Both "understood Christian tradition as a fluid movement in which the established doctrine of the past was creatively joined to the current moment in the development of Christian faith."[4] Both

> assumed that the theologian's primary responsibility was to the ecclesiastical community to which his vocational efforts were devoted. In the shared experience of the community the theologian encounters the unfolding truth of revelation — for Schleiermacher, pious feeling; for Drey, the idea of the kingdom of God — against which the validity of individual efforts

at theological construction must be measured. But though responsible to the communal experience of faith, the theologian necessarily relies on his own sensibilities and talent in attempting to articulate validly the current experience of the Church.[5]

In this connection, John Thiel has suggested that both Schleiermacher and Drey consciously or unconsciously patterned their understanding of the theologian's vocation on the current notion of the Romantic hero.[6] The Romantic hero (1) stood in a privileged relation with the supernatural, (2) was related as an extraordinary member to the ordinary members of society, and (3) had to live up to an inherited heroic ideal. This threefold relationship — to the "gods," to society, to his own identity — carried over to the theologian. He (1) stood "in a privileged relationship to the evolving immediacy of divine revelation in ecclesial experience,"[7] (2) was distinguished from the Church at large by his abilities and sensibilities, and (3) had to struggle constantly in pursuit of his ideal, lest the development of the tradition languish or wander aimlessly.

Schleiermacher and Drey conceived "the theologian as a defender of the freedom of religious imagination" against "those who would confine Christian tradition to the definitions of an objective, normative authority resistant to historical, and therefore truthful, development."[8] The obstacles? For Schleiermacher, biblical authority and Protestant scholasticism; for Drey, an uncritical regard for the teaching authority of the Church.

It is this paradigm-shift that may best explain the tension between magisterium and theologians in the nineteenth and twentieth centuries. The Romantic paradigm of theological responsibility found itself in conflict with the classical paradigm "as defined at Trent, affirmed at Vatican I, and promulgated throughout the Modernist controversy and its aftermath until Vatican II."[9]

Between the two Vatican Councils the magisterium simply rejected the Romantic paradigm — and nowhere as forcefully as in Pius X's *Pascendi dominici gregis* (1907). Horrified by Modernism's commitment to a developmental understanding of religious truth, Pius condemned the Romantic paradigm passionately — in fact, caricatured it. Pius could not distinguish the Modernist celebrating theological talent from the age-old heretic asserting his solitary speculations over against the universal faith. Modernist pride, *Pascendi* fulminated, "leads them to hold themselves up as the rule for all," leads them to the presumptuous judgment "We are not as the rest of men."[10]

No doubt, a number of Modernist positions and presuppositions — on Sacred Scripture, in philosophy, in theology — merited ecclesiastical censure. In its extreme form — denial of the supernatural as an object of certain knowledge, exclusive immanence of the divine and of revelation, total emancipation of scientific research from church dogma — Modernism was a threat to Catholic Christianity. On the other hand, the condemnation showed no appreciation of values many so-called Modernists represented: faith as personal encounter, religious experience, relation between psychology and religion, sense of mystery, pastoral function of theology, less mechanical role for authority, new insights into development of dogma, fresh stress on the organic nature of the Church and the importance of the laity, greater respect for scriptural scholarship and natural science, a newer framework for church-state relationships, a call to abandon a Catholic cultural ghetto.[11]

More harmful still was the aftermath of the condemnation. The encyclical *Pascendi* called for vigilance committees in every diocese, ordered the dismissal of every teacher "found to be tainted with Modernism." Informers were encouraged; harsh censorship was imposed; a kind of secret society (Sodalitium Pianum), directed by an Italian monsignor, ferreted out suspected Modernists. Benedict XV put an end to most of these excesses, but the effects on Catholic scholarship were disastrous. For half a century, Catholic scholars were in a holding pattern — out of sheer fear.

In my early Woodstock days, I must confess, I was not aware of this. I took it for granted that the operative method, the thesis method, of teaching and learning theology was the theological "way to go." By thesis method I mean a conclusion stated at the very beginning, proven primarily from affirmations of the magisterium, confirmed by scriptural texts interpreted by dogmatic theologians, bolstered by selected passages from the Fathers of the Church in a doctrinally biased anthology (M. J. Rouët de Journel's *Enchiridion patristicum*). Adversaries were rarely read by the students — in fact, such reading was usually prohibited; these fine gentlemen languished in a "hell" section of the Woodstock Library, available only with special permission.

When I began to teach at Woodstock after three doctoral years at Catholic University, I rather hoped that with my fairly rich background in early Christianity I might enrich the patristic section of the thesis method by revealing the contexts in which early Christian doctrines were shaped (e.g., the early persecutions and the Constantinian "peace"), opening up controversies that agitated the maturing Church (e.g., Arianism, the baptism of "heretics," Cyril of Alexandria and Nestorius on the person of Christ), indicating more professional ways of dealing with early Christian texts, adding to the usual literary proofs the evidence of liturgy (e.g., the prebaptismal and postbaptismal catecheses of Cyril of Jerusalem and Ambrose of Milan) and archeology (e.g., the Eucharistic stele called the Epitaph of Abercius). Not once was I invited into a dogma class. I did indeed offer "secondary" courses: Introduction to Patrology, Development of the Doctrine of Original Sin, Mariology in the Patristic Age, and so on. But such courses were never integrated into the dogmatic cycle.

I have never forgotten the evening after my first exams as a professor. At early dinner for examiners, I mentioned my surprise that a young Jesuit examinee, after citing the Council of Florence for proof of a thesis, did not know when the council had met. "Was it before Trent [1545–63] or after?" "I don't know." "Was it before Nicaea I [325] or after?" "I don't know." A much older colleague, an Old Testament scholar, broke into my jeremiad: "You had no right to ask him that question. He's not responsible for it." Dogma then hung in midair, unaffected by history.

This is not to "trash" undergraduate theology at Woodstock before Vatican II. For those of us who were privileged to pursue graduate studies in theology later on, it was a well-organized, thorough beginning, open to developments we could not have anticipated at the time; for those not so fortunate, it left ever so many with several hundred theses and a method, much of which would fairly soon pass into history.

A Three-headed Creature

The history I have just sketched led me in the early '70s to a startling realization. I am something of a theological monstrosity: I am a three-headed creature. My Jesuit education fashioned a Scholastic (neo or not, I know not); my graduate specialty swept me back to a patristic mind-set; in the '60s our young students, at Woodstock and elsewhere, flung me violently into the present. Every so often I wonder, what sort of triune beast am I? An authentic schizoid leading a triple life? Or downright dishonest and living a triple lie? In my manic moments (like now) I find these three movements, this oscillation from Aquinas to Origen to Whitehead and back again, exhilarating, liberating. Why such joy and sense of freedom? Because this type of intellectual involvement has made me less defensive, less rigid, more open to all kinds of experience, has increased immeasurably my ability (in Carl Rogers' words) "to toy with elements and concepts,"

> the ability to play spontaneously with ideas, colors, shapes, relationships — to juggle elements into impossible juxtapositions, to shape wild hypotheses, to make the given problematic, to express the ridiculous, to translate from one form to another, to transform into improbable equivalents. It is from this spontaneous toying and exploration that there arises the hunch, the creative seeing of life in a new and significant way.... [12]

This prefatory prattle has a purpose. It leads inexorably to a threefold division, three movements to my song and dance, each with its own tempo. The first movement, allegro, has to do with the experience that was Scholasticism. The second movement, andante, picks up the contemporary experience. The third movement, adagio, plays back the experience I call patristic, the experience between the New Testament and the Middle Ages.

Scholastic Experience

Several decades ago I was convinced that I had witnessed the death and burial of the theology that first nurtured me. That Scholastic theology should crumble, that the perennial would prove impermanent, this had for me all the aura of the inevitable. Inevitable because a new man, a new woman, had been born, had shaped and been shaped by a new world. The tragedy is, few Catholic theologians saw the cloud when it was no bigger than a human hand. One who did, back in the '60s, was a perceptive Dominican, Fergus Kerr. His analysis of "Theology in a Godforsaken Epoch"[13] began with a presupposition:

> All Catholic theology occurs in the first place within the context of some Church-mediated experience of God. This does not mean reducing theology to spirituality or to the conceptual elaboration of personal piety. It is simply saying that theology requires a starting-point, a source of intelligibility, which is encounter with God himself: for without some prior relationship to its "object" theology can never be anything more fundamental than the philological investigation of more or less ancient

documents.... Doing theology at all depends on hearing the word of God: God must be allowed to speak to us before we can begin to speak about him.[14]

But the way God was speaking to the new man, to the new woman, was radically different from the way God spoke to the old, from the way God had spoken to me. A new epoch had come to birth. And what is the genius of an epoch? What makes it unique, original, unrepeatable? In Kerr's vision,

> It is... the consensus about ideals and standards in human experience which is registered and communicated in the ano-nymity of the common language of a generation. It is a consensus about what is meaningful at all, about what counts as sense in the first place.... It is a consensus about what is... obvious and simply beyond argument; it is a consensus manifested in one's sense of priorities, in one's sense of what counts as relevant, worthwhile and significant, or pointless and ridiculous. It is one's perception in community of the total-ity of meaning which constitutes the context in which words like "real," "true," "beautiful," "Nature," "history," "love," "God," etc., can have any sense [i.e., direction] in the first place.[15]

It is this sense of what is meaningful "which generates an epoch — and it is this which changes. It is only in this total context that we can have any experience at all, that we can talk and think and make love and make bombs and do theology. It is this instinct for what matters, this preliminary sense of direction, which changes from one epoch to another."[16]

In this new epoch, in the '50s and '60s, God seemed far less accessible than before to traditional Catholic categories of experi-ence. I mean the poetry that saw Christ's "blood upon the rose, and in the stars the glory of His eyes" (Joseph Mary Plunkett); the way a whirlwind would reflect God's power, a mountain mirror God's majesty, surging waves God's irresistibleness, a star-flecked sky God's breath-taking loveliness. I mean the institutions, from papal pronouncements through corporate liturgy to private confes-sion, that would mediate "the holy," a sense of God's presence, to untold millions. I mean, in a special way, our traditional theology. Not only did theology fail to make God more intelligible, more vis-ible, more palpable, more available; sometimes it hid God's face, made it more difficult to discover divinity.

Oh yes, a fresh theology was being born, where the moving forces, the thrilling ideas, were person and community, commitment and action, responsibility and response, encounter and experience, liberty and love, and so on and so forth. But a theology thus oriented, so structured, called for a manner of philosophizing adequate to its specialized demands. And here, as I saw it then, traditional Scholasticism was weighed in the balance and found wanting. Robert Johann, first-rate metaphysician and no iconoclast, saw the problem clearly and expressed it incisively.[17]

First, traditional Thomism was built solely on cognitive experience: man/woman is essentially a knower. But "an age like our own, increasingly concerned with man's temporal destiny and inclined to view theory only as a function in the process of man's temporal development, will find this identification of human perfection with abstract knowledge quite unacceptable."[18]

Second, the experience that founded traditional Scholastic philosophy was limited to the experience of making judgments, and so the philosophy that resulted was a philosophy of natures. "To an age, however, that has newly discovered the person and is passionately concerned with the emphatically personal realms of responsibility, identity, liberty and love, such a limitation will appear intolerable."[19]

Third, traditional Scholastic philosophy seemed "unable in principle to fulfil the traditional aspiration of philosophy, namely, to grasp the whole of the real and the real as a whole." For it came to grips "only with the objective face of the real. Being as subject [eluded] its grasp."[20] And so Johann found it less than surprising that contemporary man and woman, searching desperately for wholeness, were not attracted to a philosophy that could not in principle provide what they were seeking.

In this context I was tempted to ask: Cannot Scholasticism so broaden its base of experience as to incorporate the experience that was so meaningful to modern men and women? I believe I concluded, regretfully indeed, perhaps hastily, that this would be too much like attaching contemporary insights like some tail to Scholasticism's posterior. I say "regretfully" because I owe so much of what is best in my thinking to the philosophy and theology I imbibed at Woodstock. In fact, I find it imperative to remind those for whom Scholasticism is an obscenity that the philosophy which fell from the lips of Aquinas has still the power to thrill the new age. I have in mind one remarkable paragraph I memorized years ago:

There are two ways of desiring knowledge. One way is to desire it as a perfection of one's self; and that is the way philosophers desire it. The other way of desiring knowledge is to desire it not [merely] as a perfection of one's self, but because through this knowledge the one we love becomes present to us; and that is the way saints desire it.

Such, as I experienced it, was Scholasticism at its best. Contemplation yes, but aware that knowledge is never thoroughly human, nowhere authentically Christian, unless it is impregnated with love: love for God's creation, for God's people, for God's very self. Cold knowledge of nature's forces, without reverence for the work of God's hands, risks making each atom a perilous possession, each moon walk a step to destruction; the ceaseless rape of our earth demonstrates this. Sheer knowledge, empty of love, can only turn a marriage barren. Unless we love, St. Vincent de Paul told his followers and us, the poor will never forgive us for the bread we give them. And all our discovery of God — whether it be a rose that reveals or the Son of Mary — will end in frustration if it does not end in oneness, in a person-to-person relationship between a human being and a living God.

Since recording these paragraphs on "the death and burial" of Scholasticism (originally penned in the early '70s), I have been compelled to modify somewhat the harshness of that appraisal. In 1993 Jesuit Gerald McCool, longtime professor of philosophy at Fordham University, delivered a significant lecture at Rockhurst College, Kansas City, Missouri, in which he detailed the new forms that the tradition of Aquinas has taken on and indicated the contribution contemporary thinkers hope to make to philosophy and theology by drawing on that heritage.[21] McCool admitted that Vatican II deprived Aquinas of the unique place of honor in philosophy and theology accorded to him by Leo XIII, and that in the postconciliar period the neo-Thomist movement declined sharply in influence and visibility.

It is not true, however, as we sometimes hear, that during the last three decades St. Thomas all but vanished from the intellectual scene. It would be more accurate to say, I believe, that although less prominent than it was in the heyday of neo-Thomism, the tradition of St. Thomas has preserved its vitality by taking on other forms. Some of these new forms are linked historically to the older neo-Thomist movement while others, in whole or in part, are of independent origin.[22]

McCool looked at five contemporary disciples of Aquinas. Two
were theologians: Karl Rahner and Bernard Lonergan, transcendental Thomists both. Three were philosophers: personalist Thomists
William Norris Clarke and Karol Wojtyla (John Paul II), and Alasdair MacIntyre, who alone of the five dispensed with metaphysics
and made his case for Thomas' ethical tradition on historical and
linguistic grounds. After an incisive and insightful penetration of
their similarities and differences, McCool concluded with two paragraphs that have compelled me to suspect that my death notice of
Scholasticism was highly exaggerated.

> We can call these disciples post-modern representatives of
> Thomas because the problems which they address in their
> contemporary versions of his tradition are post-modern ones:
> the collapse of self-grounding Cartesian philosophical rea-
> son — the foundation on which modern Enlightenment culture
> rested — and the problem of integrating contemporary histor-
> ical and scientific data into a coherent world view despite the
> plurality of contemporary conceptual systems. The differences
> which set each one of them apart from the others are notable,
> since each one of these thinkers has worked in independence
> of the others and with no desire to link his work to the older
> neo-Thomistic movement. That very independence may cause
> us to overlook the degree to which their common master has
> remained alive and operative in their contemporary speculative
> systems; and it can make us forget as well how dependent all
> of them have been on their historical and speculative heritage
> from neo-Thomism. In their own way they still remain carriers
> of an ongoing intellectual tradition.
>   Since Vatican II, Thomas may have taken up with different
> company. His tradition bears the mark of that and, although
> still linked to its past, it is changing. In other words, *it is still
> alive;* for one thing that the tradition of St. Thomas failed to
> do in the last three decades was to die.[23]

I was particularly fortunate in that my most profound (not my
only) inspiration at Woodstock — and within the Scholastic experience — was John Courtney Murray, who lectured on Trinity and
on grace.

Two short sentences lay at the heart of Murray's theology and
life. I first heard them in class, when he was schematizing his vision
of theology. He took the sentences from Aquinas, who had borrowed them from an unidentified sixth-century author who claimed

to be the Dionysius the Areopagite converted by Paul's preaching (Acts 17:34). The first sentence: "Amor est vis unitiva et concretiva."[24] Love makes for oneness; the lover produces another self. In Murray's striking translation, "Love is a centripetal force." The correlative sentence: "Amor facit extasim."[25] Love carries the lover outside himself, outside herself; the lover becomes selfless. In the Murray version, "Love is a centrifugal force."

The pertinence of these two sentences for a systematic theology built, as Murray's was, on Thomistic lines is clear enough. They summed up the heady synthesis of his beloved Aquinas: (1) God in God's secret life, (2) man/woman as they come forth from God, and (3) man/woman as they return to God through Christ. For all that his mind roamed freely above the pedestrian level, Murray's theology was never an abstract, sterile profession. It consistently enfleshed the intuition of Aquinas: The profoundly Christian way of desiring knowledge is to desire it not primarily as a perfection of one's self, but because through this knowledge what we love becomes present to us — God, the people of God, the things of God. And, as the years moved on, Murray's "problem of God" took him from biblical theism to postmodern atheism.[26]

Passionately in love with truth, Murray was even more enchanted by our understanding of truth. He never claimed that we could change the truth; he did claim that our grasp on truth changes. He held stoutly to objective truth, but he saw no substance in disembodied propositions, in truth "somewhere out there," independent of a mind, isolated from history, lifeless syllables not incarnate in a person. He was among those Vatican II *periti* primarily responsible for the shift in Catholicism from the so-called classical mentality, where truth floats serenely in space, unaffected by persons and events, to historical consciousness, where truth is ever writhing in the anguished, quicksilver grasp of a living man or woman.

Two by-products of Murray's historical consciousness merit mention here. There was, first, his insistence that the search for certainty is less significant than the quest for intelligibility. He was persuaded that an all but compulsive concentration on certitude had too long afflicted the Catholic conscience and straitened the Catholic intelligence.[27] A second by-product was his ability to avoid what he called "the intellectual and moral vice that is known as the selective perception of reality." He had an uncommon genius for perceiving the several facets of any problem, for putting the partial visions and their advocates into fruitful confrontation: the prophet and the politician on selective conscientious objection, the theologian and

the historian on the issue of state religion. Explicit in his approach
was Clement of Alexandria's insight late in the second century and
early in the third: "There is only one river of truth, but many streams
fall into it on this side and on that."

Correlative with his nuanced approach to truth was Murray's
profound affirmation of freedom. He had a prophetic conviction,
rare among Catholics of his generation, that the essential definition
of the human person as a rational animal is not enough to define
the person existentially in our time. In this new era, he insisted, at
this point in the evolution of man/woman and society, you cannot
define a human being adequately unless you bring in the dimension of freedom. And so he fought, with ultimate success, to have
the Church declare unequivocally that religious freedom is a human
right, that this right has its foundation not in state or society or religion, or even in objective truth, but in the very dignity of the human
person. And so he sought, without success, to have the Congress
acknowledge the right of discretionary armed service, recognize the
legitimacy of selective conscientious objection.

Murray's approach to truth and freedom made for suspicion,
misunderstanding, condemnation. These never sat lightly on his
shoulders. Not simply because he was so wonderfully human and
sensitive; more importantly because he was so agonizingly aware
how much the Church and humanity had suffered from an overem-
phasis on "truth out there" and its imperious claims on the free
person.

Contemporary Experience

Scarcely sterile, this sort of Scholastic experience. And still there
came the season when it did not satisfy. Failed to satisfy not only
those newly born into the new world, but even the children of World
War I who cut their teeth on Thomas or were suckled by Suárez.
For me, as for many, it was a sticky, bloody process. It is not easy to
confess that the range of your experience is frightfully narrow. But
for me, as for many, it became agonizingly clear that this philosophy
had to be radically restructured, that without such root renewal we
graying theologians would go on talking to ourselves and not to the
world whose air we were breathing.

Where did we discover this richer experience? I can speak best
for myself. I found it largely in contemporary philosophers who
balanced my traditional stress on abstract essence with an even
greater emphasis on human existence, often insisting that living in

the doctrine of Christianity is more important than speculating on it. The influences on me were several, quite varied in their weight. There was controversial Jesuit Pierre Teilhard de Chardin (Was he a philosopher?), especially what Cardinal Feltin called his marvelous, seductive "global vision of the universe wherein matter and spirit, body and soul, nature and supernature, science and faith find their unity in Christ."[28] Quite possibly, however, Teilhard moved me at the deepest level with *The Divine Milieu,* the mirror of an incredibly profound and affecting spiritual life. There was Danish Lutheran Søren Aabye Kierkegaard, defining my self as freedom, yet dependent on God; stressing decision and choice, fear and trembling, dread and despair. There was philosopher and playwright Gabriel Marcel, with his claim that "to be" is to participate in being; I must avoid transforming being into having; "I *am* my body." There was Jewish Martin Buber, whose existentialism began not with the self but with the relations between selves. His influence on Catholics like myself stemmed largely from his emphasis on the dialogue between man/woman and the Eternal Thou; God is not primarily an object of knowledge.

Slowly and painfully I laid hold of the experience which Johann defined as "the dynamic interrelation of the self and the world, grasped, not objectively, but from within, insofar as the self, as self, is present to both itself and the world as co-constituents of an open yet all-inclusive whole."[29] I began to open up to the experience in which the world "is not merely the world of things" but "also, and more importantly, the world of persons, of other selves."[30] I touched, perhaps for the first time, that experience which is "never a closed circle" but "always open to further development."[31] Without rejecting the experience that is expressed and formulated in judgments, I reached out for the experience that is "knowledge in action, in terms of which the world is present, not as expressly known, but as lived in."[32]

It was with uncommon excitement that I discovered this richer experience in Alfred North Whitehead.[33] In the first place, I was fascinated by his insistence that "the living organ of experience is the living body as a whole."[34] Not simply the five sense organs as *the* avenues of communication with the external world; the living body as a whole. In the second place, I was profoundly shaken by his attack on "the presupposition [*my* presupposition] that the sole way of examining experience is by acts of conscious introspective analysis. Such a doctrine of the exclusive primacy of introspection is already discredited in psychology."[35] In this connection, there is one Whitehead paragraph that has proved extraordinarily enriching:

> In order to discover some of the major categories under which we can classify the infinitely various components of experience, we must appeal to evidence relating to every variety of occasion. Nothing can be omitted, experience drunk and experience sober, experience sleeping and experience waking, experience drowsy and experience wide-awake, experience self-conscious and experience self-forgetful, experience intellectual and experience physical, experience religious and experience sceptical, experience anxious and experience care-free, experience anticipatory and experience retrospective, experience happy and experience grieving, experience dominated by emotion and experience under self-restraint, experience in the light and experience in the dark, experience normal and experience abnormal.[36]

In the third place, I have been broadened by what Whitehead called "the main sources of evidence respecting this width of human experience." Three main sources of evidence: "language, social institutions, and action."[37] My experiential past placed strong stress on language, e.g., concepts, definitions, deductions, but not stress enough on the "flashes of insight beyond meanings already stabilized in etymology and grammar,"[38] the "meanings miraculously revealed in great literature,"[39] the sciences seeking "linguistic expressions for meanings as yet unexpressed."[40] My experiential past was indeed involved in institutions, e.g., structures like the Roman magisterium, regulated ritual like the liturgy, organized life-styles like the seminary, but not richly enough to include so much that was seen as secular or just non-Roman. Action could hardly escape my experience; but there was excessive emphasis on the age-old maxim *agere sequitur esse,* "what I do is the consequence of who I am"; not enough emphasis on the contemporary insight (to coin a Latinism) *agere efficit esse,* "what I do is creative of who I am." We fashion our future, our own and the world's.

Understand me. I am not asserting that all experience is religious experience (I shall speak of religious experience in some detail in the chapter on spirituality). Some experiences are religious, others are not. My point, however, is this: As with the sacred and the secular, so with the religious and the nonreligious — we are not as quick as once we were to draw the dividing line.

Let me turn quite concrete. Over the years, together with other

Catholic theologians, I became increasingly dissatisfied with the traditional concept of divine revelation that closed God's public self-disclosure with the apostolic age. Granted, the public revelation through Jesus and his apostles was a privileged moment in God's break-through to the world. Still, a God who spoke of old but speaks no more (save privately, to the individual heart) makes the human response, man's/woman's experience of God, somewhat questionable. One large reason why Christianity is ceaselessly contemporary is the thrilling fact that God is disclosing Godself *now*. And disclosing Godself in persons and events and situations that do not demonstrably touch the divine, that have no clear-cut connection with Christ.

I was probably edging onto 50 before I began listening to what the Spirit might be saying outside the formal structures of Roman Catholicism. I heard the Spirit speaking not only through individual Protestants but through the institutions called Protestantism, no longer simply obstacles to the influence of Christ but channels of grace to their constituencies, to me. I heard the Spirit speaking through the Jewish community; for I was intrigued, profoundly moved, by the inflexible affirmation of St. Paul, "God has not rejected His people whom He foreknew" (Rom 11:2). I heard the Spirit speaking in the arts — from an unbeliever's *Man for All Seasons,* through Peanuts' latest reflection on the human comedy, to Samuel Beckett's "Two times anything equals zero." I heard the Spirit speaking through the university: through philosophies like personalism and process, existentialism and linguistic analysis; yes, even through the campus violence that bloodied the '60s but expressed so tragically a cry of the heart. I heard the Spirit speaking through the black community's struggle for freedom, heard God cry once again, "Let my people go!" I heard the Spirit speaking through untold millions crying to me that they could not discover God in creation or abstraction; as they stood mute and unresponsive before a God who did not weep when they bled; as they insisted that, if they were to find God at all, they must somehow find God in living men and women — in those we so facilely call God's images.

I am still uncertain just where secular experience ends and religious experience begins. Yet this much seems certain. For all their doubting and questioning, today's men and women are more open than yesterday's to a ceaseless, ubiquitous activity of God in God's world. They are ever on the edge, therefore, of a response to the Real, of a yes to God, a yes to their sisters and brothers. Within Catholicism itself, the traditional search for certainty has been relentlessly replaced by the quest for understanding. The paradoxical result? Less attachment to incontrovertible propositions, more profound attachment to the God to whom all propositions point; less clarity on the meaning of experience, greater conviction that religious experience cannot be "cabined, cribbed, and confined" by law or system.

Patristic Experience

Thus far two movements, the Scholastic and the contemporary. It is high time I moved into my area of specialization, patristic theology. An instant objection: If today's experience is so broad and all-embracing, why go back 1,500 years and more? Granted that Christian antiquarianism is a respectable, if musty, occupation, reasonably remote from the grosser occasions of sin, why raid the past for another footnote, another "cf. ibid.," to what is being mined so excitingly, so maturely, in the present?

For this chapter's purposes, I have uncovered in patristic theology several facets of religious experience which were lost or downplayed in Scholastic thought and have only begun to surface again in our time. It is not a question of living in the past, but of allowing the past to be in part programmatic for our future.

A first facet of patristic thought is congenial to our experience: There is no gap between theology and spirituality. The gap was to be created later, in another Christian millennium, when theology became system — what Webster defines as "an organized or methodically arranged set of ideas; a complete exhibition of essential principles or facts, arranged in a rational dependence or connection."[41] I shall detail this later, in the chapter on spirituality. Suffice it to note here that, for the Fathers, theology was a search not only for the truth of God, but for God's very self. Moreover, the search was carried on not by reason alone, not simply by that particular activity of intelligence whereby one can infer new propositions from previous propositions; the whole person comes into play, is put to work on God's revelation, because it is the whole person that must respond to the revealing God. And so patristic theology is a spirituality. Not only does knowledge have love for its finality — love of God and God's humans and God's earth; love deepens knowledge; and at their most profound, knowledge and love become one, because knowledge is union.

Why this kind of theology? Several factors explain it. (1) Most of patristic theology grew out of live problems, from the Docetic denial of Jesus' genuine humanness, through Jerome's coarse argument with a bartender on monasticism and the cult of martyrs, to the *City of God* that Augustine fashioned from the fall of the Empire. (2) Some of patristic theology was written in blood: Ignatius of Antioch chained to ten legionnaires, Origen stretched in agonizing stocks, Athanasius hiding in boats and tents, Chrysostom exiled to die. (3) Rarely could the Fathers divorce their search for God's truth from the living people for whom God spoke that truth. Even sailors sang the Arian song on the Alexandrian docks. (4) The context of patristic theology was what Dom Rousseau called an "eschatological tension."[42] Theology is situated in a constant aspiration, a ceaseless yearning, for its ultimate term, the final triumph of the kingdom of Christ. Patristic theology is not timeless, extratemporal, static; it is a theology of time, in time, dynamic, dramatic.

A second facet of patristic theology was the Fathers' experience of Scripture. I know, they did not have our basic tools; even Jerome could have profited from large chunks of *Redaktionsgeschichte*. The mind of Mark or Micah can be lost in the hermeneutic of four scriptural senses, as represented in a medieval distich:

> Littera gesta docet, quid credas allegoria,
> Moralis quid agas, quo tendas anagogia.

The literal sense tells us what happened; the allegorical sense, what we must believe; the moral sense, what we must do; the anagogical sense, where we are headed. The Alexandrian symbolism that found the features of Christ in just about every line or segment of Scripture, the Augustinian principle that "in the Old Testament the New lies hidden, in the New Testament the Old lies open" — such exegesis often did violence to the authentic autonomy of the Hebrew Bible. And still I continue to nod assent to what first-rate Scripture scholar Pierre Benoit wrote more than a half century ago:

> We are not merely Westerners; we are moderns, who have passed through the crisis of rationalism and are still imbued with its scientistic positivism. Despite us, in us rational truth has supplanted religious truth. Hence that itch for material precision, that passion for dwelling on the detail of some fact, the while we forget its value as sign — the only thing that ultimately matters. We "strain out the gnat and swallow the camel" (Mt 23:24). This insistence on the critical is useful, but in its subordinate place; it ought not be a myopia which hinders one's view of the horizon. "This must be done, but without

leaving the other undone" (Mt 23:23). The sacred writers of
old, who saw in everything the problem of God, grasped the
inner meaning of history better than we, even though they were
not as successful in mastering its exact details. And the Fathers
of the Church, Greek and Latin though they were, possessed
nevertheless that religious sense which made them go straight
to the essential, without being troubled to the same extent by
deficiencies that are secondary. It is this feeling for the faith
that we must recapture if we too want to understand what the
Bible is trying to tell us. Then it will be that many of the false
problems will vanish. We shall find in the Bible the truth in its
totality, because we shall be searching for it there alone where
God put it.[43]

Theology for the Fathers, like tradition for the Fathers, was their
experience of Scripture within the Church. We have, of course,
gone beyond their exegetical method; but we can still appropriate
with profit their familiarity with Scripture, their love for Scripture,
their search for Christ in Scripture — the blunt assertion of Jerome,
"Ignorance of Scripture is ignorance of Christ."

Scripture within the Church — this suggests a third fascinating
facet of patristic thought: the early Christian experience of church.
How express that experience? Karl Delehaye summed it up in a
striking phrase: "The Church is the great We of the faithful."[44] The
Church is primarily a communion, not a pyramid but a body. This
one communion shares jointly in Christ's light and life; this one
communion jointly communicates Christ's truth and grace to men
and women.

This experience of the Church as communion was not so much a
thought-out theory as a lived-out reality. It was indeed conceptual-
ized. It was expressed warmly in the patristic imagery of the Church,
the whole Church, as mother, with all the faithful responsible for
the common life of the community.[45] It emerged in typical rhetoric
from Augustine, especially his reflections on the Church as a community of life with the triune God and with the whole company of
Christian believers. But to me the most attractive aspect of patristic
ecclesiology is that the conceptualization emerged not simply from
a reflection on Scripture (e.g., St. Paul on the Body of Christ) but
from a living experience of Christian oneness.

I am not looking at the early Church through rose-tinted glasses.
There were heresies, sects, schisms; but the Christian Church during the patristic era could suffer these without devastating rupture

to its oneness. There were different theological currents, schools, tendencies; but all coexisted within the one Church. There were geographical and cultural mentalities, but not to the destruction of the one body. Despite divergences in race and culture, in language and mentality, in exegesis and theology, Basil of Caesarea could write: "The faith we profess is not one thing in Seleucia, another in Constantinople, another in Zela, another in Lampsacus, and still another at Rome. The faith that circulates today is no different from the faith of yesterday; it is always one and the same."[46] Hyperbole? Perhaps, but a rich basis in reality.

This oneness was not an abstract unity parroted by bishops in council. It was a life, and its foci were the local church and the Eucharist. Five decades of research keep me from misrepresenting the early Church as a heavenly Jerusalem, where the saints of God without wrinkle or spot danced to a single tune in undisturbed harmony. But I have come away time and again from the Church of the Fathers mightily moved by its stress on the We. This was to be expected in the persecuted Church, from Nero to Diocletian, if only because the blood of martyrs is indeed the seed of Christians, and because fire and sword seem specially suited to separate the wheat from the chaff. The We was imperiled in an established Church torn internally, where "Christian" emperors like Constantine could control ecclesiastical policy, a Cyril of Alexandria could call a Nestorius "the new Judas," and venerable sees like Rome and Constantinople could challenge one another with unchristian coldness. And yet, somehow, the We of Christians characterized the patristic era; the magic word was not authority but community; and the Eucharist was still capable of linking hostile hands in love, still the most powerful force for building up the Body of Christ.

For me, the patristic experience bears eloquent witness (not proof but witness) to three facets of intelligent Christian living. (1) Theology is the search, the struggle, of the whole person for a living God. (2) This God who speaks to us now in such varied accents spoke a definitive word once before in syllables we have not yet exhausted. (3) The I that is every Christian will never be satisfied save in the We that is all Christians. This is not something the Fathers *said;* their relevance is that they *lived* it.

Largely in consequence of this threefold experience — patristic, Scholastic, and contemporary — I was brash enough to try to summarize, in the wake of Vatican II, the broad lines of direction a theology in tune with the times must take. This in 1966, at an international theological conference at the University of Notre Dame.

> Such a theology will be at once more authentically *biblical and historical*; for it will wrestle with the once-for-all-given (not as isolated proof-texts, but as the biblical "event" in its original contexts) and the progressive (and retrogressive) efforts of the Christian ages to grasp it and express it and live it and touch it to new generations.... Tomorrow's theology will be more *anthropological,* in that it will search out man [*sic*] as he is, with flesh and bones, inwardly divided because at once sin-full and still God's image, alternating between hope and despair, love and hate, life and death. It will be more *pastoral,* not in the sense of "instant application," fast-working bromides for confessor and counselor, rather in that its burning questions will rise in significant measure from the anguish of contemporary man, and will never lose from sight the People of God in whose service theology operates — yes, even the vast and growing majority of men who know not Christ and care not. It will be more *ecumenical,* in that "Protestants and Others Disunited" will not be primarily adversaries but co-operators in a common concern, the effort of faith not simply to understand but to unite in love. It will be more *eschatological,* not in a lyric leap to a more abiding abode, but in its awareness of a pilgrim people in movement now and tomorrow and every day, through the demonic and the salvific, to the consummation of their corporate oneness in Christ.[47]

International Theological Commission

A further significant development of my theological experience began in April 1969. A document signed by Cardinal Amleto Cicognani, the Holy See's Secretary of State, declared that Pope Paul VI had appointed me to the International Theological Commission (ITC), recently set up in response to a proposal of the 1967 Synod of Bishops. Thirty scholars from 19 countries had been selected by the pope after consultation with episcopal conferences throughout the world.

Who were they? From Argentina, Lucio Gera; from Austria, Franz Lakner, S.J.; from Belgium, Philippe Delhaye and Gérard Philips; from Brazil, Roberto Mascarenhas Roxo; from Canada, Bernard Lonergan, S.J.; from Chile, Jorge Medina-Estevez; from the

Congo, Tharcisse Tshibangu; from France, Louis Bouyer, C.O., Yves Congar, O.P., André Feuillet, S.S., Marie-Joseph Le Guillou, O.P., and Henri de Lubac, S.J.; from East Germany, Heinz Schürmann; from West Germany, Karl Rahner, S.J., Joseph Ratzinger, and Rudolf Schnackenburg; from Holland, Joseph Lescrauwaet, M.S.C., and Andreas Maltha, O.P.; from Italy, Carlo Colombo and Cipriano Vagaggini, O.S.B.; from Japan, Peter Nemeshegy, S.J.; from Lebanon, Ignace Khalife, S.J.; from Poland, Stanislav Olegnik; from Spain, Olegario Gonzalez de Cardedal; from Switzerland, Hans Urs von Balthasar and Johannes Feiner; from the United States, Barnabas Ahern, C.P., and Walter Burghardt, S.J.; from Yugoslavia, Tomislav Sagi-Bunic.

Not all or only the most competent, renowned, or genuinely progressive theologians and/or biblical scholars had been chosen; e.g., Hans Küng and Edward Schillebeeckx were not there, yet I was (*Time* magazine graciously referred to me as "a thoughtful progressive"). The group represented a spectrum of scholarly approaches — deliberately so.

The ITC had (and has) for its function to be at the service of the Holy See, and especially the Congregation for the Doctrine of the Faith (CDF), on doctrinal problems urgent at a given time. Not particular situations like the orthodoxy of a book or an author. The specific issues could be determined by the pope or the CDF, or even by the commission; they would be researched in collaboration, with the help of other theologians and other disciplines; a plenary session would be held in Rome each year. Early problems studied by the commission included collegiality, pluralism, and Christian ministries. The Cardinal Prefect of the CDF (then Franjo Seper) is ex-officio president of the commission. The members, chosen for their theological competence and fidelity to the Church's magisterium, are appointed for five-year terms.

Our inaugural meeting took place October 6–8, 1969, Poland's Olegnik the only absentee (prevented, if my memory serves me, by the political situation). It was organizational, exploratory. Highly competent simultaneous translation (into French, German, and English), meals in common, and delightfully warm October weather helped enormously. (My one problem was dinner at midday; my solution was to surrender it in favor of a walk through a section of Rome with cheese and wine at an outdoor café.) We used the language each found easiest. I, for one, spoke in English; Rahner used Latin — a blessing, for he was unexpectedly intelligible in Latin. I recall that Gustave Weigel once asked Rahner, half in jest, why he wrote those impossibly long 60-line German sentences. Karl replied in all seriousness: "I have never written a German sentence longer than 33 lines." Thirty-three lines, with the main verb, the heart of the matter, at the end! Cardinal Seper chaired the sessions with a fine feeling for freedom of speech and the inexorable clock; CDF's learned and creative Msgr. Charles Moeller assisted him without (unfortunately) being permitted to participate in the discussions.

Understandably perhaps, some misleading media reports about the first meeting had to be punctured. Paul VI did *not* confront us with "the gravest warning he has ever directed against critics of his authority" — despite "Vatican observers." In measured, almost tired tones he balanced, in the Pauline mode, a firm reaffirmation of traditional papal claims with an assurance that the freedom necessary for theological inquiry would be respected. We did *not* then retire, in cloak-and-dagger style, to some secluded, inaccessible spot. We lived and discussed at the Domus Mariae, a large, busy conference center where such novelties as women and reporters were part of the daily scene. We were *not* bound by "pontifical secrecy." The agenda and the manner of its presentation precluded this; we were held only to the discretion required of responsible individuals in complicated, delicate matters.

True, the Experimental Statutes tried to lay pontifical secrecy upon us, as if no single word uttered in our formal meetings could be communicated to the world outside. But many of the members protested against this, and it became clear that, given *what* we were discussing and *how* it came to us, pontifical secrecy did not apply across the board. In this connection my own bold, perhaps brash intervention of October 8 represents what many of the theologians felt. I do best to reproduce that intervention verbatim.

> I should like to make three main points. First, *many things said and done by this Commission are not to be revealed,* should not be made public, must be regarded as private. For example: who said this or that; personal differences or exchanges; tentative hypotheses, presentations of theological impressions or convictions which may be defective because I do not have the sources at my disposal here, and which I may change tomorrow; confidential reports from Cardinal Seper; some work we shall be doing where premature disclosure would be detrimental to, would harm, the task itself, would be prejudicial to the very purpose of our work; a final decision before it has been officially released, etc.

Second, *the solution is not pontifical secrecy.* This for at least five reasons:

1. The good which we accomplish for the Church will depend in some measure, to some degree, on the *confidence* we inspire — the confidence the Christian people have in us. But we begin our work under something of a shadow, a cloud. In the popular mind we are not like Melchizedek: without father, without mother, without genealogy. We have an ancestry: Congregation for the Doctrine of the Faith, Holy Office, Inquisition. Already in many minds we are (*sit venia verbo* ["pardon the expression"]) theological bastards.

2. The *climate* of today's world calls for greater openness, less secrecy, in the interests of honesty, in the interests of a people's right to know, in order that they may act responsibly. Hence the principle, in politics and religion and everyday living, "no more secrecy than is absolutely required."

3. The memory of *Vatican II* is still fresh in many minds. People remember the vast gap, the contradiction, between the rule of secrecy and the reality. And they are cynical. After reading our Experimental Statute on secrecy, I happened to be in Rome. I asked someone what pontifical secrecy meant, because my own research (e.g., in the *Acta apostolicae sedis*) had proved unsatisfactory. He answered: "Pontifical secrecy means that, in accordance with the traditional manner of acting of Vatican monsignori, you never sell any secrets cheaply." Humorous yes, but also tragic.

4. In somewhat the words of Peter at the Jerusalem Council (Acts 15:10), do not "place upon our necks a *yoke* which our fathers were not able to bear." I have to go back to a theological faculty, to an association of theologians of which I was president [the Catholic Theological Society of America], to the North American Academy of Ecumenists of which I am president, to the Baltimore Archdiocesan Commission for Christian Unity, to the Lutheran-Catholic dialogue, to the American bishops, with whom the American theologians are trying to establish more than an armed neutrality. Many of these will be either puzzled or hurt or scandalized or suspicious if I tell them as little as Bishop Colombo [sitting nearby] was able to tell the press yesterday. To do the work of the commission, I need the collaboration of my colleagues — Catholic and Protestant and unbeliever, theologian and sociologist and journalist. I cannot get this by asking for something and giving nothing. Theology

is now a work of incredible collaboration. An atmosphere of secrecy will destroy any such possibility for me.

5. The *press* will be on my neck. Already it is: Two called this morning. If I do not tell them the truth — not all, but some of it — they will be forced to use rumors, half-truths, "Vatican observers," etc., to the harm of the Church. Look at yesterday's *Herald Tribune* (Paris), *Daily American* (Rome), and *Il Messagero*.

Third, in harmony with the above, *I ask the Holy See: Are you willing, ready, to trust us?* And, supposing that you are, I propose that we adopt the following rule: "The members of the Theological Commission will exercise the normal prudence expected of responsible men when dealing with delicate, critical, complicated issues, where the interests of human beings and of the Church can be compromised by irresponsible or premature publication of the views and activities of the commission."

We had arrived at the Domus Mariae armed with a book of 155 pages. It contained two position papers: Rahner on *what* the more compelling contemporary issues are, Philips on *how* we ought to go about it all, together with recommendations of the various members on the what and the how. Rahner's paper was especially valuable for putting our work in the framework of the CDF: What was its *modus operandi* in the past, and how should it function now? Philips wrote of the "spirit" that should inform our efforts (e.g., openness to the future), and from his vast experience at Vatican II he was able to formulate a set of remarkably efficient guidelines. I sum up Rahner's presentation here because it was a wondrous wedding of insight and courage.

The ITC, he said, is intimately linked to the CDF. It must indeed exercise its own function (and this calls for spontaneity, responsibility, co-operation), but its function is always ordered to the work of the CDF. It is not a *mere* instrument, but it is an instrument. Hence the urgent question: What is the CDF and what ought its function be today? Obviously, it has to defend the faith against error and peril. But this response is too abstract, and the CDF's past *modus operandi* does not reveal how it ought to function now. On the answer to this basic question, Rahner noted, our choice of ITC themes depends. Some difficulties hinder an adequate response.

The first difficulty is the CDF's traditional methodology. It defended the faith, yes, but without awareness of the different philosophical presuppositions and cultural mentalities behind the condemned ideas and theses. As a result, the faith was defended in a sterile, repressive fashion, without positive assimilation of what was good and fruitful in the new. Consequently, CDF's (actually, the Holy Office's) history in the last century is a history of disasters and lost opportunities. Legitimate authority and function, of course; but the men in power too often acted like *beati possidentes* — they knew it all. Better to defend the faith defectively than to betray it even slightly, yes; but deplorable aspects and numerous errors of the CDF could have been avoided: on the Bible, on modern science, on psychology, on the social sciences.

Second, the traditional CDF methodology is today largely ineffective within the Church. The former alternatives — either submit or get out — are increasingly not recognized as the only alternatives. Increasingly, Catholics do neither; they opt for partial participation. There is a growing difference from the past in the relationship between the theoretical and practical intellect. In Germany the majority of the younger clergy do not think that every dogma is absolutely true. Nor does that attitude bother them, because they have little concern for sheerly theoretical truth in abstraction from its existential efficacy. Here we have a mighty transformation in the sociology of thinking. The axiom "submit or get out" is not admitted, nor are there practical ways of implementing the axiom.

Third, in the past the CDF tried to give its attention to *all* the errors and *all* the dangers to the faith. This was done — at least the decisions were given — by a small group of theologians, almost all living in Rome, whose competence was not always beyond challenge. The manner in which the CDF defended the faith presupposed a type of unity between the faith and theology which no longer exists — nor can it. We are more consciously aware today of how diverse are the presuppositions (philosophical, cultural, scientific) that make for different theologies with respect to the one faith. The CDF can no longer suppose and use one common philosophy in its operations. Nor can it, with its small complement of members, know and appraise these different theologies, or use a universally understandable and apt language to settle the controversial issues it confronts. Hence the diverse reactions to controverted theological affirmations. Of old, a condemned proposition was understood in the same sense by both parties; today such understanding is far more difficult to achieve.

What follows for the activity of the ITC and the CDF? For our selection of themes? On general lines, Rahner offered two recommendations. First, we must recognize our ignorance with regard to

procedure, because we do not really understand the new situation
in which the Church and its magisterium exist; we do not grasp the
reasons behind the new sociology of thinking. We are still judging
the present (principles, thinking, activities) by the past, and propos-
ing remedies accordingly. What we do not know is not simply *how*
to propose and preach Christian truth, but *what* to propose and
teach.

Second, a fresh methodology is demanded. We can no longer
settle questions by appealing to the doctrine and practice nearest
chronologically to our time — the period just prior to our own. New
methodological approaches are necessary — e.g., historical and exegetical — respecting the milieu of texts; we must recognize that past
unanimity does not suffice to prove that a proposition is revealed
doctrine.

As for special themes, Rahner first suggested four that were rather
broad. (1) In defending and preaching the faith, what are the possibilities, limits, and methods appropriate for the Church and her
magisterium now as contrasted with the past? (2) Who belong to
the Church — e.g., in the light of current discussions on how to determine a person's belief or unbelief? (3) The juridical vs. the moral
in the Church, so that the limits of public authority in the Church
vis-à-vis the individual conscience might appear. (4) The concrete
constitution of the Church and of particular churches — e.g., what
is of divine right, and how is that which is of human right to be
exercised?

As for more specialized themes, Rahner recommended five, without developing any of them: mixed marriages, *communicatio in
sacris,* infant baptism, indissolubility of Christian marriage, and
clerical celibacy.

The discussion that Rahner's position paper evoked carried over
into several sessions. It was a freewheeling affair, which only *seemed*
to be getting nowhere. All the while the participants were learning
to talk to one another; aspects of problems were suggested, debated, nuanced, and clarified; we were zeroing in on those areas
that seemed uncommonly significant, and on what we as a group of
theologians were competent to do. Cardinal Seper was understandably anxious for us to get practical and decide on specific issues for
our collaboration. But a theologian is hard to push; and 29 theologians are difficult to the 29th power. An example of such theological
slowdown was my own intervention soon after Seper's request —
observations which have only increased in pertinence after a quarter
century.

I am in sympathy with Cardinal Seper's desire that we select specific themes. And yet, I think this desire harmonizes with what we were doing this morning. Rahner and others have called our attention to a problem that underlies, is intimately involved in, *any* theme we select. Perhaps it should be a theme in itself; perhaps it will be sufficient to keep this in mind whatever theme we choose. But it is critical, inescapable. I mean the problem of different cultural mentalities. By a cultural mentality I mean (1) a point of view, (2) a way of thinking, (3) certain presuppositions, (4) a set of values, (5) a language and rhetoric which express all these and which alone adequately express them. And I mean different mentalities not only as between, say, Africa and America, but also changing mentalities within a single country.

Take our situation in the United States. Not only outside the Catholic Church, but inside. Not only in the colleges and universities, but in the seminaries. Not only in Jesuit seminaries, but in diocesan as well. For many of our young men and women (perhaps most), the center of reality is not a divinely ordered cosmos, but *the human person.* What strikes them every moment of the day is not permanence but *change* (hence their aversion to an unchangeable church, dogma, infallibility, moral absolutes). The important *revelation* for them is not so much the revelation given yesterday through Christ, as the revelation given today through man and woman and their technological world — and the revelation to be given tomorrow. The *unity* they seek is not the unity of the churches but the unity of human persons (hence their impatience with the ecumenical movement, Rome's gradualness, arguments about intercommunion). Their *philosophy* is not Scholasticism (often this is a dirty word) but one or other or all of the philosophies of experience. They do not live on yesterday's beliefs, but are ready to risk their existence from day to day, make up their existence from day to day. *Faith,* for them, is not a set of propositions to which they assent, but a loving commitment to Christ, through the people they serve, despite certain propositions of the Church — which they may accept or deny or disregard. *Authority,* for them, is not so much something you *have* because God or people have given it to you, but something you *earn* by the manner in which you lead. The *morality* of an act is determined not so much by what some institution outside of them says it is, but by their own personal evaluation of all the circumstances here and now. *Rome* — pope, congregations, soon the ITC — Rome is suspect, because it gives the impression of being cold, legalistic, indifferent to individuals, tied to the past; because, to reverse Nero, Rome is fiddling while people are burning. This is not "Americanismus"; this is a mentality widespread in the West.

Don't think we will touch these young people because we come to the conclusion that dogma can change, or that Mary was not a virgin physically, or what have you in the area of doctrine. There is a more basic problem: they are not listening. Before they will listen to us, we must listen to them. (In this connection, why not a 31st member, age under 30? [Today I would add, why not a woman?]) Countless good Catholics did not accept *Humanae vitae,* not only because many disagreed with the conclusion, but because the style was unsuited to a new mentality. The encyclical did not "speak to" them.

In brief, therefore, either make this neuralgic problem a theme in itself, or make sure it underlies any theme we choose.

During my 11 years on the commission, my problem never became a theme in its own right and never really underlay any of the themes we discussed. The themes, however, were significant (e.g., ministry, Christology, liberation theology, the Christian moral conscience), argued by some of the finest minds in the Catholic theological fraternity. The positive features of the ITC were obvious: varied fields of specialization, different cultures, fascinating personalities, several ways of approaching theological issues. Disadvantages? A rather tightly knit group: all Roman Catholic, all "approved," all male. I recall vividly that, in the week given over to liberation theology, no member of the commission was in a position to offer a spirited defense of this rapidly developing movement, and no liberation theologian, e.g., Gustavo Gutiérrez, was invited to join us and improve our understanding "from the inside."

Almost two decades have fled since I served on the ITC, and memory threatens to play me false. Still, I agree with Peter Hebblethwaite that after the first few years there was "a certain *malaise* among members of the ITC."[48] He mentions the complaint that Cardinal Seper "refused to relinquish control over doctrinal matters" and that the ITC was being subordinated to the CDF.[49] But by the very conditions imposed on our existence, we were to be at the service of the Holy Father and the CDF. We knew that, much as some of us found it a hindrance to our effectiveness. It was Rahner who put into words what upset some of the ITC. He resigned because the ITC was "stewing in its own juice."

> I would have liked the ITC to be seriously considered on the questions that concerned the CDF. The Prefect at that time, Cardinal Seper, clearly did not want this. So the ITC ended up by being a theologians' club where intelligent theologians intelligently (impotently) dialogued with one another. I felt I didn't need to go to Rome for that. I could do it just as well with my colleagues in Germany. . . . I can eat ice-cream in Germany too, excellent though the ice-cream in Rome may be.[50]

I agree with Hebblethwaite that "the ITC felt under-used."[51] And we did indeed live so far apart that effective collaboration was close to impossible. The five-person subcommission on pluralism in my time was a prime example. Joseph Ratzinger was in Bavaria; Hungarian Jesuit Peter Nemeshegy lived in Japan; Oratorian Louis Bouyer was shuttling between the United States and France; Tomislav Sagi-Bunic was in Zagreb, Yugoslavia; my home was the United States.

University Theology

When I was appointed to the International Theological Commission in 1969, I was still teaching patristic theology at Woodstock College in Maryland. But in the '60s significant changes were taking place. When I began teaching in 1946, Catholic theology in the United States was largely a seminary theology. There were indeed faculties of theology in Catholic colleges and universities, but the scholarly production emanated predominantly from the seminaries.

One concrete proof: publication. Take the journal of my predilection, *Theological Studies,* on which I served as managing editor from 1946 to 1967, and as editor-in-chief from 1967 to 1990. During the first decade of its existence, 1940–49, published contributions from seminaries (mostly but not exclusively Jesuit) totaled 144; of the remaining 41, 29 stemmed from various other educational institutions here and abroad (17 of these from the Catholic University of America), while 12 were authored (unsigned) by the then editor, William J. McGarry, S.J., in residence in New York City at the editorial offices of the weekly *America.*

The second decade, 1950–59, was not significantly different in numbers: 147 contributions from seminaries, 38 from elsewhere —

only six that year from Catholic University, but gratifying representations from Oxford, Montreal, Paris and Solesmes, Glasgow, Hiroshima, London, Rome, and Jerusalem.

The third decade, 1960–69, moved gradually but indubitably in the direction of greater university participation. For the whole decade, there were 109 contributors from seminaries, 93 from other institutions. But of these categories, in the first five years the numbers were 60 and 32 respectively, in the last five years 49 and 61. The year 1967 was helpful in this regard because the September issue commemorated the 450th anniversary of Luther's 95 theses, with non-Roman representation. But more broadly, 1967 provided contributions from Toronto and Tokyo and from universities as varied as Munich and Marquette, Yale and Cambridge, Stanford and Santa Clara, Iowa and Fordham, Detroit and Georgetown.

The fourth decade, 1970–79, revealed significantly what the previous decade had strongly suggested. This time only 85 contributors stemmed from seminaries, 146 from colleges, universities, and other situations. The latter included Ivy League's Harvard and Yale, Cornell and Brown; Johns Hopkins and Howard, Georgetown and New York University, Loyola of Chicago and the University of Chicago, Detroit and Florida State, Wayne State and Wisconsin, Southern Methodist and St. Louis, SUNY at Stony Brook and Massachusetts General Hospital, Dayton and Detroit, Marquette and Le Moyne, Catholic University and Canisius, Seattle and St. Bonaventure; Fordham, Notre Dame, and Rutgers; north of the border, Alberta, Manitoba, and Montreal's Concordia; across the seas, Oxford and Cambridge, Sankt Georgen, Munich, Paris' Institut Catholique, and Rome's Biblical Institute and Gregorian. Plus an Indian mission.

The fifth decade, 1980–89 (closing my editorship of the journal), continued the "turn to the university." During those ten years 63 contributors stemmed from seminaries, 199 from colleges, universities, and other situations. Typical was the 50th-anniversary volume (1989): Only five of the 28 contributors hailed from seminaries. The variety of place names grew even larger. Besides names already mentioned, we published pieces from Vanderbilt and Princeton, Baltimore Loyola and New Orleans Loyola, St. Thomas in Houston and Loyola Marymount in Los Angeles, Indiana University and Creighton in Omaha, Wheeling in West Virginia and Cornell in Ithaca, Gonzaga in Spokane and Emory in Atlanta, the Johns Hopkins School of Medicine, Saskatchewan in Canada and King's College in London, Hull in the United Kingdom and Rome's North American College, Angelicum, and Oriental Institute, plus pieces from Sydney and Melbourne and North South Wales, Alberta and West Africa, the Ateneo de Manila and a number of other places.

This passage of theology from the old-time seminary to the university (and to the theological schools that are consortia and/or connected to universities) has opened theology in ways that I could hardly have envisioned when Woodstock moved to New York City in 1969, even when it closed once and for all in 1974. Not only had Catholic priests increasingly undergone graduate theology or religious studies in non-Catholic institutions; the theology departments of Catholic colleges and universities were transformed by the emergence of the laity, women as well as men. No longer could the Jesuit superior of the Maryland Province appoint a Jesuit to the theology faculty of Georgetown or Scranton or Wheeling or Philadelphia's St. Joseph's or Baltimore Loyola; each potential professor had to be tested by the department in question, subject not only to accepted standards of competence but to all the multiple personalities and internal politics that shape and shake and sometimes shame an academe that prides itself on its objectivity.

In consequence, Catholic theology finds itself inevitably involved in what Avery Dulles called "a widespread perception that we are moving, or have already moved, into a period radically unlike the past few centuries, necessitating an abrupt shift of theological style comparable in magnitude to the shift that occurred with the dissemination of printed literature in the sixteenth century."[52] Dulles has charted the movement of theology from a precritical era (the patristic and medieval periods, when the criticism that did exist was not leveled at the canonical sources themselves) to the critical period (when the new science heralded by Francis Bacon and Galileo and the methodical doubt stimulated by such as Descartes rejected what could not be verified by self-evident facts and principles) to the postcritical age (emerging among philosophers like Michael Polanyi, sociologists such as Robert Bellah, theologians like George Lindbeck and Dulles himself).

I am profoundly impressed by Dulles' critique of the critical era — in large part, no doubt, because he articulates with characteristic insight and precision so much that I have felt but have been unable to systematize. He draws attention to "five flaws":[53] (1) the critical program's bias toward doubt, insensitivity to the genuinely responsible nature of firm religious commitments; (2) its failure to recognize that doubt itself rests on a fiduciary basis, presupposes beliefs that can themselves be doubted; (3) the fact that universal doubt is unrealizable, would destroy any effort to construct an edifice of knowledge; (4) the program's neglect of the social dimension of knowledge, the significance of predecessors and colleagues; (5) "most fundamentally," its neglect of precritical orientations, knowledge's tacit dimensions, Pascal's "reasons of the heart," Newman's "instincts of an educated conscience." I also feel strongly in tune with Dulles' conviction that his type of postcritical theology can claim as a significant merit

> its ability to maintain a dynamic equilibrium between continuity and innovation. Looking on tradition primarily as the bearer of tacit knowledge, it recognizes that fidelity to the tradition may be consonant with certain innovations in the formulation of doctrine. While critical theology was unduly allergic to the authority of tradition, and while countercritical theology was unduly suspicious of originality, each is given its due in postcritical theology. Postcritical theology has its home within the Church as a community of faith, but it dares on occasion to break through the accepted frameworks in its passionate exploration of the mystery to which the Church bears witness.[54]

More recently, Dulles delivered a penetrating lecture on "The Future of Seminary Theology" at an academic convocation marking the centenary of St. Joseph's Seminary in the Archdiocese of New York.[55] After a brief critique of university theology and an incisive insistence that "Catholic theology must always be a reflection on the faith of the Church, practiced within the community of faith, with a view to serving and enhancing the spiritual life of that community,"[56] Dulles focused on seminary theology, its strengths and its limitations. Its strengths he found precisely where university theology is most precarious: (1) doctrinal purity, certified by Scripture, tradition, and the magisterium; (2) a gospel spirituality, so that theology is practiced within a community of prayer and the student sees reality through the eyes of Christ; (3) a liturgical dimension, where participation in the sacraments inserts the student in a living way into the paschal mystery studied in the classroom. The limitations are not negligible. The focus on pastoral ministry limits profound exploration of new, difficult, unanswered questions. Emphasis on sound doctrine and the accumulation of a satisfying faith heritage can induce an anti-intellectualism unconcerned about rapid developments in science and technology, intolerant of careful study, patient dialogue, tentative answers. Immersion in unalterable truth can lead professors and students to disregard doctrinal development, live and teach that what the Church proclaims now was always thus. Priests formed in nonhistorical orthodoxy have been paralyzed by the changes of the '60s.

Dulles was aware of a neuralgic need that I have experienced firsthand in touring the dioceses with my project Preaching the Just Word. The ideal that Harvard's James Bryant Conant recommended, i.e., to inoculate students with "the virus of a self-perpetuating education," is by no means carried into universal practice. If Catholic theology is the Church's ceaseless effort to understand what God has said and what God might be saying now, the failure of priests to continue the struggle to understand is not only a personal loss but a pastoral peril. For better or worse, as a friend recently remarked, most of our Catholic faithful imbibe their theology in largest measure from the weekend homily. I shall discuss this at greater length in the chapter on priesthood.

Methodologies

Dulles' stress on a "shift of theological style" is particularly noticeable in methodologies. By methodology I mean, very simply, how does one go about doing theology? During my undergraduate theology more than five decades ago at Woodstock in Maryland, and for several decades afterward, the Catholic methodology was clear, consistent, accepted. It was formulated in 1950 by Pius XII in his encyclical *Humani generis:* "The task of theologians is to show how doctrines taught by the living magisterium are found either explicitly or implicitly in Scripture and in divine 'tradition.' "[57] And so the proofs of each thesis ran, in descending order, as follows: from the magisterium, from Scripture, from the Fathers, from the theologians, from reason.

This has changed radically. The present situation in theology, including Catholic theology, is an ever-increasing pluralism. So many methodologies that it is impossible to detail them. Robert Browning might sing of love, "How do I love thee? Let me count the ways."[58] Not so for methodologies. Consequently, David Tracy did me an initial service in 1975 when he attempted to uncover five basic models in contemporary theology, in the chronological sequence of their emergence.[59]

1. *Orthodox model.* The theologian's task is to "express an adequate understanding of the beliefs of his particular church tradition."[60] The spectrum is wide: from fundamentalist through biblical to systematic. But in each case the theologian is not impressed by

the counterclaims of modern scholarship. He or she is a believer, is addressing believers, has for function not so much proof as understanding of accepted mysteries. A good example for Tracy is the Vatican I model for theology.

2. *Liberal model.* On the one hand, the liberal theologians are "committed to the cognitive claims and the fundamental values of the Christian vision."[61] On the other hand, they accept "the distinctively modern commitment to the values of free and open inquiry, autonomous judgment, critical investigation of all claims to scientific, historical, philosophical, and religious truth."[62] How maintain both commitments? By showing "how a proper reinterpretation of modernity's most basic value commitments and proper reinterpretation of Christianity's historic claims to truth and value can be — indeed must be — reconciled."[63] The clearest example here, the paradigm, would be Schleiermacher.

3. *Neo-orthodox model.* Perhaps not a radically new alternative; rather a critical moment in the larger liberal tradition. It did not reject liberalism out of hand; it criticized it on two fronts: its inability to account for the negative elements in human existence (tragedy, terror, sin) and its unacceptable reinterpretation of the event of Jesus Christ, specifically its inadequate explication of Christianity's central belief, i.e., justification. The neo-orthodox response: explicit recognition of the unique gift of faith in the Word of God. Here the neo-orthodox join the orthodox; but, unlike the orthodox, their faith "is radically experiential and claims, in effect, like the liberal's, to illuminate all human existence."[64] Exponents would be Karl Barth and Karl Rahner.

4. *Radical model.* Its problem with the preceding three models? "A conscience committed to the struggle for human liberation cannot really affirm a radical faith in and dependence upon the God of orthodox or liberal or neo-orthodox Christianity." The solution? "This Wholly Other God must die in order that the authentically liberated human being may live." The Christian God can only "alienate human beings from one another, from the world, and from their authentic selves." What essential assertion of traditional Christianity must be maintained? The affirmation of "a life which, in its commitment to liberation and to others, may serve to humanize the world: a life like that made present...in Jesus of Nazareth and in the liberating event of the death of God in the contemporary world."[65]

5. *Revisionist model.* Recognizing strengths and limitations in the preceding four models, the revisionist "is committed to contin-

uing the critical task of the classical liberals and modernists in a genuinely post-liberal situation," will "try to rectify earlier theological limitations both in the light of the new resources made available by further historical, philosophical, and social scientific research and reflection and in the light of the legitimate concerns and accomplishments of the later neo-orthodox and radical theological alternatives." The central task of theology today is "the dramatic confrontation, the mutual illuminations and corrections, the possible basic reconciliation between the principal values, cognitive claims, and existential faiths of both a reinterpreted post-modern consciousness and a reinterpreted Christianity."[66] The revisionist claims that "contemporary Christian theology is best understood as philosophical reflection upon the meanings present in common human experience and the meanings present in the Christian tradition."[67] A prime proponent of the revisionist model? Tracy himself.[68]

Though impressed by Tracy's schematization, I resonated even more to Avery Dulles' observation that he did not find himself comfortable in any of these "models."[69] Moreover, I too was reluctant to subscribe to two highly important characteristics that specified Tracy's revisionism: that the revisionist theologian (1) cannot be definitively committed to any particular doctrine, church, or religion and (2) is committed to the faith of secularity, to the same faith shared by his secular contemporaries.

In fairness, I must point out that Dulles found Tracy's later volume, *The Analogical Imagination,* correcting *Blessed Rage* on important points.[70] Tracy no longer called for a revision of doctrine in which the "faith of authentic secularity" would be a controlling principle. He recognized that praxis itself can be an inner moment of systematic reflection. The theologian of faith may properly appeal to a religious tradition for warrants. Tracy admitted that *Blessed Rage* did not do justice to Thomist and neo-Thomist positions. He removed some ambiguities in Christology, stated clearly that Christianity rests on the Christ event as God's decisive word and manifestation, but apparently continued to "hold that fundamental theology, as distinct from systematics, need not explicitly concern itself with the real existence and character of Jesus."[71]

At this point let me sketch four methodologies that have actually served to deepen my understanding of theology since the Second Vatican Council. I mean Bernard Lonergan's and Karl Rahner's methodologies, liberation theology, and feminist approaches.

Bernard Lonergan

Much as I admire David Tracy, I would say that I was more
influenced by Jesuit Bernard J. F. Lonergan. Here was an impressively original thinker who for four decades consistently confronted
theologians with a profound reappraisal of theological method:
What does the theologian do, and how ought he or she to do it?
Focus briefly on his *Method in Theology*.[72] The basic framework is
"transcendental method." The expression is daunting, save to the
initiated. In fact, it intimidated *me* until I read a singularly clarify-
ing explanation in a review of *Method in Theology* by (who else?)
Avery Dulles. This single paragraph can well serve as an engaging
introduction to Lonergan for the fainthearted.

> L. holds that the human mind is governed by an unrestricted
> dynamism toward the fulness of truth, reality, and goodness,
> and that from this dynamism one can distil the transcendental
> notions of the true, the real, and the good. These notions, taken
> in reference to L.'s four levels of intentionality (experience,
> insight, judgment, and decision), yield four transcendental
> precepts: be attentive, be intelligent, be reasonable, and be
> responsible. The criteria used in transcendental method are
> thus rooted in the very nature of the human mind. By obey-
> ing the transcendental precepts man progressively expands his
> horizons and undergoes a series of conversions — intellectual,
> moral, and religious — culminating in the experience of the
> love of God.[73]

But even before *Method* appeared, I was entranced by Lonergan.
Back in 1964, a complete issue of the journal *Continuum* in Lonergan's honor offered me an opportunity to sketch my appreciation
of him as a theologian.[74]

Lonergan's *Insight* (1957), moving with discouraging ease from
mathematics through the physical sciences to common-sense wisdom, explored the process whereby human intelligence reaches
understanding in the major fields of prephilosophical knowledge,
then in the realm of philosophical or reflective understanding, to
reveal the dynamism behind every intelligent inquiry. He attempted
to uncover the permanent structure of human knowledge. It was
a profound rethinking of Aristotelian-Thomistic epistemology, in
terms more acceptable to contemporary scientific intelligence. A daring enterprise, where a profound grasp of the philosophical past
is impregnated with a keen awareness of our scientific present, to

foreshadow a theological future that might command the respect of even the post-Christian mind.

Lonergan's five famous *Verbum* articles in *Theological Studies* (1946, 1947, 1949) should be set in a similar context. Here he sought (1) to determine the introspective psychological data involved in the Thomist concept of an "inner word"; (2) to review the metaphysical categories and theorems in which these introspective data were expressed by Aquinas; (3) to follow the extrapolation from the analysis of the human mind to the account of the divine intellect as known naturally; and (4) the central issue of his inquiry: to study the procession of the divine Word. He tried to *understand as Aquinas understood.*[75]

Lonergan's works on the Trinity (1957, 1964) and on the Word Incarnate (1961) showed impressively, with emphasis on Nicaea and Chalcedon among others, how doctrinal evolution is a complex historical process involving three movements or dimensions of movement: the transcultural, the theological, and the strictly dogmatic. As transcultural, the movement involves transposition not merely from one use of words to another, but from one underlying mentality to another. As theological, the movement takes a precise direction — toward theological *understanding* in a highly particularized sense: analytical reduction from what is first, or immediate, in the order of human experience, to what is first, or immediate, in the order of things as they are in themselves, objectively.

Lonergan's lectures and institutes likewise fastened on the fundamental. An instance in point is the institute he conducted in the summer of 1962 at Regis College, Toronto, on the method of theology.[76] A central theme was the problem created for the theologian by a new ideal of science (dealing with probabilities, change at the instant, statistical laws, empirical intelligibility, particulars), by a new mentality and method of approach in people themselves, by phenomenology and existentialism and personalism, by a shift of the human person from rational animal to symbolic animal, by the demand for a praying theology rather than a thinking theology. Once again Lonergan's quest looked to integration — and this in the preconceptual operations of the subject, in the elemental drive of human intelligence. He plunged deep into the forms of meaning (linguistic, intersubjective, aesthetic, symbolic), into the general problem of *another's* meaning with which hermeneutics deals, into the history of meaning which shifts our viewpoint from what any one author meant to what was going on in the total process.

Integration and synthesis — this, I gathered, was cardinal in Lonergan's vision. For, as Frederick Crowe observed in appraising *Insight,*[77] Lonergan's long-range enterprise had for its purpose to help fashion a theology that would do for our age what St. Thomas did for his. The program had three fairly recognizable stages: (1) to appropriate the mind of Aquinas as a structured dynamism productive not only of the ideas he actually had seven centuries ago, but also of the prolific, exciting new ideas he would have, did he live now; (2) to bring to this acquisition the method to be gleaned from seven more centuries of intellectual fermentation on philosophy, cognitional activity, and theology; (3) to set these forces to work in evolving a theology that would integrate the vast treasures of knowledge presently available but dreadfully disorganized, and would lift the minds of man and woman to new heights in their ascent toward the mind of Christ.

Lonergan did not live to achieve the integration and synthesis he envisioned; he died in 1984. Nevertheless, I suggested three decades ago that we can apply to him what he said of Aquinas back in 1942:

> It is not to be regretted that St. Thomas did not adopt a specialist viewpoint, for it is the nemesis of all specialization to fail to see the woods for the trees, to evolve *ad hoc* solutions that are indeed specious yet profoundly miss the mark for the very reason that they aim too intently at a limited goal. There is a disinterestedness and an objectivity that comes only from aiming excessively high and far, that leaves one free to take each issue on its merits, to proceed by intrinsic analysis instead of piling up a debater's arguments, to seek no greater achievement than the inspiration of the moment warrants, to wait with serenity for the coherence of truth itself to bring to light the underlying harmony of the manifold whose parts successively engage one's attention. Spontaneously such thought moves towards synthesis, not so much by any single master stroke as by an unnumbered succession of the adaptations that spring continuously from intellectual vitality.[78]

Karl Rahner

A second example of contemporary Catholic methodology that has influenced my thinking is Karl Rahner. Obviously not *ein Amerikaner,* but his has been for decades the most pervasive influence on North American Catholic theology. In 1968, in the course of my presidential address to the Catholic Theological Society of America, I remarked that other worlds of ideas were dominating our American Catholic thinking instead of stimulating it; "they *are* our theology, not part of theology's history. The ultimate Catholic argument used to be *'definitur in Concilio Tridentino'* ['defined in the Council of Trent']; today it is more likely to be 'as Karl Rahner says so well.'" [79]

On the subject of his methodology, Rahner often expressed reserve. Once, at a friend's request, Jesuit Leo O'Donovan brought Rahner her study of his theological method. Rahner "asked with a smiling frown whether indeed he *had* one." [80] He did indeed, but interpretations vary. Following O'Donovan, who studied under Rahner, I shall stress four facets of that method.

1. Rahner's method is twofold. It is not simply transcendental but at once transcendental and historical; the two are interdependent. In Montreal in 1969, for example, "he made it perfectly clear that he considered transcendental theology as a method to be only part of theology and that, as a result of the historical reflection which is essential to theology, it has a scientific character prior to any explicit transcendental analysis." [81] This dialectical union of perspectives is strikingly apparent in Rahner's doctrine of the Trinity, where we find his axiomatic thesis that the economic Trinity is identical with the immanent Trinity, and vice versa.

2. Rahner's method is anthropological: "He has consistently sought to root the grace of God in the soil of human experience, recalling again and again that unless we appreciate the scope of the human we cannot appreciate how God's own life may be its innermost origin and ultimate goal." [82] But it is not exclusively anthropological. For Rahner, "all genuine knowledge of humanity in its historical experience pivots on the imagination and its symbols. Just as history has been essential to Rahner's method from the beginning, so too has been the image." [83] We must learn to imagine and reimagine our human situation.

3. The foundations of Rahner's method do have a philosophical character. Nevertheless, it is not a theological method built on a philosophical foundation but "a religiously inspired theology which has generated a philosophy within itself in order to foster its own development." [84]

4. Theology is, for Rahner, a way of opening Christian life to deeper and more active faith. Theology will not serve truth unless it is guided by love. But such Christian reflection and love involve a surrender to the mystery that is God. [85]

Liberation Theology

A third methodology with considerable effect on me has been liberation theology. Its methodology is complex, not to be caricatured by oversimplification. But back in 1973 a brief summation from Gustavo Gutiérrez left its imprint on me.

> Theology is reflection, a critical attitude. Theology *follows;* it is the second step. What Hegel used to say about philosophy can likewise be applied to theology; it rises only at sundown. The pastoral activity of the Church does not flow as a conclusion from theological premises. Theology does not produce pastoral activity; rather it reflects upon it.[86]

Put another way, liberation theology seeks to understand faith from within the historical praxis of the Christian community. It is a critical reflection on the living faith of the community. With roots in the poverty of Latin America, it begins with a social analysis of actual poverty and oppression, then extracts from this various implications for the Church and Christian living. Gutiérrez put it pithily a decade later: "Theology comes after involvement."[87] So too for Juan Luis Segundo: Liberation theology is "a second step."[88] The first step is commitment to liberation. What this means is that "it is impossible to know what a specifically Christian contribution to liberation might be prior to a personal commitment to liberation."[89] But I could not help adverting to an important difference one scholar noted between Gutiérrez and Segundo:

> Whereas Gutiérrez speaks of commitment in terms of solidarity with the poor and involvement with the masses, and thus regards the task of fostering a critical consciousness among the people of God as a principal concern of liberation, Segundo emphasizes commitment as effective participation in an enlightened minority, an elite whose historical mission is to function as a core revolutionary vanguard in transforming the world.[90]

In a small way I had the privilege of introducing Gutiérrez to North American readers. At a Miami meeting in 1969 of North and Latin American bishops, I heard him discuss liberation theology in an impressively gentle yet passionate fashion. As a *peritus,* I found occasion to defend his position on the criteria for even violent resistance to oppression as conformable to contemporary Catholic moral theology under certain specific conditions. I asked him to put together for *Theological Studies* some "Notes for a Theology of Liberation." He did.[91] The article, as I stated in an introductory paragraph, was theological dynamite; not every theologian would sing amen; but the Church could not avoid this challenge from a socioeconomic situation where the rich grow richer and the poor become poorer. The last sentence of Gutiérrez's article still challenges me: "Adapting Pascal, we can say that all the political theology of hope, of liberation, of revolution, is not worth as much as one act of faith, hope, and charity leading to an active effort to liberate man from all that dehumanizes him and keeps him from living according to the Lord's will."[92]

Feminist Theology

A fourth methodology, one that increasingly claims my attention, arises within feminist theology. Feminist scholarship within a Christian context "is united in its attention to the interpreted experience of women as a source for religious and theological reflection, especially as those analyses, whether secular or religious, reflect the collective experience of women, in whatever groups of race, age, class, nationality."[93] This scholarship can be divided into reformist and revolutionary approaches. The reformist uses the experience of women as a corrective, the revolutionary as a fresh starting point and a norm, creating new symbols and traditions.[94]

Early on, I was attracted by one of Anne Carr's critical requirements for reformist theology. She stressed the need to ground a fresh understanding of theological tradition by seeing it from the perspective of contemporary questions. The use of hermeneutical and critical theory held strong possibilities for exposing the distortions of the past and for seeing something more.[95]

In its early existence, most of reformist theology focused understandably on negation; I mean analysis of the distorted traditions about women through the centuries. I could empathize with that emphasis; for in my patristic research I had uncovered endless evidence of an inadequate anthropology in regard of woman that affected the theology of many an early Christian writer. (I shall expand on this in chapter 10 on women.) But in the last decade or so, I have been profoundly impressed by the way reformist theology has addressed central symbols of Christianity from a systematic perspective. One splendid example is Elizabeth Johnson's article on "The Incomprehensibility of God and the Image of God Male and Female."[96] She brought the classical doctrine of God's incomprehensibility to intersect with the theological proposal, arising from the experience of women today, to image God male and female. She analyzed three approaches to the use of female imagery for God. The "traits" and "dimensions" approaches she judged inadequate, while the "equivalent imaging of God male and female" she felt held the best promise for both the renewal of the doctrine of God and the liberation of humans.

Even more broadly influential on my theology is Johnson's award-winning book *She Who Is: The Mystery of God in Feminist Theological Discourse.*[97] It is a profound, creative, imaginative contribution to the endless question, how may we speak rightly of God? In shaping this new discourse about God, she draws on a number of key resources, in particular women's interpreted experience and a critical retrieval of elements in Scripture and the classical tradition — "building blocks for a liberating naming toward God."[98]

It is not only systematic theology that feminism has challenged to new ways. Feminist hermeneutics is significantly changing the face of biblical studies.[99] Beginning with exegesis, feminist interpretation highlights neglected texts (e.g., depictions of the Deity as midwife and mother; the Hebrew midwives with whom the Exodus originates) and re-examines familiar ones (e.g., Genesis 2–3, revealing equality rather than male domination/female subordination). Then the contours and content of a feminist biblical theology begin to emerge: a creation theology that undercuts patriarchy; the presence and absence of the female in Scripture; differences between the orthodoxy of the establishment and the religion of the people; the Bible itself subverting androcentric idolatry in language for God; rejection of facile formulations and dogmatic positions; the entire Bible as authoritative, though not necessarily prescriptive.

Without subscribing to every feminist position, I have no hesitation in asserting that Scripture and theology are increasingly richer for the new face with which our sisters have gifted them. What amazes me is that for 19 centuries Catholic scholarship searched largely without them in our efforts to grasp what God was saying then and what God might be saying now. Another strong if needless proof that theologians and biblicists as well as the magisterium are in large measure captive to their culture.[100]

Hans Urs von Balthasar

In the twilight of my existence I regret that I have not taken greater advantage of Hans Urs von Balthasar. Not only because this incredibly learned and profound Swiss theologian has produced a massive trilogy unparalleled in our century. More importantly for me, here is a theologian who "restored 'beauty' to the heart of the theological enterprise. For the first part of the trilogy [*Herrlichkeit* (*The Glory of the Lord*)] views God's revelation 'aesthetically': under the form of the beautiful."[101]

> The revelation of the glory of God on the face of Christ recapitulates and transforms all the intimations of beauty found in nature and history and enraptures the beholder. The believer's proper response is neither demonstration nor defense, but worship and contemplation. Balthasar's stated aim is to provide "a kneeling theology," whose poles are "adoration and sanctity, or love of God and neighbor."
>
> This reforging of the links between theology and spirituality, between study and sanctity, is what makes Balthasar's thought so compelling. Yet it does not entail any retreat from the world, any lessening of commitment to action. . . . His theology allows no simplistic separation between orthodoxy and orthopraxis, contemplation and commitment. Rather, "the deeper that action is meant to penetrate, the deeper must be the contemplation that precedes and follows it."[102]

THREE

From Luther to Paul VI
Isolation and Ecumenism

Ecumenism has been a significant part of my priestly and human existence. But my involvement was a very gradual insertion, influenced by historical factors — situations, events, people — that were part of my theological environment. For till mid-century, perhaps till 1962–65, Roman Catholicism was perched at best on the edge, the periphery, of the ecumenical movement, the struggle for the unity of Christ's Church. After all, did not we Romans already possess, imperfectly perhaps but surely fundamentally, the unity for which Jesus prayed in John 17? The sects — not "churches" strictly speaking — could achieve genuine Christian unity only by a "return to Rome," by coming home.

Such, on the whole, was my introduction to ecumenism. As early as 1919, a Protestant committee visited Pope Benedict XV to extend an invitation to the Catholic Church to take part in the Lausanne Conference on Faith and Order; in 1926 Episcopal Bishop Charles Henry Brent went personally for the same purpose. On both occasions the visitors were received with courtesy and friendliness, but the answer was clearly no.[1]

Four Roman documents from the first half of the twentieth century exemplified for me the official Catholic position. On July 8, 1927, the Holy Office issued a response to a question either sent to it or formulated by it: "May Catholics take part in or promote congresses, meetings, lectures, or societies which have for purpose to unite into a religious federation all who in any sense whatever call themselves Christians?" The reply: an unconditioned no.[2] On January 6, 1928, in his encyclical *Mortalium animos,* Pius XI forbade all participation in the ecumenical movement; he called it "panchristian."[3] Why?

> The reasons are: the postulates of the union deny that the *una sancta* already visibly exists in our world and affirm that she must be brought into existence; it is implicitly affirmed that

66

union can be achieved without unity of doctrine; the Catholic Church is not considered to be the Church of Christ but one of many communities in that Church, which is not coextensive with her. These postulates involve relativism of dogma, modernism in theology, and indifferentism in theology. Any meeting or association based on such principles contradicts the total faith of Catholicism, so that no Catholic can in logic or charity take part in them.[4]

On June 5, 1948, shortly before the World Council of Churches met in Amsterdam, the Holy Office issued a *monitum* (admonition) to the effect that, in harmony with canon 1315 #3 of the Code of Canon Law, no Catholic may take part, without leave of the Holy See, in "mixed congresses of Catholics and non-Catholics" wherein matters of faith are discussed. The general prohibition then focused on " 'ecumenical' congresses, as they are called," and the *monitum* went on to forbid "common services of worship."[5]

Did the *monitum* forbid all manner of intellectual discussion between Catholics and non-Catholics? An instruction of the Holy Office dated December 20, 1949, attempted to cut through differing interpretations of the *monitum*.[6] Reunion means acceptance of Catholicism by non-Catholics. Nevertheless, current non-Catholic ecumenism is a joy to Catholics and "an inducement to lend their assistance to all who are sincerely seeking the truth, by entreating light and strength for them from God in fervent prayer."

The instruction contemplated two types of meetings: (1) open, bringing together Catholics and non-Catholics to discuss their credal views and differences on a basis of equality and reciprocal freedom; (2) closed, restricted to representative theologians of different denominations. Since such meetings involve ambiguity — potential good for Catholic witness, danger of fusionism and indifferentism — they demand episcopal organization, oversight, and supervision on the local level, permission of the Holy See if interdiocesan, national, or international.

International Conference on Patristic Studies

The admonition and instruction touched my life in 1951. That year an intriguing dream of Oxford's F. L. Cross came to fruition: the quadrennial International Conference on Patristic Studies, a gathering of scholars from East and West and from all Christian denominations, to share their expertise and projects. What is not generally known is that the dream almost turned into a nightmare.

Invited to participate in the first assembly, I received the requisite Jesuit permission from the provincial superior of the New York Province, Father John McMahon. Soon after, I discovered (I do not recall how) that the Holy Office had indicated that, since this was an international ecumenical meeting on religious/theological issues, it fell under the mantle of the 1948 admonition and the 1949 instruction: Permission to attend had to come from the Holy See. Assisted ably by Jesuit John Reed, professor of canon law at Woodstock, I framed a formal petition to the Holy Office. Weeks passed; no word from Rome. As the September date drew near, Father McMahon graciously allowed me to fly to Oxford in expectation of Roman approval, but I was not to take part without such express permission.

The evening of the inaugural reception brought hundreds of scholars to Christ Church, Oxford — a breath-taking gathering of some of the finest patristic scholars in the world. But in the midst of this unique emotional assemblage of recent "enemies," there was Catholic confusion. Before my arrival, most Catholics had no idea that anyone needed anyone's permission; few if any suspected that the Holy Office was involved. Priest/scholars from the diocese of Birmingham that embraces Oxford were under the impression that they needed only their own ordinary's permission. A French Jesuit suggested that he and I cable Jesuit headquarters in Rome asking, "What do we do?" (I told him I had done a number of imprudent things in my life; this would have been "too much.") Heythrop College, then the house of philosophy and theology for the English Province of the Society of Jesus, had indeed cabled for permission for a handful of its faculty to attend, giving names. The answer: Maurice Bévenot (not on the request list) may attend. Maurice had, I believe, attended the World Council's Amsterdam meeting as a Vatican observer; he was safe. Dr. Cross had tried to explain to the Holy Office that this conference was concerned with the facts of history, was not a theological debate. No success. With my own provincial's instructions on participation, I could only leave Christ Church sadly and spend the next few days isolated in London. Four years later, typically, the Holy Office had nothing to say about the Second Oxford Conference.

That 1955 gathering, again at storied Christ Church, captivated me — present this time in the flesh for all sessions. A youthful 41, I saw, listened to, pressed flesh with "the greats" of patristics:

Aland and Daniélou, Molland and Mohrmann and Marrou, Quispel and Capelle, Bouyer and Boyer and Botte, Grillmeier and R. M. Grant, Jouassard and Sagnard, Hanson and Metzger, Beryl Smalley and Ortiz de Urbina. These and a host of others gave the conference its unmistakable air of distinction and internationalism. Ten major addresses, 40 papers with open discussion, and 115 shorter "communications" were crowded into four rather breathless days as summer passed over into autumn.

Less familiar, even to patristic scholars, was another meeting that took place September 25, the Sunday after the international event closed. On the initiative of Bruno Brinkman, S.J., the Jesuit delegates to the Oxford assembly were invited to spend the weekend at Heythrop College, situated some 16 miles to the north of Oxford.[7]

From Belgium came George Dejaivfe, director of the Museum Lessianum, and Roger Leys, author of an important book on the image of God in Gregory of Nyssa; from Holland, P. Smulders, professor of patrology at the Canisianum. Rome gave Charles Boyer, acknowledged authority on Augustine; I. Hausherr, specialist in the mysticism of the Eastern churches; Ignacio Ortiz de Urbina, known for his work on the Nicene Creed and early Eastern Mariology; and Joseph P. Smith of the Oriental Institute, translator of Irenaeus' *Proof of the Apostolic Preaching* for the Ancient Christian Writers series. Frenchmen very much in evidence were F. Graffin, editor of the series of texts and translations Patrologia orientalis; Claude Mondésert, editor of the still youthful Sources chrétiennes; Jean Daniélou, who had already begun to illumine the typology of Christian antiquity and done so much to rehabilitate Origen; and Edouard des Places, who edited Plato's *Laws* for the Budé series. Spain was represented by Santiago Morillo of the Centro Estudios Orientales in Madrid; Germany by Heinrich Bacht and Aloys Grillmeier, the learned editors of the monumental three volumes on the Council of Chalcedon. Three Americans were on hand: Edgar R. Smothers, then preparing an edition of Chrysostom's homilies on Acts; George P. Klubertanz, professor of philosophy at St. Louis University; and myself. The English Province was well served by Thomas Corbishley, master of Campion Hall, Oxford; Anthony A. Stephenson, whose articles in *Theological Studies* had occasioned much favorable comment; and several members of the Heythrop faculty, including Maurice Bévenot of Cyprian fame and J. H. Crehan, expert on early Christian baptism and the Creed.

At Heythrop we reviewed what had transpired in each of the 40 sessions at Oxford on ten themes: biblical exegesis, the Constantinian epoch, Christology, monastic origins, early liturgy, Hellenistic philosophy, literary criticism, Judaism, spirituality, and patristic ideals and their contemporary significance. What was even more striking than the sheer review, I still recall, was the air of unfeigned, uncompelled charity that dominated our discussion. Despite the fact that three languages — French, German, and English — were in constant use, and at least eight nationalities were represented, there was in the group an absence of tension, a pervasive feeling of oneness, that was genuinely touching and would have delighted the heart of Ignatius. I felt that the English Jesuits merited a warm word of commendation for the spontaneity and relative ease with which they shifted so often to the French language.

That same evening five reports proved uncommonly stimulating. Daniélou sketched the extensive, enviable activity of French Jesuits in patristics. Grillmeier surveyed the significant accomplishments of the Society in Germany. I summarized the relatively scant contribution of American Jesuits to the understanding of early Christianity. Corbishley pointed out that in the context of English Catholicism — where the intellectual activity of the Society was necessarily engaged, in great measure, though not exclusively, with the popular and semipopular presentation of the faith — the notable achievements of scholars like Bévenot and Crehan gave solid hope for a patristic future. Ortiz de Urbina gave an encouraging report on Jesuit patristic efforts in Spain, despite the loss suffered in the death of José Madoz. At that time Spain had given several patrologists to Rome, notably Ortiz himself and the promising Antonio Orbe, who has since more than fulfilled expectations, e.g., on Irenaeus and in Valentinian studies within Christian Gnosticism.

I must confess that two resolutions taken at Heythrop were never implemented: (1) formation of an Institute of Jesuit Patristic Studies (suggested by Grillmeier), a center or clearing house for Jesuit efforts, to avoid duplication and facilitate collaboration; (2) a substantial volume (my suggestion) covering rather exhaustively the patristic notion of tradition, a cooperative effort of ten or more Jesuit patrologists, to be published simultaneously in at least four languages: French, German, English, and Spanish.

· Ecumenical Activity in the United States

For almost two decades it was my good fortune to be involved officially in matters ecumenical, specifically in relation to non-Roman Christians. The first small but important beginnings go back to the '60s: From 1962 to 1970 I was a member of the Baltimore Archdiocesan Commission for Christian Unity, the first such commission to be set up in the States. From 1965 to 1976 I was part of the U.S. Dialogue Group, Lutheran-Roman Catholic Conversations. From 1968 to 1976 I was graced with membership in the Faith and Order Commission of the World Council of Churches; from 1971 to 1975, in the Faith and Order Commission of the National Council of Churches. From 1968 to 1973 I was a consultor to the Holy See's Secretariat for Christian Unity. I was the first president of the North American Academy of Ecumenists (1967–70) and, I believe, the first Catholic to be elected president of the American Theological Society (1974–75). From 1965 to 1980 I was privileged to be a member of the Academic Council that set up the Ecumenical Institute for Advanced Theological Study in Jerusalem (Tantur), a highly imaginative undertaking that owes its existence and prosperity in largest measure to the diplomacy, persistence, and financial resourcefulness of the then president of the University of Notre Dame, Theodore M. Hesburgh, C.S.C.

The result? A new way of doing theology. Prior to the '60s, my theological contact with Protestants was utterly impersonal: I met them in textbooks, as adversaries to our theses in theology, rarely read them, knew their positions from summary Catholic presentations. Meeting them in the flesh, particularly in the Lutheran-Catholic Dialogue, was something of a shock. For the first time, I was genuinely struck by the realization that there are Protestants smarter than I am!

There was Arthur Carl Piepkorn, professor of systematic theology at Concordia Seminary in St. Louis, who was to suffer so intensely from Missouri Synod crises. Ecumenism was lodged in his genes. He told me that, as he grew up, one devotion within his family was the rosary, though understandably with some "mysteries" different from the official Roman Catholic version. Arthur Carl came to each session with a bottomless satchel of Lutheran and Catholic source books, from which he constantly quoted verbatim *as he was reaching for them*. There was Warren Quanbeck, professor of systematic theology at Luther Theological Seminary in St. Paul, a genial Protestant observer at Vatican II who returned from the council with high respect for the proceedings and a barrelful of Roman limericks. There was John Reumann, professor of New Testament at the Lutheran Seminary in Philadelphia, whose NT dialogues with Jesuit Joseph Fitzmyer and with Sulpician Raymond Brown were ceaseless sources of information and delight. There was Joseph Sittler, professor of theology at the University of Chicago Divinity School, whose open exchanges with John Courtney Murray were fascinating models of the art of literate conversation. There was cochair Paul Empie, general secretary of the U.S.A. National Committee of the Lutheran World Federation, the delightful gadfly who kept us from flying into the theological blue yonder, always had the Christian people in view. Empie, like Piepkorn and Quanbeck, Sittler and Murray, died much too early.

Here was ecumenical dialogue at its most theological — made possible because all the participants were theologians or Scripture scholars or church historians. And each subject of conversation — e.g., baptism, Eucharist, ministry, papal primacy — was offered to the outside world in a volume that contained the formal papers, a common statement, and statements by each of the two groups. A fine example of the closer understanding effected by such dialogue can be found in the fourth published volume, *Eucharist and Ministry.* Among the "Reflections of the Lutheran Participants" we read in bold type:

> As Lutherans, we joyfully witness that in theological dialogue with our Roman Catholic partners we have again seen clearly a fidelity to the proclamation of the gospel and the administration of the sacraments which confirms our historic conviction that the Roman Catholic church is an authentic church of our Lord Jesus Christ. For this reason we recommend to those who have appointed us that through appropriate channels the participating Lutheran churches be urged to declare formally their judgment that the ordained Ministers of the Roman Catholic church are engaged in a valid Ministry of the gospel, announcing the gospel of Christ and administering the sacraments of faith as their chief responsibilities, and that the body and blood of our Lord Jesus Christ are truly present in their celebrations of the sacrament of the altar.[8]

Among the "Reflections of the Roman Catholic Participants" we read, again in bold type:

> As Roman Catholic theologians, we acknowledge in the spirit of Vatican II that the Lutheran communities with which we have been in dialogue are truly Christian churches, possessing the elements of holiness and truth that mark them as organs of grace and salvation. Furthermore, in our study we have found serious defects in the arguments customarily used against the

validity of the eucharistic Ministry of the Lutheran churches. In fact, we see no persuasive reason to deny the possibility of the Roman Catholic church recognizing the validity of this Ministry. Accordingly we ask the authorities of the Roman Catholic church whether the ecumenical urgency flowing from Christ's will for unity may not dictate that the Roman Catholic church recognize the validity of the Lutheran Ministry and, correspondingly, the presence of the body and blood of Christ in the eucharistic celebrations of the Lutheran churches.[9]

One of the (not unexpected) frustrations of the Lutheran-Catholic Dialogue is that such recommendations are not often acted upon by higher authorities. Still, the recommendations are there for all to see — in bold type. A second frustration, as I experienced it, is that the theological discussions only rarely get translated for and into the parishes. If theology is the Church's ceaseless effort to understand ever more clearly and profoundly what God has said in the past and what God is saying now, our leaders and our people are not served adequately when the conclusions of competent and committed Christians-in-dialogue are overlooked, ignored, or simply unknown.

Gustave Weigel

For all my debt to Protestant ecumenists, the ecumenist I admired most, whose friendship I was particularly privileged to share at old Woodstock in Maryland, was Jesuit Gustave Weigel (1906–64). It began in 1948, when Gus came to teach at Woodstock. He had enjoyed an uncommonly fruitful apostolate in Chile from 1937, after completion of his doctoral studies at the Gregorian University in Rome.[10] Not only did his leadership at the Catholic University of Santiago help to revitalize the Church in Chile; his contacts and friendships were many and broad: with the American ambassador to Chile, Claude G. Bowers, who wrote that Gus had "become an institution in Chile"; with the Chilean hierarchy; with priests; with all manner of laity. Still, there was a good deal of tension, of jealousy among some Chilean Jesuits over El Gringo, who carried on his apostolate with such unaccustomed freedom. On a visit to the States, he received a letter dated January 17, 1948, from Father Vincent McCormick, American assistant to the Father General, John Janssens. The letter read in part: "Our Superiors in Chile do not wish you to return ... because they do not approve of your method of conduct."[11]

Although Gus never aired his reactions in public, the bitterness in his heart comes through in one paragraph of a letter he wrote to a Chilean friend, Alberto Hurtado, recently beatified:

> You see that I am very bitter.... The dirty thing that was done will never be right as far as I am concerned. God in His own wisdom knows what He is doing and I have faith in Him — but only God can make good come from evil. The men who do the evil must pay, even to the last centavo. I am not interested that they pay; I do not wish to see them suffer. I have suffered too much in this whole question and I have no desire that others go through all this.[12]

Santiago's loss was Woodstock's gain. For years I shared the same third-floor corridor at old Woodstock College in Maryland with Gus Weigel and John Courtney Murray: 15 years with Gus, 21 with John. Similar they were, but hardly the same. Kindred spirits indeed: fascinated by life and in love with ideas; at home in an impressive number of intellectual disciplines and at ease with non-Romans and unbelievers; powerful rhetoricians and profound but witty conversationalists. Still, quite different: Gus of the peasant frame, John of the distinguished gait; Gus the "quick read" and intuitor, John the tireless scholar; Gus the descendant of Plato and fascinated by Paul Tillich, John the heir of Aquinas and captivated by Bernard Lonergan; Gus the more earthy, John the eagle soaring. Gus dead in a bathtub, John in a taxicab!

Together with colleagues like ecclesiologist Avery Dulles and biblicist Joseph Fitzmyer, they lent Woodstock an intellectual prestige then unmatched among Catholic seminaries and schools of theology. Besides, Murray and Weigel played prominent parts at Vatican II — Murray as an official *peritus,* Weigel especially as translator and interpreter for American Protestant observers — and infused unaccustomed vitality into a hesitant, suspicious, suspected Catholic ecumenism.

In relation to Vatican II, Weigel's activity was puzzling. Before the council opened, as consultant to the Secretariat for Promoting Christian Unity, he was assigned to a subcommission studying the priesthood of the faithful and the role of the laity in the Church — a topic that included religious freedom and religious tolerance. But Gus found the meetings frustrating. He did not like working in groups, and he felt that the conservatives were powerful enough to assure the failure of the council. As friend Murray wrote, "Not for him was the bruising business of composing a text in collaboration with other minds. I chided him, for instance, for his disinclination to put an American hand to the drawing up of the two pre-conciliar texts on religious freedom. He simply remained disinclined."[13]

Theologically Gus Weigel was not a trail blazer; ecumenically he was a Catholic pioneer. His ecclesiology was quite conservative and traditional, his approach to non-Catholic Christians largely liberal and engagingly human. As his biographer Patrick Collins has pointed out,

> Weigel himself was aware that his work was transitional, that others would come after him to carry the movement on to more advanced stages, and that his own part in the work would be simply taken for granted. Though ecumenism continues, especially among theologians in dialogue, the spirit of newness and hope that accompanied the rise of the movement in this country has for the most part faded. It is, then, not surprising that few young people remember the one whose deep, lovable humanity and profound Christian faith were largely responsible for first bridging the gaps between Protestants and Catholics in this country.... [14]

Yes, we desperately need Weigel's realistic stress on convergence rather than conversion (unlikely) or compromise (unacceptable); his utter trust in God as ultimately the architect of unity; his total gift of self to the other whoever he or she might be; his humble acceptance of human limitation, of deep frustration, of temporary defeat. I recall the delight he took in Thomas Carlyle's remark on Lady Margaret Fuller's dictum that she accepted the universe: "Gad! She'd better." And yet he was not a fatalist or a quietist. You do not accept the universe, he insisted, if you do not accept it as dynamic, in evolution; if you do not move with it, help it to move; if you do not blend necessity with freedom, in a humility that recognizes limitation without being crushed by it. His life reveals, in Avery Dulles' words, "a talented, energetic man in a hurry, quick to make judgments of persons and issues, always interesting, often wrong but often uncannily right."[15]

Carl Henry, gifted editor of the fundamentalist fortnightly *Christianity Today*, recaptured Gus uncommonly well when he wrote several weeks after his dear friend's unexpected death:

Father Weigel and this writer attended major ecumenical assemblies and conferences in the role of observer. But one meeting with him stands out, a simple luncheon in a modest Washington restaurant. We had spoken frankly of our own religious pilgrimages and had exchanged theological agreements and differences. Then suddenly, at a point of important dogmatic difference, Dr. Weigel reached a hand across the table and clasped mine. Calling me by name, he said, "I love you." The editor of *Christianity Today* has met scores of Protestant theologians and philosophers of many points of view. None ever demonstrated as effectively as Gustave Weigel that the pursuit of truth must never be disengaged from the practice of love.[16]

Vatican II

As for myself, I came early to a broad conviction about the significance of the Second Vatican Council not only for Roman Catholics but for religion and reality outside our frontiers. The council was significant, I concluded, because it inserted (or reinserted) the Catholic Church into history, into Christendom, and into the world.[17]

The council inserted Catholicism into *history;* for on the whole it reveals a shift from classicism to historical consciousness. John Courtney Murray captured the difference with admirable lucidity and phrased it with remarkable brevity:

The meaning of these two terms would require lengthy explanation, both historical and philosophical. Suffice it to say here that classicism designates a view of truth which holds objective truth, precisely because it is objective, to exist "already out there now" (to use Bernard Lonergan's descriptive phrase). Therefore, it also exists apart from its possession by anyone. In addition, it exists apart from history, formulated in propositions that are verbally immutable. If there is to be talk of development of doctrine, it can only mean that the truth, remaining itself unchanged in its formulation, may find different applications in the contingent world of historical change. In contrast, historical consciousness, while holding fast to the nature of truth as objective, is concerned with the possession of truth, with man's affirmations of truth, with the understanding contained in these affirmations, with the conditions — both circumstantial and subjective — of understanding and affirmation, and therefore with the historicity of truth and with progress in the grasp and penetration of what is true.[18]

In the case of the council, historical consciousness means an acceptance of the fact that in no single facet of her existence is the Church of Christ a sort of Platonic idea serenely suspended in midair; a recognition of the fact that in every phase of her pilgrim life the Church is inescapably involved in the ebb and flow of history. Not only in the external forms of her worship, but in her inner grasp on God's revelation; not only in accidentals and at the outer edge of her life, but in essentials and at the inner core of her being. It is a rejection of the council's most insidious enemy — not Curialism or triumphalism, not Romanism or reactionism, but what Michael Novak in an inspired moment called "nonhistorical orthodoxy," an orthodoxy "suspended, as it were, outside of history."[19]

Nonhistorical orthodoxy claims to be not only one theology among many but "the wholly perfect and absolute expression of faith."[20] It "combines triumphalism about the glories of the Church with pessimism about the contemporary world."[21] It "encourages loyalty to the ideal Church, without worrying about how to make the actual Church efficacious in the present world.... The order of fact, history, is the enemy...."[22]

It was, and is, my conviction that the most significant struggle from the opening of the council to its close was the struggle between nonhistorical orthodoxy and the effort to situate the Church in the totality of her existence at the heart of history. And it is my contention that in large measure the council moved from the mentality of classicism that has dominated the Church's past to a historical consciousness that will be her irreversible future. The proof lies primarily in the Pastoral Constitution on the Church in the Modern World, as well as in the Declaration on Religious Freedom, of which John Murray was the principal architect.

The Freedom decree had for achievement, as Murray delighted to phrase it, that it brought the Church into the nineteenth century, "abreast of the consciousness of civilized mankind."[23] And yet, it is of incalculable import for her *future.* Doctrinally, it raises to a new pitch of urgency the issue of development. If the mentality of classicism, with its emphasis on immutable truth somewhere out there, seemed to leave little room for real change, for genuine evolution, does historical consciousness leave any room for the irreversible? Specifically with reference to religious freedom, has Vatican II done no more than discard transient, fugitive elements in the tradition, or is it more faithful to history to affirm that the council discarded the tradition? Not easy to answer.

Second, Vatican II inserted the Catholic Church into *Christendom.* It set Catholicism squarely within the ongoing movement toward unity, and it suggested a vision of ecumenical theology that was revolutionary. Here two documents were crucial: the Constitution on the Church and the Decree on Ecumenism; but in both the basic theological insight is Vatican's explicit recognition of non-Roman congregations as churches or ecclesial communities.[24]

The Constitution on the Church seems to speak literally of bonds with *individual* non-Catholic Christians. The official *relatio,* however, makes it clear beyond dispute that the expression "within their own churches or ecclesial communities" was included for a quite specific reason: to reveal the council's conviction that the bonds of union previously mentioned (e.g., Scripture, religious zeal, living faith, baptism, and perhaps other sacraments), these elements held in common, look not only to individuals but to the communities of non-Roman Christians precisely as communities. And this conciliar conviction the Decree on Ecumenism confirms.

A nuance, yes; but a historic nuance. It gave a magisterial *coup de grâce* to a stance that had consistently characterized Catholic thinking on Protestants and Protestantism. Put perhaps too simply, the position came down to this. The grace of God is undeniably operative outside the visible structure of Roman Catholicism. It is there for any perceptive person to see. There are Protestants who put Catholics to shame: in their total commitment to Christ, in their love for God's Word and God's children, in their anguished quest for peace on earth and justice for all, in their willingness to starve and burn and die for the gospel. God's grace is there; but (so the thesis went) it touches these Christians as individuals, not in any sense because they are living members of the Lutheran *Church,* of the Presbyterian *Church,* of the Methodist *Church.* Quite the contrary. The striking thing is that God's grace is operative in these good people, in these love-laden Christians, *despite* their adherence to heresy, *despite* the fact that they have in good faith become part of a community whose existence objectively contradicts God's saving will, the divine redemptive design for God's people.

Given that basic premise — Protestant churches exist contrary to God's will — the conclusion seemed to many of us before the council rigorous and inevitable: Protestantism as an institution and Protestantism as a ministry are rather a hindrance than a help to the salvific activity of God's Spirit. Not that Protestants have not played a genuinely prophetic role while remaining Protestant. Figures like Wesley and Kierkegaard, Adolphe Monod and Louis Meyer, Karl Barth and Emil Brunner were convincing evidence to the contrary. But all this could be, and was, explained on an individualistic level, in isolation from the errant community: God's Spirit whispers where it is God's will to whisper. Grace-filled individuals? Of course; any other conclusion would defy everyday experience, would put proud limits to a God who will not be circumscribed by humans. But grace-filled communities? Such pluralism seemed to contradict the divine design for salvation, the one community to which the saving Christ has committed his saving word and his saving sacraments.

This attitude within preconciliar Catholicism, not altogether universal but devastatingly widespread — this attitude in its naked, unrefined form is incompatible with Vatican II. A remarkable, unexpected development emerged from the council. The grace of Christ is at work, richly and incessantly, not only within Protestants but within Protestantism, not only within Anglicans but within Anglicanism, not only within the Orthodox but within Orthodoxy.

This nuanced attitude of contemporary Catholicism toward separated Christians proved to be of far-reaching theological and practical import. In the first place, it was the profound basis for the kind of dialogue envisioned in the Decree on Ecumenism: dialogue not merely between Christians but primarily between the *churches* — dialogue (hold your Catholic breath) "where each can deal with the other on an equal footing."[25] Second, it was the profound basis for an authentically ecumenical theology, where separated Christians are no longer in the first instance adversaries of particular doctrines but partners in a joint enterprise, co-operators in a common concern — the effort of the Christian intelligence to achieve, under grace, an ever-deeper understanding of the faith once committed to the saints.

Now this development affected, to a critical degree, my priestly/theological existence. Once I recognized such grace-filled communities, I could disregard non-Roman theology only at the risk of impoverishing my own. Not simply because of the charismatic element so evident in more prominent prophets, the Barths and Brunners, the Tillichs and Niebuhrs, the Minears and Haroutunians, the Temples and Butlers, the Outlers and Lindbecks, the Florovskys and Schmemanns, the individuals who graced non-Roman pulpits and chairs of theology. Not simply their remarkable erudition and personal insights. I dared not disregard these prophets precisely because their prophetic voices echoed from within a graced *community*. It was henceforth the communities I had to take seriously — and precisely as a theologian. I mean the various communities in the totality of their ecclesial existence: the graced word from the pulpit and the graced faith in the pews, the graced life of the housewife and the graced mind of the theologian — and all these as vital facets that fashion and are fashioned by a community of grace and of salvation.

Further, it was these communities, in the totality of their ecclesial reality, that *every* Roman Catholic had to take seriously from 1965 on. It would no longer do to say, "Some of my best friends are Protestants," much as this might represent a thaw in a traditionally glacial situation. It simply is not enough — not theological enough, not ecumenical enough, not Christian enough, not Catholic enough. Roman love must go out to the non-Roman community in its communal aspect. Not that with Vatican II Methodist theology or even Methodist faith had suddenly become indistinguishable from Catholic theology or Catholic faith, but because the community that is Methodism is alive with the presence of Christ, is a grace-filled community where the redemptive purposes of a God who wants all men and women to be saved are being worked out through the outpouring of the Holy Spirit.

Obviously, with Vatican's nuance a serious theological issue had reared its head. How can the Catholic theologian reconcile with his or her traditional understanding of "one true Church" the recognition by the council of other Christian churches, not simply as sociological phenomena but as ecclesial realities, not primarily as obstructions to the redemptive activity of God in Christ but as structures splendidly fruitful for the grace that saves?

Here a struggle commenced within me — intellectual and emotional. For I too was a child, a product, of my time, my education, my environment: "One true Church" = Roman Catholic Church. In the '60s Catholic theology, confronted with a significant development in the Catholic vision of the Church, had only begun its fundamental function: investigation, penetration, clarification, synthesis. Catholic ecclesiology had to confront five apparent antitheses that emerged from Vatican II: (1) "the Church of Christ *is* the Catholic Church" vs. "the Church of Christ *subsists in* the Catholic Church"; (2) institution vs. communion within the one reality that is the Church; (3) membership in the Church vs. various degrees of incorporation into the Church; (4) incorporation into the Church vs. incorporation into Christ; (5) the Church as holy vs. the Church as sinful and always in need of reform.

In a sense, the critical question for a Catholic is: Why remain a Catholic? Put simply — perhaps all too simply — I remain a Catholic because I believe, am convinced, that on the level of institutional existence — in the areas of revealed doctrine, of worship (including sacraments), and of moral principle — the Roman Catholic Church has preserved *more perfectly* than any other Christian community the will of Christ for his Church. Is it possible that at any given moment another community may be living more perfectly the twin law of love — love God above all else, love your sisters and brothers like other selves — the love that is the ultimate purpose of the institution? Of course. Hence the conflicts that inevitably arise within any Christian community: Do I stay because of the institutional factor and work toward deeper love from within the system, or do I leave because "I can do no other"?

In any event, the historic nuance of Vatican II made possible the remarkably open and progressive attitude that characterized the last paragraph of the Decree on Ecumenism: "This most sacred synod urgently desires that the initiatives of the sons [and daughters?] of the Catholic Church, joined with the initiatives of [our] separated brethren, go forward without obstructing in any manner the ways of divine Providence and without prejudging the future inspirations of the Holy Spirit."[26]

A third facet of fundamental significance: Vatican II inserted the Catholic Church into the *modern world*. For the first half of my life, a widespread Catholic attitude was a "fortress mentality." Catholicism was an island beset and besieged by the modern world. This modern world was in a sense good, as all of God's creation is in a sense good. But it was a dangerous thing, doubly dangerous because so seductive — in its unrepentant state a stumbling block to the Christian.

This pessimistic outlook was not utterly unreasonable. On the political level, the nineteenth century saw the movement away from the sacral conception of society and state to the secular conception — a movement whose term in Continental Europe was the laicized state of rationalist or atheist inspiration. On the intellectual level, the nineteenth and twentieth centuries saw the movement away from classicism to historical consciousness; but the concrete term of this movement as it confronted the Church was Modernism, described by Pius X as a "conglomeration of all heresies," with the objective character of truth part of the wreckage. In Scripture, there was the movement away from the historical Jesus, away from the historicity of the Gospels, away from the inerrancy of the Book. In the sciences, evolution seemed to negate the creative activity of God. And so on and so forth, in economics and the arts, in education and psychiatry — all the significant movements appeared to threaten or to disregard the one true God and the one true Church.

What the Catholic Church (with the exception of a handful of individuals) did not do was in each instance the very thing that was demanded. I mean a work of discrimination: to discern the signs of the times, in order to discover, beneath the transitory historical forms assumed by each new movement, the valid dynamisms that were at work. One example. In the movement away from the sacrality of society and state, the true underlying direction was toward a proper and legitimate secularity. But what appeared on the surface was not progress but simply revolution.[27]

I am not asserting that from Leo XIII to Pius XII the Church had not even begun to discern the signs of the times, the deeper currents of history. It had indeed begun. But before John XXIII and Vatican II the work of discernment was partial, fragmentary, focused on isolated facets of the various problems. In 1962 the time was ripe for two singular developments: (1) an unqualified affirmation of the Church's *love* for the world outside her institutional limits, and of her yearning to *serve* it; (2) an effort to discern, beneath transitory historical forms, the valid dynamisms at work in the *entire* world.

To my mind, no document affirms this development more forcibly or more emotionally than the last section of Paul VI's address opening the second session of the council on September 29, 1963. He was addressing himself to the fourth aim of the council: "The Church will build a bridge to the contemporary world." He noted that the conciliar fathers, in response to John XXIII's open-door policy, had unexpectedly determined "to treat no longer of your own limited affairs but rather those of the world, no longer to conduct a dialogue among yourselves but rather to open one with the world." He confessed that he was tempted to be frightened, to be saddened, to defend and condemn; for he was a realist, and his eyes were not blind to the (then) Iron Curtain, to the spread of atheism, to the emptiness, sadness, and despair in so many human hearts. He was tempted to dwell pessimistically on these aspects of contemporary society, but he refused to: "Not now," he said — not while love was flooding his heart and the heart of the Church assembled in council. Rather he went on to say: "Let the world know this: the Church looks at the world with profound understanding, with sincere admiration, and with the sincere intention not of conquering it, but of serving it; not of despising it, but of appreciating it; not of condemning it, but of strengthening and saving it." Paul went on to address "some categories of persons with particular solicitude": the poor and needy, the suffering and sorrowing; men and women of culture and learning, scientists, artists; workers; leaders of nations; "the new generation of youth desirous of living and expressing themselves; the new peoples now coming to self-awareness, independence, and civil organization; the innumerable men and women who feel isolated in a troubled society that has no message for their spirit." To all he offered words of hope, encouragement, confidence, comfort; to all he presented the Church as a servant.[28]

On finishing, Paul "tried to read greetings in various languages. His voice was hoarse. He was emotionally drained. He read a few lines in Greek. Then he said with a tired gesture to his master of ceremonies, Archbishop Enrico Dante, *Basta!* 'Enough.' He waved aside the other pages and rose to leave. The ovation was thunderous...."[29]

It was in harmony with this vision, this Christian optimism, that the council fashioned its Constitution on the Church in the Modern World. The conciliar fathers were in large measure aware of the world's suspicion: Catholicism makes for inhumanity, for a monstrous indifference to secular interests, a callous isolation from the common cares of the world. That is why the constitution opens with the anguished sentence, "The joys and the hopes, the griefs and the anxieties of the men and women of this age, especially those who are poor or in any way afflicted, these too are the joys and hopes, the griefs and anxieties of the followers of Christ."[30]

John Courtney Murray

The Holy Spirit works in wondrous ways, unexpected ways. There I was, on a bleak spring day in 1955, standing helplessly in John Murray's room at old Woodstock College, watching him sift out the books on his shelves. *These* books would stay: They dealt with grace and the Trinity, with education or social issues, with the old humanities and the new atheism. But *those* would go — back to the Woodstock Library: They dealt with religious freedom, with church and state, with Catholicism and the American proposition.

Those would go because Murray saw no further use for them. His research was indeed incomplete, far from finished; but before he could publish further in those fields, before he could present his ideas to his peers for challenge and criticism, they would have to undergo a prior critique — in Rome. And recent experience had revealed a Rome officially and powerfully hostile to him and his ideas.

With his love for the Church of Christ and the Society of Jesus, Murray felt he could not disobey. But with his love for truth and the human person, he did not see how he could operate honestly in such chains. So he cleared his room — as he wrote later, "in symbol of retirement, which I expect to be permanent. And all other practical measures will be taken to close the door on the past ten years, leaving all their mistakenness to God."

It was a bleak day, and my heart ached as I could only stand and look and listen — and wonder. His life's work seemed a shambles. I thought of St. Francis Xavier writing in frustration from India to King John of Portugal: "It is a sort of martyrdom to . . . watch being destroyed what one has built up with so much labor."[31]

Ten years later, December 7, 1965, Pope Paul VI affixed his signature to Vatican II's Declaration on Religious Freedom (*Dignitatis humanae, DH*) — a document that carried the imprint of Murray's mind, sealed with conciliar sanction some of his most significant and controversial research, stamped with authority the work he did as "expert" at the council. About the same time, in what John told me was one of the most moving moments in his experience, he stood proud and tall at the main altar in St. Peter's with theologians of similar stature and suffering, like Yves Congar and Henri de Lubac, and by papal invitation celebrated with Paul VI the Eucharist of our reconciliation with God and one another.

DH has often been styled the council's "American document." Here we must be careful. For one thing, *DH,* approved by a definitive vote of 2,308 to 70, was an act of the universal Church. For another, it was not the product of American participants alone. Such an interpretation would overlook the crucial contributions of men like Jan Willebrands and Charles Moeller, Carlo Colombo and Yves Congar, Jérôme Hamer and Pietro Pavan, Augustin Bea and Emile Joseph De Smedt. It would forget that the most significant drafts on religious freedom set before the council emerged officially from the Secretariat for Promoting Christian Unity — a group whose competence to present texts with a theological content was disputed until John XXIII on October 22, 1962, put SPCU on the same level as the other commissions and authorized it to lay drafts and schemata before the council. Nevertheless, I have been happy to make my own the remarks of one of the document's architects, Pietro Pavan, at a symposium organized by the Woodstock Theological Center to celebrate *DH*'s tenth anniversary:

I took part in the Second Vatican Council from beginning to end. At the preparatory stage I was a member of two pontifical commissions, the Theological Commission and the Commission on the Lay Apostolate. In the four sessions...I was a *peritus*. I am therefore in a position to say with full assurance that the impact of the American episcopate — above all, all the bishops of the United States — was decisive (1) in bringing about the Declaration on Religious Freedom and (2) in ensuring that its main line of argument should be the one which it now exhibits.[32]

In fact, the religious-freedom issue would have been removed permanently from the council's agenda, had it not been for strong American intervention.[33]

When Vatican II opened, Murray was not there. In his own ironic word, he had been "disinvited." But before the second session opened, a powerful prelate intervened.[34] New York's Cardinal Francis Spellman requested of Rome that Murray be named a *peritus* ("expert"). According to the cardinal's secretary at the time, Patrick V. Ahern, the request was politely but firmly turned down by Cardinal Alfredo Ottaviani, who headed the screening committee involved. Spellman replied sharply: I would not certify Father Murray if I were not sure of his credentials and his orthodoxy. In effect he said, you are questioning my judgment. Ottaviani responded: Thank you very much; the matter has been brought again before the screening committee; unfortunately....

> Cardinal Spellman's response to this letter has vanished from the archdiocesan files, as has the other correspondence in the matter — victims, Bishop Ahern believes, of the cardinal's determination to expunge the record of unpleasantness that might "give scandal." But the bishop has no difficulty recalling the nature of the letter. "It came down to something like, 'Father Murray is going as my personal *peritus*,' he said. 'And if he doesn't go, I don't go.' Then, of course, the final reply came back to the effect that Father Murray would be most welcome. I don't think there's any doubt that Cardinal Spellman singlehandedly got Father Murray into the Council."[35]

The full story of Murray's influence on *DH* has still to be written. Early on he addressed a significant commission decisive for the fate of the religious-freedom issue — a group that included such VIPs as Ottaviani and Karl Rahner, Msgr. Joseph Fenton and Cardinal

Michael Browne (the same Browne of whom Murray said in a 1964
lecture at Georgetown University that he "proved more unsinkable
than his famous Irish cousin Molly"). He called it "a glorious victory for the Good Guys."[36] He was commissioned by the Secretariat
for Promoting Christian Unity to do an analysis of the comments
sent in by the bishops on religious freedom.[37] He fashioned preliminary drafts of the document, addressed American and other
national groups of bishops, shaped interventions for many a U.S.
bishop, eloquently interpreted the issues for reporters at the daily
press panels. His lodgings at the Casa Villanova "became the Council's intellectual crossroads. Cardinal and bishop, priest and layman,
European and American, liberal and conservative were all part of
the cast which lived, worked, prayed and talked there. 'To be anything in Rome is to be at the Villanova,' [John] Cogley wrote in
Commonweal."[38] Little wonder that Pavan has written:

> In the drafting of [the third schema — separate from the
> schema on ecumenism] as well as in subsequent redraftings
> down to the time when the Declaration *Dignitatis humanae*
> took its final shape, an outstanding part was played by John
> Courtney Murray, S.J. He was distinguished at all times for
> his unique grasp of the subject, for his wisdom, his nobility of
> mind, his loyalty to the Church, and his love of truth.[39]

And still, even during the council, Roman obstacles threatened
Murray's full participation. The courageous Redemptorist Bernard
Häring, who played so pioneering a role in the revamping of
Catholic moral theology, recently revealed a discussion, within a
subcommission of the council's Doctrinal Commission, on a draft of
the projected Declaration on Religious Freedom prior to its submission for public discussion. He reports that the task of co-ordinating
secretary fell to him and that "the subcommission did not water
down the text, but rather strengthened it."

> In view of this situation Cardinal Ottaviani, the President of
> the Doctrinal Commission, tried delaying tactics. Since the ad-
> monitions from our side accomplished nothing, we had to
> request a decisive action by Pope Paul VI that forced Cardi-
> nal Ottaviani to place the text on the table for discussion in
> the full Commission as soon as possible. For this the bishops
> brought Father Murray along. Nevertheless Ottaviani refused
> to let him speak, despite loud protests from bishops. Since I
> had been chosen as speaker for this draft, I could not be re-

fused the opportunity to speak. Ottaviani responded angrily that one did not need this whole text since there was already too much freedom in the Church. Now my patience was tested to the limits. I said: The fact that the head of the Holy Office answers thus is sufficient proof of the pressing need of this declaration and the necessity to allow the theologian whom he had so long condemned to silence the opportunity finally to speak. Ottaviani grimly relented. It was a pleasure to experience how magnificently Murray presented his viewpoint in beautifully fluent Latin and with sovereign dignity. The subsequent vote resulted in the overwhelming majority approving the strengthened text and passing it on to the Council.[40]

I introduce Murray and religious freedom into this chapter on ecumenism because unborn millions of any and no religion will never know how much their freedom is tied to this man whose pen was a powerful protest, a dramatic march, against injustice and inequality, whose research sparked and terminated in the ringing affirmation of an ecumenical council: "The right to religious freedom has its foundation" not in the Church, not in society or state, not even in objective truth, but "in the very dignity of the human person."[41] Unborn millions will never know how much the civilized dialogue they take for granted between Christian and Christian, between Christian and Jew, between Christian and unbeliever, was made possible by this man whose life was a civilized conversation. Untold Catholics will never sense that they live so gracefully in this dear land because John Murray argued so persuasively that the American proposition is quite congenial to the Catholic reality.[42]

Argued persuasively.... John Courtney Murray had a remarkably high regard for "conversation." Conversation in its original Latin sense: *conversari,* living together and talking together. This, for him, lay at the heart of a civilized society — domestic, religious, civil. Can we live with our differences? Can we exchange words for violence, ideas for insurrection? Can we make our very differences fruitful for the future?

You might say this was Murray's own life. At home — the old granite building called Woodstock College in Maryland, where Murray and his dear friend Gustave Weigel introduced this budding theologian (actually young professor of patristics) into theology's realm of religious imagination ... by conversation. In Rome — during Vatican II, in his lodgings at the Casa Villanova, which became, as I noted above, the council's "intellectual crossroads" ... through conversation. In the homes of the influential — Henry Luce, Clare Boothe Luce, Thomas Watson, Thomas Murray, Cardinals Stritch and Mooney... through conversation.

One significant theological area that in the years ahead should demand Murray's type of intelligent conversation, of persuasive argumentation, stems from *DH* itself. The declaration was, as Murray saw, "the most controversial document of the whole Council, largely because it raised with sharp emphasis the issue that lay continually below the surface of all the conciliar debates — the issue of the development of doctrine."[43] In basing religious freedom on the dignity of the human person, in discarding the post-Reformation and nineteenth-century theory of civil tolerance of false religions, in claiming from the state "nothing but freedom," in dismissing into history the legal institution of state religion, in the philosophy of society and state that undergirds the document, has Vatican II done no more than discard transient, fugitive elements in the Church's tradition, or is it more faithful to history to affirm that the Church has discarded "the tradition"?

Murray was convinced that in *DH* the council was bringing forth from the treasury of truth "a doctrine that is at once new and also in harmony with traditional teaching."[44] In so speaking, he was raising implicitly one of the most explosive questions in contemporary theology: How much discontinuity is compatible with Catholic continuity? Not, *is* discontinuity compatible, but how much? The question, I submit, cannot be answered in the abstract. The solution lies in the Church's life: Where in fact are the discontinuities, and how Catholic are they? Concretely, what is the evolution from 1832 to 1965, from Gregory XVI's *Mirari vos* to Vatican II's *Dignitatis humanae*? Is it a movement simply from obscurity to greater enlightenment, a better understanding of our genuine tradition, or must we say that, in the area of religious freedom, Catholicism now rejects what in the nineteenth century it held as "doctrine"? Here is a neuralgic issue for a doctoral candidate tearing his shaggy mane in search of a dissertation topic.

Toward the 25th anniversary of Murray's death, Catholic University theologian Joseph Komonchak described his singular gifts in terms that Murray had used of Christ responding to the challenge "Is it lawful to pay taxes to the emperor?" (Mt 22:17). Two qualities: the coldness of perfect clarity and the warmth of a love of truth.[45] "If," Komonchak concluded, "we are still striving to realize a world in which we can peacefully be both Christians and citizens, in good part we owe it to the example John Courtney Murray gave of how to place an intellect in the service of God and the church."[46]

A couple of months after Murray's death, his dear friend the political analyst Emmet John Hughes tracked down the young taxi driver who picked Murray up in Queens on the morning of August 16, 1967. Howard Klein never heard John Murray say more than "Good morning. 106 West 56th Street, if you please." Less than ten minutes later he brought Murray's body to the nearest hospital — dead on arrival. Let Hughes tell the moving story.

We drove over the route of those last frantic minutes. He patiently told me of how he felt when he saw his passenger stricken and how the tall man slowly fell over like a statue. We sat together in the front of his cab, and when he had finished all his details, he hesitated and finally said:

"Just one thing has bothered me. This was a big man, because I've heard and read about him since. But he was a Catholic all his life, of course, and lived with Catholics and was surrounded with priests, naturally. Yet the poor guy had to die with a Jew near him, nobody else. Jeez, I just hope he didn't mind."

There was only one answer to this: "Believe me," I said, "if he heard you say any such thing, he would be answering you right now: 'My dear friend, some of my best friends are Catholics — and most of my enemies.'"

He laughed — and then suddenly leaned over the front seat, looking to the back, and said smilingly: "Hey you, Father, I got a friend of yours here." He saw my puzzlement and quickly explained: "It sounds crazy, I know, but ever since that day, when I get into the cab in the morning I say hello to him, and at the end of every day I get out saying, 'Good night, Father.'" A little incredulous, I could only ask him why. "I can't tell you. I don't know what I believe. I don't even go to the synagogue much. I just have the feeling he was someone really special."[47]

He was.

My Jewish Sisters and Brothers

Quite some years ago I was startled by an affirmation of Rabbi Abraham Joshua Heschel: Much of what the Bible demands can be summed up in a single word — remember! It was then I began to discover in ancient Israel a community of faith vitalized by memory, a people that knew God by reflecting not on the mysteries of nature but on its own history. To actualize was to retain within time and space the memory and the mystery of God's saving presence. And isn't that what Christian existence is all about — a living memory? Each day we Christians memorialize, we re-present, the passion and resurrection of Jesus Christ, celebrate the death of the Lord until he comes.

Not long after, Johannes Metz compelled me to distinguish my memories. There are memories that simply make us feel good, because they glide over all that is oppressive and demanding. And there are memories that are dangerous, because they make demands on us, reveal perilous insights for today, illuminate harshly the questionable nature of things with which we have come to terms.

My Jewish memories of the far distant past make no demands on me; they are delightfully simple, free of anxiety and complexity. I grew up in a multiracial Manhattan neighborhood, unaware of the Great Gatsby and the roar of the '20s, amid Italians and Irish, Jews and Germans. Where epithets like Dago and Mick, Kike and Kraut revealed not racial animosity but lack of imagination. Where Moishe was no more responsible for the crucifixion of Christ than I for a pogrom in Poland; Moishe was my friend! Where this pre-teen sat with his German father and mother in the rear of Jacob Rosenbluth's grocery and listened to two immigrant couples swapping very human anecdotes and trading in love, breathed the garlic and onions that hung from the ceiling and guaranteed both Jew and Gentile against winter colds.

My existence as a Jesuit priest from 1941 changed all that, made for different memories, memories dangerous and demanding, memories harsh in the pitiless light they cast. True, my adult relationship with America's Jews has been episodic rather than continuous. But the episodes have invariably influenced my life profoundly. Let me muse on the most significant — in no particular order.

In March 1966, several months after the close of the Second Vatican Council, I was privileged to share in an International Theological Conference hosted by the University of Notre Dame. The conference brought together Roman Catholics, Orthodox, Protestants, Anglicans, and Jews who had worked over, prayed over, worried over, even written the council documents, to discuss what had actually happened, what was said and why, what it meant, and where it seemed to lead for the future.[48] The very litany of my fellow participants is striking: Barnabas Ahern, Christopher Butler, Carlo Colombo, Yves Congar, Henri de Lubac, Godfrey

Diekmann, Joseph Gremillion, Bernard Häring, George Higgins, François Houtart, George Lindbeck, Mark McGrath, Jorge Medina Estevez, John Meyendorff, Paul Minear, Charles Moeller, John Courtney Murray, James Norris, Albert Outler, Gerard Philips, Karl Rahner, Joseph Sittler, Thomas Stransky, Marc Tanenbaum, Roberto Tucci. Half a hundred press representatives were present; TV carried the conference to ten major cities.

It was one of the most absorbing weeks in my extended theological and human experience. But perhaps the most soul-searing presentation for me was Rabbi Tanenbaum's paper apropos of Vatican II's "Jewish declaration."[49] For, although he "welcomed the Declaration as an important contribution to improve the future relations between Catholics and Jews,"[50] he was still convinced, from his study of history, that "Fundamentally, Christianity has never made up its mind as to where it stands in terms of its common patrimony with Judaism and its daily attitudes and relationships and behavior toward Jews."[51] The single paragraph that has left an inerasable mark on my mind and heart runs as follows:

> One must confront ultimately how as recently as the past twenty-five years — in a country which, when it vaunted its great values and its great moral traditions, spoke of itself as a country of ancient Christian culture, which was in fact the seat of the Holy Roman Empire for almost a millennium beginning with Charlemagne — it was possible for millions of Christians to sit by as spectators while millions of human beings, who were their brothers and sisters, the sons of Abraham according to the flesh, were carted out to their death in the most brutal, inhuman, uncivilized ways. And one must confront as one of the terrible facts of the history of this period the conversation that took place between Adolf Hitler and two bishops in April 1933, when they began raising questions about the German policy toward the Jews and Hitler said to them, as reported in the book, *Hitler's Table-Talk,* that he was simply completing what Christian teaching and preaching had been saying about the Jews for the better part of 1,900 years. "You should turn away from them as a pest and a plague of the human race," said St. John Chrysostom, and 1,500 years later thousands of his disciples implemented his teachings, literally.[52]

Little wonder that Tanenbaum deplored "the absence in the Declaration of any note of contrition or repentance for the incredible sufferings and persecutions Jews have undergone in the Christian

West." In various declarations, he noted, the Church did ask forgiveness from Protestants, Eastern Orthodox, and Muslims, "but
not from the Jews. Many Jews, especially those who lived through
the Nazi holocaust, asked with great passion, 'How many more millions of our brothers and sisters will need to be slaughtered before
any word of contrition or repentance is heard in the seats of ancient
Christian glory?' "[53]

During the same conference a particularly revered rabbi inserted
himself into the discussion on Tanenbaum's paper. Looking for all
the world like a prophet out of the Hebrew Bible, Abraham Joshua
Heschel pleaded for dialogue in language and love I have never
forgotten:

> What divides us, what unites us? Now we disagree in law, in
> creed, in commitments that lie at the very heart of our reli-
> gious existence. We say "no" to one another in some doctrines
> essential and sacred to us. What unites us? Our being account-
> able to God, our being objects of God's concern, precious in
> his eyes. Our conceptions of what ails us may be different, but
> the anxiety is the same. The language, the imagination, the
> concretization of our hopes are different, but embarrassment
> is the same, and so is the sigh, the sorrow. And the neces-
> sity to obey? We may disagree about the ways of achieving
> fear and trembling, but the fear and trembling are the same.
> The demands are different, but the consciences are the same
> and so is arrogance, iniquity. The proclamations are different,
> the callousness the same. And so is the challenge we face in
> many moments of spiritual agony. Above all while dogmas,
> while forms of worship are divergent, God is the same. What
> unites us? A commitment to the Hebrew Bible as Holy Scrip-
> ture, faith in the creator, the God of Abraham, commitment
> to many of his commandments, [to] justice and mercy, a sense
> of contrition, sensitivity to the sanctity of life, to the involve-
> ment of God in history, to the conviction that without the holy
> the good will be defeated, and the prayer that history may not
> end before the end of days, and so much more. Maybe then it
> may come very soon when the Hebrew Bible will be called the
> Hebrew Bible — without the adjective "old." [54]

A second episode, February 21, 1964. It was a "first" on both
sides. The Reform Synagogue in White Plains, New York, had never
before welcomed a Catholic priest to its holy place, and I, for my
part, had never entered a synagogue, much less spoken therein.

At that time Catholic-Jewish relations were just beginning to improve. Pope Paul VI had visited Israel seven weeks before, but 20 months were to elapse before Vatican II issued its declaration on non-Christian religions.

I was there to give a message that would be my own and still a word from the Catholic community. The task was extraordinarily difficult, for we were more than strangers: I represented an institution that to many of my listeners was hostile to Judaism, bore a large responsibility for the traditional plight of the wandering Jew and the ghetto Jew. We were severed by Jesus, by our histories, in our day-to-day living. I could hardly ask my listeners to "forget it"; to the Jew, as Elie Wiesel put it, "whoever forgets becomes the executioner's accomplice."

I decided to make a small beginning toward reconciliation by focusing on the famous Suffering Servant passage in Isaiah 52:13–53:12. I had read that for the last eight centuries most Jewish interpreters had seen in the Servant the Jewish people, had seen in his sufferings not only the agony of the Captivity but the sufferings of the whole Jewish people. I wanted to suggest the redemptive power of Jewish suffering — for them and for me.

It was, at best, a magnificent failure. From certain reactions, then and later, especially from the young, I was forced to conclude that a theology of redemptive suffering makes little or no sense if your history includes (among much else) the Holocaust. It was a disturbing experience that has served me well in dialogue with individual Jews and small groups. Not only are my eyes more open to the complexities of our historical and theological problems; my heart has expanded in love and compassion for living, loving people "of [whose] race is the Christ" (Rom 9:5).[55]

Interestingly, a recent article on the Center for Jewish-Christian Learning at the University of St. Thomas in St. Paul, Minnesota, confirmed my White Plains experience.

> Christians have always believed, and Vatican II reaffirmed, that suffering yields sanctity. The Jewish people, in contrast, see no value, spiritual or otherwise, in suffering. Its value is that, as we use our free will to eliminate it, there will be less. "Suffering, as such, does not confer privileges," said Elie Wiesel in his appearance at the center. "It is not because I suffer that I have certain rights.
>
> "But the main reason why we talk is not for the dead — it is too late for the dead. We are talking for the next generation,

for the children. It is not too late for the children.... Our past
may become our future unless we are careful."[56]

"Unless we are careful...." Yes indeed. I remember, from my
years as theologian-in-residence at Georgetown University, a letter
from a student to the school newspaper *The Hoya*. He claimed, seriously, that the Holocaust never took place; it is fiction, fabrication,
pure and simple. And he is hardly alone.[57]

A third episode, an article in *Commonweal* four decades ago. I
had come to know the author, Arthur A. Cohen, in the years immediately preceding, when he was instrumental in publishing a book
I coedited with a remarkably imaginative Jesuit, William F. Lynch,
*The Idea of Catholicism: An Introduction to the Thought and Wor-
ship of the Church* (Meridian Books, 1960). Arthur was a deeply
committed Jew, an observant Jew (I recall vividly the details of travel
and diet connected with a lecture I arranged for him at Woodstock
in Maryland on a *Friday evening!*), a profound analyst of America's
religious, specifically Jewish situation. Here I reproduce a single sentence from that article: If "American society is ... , as some Christian
thinkers argue, an essentially Christian society ... then Jews might
prefer a return to the ghetto which, however socially isolated, was
spiritually free."[58] It was a sentence for me to ponder, to agonize
over. What have we done to our sisters and brothers? What are we
doing now? What ought we to do?

A fourth episode. A sympathetic Jew, Schalom Ben-Chorin, posed
a pungent problem for me, a problem for all Christians: "We must
... question, in the light of the Bible, whether the message of the
Old Testament which the New Testament claims has been fulfilled,
has in fact been fulfilled in history.... And here, my dear Christian
readers, we give a negative reply. We can see no kingdom and no
peace and no redemption."[59]

The problem? If a Jewish friend like Leon Klenicki were to press
me for evidence that the Messiah has come, what signs would I point
to? Where is the kingdom, the peace, the redemption promised in
the Prior Testament? If I believe, with the Preface for the feast of
Christ the King, that the kingdom of Christ is "a kingdom of truth
and life, a kingdom of holiness and grace, a kingdom of justice, love,
and peace," where is it? Can these possibly be the Messianic times?
When three out of every four human beings do not know Christ?
When one out of four goes to bed hungry? When violence roams
every large city and death never takes a holiday? When Christians
wage war on Christians in a Christian country? When six million

of God's chosen people perish in gas ovens, of planned starvation, of medical experimentation? When 1.5 million developing humans are each year forcibly prevented from seeing the light of day in this "land of the free"? *This* is the new covenant in Christ's blood? *This* is "the day of the Lord"? *This* is a world redeemed from sin? *This* is what the Prior Testament was preparing for?

A problem indeed. In preaching I have, of course, offered two palliating observations.[60] First, the kingdom of God and of Christ is not here purely and simply; it *is* here and it is *not* here. As Vatican II put it, the Church "becomes on earth the initial budding forth of that kingdom."[61] We are still fashioning the kingdom, the rule of Christ over human hearts; and we fashion the kingdom as a pilgrim people, through tears and trembling, through sin and selfishness, through suffering and death. Second, the most significant facets of Christ's kingdom are invisible, beyond the power of sense to perceive. The kingdom is primarily within us, above all a kingdom of holiness and grace.

Helpful, but not completely satisfying. The kingdom should reveal its effects now, in our everyday world of flesh and blood. My theology explains why the Church is not perfect; it does not explain why the Church is not holier than it is, why Christians are not more visible sacraments to the world, more transparent signs that Christ is here. It does not explain how so many in a redeemed world can be as ruthless, as pitiless, as loveless as the unbelievers St. Paul castigated.

One solution I find transparent but difficult to bring about: thousands of Christians like Dorothy Day. From jails and soup kitchens, through the *Catholic Worker* and houses of hospitality, in voluntary poverty and with unconfined faith, she gave her life literally to the poor and the destitute, lived and ate with these down-and-out images of Christ. At her funeral in 1980, former yippee Abbie Hoffman remarked, "She is the nearest thing this Jewish boy is ever going to get to a saint." And in the overflow outside the church, "a drifter who gave his name as Lazarus" said "with tears oozing down his seamed cheeks: 'That fine lady gave me love.' "[62]

A fifth episode. It happened at a 1974 international symposium on the Holocaust held in New York's Cathedral of St. John the Divine. In the discussion period after remarks of mine on a paper by Rosemary Radford Ruether on "Anti-Semitism and Christian Theology,"[63] young Jew after young Jew assailed me with savage denunciations, so furiously that the chairman had to protest. Only later did I realize it was not so much I personally that was under attack. My Roman collar was a symbol. It summed up and summoned up every Jewish ghetto ever structured by Christians, every forced baptism, every Crusade to "liberate" the Holy Places, every Good Friday pogrom, every forced exodus like 1492, every Dachau and every Auschwitz, every death for conscience' sake, every back turned or shoulder shrugged, every sneer or slap or curse.

A sixth episode is a lecture I gave in the mid-'80s at a symposium on the Jewish-Christian problematic at Seton Hall University in South Orange, New Jersey, sponsored by the remarkable Jewish convert and priest John Oesterreicher, who died in the summer of 1993.[64] The lecture is significant for me because for the first time I was forced to put together in detailed fashion, for myself and Catholic preachers in general, my understanding of (1) the Prior Testament, (2) the New Testament, and (3) the signs of the times.

In harmony with the Catholic theology of the '30s and '40s, the "Old Testament" was presented to my untutored Jesuit ears on two different but related levels. First, with a deep bow to Augustine of Hippo, the New Testament was seen to be hidden in the Old, the Old come to light in the New. Second, the Old Testament offered proof-texts for many of our theological theses, e.g., Genesis 3:15 for Mary's immaculate conception, Isaiah 7:14 for Jesus' virginal conception. On both levels we were heirs to a centuries-long tradition: the effort of early Christian Alexandria, Origen in particular, to find Christ throughout the Hebrew Scriptures — a practice that enjoyed high favor till fairly recent times.[65]

Although the stress on spiritual senses may have seen its biblical and theological day, and the modern emphasis rests on the literal or primitive and primary sense of the author(s), Vatican II could still declare, "God, inspirer and author of the books of both Testaments, has wisely arranged that the New Testament be hidden in the Old and the Old be made manifest in the New."[66] And a bit more fully, "...the books of the Old Testament with all their parts, caught up in the proclamation of the gospel, acquire and disclose their full meaning in the New Testament...and in turn cast light on it and explain it."[67]

It was not and is not within my competence to settle a still unsettled question: What precisely is the unity of the two Testaments? Still, I am striving to see clearly, and express faithfully in my preaching, what the Prior Testament is saying on its own terms. Guided by John McKenzie,[68] I have discovered universal values therein: a ceaseless insistence on one only God, splendidly personal; an unparalleled insight into the human person and the human condition;

a precious presentation of the common experience of suffering; a rich record of inner freedom in the context of divine sovereignty; a touching wedding of pain and mortality with delight in the sheer pleasure of breathing and moving, of integration with nature and with one's fellows; insistence that, despite ambivalence on an afterlife, mere survival is not an absolute, life is not worth living if the price is moral integrity, human dignity at times demands a yes to death and its darkness.

I cannot tell the Jews how to read a Book that is peculiarly theirs. In fact, it is only by understanding historical Jewry that I have come to know Jesus as a man. McKenzie has phrased it splendidly:

> When the Word becomes flesh, a man is born; this man is a member of a particular human community and of a particular generation of mankind by nativity. Much of what he is has already been determined by the place and time of his nativity. The Word could not become universal man; he is qualified by those adjectives which we use to distinguish one human group from another. Jesus was a Palestinian Jew of the 1st century of our era; he neither lacked nor sought to escape the determinations that this historical fact laid upon him. It follows that he cannot be known unless these determinations are known. We do not imply that he cannot be known at all; we do imply that he can be known better if he is known in his historical reality.[69]

As for the New Testament, I have come to recognize how difficult and delicate is the issue of anti-Semitism. At one pole, uncounted Christians dismiss out of hand, a priori, any intimation of anti-Semitism in books that presumably are divinely protected not only against sin but against error in matters religious. At the other pole, Jews on the whole find the Gospels and Paul obviously biased against "the Jews," the source of most of the anti-Semitism that has cursed the earth from the earliest Christian communities through the medieval ghettos down to the gas chambers of Dachau and Auschwitz.

Much of my effort at fresh understanding profited from the impressive research of others. I was enormously aided by John G. Gager's *The Origins of Anti-Semitism: Attitudes toward Judaism in Pagan and Christian Antiquity*.[70] Specifically, Gager showed me the French historian Jules Isaac inaugurating a new era in research in 1948 with his *Jesus and Israel*. When his wife and daughter were murdered by the Nazis in 1943, Isaac started, aged 66, two projects that would end only with his death 20 years later: the Christian origins of anti-Semitism, and Jewish-Christian co-operation. One of his main theses: The Jews of Jesus' time neither rejected him nor crucified him; and Jesus did not reject Israel.

The net effect of Isaac's work has been twofold: (1) to lay the blame for anti-Semitism squarely at the door of Christianity; (2) to buttress the argument that anti-Semitism, while exclusively a Christian product, results from a misinterpretation by Christians of their own scriptures and founder, and stands in fundamental opposition to the historical origins and basic tenets of Christianity.[71]

Gager showed me Marcel Simon's *Verus Israel,* which dominated the postwar era till quite recently. Although Simon faults Isaac for failing to distinguish adequately between anti-Semitism and anti-Jewish apologetic, he agrees with Isaac fundamentally in recognizing "that there is no clear line of separation between anti-Jewish polemic and anti-Semitism and that systematic hostility toward Jews is to be found from the very beginnings of Christianity."[72]

Gager opened for me the most telling research after Simon. There is the French scholar F. Lovsky, arguing that "With the possible exception of the Gospel of John, anti-Semitism as such is not to be found in the New Testament." He attributes "the increase of anti-Semitic views in Christian circles of the second, third, and fourth centuries to the impact of popular anti-Semitism throughout the Greco-Roman world."[73] There is Gregory Baum, convert from Judaism, at first distinguishing "sharply between the legitimate, theological anti-Judaism of the New Testament and modern, racial anti-Semitism,"[74] then, in his introduction to Rosemary Radford Ruether's *Faith and Fratricide,* citing her work "as one among several factors that had forced him to abandon his earlier attempts to defend the New Testament against the charge that its writings reflect a fundamental hostility toward Jews and Judaism."[75] And there is Ruether herself, who "not only embraces [Isaac's] basic position on the Christian sources of modern anti-Semitism but moves beyond it on the issue of the inseparability of anti-Semitism and early Christianity."[76]

As I write, I find myself agonizingly torn by the evidence and the conflicting conclusions first-rate scholars have drawn from the evidence.[77] What I have tried to do in the practical order, particularly in preaching, is to be intelligently aware of a handful of specific trouble spots in the New Testament: Luke's use of "the crowds" where Matthew and/or Mark specify the authorities; John's expression "the Jews" in clearly hostile contexts; "the mob" at Jerusalem in the Passion accounts. And there is the confrontation between Paul and Diaspora Judaism. What went so tragically wrong that, despite some Jewish acceptance, Paul turned from "the Jews" to the Gentiles? I do not know. But I do resonate to the conviction of a fine Catholic biblical scholar after careful analysis of the evidence: "the oft-repeated statement that the Jews rejected Jesus and had Him crucified is *historically* untenable and must therefore be removed completely from our thinking and our writing, our teaching, preaching, and liturgy."[78] That conclusion preceded by several months the strong affirmation of the Second Vatican Council:

> True, authorities of the Jews and those who followed their lead pressed for the death of Jesus (cf. Jn 19:6); still, what happened in his passion cannot be blamed upon all the Jews then living, without distinction, nor upon the Jews of today. Although the Church is the new people of God, the Jews should not be presented as repudiated or cursed by God, as if such views followed from the holy Scriptures. All should take pains, then, lest in catechetical instruction and in the preaching of God's Word they teach anything out of harmony with the truth of the gospel and the spirit of Christ.[79]

Finally, let me muse briefly on two "signs of the times" that touch me to the Jewish people — yesterday, today, and tomorrow. By "signs of the times" I mean events, situations, movements that at given moments, at certain times, reveal to us what God wants of us. Not always easy to diagnose, to interpret, but at the very least they compel us to stop and think, to look and listen. Such was the rebellion of the blacks three decades ago, a nonviolent "We shall overcome" that forced much of America to face a revolutionary fact: At this point in the evolution of humanity and society, to define the human in Aristotelian terms as "rational animal" is not existential enough; you are not human if you are not free. Such, too, I shall suggest later, is the feminist movement of today. Our eyes are opening to a centuries-old global sin, Adam's ceaseless rape of Eve. Here and elsewhere we must listen for God's voice; else we are in terrible danger of human folly. Folly? Historian Barbara Tuchman defined it for us: "persistence in ignoring the signs, the refusal to draw anything from the evidence."[80] Here two signs: the Holocaust a half century ago and Catholic questioning today.

In the march of human folly, some say the Holocaust never happened. But it did; dear God, it did. What does it say? For some Jews, it says that "God died in Auschwitz"; for other Jews, how can you *not* believe after Auschwitz?[81] What might it say to the Christian? More pungently, what does it say to me?

On April 22, 1985, I preached by invitation in Georgetown University's Dahlgren Chapel at a service commemorating Armenian genocide and Jewish Holocaust.[82] I confessed that the Holocaust had made for memories dangerous and demanding, harsh in the pitiless light they cast on my human and Christian existence. What memories?

I remember the prince of patristic preachers, John Chrysostom, taking Christians of Antioch to task for thinking of Jews with respect: "The synagogue is not only a brothel and a theater; it also is a den of robbers and a lodging for wild beasts.... God is not worshipped there. Heaven forbid! From now on it remains a place of idolatry."[83]

I remember the conversation between Hitler and two bishops in April 1933, "when they began raising questions about the German policy toward the Jews and Hitler said to them, as reported in the book, *Hitler's Table-Talk,* that he was simply completing what Christian teaching and preaching had been saying about the Jews for the better part of 1,900 years."[84]

I remember the anguished Jewish protest over the absence in Vatican II "of any note of contrition or repentance for the incredible sufferings and persecutions Jews have undergone in the Christian West."[85]

I remember a powerful Catholic priest in the '30s castigating "the Jews" for their immoral influence on our culture, remember many a Christian still convinced that "the Jews" control our banks and our entertainment, to the detriment of our way of life.

I remember that it is only a handful of years since Catholics stopped praying on Good Friday "for the perfidious Jews," substituted a warm prayer "for the Jewish people, the first to hear the word of God, that they may continue to grow in the love of His name and in faithfulness to His covenant."

I remember that a generation of Gentiles has grown up for whom Holocaust is a word and little more — as vague and transient as the War of 1812, or the Battle of San Juan Hill, or the San Francisco earthquake; and I remember Elie Wiesel's warning: To forget is to become the executioner's accomplice.

I remember how Jews reacted to a 1985 document from the Vatican's Commission for Religious Relations with the Jews, "Notes on the Correct Way To Present Jews and Judaism in Preaching and Catechesis in the Roman Catholic Church."[86] Despite quite favorable reactions by Eugene Fisher, executive director of the (U.S.) National Conference of Catholic Bishops' Secretariat for Catholic-Jewish Relations, and by Msgr. Jorge Mejia, secretary of the Vatican commission that issued the document,[87] the International Jewish Committee on Interreligious Consultations found certain formulations "a retreat from earlier Catholic statements." Not only was the document "published without prior consultation with the Jewish community." It defines Judaism "not in terms of its self-understanding... but only in terms of Christian categories" which seem "triumphalistic." Formulations about Jews and Judaism, about the Holocaust and Israel, appear "regressive." The Vatican "Notes" on the genocide and the state "are totally inadequate in providing Catholics with sufficient guidelines on how to teach, preach, and understand these major events that have so decisively shaped the way Jews define themselves." Nor are they successful in the effort to remedy the "painful ignorance" of Christians about Jewish history and traditions, which are seen not as having independent value, but simply as preparatory — and that alone is why Catholics should "appreciate and love Jews."[88]

A second sign of the times is a growing Catholic theological uneasiness with traditional doctrine on the role of the Jews in the history of salvation. I myself have become increasingly unhappy with a theology of sheer preparation for Christ; and yet I am unable to express satisfactorily an attractive thesis that presents Judaism as having permanent salvific validity in God's promise. I am still struggling with two pertinent issues.

First, a broad Christological question: In what sense is Jesus Christ our Savior? I find quite unchristian the rigorously conservative thesis that a man or woman can be saved only through explicit personal knowledge of and commitment to Jesus as the Christ. But shall we say then that salvation is indeed attainable only through the grace of Christ, *but* that this grace is offered and available to all — the theories of "anonymous Christian," "latent Church," "supernatural existential"? Can we go further: Jesus Christ is the normative way to God and salvation, but not the exclusive mediator for all humankind — central but not unique?[89]

Second, how shall we understand Romans 9–11? Here is a people whose gifts and call are "irrevocable" (Rom 11:29), and yet "a hardening in part has come to Israel [or: a hardening has come to Israel in part] until the full number of the Gentiles comes in, and so all Israel will be saved" (vv. 25–26). Tantalizingly broad but highly attractive is a "solution" that goes back two decades:

A consideration of the situation in the light of Paul's statements not only leads to a complete abandonment of the traditional theories of rejection and substitution, but also makes it possible and necessary to give *a positive interpretation* of the present existence of the Jewish people. To be able to fulfil their function for the Christian community, the Jewish people must preserve their identity and autonomy.[90]

This conclusion compels a summary of Fitzmyer's extensive treatment of Romans 9–11.[91] Paul's gospel of uprightness through faith in Christ has raised a specific problem: the relationship of Israel to this mode of justification or salvation. How do the Jewish people fit into God's new plan?

For Paul, the problem that caused his anguish started with God. "His promises to Israel all stem from his gratuitous election of it as his people; hence his word has not failed. Paul insists: Israel's rejection does not mean that God's word has failed."[92] "The promises made to Israel have been faithfully kept; God has proved true to them. The purpose that God had for Israel has not become a dead letter."[93] What happened to Israel is not contrary to God's direction of history; Israel's indocility was foreseen. God does not act arbitrarily; God's merciful foresight included not only Israel's infidelity but the call of the Gentiles; for God had promised Abraham, "All the nations of the earth shall be blessed in you" (Gen 18:15).

A second step: Israel's failure derives not from God but from Israel's own misstep. Four stages to Paul's argument:

> (1) Israel has preferred its own way of uprightness to God's way (9:30–33); (2) Paul expresses his sorrow that Israel has failed to recognize Christ as the end of the law, through whom uprightness has now been made attainable (10:1–4); (3) the old way of obtaining uprightness was difficult and arduous, whereas the new way is easy, within the reach of all and proclaimed to all, as Scripture shows (10:5–13); and (4) Israel has not taken advantage of this opportunity offered by the prophets and the gospel, so the responsibility lies with it (10:14–21).[94]

Still, God has not rejected His people; Israel's disbelief is only partial, temporary, providential. Its threefold purpose: "(1) to allow salvation to come to the Gentiles; (2) to make Israel jealous of such Gentiles; and (3) to allow their eventual share in salvation as a sign of their coming from death to life."[95]

Aware that his solution to the problem of Israel is not satisfactory, Paul begins to speak of the "mystery" of Israel — mystery in the sense of a secret hidden in God, now revealed, not completely comprehensible. "All Israel will be saved" (11:26). But how? Over the centuries scholars have discussed, debated, disagreed. Two basic explanations dominate today. The first is theological: Israel will be saved by God, an act of mercy independent of acceptance of Jesus as Messiah or of a mass conversion to the Christian gospel. It will be Yahweh bringing His covenant with Israel to its fruition. The second explanation is Christological: Israel's salvation will come about through Christ. This interpretation is used in two different senses. (*a*) For some interpreters, the parousiac Christ will pardon the hardening of all Israel without conversion to the gospel. (*b*) For others, the whole thrust of Romans demands that the justification of *all* human beings depends on faith in Christ Jesus, without which there is no salvation.

It is this latter form of the Christological interpretation that Fitzmyer sees as the only one tenable: " ... Christ has to be understood as 'the deliverer' of Israel (11:26b), and the 'covenant' (v 27) is that of Jer 31:33, as realized in the ministry, death, and resurrection of Jesus Christ.... " Why? Because two different kinds of salvation "would seem to militate against [Paul's] whole thesis of justification and salvation by grace for *all* who believe in the gospel of Christ Jesus (1:16). For Paul the only basis for membership in the new people of God is faith in Christ Jesus."[96]

A hard saying? Yes indeed. But evoking a further, neuralgic question: How binding is Paul's conviction on Christians? Is it God's Word ... or Paul's word? Is it revelation or theology?

As I struggle to understand, I realize increasingly how indispensable is dialogue between Jews and Christians. I mean face-to-face encounter between individuals and between the communities; conversation that is not only exchange of ideas but a search for closeness, oneness, intimacy with an all-too-strange other; witness to the truth as each sees it, but without the oppressive proselytizing that offends against the freedom of God's children.[97] All the while, musing with Paul on the mystery of our estrangement, "I have great sorrow and unceasing anguish in my heart" (Rom 9:2).

In my sorrow and anguish I am stimulated by a challenging story told by a rabbi of Zans. A man had been wandering about in a forest for several days unable to find his way out. Seeing another man approaching, he asked him, "Brother, will you please tell me the way out of the forest?" Said the other, "I don't know the way out either, for I too have been wandering here for many days. But this much I can tell you: The way I have gone is not the way."[98]

And so with us. The way we have been going may not be *the* way. Is it too much to ask that we join hands and look for *the* way together?

Tantur

Finally, an ecumenical involvement with beginnings not widely known. Back in April 1963, Pope Paul VI asked his good friend Father Theodore Hesburgh, then president of the University of Notre Dame and of the reconstituted International Federation of Catholic Universities, to stop off and visit with him.[99] At lunch the pope revealed to Hesburgh his long-nourished dream of a time when all branches of Christianity would be united and he would play a role therein. Similarly, as Vatican II was drawing to a close, Protestant biblicists and theologians like Oscar Cullmann and E. K. Skysdgaard were lamenting the apparent end of so singular a type of dialogue. All agreed that there should be a place where Christian theologians could live and study together.

As for the place, Assisi seemed to Paul too romantic, Geneva too Protestant, Canterbury too Anglican, Istanbul and Moscow too Orthodox. The most appropriate locus seemed to be Jerusalem; there Paul decided to build a permanent ecumenical institute.

Outlining his dream, the pope smiled at Hesburgh: "Now that you're the head of the Federation of Catholic Universities, it would be nice if you could take on the responsibility of this ecumenical institute for me." Despite his immediate protests, Hesburgh was increasingly attracted to the idea, and as they discussed possibilities for the building, he found himself "hooked." Later, driving through various possible sites in the Holy Land with Father Pierre Duprey, he found irresistible a remote hilltop ringed with olive and pine trees, 35 acres, the highest point between Jerusalem and Bethlehem. The property, known as Tantur, belonged to the Knights of Malta, but a small group of Salesian priests was living on it. The Vatican purchased the property and leased it to Notre Dame for 50 years at a dollar a year.

Hesburgh established an ecumenical advisory council, 30 representatives of all Christian churches; I was graced with membership in that group. With him as guiding light, remarkably efficient chairman, and fund-raising genius, we met each year in highly attractive places: Lake Como, Bellagio, Venice.... It took seven years before the buildings were constructed and the plans for action were in place; the institute opened in 1970. Since then more than 2,000 Protestant, Orthodox, Anglican, and Roman Catholic theologians, men and women of varying ages, have lived, studied, and prayed there together. "The dream of Pope Paul VI lives on today at Tantur in Jerusalem, working to achieve Christian unity at a place where Christianity began."[100]

FOUR

From Prior Testament Prophet to New Testament Preacher

The Art and Craft of Preaching

In his Afterword to a book about the remarkable priest-activist Jack Egan, Martin Marty of the University of Chicago told how a poet began her course on preaching after having heard homilies by her students: "How can your Gospel be so interesting, and you who speak it so G— D— dull?"[1]

The question, as pertinent as it is impertinent, recalls to my mind a book authored in 1986 by George Dennis O'Brien, then president of the University of Rochester, with the engaging title *God and the New Haven Railway and Why Neither One Is Doing Very Well.*[2] At one point the normally good-humored president is disturbed about the split between proclamation and ongoing life. He notes that most people on the train platform are not likely to see church service as "one of the livelier, more salvational times of week." Their appraisal is more likely to be "Saturday Night Live, Sunday Morning Deadly."[3] Along similar lines, a university professor of literature suggests that the time has come to speak truthfully to the Church about the quality of its rhetoric. "Discourse in the church," the lady laments, "is so dull. In sermons, in social-action statements, in all the communication we hear within the church, the guiding principle seems to be blandness."[4]

A quarter century ago, I was struck by a startling sentence from a remarkably learned French Dominican, Yves Congar: "I could quote a whole series of ancient texts, all saying more or less that if in one country Mass was celebrated for thirty years without preaching and in another there was preaching for thirty years without the Mass, people would be more Christian in the country where there was preaching."[5]

That observation, from a circumspect scholar, should be taped to every rectory refrigerator. For, despite Vatican II's insistence that "priests...have as their *primary duty* the proclamation of the gospel of God to all,"[6] despite the flat confirmatory assertion of the U.S. Bishops' Committee on Priestly Life and Ministry, "The other duties of the priest are to be considered properly presbyteral to the degree that they support the proclamation of the Gospel,"[7] the view from the pew is discouragingly critical. I am not suggesting that the gospel is proclaimed only from the pulpit; evangelization is far broader than formal preaching by presbyters. Still, the occasion when the vast majority of committed Catholics regularly gather together is the weekend liturgy, where the priest celebrant faces a captive audience. And yet, despite a fair number of effective preachers, all too frequently our people are not confronted with a word that nourishes while it challenges, heals while it bruises. The criticism is further fueled by an increasingly educated populace no longer silent before homiletic pap and bromides, and by articulate Catholic women who are even more thoroughly convinced of their calling to the pulpit when they must submit to our contemporary constipation of thought and diarrhea of words. And all the more eloquent is the mute witness of untold thousands of "ordinary folk" forsaking our liturgy for the impassioned preaching of the Pentecostals.

Background

I am convinced that our contemporary homiletic doldrums can be traced, at least proximately, to a mid-century situation. In my early years as a priest, the liturgy of the word played an insignificant role in Sunday worship. A pithy proof? A Catholic could miss the whole liturgy of the word without having to confess it. Gloria, biblical readings, Gospel, sermon, Creed — you could join the congregation after all these were said and done and still "hear Mass," fulfil your obligation. No manual of morality would do more than rap your knuckles lightly. For the "essential" parts of the Mass were Offertory, Consecration, and the priest's Communion. And so the burning moral issue was: How much of the Offertory could you miss and still say you were present for the Offertory?

Why this choice bit of casuistry? Because the sole stress was on the Sacrifice. One word alone was all-important: the consecratory word. Here was *the* Real Presence; here was the efficacious word, objectively infallible, utterly trustworthy, limpidly clear. No worry about the person, about reader or preacher, songstress or danseuse. No need for priestly lips to be touched by live coals; enough that they whispered distinctly "This is my body." I recall that, as I was growing up in St. John the Evangelist parish in New York City, each Sunday Mass had its quota of what we adolescent altar servers called "sharpshooters": men on one knee in the back, just waiting for the sermon — the signal to sneak out for a smoke.

Today's liturgical attitude is refreshingly different. In Vatican II's wake, there is fresh stress on the whole "word" as a locus where God transpires, comes to light. Music, readings, homily, dance — God is there (or can be there), a real presence. With Communion now taken for granted by the vast majority of Sunday worshipers, the liturgy of the word has assumed uncommon significance. A responsorial psalm is sung by a choir with the congregation; lectors are trained (sometimes) to read intelligently; people come to church hoping (at times against hope) that their minds and hearts will be fed by the homily.

Given these new emphases, it was my fond hope in the late '60s that the Catholic homily would "take off." With Scripture opening to new Catholic life, with liturgy moving from me-and-Jesus to a fresh sense of community worship, with young priests shaped in the shadow of Vatican II, with the laity in the mood for God's revivified Word, there was good reason to expect a second spring in homiletics. It has not transpired. Some advances indeed: preaching programs such as that sponsored by the Aquinas School of Theology in St. Louis; the Catholic Coalition on Preaching; the Catholic Association of Teachers of Homiletics; the stimulus provided by the U.S. bishops' document *Fulfilled in Your Hearing;* increasing awareness of the unique importance of the homily among a number of priests; all manner of published "Homily Hints"; a Notre Dame program to improve preaching through the generosity of the late John Marten, for which I was privileged to be the first senior lecturer; the emergence of permanent deacons and of first-rate preachers among the nonordained; and much else besides. Despite all this, problems have continued to plague the preaching ministry in the three decades since the Second Vatican Council closed.

Problems

Scripture

First, fear of Scripture. For all too many priests, the Bible is an expanding mystery. They sympathize with the plaint of a priest echoing Mary Magdalene at the tomb of Jesus: "The exegetes have taken away my Lord, and I know not where they have laid him." What Jesus himself actually said has been increasingly debated. And this not simply because Scripture scholars disagree, because the Jesus Seminar finds little of Jesus' *ipsissima verba* in the Gospels. After all, in 1964 the Biblical Commission of the Catholic Church issued an "Instruction on the Historical Truth of the Gospels" which explicitly listed "three stages of [the Gospel] tradition": (1) what Jesus himself actually said and did, the *ipsissima verba Iesu;* (2) the testimony of the apostles, the accommodations they made to the needs of their listeners, passing on what Jesus had actually done "with that fuller understanding which they enjoyed" in consequence of their Easter and Pentecost experiences; (3) the writings of the evangelists selecting some things, synthesizing others, explicating still others "as they kept in mind the situation of the churches."[8]

Such distinctions trouble the serious nonprofessional preparing a Sunday homily. Add to that certain turnabouts in traditional Catholic interpretations due to the historical-critical method: Mary is no longer in Genesis 3:15, Jesus in Isaiah 7:14; the priest is no longer prefigured in Melchizedek, the Mass in Malachi; the Song of Songs is secular eroticism and would be banned in Boston.[9] Add to that the recent stress on social analysis,[10] biblical theology from feminist perspectives,[11] the narrative approach that reveals the complexity of human lives and choice, as well as the dynamic response of readers to the story[12] — and the Catholic preacher, especially one ordained before Vatican II, may well develop an inferiority complex in the face of a biblical revolution. How in heaven's name can the ordinary down-to-earth padre ever really know what God is telling us?

The problem is not artificial; for the Word of God is like no other book in creation, hardly self-explanatory. And still, Scripture remains indispensable for the preacher, an incomparable way in which God speaks to us, reveals Godself, challenges us, graces us. Here we come to know Christ as nowhere else. That is why St. Jerome could claim that ignorance of Scripture is ignorance of Christ. Difficult as it is, Scripture is still the single most important source for any Christian preacher. Not even dogma supplants Scripture in dignity or content. As Vatican II confessed when dealing with divine revelation, "the magisterium is not above the Word of God, but serves it.... "[13] And in the same document:

> Like the Christian religion itself, all the preaching of the Church must be nourished and governed by Sacred Scripture. In the sacred books, you see, the Father who is in heaven comes

to meet His children with extraordinary love and speaks with them. So remarkable is its power and force that the Word of God abides as the support and energy of the Church, the strength of faith for the Church's children, the food of the soul, the pure and perennial source of spiritual life.[14]

I myself am not an expert in Scripture. What I did discover, for my homiletic consolation, is that I did not need to be. What is necessary? God's written Word must take hold of me as God's spoken word took hold of Isaiah and Jeremiah, of Ezekiel and Hosea; as the spoken word of Christ mesmerized Matthew and Magdalene, captured Simon Peter and the Samaritan woman. How? Basically, the word I study has to be the word I pray, and the word I pray the word I live.

For most of us, there is no substitute for study of the Word. I know that my dear forebear Ignatius Loyola had a single illumination — of God One and Three, the world's fashioning, and the bodying forth of the Son — that outstripped, by his own admission, all he learned or was given by God in 62 years. But *I* cannot count on such a self-manifestation of God. I must have recourse to the source God invented for all of us, the self-disclosure that is God's written Word. It exists not to while away some disenchanted evening, but to transform me, to turn me inside out, to fashion a new creature. If that is so, then the more I know about it and the deeper I plunge into its depths, the more likely I am to experience its incomparable power. Martin Luther did. His study of Scripture between 1513 and 1517 — the Psalms and Romans, Galatians and Hebrews — transformed not only his theology but his life and his preaching.[15]

Even more impressive to me, Luther recognized and regretted how inadequate sheer scholarship soon proves itself. At the close of his Christmas sermon in 1522 he cried out despairingly:

O that God should desire that my interpretation and that of all teachers should disappear, and each Christian should come straight to the scripture alone and to the pure word of God! You see from this babbling of mine the immeasurable distance between the word of God and all human words, and how no man can adequately reach and explain a single word of God with all his words. It is an eternal word, and must be understood and contemplated with a quiet mind.... No one else can understand except a mind that contemplates in silence. For anyone who could achieve this without commentary or interpretation, my commentaries and those of everyone else would not only be of no use, but merely a hindrance. Go to the Bible itself, dear Christians, and let my expositions and those of all scholars be no more than a tool with which to build aright, so that we can understand, taste and abide in the simple and pure word of God, for God dwells alone in Zion.[16]

Luther confirmed me in my conviction that though for most of us there is no substitute for study of the Word, for recourse to the source God invented for all of us, scholarly tomes and commentaries are only a beginning. The Bible is not Blackstone's *Commentaries* or Einstein's theory of relativity; it is a book to be prayed. Not only does it inform the intellect; it ought to form the whole person. This is impossible in a classroom; it demands a prie-dieu, forces me to my knees.

That is why I have rarely had recourse to "homily hints." For all their immediate value, for all their ability to rescue the storm-tossed pastor, for all the biblical information and practical suggestions they offer, such resources are not likely to reshape the preacher's spirit, mold the core of his or her being. This calls for Luther's contemplation, not necessarily "with a quiet mind" but surely with Ignatius Loyola's ceaseless prayer to see Jesus more clearly, so as to love him more dearly and follow him more nearly. For (as we shall see shortly) the homily is prayer, the homily is liturgy, the homily is worship. But for the homily to be worship, the homilist must be a worshiper, habitually; and this calls for talking with God, listening to God, wrestling with God; it calls for "God's love poured into our hearts through the Holy Spirit that has been given to us" (Rom 5:5). It demands the close union of the preacher with Christ expressed in the Pauline "in Christ," "an inclusion that connotes a symbiosis of the two."[17]

Theology

A second persistent problem: ignorance of theology. By "theology" I mean not primarily an abstract, abstruse science. I mean the Church's ceaseless effort to understand what God has said and done, what God might be saying and doing now. Back in the '70s, while teaching historical theology at the Catholic University of America, I was asked to give a convocation address there at the beginning of the school year to students (mostly seminarians) engaged in master's programs in theology. Before lyricizing the glories of theology, I thought it realistic to tell them why it would be enormously difficult for the faculty to "sell" theology to them. Three reasons.

First, for many of you, theology is a requirement for ordination. So much so that, if tomorrow the pope were to impose four years of chemistry instead of theology, some of you might react, "I don't care for chemistry any more than for theology, but if that's what it takes to be ordained, 'thy will be done.' "

Second, for many of you, this is not where the action is. Real life is not in the classroom; it's out there — on our jungle streets and our hospital beds, on battlefields and the docks, in broken homes and breaking hearts. While we descant on the Christ of Chalcedon, Christ will continue to be crucified in Belfast and Beirut, in countless wombs and homes for the aged. We're *talking* about love and hate, about sin and grace, about war and peace. The reality is out there.

Third, perhaps most difficult of all, as priests you will get three square meals a day whether you know theology or not. Across the road is the law school library; students have to be thrown out at midnight. Why? Because their livelihood depends on what they learn. Not so for you. In fact, you can be theologically illiterate and become a bishop.

Add to that the undeniable fact that many of our theological seminaries were not halls of inspiration.

I am not advocating for preachers an ivory tower or medieval bower where in splendid isolation they can contemplate a theological navel. Theology, for me, was terribly unreal until it turned into a search — a searing search — for God and the human person, through systematic reflection on experience.

In theology I have been searching for God. Not for a God who dwells only in light inaccessible, outside time and space. Rather for a God who has a history — a history shaped by every star and every stone, each blade of grass, each deer in flight or bird on the wing, each human heart. For a God who speaks, not only from a burning bush millennia ago, but in the passionate revolt for freedom in Eastern Europe, in South Africa, in North America. For a God whose pulsing image is every one of us. For a God who *became* one of us, who wore our fragile flesh from a feeding trough to twin beams of bloody wood, wears our flesh gloriously now. And in theology I have been searching for man and woman. For, in the felicitous phrase of second-century Bishop Irenaeus of Lyons, "God's glory is man/woman alive!" Searching, therefore, for what it means to be human, what it means to live — yes, what it means to die.

Where must I the preacher seek for God, where seek for man and woman? In the stuff of theology's search, its data: in experience. *My* experience indeed, for it is I who am searching. But not in some narrow sense, as if my latest eructation is the wind of the Spirit. No, the Catholic experience must be catholic, must include the community experience that spans ages and continents. And so I have felt the Hebrew experience of Sinai and the desert, of exile and return; the New Testament experience of God's break-through to earth in the flesh of God's Son; the conciliar experience from Nicaea I to Vatican II; the experience of theologians from Origen through Aquinas to Rahner and Lonergan, mystics like Tauler and Teresa.

I have shared the experience of non-Roman Christian communities, their pens and pews and pulpits, and there I have found Christ in fresh dimensions, heard the whisperings of God's Spirit. I have discovered the "Song of the Lord" in the Hindu *Bhagavad-Gita,* with its four ways of oneness: for the intellectual, the way of intuitive oneness; for the meditative, mental concentration; for the emotional, devotional self-giving; for the active, service in the spirit. I have listened to our one Lord speaking through the Jewish community as it alternately affirms and denies that "God died in Auschwitz." My theology, and so my preaching, has been leavened by the arts, from Tchaikovsky's *Swan Lake* ballet, through Peanuts' latest reflection on reality, to Samuel Beckett's frightening "Two times anything equals zero" and *Godspell*'s glorious "God is dead; long live God!" I have come to agonize over the experience of living man, living woman, as they cry to me that they cannot discover God in my abstractions, as they stand mute before an immutable God who does not weep when they bleed, as they insist that, if they are to find God at all, they must somehow find God in one another — yes, in me.

To do theology this way is to take a frightful risk; for I wrestle with God and I wrestle with humans — perhaps even, as Murray and de Lubac, Congar and Küng wrestled, with Rome. My life may well resemble Nikos Kazantzakis' *Report to Greco:* "the red track [to Golgotha] made by drops of my blood, the track which marks my journey among men, passions, and ideas." I am often lonely, for despite the dialogue and collaboration, my deepest reflection takes place alone. I often wonder whether it's worth doing, for I am interpreting John on loaves and fishes while ten thousand of the world's hungry die each day. I argue abstract love over Budweiser or Burgundy (actually a vodka gimlet) while Arabs and Israelis are locked in hate, unnumbered adults and children redden Rwanda with their blood, and six of my brother Jesuits are assassinated in San Salvador. I try to recapture the meaning of God's presence while thousands of my fellow Americans are experiencing God's absence. I frequently feel frustration; for to hard questions there are no easy answers, pop theology is an illusion, and at times I must rest content if I uncover not the answer but the real question.

Succinctly, the attitude of a theologian was touchingly phrased by that remarkable theologian-in-a-wheelchair Yves Congar in his slender book on Archbishop Lefebvre: "As for me, I want to gather up every small fragment of truth, wherever it is to be found, with the same care that I would use in picking up a tiny piece of a consecrated host."[18]

Why drag theology into the pulpit? Briefly and bluntly, because without theology I have precious little to say. Let me get uncomfortably concrete — two examples: God's providence and the reality of Jesus.

In the pulpit I talk about God. But what do I tell my patient people? Reassure them that God loves everybody, no matter how inhuman their situation? Simply repeat ever more loudly the words of Jesus, "Do not worry about your life, what you will eat or drink, or about your body, what you will wear. Strive first for God's kingdom...and all these things will be given to you as well" (Mt 6:25, 33)? Keep repeating this, even when thousands of swollen bellies scarring the sands of the sub-Sahara cry mutely "Not true!"? Or must I not struggle with the agonizing problem of a God who lets bad things happen to good people when He (or She) could prevent it? Ought I not at least relive the anguish of Job as he struggles with God — bewildered, confused, not understanding why all this is happening to him when he hasn't done anything to deserve it, when he loves Yahweh, wants only a more intimate relationship? As his wife tells him, "Do you still hold fast to your integrity? Curse God, and die" (Job 2:9). As his friends insist that Job must have offended God, otherwise God would not treat him like an enemy. As Job curses the day he was born, begs God to just leave him alone, let him have a little comfort before he joins his ancestors in Sheol. As Yahweh reveals Godself to Job, not to explain the mystery of suffering, not to justify the ways of heaven — simply to let Job find God. What do I say when sheerly human wisdom is bankrupt?

Very simply, do I have a theology of divine providence that can speak persuasively not to an abstract mystery of evil but to living men and women who believe what is beyond belief, who hope against hope, who do love somewhat as Jesus loved, and "all these things" Christ promised are denied them? It is not only the pagan who is afflicted with AIDS, not only the child of unbelievers who is born with Down's syndrome, not only Muslims who are destroyed by muscular dystrophy, not only sinners who are schizophrenic, not only the violent who are blasted to bits by the winds of war. What does my theology, my organized search for God, say to the crucified in my congregation, to the pain-ridden in my pews? I may not have *the* answer, but literally "for Christ's sake" I had better have something solidly Christian to say.

Another example. In the pulpit I am expected to be speaking about Jesus the Christ. But who will I say that he is? Will I sputter polysyllables like "God-man consubstantial with the Father, consubstantial with us"? Can I be content with the classical "descending" Christology — a Christology largely separated from soteriology, "a discussion of who Christ is prior to any discussion of how he has made and is making a difference"?[19] I recall how bluntly Georgetown University's Monika Hellwig put the problem:

> Because of its timeless character, rather detached from the events of human societies in their constantly changing history, classical Christology seems rather to explain than to challenge what is going on in the human community. Jesus emerges as the Pantocrator in the world as it already is, with all its injustices, false values, oppression and exclusion of less powerful groups, enduring conditions of cold war, and so forth. Attitudes that take these things for granted as the state of the world until the end time are linked with a too exclusive concentration on the divinity of Jesus as his essential identity, thereby placing him above all these things, and placing the salvation he mediates in that other, eternal realm which is where he really belongs. That realm, incidentally, is the realm of spirit. Risen bodies are quite awkwardly located there, and mortal bodies not at all. As long as salvation belongs exclusively in that realm, famine, disease, homelessness, persecution, even torture are not immediately relevant to the project of redemption. Moreover, it can quite easily be assumed that the social structures causing all this human suffering, and the relationships between peoples which the structures embody, are also not of immediate relevance to salvation. To Jesus in person these problems are related through the individual who suffers them, because the

humanity of Jesus (seen as very passive) provides the model of patient and uncritical endurance under all circumstances.[20]

The point I am making is this: Whatever I proclaim about Jesus will stem, consciously or unconsciously, from a Christology. Will the last word about Jesus stem from the Council of Chalcedon in 451, or will my preaching enrich an essentialist Chalcedon with the gains of biblical, existentialist, liberation, process, political, and feminist theologies? Each preacher must face this contemporary challenge, because each must face the perennial question posed by Jesus, "Who do you say that I am?" (Mt 16:15). I owe it to the people before me to inform them who Jesus was then and who Jesus is now. A frightening demand, for my answer may well shape their Christian living — or misshape it.

Liturgy

A third problem stems from the liturgy, particularly the Eucharist. The problem has its origin in an attitude widespread when the bishops assembled for the Second Vatican Council, an attitude summed up in a 1958 article I shall not dignify with documentation: "The sermon is accidental to the Mass, and although it is important, its omission does not affect the integrity of the great act of worship." In response, three affirmations: The homily is liturgy; the homily is worship; the homily is prayer.[21]

The homily is liturgy. It is not an extraneous activity inserted into something more properly designated as liturgy, interrupting liturgy, akin to the TV commercial, useful (as in an earlier time) for parochial announcements or as a spur to greener giving. The homily, Vatican II declared, is "part of the liturgical action."[22] It is integral to the liturgical action. Here "integrity" does not mean substantial fulfilment of a Sunday obligation — whether you must attend another Mass if you had to leave during the sermon. It has to do with wholeness; it concerns the constituent parts that together compose something whole and entire. Theologically, the liturgy of the word (including the homily) and the liturgy of the Eucharist make up one unified liturgical celebration. Such was the Lord's Supper from the earliest days of the Christian community. Christians could not genuinely participate in the Lord's Supper unless they heard what it meant and stood present to share in it by faith.[23] Luther himself wanted the reality of "the Word" preached in the sermon always associated with the sacramental celebration; Calvin wanted the Sunday service in Geneva to be a combination of Eucharist and sermon; so too the early English Reformers.[24] In Jungmann's strong sentence, the homily "should emanate from the consciousness that although it is freely created by the liturgist, it is liturgy itself."[25]

The homily is worship. Here Vatican II was pointed and pellucid: "The two parts which, in a certain sense, go to make up the Mass, namely, the liturgy of the word and the liturgy of the Eucharist, are so closely connected with each other that they form but one single act of worship."[26]

In a typically perceptive article on the problem of liturgical preaching, Yves Congar located three links between word and worship.[27] First, Christian worship is a re-presentation of God's saving acts in shaping a covenant with us. But the liturgy's insights are more or less veiled; texts and forms tend to be immobilized; the connection between the Church's sacraments and Christ's pasch is not instantly recognizable. The homily extends the immemorial symbols to a particular time, place, and people, expresses them anew, makes them come alive.

Second, worship is a witness to faith — faith being my response to God's action communicated through God's Word. The peril of liturgy is that it can be impersonal. The homily personalizes what the rite expresses in a common and general way. It should rouse the faith of this people more personally than is possible for liturgical symbols and ritual actions.

Third, worship is a spiritual sacrifice: I accept gratefully God's Eucharistic gift and unite it to the offering of my concrete existence, my total life. The specific function of the homily is not only to explain the liturgical mystery, but to bring the faithful into the mystery "by throwing light on their life so that they can unite it to this mystery."[28]

Conclusion: The homily is prayer. But if preaching is prayer, then the preacher must be a pray-er. Not simply that my hearers can count on me for x-number of spiritual exercises on any given day; my whole life must be a prayer. Concretely, the context, the setting, the framework of all I think and say and do should be a relationship of love with Father, Son, and Holy Spirit. I must be habitually a worshiper, letting God speak to me, responding to God, yes wrestling with God.

The point is, a homily is not primarily a performance, a spectacle, a one-act, one-person play. I am not playing a role: Laurence Olivier or Kenneth Branagh becoming Henry V, Paul Scofield recapturing Thomas More. When I say, "It is no longer I who live, Christ lives in me" (Gal 2:20), I am not putting on Christ for the homiletic moment, only to remove the putty and the paint in the sacristy. If I am a consummate actor, I may play the impostor on occasion for a time, preach effectively even when divorced from the Lord Jesus, fool all of the people some of the time; but it will not last. I will grow tired of playacting, ashamed of sham.

Words

Fourth, a word about words. One word is not as good as another. I am confessedly and unashamedly a weaver of words. The fascination with words that marked my classical studies took on more substantive flesh when first I touched theology at old Woodstock. In the Hebrew Testament I found the word wondrously alive. As John L. McKenzie was to phrase it years later, the spoken word for the Israelites was

> a distinct reality charged with power. It is charged with power because it emerges from a source of power which, in releasing it, must in a way release itself. The basic concept of the word is the word-thing. The power of the word...posits the reality which it signifies. But in so doing it also posits the reality which speaks the word. No one can speak without revealing himself; and the reality which he posits is identified with himself. Thus the word is dianoetic as well as dynamic. It confers intelligibility upon the thing, and it discloses the character of the person who utters the word.[29]

That is why *God's* word is particularly powerful.

In the New Testament, I discovered, the word as a distinct reality charged with power is fulfilled to perfection. God expresses Godself not only in human syllables but in a Word that is itself a person. The same personal Word God utters from eternity, God uttered on a midnight clear — to us. "In Jesus Christ is fulfilled the word as a distinct being; as a dynamic creative entity; as that which gives form and intelligibility to the reality which it signifies; as the self-revelation of God; as a point of personal encounter between God and man."[30]

The word, I learned from the Letter of James, is a perilous thing. "We use it to bless the Lord and Father, but we also use it to curse men and women who are made in God's image" (Jas 3:9). And still, in St. Paul's eyes, the word is an indispensable thing. "How are men and women to call upon him in whom they have not believed? And how are they to believe in him of whom they have never heard? And how are they to hear without a preacher?" (Rom 10:14).

Words, I learned from experience, can be weapons, and words can be healing. Words can unite in friendship or sever in enmity. Words can unlock who I am or mask me from others. Two words, "Sieg Heil," bloodied the face of Europe; three words, "Here I stand," divided the body of Christendom. Words have made slaves and freed slaves, have declared war and imposed peace. Words sentence to death ("You shall be hanged by the neck") and words restore to life ("Your sins are forgiven you"). Words covenant a life together in love, and words declare a marriage dead. Words charm and repel, amuse and anger, reveal and conceal, chill and warm. Words clarify and words obscure. A word from Washington rained down atomic hell on Hiroshima; words from an altar change bread and wine into the body and blood of Christ.

With all this, I feel no shadow of guilt in being a weaver of words. A word is real; a word is sacred; a word is powerful; a word is...I.

More recently, my high regard for words received an unexpected confirmation. It came from that remarkable symbol of Czechoslovakian courage Václav Havel, from his acceptance speech when awarded the Peace Prize of the German Booksellers Association at the Frankfurt Book Fair on October 15, 1989, shortly before becoming his country's president. Entitling his speech "A Word about Words," he claimed one thing as obvious: "we have always believed in the power of words to change history."[31] One paragraph, illustrated from history, from Gorbachev and Li Peng and Ceausescu, from the French Revolution and *perestroika*, stated:

> No word...comprises only the meaning assigned to it by an etymological dictionary. Every word also reflects the person who utters it, the situation in which it is uttered, and the reason for its utterance. The same word can, at one moment, radiate great hope; at another, it can emit lethal rays. The same word can be true at one moment and false the next, at one moment illuminating, at another, deceptive. On one occasion it can open up glorious horizons, on another, it can lay down the tracks to an entire archipelago of concentration camps. The same word can at one time be the cornerstone of peace, while at another, machine-gun fire resounds in every syllable.[32]

Havel warned his hearers, from harrowing experience, of "the fiendish way that words are capable of betraying us — unless we are constantly circumspect about their use. And frequently — alas —

even a fairly minor and momentary lapse in this respect can have tragic and irreparable consequences, consequences far transcending the nonmaterial world of mere words and penetrating deep into a world that is all too material."[33] "Peace" is the living example: "I know what the word has meant here for all those forty years: ever mightier armies ostensibly to defend peace."[34] He concluded that the task of guarding against insidious germs of arrogance in words seemingly humble is not just linguistic but "intrinsically ethical. As such, however, it is situated beyond the horizon of the visible world, in that realm wherein dwells the Word that was in the beginning and is not the word of man."[35]

Lest this section end on a discouraging note, let me confess that I continue to be moved, even influenced in my preaching, by the beauty of words in contemporary literature. One example: the memoir of Frank McCourt titled *Angela's Ashes*. The family has returned from Depression-era Brooklyn to the slums of Limerick. At one point the mother, Angela, says that in America what she missed most of all was the River Shannon: "The Hudson was lovely but the Shannon sings."[36]

Imagination

How do words take flesh? Through imagination. The scholar of mythology Joseph Campbell did not think much of us clergy; he said we have no imagination. Part of the reason, at least for Catholics, is our older education. Imagination was identified with "bad thoughts," and bad thoughts were sexual phantasms, and these we confessed ashamedly. Perhaps more significantly, as Carmelite William McNamara has complained, all through school we were taught to abstract; we were not led to contemplation, to immediate communion with reality, to loving admiration, experiential awareness. We were not taught to simply "see."

What do I understand by imagination? The capacity of the human person, the capacity we all have, to make the material an image of the immaterial or spiritual. Over the years I discovered the creative power of imagination especially in three areas highly significant for effective preaching: (1) in story — a constellation of images, a narrative where we recognize our own pilgrimage; (2) in symbol — "an externally perceived sign that works mysteriously on the human consciousness so as to suggest more than it can clearly describe or define";[37] (3) in the fine arts — including motion pictures. A word here on the first two.

First, story. Theologian Sallie TeSelle put it well: "We all love a good story because of the basic narrative quality of human experience: in a sense *any* story is about ourselves, and a *good* story is good because somehow it rings true to human life."[38] Let one example suffice, a Jewish parable that impressed me powerfully not many months ago, especially in its unexpected ending. It runs like this:

Once upon a time, two families came to a rabbi wanting him to settle a dispute about the boundaries of their land. He listened to the members of one family as they recounted how they had received this land as their inheritance from their ancestors and how it had been in their family for generations. They had maps and papers to prove it. Then the rabbi listened to the other family. Its members described how they had lived on the land for years, working it and harvesting it. They claimed that they knew the land intimately and that it was their land. They didn't have the papers to prove it, but they had the calluses and sore backs and the harvest and the produce of the land.

The rabbi looked at them both and backed away from between them. They turned on him and said, "Decide, rabbi, who owns this land." But the rabbi knelt down on the land and put his ear to the ground, listening. Finally he stood up and looked at both families. He said: "I had to listen to both of you, but I had to listen also to the land, the center of this dispute, and the land has spoken. It has told me this: 'Neither one of you owns the land you stand on. It is the land that owns you.'"[39]

Second, symbol. Not every sign is a symbol. A mere indicator ("This Way to Washington") or a conventional sign (a word) is not a symbol. "The symbol is a sign pregnant with a depth of meaning which is evoked rather than explicitly stated."[40] It might be an artifact: a totem, a crucifix, the brazen serpent. It might be a person or an event: Moses leading the Israelites out of Egypt, Jesus Christ crucified and risen. It might be a theme: the Suffering Servant in the Prior Testament, the kingdom of God in the New. It might be a story: parable, allegory, myth.

A decade ago I did something quite unusual that has proven wonderfully productive for my own preaching. I invited two dear friends of mine, young married women, to dinner at a District of Columbia restaurant. On one condition: In-between bites of their favorite foods, they were to suggest whatever contemporary cultural symbols came to mind.

The results were astonishing. Some of the symbols fit well together, others were contrasting or contradictory. Most were secular, some explicitly or potentially religious. Suggested were heavy metal and MTV; the computer, car phones, and crack; Michael Jackson and Jesse Jackson; freedom and human rights; Madonna or Mother Teresa; Rambo and Dirty Harry's "Make my day"; a comic-strip Peanuts and a President's jelly beans; yuppie or Alzheimer; Walkman and the boob tube; Sandra Day O'Connor or *Playgirl;* Sushi or Mexican beer; Super Bowl and Big Mac; prochoice or prolife; Mike Tyson and Steffi Graf; a wasted *Challenger* or a Mars-bound *Discovery;* Wall Street and Häagen Dazs; the "Army: Be All You Can Be" or the Community for Creative Non-Violence; the recreational hobo or the homeless on D.C.'s winter grates; black power and ERA; Star Wars and strawberry daiquiris; Marcel Lefebvre or John Paul II; Bill Cosby or "The Young and the Restless"; God as mother, God as lover, God as friend of the earth; AIDS and the compassionate Christ.... Fifty and counting. There was more, ever so much more — symbols my shortsightedness stopped me from seeing, symbols the younger and still more restless than I could surely spy.[41]

Symbols come and symbols go; and so another dinner is in order. But that singular experience and its aftermath have lent vivid confirmation to a conviction long dear to my heart: Unless our preaching is molded in large measure by this type of contemporary context, we will be whistling down the wind — Shakespeare's "sound and fury" perhaps, but "signifying nothing." Preach as part and parcel of this concrete world, aware of its paradoxes and contradictions, attuned to its limitless potential for good, saddened or enraged by so much folly and insensitivity, alive to the grace of God with whom nothing on earth is impossible, and the American words will come. But don't start with the words; start with the reality, the real-life symbols that surround us, the symbols within which, sense it or not, our own lives are shaping.

From these experiences two conclusions forced themselves on me. First, imagination is not at odds with knowledge; imagination is a form of cognition. In Whitehead's words, "Imagination is not to be divorced from the facts; it is a way of illuminating the facts."[42] True, it is not a process of reasoning. Notre Dame of Paris is not a thesis in theology; C. S. Lewis' famous trilogy does not *demonstrate* the origin of evil; Gerard Manley Hopkins was not analyzing God's image in us when he sang that "Christ plays in ten thousand places, / Lovely in limbs, and lovely in eyes not his / [plays] To the Father through the features of men's faces."[43] And still, imaging and imagining is a work of our intellectual nature; through it our spirit reaches the true, the beautiful, and the good.

Second, the imagination does not so much teach as evoke; it calls forth something from me. And so it is often ambiguous; the image can be understood in different ways. I frequently recall with relish the reporters who asked Martha Graham, "What does your dance mean?" She replied: "Darlings, if I could tell you, I would not have danced it!" Something is lost when we move from imagining to thinking, from art to conceptual clarity. Not that imagination is arbitrary, that *Swan Lake* or Luke's Infancy Narrative or *Hamlet* or the Transfiguration is whatever anyone wants to make of it. Wilder was right: "Inebriation is no substitute for paideia."[44] And still it is true, the image is more open-ended than the concept, less confining, less imprisoning. The image evokes our own imagining.

All this is uncommonly important for effective preaching. In the '80s a thesis gaining some support claimed that, given the increasing ignorance of our people, especially the young, in matters Catholic, we should scrap the Vatican II homily and get back to instructional sermons. With elementary Catholic education vanishing, the only viable way to teach is via the Sunday sermon. Give the faithful the dogma, the doctrine, and give it with consummate clarity, with unquestioning certitude. The call for such instructional preaching has been intensified more recently by the publication of the *Catechism of the Catholic Church;* for in Part 2, "The Celebration of the Christian Mystery," we read that the "privileged place for catechizing the People of God is in the liturgy" (no. 1074). Missing is Vatican II's kerygmatic or mystagogic emphasis on the biblical homily. In consequence, some U.S. bishops have urged the Committee on Pastoral Practices of the National Conference of Catholic Bishops to produce a preaching guide that would parcel out the content of the *Catechism* over a three-year period, corresponding to the three-year liturgical cycle of Scripture readings. Besides, publishing houses and diocesan liturgical offices have begun providing priests and deacons with preaching guides based on the *Catechism.*

I have serious problems here. I grant that many Catholics are distressingly ignorant of God's self-revealing, do not know what the Son of God took flesh to tell us. They should come to learn this. But not by straightforward indoctrination in a homily, a kind of catechism or laundry list of dogmas to be believed, doctrines to be accepted. This might be advisable if the task of the liturgy were simply to *recall* God's saving works, *remember* the mystery that is Christ. Then I might merely explain lucidly what it all means.

But since the homily, like the liturgy of which it is part and parcel, should proclaim, re-present, make effectively present "God's wonderful works in the history of salvation," make "the mystery of Christ present and active" within the faithful,[45] indoctrination is inadequate.

Why? Several reasons.[46] For one thing, liturgical experts like Gerard Sloyan have pointed out that programs of instructional sermons understand neither the liturgy nor catechesis. They would "rob Catholics of their biblical heritage yet again and only doubtfully instruct them."[47] The liturgy is not a lecture, the pulpit not a classroom. Yes, we should learn from the liturgy, gain insights from the homily. But, even for sheer effectiveness, not in catechetical style, not by indoctrination.

Why not? Because indoctrination plays upon one faculty of the human person: the intellect's ability to grasp ideas, concepts, propositions. It pays little heed to an old Scholastic axiom, "Nothing is present in the intellect that was not previously present in the senses." Our ideas are triggered by sense experience. On the whole, then, the more powerful the sense experience, the more powerfully an idea will take hold. If I want to sell you on Beef Stroganoff or Hasenpfeffer, I don't hand you a recipe; I let you smell it, taste it, savor it. If I want you to "see" the Holocaust, I won't just say "six million were exterminated"; I'll let you see the gas ovens in Auschwitz, the mountains of human bones in Dachau. It is not enough to show you the score of Handel's *Messiah;* you must drink it in with your ears. It is one thing to hear "I love you," quite another to experience love's touch.

That is why, I have insisted for years, the effective homily is a fascinating wedding of all those ways in which the religious imagination comes to expression: vision and ritual, symbol and story, the fine arts. This is the homily at its best, the homily that makes God's wonderful works come alive, immerses in the mystery, evokes a religious response.

A response — there's the magic word. For the homily is truly a homily not when the believer assents to a proposition, declares "I do believe there are three persons in one God," but when the believer asks, "What do you want from me, Lord?" And the most effective approach to such a response is not ratiocination, not demonstration; it is imagination.

The evidence for imagination's incomparable power surrounds us. We keep saying, "A picture is worth a thousand words." Americans spend billions each year on movies, theatres, concerts. Our children's supreme educator, for good and/or ill, is TV. Even the commercials, that sell products from head to foot allegedly essential for human existence, sell us with the greatest array of imaginative talent since the creation story in Genesis 1 and John's visions on Patmos.

And we — Sunday after Sunday we dull the magic and mystery of Jesus with unappealing, soporific abstractions. Our lack of imagination contrasts sharply with what a reviewer once said of Msgr. Ronald Knox, English convert, satirist, master of style: "One can look in vain in his *Sermons* for such unctuous phrases as 'Holy Mother the Church,' which some preachers use as carelessly and frequently as sailors use obscenities to conceal their inability for sustained communication."[48]

Read Presbyterian novelist-preacher Frederick Buechner's *Telling the Truth: The Gospel as Tragedy, Comedy, and Fairy Tale,*[49] and see the Christian gospel come alive, feel it split your sides and wrench your heart, capture your imagination as graphically as do Bergman and Bradbury, Shakespeare and Spielberg. Listen to him as he pleads:

> Let the preacher stretch our imagination and strain our credulity and make our jaws drop because the sad joke of it is that if he does not, then of all people he is almost the only one left who does not. Scientists speak of intelligent life among the stars, of how at the speed of light there is no time, of consciousness as more than just an epiphenomenon of the physical brain. Doctors speak seriously about life after death, and not just the mystics anymore but the housewife, the stockbroker, the high-school senior speak about an inner world where reality becomes transparent to a reality realer still. The joke of it is that often it is the preacher who as steward of the wildest mystery of them all is the one who hangs back, prudent, cautious, hopelessly mature and wise to the last when no less than Saint Paul tells him to be a fool for Christ's sake, no less than Christ tells him to be a child for his own and the kingdom's sake.[50]

A neuralgic question for all of us. Why is it that the Catholic priest, carrier of the most fascinating, most amazing, most significant story in the history of humankind, is not captivated by it, does not shiver and shake when he thinks of it, does not sweat blood preparing to preach it, rarely preaches with the profound passion of the Protestant pastor, cannot bring his people to laugh with him and weep with him as he retells in a contemporary idiom the perennial Parable that is Jesus gloriously alive? Does it go back to the seminary, to the way we theologians deaden a living tradition, or is it a malaise that afflicts the priest because the grime and the grit of parish existence extinguish an enthusiasm that indeed was once aflame?

The priest, Urban Holmes insisted, is "one who incites people to imagine."[51] Andrew Greeley, sharp critic of contemporary priestly preaching, would agree. For him, "perhaps the most important" requirement or characteristic of effective preaching is imagination.

> Preaching is creative work. If a priest permits his creative imagination to atrophy so that it becomes a vestigial organ, then he will fail on Sunday morning. I have often argued, usually in the face of derisive laughter, that no one should be ordained who has not displayed some development of creative imagination: short stories, poems, painting exhibitions, photo shows, or storytelling interludes. I would settle for anything that demonstrates that the future priest has some spark of the creativity, with which we are all born, still on fire within him. It is virtually impossible for the priest who does not read, write, think, or imagine to do well in the most important part of his work — the homily.[52]

Preparation

Lack of preparation is, I keep insisting, the kind of devil that cannot be overcome even by prayer and fasting. Here I resonate to a story told to me some years ago at Belmont Abbey in North Carolina by the famed Baptist biblicist and preacher Dale Moody. A student in his Spirit course at the Louisville seminary was not meeting the professor's expectations. So Dr. Moody called him in and (in a delightful drawl I cannot reproduce here) said: "Son, you're not doin' all that well in my course on the Holy Spirit. You been studyin'?" "Dr. Moody," the young man replied, "I don't have to *study* about the Spirit; I'm *led* by the Spirit." "Son," Moody asked, "that Spirit ever lead you to the library? If He doesn't soon, you're in deep trouble!"

I average four hours of preparation for every minute in the pulpit. A priest in the South, reading this in an interview in the *U.S. Catholic,* wrote to the editor: "Anyone who has so much leisure can have nothing of importance to tell the rest of us." To this retort let me simply respond that in my book "preparation" of a homily includes not only the time spent at a computer but much that a priest *experiences* during his day. I mean his morning meditation, the people he meets on the street, the hospitals and/or jails he visits, the newspapers and books he reads, the TV he watches. The problem is, so little of this enters the pulpit; hence the abstractions, the timeless truths, the failure to touch living, breathing, struggling people.

One example. In early June 1997, two weeks before a wedding, I still had no idea what of significance this celibate male might say to a man and a woman about to link their love for life. Restless, frustrated, I was punching my remote control from channel to channel. For some reason — coincidence or providence — I stopped in the middle of "Touched by an Angel." The scene: only minutes before a wedding ceremony. The bride-to-be had panicked, was paralyzed by anxiety. How could she possibly say "for ever"? All her experience protested, "Nothing lasts for ever." Especially when her own mother and father had divorced.

At that moment the efficient lady in charge of all arrangements suddenly remembered, uttered aloud, the one thing she had forgotten: one invitation. An invitation to...God. Taking up on this, the angel (Della Reese, I believe) said to the bride, "Anybody can have a wedding, but it takes so much more to have a marriage." Touched by an angel, I turned from tube to IBM Word. The homily expanded on those two insights: an invitation to God, and the "so much more" it takes to have a marriage. Those two insights fused beautifully with the three liturgical texts that had been chosen by the couple: the total, the sensuous, the erotic love that is "a flame of the Lord" in the Song of Solomon 8:6–7; the chilling challenges to love, especially the call to forgiveness, in Colossians 3:12–17; and the love in John 15:9–17 that turns a couple together outward — the recessional that is a movement from church to world, from altar to people, from Christ crucified on Calvary to Christ crucified at the crossroads of our country.

Very simply, our homily is all around us: the Word of God touched to the experiences of our people. Here is my preparation. Forty hours indeed. But not hours stolen from prayer, from pastoral ministry, from relaxation. All are grist for the homilist's mill. But only if we are on tiptoe of expectation, ready for every surprise of our surprising Spirit.

Fire in the Belly

Some years ago *Time* magazine reviewed a production at the Met of Puccini's opera *La Bohème*. To credit the reviewer, the lady who played Mimi had only a moderately fine voice, but she was a splendid actress; the gentleman who played Rodolfo had a glorious voice, but his acting was egregious. At the close of the final scene, the tear-wrenching dying of Mimi, the reviewer remarked, "His [Rodolfo's] was the only dry eye in the house."

Passion is not an option for the preacher; his dare not be the only dry eye in the church. Passion is a must; for passion simply means I feel deeply. Passion is prophet Hosea proclaiming in God's name, "A spirit of whoredom has led [my people] astray, and they have played the whore, forsaking their God" (Hos 4:12). Passion is Jesus driving buyers and sellers from the temple, overturning the tables of the money changers. Passion is Martin Luther King Jr. excoriating violence while a bullet tears his flesh on a Memphis balcony. Passion is Children's Defense Fund president Marian Wright Edelman sending an open letter to President Bill Clinton blasting both the Senate and the House welfare bills as "fatally flawed, callous, anti-child assaults."[53] Passion is the rage we feel when we read of Serbs butchering 8,000 Muslims near Srebenika. Passion is the sense of outrage I experience when elderly men and women have to rummage for food in garbage cans. Yes, passion is the consuming love that links a husband and wife as little else can.

Save possibly for a consummate actor, pulpit passion, fire in the belly, is not an emotion a preacher can fake, manufacture at will. In a sense, it surges up in despite of us. Reason can exercise some control, but often reason cannot simply suppress it. For which I thank God . . . passionately. I do not want to be in perfect control when I preach, especially when I am castigating biblical injustice, infidelity to relationships, to responsibilities, that stem from our covenant with God in the blood of Christ. I want people to sense that when I speak of the violence in my District of Columbia, violence that in five years took the lives of over 200 children, violence that has children preparing not their futures but their funerals, I feel for them, I fear for them, I weep with them. I want people to see that when I pour out statistics on children — one out of every four grows up in poverty in the richest country on earth, the younger you are the poorer you are — I am outraged, I grow black with anger. I want people to feel that whether I am praising them for work with the oppressed and marginalized or challenging them to risk even more for Christ and his crucified images, I love them with a crucifying love. I want people to sense that my homilies are not primarily head trips, cool, calm, collected analyses of a world in danger of losing its soul.

For all my way with words, Cartesian clarity is not enough. The homiletic word flings forth a challenge; it is a summons to decision; God wants a reply. But if I want to persuade, my whole person must be aflame with what I proclaim. If I am to move, the words I utter must be chosen not only with care and love, but with sweat and fire. To challenge, the word must come alive; *I* must come alive. How do the passionate preachers get that way? Some by heart-rending experience with the poor, with the downtrodden and the forgotten, with the AIDS-afflicted and the drug-addicted. Most of us, like myself, profit at second hand, from TV and the local newspaper, even from music and poetry. That is why, before I actually compose, before I bring my ideas together in organized fashion, I listen to Beethoven or Tchaikovsky, Marilyn Horne or Whitney Houston — most recently, Carreras, Domingo, and Pavarotti in concert; I read poetry aloud, Shakespeare or Gerard Manley Hopkins, Elizabeth Barrett Browning or Maya Angelou. Something to turn me on, so that the end result will not sound like a Roman rescript or a laundry list. With increasing zest I listen to the prophets of Israel — today and yesterday. Let me tell you how.

Prophet and Preacher

A significant influence on my preaching has been the revered Rabbi Abraham Joshua Heschel. I first made contact with him at Notre Dame's 1966 International Theological Conference (about which I wrote at some length in chapter 3), when he spoke on the need for dialogue: What divides us, what unites us? My next contact was through his written word. It was 1972. I was spending a week of retreat in Sedona, Arizona, at the Spiritual Life Institute of America, founded and directed by the Discalced Carmelite William McNamara, whom I have elsewhere described as a wondrous wedding of Irish wit and Isaian woe. There I came across some of the authors who express SLIA's vision or some facet thereof: Merton and Maritain, Aelred Graham and Gerald Vann, Josef Pieper and Nikos Kazantzakis, Teilhard de Chardin, John of the Cross, and C. S. Lewis. And there lay Heschel's *God in Search of Man*.[54] For Heschel, I discovered, the problem of God is really the problem of man and woman. It is their meaning that "cries for an answer, and worship is an answer. For worship is an act of man's relating himself to ultimate meaning. Unless man is capable of entering a relation to ultimate meaning, worship is an illusion. And if worship is meaningless, human existence is an absurdity."

My next contact was a 1982 article in *America*. It seems that several years before his death in 1972, Heschel suffered a near-fatal heart attack from which he never fully recovered. A dear friend visiting him then found him woefully weak. Just about able to whisper, Heschel said to him: "Sam, when I regained consciousness, my first feeling was not of despair or anger. I felt only gratitude to God for my life, for every moment I had lived. I was ready to depart. 'Take me, O Lord,' I thought, 'I have seen so many miracles in my lifetime.'" Exhausted by the effort, Heschel paused, then added: "That is what I mean when I wrote [in the Preface to his book of Yiddish poems]: 'I did not ask for success; I asked for wonder. And You gave it to me.'"[55]

Worship and wonder. What more could I expect from Heschel? His book *The Prophets*[56] — especially the opening chapter, "What Manner of Man Is the Prophet?" This discovery, in the mid-'80s, tossed fresh fuel into my homiletic flames. For Heschel's presentation of the (male) biblical prophets persuaded me to compare the ancient prophet with the modern preacher.[57] He exposed seven facets of prophetic preaching; five I found splendidly adaptable to our homiletic situation.

1. The Hebrew prophet is extraordinarily sensitive to evil, to injustice — so much so that at times he seems to pay excessive attention to trivialities, what *we* might deplore but have learned to live with. "To us a single act of injustice — cheating in business, exploitation of the poor — is slight; to the prophets, a disaster. To us injustice is injurious to the welfare of the people; to the prophets it is a deathblow to existence; to us, an episode; to them, a catastrophe, a threat to the world...."[58]

2. In consequence, this "man who feels fiercely,"[59] who is stunned by human greed, whose prophecy is the voice God has lent to the silent agony of the plundered poor, this man in whose voice God rages, this man rarely sings, he castigates; his images do not shine, they burn; his words do not mean to edify, they are meant to shock.

3. The Hebrew prophets were iconoclasts. They challenged sacred institutions, sacred beliefs, sacred persons. To those who kept mouthing, "This is the temple of the Lord, the temple of the Lord, the temple of the Lord," Jeremiah responded, "Do not trust in these deceptive words" (Jer 7:4). The temple would not save them, would not assure Yahweh's protection. For this, they had to amend their ways. As long as faithfulness was far from the people, sacrifices were not pleasing to the Lord. And to the kings who were anointed to shepherd Israel Ezekiel cried out, "The weak you have not strengthened, the sick you have not healed, the injured you have not bound up, the strayed you have not brought back, the lost you

have not sought, but with force and harshness you have ruled them" (Ezek 34:4).

4. The Hebrew prophets were embarrassed, lonely, frustrated. Embarrassed because, while others were predicting peace and prosperity, they threatened disaster and destruction. Lonely because they alienated simply everyone: the pious as well as the wicked, believers as well as cynics, priests as well as princes, judges as well as false prophets. Little wonder that Jeremiah laments, "Cursed be the day on which I was born!" (Jer 20:14). Frustrated because "For 23 years I [Jeremiah] have spoken persistently to you, but you have not listened" (Jer 25:3).

5. The prophets' words were charged with divine power because they had experienced God's own pathos.[60] They were not particularly interested in God's essence; their God was not the Wholly Other. They had experienced God "as living care":[61] the God of the covenant, a God involved in history, a God who has a stake in the human situation, a God who is intimately affected by events. The human person is not only an image of God but a perpetual concern of God, "a consort, a partner, a factor in the life of God."[62] The prophets not only heard God's voice; they felt God's heart. How, then, could they ever speak dispassionately, serene and unruffled?

I have argued time and again that Heschel's prophets, from Isaiah to Malachi, can be, should be, a pattern for our own prophetic speech. First, many of us have lost, or have never had, the neuralgic sensitivity to evil and injustice that ought to mark every prophet. Some surely share that sensitivity; but it is usually those who have experienced firsthand the sorry existence of the poor and the imprisoned, the hungry and the downtrodden. More of us simply deplore injustice; we are against sin; we take up collections for the homeless Haitians or Kosovars. Moreover, there is so much evil, so much injustice, over the globe that we grow used to it; with TV's remote control we can wolf our pizzas and slurp our Schlitz to the roar of rockets and the flow of blood.

When that happens, our preaching will not reflect a second facet of Hebrew prophecy: We will not "feel fiercely." When I began to preach five decades ago, the Catholic stress was on the clear and distinct idea. Our seminary education, in philosophy and theology, emphasized objectivity. We were dispassionate searchers for truth, cool critics of error and heresy — beetle-browed, lynx-eyed, hard-nosed, square-jawed. Imagination was for poets. We did not show our emotions. Emotions were for women, and women could not be ordained.

For effective preaching the analytic mind is not enough by half. Not that we should rant and rave in the pulpit. I mean rather that our people should sense from our words and our faces, from our gestures and our whole posture, that we love this sinning, struggling community with a crucifying passion; that we agonize over our own sinfulness, our failure to be holier than we are; that we weep with the refugees whose tears water the ways of Rwanda; that we too are awfully vulnerable, prey to the loneliness that ravages the human heart; that we too must at times cry out "I believe, Lord; help my unbelief"; that the heavy-burdened can look to us not so much for answers as for empathy; that our celibacy has not turned us into crotchety old bachelors but opens us warmly to all who need the touch of our hand; in a word, that we too share the dread-full human condition. And, not least, that we who are priests joy in our priesting, would not exchange it, literally, for "the world."

Third, the Christian preacher must prove a ceaseless challenge to the community. Iconoclasts? Yes, in the sense that our task, in part, is to shatter false images, destroy idols. That these parade in the cloak of the sacred — institutions, beliefs, persons — only makes our task more sensitive, more delicate; it does not remove our responsibility.

Not ours, like Savonarola, to castigate, condemn, flay the people before us. But must we not insist to them, with Jeremiah, that the temple of stone in which they worship does not save; that though the Church is a community of salvation, only Jesus saves; that the more important temple is this flesh of ours which is the living temple of the Spirit? Must we not constantly preach that the faith which is a firm acceptance of revealed propositions is sterile without the faith which is a total self-giving to the revealing God? Should it not leap forth from what we say and how we say it that the shepherds, whether pope or pastor, are servants, often "unprofitable"; that it is not only the laity but ourselves who are ceaselessly summoned to conversion, that our homilies are directed in the first instance at our own lives? Is it impertinent for modern prophets to apprise the people of the Baals in their midst — perhaps especially the resurgent rugged individualism that imperils the Pauline doctrine of a single body in which no one can say to any other, "I have no need of you" (1 Cor 12:21)?

Fourth, it is the rare preacher who is rarely lonely — especially the celibate. For all the TLC in our lives, we walk very much alone. Not Trappist solitude; my preaching has to be born of people and their needs. But the task of hearing what God is saying to me — in the word I read on the sacred page, in the word that is the Church's reflection on God's revelation, in the word God speaks to the depths of my heart, in the voices of the world around me — is a lonely toil. For to hear is not enough; I must struggle with that word, at times wrestle with God, lay hold of the word not only with cold intellect but with my rebellious emotions. Most taxing task of all, I must live the word I preach.

Fifth, our words, like the words of the prophets, should be charged with divine power. Not primarily because we have been ordained to preach (I do not discount sacramental grace) but because we have experienced God. I shall say more on this in the chapter on spirituality. For my present purposes, I recommend several sentences Karl Rahner has put on the pen of Ignatius Loyola:

> I was convinced that first, tentatively, during my illness in Loyola and then, decisively, during my time as a hermit in Manresa I had a direct encounter with God.... I am not going to talk of forms and visions, symbols, voices, tears and such things.... All I say is I knew God, nameless and unfathomable, silent and yet near, bestowing Himself upon me in His Trinity. I knew God beyond all concrete imaginings. I knew Him clearly in such nearness and grace as is impossible to confound or mistake.... I knew God Himself, not simply human words describing Him.... This experience is grace indeed and basically there is no one to whom it is refused.... [63]

With Heschel, I am speaking of an experience not of a God dwelling only in some sort of outer space, but of a God intimately involved in our history, a God who became one of us. Here my background in Scholasticism makes for problems. How experience as "living care" a God whom we conceive as Immovable Mover, a kind of Christian Buddha staring unblinkingly into space? I am not ready to deny divine immutability. But this I dare say: We shall be effective preachers to the extent that we experience and preach a living God, a loving God. Loving not only because God gave a unique Son to crucifixion for us almost two millennia ago, but because right now what happens to me happens somehow to God. I must experience and preach a God who "not only rules the world in the majesty of His might and wisdom, but reacts intimately to the events of history ... does not stand outside the range of human suffering and sorrow [but] ... is personally involved in, even stirred by, the conduct and fate of man."[64]

The Cost of Preaching

What shall a man or woman "give in exchange" for effective preaching? I began to learn in the early '80s, when I first came across a soul-stirring book by Dietrich Bonhoeffer, the German Lutheran pastor who was hanged in 1945 for conspiring to overthrow Hitler. First published in 1937, *The Cost of Discipleship* contained a phrase that was to echo through much of the Western world: "cheap grace and costly grace."

Bonhoeffer was troubled by a puzzling problem. How could it be that the Church and the preacher were using so ineffectively the most precious gift they possessed, the word of the nearby God? How explain the chasm that yawned between the Church's mandate to preach the word publicly and the dismaying absence of credibility in the preacher and his preaching? He looked for, struggled for, renewal of the word's authority not through a fresh doctrine of ministry but through discipleship alone. And renewal of discipleship meant a renewed concentration on a root Reformation principle, *sola gratia,* "grace alone." Not cheap grace; costly grace.

> Cheap grace means grace sold on the market like cheapjacks' wares. The sacraments, the forgiveness of sin, and the consolations of religion are thrown away at cut prices. Grace is represented as the Church's inexhaustible treasure, from which she showers blessings with generous hands, without asking questions or fixing limits.... The essence of grace, we suppose, is that the account has been paid in advance; and, because it has been paid, everything can be had for nothing.... What would grace be if it were not cheap?
>
> Cheap grace means grace as a doctrine, a principle, a system. It means forgiveness of sins proclaimed as a general truth, the love of God taught as the Christian "conception" of God. An intellectual assent to that idea is held to be of itself sufficient to secure remission of sins....
>
> Cheap grace is the preaching of forgiveness without requiring repentance, baptism without church discipline, Communion without confession, absolution without personal confession. Cheap grace is grace without discipleship, grace without the cross, grace without Jesus Christ, living and incarnate.
>
> Costly grace is the treasure hidden in the field; for the sake of it a man will gladly go and sell all that he has. It is the pearl of great price to buy which the merchant will sell all his goods. It is the kingly rule of Christ, for whose sake a man will pluck

out the eye which causes him to stumble, it is the call of Jesus Christ at which the disciple leaves his nets and follows him.

Costly grace is the gospel which must be *sought* again and again, the gift which must be *asked* for, the door at which a man must *knock*.

Such grace is *costly* because it calls us to follow, and it is *grace* because it calls us to follow *Jesus Christ*. It is costly because it costs a man his life, and it is grace because it gives a man the only true life. It is costly because it condemns sin, and grace because it justifies the sinner. Above all, it is *costly* because it cost God the life of his Son: "ye were bought at a price," and what has cost God much cannot be cheap for us. Above all, it is *grace* because God did not reckon his Son too dear a price to pay for our life, has delivered him up for us. Costly grace is the Incarnation of God.[65]

I am convinced that within the Catholic Church preaching remains at a low ebb, is less effective than it should be, primarily because preachers of the Word, specifically those ordained to preach, either see the sermon as a product that comes cheap or, recognizing its high cost, are reluctant to pay the price. Effective preaching, preaching that moves hearts and changes minds, is costly because, like grace, it costs me my life. Literally. An outrageous thesis? Hardly. I preach at a great price because preaching costs me my mind, my spirit, my flesh and blood.[66]

Preaching costs me my *mind*. Ceaselessly I confront the preacher's predicament: how to grasp accurately "the Word of God," a God who communicates with me in words and language God does not personally employ, a divine mind translated by syllables that are not divine and are conditioned by time and culture. Sunday after Sunday I face "the three stages of tradition by which the doctrine and the life of Jesus have come down to us": (1) what Jesus actually said and did, (2) the preaching of the apostles interpreting Jesus' words and deeds "according to the needs of their listeners," and (3) the Gospel authors selecting what they needed and "adapting their narration of them" to current situations.[67] This is the kind of knowledge that makes a bloody entrance. I have to study. Only through intellectual discipline can most of us, people without extraordinary charisms, become effective preachers. For at least three good reasons.

First, it is through disciplined study that I increasingly comprehend what I mean when I say, "The Word of the Lord." Not every sentence I declaim from Scripture is God's revelation. In fact, there are books in the Bible where it is difficult to find any revelation at all. And still all the books of Scripture "were written under the inspiration of the Holy Spirit and therefore have God for author."[68] We are indeed far from a totally satisfying theory of scriptural inspiration, but I find it reassuring and exciting that whatever I announce from Genesis 1:1 to Revelation 22:21 is there because, for God's own good reasons, God wanted it there and, in the mysterious fashion proper to divinity, the Holy Spirit arranged that the human writer(s) put it there.

Second reason: It is largely through disciplined study that I can preach a genuinely biblical homily. Not a homily that "uses" a Scripture phrase as a superficial springboard or to bolster ideas already elaborated. Rather, a homily that moves seriously and credibly from what the text meant then to what it might be saying now. A homily, e.g., on Matthew 22:1–14 (the wedding banquet) that sees Matthew's version of the parable(s) emerging from his community experience: infighting, lack of love, the agonizing question of Christian identity. A homily that adapts Matthew's experience to our contemporary Catholic community, where the preacher can say with Matthew: (1) You do indeed have a Catholic identity, shared in part with other Christians, different in that you express your commitment to Christ through a body of beliefs, a system of sacraments, an order of authority that other Christians cannot totally share. (2) You have a wider mission than to your own local community; the world is your parish. (3) Whatever your mission is, it will fail if you cannot live with your divisions, if the hurts that tear you and the divisions that rend you cannot be made redemptive, if you cannot bind the wounds that keep you from experiencing, from tasting, the banquet of salvation in this particular "royal hall."[69]

A third reason: Disciplined study helps me to lay hold of the Church's authentic tradition. By tradition I mean "Scripture within the Church." On this point I have often recommended two instructive paragraphs from Vatican II:

> And so the apostolic preaching, which is expressed in a special way in the inspired books, was to be preserved by a continuous succession of preachers until the end of time. Therefore the apostles, handing on what they themselves had received, warn the faithful to hold fast to the traditions which they have learned either by word of mouth or by letter (cf. 2 Thess 2:15)....Now what was handed on by the apostles includes everything which contributes to the holiness of life and the in-

crease in faith of the People of God, and so the Church, in her teaching, life, and worship, perpetuates and hands on to all generations all that she herself is, all that she believes.

This tradition which comes from the apostles develops in the Church with the help of the Holy Spirit. For there is a *growth in the understanding* of the realities and the words which have been handed down. This happens through the *contemplation and study* made by believers, who treasure these things in their hearts (cf. Lk 2:19, 51), through the intimate understanding of spiritual things they experience, and through the preaching of those who have received through episcopal succession the sure gift of truth. For, as the centuries succeed one another, the Church constantly moves forward toward the fullness of divine truth until the words of God reach their complete fulfillment in her.[70]

I have been singularly blessed, for I have been privileged to study intimately how the Church has grown in understanding: understanding of itself, of its mission, of its message. I do not expect the parish priest to be a professional theologian. I do expect him to continue, in fact to intensify, the struggle he initiated in the seminary — an ongoing effort to grow with the Church. His enemy is time. His enemy is the explosion of knowledge — in Scripture, in history, in theology. His enemy is the complexity of today's human issues, from world hunger through genetic engineering to the morality of contemporary war. Still, no preacher dare abandon the struggle to understand, for to forsake it is to risk condemning our preaching to sterile abstractions; it is to settle for "cheap grace."

Effective preaching lays a heavy cost on my *spirit*. Actually, "spirit" includes what I have said about the mind, but it goes beyond my ability to grasp an idea; spirit is my whole intellectual nature — my imagination, my emotions and passions, my creativity. Take imagination. For most Catholic preachers, imagining takes more effort, induces more spiritual sweat, demands more courage than the clear and distinct idea. Once I start saying, "the kingdom of heaven is like...," once I break through the surface to the reality beneath, once I plunge into the world of intuition and wonder, of festivity and play, I'm in C. S. Lewis' Narnia, the kingdom of the imagination, where reigns the lion Aslan, the unsafe, untamed Christ; where the courtly mouse Reepicheep convinces me that danger is something I meet head on; where the pessimistic marshwiggle Puddleglum surprises me with his "Suppose we *have* only dreamed all these things. Then all I can say is that . . . the made-up things seem a good deal more important than the real ones."[71]

In point of fact, I revel in it, this kingdom of the imagination. But for all its fascination, for all its delight, there is a recurring insecurity here. It's like walking on the moon; you're never quite sure what lies ahead. You open all sorts of doors, open yourself to the unexpected; and the unexpected can be startling, even frightening. And you open yourself to being misunderstood; for the imagination, remember, is more open-ended than the concept, capable of different understandings.

Effective preaching takes its toll on the emotions, on the passions. Can I possibly assail the assault on the womb (1.5 million developing humans in the United States forcibly prevented each year from seeing the light of God's day), deplore the rape of women and slaughter of innocents in Bosnia, Rwanda, and Kosovo, mention the 30-odd million refugees who water the world's roads with their tears, without losing my cool? A justice of New York State's Supreme Court tells us, "A society that loses its sense of outrage is doomed to extinction."[72] Not outrage for a passing moment in the pulpit. Outrage that surges up as I read another front-page article on the hungers of our children, tears that well up as I touch the hurts of God's broken images each day on the streets of our nation's capital. I cannot compose a homily the way I stucco a wall — completely calm, cool, and collected.

More generally, I have a love-hate relationship with each homily. To see me at my word processor is to shake your head in wonder. From the first phase of mulling to the final phrase of text, I am a man possessed. My homiletic life exemplifies a sentence in the preface of Richard Bach's delightful allegory *Illusions: The Adventures of a Reluctant Messiah:* "Once in a while there's a great dynamite-burst of flying glass and bricks and splinters through the front wall and somebody stalks over the rubble, seizes me by the throat and gently says: 'I will not let you go until you set me, in words, on paper.' "[73]

I love it because preaching calls into play just about everything I have studied and taught, experienced and been graced with, through more than half a century of Jesuit existence. Classical studies and history, foreign languages and English literature, philosophy and theology, Scripture and patristics, spirituality and prayer, community living and extensive traveling, Hollywood and Broadway, music and the dance, dialogues Jewish and Protestant, friendships with all manner of folk from teenagers to the aging — all this and so much more is grist to my homiletic mill. I could not ask for a richer set of resources. All of these are caught up into this moment, this hour, these weeks — instruments of beauty and goodness and truth ready to be shaped into a singular symphony.

But the love is saturated with frustration. I frequently feel what St. Augustine of Hippo felt: "For my part, I am nearly always dissatisfied with my discourse. For I am desirous of something better...; but when I find that my powers of expression come short of my knowledge of the subject, I am sorely disappointed that my tongue has not been able to answer the demands of my mind."[74] Conceiving mystery correctly (from an ageless Trinity to a ceaseless Evil) and expressing it in language acceptable to Rome's Congregation for the Doctrine of the Faith is painful enough, laborious, exacting. More frustrating still is the task of translating the technical truth, molding it in such a way that a fresh vision of God and human living takes hold of minds theologically untrained, of hearts yearning to be stirred, of eyes pleading to see Jesus.

Finally, effective preaching costs me my *flesh and blood* — while I prepare, for some hours before delivery, and after all has been said. The days and weeks of composition differ significantly from my research into the Fathers of the Church. My body tenses, muscles tighten, nerves give me fits — as they rarely did in patristic research. There I was hardly harassed by a clock; I could set my own pace; I was not aware of men and women whose relationship to God and to fellow humans might be altered by my research. Weariness, yes; perplexity, often; anxiety, at times; but spasms of the colon, acid in the esophagus, rarely.

The hours before delivery have been, continue to be, in very truth nauseating. Especially if, as often, the congregation is entirely new to me (Good Friday homilies in Seattle's cathedral on the Seven Last Words of Christ) or the occasion uncommon, even somewhat awesome (a baccalaureate homily on Georgetown's campus before ten thousand from a hundred countries; a unique homily on the shores of Guam, celebrating the beatification of Blessed Diego of the Marianas). Here the spastic colon and the hiatal hernia have a field day, and the hours of darkness preceding are a night of the loose bowel.

Nor does my thorn in the flesh cease to be active once the homily is over. Once I relax totally, sit down with a grateful and satisfied "aaah," it is often a signal for the flesh to take revenge. All energy may vanish, stomach spasms strike with dismaying regularity, food refuses to sit comfortably within the system.

I often ask myself: Is this a natural price perfectionists must pay?

Or does a less than Christian pride, excessive human ambition, a thirst for the world's applause play a role in my striving for a perfect production? Were I seeking God's glory alone, would "the slings and arrows" I endure be less "outrageous"? Possibly; I cannot say yes or no with any conviction. I only know that the effectiveness of my preaching often seems directly proportionate to the agony of mind, spirit, and flesh I endure. I like to think that even more powerful than my yearning for approval is my anxiety to get inside this congregation, lift living people out of a routine existence, strengthen the hearts of the heavy-burdened, inspire a fresh vision — and I am psychically and physically sensitive to the possibilities of mucking up. A bad sermon is not simply laying another egg. All too many of the faithful leave us if they do not hear from our lips as from the lips of Jesus "words of grace" (Lk 4:22) — captivating eloquence and words conveying God's merciful favor.

In summary, my own experience and the experience of countless others convinces me that it is difficult for most humans to shape a work of art with hands alone or tongue. The whole man, the whole woman, must be absorbed into the creation. Not with serene objectivity, like a zoologist peering through a microscope. More like Welsh poet Dylan Thomas, "alternately ecstatic and morbid," obsessed "with death, religion, sex, and the sound of words," high-spiritedly in love with life.[75]

Mentors Who Molded Me

What preachers lie behind me, sensibly or insensibly molding my homilies?[76] The first, and at that time quite remote, influence arose more than a half century ago, in my Jesuit juniorate — classical studies on a college level. We read "The Second Spring," a sermon preached by John Henry Newman, then a convert of seven years, as the second session of the First Provincial Synod of Westminster opened at St. Mary's College, Oscott, July 13, 1852.[77] Two years before, Rome had restored a diocesan hierarchy to an England whose Catholic situation had been remarkably transformed for the better in the seven decades preceding. Preaching before Nicholas Cardinal Wiseman, the bishops of England, and a number of distinguished children of the Oxford Movement and descendants of the English martyrs, Newman had his listeners in tears as he sketched the glories of the ancient Catholic Church of England, its death, and its second life only then beginning. It was a historic moment, even though the sanguine hopes of the preacher and his congregation for the rapid conversion of England did not materialize. A historic moment, and a remarkable sermon, which merits study and meditation as a piece of homiletic art.

Newman's theory of preaching? (1) Be earnest, that is, intensely aware of the purpose of preaching, to minister a spiritual good. (2) Be definite, for definiteness is the life of preaching: a definite hearer, a definite topic, a definite speaker; nothing which is anonymous or simply of yesterday. (3) Be personal, for people are moved not simply by what is said but by who says it; the preacher persuades by what he is as well as by what he delivers.

But in my early Jesuit days it was not so much Newman's ideas that captivated me as his mastery of language. The words he chose always seemed so right; he could sustain, as few since, the periodic sentence; and the language was instinct with love. We imitated him, not to plagiarize but to get his feel for words, for style, for the ordering of a clause, a sentence, a paragraph; how to use language with reverence, with care, with discrimination, with feeling.

A second strong influence on my preaching stemmed from the early Christian theologians, the patristic literature that has been my specialization and love since the Jesuit juniorate. It was specifically in graduate studies under Johannes Quasten at the Catholic University of America that several facets of "the Fathers" took on pertinence for my preaching. I came to realize how astonishingly large a proportion of the patristic legacy was transmitted in sermons, in face-to-face contact with a believing, worshiping community. For those theologians, theology was not an arcane discipline, done in ivory towers or behind ivied walls. Their theology was itself a spirituality, to be communicated in vibrant speech to pulsing people. And that theology/spirituality was profoundly rooted in Scripture.

From scores of patristic preachers, five have served me particularly well. There is Leo the Great (pope 440–61), lucidly clear and admirably succinct, sentences neatly balanced, antitheses and wordplays delighting eye and ear, making Christ come alive in ever-fresh ways. There is Origen (ca. 185–253), strikingly original thinker who may have preached nearly every day (so his biographer Pamphilus), homilies with four characteristics: (1) a liturgical dimension, giving flesh to the Word in the community of faith and worship; (2) a prophetic quality, not only instructing minds but converting hearts; (3) essentially scriptural, often a running exposition of the text; (4) direct, familiar, conversational.[78]

There is Augustine, who constantly astonished and delighted, though he had a weak voice and tired quickly. Most of his sermons were more spontaneous than they seem: delivered first, written down then or afterwards by someone else. Logical construction was not his forte. He played perpetually on words, punned shamelessly, was inordinately fond of assonance, alliteration, antitheses. He encouraged reactions from his audience, found applause stimulating, provocative: "What is there to cheer about? We are still battling with the problem and you have already started to cheer!"[79] He saw the sermon as not only education but entertainment: "You must not believe, brothers and sisters, that the Lord intended us to be entirely without theatrical spectacles of some kind. If there were none here, would you have come together in this place?"[80] More substantially, Augustine's sermons are essentially biblical in character; he is proclaiming biblical truth; he lives in Scripture; the Bible has shaped him. And here Augustine's theory of knowledge is pertinent. No man or woman really instructs another; the real teacher is God. And so Augustine plants the word of God from God's Word and lets God make the twig bear fruit, the leaf burst forth.[81]

There is John Chrysostom. The eighteen large volumes of his works in Migne (*Patrologia graeca* 47–64) are for the most part sermons. The remarkable purity of his language, the style the classical scholar Wilamowitz-Moellendorff called "the harmonious expression of an Attic soul," and his startlingly direct, down-to-earth applications can make us forget that most of his sermons are exegetical homilies on the two Testaments. They home into the literal sense; they invariably extract a spiritual message; and they confront the congregation where the people actually live. I have long been impressed by and profited from Chrysostom's passionate attachment to St. Paul. It grieved him sorely that some Christians were not only ignorant of the man, but did not even "know for certain the number of his epistles." I realize that in our day biblical criticism has made us intelligently uncertain of the exact number; but we can blame only ourselves for not knowing and loving Paul as Chrysostom did, for not preaching the Pauline Christ with some of his infectious enthusiasm.

Finally among the Fathers, I owe much to Gregory the Great (pope 590–604), specifically his *Pastoral Care,* a practical work that in the Middle Ages was for the secular clergy what the Rule of St. Benedict was for the religious orders. I found it highly useful for the four problems Gregory set himself to discuss: (1) the person and motives the pastoral office demands, (2) the virtues of a good pastor, (3) how to preach to different types of people, and (4) the need for recollection, "return to oneself." In Part 3 he details, with pastoral concern and psychological acumen, 36 contrasting sets of people (e.g., men and women, young and old, joyful and sad, meek and choleric, taciturn and loquacious, gluttonous and abstemious) that must be distinguished by the preacher and teacher. Whence came this knowledge? From uncommonly wide experience: in world and monastery, as papal nuncio and pope, with soldiers and generals, merchants and kings, rich and poor, lofty and lowly, manic and depressive, priests and bishops and patriarchs. Much of his career and personality, his ability and humility, reminds me of good Pope John XXIII.

As for Protestant influences, the first to impress me were theologians. Close contact for more than a decade with Lutherans such as Joseph Sittler, Arthur Carl Piepkorn, Warren Quanbeck, and George Lindbeck moved the "adversaries" of my undergraduate theology to friends deeply devoted to our common Lord, profoundly spiritual, in love with liturgy, engagingly human. A good bit later the Protestant theologian was supplemented by the Protestant preacher.

Three preachers in particular. First and foremost, Frederick Buechner, convert from agnosticism and Presbyterian minister, first-rate preacher and seasoned novelist. Mulling over two collections of his sermons from the '60s, The *Magnificent Defeat*[82] and *The Hungering Dark,*[83] I was constantly arrested, delighted, amazed at what David Read called his "fresh language, poetic vision, unexpected twists, deeply personal witness to Christ."[84] I would add, perhaps under "unexpected twists," Buechner's grasp of the comic, the humorous, in Scripture.[85] If the tragic is the inevitable, the comic is the unforeseeable, the incongruous: God choosing the Jews; Sarah and Abraham laughing uncontrollably "at the idea of a baby's being born in the geriatric ward and Medicare's picking up the tab"; the Prince of Peace who looks like the prince of fools. Perhaps in particular, I continue to resonate to remarks Buechner made in a 1983 address celebrating the rededication of the library at New York City's Union Theological Seminary: "Words are our godly sharing in the work of creation, and the speaking and writing of words is at once the most human and the most holy of all the businesses we engage in." He went on to say, "The ultimate purpose of language, I suspect, is so that humanity may speak to God."

Then there is Lutheran theologian Joseph Sittler, with whom I spent uncommonly profitable days within the Lutheran-Roman Catholic dialogue. I have relished his little book *The Anguish of Preaching,*[86] particularly his insights into what can be taught the preacher (disciplines correlative to preaching) and what cannot (preaching itself). I heard him preach no more than three times, at a convocation hosted by Bangor (Maine) Theological Seminary in 1968. His spoken word, even when unrehearsed, lent delight to the ear: measured syllables, rhetorical balance, lovely cadences, all with a view to gentle yet forceful Christian persuasion. I cannot overestimate my indebtedness to him for his wonderful wedding of God's Word imaginatively recaptured and his sense of the sacredness and power of our own feeble syllables. And this simply the outer garment for Sittler's startling insights into God's Word. Take two sentences from one of those sermons, "The Nimbus and the Rainbow," a reflection on the story of Noah and the ark within the American furor over the rape of nature.

> The bow of God's promise and power and grace is over the city. Absolutely according to man's decision the city can become a theatre of grace in which humanity can be richly realized, or it can become a humanly intolerable hell, a stifling intersection of procedures for industrial convenience and, in Chicago's instance, conventioneers' frivolity.[87]

To grasp the significance of Sittler's concern, one must realize how intensely Sittler campaigned for "a doctrine of grace elaborated as fully under the article of God the Creator as a doctrine of grace has been historically developed under the article of God the Redeemer."[88]

Most recently I have been stimulated by the sermons (published Sunday after Sunday) of David H. C. Read, for three decades minister of the Madison Avenue Presbyterian Church in New York City, cofounder with me and Robert Birge of the ecumenical journal *The Living Pulpit*. His sermons reflect his rich experience of our human condition, especially as a World War II chaplain, a prisoner for five years.

> Being taken prisoner means being stripped down. Suddenly everything you have come to rely on is gone. Your possessions, your job, your plans, those dearest to you, your country — all these are, in a peculiar way, no longer there. There's just you — and God? ... [H]unger and thirst can drive almost every other thought from the mind. I had a little Greek Testament with me when I was captured, and I read it on the road. But a friend marching beside me remarked one day that he didn't see me reading it when we were passing through a village

where French women were thrusting bread into our hands as we passed.... All the texts on which one has preached ... these suddenly seem either mere pulpit rhetoric or the most important words in the world. I knew then and ever after that they are real — even when the darkness falls and the foundations quiver.[89]

Link such profound experience of living and dying to Read's love for Christ and the Word and the Church, to his insatiable yearning to plunge deeper and deeper into the Mystery that is God and the mystery that is God's every creation, to a rhetoric that can glow with the icy logic of the philosopher or the consuming fire of the prophet — and you have a preacher, if not for all seasons, surely for our post-Christian culture.

How summarize what I owe to the Protestant pulpit? It centers, I suspect, on biblical preaching. Not that my earlier, pre-Vatican II sermons were unscriptural; rather that the biblical heritage in my preaching was transmitted through, all but hidden in, the Church's doctrine. I rarely wrestled with the text myself; that had all been done for me. What was lost in such transmission was a personal experience of the Word. It's the difference between seeing a movie, say *Schindler's List,* and reading a summary of the plot and its meaning; between an experience of the symbols and an explanation thereof.

Not that the Protestant pulpit did it all for me. The biblical resurgence within Catholicism in the wake of Pius XII's *Divino afflante Spiritu* (1943) and the scriptural focus exemplified by Vatican II have surely touched me more directly. Still, I find it a fine thing in retrospect that our Protestant brothers and sisters have kept thrusting the text in our faces and urging us to "take and read." Not the average TV evangelist; rather the Protestant scholars and preachers who have struggled with God's Word, have not found therein fast-acting placebos for the predestined, have linked what the Word meant then to what it might be saying now, have tried to translate that Word into syllables that speak to the heart of our cultures, to the root of our experiences.

For all this, good friends, much thanks.

An Ecumenical Epilogue

In the early '90s Baylor University, a Baptist institution in Waco, Texas, instituted a methodical two-year homiletic survey coordinated by sociology professor Larry Lyon. The background of the survey was a desire to invite great preachers to campus as part of the university's celebration of its 150th anniversary (1996–97). The inability of an anniversary panel to agree on whom to invite resulted in a two-pronged search in the world's major English-speaking countries designed to uncover (1) certain indispensable characteristics of effective preaching and (2) the 12 most effective preachers in the English-speaking world.

For the first phase, 333 questionnaires were sent to professors of homiletics in the world's major English-speaking countries. Responses from 151 provided Dr. Lyon with 700 suggested qualities, 93 percent of them fitting neatly into seven broad categories: biblical/exegetical, relevance, preacher's persona, theological/orthodox, sermon structure, effective communication, and delivery/style. For the second phase, surveys then went out to the original set of homiletics professors, to editors of Christian periodicals, to the 15 preachers named by *Ebony* magazine in 1993 as most effective African-American preachers, and then to each preacher who received a nomination. From 341 responses came 1,548 nominations. The top 12 were named as Baylor's most effective preachers in the English-speaking world. The list, in alphabetical order:

Walter J. Burghardt, S.J., senior fellow, Woodstock Theological Center, Washington, D.C.

Fred Craddock, professor emeritus of preaching and New Testament, Candler School of Theology, Emory University, Atlanta, Ga.

James Forbes Jr., senior minister, Riverside Church, New York, N.Y.

Billy Graham, evangelist, Billy Graham Evangelistic Association.

Thomas G. Long, professor of preaching and worship, Princeton Theological Seminary, Princeton, N.J.

Lloyd Ogilvie, chaplain of the United States Senate.

Haddon Robinson, professor of preaching, Gordon-Conwell Theological Seminary, South Hamilton, Mass.

John R. W. Stott, rector emeritus, All Souls Church, London, England; chaplain to the Queen 1959–91.

Charles R. Swindell, president, Dallas Theological Seminary, Dallas, Tex.

Barbara Brown Taylor, rector of Grace-Calvary Episcopal Church, Clarkesville, Ga.

Gardner C. Taylor, pastor emeritus, Concord Baptist Church of Christ, Brooklyn, N.Y.

William H. Willimon, dean of the chapel and professor of Christian ministry, Duke University, Durham, N.C.

The diploma recognizing my role in the ministry of Christian preaching touched me at an uncommonly deep level. It reads:

> In recognition of our shared ministry,
> Baylor University recognizes Dr. Walter J. Burghardt, S.J.,
> for his dedication to the proclamation of the Gospel
> and exemplary service to the Kingdom of God.

In a *Newsweek* article on the survey and its results,[90] religion editor Kenneth Woodward noted "some obvious choices": Graham, Forbes, and Gardner Taylor, "the granddaddy of current African-American preachers"; and one surprise: "Roman Catholics, seldom noted for their preaching, are represented by Jesuit Walter J. Burghardt." Referring apparently to the ages of most of the 12, he observed that "Baylor's dozen is more like a preachers' hall of fame than a team of active all-stars."

In point of fact, the "all-stars" are almost without exception extraordinarily "active." Still, Woodward raises a critical question: Where are the effective junior preachers? I am not surprised that the newly anointed 12 were the graying and the balding. The passage of the years, our long-lasting involvement in teaching and writing, and our preaching opportunities across a country afford us an exposure and a recognition rarely open to the younger, more localized, area-bound clergy. My project Preaching the Just Word and my ecumenical travels have put me in touch with a fair number of younger preachers, Protestant and Catholic, splendidly gifted with the qualities Baylor commended. They are out there, but they need a homiletic Internet to advertise them.

On the other hand, surveys and lay rumblings suggest a widespread failure among younger clergy to realize, or at least to actualize, the incomparable potential of preaching. I have said enough above to make clear my conviction that none of the usual excuses — time, other demands, native incompetence, lack of appreciation — can justify a low priority allotted to preaching the gospel. St. Paul was right on target: "Faith comes from what is heard, and what is heard comes through the word of Christ" (Rom 10:17). And the word of Christ, for better or worse, comes through the word of the preacher.

FIVE

From Cain to Antichrist

Social Injustice and the Just Word

Till the late '80s, most of my priestly life was expended on theology — teaching at Woodstock College and the Catholic University of America, writing articles for various journals, editing the journal *Theological Studies* and coediting the series of translations Ancient Christian Writers, preaching on radio and various festal occasions, engaging in ecumenical pursuits such as the Lutheran-Roman Catholic dialogue and Faith and Order. But over the past quarter century, almost imperceptibly, something new kept entering my life. It may have begun in 1970, when I moved with Woodstock from the isolated, insulated 650 acres of the seminary's Maryland woodland to the concrete jungle of New York City. It crept more insidiously under my skin when I moved to our nation's capital: to Catholic University in 1974, to Georgetown University in 1978, to St. Aloysius Church and Gonzaga College High School in 1993.

Concretely, it meant coming closer to the face of Cain. I mean the Cain who slew his brother, and when the Lord asked him, "Where is your brother Abel?" responded, "I do not know. Am I my brother's keeper?" (Gen 4:8–9). I mean a slowly growing awareness of another aspect of America to which I had been exposed mostly by the media, only at a comfortable distance. I mean the cry of the poor.

To hear that cry, I had to go back to Scripture, had to discover who "the poor" are in God's inspired Word.[1] Not only the poverty-stricken, those without money enough to lead a decent human existence. Poor was the leper, ostracized from society, excluded from normal association with others, compelled often to live outside his town. Poor was the widow, who could not inherit from her husband, was an obvious victim for the exactions of a creditor, often had no defender at law and so was at the mercy of dishonest judges. Poor were the orphans with no parents to love them. Poor was the sinful woman who bathed Jesus' feet with her tears, the woman caught in the very act of adultery, to be stoned according to the law of Moses.

148

Poor was wealthy toll collector Zacchaeus, a henchman of the Romans, a social outcast because of his job, no longer a true son of Abraham. Israel's poor were the oppressed, those of a lower class preyed upon by the powerful. The poor were all those on whose behalf the Lord castigated His chosen people through the prophets:

> Cease to do evil,
>   learn to do good;
> seek justice,
>   rescue the oppressed,
> defend the orphan,
>   plead for the widow.
>   (Isa 1:16–17)

The Cry of The Poor Today

Who are the poor that cry out to us in our time? Let me sketch five groups, quite aware that these five do not cry alone.[2]

Children

First, the most vulnerable of all: our children. TV trumpets our love for children, yet one of every four little ones grows up hungry in the richest nation on earth,[3] each year 40,000 do not live to see their first birthday, each year 1.5 million developing humans are forcibly kept from seeing the light of day. We proclaim our young as the flower of our future, yet every 26 seconds a child runs away from home, every 47 seconds a child is abused or perilously neglected, every 67 seconds a teenager has a baby, every 7 minutes a boy or girl is arrested for drug abuse, every 36 minutes a child is killed or injured by a gun. We piously dedicate this decade to unparalleled American education, second to none in science, yet uncounted Johnnies still can't read, 25% of our teenagers drop out of school, and every day 135,000 children go to school with a deadly weapon.[4] The head of Covenant House, Sister Mary Rose McGeady, dedicated her 1991 book *God's Lost Children* "to the 1,000,000 homeless children who slept on America's streets last year, scared, cold, hungry, alone, and most of all, desperate to find someone who cares."[5]

Not a genteel, graceful poverty; not the dignified poverty of Jesus, Mary, and Joseph. This is the poverty that batters the body and crushes the spirit. This is the poverty that makes for death; for low-income children are two times more likely than others to die from birth defects, four times more likely to die from fires, five times more likely to die from infectious diseases and parasites, six times more likely to die from other diseases. This is the poverty that makes for disease and illness; for this brand of poverty stunts growth, destroys the body's iron, facilitates asthma and chronic diarrhea, child abuse and drug addiction. This is the poverty that afflicts intelligence; for it slows the mind, affects test scores, lowers attention span, increases school dropouts. This is the poverty that leads to violence, to crime, to senseless killing for a pair of Reeboks. This is the poverty that breaks up families, makes our streets concrete jungles, crowds our jails with juvenile delinquents.

And as I gaze over the earth, I discover that the number of children who are projected to die in the '90s alone, most from diseases we know how to prevent, may reach one hundred and fifty million! Almost as staggering as the national debt and the scandal of Savings and Loan. More staggering because here are the most vulnerable of humans, as defenseless as the child in the womb.

In my own back yard, the District of Columbia, a dismaying trend came to light recently. Children in our nation's capital were planning their own funerals: how they wanted to look, how be dressed, where be waked. Not out of curiosity, not from a Christian consciousness of death's significance. They simply did not believe they would be around very long, had every reason to expect they would not grow up. Where they play, coke and crack are homicidal kings. In one five-year period 224 of their childhood friends had died from gunfire. Some were deliberate targets, others just happened to be there, at least one lay in a cradle. And so the living little ones have begun planning for the worst, as if their own murders are inevitable, as if their own dreams will surely be just as cruelly cut short.[6]

Elderly

Second, the cry of the elderly. We inhabit a culture that canonizes youth and beauty, activity and productivity, strength and sexual prowess. The ideal of aging? Not to seem to age at all. Bob Hope and Eva Gabor, Paul Newman and Joanne Woodward, Jimmy Carter and Angela Lansbury, Sargent Shriver and Cecily Tyson — here is eternal youth. If after 60 or 65 you can continue a productive career, if you can still stroke a tennis ball, straddle a Honda, or satisfy a sexual partner, then your aging is ideal.

Most Americans, however, do not age so gracefully, so creatively, so productively. Most sexagenarians, practically all septuagenarians, are "retired." In our culture, to be retired is to be literally "useless"; the aged rarely serve a practical purpose; they don't "do" anything. Not only are they irrelevant to big business, big labor, big government, big military, big education; they are a drain on the economy. Whether glowing with health or in a permanent vegetative state, they use up medical resources, medical miracles, that could benefit the useful members of society. The "new boys [and girls] on the block," economic man and economic woman, draw their knowledge and wisdom from computers, not from the hoary stories of the aging. Honor them, naturally — till they become an economic liability meriting a merciful injection. Respect for elders, of course; but life in the same house with grandpa and grandma? It simply would not work; too wide a gap between the generations; the old folk are not "with it." On the whole, a nursing home makes better American sense. And there they sit, watching and waiting: watching TV's "Married — with Children" and waiting for someone they carried in their womb to visit and "watch one hour" (Mt 26:40) with them.

AIDS-afflicted

Third, the AIDS-afflicted. It was in the late '80s that I first heard their cry with Christian ears. I heard it in Nashville, Tennessee. An Anglican minister was addressing the 73rd Assembly of the Catholic Health Association of the United States. To an audience that often wept openly Canon William Barcus uttered a cry that still rings in my ears:

> I stand here with you — as a brother to you, a churchman, a man with AIDS. A man who regrets nothing of the love and goodness he has known, who stops now to notice flowers, children at play.... A man who loves his church from his heart, from every molecule in him.

In the course of his address Canon Barcus recalled a 1944 photo essay in *Life* magazine.

> It was about the red foxes of Holmes County, Ohio, who lived in the woods and ate mostly mice and crickets, but sometimes also chicken and quail. This, the story explained, "made the brave men of Holmes County angry because they wanted to kill the quail themselves." So one Saturday about 600 men and women and their children got together and formed a big circle five miles across. They all carried sticks and started walking

through the woods and fields, yelling and baying to frighten the foxes, young and old, out of their holes. Inside this diminishing circle the foxes ran to and fro, tired and frightened. Sometimes a fox would, in its anger, dare to snarl back, and it would be killed on the spot for its temerity. Sometimes one would stop in its anguish and try to lick the hand of its tormentor. It too would be killed.

Sometimes, the photo showed, other foxes would stop and stay with their own wounded and dying. Finally, as the circle came closer together, down to a few yards across, the remaining foxes went to the center and lay down inside, for they knew not what else to do. But the men and the women knew what to do. They hit these dying wounded with their clubs until they were dead, or they showed their children how to do it. This is a true story. *Life* reported and photographed it. . . .

I stand before you today [Barcus continued] as one weary of running, as one wounded myself, and I say to the churches, the churches first, and then to the government, the silent government, and then to the world: "What have you done to my people? What have you done to your own people — beautiful people . . . ?"

My people are being destroyed, and your people, and all our people together. Not only by an illness called AIDS, but by a darker illness called hatred. . . . The Christ, Jesus, the compassionate lord of life and lord of more forgiveness and lord of more hope is the one we have vowed to follow and be ultimately guided by. We must tell that to our smugly self-righteous brothers and sisters. . . . For if we do not, their souls will perish in the circle of misunderstanding and scorn they teach so many as they club and scream their disdain for the outsider, the misunderstood, the different. . . . Sadly . . . too many with AIDS have wondered if they had any alternative but to go to the center of the circle and lie down and die. Where are you in that circle? Where are we? Where would Christ be? . . .

For all of us within an awakening church . . . I say to the world, "Help us. Join us." To you as church . . . I say from long despairing peoples of all kinds, "Help us. Please help us. Be the gospel alive!"[7]

All too many of us find it dreadfully difficult to be "the gospel alive" where AIDS is at issue. All too many see in AIDS God's revenge on the promiscuous.

Women

Fourth, the cry of women. In its 1994 human-rights report, our State Department focused for the first time on the treatment of women.[8] The findings are grim. The report on 193 countries paints a stark, dreary picture of rampant day-to-day discrimination and abuse: forced prostitution, ritual mutilation, inferior education, backbreaking farm work, legal inequities regarding adultery, the blind eye of government. In the United States, women earn 70 percent of what men do on average; in 1993 there were more than a million attacks on women by their husbands or companions. It has taken our country longer to legislate against sexual abuse than to condemn black slavery.

The feminist movement cries for "the empowerment of women for the transformation of social and religious structures beyond patriarchy — that model of social organization that assures men, predominantly white men, have control and dominant power within social and religious structures."[9] Women cry that for all too long their voices and their experience have been silent not only in government and industry, in the home and the school, but in the churches and religious life, in the interpretation of Scripture and the understanding of theology, in every area where ideas are generated that change the world and decisions are made that affect the way women think, the way they live, the way they worship.

Women cry aloud against the "feminization of poverty" in the United States, sometimes termed more accurately the "pauperization of women and children."[10] They cry out against the powerlessness of women to shape the world, their world, in any but a masculine mold.[11] They cry out against a division of labor within the family that is gender-based, does not take into consideration a woman's gifts, talents, education, or desires, a division of responsibility that "disenfranchises men from the full potential of their fatherhood while it disenfranchises women from the full potential of their personhood."[12] They cry out against a Catholic education that trains women for the professions, yet still holds out as the ideal the full-time mother. They cry out against the multiple demands made on them by the family, the workplace, and the common good, demands that create needless stress, corrosive frustration, even profound guilt.[13] They cry out in one "Women's Creed":

> We look forward to the future in faith and hope, working for
> the day when we and all our sisters no longer have to fit a

stereotype, but are free to use all our gifts and to share in all the benefits of human life and work. We look forward to the age of peace, when violence is banished, both women and men are able to love and to be loved and the work and wealth of our world is justly shared.[14]

African Americans

Fifth, the cry of our black sisters and brothers. Their cry echoes the cry of Yahweh to Pharaoh, "Let my people go!" Rather than recite impersonal, barren statistics, I prefer to recall black Sister Thea Bowman, stricken with breast cancer and bone cancer, racing her wheelchair across the country to spread her gospel of love, her gospel of life, "I'm not going to die. I'm going home like a shooting star." In 1989 she spoke her mind passionately to the bishops of the Catholic Church in the United States:

> ... despite the civil rights movement of the '60s and the socio-educational gains of the '70s, blacks in the '80s are still struggling, still scratching and clawing as the old folks said, still trying to find home in the homeland and home in the church, still struggling to gain access to equal opportunity.
>
> A disproportionate number of black people are poor. Poverty, deprivation, stunted physical, intellectual and spiritual growth — I don't need to tell you this, but I want to remind you, more than a third of the black people that live in the United States live in poverty, the kind of poverty that lacks basic necessity.
>
> I'm talking about old people who have worked hard all their lives and don't have money for adequate food or shelter or medical care.
>
> I'm talking about children who can never have equal access and equal opportunity because poverty doomed them to low birth weight and retardation and unequal opportunity for education....
>
> Black children are twice as likely as white children to be born prematurely, to suffer from low birth weight, to live in substandard housing, to have no parent employed.
>
> ...One of every 21 black males is murdered. A disproportionate number of our men are dying of suicide and AIDS and drug abuse and low self-esteem.[15]

Cries of the poor indeed. But, as I said, these do not cry alone. I have begun to listen to the Hispanic communities, in many ways second-class citizens politically, barely tolerated by many Anglo worshipers. I have heard the tearful groanings of our Native Americans, driven from the land they revere, homeless in their own homes, without work, without hope, wracked by alcoholism. I have long shared the anguish of our Jewish sisters and brothers, fearful as they hear Americans arguing that the Holocaust which consumed six million of their dear ones is a gigantic hoax, never really happened. I taste the tears with which multimillion refugees water the highways of the world. I shudder to recall that each week 500 men, women, and children are murdered or maimed by land mines mostly made in the developed world and sold in the developing world. I close my ears in horror and shame to the cries from scores of death rows, while most Americans clamor for the gas chamber, the rope, the fatal injection, one life for another. It is now not the Lord but God's people who cry, "Vengeance is mine!"

The Dream

It is in this context that my dream was born. Nothing quite as mind-blowing as the dream of Martin Luther King Jr. Still, not insignificant for the future of our Church, our Christianity, our country, our way of life, our profound spirituality.

It was springtime 1990. I was in my 12th year as theologian in residence at Georgetown University, in my 23rd year as editor of the scholarly journal *Theological Studies,* my 44th year on the editorial staff. I knew I would be resigning both positions soon. I was inching toward 76. Where should my focus be for however many years God would grant me — something that would creatively engage my background, my talents, my interests? Background? Theology. Talents? Communication: preaching, lecturing, writing. Interests? Ideas and people.

The impetus came from Jesuit James L. Connor, director of the Woodstock Theological Center (WTC), a research institute founded in 1974 by the New York and Maryland Provinces of the Society of Jesus to examine contemporary social problems from the perspective of the Judeo-Christian tradition. With his customary shrewdness Father Connor had just raised me from a largely inactive associate fellow of the Center to the exalted state of senior fellow. It proved to be the seed plot of my dream. The WTC, located at Georgetown University, was doing splendid work in touching theology to social, economic, and political issues — research, books and articles, conferences and workshops. But this approach, indispensable though it is, reaches only a relatively small number of people. How could we expand the Center's influence, stimulate American Catholicism as a whole to live and spread Catholicism's best-kept secret, its social gospel?

It was then that it hit: preaching! Where do American Catholics gather regularly in largest array, even more than for pro football? At weekend liturgy. A captive audience, millions of potential listeners, even if only 30 percent of Catholics share the liturgy two Sundays or more each month. The liturgy of the word, but concentrated on the second great commandment of the law and the gospel, "Love your neighbor as yourself." The neighbor? The child unborn or abused, the world of business and economics, 37 million without access to healthcare, the hungry and the homeless, the refugee and the imprisoned, the victims of poverty and racism, women. And intimately linked to people...the earth we rape and ravish.

But the dream had a nightmarish aura: Catholic preaching has been dull as dishwater. Not entirely, but in discouragingly large measure. If our homilies were to revive the social gospel, our homilists had to be set aflame. But how? One of our consultants, New York's Father Philip Murnion, experienced director of the National Pastoral Life Center, insisted that the project would fail if the primary stress were laid on information, data, skills, and strategies, important as these are. Even more important is a spirituality undergirding the data and skills, a conversion that turns the preacher inside out, puts "fire in the belly." In consequence, we seized on a method: retreat/workshops, five days in length. Retreat indeed, for the week would have rich time for meditation (pertinent themes from the Spiritual Exercises of St. Ignatius Loyola in the context of social-justice issues), Eucharist, examination of conscience, scrutiny, reconciliation. Workshop, for teams of five or six would guide each week, experts in various categories: not only social-justice theory and action, but Scripture, spirituality, the Spiritual Exercises, liturgy, the cultures into which we preach, the art and craft of preaching. Not two separate areas. No, the spiritual would interpenetrate the intellectual, the intellectual deepen the spiritual.

Over the years, blanket the country; send the retreatants back to their areas, to their parishes, yearning to spread the good news to their congregations, to other preachers. Not to solve complex issues in a homily, but to raise consciousness, raise awareness, so that the faithful in the pews are moved, excited, gather to ask three questions: (1) What are the justice issues in our parish? (2) What resources do we have at our disposal? (3) What concretely shall we do? In other words, resolve to tackle in organized fashion the social issues that haunt a particular parish, challenge its Christian commitment to love as Jesus loved.

We would begin with ordained priests, because it is they who regularly address the captive audience — more accurately, the faithful thirsting for fresh insight into God's Word. Gradually we would involve permanent deacons, then all who preach, male and female, clergy and laity.

Problems

I realized from the beginning that Preaching the Just Word faced serious obstacles. A remarkably creative Old Testament scholar, Walter Brueggemann, put the problem in fine perspective when he addressed what he termed "scandal" in the preaching of social, political, and economic issues.

> In Luke 7, after John the Baptist raises his christological question through his disciples whether Jesus is the Christ, and after Jesus answers with specificity that "the blind see, the lame walk, lepers are cleansed, the dead are raised, and the poor rejoice," Jesus adds, "blessed is the one who is not scandalized by me" (v. 23). Or as I have rendered it, "Lucky are you, if you are not upset." The theological scandal of biblical faith, especially when rendered into political, economic issues, is indeed upsetting.
>
> How is a pastor to give voice to this scandal in a society that is hostile to it, in a church that is often unwilling to host the scandal, and when we ourselves as teachers and pastors of the church are somewhat queasy about the scandal as it touches our own lives? How can the radical dimension of the Bible as it touches public reality be heard in the church?[16]

The problems stem from the pews and from the pulpit. From the pews, because all too many Christians, Roman Catholics included, do not believe that justice issues, the "social gospel," belong in the pulpit. Many a Catholic, like myself, grew up with the catechism imperative, "God made us to praise, reverence, and serve Him in this life and to be happy with Him for ever in the next." From this all too many concluded that the Church, precisely as Church, has no commission to right human injustice. The Church is a spiritual institution, and its mission is sheerly spiritual; it is a channel that links the human person with God. Oh yes, if poverty and politics, injustice and inhumanity stand as barriers to God's grace, the Church must struggle against them. But, it is alleged, not as a direct facet of its mission — only as obstacles at the outer edge of its vocation. The Church's commission is to gather a band of true believers who will prepare themselves by faith and hope for the redemptive action by which *God* establishes the kingdom when the curtain falls on history.

A vivid example of this attitude struck me early in my life at Georgetown. In May 1979, passions flamed in our nation's capital. Mass was about to begin in St. Matthew's Cathedral — a Mass to mark Argentina's national day. Unexpectedly, the assembled Argentinians — embassy officials, military leaders, others — were addressed from the sanctuary by a priest protester. For six years this missionary had ministered to a Buenos Aires shantytown; he told how he had been imprisoned and tortured, how priest friends had simply disappeared; he wanted the congregation to join him in a prayer for reconciliation. But at that moment "the organist drowned him out... the microphone went dead... the rector of the cathedral told [him] to move on."[17]

The trouble seemed over; the 40 or so demonstrators moved from church to street and the liturgy opened. But the preceding was only the prelude. The homilist, head of the Spanish Secretariat of the Archdiocese, Capuchin Sean O'Malley (now bishop of Fall River, Massachusetts), appeared in symbolic purple. Instead of the usual eulogy, he quoted statements by John Paul II and the bishops of Latin America about repression, torture, and disappearances, about the attempt of governments to justify such activities on the basis of national security. He began to focus on the people who had vanished under the Videla regime and quoted Scripture on Herod's slaughter of the innocents.

At that juncture the congregation (300 or more) stormed angrily out of the church, led by a high-ranking general. Some damned the homilist for "turning a religious event into a political one." Another said, "Priests have no place in politics. He should have given a sermon on another subject, like the love of God." But the archdiocesan director of communications said "he had no objection to the way the sermon was handled.... 'We hope our priests are teaching the truth' he said. 'Whether what they say is offensive and bothers the conscience of some people should not be the issue. The issue should be whether it is the truth.' "

But it is not only the average layperson without scholarly pretensions who has difficulty with a social gospel. I recall a distinguished professor in a British university insisting that Jesus taught a personal rather than a social morality and arguing that by nature Christianity is exclusively concerned with "the relationship of the soul to eternity." Not impertinent here is a learned professor of political philosophy in a Jesuit university strenuously opposing the Church's persistent opposition to aspects of democratic capitalism — "the last great hope for the poor."

Two other episodes have touched me more directly. In a 1990 autobiography Jesuit George H. Dunne recalled a retreat he had given as a young priest in 1943 to Jesuit theological students in California. During his conferences Father Dunne dealt at times with social issues — racial segregation, New York's rat-infested tenements, exploitation of migrant farm workers, the Spanish Civil War, the anguish of the poor. And "with millions of Jews dying in gas chambers," he found it impossible to "speak about love of neighbor without talking about the evil of anti-Semitism."

Not long after, Father Zacheus Maher, official representative of the Jesuit Superior General for the United States during World War II, wrote to Dunne deploring that instead of following the Spiritual Exercises of St. Ignatius, he had substituted a series of "brilliant talks on social subjects." "Such subjects," Maher stated flatly, "have no place in the Spiritual Exercises."[18] This, incidentally, is the same Maher who, when I was pursuing my tertianship (year of spiritual renewal after theology) at Auriesville, New York, in 1942–43, addressed a letter to all the Jesuits in the United States condemning a splendid brochure, informative and up-to-date, on *Catholic Youth and Chastity* authored by a remarkable Jesuit moral theologian, Gerald Kelly, and a medical doctor. On that occasion Maher deplored the tragedy that our Jesuits, especially the recently ordained, were "soiling their hands and their hearts" with this pamphlet. It is not only the Lord who can read human hearts at a distance.

A second direct experience that is lodged unforgettably in my memory took place in the late-'80s in a Jesuit community during refreshments before dinner. While preparing my own libation, I was intrigued by a conversation nearby in the German language between a community member, professor of economics, and a visiting German Jesuit working in Latin America. The visitor was lamenting the wretched condition of the poor in Latin America; he called it *ungerecht* ("unjust"). No, replied the professor, not *ungerecht* —

unglücklich ("unfortunate"). And you still believe Jesuits are shaped in a single mold?

What accounts for this attitude? Without laying the whole blame at a single door, I am persuaded that one significant factor is massive American Catholic ignorance. Most of our educated Catholics, including clerics, lack a sense of Catholic tradition. Not tradition as some musty museum piece; rather, tradition as the best of our past, infused with the insights of the present, with a view to a richer, more catholic future. In this context Lawrence Cunningham, now at the University of Notre Dame, found himself frustrated when he was professor of religion at Florida State University

> because students lack any sense of the historical perspective of Western culture in general and the part Catholicism played in the formation of that culture in particular. They...have no sense of the kind of church which existed before the Second Vatican Council. Students have this strong conviction that what is important happens now and the "now" has little or no link with the past. They tend to see the life of the church rather as they see the surface of a video game screen: active, immediate and graspable as a whole.[19]

Cunningham's experience can be transferred to American Catholicism in general. The results are tangible: a generation of "educated" Catholics who know Augustine only as a born-again Catholic who foisted on us a hellish doctrine of original sin and a pessimistic view of marriage; who cannot spell Chalcedon, even though three decades ago Harvey Cox was arguing that apart from the Council of Chalcedon technopolis is unintelligible;[20] who can anathematize Aquinas and scuttle Scholasticism without ever having read a word thereof; who sneer at the mere mention of "medieval," as if the Middle Ages were in all respects darker than our own; who couldn't care less about a papal pronouncement, much less peruse it. During a half century of theology I have watched our incredibly rich tradition pass slowly but surely into museums or at best into the hands of appreciative Protestant sisters and brothers.

This lamentation is not irrelevant to social justice and its proclamation. Our postimmigrant church is incredibly ignorant of 20 centuries of rich social doctrine: from Jesus' proclamation of "good news to the poor" (Lk 4:18) to John Paul II's warning against an unbridled capitalism; from the insistence of early Fathers of the Church that God's good earth was given to all men and women, not to a favored few, to the U.S. bishops' pastoral plea for "economic justice for all."[21]

Compounding the problem from the pews is the problem from the pulpit. Compounding the problems noted in my chapter on preaching is the very scope, the enormousness, of the issues involved. How is it possible for a homilist to handle with competence issues as complex as insider trading, the rape of the earth, unequal opportunities for education, the war on the womb, parental neglect and sexual abuse, injustice to women in church and society, a billion of God's images falling asleep hungry, coke and crack kings of our streets, black and white in a tenuous truce?

Implementation

Nevertheless, all the experts we consulted agreed that the project is crucial. Some have since added that it may well be the most important Catholic project of this decade. But how in the concrete do we go about it? Five-day retreat/workshops. Retreat because prayer, meditation, contemplation, liturgy, scrutiny, penitential rite are integral elements in the program, integral to the shaping of a spirituality, integral perhaps to conversion.

Meditation

A rich example is the morning meditation, based on selected themes from the *Spiritual Exercises* of St. Ignatius Loyola, crucial meditations that not only provide a taste of the Ignatian thrust but also move the retreatant out of a sheerly individualistic, me-and-Jesus spirituality into an experience of a God-given community, the human family. How does the retreat scheme unfold day by day?

Monday: creation, call, covenant: God forms a family.
Tuesday: sin as the sundering of family relationships.
Wednesday: call to labor with Christ to reconcile our divided family.
Thursday: cost and heart of this reconciliation: Christ's passion, a social event in cause, motivation, and effect.
Friday: our sending forth as Pentecost in the risen Lord.[22]

1. It begins with *creation*. God did not have in mind isolated units, autonomous entities, scattered disparately around a world, totally independent each of every other — entities that might one day decide through a social contract to join together for self-protection,

self-aggrandizement. God created, continues to create, a people, a human family, a community of persons, a body. Such was the vision of Vatican II: "God...has willed that all men and women should constitute one family."[23] "God did not create man and woman for life in isolation, but for the formation of social unity."[24] "This solidarity must be constantly increased until that day on which it will be brought to perfection. Then, saved by grace, men and women will offer flawless glory to God as a family beloved of God and of Christ their brother."[25]

The problem? Our culture promotes airtight compartments, each insulated from every other. Individualism, Robert Bellah insists, lies at the very core of North American culture. Self-promotion goes back to Eden, but it has become socially legitimized. Modern imagination has been schooled to think "me" prior to "we," "me" over against "you." An astounding paradox: While communication explodes, community continues to disintegrate. In consequence, the grace we need and want from this meditation is a new imagination, the mind and heart of Christ Jesus (Phil 2:6–11). We want to look around and instinctively see ourselves within the family, members of a body, participants in a community. That, we shall see, is the profound meaning of the Incarnation: the imbeddedness of the God-man within this historical, human family of ours.

2. *Sin* is the sundering of community. The whole of Scripture from Genesis to Revelation is the story of struggle for community, of lapses into disintegration, division, enmity. If biblical justice is (as we shall see) fidelity to the demands of relationships, then sin is a refusal of responsibility; sin creates division, alienation, dissension, marginalization, rejection; sin dis-members the body.

In this context it makes sense to say that there is no such thing as a sheerly "private" sin or a sin confined to "two consenting adults." All sin is social, just as all grace and goodness is social. Presbyterian novelist/preacher Frederick Buechner has expressed this with characteristic imagination when comparing humanity to an enormous spider web:

If you touch it anywhere, you set the whole thing trembling. ...As we move around this world and as we act with kindness, perhaps, or with indifference, or with hostility, toward the people we meet, we too are setting the great spider web a-tremble. The life that I touch for good or ill will touch another life, and that in turn another, until who knows where the trembling stops or in what far place and time my touch will be felt. Our lives are linked. No man [no woman] is an island....[26]

3. There follows our call to *reconcile* those who are divided, to reintegrate the body, to heal divisions in the family. It is our share in the Incarnation, in redemption, in the mission of Jesus, his prayer that all may be one, his plan to reconcile simply everything in himself, to break down the wall that divides Jew and Gentile, slave and free, male and female. It is thrillingly summarized by Paul in his second letter to the Christians of Corinth (5:17–20):

> If anyone is in Christ, there is a new creation; everything old has passed away; see, everything has become new! All this is from God, who reconciled us to Himself through Christ and has given us the ministry of reconciliation; that is, God was in Christ reconciling the world to Himself, not counting their trespasses against them, and entrusting the message of reconciliation to us. So we are ambassadors for Christ, since God is making His appeal through us; we entreat you on behalf of Christ, be reconciled to God.

Take the call of Simon Peter (Lk 5:1–11). Simon is cleaning his nets; Jesus gets into Simon's boat, teaches the crowds, then asks Simon to "put out into the deep water...for a catch" (v. 4). Simon does, even though a whole night of fishing has been totally frustrating. Then the miraculous catch, Peter's "Go away from me, Lord, for I am a sinful man" (v. 8), Jesus' "Don't be afraid; from now on you will be catching people" (v. 10).

Here there are hidden depths. (1) The mission is not pole fishing, one on one; it is net fishing, gathering people, a community of women and men, reconciling. (2) It is the mission of one who has been reconciled. Peter has urged Jesus, "Go away from me," be distant, let's live divided. Jesus gets right to the root of Peter's problem: "Don't be afraid." (3) Peter bonds with Jesus, joins and follows him in a surrender that is trust or faith. He risks his self-control, exchanges it for companionship, even while still *feeling* fear. (4) It is in and out of this continuing, lived experience that Peter can be Jesus' instrument of reconciliation for others. "I have prayed for you [Peter] that your own faith might not give out. Indeed, you yourself will turn back [will repent of your denial of me]; then reinforce your brothers" (Lk 22:32). (5) An indispensable moment in being reconciled and in being reconciler is acknowledgment of our own sinfulness, alienation, division, in whatever form.

4. Jesus' mission culminates on Calvary, finds its fullest expression in his death, which is also and simultaneously his resurrection. So, if we would understand our mission, we must struggle to understand the *crucifixion* — understand not only with the head but in the heart.

The crucifixion is a social reality, a social event — in its origins, in its actuality, in its outcome. It can be misleading to say "Jesus died for *my* sins." Jesus died for *us*, for us as a family, i.e., that we might *become* family. He died for the failures or refusals of individual members of God's family to fulfil the responsibilities inherent in their relationships. That intent was graphically expressed when the chief priests and Pharisees called a meeting of the council to express their concern over a Jesus performing all sorts of signs, threatening to attract a huge following, with the Romans poised to destroy temple and people. Recall the response of high priest Caiaphas: "You know nothing at all! You do not understand that it is better for you to have one man die for the people than to have the whole nation destroyed." Evangelist John adds: "He did not say this on his own, but being high priest that year he prophesied that Jesus was about to die for the nation, and not for the nation only, but to gather into one the dispersed children of God" (Jn 11:47–51).

As we look at the crucifix (Ignatius' "How have you come to this?"), we think back on the way Jesus appealed to all strata of society (rich and poor, those "in" and those "out," the managers and the managed) to enter into the kingdom (a social reality), to be integrated with all the others, incorporated into one body, to be servants of one another. The victim of society's rejection, he was forming society, a new society, where no one can say to any other, "I have no need of you" (1 Cor 12:21). By crucifixion: "When I am lifted up from the earth [in crucifixion[27]], I will draw all people to myself" (Jn 12:32). We read the four Suffering Servant songs in Isaiah, and we recall that, in the Christian understanding, here is the Suffering Servant par excellence. And such is our mission: to reconcile through the cross, through his cross and our cross. Hence the Oscar Romeros of our world, the Dorothy Days, the Jesuit martyrs of El Salvador and their lay associates. In his broken flesh Jesus has created "one new humanity" (Eph 2:15).

5. The fifth day is the retreatants' Pentecost. Sunday evening they were called together; Friday morning they are *sent forth*. We pray that the Holy Spirit may fill "the entire house" (Acts 2:2), give each and all the light, wisdom, energy, and power (Greek *dynamis*, dynamite) to move out and proclaim the just Word. "As the Father

has sent me, so I send you" (Jn 20:21). Important here is Vatican II's Decree on the Missionary Activity of the Church:

> The pilgrim Church is missionary by her very nature.... It has not pleased God to call men and women to share God's life merely as individuals.... God wills to mold them into a people in which God's children, once scattered abroad, can be brought together.... On the day of Pentecost...there occurred a foreshadowing of that union of all peoples in a universal faith. That union was to be achieved by the Church of the New Covenant, a church which speaks all tongues, lovingly understands and accepts all tongues, and thus overcomes the divisiveness of Babel.[28]

Our Eucharistic recessional, therefore, is not primarily a swift movement to the dining room; it is a movement from church to world, from altar to people, from Christ crucified on Calvary to Christ crucified at the crossroads of our world. And so, as retreatants depart, they should ask four questions of themselves: To whom am I going? What am I going to? How will I go? With whom will I go?

Very simply, Ignatian meditations, like the full-fledged Ignatian retreat, are social from beginning to end, from the Genesis creation of man and woman in God's image to Revelation's touching plea of God's people, "Come, Lord Jesus" (Rev 22:20). This is not to ignore the first great commandment, "Love God above all else." It is rather to recognize, with so much of the New Testament, that if I say "I love God" and fail to love each sister and brother like another self, in concrete action, I am a liar (1 Jn 4:20). Loving others, Jesus declared, "is like" loving God (Mt 22:39).

Biblical Justice

Our first movement on the workshop level is the effort by a biblical scholar to clarify what that all-important word "justice" should mean for us. We have been uncommonly blest in the biblical scholars who have graced our project: James Walsh, S.J., of Georgetown University; John R. Donahue, S.J., of the Jesuit School of Theology at Berkeley; several experts from Chicago's Catholic Theological Union: Carroll Stuhlmueller, C.P. (recently deceased), and Sisters Carolyn Osiek, R.S.C.J., and Barbara Reid, O.P.; Raymond Collins, dean of Catholic University's School of Religious Studies; Dennis

Hamm, S.J., of Creighton University in Omaha; Richard J. Clifford, S.J., of the Weston Jesuit School of Theology in Cambridge, Massachusetts; Old Testament expert Lawrence Boadt, C.S,P., now president of the Paulist Press. What have we and our participants gathered from such presentations? Let me try to summarize the richness of our biblical experience, if only because it has reshaped my own preaching, not to mention my involvement in justice issues.

Before Vatican II no Catholic treatise on justice would have started with Scripture. It would have taken as its springboard the ethical definition of justice: Render to each what is due to each. Only with Vatican II, and particularly with the 1971 Synod, Justice in the World, did justice become a call to the Christian from the God of the two Testaments.[29]

When Micah declared to Israel, "What does the Lord require of you but to do justice?" (Mic 6:8), he was not imposing on God's people simply or primarily an ethical construct: Give to each man, woman, and child what each has a strict right to demand, because he or she is a human being, has rights that can be proven from philosophy or have been written into law. What, then, was the justice God wanted to "roll down like a river" (Amos 5:24)? Biblical scholar John R. Donahue expressed it with admirable succinctness back in 1977:

> In general terms the biblical idea of justice can be defined as *fidelity to the demands of a relationship.* In contrast to modern individualism the Israelite is in a world where "to live" is to be united with others in a social context either by bonds of family or by covenant relationships. This web of relationships — king with people, judge with complainants, family with tribe and kinfolk, the community with the resident alien and suffering in their midst and all with the covenant God — constitutes the world in which life is played out.[30]

In similar vein, a Jewish scholar has called biblical justice "substantive justice," because it is concerned with the full enhancement of human and, above all, social life; and so it suffuses all human relationships and social institutions.[31]

In this context, when is God just? When God acts as God should, e.g., defending or vindicating God's people, punishing violations of the covenant; when God is faithful to God's promises. When are people just? When they are in right relationship to God, to other humans, yes (as we shall see) to the earth.[32]

Put simply, justice was a whole network of relationships, and the most profound basis of these relationships was Israel's covenant with God. The Israelites were to father the fatherless and mother the motherless, were to feed the stranger, the sojourner, not because the orphan and the outsider deserved it, but because this was the way God had acted with Israel. A text in Deuteronomy is telling: "Love the sojourner [the stranger, the resident alien], for you were sojourners in the land of Egypt" (Deut 10:19). In freeing the oppressed, they were mirroring the loving God who had delivered *them,* the Israelites, from oppression, had freed them from Pharaoh.

Justice in Jewish tradition, then, was not a question simply, or even primarily, of human deserving, of human law. The Jews were to give to others what they themselves had been given by God, were to act toward one another and toward the stranger as God had acted toward Israel — and *precisely because* God had acted this way. Their justice was to image not the justice of man and woman but the justice of Yahweh. For Israel, the practice of justice thus understood was an expression of steadfast love — God's love and their own. Not to execute justice was not to worship God.

Given that context, I find perilous a proposition that pervades much of Christian culture in the United States. It asserts that Christianity, by its very nature, is concerned exclusively with the relation of the soul to eternity, the individual with God; that in the societal area the essential realization religion should provide is the worthlessness of human expectations of a better life on earth. The Son of God, we are told, took our flesh not to relieve our suffering but to forgive our sins.

The thesis does violence to Scripture. Those who read in the sacred text a sheerly personal, individualistic morality have not understood the Torah, have not sung the Psalms, have not been burned by the prophets, have not perceived the implications and the very burden of Jesus' message, and must inevitably play fast and loose with St. Paul.

The social focus of God's Book is evident on the first page. As I indicated above, God's creative intent centered not on isolated individuals but on a people, a community, a family. In that divine vision, women and men "are God's representatives and conversation partners in the world, with a fundamental dignity that must be respected and fostered. They are to exist in interdependence and mutual support and are to care for the world with respect, as for a gift received from God...."[33]

This divine idea began to take concrete shape when God, bringing an oppressed mass out of Egypt, created a *people* which was to gather in prayer and thanksgiving (cult) and to live according to God's constitution (*torah*). Those who were no people God made into a people. The Exodus, therefore, was not simply a liberation from slavery; it was the formation of a new social order — what Norbert Lohfink called "a contrast society."[34] God summoned the entire community to response and responsibility (see Deut 6:20–25). This covenant was a symbol of proper relationships — to God and among men and women. What did the covenant command? The two great commandments that embraced the whole of the law and all of the prophets: "You shall love the Lord your God with all your heart, all your soul, all your might" (Deut 6:5); and "you shall love your neighbor as yourself" (Lev 19:18).

The Hebrew prophets? I find them obsessed, haunted, by the poor, the oppressed, the marginal. Through Isaiah and Hosea, through Amos and Micah and Jeremiah, Yahweh ceaselessly proclaims to Israel that the Lord rejects precisely those things the Israelites think will make God happy. Yahweh is weary of burnt offerings, delights not in the blood of bulls or lambs, finds incense an abomination, hates their appointed feasts, will not listen to their prayers and to the melody of their harps, does not want rivers of oil, thousands of rams, even their first-born. Why not? Not because these are unacceptable in themselves; rather because two essential ingredients are all too often missing: steadfast love and justice.[35] One passage from Isaiah (58:6–9a) says it all in powerful rhetoric:

> Is not this the fast that I choose:
>   to loose the bonds of injustice,
>   to undo the thongs of the yoke,
> to let the oppressed go free.
>   and to break every yoke?
> Is it not to share your bread with the hungry,
>   and bring the homeless poor into your house;
> when you see the naked, to cover them,
>   and not to hide yourself from your own flesh?
> Then your light shall break forth like the dawn,
>   and your healing shall spring up quickly;
> your vindicator [vindication?] shall go before you,
>   the glory of the Lord shall be your rear guard.
> Then you shall call, and the Lord will answer;
>   you shall cry for help, and He will say, Here I am.

This is the tradition that sparked the ministry of Jesus. It was summed up in the synagogue at Nazareth, in what Luke presents as

Jesus' programmatic summation of his mission: "The Spirit of the Lord is upon me, for [the Lord[36]] has anointed me, has sent me to preach good news to the poor, to proclaim release for prisoners and sight for the blind, to send the downtrodden away relieved..." (Lk 4:18; cf. Isa 61:1–2).[37] For Jesus, too, the just man or woman is not primarily someone who gives to another what that other *deserves*. Jesus inaugurates a new covenant, where (in harmony indeed with his tradition) the most significant relationship is the monosyllable that says it all: love. And astonishingly, where loving one's neighbor, already commanded in Leviticus (19:18), is said by Jesus to be "like" loving God (Mt 22:39). "Love your neighbor as yourself" is not a psychological balancing act: As much or as little as you love yourself, that much love or that little love you must shower or trickle on your neighbor. It means I am to love my neighbor as if my neighbor were I, as if I were in my neighbor's place, as if I were standing in his or her shoes. This is what our covenant demands — what Jesus summed up when he said, "Love one another as I have loved you" (Jn 15:12).

The Catholic Tradition

But biblical justice, I discovered, is not locked into ancient Israel. It grows, is modified, deepens as it comes into contact with different ages and cultures, fresh situations and problems. We call it "tradition." But not tradition as some musty museum piece, "This is the way we've always done it." Rather, tradition as the best of our past, infused with the insights of the present, with a view to a richer, more catholic future. Here too our presenters have enriched us with the fruits of profound experience: e.g., John Carr, director of the Office of Social Development and World Peace within the United States Catholic Conference in Washington, D.C.; Ronald T. Krietemeyer, director of the Office of Social Justice in the Archdiocese of St. Paul/Minneapolis; and Frederick Perella, active for 15 years with the Campaign for Human Development in the Archdiocese of Hartford, Connecticut.

From the tradition a number of principles of Catholic social teaching have emerged. First, the center of that teaching rests in the dignity of the human person — a dignity rooted in the image and reflection of God in each human person. From that unique dignity flow significant rights. Not only the right to life but related rights necessary for each one's integral development as a person: work, food, housing, respect, etc.

Second, God's human images have not only rights but responsibilities. A peril lurks in the centrality allotted to rights in an age like ours where an understandable clamor for human rights threatens to drown out the less attractive warning about responsibilities. Catholic doctrine insistently pairs rights and responsibilities. If biblical justice, the core of God's demands on a covenant people, is fidelity to relationships, then each of us has responsibilities: to love God above all else; to love our sisters and brothers like other selves; to cherish every facet of God's creation, from rich earth to giant redwood, from the microscopic amoeba through the prowling panther to the shooting star, as a precious gift.

Third, the heart and soul of community is the family. Catholicism has never wavered in visualizing the family as the building block of civilizations and cultures, as the primordial natural community, as the church in miniature. In consequence, the family deserves special protection, particularly in a culture where the traditional family structure is threatened; in an America where half the marriages break up and single-parent families are mushrooming; in a climate where increasingly people are questioning whether anyone can realistically say "for ever." Protective measures must include (but often do not) the rights of the unborn, of children, of the aging, the right to a family wage, to decent housing, to education.

Fourth, a preferential option for the poor, the disadvantaged, the forgotten. Not because they are necessarily holier; only because they stand in greater need. This is what the God of Israel demanded of kings; what Jesus preached in his preference for the sinner and the sufferer, the outcast and the oppressed; what the Fathers of the Church proclaimed to powerful princes and powerless people. The expression may be recent; the reality is as ancient as the Exodus.

Fifth, solidarity. For, "if interdependence is an accurate description of our modern world, then solidarity is the appropriate Christian response to this reality."[38] In the context of God's creative intent, we humans are called to overcome barriers of race and religion, of ethnicity and gender, of economic status and nationality. And within Christianity itself, we "are all one in Christ Jesus" (Gal 3:28). We are one body, and within this body no one dare say to any other, "I have no need of you" (1 Cor 12:21). In his encyclical *On Social Concern* John Paul II spoke of interdependence as "a moral category" to which

the correlative response, as a moral and social attitude, as a "virtue," is solidarity. This then is not a feeling of vague compassion or shallow distress at the misfortunes of so many people, both near and far. On the contrary, it is a firm and persevering determination to commit oneself to the common good, that is to say to the good of all and of each individual, because we are all really responsible for all. . . . [39]

The sixth principle, for sheer age and emphasis, is something of a newcomer on the justice scene: care for the earth. Why such a lag, within the magisterium as well as theology? One explanation has intrigued me for over a quarter century. Lutheran theologian Joseph Sittler insisted that our basic ecological error is that we Christians have separated creation and redemption. The reason why we can worship nature in Vermont and at the same time manipulate nature in New York is because, in our view, the redemption wrought by Christ leaves untouched the creation wrought by God. And once we wrench redemption from creation, once we put nature out there and grace in here, as long as we omit from our theology of grace humans' transaction with nature, it is irrelevant to Christians whether we reverence the earth or ravish it. [40]

Fortunately, the past several decades have witnessed an ecological awakening within Catholicism. The sources are several. There are the feminist theologians who have been emphasizing, on the one hand, the connection between patriarchal culture, the technological dream of progress, and the environmental crisis, and on the other hand, an idolatrously one-sided masculine idea of God; women who see "no liberation for them and no solution to the ecological crisis within a society whose fundamental model of relationships continues to be one of domination." [41] There are Catholic ecologists like Thomas Berry, who has argued that if we lose the environment, we lose God. [42] Among his 12 principles for understanding the universe and the role of the human in the universe process, these three have centered the ecological issue for me more powerfully than any other:

2. The universe is a unity, an interacting and genetically related community of beings bound together in an inseparable relationship in space and time. The unity of the planet earth is especially clear; each being of the planet is profoundly implicated in the existence and functioning of every other being of the planet.

7. The earth, within the solar system, is a self-emergent, self-propagating, self-nourishing, self-educating, self-governing, self-healing, self-fulfilling community. All particular life sys-

tems in their being, their sexuality, their nourishment, their education, their governing, their healing, their fulfillment, must integrate their functioning within this larger complex of mutually dependent earth systems.

12. The main human task of the immediate future is to assist in activating the inter-communion of all the living and non-living components of the earth community in what can be considered the emerging ecological period of earth development.[43]

For me personally, perhaps the most thought-provoking and inspirational single volume by a theologian in the ecological arena has been John F. Haught's *The Promise of Nature*.[44] This highly respected Georgetown University scholar believes that process theology comes closer than any other theological alternative to "giving us a framework within which to pull together the insights of science and religion into a cosmology that encourages in us an evolutionary adventurousness as well as a preservative care that might inspire appropriate ethical attitudes toward nature."[45] With the help of science, we can see religious searching as "expressive of the adventurous nature of the universe itself," need not "feel 'lost in the cosmos' in order to embrace the homelessness that religion requires."[46] Religion's essential role in the earth's ecology will take shape primarily in our "unembarrassed cultivation of its inherent sacramentalism and the genuine reverence toward nature that this implies" — a sacramentalism that needs to be nourished by mysticism, silence, and action.[47] Add to all that two challenging statements in the face of traditional theologies: (1) What happens to the cosmos, somehow happens to God. (2) Death sets the person "free from its limited relationship with a proximate terrestrial environment in order to allow a less restricted relationship to the entire cosmos."[48] Here Haught has compelled me to probe ever more deeply into the person (the human as well as the divine) not primarily as an independently conscious substance but as essentially *relational*. "Personality means the capacity for continually intensifying the depth and breadth of relationship to other persons, nature and God."[49]

The earth, nature, things, the nonhuman have commonly entered documents of the Catholic magisterium in their relationship to the development and progress of woman and man.[50] John Paul II, however, has carried ecology beyond Vatican II, beyond his predecessors. For in his message for the World Day of Peace, January 1, 1990, "Peace with God the Creator, Peace with All of Creation,"[51] he set the ecological crisis within the broader context of the search for peace within society. He linked two principles essential for a solution to the ecological crisis, for a peaceful society: an ordered universe and a common heritage. "Theology, philosophy and science all speak of a harmonious universe, of a 'cosmos' endowed with *its own integrity*.... On the other hand, the earth is ultimately a common heritage, the fruits of which are *for the benefit of all*."[52] He insisted that the Christian vision is grounded in religious convictions stemming from revelation: not only the story of creation and the sin that resulted in earth's rebellion against the human, but a subjugated earth's mysterious yearning for liberation with all God's children (Rom 8:21–23) — all things made new in Christ (Rev 21:5).

As John Paul saw it, the solution to so profound a moral problem calls for responsibility: a new solidarity between developing nations and the highly industrialized; a world's address to the structural forms of poverty, to exhaustion of the soil, to uncontrolled deforestation; a serious look at life-styles, consumerism, instant gratification. The pope called for contemplation of nature's beauty, recognition of its restorative power for the human heart. He made bold to assert that Christians must "realize that their responsibility within creation and their duty toward nature and the Creator are an essential part of their faith."[53] In conclusion he commended to our imitation St. Francis of Assisi, who loved all of God's creatures — not only the poor but animals and plants, natural forces, even Brother Sun and Sister Moon.

Liturgy and Justice

Significant for my project from the beginning has been the relationship between justice and liturgy. A bit of history first. Back in the early years of the twentieth century, Belgian Father Lambert Beauduin, who had discovered the ecclesial importance of the liturgy under Dom Columba Marmion, was struck by a creative idea: The liturgy creates Christian community, is the source and center of all Christian life. The insight was not original. In 1902, for example, Pope Leo XIII had called the Eucharist "the soul of the Church.... From the Eucharist the Church draws and possesses all its vigor and glory, all the gifts with which God has embellished it, all the blessings it has. That is why the high point of the Church's solicitude lies in this, that the Church prepare and lead the souls of the faithful to an intimate union with Christ through the sacrament of his body and blood."[54] The liturgy as creative of community would make its way into Vatican II's Constitution on the Sacred Liturgy.

Beauduin's vision, however, explicitly included the conviction that liturgy cannot be separated from social justice. In point of fact, Beauduin could not find a responsive audience in Europe for his thesis on the liturgy as the source of social justice. But a Benedictine monk, Virgil Michel, on a sabbatical from St. John's Abbey in Collegeville, Minnesota, met Beauduin, was fired by the idea, brought it back to St. John's, and a new era was born. As Benedictine Godfrey Diekmann recalled it recently, "Michel worked with Msgr. Moses Coady of Halifax, Nova Scotia, on cooperatives and credit unions. He brought Dorothy Day and Peter Maurin to Collegeville to share their ideas. He paved the way for Catherine de Hueck to send black students from Harlem to St. John's University...."[55] In 1926 he founded the liturgy magazine *Orate fratres* (now *Worship*) and simultaneously the Liturgical Press at Collegeville, and published his first two pamphlets, "Liturgy in the Life of the Church" and "Liturgy and Life." Dead at 48, Michel's work was taken over by Diekmann, then 30, originally (and still) a patristics scholar whose liturgical expertise developed almost by osmosis from Michel.

Quite some years ago J. Bryan Hehir, then involved in the United States Catholic Conference, pointed out how "The historical relationship of the liturgical movement and social ministry during the first half of this century illustrates the potential of one dimension of the Church's life to enrich the other." In those days, in the *Proceedings* of the Liturgical Conference, the names of Diekmann, Reynold Hillenbrand, Shawn Sheehan, H. A. Reinhold, and Jesuit William Leonard complemented those of John A. Ryan, Bishop Francis Haas, George Higgins, and Jack Egan. "The theme of the Church as the Body of Christ was elaborated in terms of the Church at worship and the Church in witness." From key texts, *Mystici corporis, Mediator Dei,* and the social teaching of Leo XIII, Pius XI, and Pius XII, "was fashioned a theological basis for a style of worship with a strong social consciousness and a style of social ministry rooted in the sacraments."[56]

Diekmann deserves a distraction here. In continuity with Michel, he edited *Orate fratres,* promoted the Liturgical Weeks, got to know the leaders of the liturgical movement, attended the great congresses of the 1950s, was a *peritus* to the Preparatory Commission of Vatican II, and with Frederick McManus "made a considerable impact."[57] As Dawn Gibeau put it toward the close of 1993, "Today, at 85, he stands tall as ever — 6 feet 1 inch, even after two strokes. He remains as enthusiastic about meaningful liturgy and as ebullient a teacher of patristics as when, as a council *peritus,* or expert, he helped create the liturgy document."[58] I agree. I saw him in Collegeville in 1994. With characteristic graciousness he came to my room at 8 A.M. When he left a half hour later, it was I who was exhausted: memories, ideas, plans, insights, all tumbling over one another in ceaseless succession.

With many of the early liturgical leaders Diekmann was convinced that there is an intrinsic affinity between liturgy and just living, that the liturgy itself is the pre-eminent school of justice.[59] In consequence, he participated with other like-minded liturgists in the 1963 protest march on Washington, stood about 50 yards away from Martin Luther King Jr. during the famous "I Have a Dream" address. Despite the unhappiness of the bishop of Birmingham, Godfrey joined other priests in the 1965 march on Selma, Alabama. In fact, the banner he carried then continues to brighten his monastery room. It reads, "Selma is in Minnesota, too." Not himself a social activist,

> Godfrey was one of a good number of liturgists caught in the crossfire over strategies of justice in the late sixties and early seventies, an inevitable dispute given the early liturgical movement's presumption that a social agenda would be achieved by a *slow* and *organic* development, with the laity gradually becoming empowered through liturgy to assume their position as leaders in the marketplace. This strategy, according to Andrew Greeley, became unsatisfactory to promoters of justice. Instead of waiting for the liturgy to transform the laity, priests took over! Liturgical activities of the fifties promised great results if liturgy were modernized — but no one dreamt how far things would go, and there was no structure in place, in terms of artists, musicians, scholars, resources at every level. "We need to realize," Greeley concluded, "that transformation is going to take a long, long time. Social activists demand short-term results; what Godfrey was predicting is necessarily long-term."[60]

I am afraid that the relationship between the liturgical movement and social justice is not nearly as close as it was half a century ago. A seasoned liturgical scholar, Kevin Seasoltz, has portrayed it pungently, if perhaps with too broad a brush:

The temptation on the part of liturgists is to retreat from the world's problems into a safe, comfortable, aesthetically pleasing past and to convert liturgical worship into thematic celebrations of abstract universals that supposedly please God but have little to do with responsible life in the world. The temptation on the part of social activists is to reject the liturgy as totally irrelevant, as a distraction of valuable time and energy which should be spent solving the world's problems.[61]

Granted that the Church has a vital role to play in the area of justice, can this directly affect the liturgy?[62] On principle, it should. As sacrament of Christian belief, liturgy has a twin function: It should give expression to the faith experience of the Christian people, and it should mold that experience. All "liturgies" express experience and mold it: country music in Nashville, pro and college football, marching bands and the New York City Ballet, the Nazi goose step and the Aztec two step. This is what expresses and evokes the joys and frustrations of a people, their anger and violence, their loves and hates, their pent-up emotions. If we accept the thesis of first-rate liturgiologists that Christian liturgy sacramentalizes what goes on in the rest of our lives, that the liturgical journey ritualizes the human journey, two questions challenge us: (1) In point of fact, does this liturgy express the faith experience of this people? (2) If it does, how Catholic is that expression?

A quarter century ago the dimensions of this problem were brought home to me in an article by Brian Wicker:

[The liturgical] revival [among organized Christians] had a good side — in that it stimulated mature and scholarly thought about the fundamentals of Christianity and an understanding of the depths to which secularization had gone. But it had a bad side too — the side that made it possible in some places for the Christian liturgy inside the church and the fascist liturgy outside the church to coexist, or even at times to cooperate with each other. The liturgical revival was, in its origins, a conservative or even reactionary movement, liable at times to delusions of grandeur. This gave it a certain sympathy for the trappings of fascism and made the essential atheism of the latter hard to nail down. It is perhaps not surprising that those Christians most opposed to Hitler were often those least touched by the new liturgical ideas — either intellectual protestants like Dietrich Bonhoeffer, or simple, tridentine-formed peasant-Catholics like Franz Jägerstätter. Neither is it surprising that many post-fascist secular theologies of Europe and America (including those developed under Catholic auspices) have today turned away from liturgy as a source of inspiration or hope, or have even given it up as a bad job altogether.[63]

As I recall, very few Catholics in 1979 were appalled that the liturgy in a U.S. Catholic cathedral was expected to coexist with, perhaps even co-operate with, the fascist liturgy that was Argentinian repression. As I recall, it bothered few of us that in liturgizing, ritualizing, sacramentalizing a nation's experience, the preacher was expected by devout Catholics to limit his symbols to love of *God*.

The operative question, I believe, is this: What precisely is the justice that the liturgy celebrates? Quite some years ago, Notre Dame liturgiologist Mark Searle declared that the liturgy celebrates *God's* justice. And what is that? Searle spelled it out in a perceptive paragraph:

> ...the justice of God is not to be understood...as a matter of legal enactment or as the expression of a certain divine wisdom in tailoring exquisitely fitting punishment to the crimes of the inescapably guilty. *The justice of God is ultimately God himself, just as he is.* It is a justice that is revealed in all that God does to reveal himself. In creation it is revealed by things being the way he made them and serving the purpose for which they were made. In history God's justice is manifest in the people and events that embody and fulfill his will. In short, the justice of God is satisfied when things conform to the purpose for which he made them.... [64]

How does the liturgy help created reality, creatures, to be the way God made them, serve the purpose for which they were fashioned? Not by providing Christians with principles of solution, not by telling a congregation what precisely to think about specific conflicts — affirmative action, legal and illegal immigrants, food stamps for the needy. More realistically, a celebrant who effectively celebrates the transcendent puts God's people in touch with that which transcends all their burning concerns, their particular perplexities. Good liturgy frees them to sort out the issues they have to decide, because it makes them aware of their addictions and their illusions, casts a pitiless light on myopic self-interest, detaches from a natural selfishness, facilitates Christian discernment. In that sense liturgy is not so much didactic as evocative. Let *God* transpire. Let *God* speak. In a word, good liturgy effects conversion. A prime example is Dorothy Day.

> [Dorothy] Day could not go to Communion and be insensitive to the reality that someone was hungry; she could not enjoy the warmth of Eucharistic consolation and know that she had a blanket while her brothers and sisters did not; she could not "go to the altar of God" and be aware that someone was sleeping over a grate on the sidewalk.... This is not to say that her response was merely affective and personal. It was grounded in the theological. But the rational and intellectual came after the response of the heart, the prod of merciful grace.[65]

Robert Coles' account of his first meeting with Dorothy Day is a striking illustration. A troubled graduate student, Coles sought Day out at the Catholic Worker. When he found her, she was deep in conversation with a crazed, incoherent street derelict. After registering his presence, Coles stood back waiting for that crazed conversation to end. Yet it went on and on. When Day finally pulled away from the derelict, she came over to Coles and asked him, "Now, to which of us do you want to speak?"[66]

I am also indebted to Mark Searle for pointing out how each liturgy declares or intimates the relation of justice to God, to the human community, and to material creation.[67]

1. To God; for the Eucharistic prayer begins with a soul-searing confession: "It really is proper, it is a matter of justice [*Vere dignum et iustum est*], that we should always and everywhere give you thanks." Acknowledging the absolute claim of God's justice bases our critical consciousness vis-à-vis all political and social programs; none can claim our unquestioning loyalty. It is the source, too, of critical self-awareness for all who serve the less fortunate; no messiah complex, for the cause is God's, and God's too are the power and the glory.

2. To the human community; for the liturgy is a ceaseless "we." "We stand to one another not as the rich to the poor, the wise to the ignorant, the strong to the needy, the clever to the simple; we stand rather as the poor to the poor, the weak to the weak, the loved to the loved."[68] In point of fact, the liturgical assembly reflects not the justice of the kingdom but the divisions of social groupings; this constitutes a tension rather than an achievement. And still, the tension must be preserved if we are not thoughtlessly to accept our unjust world.

3. To material creation; for when Jesus took the bread, said the blessing, broke the bread, and shared it, he showed us in striking fashion the proper use of all material things. When he took the cup, gave thanks to God, and passed it among his disciples, he demonstrated the joy in not claiming anything as our very own — even life itself. He forbade us to turn the creation committed to our care into weapons of power and destruction.

When I reflect on the wealth of meaning and the power for transformation within the Eucharistic liturgy, then contrast this with the lack of awareness, the superficiality, that pervades so many (morally good, religiously observant) Catholic celebrants, preachers, and worshipers, I weep. Weep for the injustice we do not only to the word "justice" but, more importantly, to the God of justice, to God's just Word.

Forgive us, Lord, for we know not what we are doing.

SIX

From Manresa to El Salvador

Jesuit Spirituality

More than a decade ago, Avery Dulles observed that "The gap that has developed since the sixteenth century between doctrinal theology (as something rigorously conceptual and scientific) and spiritual theology (as a practical and hortatory discipline) has done harm to both theology and spirituality."[1] Exposed though I was in my early Jesuit years to precisely this division, I was still fortunate enough to experience at the same time the approach of the Fathers of the Church.

For the Fathers, theology was not a system; it was the drama of salvation — a drama that is being acted out now, by a living God and living people. Not that mid-twentieth-century theologians denied this; they simply excluded it from their system. They were dealing with propositions, not people; with concepts, not converts. Theology was intellectual truth. For the Fathers, theology was intellectual truth, of course; but they rarely divorced their search for God's truth from the living people for whom God spoke that truth. In consequence, for all its disadvantages (e.g., it was not a system), patristic theology was warm, a living, breathing, quickening thing. Specifically, (1) it was a thoroughly biblical theology, a discovery of a vibrant Christ in the Word of God; and (2) it put not merely reason but our whole intellectual/spiritual nature to work on revelation, including intuition and imagination, emotion and passion, because it is the human person's whole intellectual/spiritual nature that is to respond to revelation.[2] A striking example, highly influential for my own spirituality, was Gregory of Nyssa, one of the most speculative of the Fathers. A perceptive commentator, Roger Leys, summed up Gregory's theology uncommonly well:

> [For Gregory] the life of the mind is to know God. And there is but one way to know Him, and that is to be like Him, to get to be in His image. To be sure, Gregory speaks also of "the ascent of the soul toward God by the ladder of creatures"; but

he has little liking for this, perhaps because of its affinity with that knowledge of God (scarcely unitive) which even the wise of this world can achieve. Rather, the knowledge of God to which he gives preference in his thinking is that of participation in His virtues, in His holiness — that knowledge which is essentially union. The gaze of purity, of goodness, of rectitude is undoubtedly a gaze "on" God, but primarily it is the gaze "of" God which communicates His divine presence to us. And how participate in that holiness of God? By following Him through faith, eyes closed, wherever He leads; by opening one's heart always to a further and deeper submissiveness; by divesting oneself of every favor already received through unceasing yearning for what is always beyond; in a word, by the ecstasy which is a going out of oneself. The image of God is not, therefore, static reality but continual growth; and far from being an object of clear vision, it keeps sinking deeper into God's unknown....[3]

Patristic theology/spirituality has served me well through six decades. And yet I am persuaded that I resonate to it in large measure because it harmonizes so admirably with the most significant influence on my spirituality and that of Jesuits in general: St. Ignatius Loyola, founder of the Society of Jesus, and his *Spiritual Exercises*. But before moving into Ignatius, I think it wise to speak of spirituality more generally.

Spirituality

St. Paul sparks a useful beginning. The spiritual person, he explains, is one whose whole being, whose whole life, is influenced, guided, directed by "the Spirit that is from God" (1 Cor 2:12). This understanding, broad though it is, I regard as basic; for over the centuries "spiritual" has been employed in all sorts of contexts. It has been used in contrast to corporeal or material, to those exercising civil rather than ecclesiastical jurisdiction. It has been applied disparagingly to writers suspected of quietism or fanaticism; it has replaced terms like devotion, piety, interior life.[4]

So then, should anyone ask what I understand by spirituality, my basic response would be: My spirituality is my Christian living as guided by the Holy Spirit. Not some ghostly apparition in outer space, but the Third Person of the Trinity, the divine Person given me by the Father and the Son, alive within me, shaping me into an image of Christ, shaping me increasingly as brother in Christ to all who are children of the Father. How does the Holy Spirit effect this? By infusing into me incredible gifts that I could not possibly produce by my naked human nature. I mean a faith which at its best is not only or primarily an acceptance of revealed propositions but a total self-giving to God; a hope which is not a gossamer optimism but a confident trust in the promises of a God ever faithful; a love which enables me to love my sisters and brothers as Jesus has loved me (1 Cor 13:13). I mean what Paul called "spiritual wisdom and understanding, so that you may lead lives worthy of the Lord, fully pleasing to him, as you bear fruit in every good work and as you grow in the knowledge of God" (Col 1:9–10). I mean what Paul termed "the fruit of the Spirit: love, joy, peace, patience, kindness, generosity, faithfulness, gentleness, and self-control" (Gal 5:22–23). I mean charisms that build up the Christian community, different gifts to different persons, but "all activated by one and the same Spirit, who allots to each individually just as the Spirit chooses" (1 Cor 12:11; cf. 1 Cor 12:4–11, 28–30; Rom 12:6–8; Eph 4:11–13).[5]

Within Catholicism there are spiritualities and spiritualities. Basically, each spirituality lives up to the description I have attempted. Each is a living-out of the Christian life under the inspiration of the Holy Spirit, through the gifts the indwelling Spirit produces in us for our personal sanctification and our contribution to the life of the community. But different social situations, different cultures, different religious communities, different personalities lay special stress on different facets of the richness, the breadth and depth, that Catholic spirituality encompasses. And so we have a cursillo spirituality, a charismatic spirituality, a lay spirituality. We have the Franciscans stressing Lady Poverty, the Dominicans emphasizing proclamation of the Word, the Benedictines laying particular weight on contemplation and liturgy, on "love of learning and the desire for God."[6] We have individuals imitating the lady mystic Julian of Norwich, Teresa of Avila or Thérèse of Lisieux, Dorothy Day or Thomas Merton. Special emphases within the one basic spirituality, to suit different needs, desires, tasks, persons.[7]

Highly important for my own involvement in justice issues is another recent emphasis. For all too long and for all too many, spirituality has been identified with our interior life, what goes on inside of us, what is a profoundly private experience. A holistic spirituality includes both the inner experience of God and its outward expression in relationships.[8] That is why I was delighted to discover several years ago a definition that attracts me mightily: Spirituality is a "process of being conformed to the image of Christ for the sake of others."[9]

Ignatius Loyola

Ignatian spirituality traces back to a profound conversion experienced by a soldier, aged 30, recovering from a dreadful leg wound suffered while he was defending a fortress against French forces at Pamplona in Spain. A short pilgrimage to the Holy Land was followed by extraordinary experiences of the Trinity, of Christ, and of our Lady that transformed Ignatius from a secular knight to a servant of the Lord Jesus. Gathering a group of like-minded men into a Company of Jesus, he established educational and charitable institutions, directed a vast missionary network, and practiced an impressive love and care of the poor, the underprivileged, the sick, and the dying.

Ignatius' union with the triune God in Christ (experiencing the Father as Father, the Son as Son, the Holy Spirit as Holy Spirit), his pastoral experience, and the promise of divine favor in Rome fashioned a spirituality and a mysticism that Harvey Egan has captured as "communal, ecclesial, and 'hyperpapal' (Hugo Rahner), but also Christ-centered, Eucharistic, and priestly. 'To be with the Trinitarian Christ in prudent and loving apostolic service to the entire world' may well serve as a summary of his spirituality."[10] Egan went on to elaborate:

> [Ignatius'] richly incarnational...mysticism finds God in all things and all things in God. His sacramental, affirmative mysticism and spirituality never separates love of God, neighbor, and world. It is a mysticism of joy in the world, an Easter spirituality that loves the earth because the Trinitarian God creates, redeems, and loves it. Ignatius' Trinitarian and Christocentric mysticism and spirituality are incarnated in a community of love for effective apostolic service, service that includes social and political dimensions.[11]

The *Spiritual Exercises*[12]

This slender volume is admittedly a classic of Christian spirituality. Not that Ignatius invented or originated the spiritual retreat or methodical prayer; simply that his Exercises made significant contributions to both. The book we have was composed over a period of years (1521–48) that saw three major influences contributing to its formulation: (1) the *Vita Christi* of Ludolph of Saxony, the *Flos sanctorum* of James of Voragine, and the *Exercitatoria* of Garcia de Cisneros, all of which he read while convalescing at Loyola after his leg was shattered during the battle of Pamplona; (2) his spiritual experiences during his conversion; (3) the mystical graces he received at Manresa, where he wrote the *Exercises* substantially: illumination of mind on the Trinity, creation, the humanity of Christ, the Eucharist, and the Virgin Mary.

It is a deceptive little book, not made for rapid reading. In reality, the *SE* is not meant to be read but to be experienced. In fact, Ignatius intended it not so much for the exercitant as for the director. Ignatius himself envisioned retreats not preached to groups but under individual direction, with the *Exercises* initiating for the retreatant a dialogue with the director, the text, Christian faith, God, and the "signs of the times." How long? Either a short session each day over a period of months, or the integral retreat of 30 days for those who can withdraw from all other occupations. For Ignatius,

> By the term "Spiritual Exercises" is meant every method of examination of conscience, of meditation, of contemplation, of vocal and mental prayer, and of other spiritual activities....
> For just as taking a walk, journeying on foot, and running are bodily exercises, so we call Spiritual Exercises every method of preparing and disposing the soul to rid itself of all inordinate attachments, and, after their removal, of seeking and finding the will of God in the disposition of our life for the salvation of our soul.[13]

SE is itself the fruit of an experience, a year-long process of conversion where the forces of good and evil struggled mightily for possession of Ignatius' soul, where he felt irresistibly impelled to shape his life Godward, and where God apparently revealed to him in a sort of synthesis the divine design for the world. It is this experience that Ignatius was persuaded could be communicated to others, could have a similar value for untold layfolk in the world, develop "comtemplatives in action."[14] In four "weeks" the exercitant meditates successively on (1) the sinful condition of the human, (2) the hidden and public life of Christ, (3) his passion, and (4) his resurrection and ascension, with a final Contemplation on How to Love Like God. All this to discover God's will in my regard, to see Christ more clearly, love him more dearly, follow him more nearly.

Highly important is the realization that *SE* is not a static reality, etched once for all in stone. Recent proponents of a philosophical hermeneutics insist that the genius of a "classic" — Sophocles or Shakespeare, Scripture or Chopin — is that the masterpiece in question invariably contains more than the original artist(s) could have consciously known or explicitly intended. According to Hans-Georg Gadamer,[15] for example, it is not only possible but is always the case that the meaning mediated by the text actually exceeds the conscious intention of the author.[16] Consequently, the classical text is never exhausted by the commentary of an individual or the interpretation of an age. There is always room for further discovery, for fresh insights, for contemporary applications that do not betray the text and still are not *in* the text. In this way the "excess of meaning" differs from the "fuller sense." For the fuller sense "is thought to be actually and independently contained in the text"; the excess of meaning "is not 'contained in the text' independently of the interpreter." Somewhat as "The score [of a great piece of music] becomes music only when rendered," so "the text becomes meaningful only when interpreted."[17]

Such, I suggest, is a fascinating facet of Ignatius' Spiritual Exercises. After four and a half centuries, we are not only continuing to grasp what was Ignatius' explicit intent in the course of the Four Weeks; we are unearthing ideas and insights that, perhaps paradoxically, were not in the pilgrim saint's mind but do go back to an author who wrote far more than he knew. When I compare the Exercises as commented and preached today with the Exercises presented to me in my noviceship (1931–33) and tertianship (1942–43), I am amazed, in awe, delighted. A word of explanation here.

In large measure I myself have developed spiritually because I have come increasingly to recognize the "excess of meaning" in various Ignatian Exercises, what new generations of researchers and spiritual directors have discovered, and I have integrated these with decades-old experiences. I shall be for ever grateful to my master of novices, Leo M. Weber, and to a fair number of retreat preachers in my earlier Jesuit years, for various ways of experiencing what Ignatius intuited and intended. But some of our Jesuit retreat masters talked too much; their "points" left all too little time for *our* meditation (admittedly, to our immature delight). And the preached retreat, to retreatants utterly unknown to the preacher, frequently left much to be desired. One mission-band veteran, a former chaplain in World War I with a Pelagian thrust (you could do anything you really wanted to do), gave us young Jesuit scholastics (I was in first-year philosophy) a veritable parish mission that painted sin in vivid colors Michelangelo would envy. An adolescent at the time, I can still remember word for word one impressive rhetorical sentence flung at us with Jovian thunder: "If you can't resist the bubble in the glass, the tinkle of the silver coin, or the smile on a woman's lips, tear that habit off and get out!"

Looking back, I regret that relatively little attention was given to the role of the senses, of emotion and passion, so important to the Ignatius of the Exercises. Far too frequently the retreat was a head trip. I suspect that several factors were at work here: the predominance of the rational in our education; suspicion of the emotions as dangerous aspects of our sinful nature (no one bothered to tell us that intellect and free will are also perilous); perhaps even the "Protestant" emphasis on that so subjective a thing called experience. More recent exponents of the *Exercises* are more holistic in their approach. I am convinced that Ignatius would react enthusiastically to a moving paragraph penned by that most rigorous of theologians Bernard Lonergan:

> ... feeling [that answers to what is intended, apprehended, represented] gives intentional consciousness its mass, momentum, drive, power. Without these feelings our knowing and deciding would be paper thin. Because of our feelings, our desires and our fears, our hope or despair, our enthusiasm and indignation, our esteem and contempt, our trust and distrust, our love and hatred, our tenderness and wrath, our admiration, veneration, reverence, our dread, horror, terror, we are oriented massively and dynamically in a world mediated by meaning. We have feelings about other persons, we feel for them, we feel with them. We have feelings about our respective situations, about the past, about the future, about evils to be lamented or remedied, about the good that can, might, must be accomplished.[18]

Some examples of the old and the new.[19] Take the First Week. On the one hand, it should always have been pellucidly clear that, for Ignatius, Christ does not make his entrance only after we have mulled over the mystery of sin and evil, over judgment, heaven, and hell; Christ is critical to the whole process of conversion, of reform. The retreatant meditates in the shadow of Christ crucified, asks three searing questions: "What have I done for Christ? What am I doing for Christ? What ought I to do for Christ?"[20] On the other hand, we have discovered what is not explicit in the text but is a legitimate understanding in the context of our culture: The reform to which the Ignatian retreat looks is not a Lone Ranger or Don Quixote or *sola fide* ("faith alone") effort but a collaborative enterprise of corporate conversion where faith expresses itself in work for justice, and justice (at least in its ethical sense: Give to each what is due to each) requires political science, psychology, and economics.

Take the Second Week. On the one hand, the meditation on the "Call of the King" explicitly envisions a lord-vassal relationship, though in a form of service that demands mutual fidelity. On the other hand, the ideal king may be imagined as any leader who can win hearts and inspire devotion. In fact, the king can legitimately be seen as my transcendent self, the living principle of generativity, fertility, and creativity. And Christ is not simply male but the androgynous male, humanity male and female, ceaselessly moving to wholeness and unity-in-difference.

Take the Third Week. On the one hand, in its theology of dying with Christ in order to enter into his life, it is hardly uniquely Ignatian, is not particularly unusual among Christian spiritualities. On the other hand, at least one interpreter has drawn somewhat subtly from Ignatius the importance of the contemplation on the burial of Christ — a contemplation that "brings us out of suffering and pain into a stillness where there is no longer any desire or fear, no rejoicing over good, no sorrow over pain." This "utter stillness and motionlessness of death," this silence, is the goal of the Week, the perfection of Ignatian indifference. Out of this silence will come an experience of the risen Christ.[21]

Take the Fourth Week. On the one hand, Ignatius did see Jesus' resurrection (with the Contemplation for Learning to Love Like God) as the climax of the *Exercises,* as not simply glorious history but ongoing redemption, Christ alive now, our joy in the risen Lord. On the other hand, he could hardly have foreseen the impact on his *Exercises* of a fresh theological understanding of the resurrection, such as was initiated by scholars like F. X. Durrwell, David Stanley, and Gerald O'Collins. But *SE* is wondrously open to all this.

Features of Ignatian Spirituality

First, an important prefatory observation. Although the Spiritual Exercises are the basis of Jesuit spirituality, it would be a mistake simply to identify Ignatian spirituality with the Exercises. This would lead us

imperceptibly to identify two distinct elements in Jesuit spirituality: the *Exercises,* and the complex history that culminated
in Ignatius' *Constitutions* for the Society of Jesus. Then,
since innocently deficient ideas still have consequences, we ar-
rive at two practical errors: pointing the *Exercises* toward a
spirituality they do not intend and depriving Jesuit spirituality of its specific character, as found most notably in the
Constitutions.[22]

In the two decades after Manresa while Ignatius wandered around
Europe and the Holy Land, in the six years (1534–40) during which
he and his companions were still searching for "the way to go"
though they had already made the Exercises, in the dozen years during which Ignatius laboriously worked out the Jesuit Constitutions,
he and his first followers "were seeking something the Exercises
had not given them."[23]

Encounter with God

Several features of Ignatian spirituality merit highlighting here. First,
integral to Ignatian spirituality is *encounter with God.* For in his Introductory Observations Ignatius insists that the director should let
God "communicate Himself in person to the devout soul," should
"permit the Creator to deal directly with the creature, and the creature directly with his Creator and Lord."[24] Back in 1978, Karl
Rahner wrote a striking essay titled "Ignatius of Loyola Speaks to
a Modern Jesuit,"[25] in which he put on the lips of Ignatius, with
remarkable insight and frankness, some account of the saint himself and the task that faces Jesuits today. One of the most striking
sections focuses on his experience of God.

> As you know, my great desire was to "help souls," as I put it in
> my day; to tell people about God.... I was convinced that first,
> tentatively, during my illness in Loyola and then, decisively,
> during my time as a hermit in Manresa I had a direct encounter
> with God. This was the experience I longed to communicate
> to others.
>   When I claim to have known God at first hand, I do not
> intend here to add to my assertion a theological treatise on the
> nature of such a direct experience of God.... I am not going
> to talk of forms and visions, symbols, voices, not of the gift of
> tears and such things. All I say is I knew God, nameless and
> unfathomable, silent and yet near, bestowing Himself upon me

in His Trinity. I knew God beyond all concrete imaginings. I knew Him clearly in such nearness and grace as is impossible to confound or mistake. . . .

God Himself. I experienced God Himself, not human words describing Him. I experienced God and the freedom which is an integral part of Him and which can only be experienced through Him and not as the sum total of finite realities and calculations about Him. This experience is grace indeed, and basically there is no one to whom it is refused. Of precisely this was I convinced.[26]

It was in such statements as those which Rahner put on the lips of Ignatius that, in the mind of his collaborator Herbert Vorgrimler and others, "the aged Karl Rahner spoke about the primal experience which completely captivated him while he was still young and which provides the key to his life and work."[27]

It is common knowledge among theologians and spiritual directors that through the centuries Catholic theology has struggled with the problem of the human experience of God, that competent historians and theologians are not at peace, that Thomas Aquinas, e.g., apparently does not state explicitly that we have an experience of God. And yet, Avery Dulles himself has graciously admitted that "The recent work of Harvey Egan . . . makes a convincing case that St. Ignatius, especially in his Spiritual Journal, must be interpreted as holding that God can be perceived as immediately communicating himself to the human spirit."[28] I find the thesis difficult to contest when I read Rahner declaring in an interview only two years before his death:

In my theology the givenness of a genuine, original experience of God and his Spirit is of fundamental importance. . . . That does not mean that the linguistic representation and interpretation of the religious experience is not something that has to occur within the Church under the supervision of her magisterium. But I believe . . . that an awakening, a mystagogy into this original, grace-filled religious experience is today of fundamental importance.[29]

Rahner's theology of religious experience, of knowledge of God, has been severely criticized. I became acutely aware of such criticism in 1985 when, as editor of *Theological Studies,* I accepted a strong article by Paul Molnar of St. John's University in Jamaica, New York.[30] His basic claim?

Both Scripture and tradition actually maintain that Christians have no direct knowledge of God. Christians cannot simply assume that their experiences are experiences of the transcendent God without making the Creator indistinguishable from the creature. Because Rahner fails to recognize and to maintain this insight, he ultimately makes God indistinguishable from the world at precisely the point where Scripture and tradition insist that God ought to be most clearly discernible.[31]

In response, Benedictine James Wiseman has addressed two questions: (1) Whence comes Rahner's insistence on an immediate experience of a hidden God? (2) In the context of the objections, is Rahner's thesis justified?[32]

Whence? From the entire Christian mystical tradition. From Gregory of Nyssa insisting at once on God's incomprehensibility *and* a "perception" or "sensation" of God's presence. From the mystics' favorite choice of *touch* to designate the initial mystical contact. From Rahner's perception that in the Spiritual Exercises Ignatius is not satisfied with a conceptual knowledge of God. From Rahner's conviction that in our time direct experience of God is of critical importance.

> I am convinced that such an immediacy between God and the human person ... is of greater significance today than ever before. All the societal supports of religion are collapsing and dying out in this secularized and pluralistic society. If, nonetheless, there is to be real Christian spirituality, it cannot be kept alive and healthy by external helps, not even those which the Church offers, ... but only through an ultimate, immediate encounter of the individual with God.[33]

But, given the objections above, is such a position justified? Here I leave the arena to systematic and speculative theologians. I wonder, simplistically perhaps, whether the issue may not center on the word "knowing." Direct, immediate knowledge of God is not identical with comprehensive knowledge. For the Fathers, the mystics, Rahner himself, our earth-bound knowledge of God is always imperfect; and still it is genuine knowledge, true experience. Are the experiences of Gregory of Nyssa, Hildegarde of Bingen, and Julian of Norwich in conflict with the testimony of Scripture and tradition? I do not believe so.

Wiseman has suggested that a more trenchant objection stems from critics such as David Tracy and Rahner's student and dear friend Johann Baptist Metz. It has to do with Rahner's transcendental method. As Metz saw it,

> the religious consciousness formed by this theology attributes but a shadowy existence to socio-political realities. The categories most prominent in this theology are the categories of the intimate, the private, the apolitical sphere. It is true that these theologians strongly emphasize charity, ... yet they regard charity only as a private virtue with no political relevance; it is a virtue of the I-Thou encounter, extending to the field of interpersonal encounter, or at best to charity on the scale of the neighborhood.[34]

Echoing Metz, Tracy has declared that, without the prophetic core represented by liberation and political theologians, "the struggle for justice and freedom in the historical-political world can too soon be lost in mere privacy."[35]

Interestingly, Rahner has admitted not developing a praxis-oriented theology à la Metz or Gutiérrez. Such theologies were not around during his most productive period, and his time was limited, his potential finite. With all that, I delight in a Rahner text that Wiseman's article has brought to my attention.

> I have nothing against liberation theology or political theology. But didn't Johann Baptist Metz let himself be a bit taken in by Ernesto Cardenal? I was present in Frankfurt when Cardenal explained that the kingdom of God had begun in Nicaragua, that there were no prisons there anymore, that everyone loved one another.... I won't have anything to do with such nonsense![36]

Eucharist

A second feature is the union of personal interior life with *liturgical life*. Egan has called this "perhaps the principal characteristic of Ignatian spirituality."[37] It involves a profound sacramental life that has its center in the Eucharist, including frequent Communion.

Within this context I have found it understandable that Ignatius' Trinitarian and Christocentric mysticism "developed almost exclusively in the atmosphere of the Mass."[38] His entire day focused on the Mass. Many mystical favors he received during the day were extensions of, or complements to, the graces he received within the Eucharist. The Mass was the milieu wherein he made important decisions that affected him personally and the Society he had founded.

The Eucharist was literally his "thanksgiving" for the grace of experiencing the mystery of the triune God in Christ. Little wonder that Ignatius encouraged frequent Communion, rare in his day.[39] Little wonder that the inquisitors at Salamanca questioned him about his Eucharistic theology.

Devotion to Our Lady

A third characteristic I discover in Ignatian spirituality is *devotion to our Lady*. If we can credit the liturgical books of the Society of Jesus, the mother of Jesus is the mother of Jesuits. The liturgical feast "The Blessed Virgin Mary, Mother of the Society of Jesus" has replaced the earlier feast "The Blessed Virgin Mary, Queen of the Society of Jesus." About to preach on the more recent feast on April 22, 1991, as part of the Maryland Jesuit Province's celebration of the 500th anniversary of the birth of Ignatius, I was curious enough to initiate research into the reason for the change. A communication (March 20, 1991) to Walter C. Deye, S.J., then executive secretary of the U.S. Jesuit Conference, from Peter Gumpel, S.J., secretary of the Liturgical Commission of the Society of Jesus, informed us that "The question of the title of the feast celebrated on April 22 in honour of Our Lady was amply discussed by the Liturgical Commission of the Society before the new Calendar was published. With regard to the title of this feast (*Queen* or *Mother* of the Society) the opinions were divided." Some members favored change from Queen to Mother because "the title *Queen* had lost its meaning in today's democratic world." Others favored retention of Queen because "this title is closely linked to the Spiritual Exercises and the entire spirituality of St. Ignatius." The majority voted for Mother, and Father General Pedro Arrupe "decided that the title of the feast should be changed" from Queen to Mother. "Not all members of the Society were happy with this decision and we know that some continue to use the old title whereas others combine the two titles": Queen and Mother of the Society.

So much for current events. One facet of the problem is certain: our Lady in the life of Ignatius.[40] No, he never said our Lady was "Mother of the Society of Jesus." He did not race around Rome waving Marian banners to arouse devotion to her. And yet, the mother of Jesus was central to his spirituality — quietly, very naturally, without ostentation.

It began at Loyola, when he was convalescing from the cannon ball that shattered his right leg and damaged the left. Our Lady appeared to him with the Child Jesus — an appearance that proved a profound conversion experience, gave him a loathing for the life he had so far misspent. At Loyola, too, he copied in blue Mary's words in the Gospels.[41]

I find especially significant Mary's shrines. The place names fashion a mosaic of Ignatian devotion. *Aránzazu,* where the pilgrim kept a prayer vigil, placed his plans and problematic future in Mary's hands. *Navarrete,* where he spent money to repair and decorate a neglected image of Mary. *Montserrat,* where he kept his vigil of arms at the feet of the Black Virgin, spent the whole night in prayer. *Manresa,* while reciting the Hour of Our Lady, when he experienced the illumination of the Trinity that so profoundly affected his whole life — and saw our Lady too. *Barcelona,* where he visited the Church of the Dormition of Our Lady. *Rome,* where he prayed at the long-sacred shrine of our Lady. *Montmartre,* in the little chapel dedicated to Mary, where on the feast of the Assumption 1534 Ignatius and six companions pronounced the vows that would orient their life to come. *La Storta,* where the Father answered his prayer to our Lady, "Place me with your Son."

There is so much more. I recall how in his bravado days Ignatius was tempted to slip a few dagger digs to a Moor who questioned Mary's virginity after Bethlehem. I recall how he would have loved a Jewish ancestry, so as to be related in flesh to Jesus and his mother. I recall that in 1541, in Rome's Basilica of St. Paul-outside-the-Walls, Ignatius and five companions pronounced their profession in the Society of Jesus "in the presence of [God's] virgin mother and the whole heavenly court." I recall how, while composing the Constitutions, he saw "now the Father, now all three persons of the Trinity, now our Lady who was interceding for him or sometimes confirming what he had written."[42] I recall the votive Masses he said in honor of our Lady, and how he slept with the rosary on him.

And for those of us who have experienced the Spiritual Exercises, we could not escape our Lady: on sin, on the kingdom, on Jesus embryo and infant and adolescent, on his passion. So insightfully when Ignatius asks all who meditate on the Two Standards to converse with our Lady, ask her "to obtain from her Son and Lord the grace to be received under his standard."[43] For in his mind Mary was "the very embodiment of the victory over Satan and the world."[44] So touchingly, the appearance of the risen Jesus to his mother — not indeed recorded in Scripture, but "Scripture supposes that we have understanding,"[45] that a risen Jesus bypassing his mother, Jesus without his mother, makes no sense.

I do not find it fanciful to suggest that, in the mind of Ignatius, the *sheerly human person* most responsible for his decision to found a Company of Jesus was the mother of Jesus.

Finding God in All Things

A fourth characteristic of Ignatian spirituality is the effort to *find God everywhere,* in all things, in all persons. It comes to focus in the closing contemplation of the *Exercises,* traditionally titled the Contemplation for Obtaining Divine Love, more recently Learning to Love Like God, as God loves. In his third point Ignatius asks me to "consider how God [i.e., Christ[46]] works and labors for me in all creatures upon the face of the earth, that is, he behaves as one who labors."[47]

What we discover in Ignatius is the ceaseless presence of Christ to our earth, the Incarnation not only in Nazareth two millennia ago but in our midst this very moment. In startlingly concrete language Ignatius compels us to revamp a narrow theology which implies that, when the risen Jesus rose to his Father, this earth somehow lost him, save for a vague something called sanctifying grace and a mysterious presence under the appearances of bread and wine. Ignatius forces us to surrender a spirituality that looks up to heaven for God's grace. No, "consider how Christ labors for me in all creatures."

How is it that 200 billion billion stars (yes, billion billion) can fly the heavens more speedily than light, the Rockies still rise in breathtaking splendor, oil gushes from the fields of Nebraska? Because an all-powerful risen Christ gives them *being.* Not once for all; each moment. How is it that more than four thousand varieties of roses can grow and perfume our earth, giant redwoods stalk the California sky? Because an imaginative Christ gives them *life.* How is it that your Irish setter can smell the game beyond your ken, gulls scavenge your ocean, the shad ascend the waters? Because a sensitive Christ gives them *senses.* How is it that a student can shape an idea, a surgeon transplant a human heart, an architect send a skyscraper soaring, a man or woman live deliriously in deathless oneness with the other? Because a still human Christ gives them *intelligence and love.* How can I believe that the Son of God died a bloody death for me, confidently expect to live for ever, give myself unreservedly to God and my sisters and brothers? Because a living Christ infuses *faith* in me, fills my flesh with *hope,* inflames my very bones with a unique *love* not of this world.

And all this, Ignatius saw, Christ does not from some majestic throne in heaven he shares with two other divine persons. He reminds Ignatius of a skilled, enthusiastic worker — very much alive, always in touch with his creation, ceaselessly concerned, today more imaginative than yesterday, terribly in love with all he shapes. Alive not only yesterday but at each moment of each creature's existence. Indeed, the world is charged with the presence of Christ, with the labor of Christ.

Little wonder that a perceptive (non-Jesuit) professor of theological studies at the Jesuits' St. Louis University could discover that the Ignatian ideal of finding God in all things is what

> allowed Jesuit spirituality to become at once worldly and humanistic, seeing God as deeply immersed in all creation and in all human endeavor. It could take for its own the words of Terence, the pre-Christian (do we still say "pagan") poet — *Nil humanum alienum a me puto* ("Nothing human is foreign to me") — because nothing human is merely human. And no enterprise, no matter how secular, is merely secular. We live in a universe of grace. From the Jesuit perspective, therefore, it followed that holiness and humanism require each other.[48]

Uncommonly gratifying to me in this regard is a decision of the U.S. Episcopal Church in August 1994. Its house of bishops added to the Church's liturgical calendar St. Ignatius Loyola; he is now included in the Episcopal prayer book. And the prayer authorized for Ignatius' feast reads in part: "Almighty God, we thank thee for calling Ignatius of Loyola to the service of thy Divine Majesty and *to find thee in all things....*"

Learning and Loving

A fifth facet of Ignatian spirituality is its ability to *link scholarship with sanctity*. On this link I should like to dwell long and lovingly, for it represents one of the most significant discoveries in my search for God, and it is intimately related to Ignatius' Exercises.

On November 16, 1989, six Jesuits of El Salvador's University of Central America were murdered with shocking brutality by soldiers of the party in power. Of them Jesuit law professor Robert F. Drinan, former Congressman from Massachusetts, wrote this insightful paragraph:

> In the history of the Society of Jesus, Jesuits have been slain for teaching the catechism, for refusing to obey the anti-Catholic

decrees of the English government or for insisting on the doctrines of the Catholic church. But the murder of the six Jesuits
in El Salvador added a new dimension to those listed on the
martyrology of the church; now the church has martyrs who
did not take on heretics or agnostics, or enemies of the church.
The church now has a new class of martyrs: Catholics who
studied things like economics and agriculture in order to bring
about a just social order as envisioned by the social encyclicals
of the church.....[49]

In this context I have long been entranced by the Benedictine
tradition in education. That tradition, which traces back to Basil
the Great and Benedict of Nursia, I found superbly summarized
in the title of a minor classic by Dom Jean Leclercq that has profoundly influenced my own efforts to link learning and love: *The
Love of Learning and the Desire for God.*[50] At a high point in his
book Leclercq is contrasting monastic and Scholastic theology.[51] For
the Schools, theology's aim was knowledge; and the way to knowledge was through the question. In the monasteries the aim was not
so much knowledge as experience; and the way to experience was
not so much the question as desire. The significant difference was
the importance the monastery accorded to the experience of union
with God.

Here the word "experience" is not something esoteric, meant for
a select few. It simply means that in study and reflection the Benedictine tradition highlights an inner illumination, a grace of intimate
prayer, what Benedict called an *affectus,* a manner of savoring and
relishing divine realities. It means that if you want to "know" God,
you need a lived faith. This personal experience is closely linked
with a whole environment, promoted by the experience of a fervent
community. It is a biblical experience inseparable from liturgical experience. It is experiencing the Church, an experience undergone in
the very midst of the Church. It presupposes the pursuit of the spiritual life in a community whose essential aim is the search for God.
It promotes the presence in the Church of spiritual men and women
rather than intellectual masters.

It was this realization that led me to shape a commencement ad-
dress in 1986 to the graduating class of the Benedictine Portsmouth
Priory School in Rhode Island under the title "Love of Learning,
Desire for God," and to close in the following vein:

One thing I can promise you with confidence.... Wherever you
go and whatever you do — on Wall Street or with the poor

in Peru, transplanting a human heart or defending a human right, correcting the bite in my teeth or inventing a new byte for your Apple, even simply studying for four more years or seven — wherever you go and whatever you do, you will know a profound joy, a deep satisfaction, which, as Jesus promised, no human being can take from you ... if. If your yearning for learning is an adventure in loving. If the creation you master, from an amoeba to the moon, makes for reverent oneness with each single thing you touch. If each man or woman you come to know becomes a brother or sister you come to love. If the Father who remains Mystery, the Son whose wounds you cannot finger, the Spirit who makes your flesh a shrine — if these are the God of your desire, the God for whom you hunger, the God who keeps you remarkably restless until you rest eternally in Them.

Learning as love, God as your desire — here is your Benedictine heritage, here your Christian future. Live it, and you will ever be surprised by joy. I can promise you that, because I have experienced it. For this experience, a son of St. Ignatius proclaims public gratitude to the sons and daughters of St. Benedict.

In 1991, the Ignatian Year that celebrated the 500th anniversary of Ignatius' birth, I was privileged to present a celebratory lecture at St. Louis University. My topic was "The Spiritual Exercises as a Foundation for Educational Ministry."[52] I presented the Exercises as a process of conversion which in an educational institution aims at altering in students, faculty, and staff (1) their world of learning, the life of the mind; (2) their world of loving, their human and religious imagination and affection; (3) their world of living, the life of social realities.

First, the world of learning. The Spiritual Exercises — perhaps more broadly, Jesuit spirituality — can keep the student from segregating learning into a pigeonhole of its own, divorced from the thrust of the spirit toward God. Not that all of learning becomes a spiritual enterprise. Vatican II made that quite clear. With Vatican I, it distinguished " 'two orders of knowledge' which are distinct," declared that "the Church does not indeed forbid that 'when the human arts and sciences are practiced they use their own principles and their proper method, each in its own domain.' " In consequence, the council "affirms the legitimate autonomy of human culture and especially of the sciences."[53]

My point was, the life of the mind is perilously impoverished if knowledge does not lead to wonder. Not sheer questioning: I wonder if Israel should make peace with Syria. In the grasp of wonder I marvel: I am surprised, amazed, delighted, enraptured, in awe. It is Mary pregnant by God's Spirit: "My spirit finds delight in God my Savior" (Lk 1:47). It is Magdalene about to touch her risen Jesus: "Master!" (Jn 20:16). It is doubting Thomas discovering his God in the wounds of Jesus. It is Michelangelo striking his sculptured Moses: "Speak!" It is Alexander Fleming fascinated by the very first antibiotic, America thrilling to the first footsteps on the moon. It is Mother Teresa cradling a naked retarded child in the rubble of West Beirut, cradling a crippled old man in the excrement of Calcutta. It is the wonder of a first kiss.

Such should be a student's reaction to the life of learning. Not a new methodology for biology or psychology; simply awe in the presence of the multifaceted, myriad miracle that is life.

> Amazement at what breadths and depths there are to being alive — from the architectural artistry of the ant and the grace of a loping panther, through the blinding speed of a white marlin and the majestic flight of the bald eagle, to the beating heart of a unique fetus, the inspired imagery of Shakespeare, the fantastic 48 measures of Tchaikovsky's *Nutcracker,* the transforming insight of Einstein.[54]

With such wonder a student may hope to touch the pinnacle of knowledge. For, as philosopher Jacques Maritain discovered, the height of human knowing is not conceptual; it is experiential. Man or woman feels God. Yes, *feels* God.

And such are the possibilities latent in the Exercises, themselves an adventure in experience, in wonder, in the kingdom of contemplation, Carmelite William McNamara's "long loving look at the real." For Ignatius' high purpose is to see us struck, surprised, stunned by the wonder of it all — from the ecstasy of Eden unspoiled, through sin's rape of the earth and earth's dwellers, to the unique love of God-in-our-flesh pinned to a cross, and our rebirth in his rising from the rock. The net effect? Ignatius' final contemplation, Learning to Love Like God, where I marvel at the ceaseless presence of Christ to our earth, Christ "laboring" in every creature.

Second, the world of loving. Here is the kingdom of affective imagination (on which I discoursed in chapter 4 on preaching), the capacity we all have to make the material an image of the immaterial or spiritual. Andrew Greeley's sociological research has persuaded him that "the fundamental differences between Catholicism and Protestantism are not doctrinal or ethical" but "differing sets of symbols."[55] Take the central symbol: God. The classical literature of the Catholic tradition assumes

> a God who is present in the world, disclosing Himself in and through creation. The world and all its events, objects, and people tend to be somewhat like God. The Protestant classics, on the other hand, assume a God who is radically absent from the world and who discloses Herself only on rare occasions (especially in Jesus Christ and Him crucified). The world and all its events, objects, and people tend to be radically different from God.[56]

In the area of religious behavior, Greeley insists, God is imaged by the Protestant as distant (father, judge, king, master), by the Catholic as present (mother, lover, friend, spouse).[57] In their approach to human society, Catholics tend to see society as a "sacrament" of God, a set of ordered relationships that reveal God's presence; society is natural and good for humans, and so the Catholic's natural response to God is social. Protestants tend to see human society as Godforsaken, therefore unnatural, oppressive. The individual stands over against society, becomes fully human only when "able to break away from social oppression and relate to the absent God as a completely free individual."[58] Most sharply distinctive of the Catholic tradition, to Greeley, is the Catholic image of Jesus' mother; for she "blatantly confirms the sacramental instinct": All of creation, particularly its life-giving and life-nurturing processes, "reveal the lurking and passionate love of God."[59]

Here too Ignatius is exciting. His Exercises, for all their appeal to the Christian intelligence, are not a head trip. They are first and foremost an experience. An experience of Catholic symbols: Adam and Eve and Eden, angels and Satan, hellfire, a virgin and a crib, Egypt and Jerusalem, the Transfiguration, bread and wine, blood and water from the side of Christ, nail marks in risen hands, an ascension into heaven. But not a cold-reason experience. Take the experience of sin's devastating impact on angels and humans, sin's ravishing of God's good earth. I do not simply *define* sin, recall a traditional definition: any thought, word, or action against God's law. I smell sin's stench. I image sin's cost, weep over it; for sin's cost is a cross, the pierced hands of a God-man.

Ignatius playing with my capacity to imagine is attempting something terribly significant psychologically and spiritually. For I am no longer looking at the life of Christ sheerly as history. The events of Jesus' earthly existence must be seen as a "today," the historical happenings drawn into my own world here and now. Here Ignatius touched a medieval tradition while convalescing from cannon wounds back at Loyola. He was profoundly impressed by what an unknown Franciscan had written:

> If you wish to draw profit from these meditations...make everything that the Lord Jesus said and did present to yourself, just as though you were hearing it with your ears and seeing it with your eyes.... And even when it is related in the past tense you should contemplate it all as though present today.... [60]

That is how I achieve not abstract knowledge but what the medievals called "familiarity with Christ," an understanding that takes hold not only of discursive reasoning but of the whole person, an imagining that leads to loving — a direct experience of God's love, a direct return of love.

Third, the world of social realities. I mean the life that moves beyond the individual in isolation to community, people interacting, impacting one another, depending on one another. In 1975 the 32nd General Congregation of the Society of Jesus declared, "The mission of the Society of Jesus today is the service of faith, of which the promotion of justice is an absolute requirement."[61] Somewhat later it went on to assert:

> We should pursue and intensify the work of formation in every sphere of education, while subjecting it at the same time to continual scrutiny. We must help prepare both young people and adults to live and labor for others and with others to build a more just world. Especially we should help form our Christian students in such a way that, animated by a mature faith and personally devoted to Jesus Christ, they can find him in others and, having recognized him there, they will serve him in their neighbor. In this way we shall contribute to the formation of those who by a kind of multiplier-effect will share in the process of educating the world itself.[62]

What our faculties and students should experience through the Exercises is that by God's design and initiative human existence is fundamentally social, societal.[63] We are "we" before we are "I" and "thou." This is central in Christian revelation and of primary importance for our contemporary culture of individualism, where we

think first of self and then how we can join others in community —
as though community did not precede the individual genetically,
psychically, socially, and spiritually.[64] Even Catholic social teaching frequently fails to position this fact front and center, because it
lays down as primary in its social ethics the "dignity of the human
person, who is made to the image of God." From there the teaching argues to the God-invested *rights* of the individual which other
individuals and institutions must respect. This misses the point of
the Genesis story (on which it is often based) that the *adam* who is
given such dignity is not an individual but "the human," our whole
race in personification.[65]

The Jesuit educational ideal is not the intellectual mole who lives
almost entirely underground, surfaces occasionally for fresh air and
a Big Mac, and burrows back down to the earthworms before people
can distract him. A college is where young men and women who
may one day profoundly influence America's way of life touch, some
for the first time, the ruptures that sever us from our earth, from
our sisters and brothers, from our very selves. Not simply in an
antiseptic classroom, for all its high importance for understanding.
Even more importantly, *experience* of rupture: experience not only
of ecology but of an earth irreparably ravaged, not only abstract
poverty but the stomach-bloated poor, not only the words "child
abuse" but the vacant stare of the child abused, not only a book on
racism but the hopelessness or hatred in human hearts. To yearn for
such experience, I know no better introduction than experiencing
the Christ of the Spiritual Exercises, the conversion consequent on
seeing Christ more clearly, loving him more dearly.

My own experience of what is central to Ignatian spirituality
should not obscure features that more knowledgeable scholars have
brought to my attention. In particular, John O'Malley has highlighted, for the sixteenth-century Jesuit, (1) conversion of heart from
sin and conversion to discipleship; (2) movement from purgation to
enlightenment to union of wills with the divine will; (3) consolation
as a criterion for judging the authenticity of every step in the spiritual journey; (4) certain Jesuit "ways of proceeding," basic indeed
but accommodated to concrete circumstances of persons in all conditions and states of life; (5) the primacy of grace and the need for
total commitment to the movements of grace; (6) a more optimistic
view of the world and human nature than was found in many other
contemporary movements; (7) service at the core of Jesuit ministry,
a spirituality that was pastoral or ministerial. "Their synonym for
'helping souls' was ministry — *ministerium, ministeria,* words pre-

eminently proper to the Society of Jesus and not 'borrowed from Protestants,' as we sometimes hear tell."[66]

Ignatian Spirituality or Jesuit Spirituality?

Thus far I have been speaking rather consistently of a spirituality that can be called Ignatian, because it represents the way Ignatius and his sixteenth-century "companions" envisioned their calling. But 444 years have passed since Ignatius died. Is the spirituality of today's Society of Jesus exactly the same as yesterday's?

The question brings me back to Vatican II, specifically to its Decree on the Appropriate Renewal of the Religious Life. One sentence from that document is particularly crucial for the spirituality of religious orders and congregations. "The appropriate renewal of religious life involves two simultaneous processes: (1) a continuous return to the sources of all Christian life and to the original inspiration behind a given community and (2) an adjustment of the community to the changed conditions of the times."[67]

In my experience no single Jesuit has done more to activate those two principles than Pedro Arrupe, superior general of the Society of Jesus for 19 years, from 1965 to 1983. Through the three general congregations held during his term, and through his own leadership, writings, and sufferings, a spirituality evolved in the Society that was profoundly rooted in the gospel and Jesuit tradition and yet responded intelligently and courageously to the challenges of our times.[68]

Basic to Don Pedro's efforts was his insistence that for Jesuits our spiritual life and our apostolic life must be integrated. The 31st General Congregation (1965) made it quite clear that the principal reason why our labors have not produced all the results we had a right to expect was our failure to adapt our ministries adequately to changed conditions. An excellent example of the way Ignatian spirituality has influenced our contemporary ministry takes us back to 1980, when Father Arrupe, shocked by the plight of refugees (e.g., the "boat people"), created the Jesuit Refugee Service. His letter of November 14, 1980, to the whole Society is highly instructive.

> ... this situation constitutes a challenge to the Society we cannot ignore if we are to remain faithful to St. Ignatius' criteria for our apostolic work.... In the *Constitutions* St. Ignatius speaks of the greater universal good, an urgency that is ever growing, the difficulty and complexity of the human problem

involved, and the lack of other people to attend to the need (*Constitutions* 623). With our ideal of availability and universality, the number of institutions under our care, and the active collaboration of many lay people who work with us, we are particularly well fitted to meet this challenge and provide services that are not being catered sufficiently by other organizations and groups.... The Society is being called to render a service that is human, pedagogical, and spiritual....I consider this a new modern apostolate for the Society as a whole, of great importance for today and the future, and also of much spiritual benefit to the Society.... St. Ignatius called us to go anywhere we are most needed for the greater service of God.... God is calling us through these helpless people.[69]

Even more significant, because it touches every Jesuit and every Jesuit apostolate, is the key Decree 4 of the 32nd General Congregation (1974–75), the "faith that does justice" of which I spoke above. The conclusion of a "Declaration: Jesuits Today" from the same congregation has become part and parcel of Jesuit spirituality.

Thus, whether we consider the needs and aspirations of the men and women of our time, or reflect on the particular charism that founded our Society, or seek to learn what Jesus has in his heart for each and all of us, we are led to the identical conclusion that today the Jesuit is a man whose mission is to dedicate himself entirely to the service of faith and the promotion of justice, in a communion of life and work and sacrifice with the companions who have rallied round the same standard of the Cross and in fidelity to the Vicar of Christ, for the building up of a world at once more human and more divine.[70]

I could not help but experience the aftermath of this fresh focus on faith/justice across the Society of Jesus. The inseparable unity of the two, Arrupe admitted in Manila, is "the concept which has been most difficult to put across."[71] Arrupe knew that on this issue some of our most loyal friends and benefactors thought us traitors to the Ignatian ideal. He knew that more than a few Jesuits thought "the faith that does justice" nonsensical, naive. He knew there were idealistic Jesuits who carried the struggle to extremes, to a violence hardly in conformity with the cross of Christ. Yet he never wavered in his core conviction, the memorable message John Paul II proclaimed in Puebla: "The Church has learned that its evangelizing mission has as indispensable part (*como parte indispensable*) action for justice...."[72]

Spirituality Shaped by Relationships

A final thought, necessarily brief. My spirituality, anyone's spirituality, is necessarily shaped by relationships: not only with God but with family and friends, with colleagues and acquaintances, with the thousands of humans I touch long or fleetingly in the course of a life. And indeed by my relationship with the rest of God's creation, with earth, sky, and sea, and their inhabitants.

Here my mind is flooded with memories of lay friends. A half century ago, during my doctoral studies at the Catholic University of America, a priest-professor who would have been at home in the no-holds-barred debates of the Reformation and Counter Reform used to insist that the proper recreational situation for priests is with fellow priests. I thank God that I have not followed his advice. My Jesuit life, my spiritual existence, has been enriched beyond adequate description by lay friends. Some have revealed to me the ecstasy and the agony of wedded life as it images the oneness of Christ and his bride the Church. Others have given their lives, carried their Christ, to the unloved and the forgotten, the oppressed and the despised, today's "widows and orphans." And I dare not forget our Sisters: not only those teachers who endured my grade-school obnoxiousness; not only scholars like Sandra Schneiders, I.H.M., who through their research have shared the distinctive spiritualities of women; but especially a host of dear friends in religious life who this half century have been the Church's missionaries to infants and the elderly, to the homeless and the AIDS-afflicted, to the sick and the dying, to the imprisoned and the inhabitants of death row, have brought God's justice to neglected areas of the Church's mission. Not to have shared the love in their friendship would have left me less a priest, less a Jesuit, less a man.

My spirituality has been expanded and deepened from contact with other religious congregations. One example must suffice. An invitation in 1996 to address a forum sponsored by the De Sales School of Theology and the De Sales Center for Lay Spirituality compelled me to look intimately into Salesian spirituality. With a wry smile, I informed my audience that St. Francis de Sales is a persuasive proof that a young man can attend a Jesuit college, have a Jesuit for spiritual director, found a Jesuit school, and still become a saint! More substantively, I discovered (largely through the research of a gifted female friend) and exploited in my lecture remarkable parallels between the Spiritual Exercises of Ignatius Loyola and Salesian spirituality.

From a Salesian spirituality too rich to be imprisoned in a single lecture I stressed three facets that supported my Jesuit tradition. (1) Every human being is called to be holy; the summons to holiness is not a call to an elite within Christianity, an apostle John, a hermit Antony, a martyr Agnes, a mystic Julian of Norwich, a cloistered Thérèse of Lisieux. Francis, like Ignatius, challenged the laity to be holy not by retiring from the world but precisely in the midst of their world. (2) In practice, this vocation to holiness works itself out through love. For Francis, the human heart was a powerful symbol of interiority, of the depths of all that is human. To "live Jesus" is to have the name of Jesus engraved on your heart.[73] He was convinced that every man, every woman, has a natural inclination to love God above all else. (3) To such love was wedded an optimism that, for Francis as well as Ignatius, stemmed in large measure from finding God not only in every person but in every creature God has fashioned.

Little wonder that a small but lovely portrait now adorns my office wall, a gift of the Salesians: Francis de Sales and Jane Frances de Chantal. The caption: "One Heart — One Soul." It reminds me of the final meditation in Ignatius' Exercises, the Contemplation for Learning to Love Like God.

My spirituality has taken wing not only from the examples of holiness and courage provided by diocesan clergy but from their insights into practical spirituality. Most recently, Father Louis J. Cameli, professor of spirituality in the graduate school of theology at the University of St. Mary of the Lake-Mundelein Seminary in Illinois, has furnished Catholics with a 12-step program, various practices with one and the same goal: to dispose a person to receive ever more fully the transforming power of the Spirit.[74] I can do little more than list or summarize his "disciplines."

1. Take satisfying and painful experiences in the Church seriously, but recognize them as passing; let them not transfix us.

2. Cultivate compassion, which helps to rescue us from intraecclesial turmoil, to see the world's great needs and the Church's mission to serve them.

3. Inhale memory (Jesus and the saints with whom we are in communion) and exhale hope (in God).

4. Renounce blaming out there and accept limited responsibility right here.

5. Make regular acts of thanksgiving: for others in the family of faith, for the graces of community, for what God has done and will do for a holy and sinful people.

6. Confess temptations (not sins) to one another: especially temptations to return to a former life, to do something other than called to do, to collapse into paralyzing sadness at the futility of it all.

7. Purify self of nostalgia and romanticism, brace for the hard work required for living in a family of faith.

8. Pray regularly with angels; the Church is more than the sum of our earthly parts.

9. Laugh, for the Church brims over with incongruity; we are living together in a divine comedy.

10. Don't lose a devotional life; we need to cultivate some sort of shared emotional faith history.

11. Pay attention to people not to accomplish some task but simply to connect with others who share the same holy mystery.

12. Embrace intercession, pray for one another, so that distance, difference, and division will melt into a sustaining love rooted in God's prior love.

Quite a program indeed, lifelong, but remarkable in its potential for bringing spirituality from outer space to a real world, to a pilgrim church, to Christians wondering what to do.

As I advance reluctantly in age, I continue to profit spiritually from the young. Twelve years as theologian-in-residence at Georgetown University (1978–90) confirmed for me the truth of Andrew Greeley's sociological conclusion about a transformation in America's Catholic teenagers that startled the pessimist and delighted the optimist.

> The New Breed of the 1980's is more likely to think of God as a mother and a lover, and of heaven as a life of action and pleasure. Its story of its love affair with God, and thus the meaning of its life, represents a dramatic change in Catholic religious sensibility, a change apparently caused by Vatican Council II and transmitted by devout mothers, sympathetic parish priests and passionately loving spouses. Because of this new vision of God and of life, the New Breed is more likely to be open to church careers, more socially committed, more insistent on high quality church performance by the church, more formal in their prayer, more concerned about racial justice, and more personally devout (but not more committed to the church's sexual teaching or to infallibility ...). Their per-

sonal devotion may sag during the alienation interlude in the middle-20's, but the rest of their religious sensibility is likely to remain unaltered.[75]

Perceptive religious educators such as Jesuit James DiGiacomo confirmed Greeley's conclusions. They found our young people seeking God in impressive numbers and with an urgency rare in the preceding decade. Many were weary of freedom without direction, suspected self-indulgence without commitment. If they resisted our adult religions, it was because "they don't want to be part of something that looks narrow, uninspiring, cramping, dying or dead. They ascribe this bad scene to the Policeman God of a rule-keeping church taught by moralistic teachers and managed by greedy clerics who preside over dull liturgies."[76]

Thus did empirical data bolster my somewhat superficial experience. It did not deny youth's vulnerability, its confusions, its rebellions. It simply corrected our myopia. It assured us that there was more substance to the adolescent of the '80s than met the aging eye.

A splendid contemporary example of a deep, outgoing spirituality is the Jesuit Volunteer Corps at home and abroad. As I write (June 1997), one young college graduate has only recently begun two years of service in Arica, Chile. She is serving in a Young Girls' Home, working with girls abandoned, with girls abused. I reproduce one story in her own words.

I was talking with a six-year old, to get to know her and her situation. I began by asking her if she had any questions for me (the young ones are a bit confused by the gringa that keeps coming in every day and talks funny). The little girl said, "Yes." Then she asked, "Como es el amor?" "What is love?" I wasn't sure what exactly she meant, so I probed a little, and she responded that she hears love talked of all the time, but she didn't know what it meant. I thought at that moment, as I looked into her sincere face with the deep brown questioning eyes, that my heart would break, because love is something we feel, and she had never felt it during her short little life. I struggled to give her Spanish synonyms that ended up being completely useless to her . . . How does one answer such a tremendous question? The simplest statement I could give her to respond to her question was "Dios es el amor." "God is love."

I told her that because God had created her, out of love, she is wonderful, beautiful, special and important, and that no matter what, God will always be there to love her. Maybe over the next two years together we can figure out together what love is and what it feels like. . . .

At the end of a week, this young volunteer found herself still struggling with the child's question. Her prayer then was "written on a page stained with tears of gratitude, sadness, confusion and joy." It reads:

Dear God, I thank you whole-heartedly for helping me through this week. Please continue to strengthen me, that I may rise up to the challenges, so that "poco á poco" I will start to understand and begin to see more vividly your face in the faces of each of those precious girls, your daughters. I give them to you to hold, dear God. Please hug them close to your loving heart. Be with them in their moments of sadness, of fear, of loneliness. Be their mother who can't be there, because she is "soltera" [unmarried] and works the land slavishly with her rough, cracked hands — still finding herself in poverty and misery. Be their father who right now is broken by addiction and violence. Answer for each of us "como es el amor" and help me to be a light on the world's journey to healing. Amen.[77]

Little wonder that this young Catholic's prayer recalls the haunting song of Jean Valjean at the close of *Les misérables,* "To love another person is to see the face of God."

Finally, I have learned ever so much from children, the children who, Jesus insisted, tell us what heaven will be like. In one of his 50 books, *A Study of Courage and Fear,* the remarkable student of children's spirituality Robert Coles told how a young black child in Mississippi drew a picture of herself, then said: "That's me, and the Lord made me. When I grow up my momma says I may not like how He made me, but I must always remember that He did it, and it's His idea. So when I draw the Lord He'll be a real big man. He has to be to explain the way things are."[78] From the lips of children. . . .

SEVEN

From Genesis to Bonhoeffer
Free Like God

All but lost in Vatican II's 17 documents is a deceptively simple sentence: "Authentic freedom is an exceptional sign of the divine image within the human person."[1]

Perhaps the most entrancing and provocative adventure of my theological activity has been my research into a single complex idea: the human person as image of God. My involvement goes back to my doctoral years (1943–46) at the Catholic University of America. Working in patristic theology under Johannes Quasten, I discovered how precious this insight was to the Fathers of the Church. Ever since writing my dissertation on the image as understood by Cyril of Alexandria, I have been digging ever more intensively and extensively into the development of the idea across the centuries. Unfortunately, I shall never complete what I have begun; the riches of the concept are simply too vast.

Still, I think it important to sketch what over the years I have come to regard as (1) a crucial facet of image theology, i.e., freedom, and (2) highly significant "moments" in the evolution of that theology. Why? Because this concept is a central facet of my own spirituality, and because it merits concerted ecumenical and interdisciplinary effort to plumb its meaning and religious relevance. What follows is not so much an effort at synthesis as it is revelatory of a significant road in my spiritual journey.

For sweet clarity's sake, I shall divide this chapter into three broad segments:

1. background: early influences on the development of image as freedom;

2. a significant patristic segment: human freedom as divine image in the theology of Christian Alexandria;

3. a précis of later important, even exciting developments, with detailed attention to Dietrich Bonhoeffer.

209

Background

Image theology did not spring full-panoplied from the head of Jove. Christian Alexandria especially had a distinguished ancestry: Genesis, Philo, Paul, and Irenaeus.

Genesis

The springboard for 2,500 years of reflection on God's image is the first page of Scripture: "Then God said, 'Let us make humankind in our image, according to our likeness.... So God created humankind in His image; in the image of God He created them; male and female He created them" (Gen 1:26–27).[2] The paradox of this Priestly passage is the puzzlement it bequeaths even to the expert. Exegetes agree only in rejecting a substantive difference between "image" and "likeness," a genuine difference in content. But once this is granted, the specific nuance, what precisely likeness (*demût*) does to image (*selem*), baffles biblicists. Does it repeat or complete, does it explain or correct? Or shall we simply submit, with von Rad, that the writer is struggling to express a mystery, and an ancient formula has come to his assistance?[3]

More significantly, Prior Testament scholars are not at peace in spelling out the content of this correspondence between Elohim and Everyman, between God and the human person. What does it mean? Should we be moved by the immediate context (v. 26: "let them have dominion"; v. 28: "fill the earth and subdue it") and conclude that humanity is God's viceroy, that the divine image is sovereignty over the nonhuman?[4] Or may we interpret the Priestly account in chapter 1 from the Yahwist account in chapter 2 (vv. 16–17: "You may freely eat of every tree of the garden; but of the tree of the knowledge of good and evil you shall not eat") and infer that what is distinctive in our relationship to God is God's command and prohibition, that Godlikeness is "creative determination of human existence through the word of God"?[5] Is it perhaps that humanity is two sexes, that the human mirrors God by being male and female? Most lyric here is Karl Barth:

> Man is no more solitary than God. But as God is One, and He alone is God, so man as man is one and alone, and two only in the duality of his kind, i.e., in the duality of man and woman. In this way he is a copy and imitation of God.... Men are simply male and female. Whatever else they may be, it is only in this differentiation and relationship. This is the particular

dignity ascribed to the sex relationship. It is wholly creaturely, and common to man and beast. But as the only real principle of differentiation and relationship, as the original form not only of man's confrontation of God but also of all intercourse between man and man, it is the true *humanum* and therefore the true creaturely image of God. Man can and will always be man before God and among his fellows only as he is man in relationship to woman and woman in relationship to man. . . . The fact that he was created man and woman will be the great paradigm of everything that is to take place between him and God, and also of everything that is to take place between him and his fellows. . . . [6]

Or should we paint with a broader brush: Image of God means "a creature whose being is not from below but who belongs by nature to the upper region"?[7] Or shall we decide, with James Barr, that this type of exegetical operation, this effort to identify "the thing" to which "image of God" refers, is a "blood-out-of-a-stone process"?[8] For Barr, there is no answer to the question as put, no reason to think the writer had any definite idea about the content or the location of the image. Important as it was for him to express the existence of a likeness between God and humankind, there were "very powerful reasons why the subject could not be more narrowly or more exactly expressed without the danger that the whole attempt might be ruined."[9]

Is there a suggestion of human freedom in the Genesis text? As we shall see, the early Alexandrians thought so. In fact, until a few decades ago it was quite fashionable for Roman Catholics to understand creation in God's image as the fashioning of man and woman to rationality and freedom. But then a more sophisticated scholarship explained that we were experiencing less exegesis than eisegesis, triggered by an anthropology, a philosophical conception of the human as raised above the human by two of God's precious prerogatives, intelligence and love. But just as I settled into my new conviction that freedom in the Priestly account is eisegesis, along came a first-rate exegete, Bruce Vawter, to challenge my burgeoning certainties. Insisting that the vocation to dominion is not a license to tyranny but a challenge to responsibility, granting that Genesis is genuinely an encouragement to ecologists, Vawter pointed out that the dominion passage in Genesis

> gives no encouragement at all to a concept of man that puts
> him at the disposal of nature, that effectively reduces him to

his former status of yoke-man to the natural forces from which Genesis declared him free. Genesis, had it known about them, would have shed no tears over the disappearance of the dinosaur and the saber-toothed tiger. Such "endangered species," it would have concluded, were encompassed within the *radah* of man, to deal with as he saw fit, or to deal with as he should see fit.... [I]n the faith of Genesis man is the norm of what an ordered world ought to be, not some cluster of supposedly higher abstractions that are presumed to govern him. If man is created in the image and likeness of God he shares in the unpredictability of God that often clashes with the inexorable predictability of nature. Man is not permitted to succumb to the cyclic routine of nature but is destined to make decisions which may be for good or ill but which in any case are his decisions that cannot be dictated by any science exact or inexact.... Genesis put its faith in man as it put its faith in God, not that it believed every decision would be equally probable, but because it preferred free decision to any mystique of nature.... [10]

In different language, this insistence on human freedom in the first creation story had already been propounded 25 years before Vawter by the distinguished Protestant exegete G. Ernest Wright. He claimed that the emphasis in Genesis 1:26–27 must "lie on the self-conscious, self-directing vitality which constitutes the sum of personal being."[11] For him, Genesis 1 and Psalm 8 make it clear that *in consequence of* the divine resemblance the human can assume lordship of created earth.

This implies a consciousness of the radical difference existing between the animals and man as personal being. Man is endowed with a freedom and capacity for self-direction which enable him to plan and execute his plans. Furthermore, as personal being he can respond to the personal direction of God and assume office as God's steward and vicegerent on earth.[12]

Genesis 1–3 revealed to Wright a relationship of dependence and responsibility. God has a right to command, it is ours to obey. And so our freedom is limited, but only within this limitation can we find what it means to be free and what it means to be alive. The freedom, therefore, is a freedom to rule the earth. In part at least, this freedom stems from the image. It is a freedom to be used properly, with a corresponding responsibility, a freedom limited by that responsibility. Freedom and election go together. Freedom "witnesses to the mystery of creation in God's 'image'"; election, "to the mystery of communion and dependence."[13]

Not all would agree. Unless I misread the literature, many an exegete would find the scriptural data too thin to support the elaborate reconstructions of a Wright (or a Barth, for that matter). Von Rad, for one, dismissed the possibility of uncovering the Genesis "image" in human personality, in a person's free ego, dignity, or free use of moral capacity.[14]

In sum, two conclusions. First, I must confess that Genesis has not clearly betrayed its image secret, even to the most refined instruments of German exegesis. And still I am grateful, for an inspired page has thrust forward a thesis rich in promise, incomparable in influence. Scholars have wrestled with it unto frustration, polemicists have exploited it beyond recognition. Yet there it stands, its fundamental affirmation a crucial challenge to any religious anthropology: Each human person, male or female, in his or her empiric wholeness, stands in a special relationship to the creating God, a unique relationship that privileges humanity vis-à-vis the nonhuman, a relationship so intimate that we are said to be "like" God.

Second, I incline to believe that, even though the word "freedom" does not appear in the Priestly narrative, Vawter and Wright have glimpsed a critical facet of humanity's God-given freedom beneath the troubling words "image" and "dominion."

Philo

In the late '70s I was fortunate to uncover a second significant but rarely exploited moment in image theory: Philo, the famed Jewish philosopher of Alexandria (ca. 13 B.C.-45/50 C.E.).[15] Most of his adult life spanned, without ever touching, the earthly existence of Jesus. Heir to Semitic and Hellenic influences, he not only transmitted to Alexandrian Christianity his major achievement, development of allegorical exegesis. He helped mightily to tradition two emphases that would resonate in Greek iconology from Clement of Alexandria to John of Damascus. I mean *logos* and *nous*.

When God fashioned the human to God's image, the pattern God used was the *nous* of the universe, the Logos.[16] That is why, for Philo, our likeness to God cannot be corporeal. It is of our *nous*, "the sovereign element of the soul," that Genesis employs "image." Philo goes on to glorify *nous* in language that recalls the vision of Augustine and Monica at Ostia. Patterned after the very Mind of the

universe, the human *nous* is like a god to the man or woman who
carries or reverences it. Logos-like, the human *nous* is Godlike.[17]
And it is precisely in the context of mind, specifically of intelligence
and understanding, that freedom enters in as a facet of God's image
in the human person.

> For it is intelligence (*dianoia*) alone which the Father who be-
> got it judged worthy of freedom (*eleutherias*), and loosing the
> fetters of necessity, suffered it to range as it willed, and gave
> it such portion of that free will (*tou hekousiou*) which is His
> most peculiar possession and most worthy of His majesty, as
> it was capable of receiving. For the other living creatures, in
> whose souls the mind (*nous*), the element set apart for liberty,
> has no place, have been committed under yoke and bridle to
> the service of men, as slaves to a master. But man, possessed
> of a spontaneous and self-determined will, whose activities for
> the most part rest on deliberate choice, is with reason blamed
> for what he does with intent, praised when he acts rightly of
> his own will.
>
> In the others, the plants and animals, no praise is due if they
> bear well, nor blame if they fare ill; for their movements and
> changes in either direction come to them from no deliberate
> choice or volition of their own. But the soul of man alone has
> received from God the faculty of voluntary movement, and in
> this way especially is made like (*homoiotheisa*) to Him, and
> thus being liberated, as far as might be, from that hard and
> ruthless mistress, necessity, may justly be charged with guilt, in
> that it does not honor its Liberator. And therefore it will rightly
> pay the inexorable penalty which is meted out to ungrateful
> freedmen.[18]

For Philo, then, men and women image God in that they have a
"portion" of God's own freedom. They are gifted with the power of
choice, can choose between good and evil. Scholars disagree on the
extent of that freedom.[19] But two facets of Philonic freedom seem
to emerge from the texts. First, although the human mind is converted by the Logos into a fragmentary extension of the divine mind,
human freedom is not absolute; only God's freedom is sovereign.
Second, there is in Philo a kind of ethical determinism. Pervasive
themes are the human person's nothingness and utter passivity.[20]
Philo echoes the Stoics in insisting that we are "instruments" for
God's action in the cosmos;[21] our virtue is not really our own;[22] only
God is *hekousios* in an absolute sense, for our existence is ruled by

necessity;[23] medical figures describe a diseased state of the soul that ultimately becomes incurable.[24] Philo has opted, quite naturally, for "the relative free will doctrine which characterized much of classical and Hellenistic Greek thought and had already in its Stoic version left its mark on some Jewish Hellenistic and rabbinic writings."[25]

In Philonic freedom the human person is "especially like" God, but the area of unlikeness is understandably, perhaps pessimistically, broad and deep.

Paul

A third influence, not only on Christian Alexandria but on the broad Christian tradition, is the New Testament. In the Gospels there is no explicit image doctrine. I say "explicit" because there are texts which do imply resemblance to God, whether on the part of Jesus (e.g., Jn 10:30) or of his followers (e.g., Mt 5:48). Also pertinent for image-as-freedom is a striking way in which the Evangelists present Jesus: He preaches freedom, his activity frees, and he is the free man.[26] Still, it is Paul who has commanded my attention here; for the image idea is part and parcel of Pauline Christology and anthropology, though overshadowed by major themes such as justification and reconciliation. The pertinent Pauline passages reveal three related lines of image thought.

First, *Christ* is the image of *God* (cf. 2 Cor 4:4–6; Col 1:12–16; Heb 1:3). This on two levels: (*a*) as *Son* of God existing before all creatures, distinct from, yet equal to, the Father, and (*b*) as *incarnate* Son, because he is the visible image of the invisible God, God's epiphany or manifestation or luminous revelation, disclosing the Father in his own person.

Second, the *human person* is the image of *God* (cf. 1 Cor 11:7–9; Col 3:9–10). Every man, every woman, reflects God's glory and shares God's sovereignty. Thus was humanity fashioned in the beginning. Paul does not say that the original universal image was destroyed, but he does suggest that racial, social, and religious differences, perhaps even sin itself, impaired or weakened or obscured this primal likeness to God.[27]

Third, the *Christian* is an image of *Christ* (cf. Rom 8:29; Phil 3:21; 1 Cor 15:48–49; 2 Cor 3:18). The original likeness, given at creation, is re-established, reaches a new level, in a new creation: conformity of the Christian to Christ. Through the activity and influence of the Spirit whom believers receive in baptism, they are progressively transformed, Christified (some would say even divinized), so as to reproduce in themselves through grace the glory (*doxa*) of the risen Christ, even ultimately to reflect the glorified body of Christ.[28]

My immediate problem is that the Pauline corpus does not explicitly link its image doctrine with the concept of Christian freedom. The closest verbal approximation is 2 Corinthians 3:17–18: "Now the Lord is the Spirit, and where the Spirit of the Lord is, there is freedom (*eleutheria*). And all of us, with unveiled faces, seeing the glory of the Lord as though reflected in a mirror, are being transformed into the same image (*eikona*) from one degree of glory to another; for this comes from the Lord, the Spirit." And I must remember that freedom, though important and illuminating, is only one (and not necessarily the most significant) of at least nine abstract nouns Paul uses to express the effects of the Christ-event: salvation, expiation, ransom or redemption, sanctification, freedom, justification, transformation, new creation, and reconciliation.[29] And yet the two themes must intersect, if only because for Paul these are simply two different formulae for describing the Christian and interpreting Christian living. The Christian is "called to freedom" (Gal 5:13) and the Christian is "predetermined to share in the image-shape of [God's] Son" (Rom 8:29).

But what is freedom for Paul? It is a liberation of the human person that delivers from a fourfold slavery: from sin, from the law, from self, from death (cf. Rom 5–8; Gal 5:1, 13).

1. The *sin* is more than a single act. It is an evil force, almost personal, a malevolent power, that tyrannizes every man or woman born into this world. It is a power hostile to God, a power that alienates from God. Its works are sinful deeds.

2. The *law*, though good in itself, indeed "holy" and "spiritual" (Rom 7:12, 14), "acted as an occasion for sin, instructing humanity in the material possibility of doing evil, either by forbidding what was indifferent... or by arousing desires or annoying the conscience with external regulations about 'forbidden fruit.' "[30]

3. The *self* is the existential human condition — in its pejorative sense, "natural, material, and visible human existence, weak and earthbound, the human creature left to itself,"[31] unable to "boast of anything before God" (1 Cor 1:29), unable to "please God" (Rom 8:8), "the human condition before the coming of Christ — or even after that coming for those who do not live in Christ."[32]

4. *Death*, inherited from Adam, is a total death, contrasted not only with physical life but with eternal, resurrectional existence. This death sin carries with it; there is no escaping it. The goal, the end, of what we do is death (Rom 6:21).

In the persuasive summary of Schlier, Pauline enslavement is self-seeking existence which goes astray in sin awakened by the law and inevitably falls victim to death.[33]

Freedom for Christians is liberation from this fourfold enslavement. It is a freedom won for us by Christ (Gal 5:1; see Jn 8:36), a freedom that makes us slaves to Christ (1 Cor 7:22), to whom alone we owe obedience. Through "the law of the Spirit [or spirit] of life in Christ Jesus" we have been set free from "the law of sin and of death" (Rom 8:2). It is to Christ's law that we are now bound (Gal 6:2; 1 Cor 9:21); but in him and his law we find freedom from all those facets of human existence that constrain and enslave (Gal 2:4; 4:22–31; 5:1, 13; 1 Cor 9:1, 19; 10:29; 2 Cor 3:17; Rom 6:18–23; 7:3; 8:2, 21). Why? Because his law is the law of love: "love fully satisfies the law" (Rom 13:10).[34]

Irenaeus

A fourth influence, especially on Christian Alexandria, was Irenaeus, native of Asia Minor (possibly Smyrna) and bishop of Lyons in the last quarter of the second century. I found him challenging because he was the first Christian to construct his theology around the image of God in the human person, with three focal stages: creation, degradation, restoration.[35] The theology is hardly systematic — understandably so in a second-century bishop.

The first stage is the formation of Adam to God's image and likeness. This work of the Trinity[36] was a gradual process. Unlike Augustine, for whom humanity's beginnings were a pinnacle of perfection, without suffering or death, without ignorance or inner struggle, Irenaeus portrays Adam as "a young being, looking to the future; the evils — even sins — of life are but growing pains. Paradise, in a way, is less in the past than in the future. The history of man is not that of a laborious ascent after a vertical fall, but a providential progress towards a future that is full of promise."[37] For Irenaeus, fascinatingly, Adam was created on the model of the incarnate Word. Christ was constituted of body, soul, and Holy Spirit; therefore the true human, perfect and living, had to consist of body, soul, and spirit — that component of the human personality which possesses the Holy Spirit.[38] When the Word became human, the Word became what His image was.[39]

The "image" in Adam consisted of natural gifts, particularly reason and free will; the "likeness," supernatural gifts, characterized by possession of the Word and participation of the Spirit.[40] Not the

image but the likeness was lost by Adam for humanity, to be restored through the Word, the model who became what His image
was and "summed up (recapitulated) in Himself the long narrative
of humans, bestowing salvation on us in a concise way, that what
we had lost in Adam...we might receive in Christ Jesus."[41]

In the context of Gnosticism, Irenaeus is insistent and clear on
human freedom. *Autexousia*[42] is lordship, dominion, over one's
actions, power to decide between this and that, in contrast to a
necessity imposed by nature or an external force such as Destiny.
In this sense the Creator is possessed of an absolute freedom: Creation is a work consummately free,[43] not a reaction of the Demiurge
to external pressure.[44] And because the Creator fashioned humanity as God's own image, the human "was free, and his/her own
master, having been made by God to be master of everything on
earth."[45] But freedom was given to woman and man for a purpose
loftier and more radical than mastery over earth or even over angels: They were to serve their Creator freely,[46] without subjection
to any creature.

Free will, Irenaeus realized, was important for the economy of salvation. To the Gnostics, only the "psychic" or "animal" were free;
the "spiritual" were naturally good, consequently predetermined by
nature to salvation; the "material" were naturally evil, consequently
predetermined by nature to damnation. Arguing primarily against
the Valentinians, Irenaeus insisted on the universality of salvation; in
consequence, he claimed, *all* human persons are free. None are good
by nature, none bad by nature; all have the same nature (*physis*),
rational and free, are capable of choosing the good and losing it.[47]
Faith itself must be free if it is to be salvific.[48] Free will is an instrument of salvation in the hands of the Spirit. "According to Irenaeus,
the whole human person must surrender freely to the action of God's
Spirit. No other attitude is rational."[49]

But freedom, for Irenaeus, is more than a psychological fact and
a condition for merit. In the economy of salvation, freedom is the
inverse of slavery.[50] The drama of Paradise ended in the enslavement
of humanity: enslavement to sin, to death, in a sense to the precepts
of the law. If this is slavery, then freedom involves an interior change
that means a spontaneous submission to God and an escape from
death. To be genuinely free is to be interiorly in harmony with God,
to be God's adopted son or daughter. The artisan of such freedom
is God, through God's Son incarnate, dead, and risen. The Word-
made-flesh is "the Word of freedom," the Liberator par excellence.
Here Réal Tremblay caught for me the essence of Irenaean freedom.

Beyond the different articulations that constitute Irenaeus' conception of freedom, there is...one characteristic common to all: interiority. In point of fact, the bishop of Lyons sees freedom in the first instance not as the concrete exercise of a dominion over the beings and things which entice the human person, but as a reality and a transformation of an interior order that has to do with the nature of the person and touches the heart. However important it be, ethics, for example, holds only second place with Irenaeus. It is simply the expression of that inner sovereignty in which it discovers its basis and its living source.

This freedom is realized definitively only by a renewed relationship of the human person with him/herself, by an ever-increasing refinement of his/her spirit and body in response to the cultural, scientific, and social progress of the world around us, or, if you wish, through a "gnosis" of different titles and colorations. This gnosis is born, grows, and expands — under the pressure of *charis* — into a new relationship of the human person with God, in the recognition and discovery of the impresses and calls left in him/her by his/her Creator and Savior....

For Irenaeus, finally, this freedom is not an earthly reality, in the sense that it would be uniquely of this world and would end with this world. Brought to realization in God, already here below it affords access to the "heritage" of the Father and prepares us to possess it tomorrow in its fulness.[51]

Christian Alexandria

My predilection for the Greek-language theologians of the early Church predisposed me to search primarily in Alexandria for a deeper understanding of God's image as freedom. Here I must limit myself to two of my favorites: Origen and Gregory of Nyssa.

Origen

Perhaps the most significant, surely the most exciting, theologian between Paul and Augustine is Origen (184/85–253/54). When he lists "the kinds of doctrines which are believed in plain terms through the apostolic preaching," he does not stop with creation and eternal retribution, with Christology and pneumatology. "This also is laid down in the Church's teaching, that every rational soul is possessed of free will and choice.... There follows from this the conviction that we are not subject to necessity, so as to be compelled by every means, even against our will, to do either good or evil...."[52]

But, for all its importance in the context of the Gnostic peril, freedom of choice is not the facet of freedom that Origen incorporates into his vision of divine imaging. Here the four cardinal stages of his image doctrine are indispensable: creation, sin, progress, and transformation.

In creation, humanity received a participation in God's Image,[53] was fashioned on the model (the *kata* of Genesis 1:27 in the Septuagint) of the Logos who in His divinity is the only immediate Image of the Father.[54] It is participation in the Logos by our logos,[55] a communication of Trinitarian life through the Word, a gift whereby the Son-by-nature makes children-by-adoption.[56] To be *logikos*, therefore, is not simply to be intelligent, rational. "Only the saint is *logikos*,"[57] because only the saint participates in the Logos on the higher level designed by God. This supernatural sharing of each *logikos* in the Logos is the loftiest element in his/her essence;[58] in this way the human mind "can know something of the nature of divinity";[59] it makes the human person "in some fashion" consubstantial with God;[60] it is the single source of human dignity.

Through sin Satan communicates to men and women the image of "the earthy," his own image, with all the vices that attend it.[61] This participation in Satan is acquired or strengthened by *alogos* action, which lessens my qualities as *logikos*. Sin assimilates me to the animal.[62] But bestial images can only obscure, cannot destroy, the image of God.[63] Though *alogos,* the sinner is not an animal. Within sinful me abides always the possibility of returning to my "better state," the state of primitive image and likeness.[64] But sin does mean that the sinner, image of God and of Satan, is inwardly divided. Under what form is the image preserved? Not as sanctifying grace, for supernatural contact with the Logos has been severed. Rather, as an inefficacious desire, a nostalgia, an inner rending in the human spirit, which can be resolved by the action of Christ.[65]

Only through Christ is the image restored — a conversion effected by the redemptive activity of the Savior and the sinner's conformation to Christ dead and risen, through contemplation and imitation.[66] But this basic restoration is only a preliminary stage, a point of departure; the "image" is inchoative divinization, divinization in potency. The phraseology of Genesis 1:27 tells Origen that humanity received in its initial stage the dignity of "image," which made it possible for man and woman to acquire by diligent effort, by imitation of God, the perfection of "likeness" at life's culmination.[67] And in this progression from image to likeness the principal agent is the Holy Spirit.[68]

Perfect likeness is achieved not in this life but beyond death, in bodily resurrection, where we uncover the ultimate meaning of our conformity to Christ dead and risen — a resurrection in which the whole Body of the Lord will share.[69] To be conformed to the glorious humanity of God is to be conformed to the Word of God, and so to God. The ultimate likeness consists above all in this: In heaven we shall be "gods," possessing in remarkable fulness the divinity in which we now share only distantly.[70] In and through the one Son all human beings will become one only Son; for the Logos will take possession of the whole *logikē* nature, to transform every soul into His own perfection.[71]

Our specific question is, how does freedom fit into Origen's image doctrine? To be *kat' eikona* — participation of our logos in the Logos — is indeed the loftiest element in our nature. But Origen does not find the essence of participation, of imaging, in freedom of choice. The purpose of human freedom is to adhere to the Logos in love; it is here that we realize our essence. But, apart from the soul of Jesus, humanity realizes that essence perfectly only in heaven. Complete freedom, freedom from all slavery to the flesh, is not possible as long as we are still in the flesh.[72] Liberty is linked to doing good, slavery to doing evil. It is the sinner who is the slave. "They are free who abide in the truth of the Word, who know the truth so as to be freed by it."[73]

The distinction suggested above is all-important: Free will, freedom of choice, is central in Origen's system for determining what "nature" a creature has, but it is not that creature's profound essence; it is not in freedom of choice that the image of God resides. Without freedom of choice we could not be what we are; but such freedom is rather the condition than the content of our being, of our resemblance to God. That content is conformity to Christ — a conformity effected by a conversion to Christ that is progressively perfected through imitation of God. The freedom that constitutes the divine image is neither "natural" nor static. It is the holiness of the children of God, and it is a dynamic domination of the interior man, the interior woman, our logos, by its model, the eternal Logos, a domination that corresponds to the progressive liberation of the soul from the enslavement of the passions. We are free in the measure that we reflect the supremely free Christ.

Gregory of Nyssa

The most important Greek Father on the issue of freedom and God's image may well be Gregory of Nyssa (335–94), a keen speculative theologian and a remarkable ascetical and mystical writer. For Gregory, perhaps more truly than for any other of the Alexandrians, the image theme is the focal point of all his work — his theology, his anthropology, his spirituality.[74] For him, there is really but one way to know God (not *about* God), and that is to get to be in God's image, to participate in God's holiness.[75]

In Gregory's vision of the image, the human person "was made like God in all things."[76] But Gregory sees no advantage in an exhaustive catalog of perfections; he is generally content with those qualities which are pertinent to a particular context: immortality, reason, freedom, individual virtues. It remains true, however, that freedom plays a particularly critical role in Gregory's image theology; for the problem of human freedom is at the very center of his understanding of God, of the human person, of the world. He confronts the contradiction in man and woman: human existence as it is now, lacerated, wounded, in contrast with that blessed and free existence of which Scripture speaks and of which humanity ceaselessly dreams. How resolve the contradiction? By an analysis of freedom.[77] And the basis of his solution to the problem of freedom is Scripture's declaration that the human person was created in God's image. The image is essentially free, like the Model, but imperfectly. The human in its present condition is not authentic human. At the end of its experience of evil, humanity will rediscover its original freedom and become again a perfect image, turned ever and totally to its Model.

For Gregory, divine freedom is a mystery-laden synthesis of absolute transcendence and the freest possible immanence. God is free because God's absolute transcendence seems to outstrip itself by a free immanence. The fundamental text on divine transcendence is this powerful, insightful sentence: "God ... always wants to be what He is, and He is absolutely what He wants to be. ... "[78] The autonomy of the pure Spirit expresses a threefold freedom: psychological (unlimited by spatial and temporal categories), moral (*apatheia* in the paradoxical sense of the fulness of pure *pathos*, the unrestricted dynamism of infinite inner living), and metaphysical (the Trinity as free transcendence par excellence). But what is new here is the Christian conception of a Trinity wherein the freedom of transcendence becomes immanence without ceasing to be transcendence, becomes a free, conscious, creative communication, exteriorizes itself in creation of the universe, creation of the human person, incarnation of the Word.[79]

Created freedom (*eleutheria*) is "likeness to what is without master and sovereign, likeness which was given us by God in the beginning."[80] For Gregory, the real human is the human before the Fall: Here is God's image, God's likeness. The human is by definition an original existential synthesis of nature and grace. That is why the resurrection (*anastasis*) is a restoration (*apokatastasis*) — not a simple return to Eden, but a development and realization of the primitive image. For humans, the only "natural" life is life in God's image.

What, concretely, is Gregory's freedom-image? Not simply freedom of choice, though this is basic to any imaging of God.[81] An image is genuinely image to the extent that it possesses all the attributes of its model; and God's intention for humanity was to communicate God's own freedom. The expression of this free structure of the image is discoverable especially in five areas: (1) absence of sexuality, i.e., of submission of the spirit to biological determinations, to passions; (2) incorruptibility and immortality, a demand of the free image for the spirit and the body; (3) *apatheia*, i.e., freedom from enslavement to passions, the inner unity of the true I, resolving the ceaseless struggle between spirit and flesh; (4) freedom of intelligence, i.e., a pure gaze of the understanding and of the spiritualized senses, for "the life of the soul is to gaze at God";[82] (5) freedom of conscience, i.e., the pure, serene, joyful, carefree conscience before the Fall, oriented to God with confidence and spontaneity, able to speak freely with God.

Sin submitted the free image to a threefold enslavement: psychological (enslavement to error and passion), social (oppressive power and tyrannous wealth on the one hand, hunger, poverty, and sickness on the other), and religious (alienation from transcendent union, idolatry, heresy).

How is human freedom made free? By a progressive refashioning. To each alienation corresponds a stage of liberation.[83] Psychological alienation is countered by revelation of authentic reality; social alienation by asceticism, interior purification of the self; religious alienation by faith, whereby the synthesis of God and man that is Christ refashions the human to its original, authentic humanity, man/woman-to-the-Image.

But freedom is not fully recovered in this life. Purification demands death, calls for an ascesis of hell, looks to a resurrection that reproduces the integrity of the authentic I, requires an *apokatastasis* that restores all, even demons, to their primitive state, so that ultimately God will be all in all. Here at last the experience of evil gives way to the experience of the infinite, where I am free like God, in that I want to be what I am and I am what I want to be; "and with each experience of the infinite my nature becomes new, an experience inescapably dynamic, an ascensive movement creative of me. The supreme paradox, 'movement and rest can be the same thing,' is resolved, because each instant appears as fulness of freedom and creator of freedom."[84]

From Alexandria, specifically from Gregory of Nyssa, I grasped the questions I must ceaselessly put to myself for a dynamic spirituality: Do I want to be what I am? Am I what I want to be?

Later Developments

My précis of later developments must be distressingly brief, concerned with "moments" that attracted me because they were pregnant with the problem of freedom, some with roots in Alexandrian theology.

From Augustine to the Twentieth Century

There is Augustine. The bishop of Hippo intrigued me because he offered the most comprehensive, the most anguished, the most profound and provocative struggle in Christian antiquity to comprehend how the human person can be image of God as Trinity, can be like a God who is at once One and Three. Out of this struggle would come certain strong convictions. Basic is the conviction that everything created bears a *resemblance* to God; without this relation the universe would cease to be intelligible, would not exist. That is why there must be "vestiges," traces, of the Trinity in all that is. But only the *mens* is properly *image* of God. *Mens* not in the sense of naked knowledge; rather, our whole intellectual nature, which is a wondrous wedding of memory, understanding, and will. And so Augustine worked through several suggestive but ultimately dissatisfying images, rejected all trinities in the order of *scientia*, opted for trinities in the area of *sapientia*, to leave us finally with three stages of Trinitarian image, each centering around *memoria Dei, intelligentia Dei, voluntas Dei*. (1) There is the ineradicable image left to our intellectual nature after original sin: a capacity for memory, knowledge, and love of God. (2) There is our intellectual nature reformed by God's grace: graced recollection, graced faith and perception, graced love. (3) There is our intellectual nature in resurrectional glory: presence of God in beatific vision, knowledge of God "as God is," love of God in fullest measure.[85]

There is Scholasticism, especially the image theology of Thomas Aquinas. Indeed, for Aquinas, God's image is formally in the intellect, is actualized in the life of contemplation. But this very life of the intellect is incredibly free, free like God, because it can transcend the world of created things, is unrestricted in scope, has the whole of reality before it; it is free to enter a relationship with infinite Reality. And so Thomas can proclaim, "The life of contemplation consists in a certain freedom of spirit (*animi*) . . . is active service."[86] Aquinas all but reproduced Augustine's three stages, without the Trinitarian context. He saw God's image in the human person in three ways: (1) a natural aptitude, common to all humans, for understanding and loving God; (2) actual or habitual, though imperfect, knowledge and love of God in the conformity that is grace; (3) perfect knowledge and love of God in the likeness of glory. "The first is found in all human beings, the second only in the just, the third only in the blessed."[87]

There is Humanism. I found it intriguing that Charles Trinkaus titled his two-volume study of humanity and divinity in Italian Humanist thought *In Our Image and Likeness*.[88] Why? Because "the new vision of man in this period found its inspiration in a revival of the patristic exegesis" of Genesis 1:26.[89] It was an awareness of humanity's dignity as a god on earth, continuator of the creating God and the incarnate, risen Lord, that "populated and cultivated the world, created culture and the arts, erected buildings and cities."[90] Out of varied sources and traditions Humanism shaped "a new homogeneous view of man knowing, willing and acting in the image and likeness of God."[91]

There was the Reformation. Here image doctrine is crucial, because image doctrine is Christian anthropology: How do you see sinful humanity? The Reformers assailed the medieval synthesis, attacked the two-storied universe of Augustine and Aquinas head on. Despite traces of a two-image theory (universal image and believers' image), Luther's more mature predilection is for a single image: righteousness. A natural knowledge and love of God? It imperils the principle of justification by faith alone; more forcibly, it is incompatible with an intellect which, unjustified, is simply not right, incompatible with a will which, unjustified, is simply not good. Genesis 9:6 is indeed a problem for Luther: The blood of fallen humans is not to be spilled, because they have been created in God's image.

Yes, he feels compelled to respond, something of image remains after sin. But the relic is not really image; that is removed entirely from sinful unbelieving humans. The relic is not really *in* sinful man and woman; the image hangs over them as a divine destiny, in God's intention for them. The image is not static, not a thing, a faculty, a power. The image is original righteousness and its restoration in Christ.[92]

The more systematic Calvin also equates image with righteousness: Man and woman are in God's image in so far as they reflect God's glory back to God in gratitude. Does anything survive of the image in the unjustified? Calvin should say no, in harmony with his doctrine of total depravity:

> When man is considered in himself and his nature, what can one say? Here is a creature cursed of God which is worthy of being rejected from the rank of all other creatures, worms, lice, fleas, and vermin; for there is more worth in all the vermin in the world than in man; for he is a creature where the image of God has been effaced, and where the good which He has put in it is corrupted. There is nothing in him but sin; we have so gone to the devil, and he does not only govern us, but has us in his possession, he is our prince.[93]

But Calvin found it impossible to be consistent. He was so sensitive to the gifts of God within man and woman that he felt the sparks of the divine could never be totally obliterated; the human person never ceases to be different from the brute, from the irrational.

I have long sensed in Reformation thought (1) a profound pessimism on the potential of created freedom, a pessimism at the other extreme from Humanist optimism, and (2) a specifically Christian liberty expressed in obedience to God and service of one's neighbor.[94]

Then there are the image theologies of the twentieth century. I mean Emil Brunner, insisting against traditional Catholicism that the original image of God has been destroyed by sin, that the sinner cannot do or even will anything that would count as good before God; arguing against the Reform that the image abides in that man and woman have never lost what has been called their verbicompetence, their capacity to understand words, a necessary predisposition for belief in God's Word. I can be addressed. I mean Karl Barth, seeing in the love relationship between man and woman a parable and promise of the bridal relationship of the Church to Christ the bridegroom. I mean Carl Jung, aware of his audacity in making the most sacred of all dogmatic symbols (the Trinity) an object of psychological study, yet seeing "man's nature as image of God [as] based upon his immediate participation in the dialectic of trinitarian life cast in terms of the fruitful and inexhaustible interplay of the unconscious and the ego-conscious which, in turn, is a description of the activity of the Spirit."[95] I mean Gordon Kaufman, arguing that God's image is to be sought in our historicity, our capacity to create ourselves, reflecting God's history when we love and care, when we do God's will, but turning our creativity into self-destructiveness, our history into the bearer of demonic powers.[96] I mean so many more, interesting, pertinent, at times fascinating; but regretfully I have no room for them here. Besides, I am awed by a Protestant martyr to freedom.

Dietrich Bonhoeffer

In the gray dawn of Monday, April 9, 1945, a German Lutheran pastor of 39 was hanged in the concentration camp at Flossenbürg. The charge: conspiring to overthrow Hitler.

The charge was true. It was leveled against a German who returned to Germany from New York in 1939 because "I will have no right to participate in the reconstruction of Christian life in Germany after the war if I do not share the trials of this time with my people."[97] A Christian who agonized over Christian complicity with Hitler on war and the Jews. A churchman who could no longer endure the Church's silence "when she should have cried out because the blood of the innocent was crying aloud to heaven."[98] An ethicist who came to see that in extraordinary situations "There is ... no law behind which the responsible man can seek cover ... there can only be a complete renunciation of every law...."[99] A theologian who wrote from prison that only by "living unreservedly in [this] life's duties, problems, successes and failures, experiences and perplexities ... [does one become] a man and a Christian."[100] A prisoner who even gave thought to suicide, "not because of consciousness of guilt but because basically I am already dead...."[101] A disciple who experienced what he had called so poignantly "the cost of discipleship."[102] A startlingly free spirit who believed that his living and dying were but "stations on the road to freedom."[103]

It was with uncommon excitement, tinged with reverence, that in the '70s I discovered Dietrich Bonhoeffer.[104] This martyr to Nazism, who walked to the gallows without fear, not only *wrote* about freedom — the freedom of God and the freedom of the human body, the free responsibility of the German people and the freedom of a secular world to be what it really is before God. He was a uniquely free person — particularly free, paradoxically, in prison. A perceptive admirer has insisted that the real Bonhoeffer can best be seen from those features which ran simultaneously through his life and thought.

> The most obvious of these features is Bonhoeffer's exuberant sense of freedom, the incredible agility and independence with which he moved, thought, and lived. The very freedom which could enable Bonhoeffer to declare himself a pacifist would later enable him to enter the movement to destroy the Third Reich. . . . He never felt a compulsion to be different, or to conform; he simply sought his own vocation and did his best to follow it. If that vocation meant, as it often did, a radical divergence from the path of his fellow countrymen, Bonhoeffer diverged. It hurt him, but he felt his freedom and the dictates of his conscience more important than the feelings and beliefs he was urged to share.[105]

I began my study of Bonhoeffer's literary legacy with a set of lectures he delivered in the winter semester 1932–33 at the University of Berlin on the first three chapters of Genesis.[106] Here the creation of the material universe is seen as a work God loved, but a work in which God did not see Godself. At the moment God fashioned it, this world was already torn away from God, was strange to God, was no longer the Creator. Alive indeed, this creation is dead, "because, while it comes out of freedom, it is itself not free but determined. . . . Only in something that is itself free can the One who is free, the Creator, see Himself."[107] Only an image in freedom would fully proclaim its Creator's honor. Soon comes a crucial paragraph:

> In man God creates his image on earth. This means that man is like the Creator in that he is free. Actually he is free only by God's creation, by means of the Word of God; he is free for the worship of the Creator. In the language of the Bible, freedom is not something man has for himself but something he has for others. No man is free "as such," that is, in a vacuum, in the way that he may be musical, intelligent or blind as such. Freedom is not a quality of man, nor is it an ability, a capacity, a kind of being that somehow flares up in him. Anyone investigating man to discover freedom finds nothing of it. Why?

Because freedom is not a quality which can be revealed — it is not a possession, a presence, an object, nor is it a form for existence — but a relationship and nothing else. In truth, freedom is a relationship between two persons. Being free means "being free for the other," because the other has bound me to him. Only in relationship with the other am I free.[108]

How do we know this? It is the message of the gospel. In creating by entering into His creation — as distinguished from the word of command that created the nonhuman — God creates freedom. "Man differs from the other creatures in that God himself is in him, in that he is God's image in which the free Creator views himself.... In the free creature the Holy Spirit worships the Creator, uncreated freedom praises itself in created freedom."[109]

If the freedom of human over against human means to be free *for* the human, human freedom over against the rest of creation means to be free *from* it. Here is the other side of our likeness to God; we rule nonhuman creation. Oh yes, I am still tied to the soil and the animal world I rule. It is my world. I belong to it. "It bears me, nourishes me, and holds me."[110] My freedom from it lies in my ruling it; "and the more strongly I rule it the more it is *my* earth."[111] The existential problem? Through technology we are the world's prisoner, its slave; our rule is illusion; we become strangers on earth. We do not rule because we are not aware of the world as God's creation, do not receive our dominion as given by God but grasp it for ourselves.

There is no "being-free-from" without "being-free-for." There is no dominion without serving God.... God, our brother, and the earth belong together.... Only where God and man's brother come to man can man find the way back to the earth. Man's being-free-for God and the other person and his being-free-from the creature in his dominion over it is the image of God in the first man.[112]

What precisely is this freedom, this relationship? Bonhoeffer's reflection on Genesis did not unravel this for me. I had to pore through the Bonhoeffer corpus for insights (1) on the meaning of the relationship that is freedom and (2) on what the Incarnation added to creation, the Redeemer to the Creator.

Ransacking Bonhoeffer's published legacy was at once rewarding and perplexing. I began with his doctoral thesis on the communion of saints (1925), meditated for hours on the small segment dealing with authority and freedom in the empirical Church.[113] At this point Bonhoeffer admitted that he had "only a relative freedom" within the Church. Its authoritative word on Bible and faith, on dogma and creed, called for obedience. Here the Church could demand of him a sacrifice of intellect, even of conscience. But the relative freedom could become absolute. When? Whenever his relative subjection to the Church stood in the way of his absolute subjection to the authority of God's Word.[114] No definition of freedom here; freedom is contrasted with submission, with obedience; it is the right to say no to the human word, even spoken by the Church. Only the Word of God could bind his mind and conscience absolutely.

In a Barcelona address in 1929, Bonhoeffer affirmed that for the Christian there is no other law than the New Testament's paradoxical law of freedom. Freedom is the gift humanity lost in Eden, the gift Jesus restores when he places us "immediately under God, new and afresh at each moment."[115] Here several strong statements startled me.

> The Christian himself creates his standards of good and evil for himself.... He acts, because the will of God seems to bid him to, without a glance at the others, at what is usually called morals, and no one but himself and God can know whether he has acted well or badly.... There are no actions which are bad in themselves — even murder can be justified — there is only faithfulness to God's will or deviation from it....[116]

Here again freedom is utter obedience to God — but to a God who directs me in solitude, above and beyond and even against what laws and traditions may dictate.

In *Act and Being* (1931) there is a pertinent passage on God's own freedom-for. In God's self-revealing, Bonhoeffer argues,

> it is a question less of God's freedom on the far side from us, i.e., his eternal isolation and aseity, than of his forth-proceeding, his *given* Word, his bond in which he has bound himself, of his freedom as it is most strongly attested in his having freely bound himself to historical man, having placed himself at man's disposal. God is not free *of* man but *for* man.[117]

Here the Word of God's freedom is Christ. "God is *there,* which is to say: not in eternal non-objectivity but... 'haveable,' graspable in his Word within the Church."[118] What makes existence free is "being in Christ, being-directed to Christ...man exists for and through Christ."[119] In contemplation of him "the slave is unbound."[120]

In his *Ethics* (1939–43) Bonhoeffer insistently linked freedom to responsibility;[121] in fact, "freedom can consist only in responsibility."[122] Often ignorant of the good, the free person commits his or her own action "to the guidance of God."[123] Although the machinery of the social order seems to put most people in the role of obedience and subservience, such ethical emasculation need not be. Everyone can experience responsibility — and "in its most characteristic form...in the encounter with other people."[124] Our relation to God is realized in Jesus, "the one who is both obedient and free.... Obedience shows man that he must allow himself to be told what is good and what God requires of him (Micah 6:8); and liberty enables him to do good himself. In obedience man adheres to the decalogue and in freedom man creates new decalogues (Luther)."[125]

In *The Cost of Discipleship* (1937) a six-page chapter has for its title "The Image of Christ."[126] (Unexpectedly, we find no explicit mention of freedom.) To be conformed to the image of Christ means to "be assimilated to the form of Christ in its entirety...incarnate, crucified and glorified."[127] By communion with Christ we recover our full humanity. The "new nature we now enjoy means that we too must bear the sins and sorrows of others."[128] But even in this life we share the reflected glory of Christ's resurrection; we progress from glory to glory, ever closer conformity to Christ. "It is only because he became like us that we can become like him. It is only because we are identified with him that we can become like him. By being transformed into his image, we are enabled to model our lives on his."[129]

Bonhoeffer's approach to image and freedom raises many a question for a Catholic theologian, e.g., his denial of any analogy of being between God and humans. I suspect that his short remarks on analogy in *Creation and Fall* conceal issues that have been divisive of Catholics and Protestants since the Reformation. What did original sin actually do to us? What effect did it have on our intelligence and freedom? Is a natural theology possible, an inadequate but authentic knowledge of God through naked reason? Can we humans do *anything* genuinely good without God's grace? Is there such a thing as a *natural* likeness to God, a freedom that images God's freedom apart from redemption in Christ? We are touching the edge of two indispensable disciplines: anthropology and epistemology. Who are we, and how do we know?

But such questions are hardly a high enough note on which to end. For all my questioning, Bonhoeffer continues to excite me. He has propounded and lived an image of God in freedom that challenges each generation. It is not utterly without ancestry; earlier theologians have touched his central themes. I may dispute his biblical exegesis, take issue with his theology, impeach his philosophy; but when the argumentative dust has settled, I find his core contention highly persuasive, have experienced it increasingly in my priestly existence. As a human being and a Christian, I mirror God to the extent that, in obedience to God's Word and in imitation of God's Christ, I am *a person for God and for others.* Here lies responsible freedom, for here is love: love of God, love of my sisters and brothers in Christ. Here lies a convict who, like the convict of Calvary, lived free and died free. And so I close on a grateful and grace-filled note, Bonhoeffer's remarkable prison poem "Stations on the Road to Freedom":

Discipline

If you set out to seek freedom, then learn above all things
to govern your soul and your senses, for fear that your passions
and longing[s] may lead you away from the path you should follow.
Chaste be your mind and your body, and both in subjection,
obediently, steadfastly seeking the aim set before them;
only through discipline may a man learn to be free.

Action

Daring to do what is right, not what fancy may tell you,
valiantly grasping occasions, not cravenly doubting—
freedom comes only through deeds, not through thoughts taking wing.
Faint not nor fear, but go out to the storm and the action,
trusting in God whose commandment you faithfully follow;
freedom, exultant, will welcome your spirit with joy.

Suffering

A change has come indeed. Your hands, so strong and active,
are bound; in helplessness now you see your action
is ended; you sigh in relief, your cause committing
to stronger hands; so now you may rest contented.

Only for one blissful moment could you draw near to touch
    freedom;
then, that it might be perfected in glory, you gave it to God.

Death

Come now, thou greatest of feasts on the journey to freedom
    eternal;
death, cast aside all the burdensome chains, and demolish
the walls of our temporal body, the walls of our souls that are
    blinded,
so that at last we may see that which here remains hidden.
Freedom, how long we have sought thee in discipline, action,
    and suffering;
dying, we now may behold thee revealed in the Lord.[130]

EIGHT

From Jesus Christ to Vatican II

Ordained Priesthood

In these personal observations on priesthood, I want to reflect on three stages of my priestly existence: (1) the early years of (shall we say?) wine and roses, the years of quasi permanence; (2) the middle years, years of unsettling change; (3) my latest years, days of reflection on the significance of permanence and change. I shall continue with some observations on the years that lie ahead: fresh theological insights on priesthood, the generally low state of priestly morale, and what I see as good reasons for confidence. I need to add a set of reflections on priesthood and ministry stimulated by approaches of the Second Vatican Council that appear less than adequate for priest-religious; and a recent discussion of priesthood that has compelled me to re-examine several facets of this sacrament I have never before had occasion to question. I shall conclude with some thoughts on preparation for priesthood, with an emphasis on academic excellence.

Early Years: Stability

On June 22, 1941, when Baltimore's Archbishop Michael J. Curley oiled my fingers and entrusted me with the elements of sacrifice, the theology of priesthood was relatively simple and the life of a priest remarkably stable.

The theology was summed up in the ritual of ordination: I was ordained to offer sacrifice for the living and the dead and to forgive sins in the name of Christ. This approach to priesthood traced back in a particularly focused way to medieval theology, with its stress on spiritual or sacramental power. Thomas Aquinas is a significant and influential example: "The power of orders is established for dispensing the sacraments ... [and] is principally ordered to consecrating the body of Christ and dispensing it to the faithful, and to cleansing the faithful from their sins."[1]

234

Priestly life exemplified the theology. When I offered my first Mass, the ritual was highly stylized, quite solemn. I had prepared, undergone preparation, for months: no gestures beyond the shoulders, consecrated fingers linked together, rigidly controlled signs of the cross, stiff-backed genuflections (right knee touching left heel) — all in the service of reverence. The language was a stately Latin, even if not always spoken in stately style (I recall that the Old Testament story of Susannah and the lustful judges — and under which tree — abetted tongue twisting). My back was to the people, save for the Gospel and sermon, people's Communion and final blessing. A powerful symbol, for the Eucharistic emphasis was exclusively on the high priest Christ. He was priest and victim, the very altar of sacrifice; the role of his minister was to decrease, so that Christ might increase.

When I preached for the first time, the Catholic sermon was a stepchild — important in principle, insignificant in reality. For an apparently good reason: The stress was strongly on the sacrifice of the God-man, not on the words of mere mortals. Proof? A Catholic could miss the whole liturgy of the word (Kyrie and Gloria, Epistle and Gospel, announcements and sermon) and not "miss Mass." No confessor would do more than slap this sinner's wrist lightly: "three Hail Marys." I recall how we altar boys at St. John's in Manhattan referred to certain worshipers as "sharpshooters." These men knelt in the back on one knee, hand on the upright knee, chin cupped in palm of hand, waiting for the sermon — at which point they would ease out for a smoke, to return for the Creed.

In those days I raised my right arm ceaselessly in absolution, for a sense of sin was pervasive. Weekly confession was common — and not usually from scrupulosity. We knew what had to be confessed. Devoted nuns made sure of that, parish missions painted the wages of sin with the vividness of Michelangelo, prayer books carried laundry lists of all possible deviations from duty. Queues for confession rivaled waiting lines for Radio City's Rockettes or Fordham's seven Blocks of Granite (part of gridiron lore).

In those days believers besought their priests for solutions — answers to every difficulty in doctrine, each morass in morality. And solutions we gave — clearly, objectively, with authority. And the solutions were accepted, even when the petitioner walked away sadly because the solution was too formidable to follow.

In those days priesthood, like law and medicine, had status. Catholics tipped their hats when priests walked by, as they tipped their hats to the church they passed. Each year thousands of young men felt called to priestly service — many of them because they wanted to be like the priests they encountered.

In those days the prayer of priests was regular, regulated: breviary and meditation, thanksgiving after Mass and examination of conscience. Little was left to individual determination or discretion. Many a night did I read Compline at a bus stop under a street lamp, fulfilling the obligation before midnight Greenwich time or sun time or daylight saving time — whichever came latest.

In those days the clergy were clean-shaven; hair dared not defile our ears, our cheeks, our chins. We wore the cassock — to the altar, to table, almost to bed; only on the golf course did we don the world's trousers. Rome expected us to be "out of this world," separated not only from evil but from much that is good; and in large measure we were. Friendships with women were discouraged; woman was indeed a soul to be saved, but a dangerous species. Jesuits rose from sleep at 5:30 (our enemies said, 5:30 twice a day), and we were supposed to be home at a civilized hour — nothing so unstructured as a personal key.

In those days the priesthood may not have been paradise, but it was studded with stability and security; it was fenced about with fidelity. You could commit yourself with confidence to a celibate existence for life, be respected for it by a people who rarely questioned it, and expect to die serenely in the warm arms of a Christ you had served as your one master. I had few complaints, surely no serious problems.

Middle Years: Change

A half century has passed, and the passage has been soul-searing. A new world has been born, a new America, and in it a new man and a new woman. We have all been changed: by World War II and Vatican II, by Vietnam and a Third World, by the abortive rebellion in Hungary and the Soviet invasions of Czechoslovakia and Afghanistan, by the assassination of the Kennedys and Martin Luther King, by the campus riots of the '60s and the waves of Watergate, by the unexpected collapse of Communism, by the anxieties of aging and the silent war on the womb.

In this new world the old Church could not live unchanged. Change has cut the Church to its marrow. We are torn within — from the kiss of peace through contraception to one true Church, from Communion in the hand to the ordination of women, from divorce and remarriage to a married clergy. Some cry: too much too soon; others: too little too late. If you grew up before 1962, you may not find it easy to recognize your church in the three decades since Vatican II closed. The thrilling vision of the council, to refashion the Church on every level in the image of Christ, has not always been matched by remarkable results. Much good, of course; and those who deny it are plagued with tunnel vision. And still, many of our people are dreadfully confused, some openly antagonistic. Churches are emptying, schools closing; church law is openly defied, Catholics create their own morality, and the pope, to many a Catholic, is a figurehead, just another guy who simply isn't with it, is trying to squeeze the universal Church into a Polish straitjacket. And we are still experiencing change: change in the way the Church thinks, the way the Church lives, the way the Church worships.

In this new world, in this new Church, the old priest could not live untouched. Thousands of priests, many of them my dear friends, many I taught at Woodstock, have found their vocations empty of meaning or too painful to endure. (In one ten-year period, something like ten thousand priests left the priesthood in this country alone.) There is a new look to priesthood; there are new demands, fresh expectations, unfamiliar confusions.

The very center of my life, the Mass, now brings me face to face with the faithful; I may no longer lay the whole burden on Christ; the buck stops here; I must come through to the worshiping community as a person. They expect me to be not a reverential robot but a vibrant celebrant. They are not satisfied with a theologically valid change of bread and wine into Christ's body and blood; they want my face, my gestures, to tell them that I believe it, that I delight in my priesthood, that I would not exchange it for any joy they possess. When I place the body of Christ in their hands, many meet my eyes, smile, expect me to respond, to reach out to them as they reach out to me. I may no longer mumble a Latin they do not understand; I must get through to them with an English that says something to them, even if repeated day in and day out. If Catholics of the '40s and '50s saw Christ first and then me in Christ, Catholics of the '90s see me first and then, perhaps, Christ in me.

When I preach, the Word is as important to them as the Eucharist; for they sense what Vatican II asserted: Christ is present not only when the Eucharistic species are consecrated; he is present when God's Word is proclaimed.[2] And so they ask that, when I speak, my mind be filled with God's revelation, my heart raptured by the Spirit, my tongue touched with fire. If God does not speak through me, I am nothing to them but St. Paul's "noisy gong and clanging cymbal" (1 Cor 13:1).

Less often now do they come to me for God's forgiveness. The reasons vary. Some say that the old Catholic sense of sin has disappeared; "sin" itself is a dated word, save for "sinful structures" like governments and churches. Others say we have grown up: We do not see sin everywhere; our consciences are more sophisticated; even the Church is more of a guide than a master. In any event, the long lines outside the box are no more, and a synod of 200 bishops in Rome had to agonize over a neuralgic question: What ever became of reconciliation?

Hardly ever do they come to me for solutions. And they can appeal, with some justice, to Vatican II: "Let the laity not imagine that their pastors are always such experts that to every problem which arises, however complicated, they can readily give a concrete solution, or even that such is their mission."[3] Counseling is now a two-way street. The faithful want to discuss: contraception and premarital sex, human rights and nuclear war, Sunday obligation and the need to confess, married priests and the ordination of women. And they are asking not simply for an official position. A turning point in my priestly existence came in the early '60s, when I had presented the Church's position on an issue to a young lady clearly, objectively, with authority. She looked at me and said quietly, "And what do *you* think?"

Today priest*hood* means little — as little as presidency or medicine or the law. These words are abstract, and our age will not confer status on abstractions. I cannot appeal to my profession, point to my collar. What matters is not priesthood but this priest; I can offer only my priestly witness. And ever so many priests are not sure what priestly witness *is*, what it means to be a priest. Was Father Robert Drinan a priest in Congress (I believe he was), or was he on leave from presbyteral activity? And what of labor-relations expert George Higgins and peace demonstrator Daniel Berrigan and priests who teach chemistry or economics or linguistics or constitutional law? And bishops who issue a pastoral on peace and war, on specific uses of nuclear weaponry.

Today our people want their priests to be one with God *and* one with them. They expect us to be awfully close to them, warmly human, and still chaste and celibate. They challenge our pretensions to poverty. Our obedience, to bishops and religious superiors, leaves them cold when it does not free us for service — to the poor and the oppressed, to the aging and the lonely. They demand that we feed their faith *and* struggle for justice.

Today we even share the insecurities of the laity: how to find and keep a job, how to retire without bitterness, how to survive in old age, how to die believing, hoping, loving.

Latest Years: Reflections

What does this movement from 1941 to 1999 say to me, say to priests? One point I shall *not* explore: Which is better, the '40s or the '90s? The question might make for an entertaining, perhaps stormy debate on an otherwise sedate priests' retreat or reunion. But this I do maintain: The movement from the '40s to the '90s gives us reason to rejoice. Not for the obvious reason: fifty-eight years of my own priesting. That could be a sheer statistic. The last half of the twentieth century, especially these last two decades, have revealed to me some thrilling truths about permanence and change in priestly existence, in my personal priesting.

For the first quarter century of my priesting I rarely questioned what precisely defined a priest. I lived off the ordination ritual that spelled out my specific priestness in 1941. I was ordained into a twin power: the power to offer sacrifice for the living and the dead, and the power to forgive sin in the name of Christ. It was only in 1971 — perhaps in the context of the wholesale departure of priests from their ministry — that I came face to face with a stunning realization: God's revelation does not provide us with a clearly articulated notion of ministerial priesthood; the Bible does not offer a clearly defined view of the essence and forms of the Christian priesthood, does not furnish a detailed and fixed concept of my ministry. A report commissioned by the U.S. bishops on the biblical theology of the priesthood summed up sobering scriptural scholarship.

> From what has been said it should be evident that we can expect to find in the Scriptures an evolution in the concept of ministry that is eminently in keeping with the nature of a pilgrim people of God.... It will mean, first of all, that we cannot use the Old Testament as a primary referent for our conception of Christian ministry.... Acceptance of the concept of evolution will mean, secondly, that even in the New Testament we should not expect to find a clearly formulated definition of Christian ministry from the beginning, or at any single point in the development of New Testament revelation. Christian

ministry was never "frozen" in any one mold but continued to develop and to be adapted in the succeeding moments of history. This does not mean that there is no normative character to the New Testament canon. But the normative character will not be seen in a definitive "canonizing" of one exercise of ministry without regard for another, or of one historical manifestation at one time or place in isolation from other such manifestations. Development itself is canonical and therefore normative.[4]

But if Scripture does not reveal a fixed concept of what we call "priest," I had to ask whether the Church's postapostolic tradition unfolded an unchanging understanding. Here I was helped by an unpublished paper written by Avery Dulles in 1971, "What Is a Priest?" Dulles made clear that in different periods of the Church's history different theologies of priesthood, different models of ordained ministry, have come into prominence. At least five merit mention here.

1. *The Jurisdictional Model.* For several centuries after the Council of Trent, in the context of a predominantly juridical view of the Church and a hierarchical doctrine of social order, the priest was seen as the one who holds the plenitude of authority in a "perfect society." The pope and bishops, and after them the pastors, are the chief priests who habitually possess that fulness of authority known as jurisdiction. The preaching and teaching offices of the clergy are assimilated to their jurisdictional role: To teach is to impose authoritative doctrine as a matter of obedience. Even admission to and denial of sacraments comes to be seen through quasi-juridical glasses.

2. *The Cultic Model.* In much patristic and medieval theology the Church was seen primarily as a worshiping or sacramental community. In terms of this model the priest came to be regarded as the hierophant, the performer of sacred mysteries. He offered to God, in the name of the community, the totally pleasing sacrifice of Christ. On some theories, the priest was seen as cultic leader; on others, as the mediator or substitute who offered sacrifice in place of the community.

3. *The Pastoral Model.* According to certain New Testament insights, recovered in large measure by Vatican II, the Church is seen as an intercommunion of persons, effected through divine love poured out by Christ and the Spirit. In this type of theology the priest comes to be viewed primarily as pastor or community leader. He brings

people together, seeks to activate in them the graces and charisms the Holy Spirit bestows upon each for the benefit of all. In this vision the attributes of the pastor are analyzed in terms of the doctrine of John 10, Acts 20, and 1 Peter.

4. *The Prophetic Model.* In modern Protestant theology, especially the kind typified by Barth, the ordained minister is seen predominantly as proclaimer of God's Word. To believers and unbelievers he/she issues a resounding call to repentance and conversion. While some proponents of this theology would shun the term "priest," as excessively freighted with cultic overtones, they still accept a high doctrine of ordained ministry, based on the conceptions of prophet and apostle found in the Old and New Testaments.

5. *The Monastic Model.* In some Christian traditions the priest has been viewed primarily as the holy man, the guru, the spiritual director. In this perspective the religious priest is often considered to be the normal case; monastic spirituality is in great part transferred to diocesan seminaries and diocesan priests. Thus practices such as meditation, recitation of breviary, community life, and celibacy are extended to all priests without exception. The priest is expected to be withdrawn from the world and its vanities and to live in a manner that anticipates the blessings of the world to come.

Now these models are not necessarily in conflict; but the choice of one model will overshadow aspects of priesthood that seem central in another model. More importantly, this quick foray into history suggests how difficult, how impossible, it is to isolate some function, something a priest and only a priest can do, and proclaim that this is priesthood, here is the ordained ministry, utterly changeless, unaffected by history, unconditioned by culture. You might end up with a function that takes up a half hour of your time, once a day, exclusive of vacation!

But precisely here lies the priestly peril; for precisely here lies the unexamined assumption: There *is* this eternal role, this immutable essence, and it is in harmony with this role and essence that a priest's life is organized for him — where he lives and what he wears, how he works and with whom he relaxes, the obligations he has taken on and the rights he has given up. It is because of these unexamined assumptions that the first draft of the working paper on ministerial priesthood prepared for the 1971 Synod of Bishops could assert so confidently: "Priestly ministry is a mystery ... which the people of God grasped from the beginning. ... " Or "From this gospel picture of priestly ministry, it is clear that a priest's involvement in political problems, even though they are serious, cannot be ordered to his goal." Or "Because of celibacy, priests can dedicate themselves more freely to the work of proclaiming the Word of God, since they have firm control of themselves." To the credit of the bishops in synod, these affirmations were toned down in the ultimate document.

Impressed though I was by Scripture and history, I still had to ask: If we do not get from God's revelation or from the Church's tradition some unchangeable notion of priesthood, where does this leave us, leave me? Is there anything we can uncover from Christ's own tenting among us and from the Christian experience of ministry? Here, to begin with, good friend and first-rate biblicist Raymond Brown rode to my rescue. The New Testament, he showed, furnishes four facets of Christian ministry which the Catholic Church sees as basic in her priests. Not all were present from the very beginning in one and the same person; but the Church has gradually brought them together to help fashion her notion of what an ordained priest is.[5]

First, the priest is a *disciple*. Always a disciple. To be a disciple means to be "called," as the first companions of Jesus were called, as John and James, Peter and yes Judas were called — to have a vocation that stems from Jesus: "Follow me." For the priest, as for the original disciples, there can be only one master: Jesus. And the response to him must be total: "Follow me, and let the dead bury their own dead" (Mt 8:21–22). Not just for today: "No one who puts a hand to the plow and looks back is fit for the kingdom of God" (Lk 9:62). Not part time: Discipleship must be a priest's whole life; there is nothing else. And so you have that harsh sentence of Jesus, "Whoever comes to me and does not hate father and mother, wife and children, brothers and sisters, yes, and even life itself, cannot be my disciple" (Lk 14:26). Exaggeration? If so, deliberate exaggeration, to make an unmistakable point: I am not a disciple of Jesus if he is not my whole life.

Furthermore, to be a disciple is to be called to hardships too cruel for most humans: to leave everything and embrace a cross, to have nothing as my own save Jesus. To be a disciple is to pattern myself after the one master — and this master is a bloodstained, crucified master who came not to be served but to serve, who warned his disciples against honors and first places, who turned savagely on Peter when he rebelled against the passion of his Lord.

Second, the priest is an *apostle*. Always an apostle. If to be a disciple means to be "called," called to follow Jesus, to be an apostle means to be "sent," as the original apostles were sent, to serve others. The keynote is service. I must focus on St. Paul's commitment, "I will most gladly spend and be spent for you" (2 Cor 12:15).

And what I as priest carry to others is always Jesus — not only his message but his presence. "We do not proclaim ourselves," Paul declared; "we proclaim Jesus Christ as Lord and ourselves as your slaves for Jesus' sake" (2 Cor 4:5). It is always Jesus who is proclaimed — by word and work, by sacraments and sacrifice. But in a special way by prayer and suffering. A priest who has forgotten how to pray is a priest who cannot preach Jesus — whatever else he may preach. And a priest, like Paul, will present Jesus to others effectively only if he bears the death pangs of Jesus in his own body. Only if I am constantly restless because, like Paul, I am "afflicted at every turn, from struggles without and anxieties within" (2 Cor 7:5). Anxieties within: I mean a loneliness that is in itself no reason for forsaking the priestly life; a lack of appreciation, especially today when priesthood has no special status; an anguish that tears my heart because I am so weak and the forces of evil are so strong, because so often my words seem wasted on the wind, because so few seem to care.

Third, a priest is what the New Testament calls a *presbyter.* The New Testament presbyters were a group responsible for the pastoral care of the churches. The qualities the New Testament prescribes for the presbyter are sober indeed, even stuffy. He must be above reproach, temperate, sensible, dignified, hospitable, an apt teacher, gentle, not quarrelsome. His task is to organize, to stabilize, to prevent dangerous innovation. "He must hold firm to the sure word he was taught, so that he may be able to give instruction in sound doctrine and confute those who contradict it" (Tit 1:9). His task calls for authority that does not dominate, that is softened by being wonderfully warm and human.

The point is, the priest does represent an institution. No matter how charismatic, how prophetic, even if called to protest the sins and corruption of institutions, of the Church itself, the priest must represent more than his personal insights. Like it or not, I am a churchman. I cannot, as a priest, stand outside my institution; I am an official part of it. Not that the institution is always right, is beyond criticism or censure. Rather that this institution is the setting where faith is born and grows; this institution is the locus and focus of worship; this institution is the community of love. This is what the priest represents.

Fourth, a priest *presides at the Eucharist.* It is not my total task, but it is a central preoccupation of priesthood. For here the priest does what St. Paul insisted must be done: "proclaim the Lord's death until he comes" (1 Cor 11:26). I have a sacramental ministry that revolves around the bread of life and the cup of the new covenant. Around this liturgy the Church has built the access of man and woman to the life that is Christ, from the water of baptism through the ashes of penance to the oil of a final anointing. In this process the priest plays a unique role — a role that comes to focus each time I proclaim, "This is my body, which will be given for you.... This is the cup of my blood."

Here, in a very real sense, is the heart of my priesthood. Even if a priest works at much else besides — in school or slum, in collective bargaining or the halls of Congress — at some point (ideally) the priest gathers God's people around an altar, around a table, to share with them a thanksgiving where the work of redemption is accomplished and in unparalleled fashion man and woman are made one with their God. In this connection I have for years been thrilled by a paragraph from a remarkable Anglican liturgical scholar, Dom Gregory Dix. He was describing in rapturous phrases the effect of Jesus' command to his special friends, "Do this in remembrance of me" (Lk 22:19).

Was ever a command so obeyed? For century after century, spreading slowly to every continent and country and among every race on earth, this action has been done, in every conceivable human circumstance, for every conceivable human need from infancy and before it to extreme old age and after it, from the pinnacles of earthly greatness to the refuge of fugitives in the caves and dens of the earth. Men have found no better thing than this to do for kings in their crowning and for criminals going to the scaffold; for armies in triumph or for a bride and bridegroom in a little country church; for the proclamation of a dogma or for a good crop of wheat; for the wisdom of the Parliament of a mighty nation or for a sick old woman afraid to die; for a schoolboy sitting an examination or for Columbus setting out to discover America;... because the Turk was at the gates of Vienna [and the enemy] on the beach at Dunkirk;... tremulously, by an old monk on the fiftieth anniversary of his vows; furtively, by an exiled bishop who had hewn timber all day in a prison camp near Murmansk; gorgeously, for the canonisation of S. Joan of Arc.... And best of all, week by week and month by month, on a hundred thousand successive Sundays, faithfully, unfailingly, across all the parishes of christendom, the pastors have done this just to *make* the holy common people of God.[6]

Moving beyond Scripture, my experience of church history led me to suspect the mid-century stress on functions, on roles. We defined an ordained priest in terms of what he could *do* which an unordained person could *not* do. And here the crisis of identity was tearing the guts of countless priests. They were searching for priesthood in terms of something specific to themselves, powers proper to priests, functions that distinguished them from the laity. These powers and functions were becoming narrower and narrower, so that they wondered if there actually *was* anything like that. And though they did discover what they alone could do ("This is my body," "I absolve you"), it seemed so narrow in scope that it took little time, little of their life. The rest of their existence (preaching, teaching, building, organizing, counseling...) was lived in the suspicion that some man or woman in the pews could do it better.

What I came to realize with increasing clarity, with progressive delight, was that through sacramental ordination I was empowered, I had engaged myself, to shape my life to the needs of the gospel *as the Church sees them at any given moment in history.* As the Church sees them. That is why Robert Drinan's ten years in Congress with episcopal permission were not a leave of absence from the priesthood. As a columnist wrote for the *Boston Globe* after Drinan was ordered by the pope to leave Congress, "Father Drinan is doing wholesale what Mother Teresa is doing retail."

So too for George Higgins reconciling labor and management, Jesuit astronomer George Coyne directing the Vatican Observatory, the late Jesuit Timothy Healy overseeing the New York Public Library system, Metuchen's Charles Cicerale advocating rights for the mentally ill, The Bronx's Joseph Dietz administering a social-service agency, Redemptorist Fredric Hang easing the lot of the homeless in Milwaukee, Claretian Thomas Joyce agitating against plant closings and for workers' ownership, Arthur Mallinson founding a Catholic Worker house in Dallas, a priest acting as treasurer in a religious community, the thousand-and-one priests teaching economics and chemistry, philosophy and psychology, trigonometry and Greek. Are they on leave? Not on your life! Are they hyphenated priests? No sir! Is it the Church that calls this priest to this specific activity? Then that activity is priestly. Are there activities incompatible on principle with priesthood? I have discovered only two: unrepented sin and perhaps subpar golf.

Now, even if we dare not identify priesthood with some single function or several, in isolation from history and historical evolution, still the Church has come to a point in development where certain functions are regarded as special responsibilities of the ordained priest. I shall mention four in generic terms, to distinguish them from a much more arguable area: the specific means different priests may take to implement these roles.

First, I have been ordained to proclaim God's Word. Not simply — in a pluralistic society, perhaps not primarily — by formal preaching. The model of proclamation may be dialogue; it may be priestly presence; it may be prophetic speech and action in the tradition of Isaiah and Jesus.

Second, I have been ordained to build up the Christian community. Here lies my responsibility for leadership. But a leader in our time is not one who commands; a leader is a man or woman who can move hearts and minds. It is mine to co-ordinate the charisms of the community as found in the individual members. I am accountable because mine is the office that looks not merely to the care of individuals but more broadly, as Vatican II put it, "to the formation of a genuine Christian community."[7]

Third, I have been ordained to serve humankind. Here Vatican II opened up new vistas: "Because the human race today is joining more and more into a civic, economic, and social unity, it is that much more necessary that priests...wipe out every kind of division, so that the whole human race may be brought into the unity of the family of God."[8] My parish is indeed the world, for the Church's mission is simply the human person. With the passage of the years I have slowly come to see what Vatican II proclaimed so simply to priests: Although I have obligations to all manner of men and women, "the poor and the lowly" have been "entrusted to [me] in a special way."[9] It is summed up in the opening words of the Pastoral Constitution on the Church in the Modern World: "The joys and hopes, the griefs and anxieties of the men and women of this age, especially those who are poor or in any way afflicted, these too are the joys and hopes, the griefs and anxieties of the followers of Christ" (no. 1). Hence the project of my final years, Preaching the Just Word. As detailed in chapter 4, it is an effort to move the preaching of justice issues more effectively into all the Catholic pulpits and congregations of the country.

Fourth, I have been ordained to preside at worship, especially the Eucharist. Here is my cultic role at its most proper. Here I effect the Church's most powerful expression of unity — the unity of the worshiping congregation within itself, with the diocese, with the universal Church, and with all humankind. Here is foreshadowed and promised the Christian hope: that the earth and all who bleed and joy thereon will be transformed into the kingdom of God and His Christ.

Here is where my whole life as a priest is coming to a final focus. I mean the words I murmur each morning or evening to the crucified images of God: "This is my body . . . [and it is] given for you."

Years Ahead: Crisis, Cross, Confidence

On May 9, 1990, at the invitation of the late, universally revered Cardinal Joseph Bernardin, I addressed the priest-jubilarians of the Archdiocese of Chicago.[10] I noted that I was speaking to them in a period of priestly peril without parallel perhaps since the Reformation. I proceeded to point out some major elements that have fueled the contemporary crisis within ordained priesthood: the ever heavier onus of celibacy, constant criticism, a gnawing feeling of ineffectiveness, closing of schools and churches, a pervasive but inadequate theology of priesthood, burnout from the burden of unrealistic expectations, fear of the insecurities now associated with priestly aging. Since that time, an especially agonizing crisis has come to the fore: sexual abuse, especially priestly pederasty, which is bankrupting dioceses, scandalizing believers and unbelievers alike, and plunging priests into profound discouragement, even anxious fear. No one, even the most innocent, can feel safe. One of the most powerful means of communication, of compassion, is too dangerous, is forbidden us. I mean . . . touch.

Cross

Then I moved from crisis to cross. For the pattern, the prototype, of priestly existence and service is the Christ St. Paul pictured in the hymn he quoted to the Christians of Philippi when he urged them to have the mind-set of Christ:

> Though his condition was divine,
> [Jesus] did not consider equality with God
> something to exploit for selfish gain,
> but emptied himself,
> taking on the condition of a slave,
> becoming like human beings.

> And being found in human form,
> he humbled himself still further
> with an obedience that meant death,
> even death on a cross.
>
> (Phil 2:6–8)

What Paul expressed so baldly and economically, Karl Rahner packed into a profound, poignant paragraph in his later years, when he was focusing on what he called "the cross erected over history."

> According to Scripture we may safely say that Jesus in his life was the *believer* ... and that he was consequently the one who hopes absolutely and in regard to God and men the one who loves absolutely. In the unity of [his] faith, hope, and love, Jesus surrendered himself in his death unconditionally to the absolute mystery that he called his Father, into whose hands he committed his existence, when in the night of his death and God-forsakenness he was deprived of everything that is otherwise regarded as the content of a human existence.... Everything fell away from him, even the perceptible security of the closeness of God's love, and in this trackless dark there prevailed silently only the mystery that in itself and in its freedom has no name and to which he nevertheless calmly surrendered himself as to eternal love and not to the hell of futility.... He who came out of God's glory did not merely descend into our human life, but also fell into the abyss of our death, and his dying began when he began to live and came to an end on the cross when he bowed his head and died.[11]

For all that he was God, this man, like us, died not with experience of resurrection but with faith in his Father; he died not with unassailable proof of resurrection but with hope of life for ever.

Impressively true, but how bring this down to day-to-day priestly living, to the crises of contemporary priestly existence? I suggested that our service as priests is most Christian, most effective, ultimately most gratifying if we follow the Crucified. To make sense of this, I offered four concrete observations.

First, the very word "follow." It is not simply synonymous with "imitate." "Imitate" has indeed precious precedent in Paul: "Be imitators of me, as I am of Christ" (1 Cor 11:1). Still, as Rahner saw so clearly, we are not expected to reproduce the life of Jesus as such. We live in different historical situations, have unique tasks that differ from those that confronted him in his historically conditioned existence. For all our dependence on him and his earthly existence, we do not reproduce him; we complete his historical individual reality.[12]

Very simply, in the lives of all graced men and women, in the life of every priest, there are realizations of faith, hope, and love which in his restricted existence Jesus did not and could not experience. He was a man, not a woman; he was a teacher, but not a scholar; he did not experience old age or Alzheimer's; he did not even live to be a Jesuit!

More accurate, then, than "imitate" is "follow," be Jesus' disciple. And if I ask where concretely, independent of time and circumstance, Christ is to be followed, we must answer with Rahner: by dying with him.[13]

Second, following the Crucified, following Jesus in our dying, is not limited to the close of our earth-bound existence, to the terminal cancer, the cardiac arrest. Dying in a theological sense begins when living begins; we share in Jesus' dying by sharing in his cross through the whole of our lives. Not only physical pain — sinusitis, ileitis, hemorrhoids — but the agonies that are rather psychological and spiritual. I mean, concretely, the agonies that nail a priest to his crosses today: celibacy, criticism, cross fire, ineffectiveness, closures, burnout, fear, aging.

In these and other instances of what Rahner called "dying in installments," we confront the question, How do I cope? Do I just protest? Do I sulk? Do I nurse my grievances? Do I despair? Do I cling all the more desperately to what has not yet been taken from me? Or do I try to put my passion in touch with Christ's, "complete what is lacking in Christ's afflictions for the sake of his body, the Church" (Col 1:24)? Do I see such "breakdowns" as what Rahner terms "events of grace"?

In asking these questions of Chicago's priests, I was not prodding them into passivity, "Pile it on, Lord!" Nor was I speaking from an ivory tower. In my middle years there was bitter anguish — from bouts with hypochondria and scrupulosity, through the sudden deaths of my dearest friends Gustave Weigel and John Courtney Murray and the lingering psychic dying of my mother, to the traumatic death in 1974 of the Woodstock Theological Seminary that had housed my head and my heart till I neared sixty.

Ignatius Loyola, on his own admission, could have accepted in 15 minutes the destruction of his lifelong work, the Society of Jesus. It took me five or six years to come to terms with Woodstock's closing, to transcend the natural resentments, to fling away those unanswerable questionings about right and wrong, wisdom or folly, to focus

in my heart what I was preaching with my lips: Only Jesus is indispensable, Jesus alone is irreplaceable. In no other under heaven
is there salvation (Acts 4:12). True, never in the foreseeable future
will the Society of Jesus establish a similar Catholic presence on
Morningside Heights in New York, with little Woodstock admired,
accepted, and utilized by Columbia University, Union Theological
Seminary, and the Jewish Theological Seminary of America — and
this in large measure for its high intellectual attainments. But no
matter: God works in wondrous ways, paradoxical ways, God's purposes to attain. And I must confess that, had not Woodstock closed, I
would hardly have enjoyed the experiences of these last two decades,
culminating in the remarkably influential project Preaching the Just
Word. Let God be... be God. It's been a humbling realization, not
easily come by.

Third, following the Crucified may demand that we priests re-
think, refine, redefine what a down-to-earth spirituality involves. In
bygone days "Christian spirituality was conceived as an ascent to a
height of what was called 'Christian perfection,' with the ways and
stages of this ascent... outlined and marked out in advance by the
theology of the spiritual life."[14] Today the more experienced among
suffering servants are less likely to see the spiritual life as a master
plan for steady progress. It makes more sense, theological and spiritual, to see myself "as someone who is led by God's providence in
[my] life history through continually new and surprising situations,
in which [I] can never say from the outset what will happen and
how [I] must cope with it."[15] Genuine discipleship is more a matter of faithful following, not ever onward and upward, rather with
the courage to expect the unexpected, to respond to the unexpected
not from 3x5 file cards but in total openness to a Spirit who, like
Augustine's Beauty, is ever ancient, ever new.

It is then that the spiritual life becomes not a fearful scaling of icy
slopes with supernal crampons and axes, but a fascinating adventure
in which we can predict only two things with confidence: (1) The
Spirit will ceaselessly surprise us, and (2) however unexpected or
even crucifying the event, God will be there.

Fourth, such following of the Crucified renders priestly ministry
at once less difficult and more difficult. Less difficult because we do
not come to our sisters and brothers primarily with an articulate
theology, with a hatful of answers to all problems. We come as we
are, aware of our own brokenness, conscious that we are *wounded*
healers, far more effective with "the foolishness and the weakness of
God" (1 Cor 1:25) than with our own wisdom and strength. More

difficult because we must let our people see us as the people of Palestine saw Jesus: not in the glory we have with the Father, but in our self-emptying, in our "condition of a slave," in our "obedience that [means] death, even death on a cross."

Confidence

Paradoxically, dying on a cross should lead to confidence. The only genuinely Christian counterpole to the dying involved in celibacy and burnout, in criticism and closures, in fear and aging, is heralded in the mind-shivering paschal proclamation from the First Epistle of Peter:

> By [the Father's] great mercy He has given us a new birth into a living hope through the resurrection of Jesus Christ from the dead, and into an inheritance that is imperishable, undefiled, and unfading, kept in heaven for you, who are being protected by the power of God through faith for a salvation ready to be revealed in the last time. In this you rejoice, even if now for a little while you have had to suffer various trials, so that the genuineness of your faith — being more precious than gold that, though perishable, is tested by fire — may be found to result in praise and glory and honor when Jesus Christ is revealed. Although you have not seen him, you love him, and even though you do not see him now, you believe in him and rejoice with an indescribable and glorious joy, for you are receiving the outcome of your faith, the salvation of your souls. (1 Pet 1:3–9)

The point is, our Christ is alive. Alive now. More alive than I have ever been. And because Christ is alive, we have been born anew into a Christian hope. Not an Anglo-Saxon "stiff upper lip, old boy." Not wishful thinking: I hope the Serbs, the Croats, and the Muslims can shape a permanent peace. Christian hope is confident expectation — confidence that a God who is ceaselessly faithful despite our infidelities will always be there for us. Such is the hope that marked the earthly Jesus, the hope that, for all the tears in Gethsemane, left Calvary's tomb empty. With such hope we priests can cope with the fears and anxieties, the discouragement and near despair that plague priesthood in a perilous age bedeviled by change and uncertainty.

What I have been stressing to my brother priests is surely known to them intellectually but may not have penetrated their Christian guts. The hope we need if we are to confront our most profound fears and frustrations is not in the power of man or woman to provide. I am not defaming the psychiatrist's couch or the philosopher's portico; these have proven their human value, can even help us become more priestly. But in the last analysis the hope we need to live like Christ, to strengthen Christ's own crucified, is a gift of God, a gift that is actually part of our Christian make-up, a gift we paradoxical priests all too often leave untapped, commend to others but somehow allow to rust within ourselves. A *living* hope.

In recent years my own priestly hope has been deepened by the example of Mstislav Rostropovich. In February 1990, this conductor of the National Symphony Orchestra in Washington, D.C., returned to Russia after 16 years of exile.[16] He returned to give concerts, but even more importantly to heal — to begin healing political and personal wounds. Two decades before, when Aleksandr Solzhenitsyn was harassed for his books on the Soviet Gulag, Rostropovich and his wife Galina took him into their home. "Slava" also composed a letter attacking the censors who had banned Solzhenitsyn's work. Before sending it, he was tormented.

> For 48 hours after I wrote that letter, Galina did not sleep but cried. She told me, "You have the right to destroy yourself, but what right do you have to destroy my life and the lives of your daughters?" But after 48 hours, Galina tells me, "Without this letter, you will not be able to continue living." We agreed to send it. I said, "They can't break us." But she was right. She said they would break us, and they did. Totally.

Exile in the United States meant dying and rising. "For me, at 47, life ended. I was born anew on May 26, 1974. There was no continuity. I was truly like a newborn. I couldn't speak the language of the place I was in. I had no place to live. I had no real friends." But with the symphony a new career began. "This experience has made me emotionally twice as rich. I found a great deal more in music than I did when I lived in the Soviet Union. I re-examined everything, and I could see everything more vividly. All composers, even Beethoven, came to mean more."

Rostropovich's rebirth in the States is my prayer for priests today. I pray that their experience of fear or frustration, of anxiety or resentment, of desolation or despair may make them "emotionally twice as rich." I pray that they may find "a great deal more in [their priestly] music" than they ever did before. I pray that, re-examining everything, they may "see everything more vividly." I pray that all they do from now on, everything they experience, may come to "mean more," have a depth of meaning hitherto untapped. In brief, I pray that they too may be born anew into a living hope. A *living* hope.

Priesthood and Ministry

For my understanding and living-out of ministerial priesthood, I have been profoundly influenced by Jesuit John O'Malley's insistence (1) that the historiographical traditions which have determined how we understand the relations between priesthood, ministry, and religious life need to be reviewed and revised, for they have failed to take into account the *experience* of the Church; and (2) that evidence of this problem is graphically supplied by decrees of Vatican II.[17]

O'Malley has noted that *Presbyterorum ordinis,* the council's Decree on the Ministry and Life of Priests, makes three basic assumptions about the priest-minister. (1) The *parish* is normative for ministry. The priest-minister deals with a stable community, wherein a regular rhythm of liturgies of word and sacrament will be celebrated. (2) The priest-minister is dealing with the *faithful.* Consequently his training will be designed to prepare him precisely for that flock. (3) The priest-minister is all but defined by *hierarchical communion with his bishop.* [18]

These assumptions, O'Malley insists, are difficult to reconcile with the traditions of ministry in most religious orders. (1) Their ministry has transcended parish, diocese, even nation. (2) Orders have had a special interest in heretics, schismatics, and infidels, and, among the faithful, in those whom the Church's ordinary ministry has failed to reach. And their instruments of ministry have carried them beyond word and sacrament in their usual senses. (3) "[T]he priests of the great orders had no hierarchical relationship with the ordinary of the place, but had a fraternal, or capitular, or 'sect-type' relationship with their own ordinary."[19]

Christus dominus, the council's Decree on the Bishops' Pastoral Office in the Church, operates under the same three assumptions. In summary:

> There is one priesthood, which cannot be defined apart from the "episcopal order." That priesthood is concerned with the "care of souls," which has meant and still seems to mean primarily the ministry of pastors of parishes under the bishop.

Although religious orders of priests have in former times on occasion been forbidden such "care of souls," or, like the Jesuits, have explicitly renounced it in favor of other ministries, they now seem by virtue of their ordination almost to be destined for it. There seems to be, moreover, at least a suggestion that all "ministry of salvation" is reducible to "care of souls."[20]

The council, O'Malley maintains, did not take sufficiently into consideration the tradition of ministry and priesthood in the religious orders. It could not, for the pertinent history had not yet been helpfully done. The council "had little choice but to reduce religious life to the practice of certain forms of spirituality, some more 'active' than others. When religious do ministry, they may enhance it with a certain 'spirit,' but for all practical purposes they function as diocesan priests."[21] Calling for further historical study that would look not simply on what the Church has said but also on how the Church has acted, O'Malley proposed ten considerations as especially pertinent.[22]

1. Account must be taken of the fact that in the vast majority of orders and congregations founded since the thirteenth century, ministry has been at the center of their self-understanding.

2. At least since that time, two quite distinct traditions of ministry have given shape to the reality of priesthood in the Church — traditions which cannot be reduced simply to differences in spirituality.

3. A certain "division of labor" has prevailed between diocesan and regular clergy. The former have ministered primarily to the faithful through time-honored rhythms of word and especially sacrament; the latter, (*a*) to the faithful, but often in ways appropriate to special groups and circumstances, e.g., schools, soup kitchens, retreats, publications, street preaching; (*b*) to non-Catholics and public sinners.

4. This division of labor is not an accident of history; it reflects two traditions manifesting themselves with uneven beat but considerable consistency. The vocabulary differs: "office" and "parish" vs. "need" and "mission"; "hierarchy" vs. "fraternity"; "apostolic" as indicating a conduit of authority vs. suggesting a style of life and ministry.

For the first, ministry seems modeled on the Pastoral Epistles, the letters of Ignatius of Antioch, and the examples of Ambrose and Augustine. For the second, it seems modeled on Jesus and his disciples in the Synoptics, the itinerant Paul of

his letters and Acts, and the example of the charismatic layman (later deacon) Francis. In the one instance, the model
of the Church as sacrament seems especially operative; in the
other, the Church as herald. The former relates more easily to
"priest" — celebrant for the community and its public servant;
the latter more easily to "prophet" — spokesperson and agent
for special points of view.... [23]

5. With bishops and diocesan clergy the force of the first tradition
remains strong, is taken as normative, and in some cases admits of
no alternative. Its central concern: the parish as locus of ministry
par excellence.

6. Should such a tradition prevail utterly, it would impoverish
the Church and its larger mission. The "special" ministry of religious is needed today more than ever, with different forms and even
greater imagination and daring. Many of the faithful, too, are falling
through the cracks of "normative" ministry.

7. Should such a tradition prevail utterly, it would deprive most
religious of the center and meaning of their lives. "Ministry is not
something one adds to one's vocation as a Franciscan or Jesuit upon
ordination to the priesthood, but something that was central and
intrinsic from one's very first moment in the order, no matter how
imperfectly this might be expressed by the ceremony of the vows." [24]

8. The suggestion that Vatican II has uttered the final word on
these sensitive subjects suggests a prideful bias toward the present,
is even far from the council's own intent.

9. Therefore we need to recover the pragmatic approach to ministry that characterized our past but seems to be smothered today by
the "normative" or by some idealized model. "It is not our 'fidelity'
that today needs testing, but our creativity." [25]

10. The future of church ministry is hidden in God's mind. Perhaps even religious life itself has no future. In any event, we have to
think more adequately, act more appropriately, on priesthood, ministry, church order, and religious life *as these institutions actually
exist today.*

Recent Questioning

A recent book by Loyola Marymount University theology professor Thomas Rausch, *Priesthood Today: An Appraisal,* [26] has
compelled me to re-examine several aspects of priesthood I have
taken for granted ever since my undergraduate years at Woodstock.

Father Rausch has evaluated three models of priesthood: the sacral, the ministerial, and the representational, with the strengths and weaknesses he sees in each.

The sacral model, dominating Catholic understanding of priesthood from the twelfth century to Vatican II, sees the priest as a sacred person, set apart by ordination, in possession of special sacramental power, a mediator between God and God's people. It is Rausch's conviction that this "sacral concept of priesthood is not evident from the New Testament; it reflects a medieval sacralization of the priest's office, and it implies an inadequate concept of sacramental power."[27]

In point of fact, I am not impressed, or even surprised, by the absence of "priestly" terminology and "special powers" for the Church's ministers in the New Testament. As indicated earlier, we should not expect to discover a clearly formulated definition of Christian ministry at any given point in the New Testament. The theology of ministry, like every other facet of theology, was never frozen in Scripture; it underwent a process of development that even now is not finished. And granted that developments such as private celebration of the Eucharist, stress on abstinence from sexual intercourse before celebration of the Eucharist, and the law of celibacy tended to separate the priest from the community and "encouraged the notion of a priestly office with distinctive sacred duties";[28] granted that reducing priesthood to Eucharistic presidency "can lead to a false view of the priest as a person possessed of special powers," can be misinterpreted as a "type of magic"[29] — I am still convinced, with Avery Dulles, that "there are valid elements in this controverted [sacral] view."

> The official representative of the Christian community needs to be united to God in prayer and faith, well versed in the Scriptures, and ready to sacrifice himself, as Christ was, in the service of others. As a focal center for the community the priest must visibly be a sign and sacrament of Christ. Catholicism has perhaps a special responsibility to keep alive this sacral dimension of priesthood.[30]

No, the sacral model of priesthood does not in itself provide an adequate presentation of priestly ministry; it must be supplemented. But excesses do not justify jettisoning valid sacral dimensions of ordained ministry.

Still, the excesses reveal the need for another model to supplement the sacral, perhaps even to overshadow it. Some scholars find this in the ministerial model stressed by the Second Vatican Council. This model emphasizes leadership within the community, but leadership as service, *diakonia*. Here three critical dimensions singled out by Rausch commend themselves. (1) The priest must be in touch with the experience of community members: listen, interpret, give expression to it. Important because it means recognizing how God is acting in the community's life, what God is saying to its members. (2) He must be able to work collaboratively with others: with professionally trained lay ministers, with religious women, with well-educated laity on parish councils and committees. He should have a gift for empowering others to act decisively, to bring about change. (3) He must be able to challenge the community as a whole, and individuals within the community. Not by sheer authority; rather by the integrity of his own existence. Challenge them to prayerful living, to contemplation, to spiritual reading, to the faith that does justice. Such is priestly service.[31]

Other scholars, Avery Dulles for example, have proposed a representational model of priesthood. By their ordination, a sacrament that authorizes them to speak and act in Christ's name, bishops and priests are enabled to represent Christ to the Church.

Rather than delve more deeply into such genuinely theological explorations of priesthood, let me end this section with a personal word. I have insisted that the Catholic priesthood, like the Church herself, is constant at bottom and constantly changing. My half century and more of priesthood have told me at least two truths about priestly fidelity. First, we must be faithful to demands that are unchanging: Apostles, disciples, and presbyters, we must preach the word and preside at the Eucharist, help shape Catholic communities and serve the wider human family. Second — what is far more difficult and perilous — we must respond to a church in motion, a church on pilgrimage, a church that has asked many of us, halfway through our lives, to change. To change the way we think, the way we worship, the way we live. And without guaranteeing that each change will bring certainty to our minds, peace to our souls, joy to our hearts. Quite the contrary. I would be amazed if changes in the Church — liturgical directives, women servers, parish councils, closing of churches and schools, drastic drop in vocations, sacerdotal dropouts and priestly scandals, a host more — did not pose problems, rouse resentments, provoke many priests to ask if this is indeed the same church that washed our foreheads and oiled our fingers.

But here they are, thousands of them — perhaps bloody but only slightly bowed. From my involvement in Preaching the Just Word, moving from rock-bound Maine through a flood-devastated Midwest to quake-threatened California, I find that most are not just living in the '90s; they are alive. An encouraging number of them have moved into a new age, a strange age, a frightening age with enthusiasm and joy, because here is their ministry as the Church sees it *now;* here is where they try desperately to respond, in new ways, to the needs of a whole little world with more colors and smells, more problems and pressures, more anxiety and despair than the very human Jesus himself experienced.

Yes, I find our priests on the whole inspiringly faithful: faithful to what a priest must always be, faithful to what a priest should be now. I like to think of them in terms the New Testament uses of a God-chosen priest who must offer sacrifice for his own sins and for the sins of the people: "He can deal gently with the ignorant and wayward, since he himself is subject to weakness" (Heb 5:2). He can deal gently. I suggest that this is particularly true as the years roll on: as the body that once gloried in its strength wastes slowly or speedily away; as the mind that was so keen and fertile dulls and forgets; as the spirit that once prided itself on its own achievements looks back on its infidelities and bends in sorrow and love beneath the gentle hand of God. Yes, it is so much easier now to deal gently.

Fifty-eight years a priest, I stand week after week thankfully and humbly in the midst of my fellow priests. From experiences ecstatic and excruciating, I can sense to some extent what have been their Tabors and their Gethsemanes, the hills of their thrills and the gardens of their agonies. But no one save God and the individual priest really knows what the call to discipleship has cost him. I would only ask each to reflect on the thousands, most of them unknown to him, who are grateful to him for the impact he has had on their lives, who thank him in their hearts for playing Christ to them with such crucifying fidelity, for years of Godlike gentleness, for living each day the Eucharistic words of Jesus on the eve of Calvary, "This is my body [and it is] given for you" (Lk 22:19).

Priestly Preparation and Academic Excellence

Thirty-two years in seminary situations (Woodstock College and Catholic University), together with addresses to seminary students across the United States, have inevitably led me to a broad spectrum of conclusions about preparation for priesthood in our time. Here I focus on a single imperative: the intellectual life of a seminarian and priest, with special stress on diocesan clergy.

I am not subordinating the spiritual; without a profound spirituality the priest perishes. Unless the newly ordained departs the seminary with a system of prayer (e.g., meditation, contemplation, the prayer of quiet) congenial to his ministry, not only that ministry but his relationship to God is imperiled. I realize, too, that priestly ministry, in harmony with the ministry of Jesus, must concentrate on the neediest, on the most disadvantaged: the helplessly young and the brutally old, the poverty-stricken and the victim of AIDS, the mangled in mind and the crucified in flesh.

Cultural Climate and Historical Background

I am simply zeroing in on a dominant force in our cultural climate — dominant politically, economically, socially. I mean the educated. I mean those who make our laws and interpret them, make policy foreign and domestic, make peace and war; those who run our halls of learning and labs for genetics, our stock exchanges and chambers of commerce, our radio and TV, our newspapers and commercials. I mean our industry giants and our computer wizards. It is a developing, disturbing, challenging culture. It is a culture that in large measure reveals, in Robert Bellah's terms, a resurgence of late-nineteenth-century rugged individualism. Much (not all) of American society is moving away from older character ideals, away from religious man/woman and away from political man/woman, away from ideals that were oriented to the public world, the community, the common good, the other. A society that exalts economic man/woman, dedicated to "prudent self-interest."

Within this cultural climate we discover a Catholic laity with a degree of education unparalleled in the Church's history, a level of learning that resulted from the emphasis put on education by the immigrant Church. In this connection I recall some penetrating remarks by Archbishop Rembert G. Weakland over a decade ago:

One can debate about the quality of the education provided in some sectors, but the thrust and drive were always present and have reaped their rewards especially in the 40 years since World War II. At times we complained that the religious education of our laity did not keep pace with the level of their secular education, that our people were expected to take their place in society, business and academia with only grade-school religious training.... [B]ut the fact remains that our well-trained laity represents the finest asset we have in the American church today and is the source of its strength and vitality.... [32]

The tragedy, sympathetic scholars tell us, is that our Catholic body in this fair country has been more conditioned by the culture than an influence upon it. I shall discuss this at greater length in chapter 9. For the present, suffice it to say that in the United States we are witnessing (1) a widespread resurgence of rugged individualism and (2) an increasingly educated, sophisticated Catholic laity that (*a*) is the most powerful source of American Catholicism's strength and vitality and (*b*) may well be indistinguishable from the rest of the population in the "prudent self-interest" that motivates its living.

How does this cultural climate touch the intellectual life of the seminarian and priest? Granted, no priest is ordained precisely to be an intellectual, a scholar. We are ordained to be mediators between heaven and earth; to be channels of reconciliation between Christ and his ever so human images; to proclaim a gospel that consoles and sears; to pour living water over sinful brows, forgive frailty in the power of God, transform common bread into the flesh of the God-man, bless the bonding of man and maid, anoint enfeebled senses; to share, like Christ, our own brokenness, "deal gently with the ignorant and wayward" because we ourselves are "beset with weakness" (Heb 5:2).

Still, we are not ministering to men and women in a cultural vacuum. A major fault of priestly ministry in the nineteenth century was isolation from the intellectual movements outside the seminary and parish. Despite clerics like Spalding, Fenwick, and Ireland, most priests were ignorant of, some even hostile to, the intellectual currents that were sweeping across America, were alienated from the mainstream of society.[33] This despite the fact that "the priest of the immigrant was to his own people nothing short of an intellectual giant, skilled in theology but, because of his educational advantages, competent also to give advice on politics, law, education, mechanics, pharmacy, banking, and social reform."[34] The problem was, the intellectual efforts of the nineteenth-century priest were in large measure defensive, calculated to preserve religious and/or ethnic loyalties against secular or Protestant inroads.

As far back as 1893, Archbishop John Ireland warned us that too many Catholic leaders of thought were "slow to understand the new age in which they ministered, and too slow to extend to it the conciliatory hand of friendship. The churchman's work was to 'bridge the chasm separating the Church from the age.' " In that same sermon Ireland exulted, "I preach the new, the most glorious crusade. Church and age! Unite them in the name of humanity, in the name of God."[35]

If the nineteenth-century seminary and ministry were largely isolated from their age, the first five or six decades of the twentieth century give slender reason for rejoicing. Here the enemy was fear — fear engendered by Rome's reaction to Modernism (see chapter 2 above). What Michael Gannon wrote of 1908 could be repeated, by and large, into 1959:

> As 1908 proceeded on its course a gradually enveloping dread of heresy settled over episcopal residences, chanceries, seminaries, and Catholic institutions of higher learning. Security, safety, conservatism became national imperatives. Free intellectual inquiry in ecclesiastical circles came to a virtual standstill. The nascent intellectual movement went underground or died. Contacts with Protestant and secular thinkers were broken off. It was as though someone had pulled a switch and the lights had failed all across the American Catholic landscape.[36]

To recognize the isolation of most Catholic seminaries of our mid-century from the intellectual world around them, one need not subscribe to Andrew Greeley's brutal characterization of his own Mundelein days: "St. Mary of the Lake Seminary ... [was] a caricature of paradise, a sick institution, presided over by sick men and training priests many of whom would fit badly into the post-World War II society and even worse into the post-Vatican II world. Later they would leave the priesthood in droves."[37] It is nevertheless true that the best of seminaries, including my own beloved Woodstock, allowed into our cloisters and classrooms only so much of the non-Catholic world as had been predigested for us, summarized for us, censored for us.

It may be argued that, as early as 1949, John Courtney Murray declared that the task of the Catholic intellectual as a "missionary" to the "thickening secularist intellectual and spiritual milieu" had for initial responsibility "that of undertaking a comprehensive analysis of the present intellectual, cultural, and spiritual situation in its totality. If we are to interpret the world, as we must, even to itself, our first duty is to understand it, in detail, with full realism, under abnegation of the easy generalities with which the world is ordinarily denounced."[38] And yet, 12 years later, in 1961, at Marquette University, the Apostolic Delegate to the United States denounced contemporary efforts to build a bridge between secular and Catholic thought. In that context Egidio Vagnozzi spieled this exquisite piece of ecclesiastical trumpery: "Even if our bishops and priests cannot all be scholars..., with the long years of their seminary training, with the large amount of reading most of them do, they are equipped to understand and evaluate anything that the intellectuals can say and write about religion."[39] Embarrassment forbids commentary.

Intellectual Excellence

With the above as context — a culture impregnated with "prudent self-interest," a Catholic laity impressively educated and sophisticated, a (mainly diocesan[40]) clergy with little influence on the intellectual currents of society — I have asked myself and seminary residents: What specific intellectual contribution can the Catholic priest offer to his cultural climate? I submit that priesthood and its theological preparation would do well to wed three facets: *a profound thirst for understanding, seasoned by experience, and communicated with imagination.* A brief word on each.

Theology is indeed a search for understanding (see chapter 2 for details). I am not decrying praxis. I am simply claiming that "doing" theology, "doing" the truth, is not mindless warfare, not merely hand-to-hand combat with the powers of oppression political, social, and economic. It is the privilege of the priest and the priest-to-be to search out *where* God has spoken and acted, and is speaking and acting now; to search out *what* God has said and done, and might be saying and doing now: from the burning bush in Midian to the gas ovens in Auschwitz, from the word that was creation to the Word that was made flesh, from the Church gathered in council to the skin-and-bones dying that defecate at Calcutta's curbstones, from the Book that somehow reveals the heart of God to the trace of God on the face of all that is.

The search that is theology — the search for what it means to live and to love, to live and to die — should be a thrilling thing; but it will thrill young minds only if their teachers are themselves thrilled, only if the search never takes place in outer space, divorced from living men and women, cut off from the cultural climate that envelops the student. I recall, gratefully and fearfully, how a highly controversial figure urged his contemporaries not to be afraid to admit that theology, "so beautiful in itself, so engaging and vast," had become a lifeless subject, so dry as to be distasteful to students subjected to it. "Cut off from your course," he told the seminary authorities,

> many of the vain questions which tire them without results and which take away from them precious time they could spend more usefully learning about things applicable to the century in which they live and in the world on which they must act. Everything has changed around you; ideas have taken and continue to take new directions; institutions, laws, morals, opinions, nothing resembles what our fathers saw. Of what use is the most intense zeal without knowledge of the society in whose midst it must perform? We must learn with another method and learn more; with another method, to understand better, in order not to fall behind those for whose guidance we are responsible.[41]

A jeremiad from a disgruntled activist of America's roaring sixties? Hardly. The famous priest-philosopher Félicité de Lamennais. The year? 1829.

I am simply asserting that for effective priestly ministry academia at its fairest, at its most responsible, is an academia seasoned by experience. I am repeating in different rhetoric what Vatican II declared in its Decree on the Ministry and Life of Priests: "[You] cannot be ministers of Christ unless [you] are witnesses and dispensers of a life other than this earthly one. *But* [you] cannot be of service to men and women if [you] remain strangers to the life and conditions of men and women."[42] That experience does not begin and end in the seminary; it takes a lifetime of living. But if a seminary's priority is protection from "the world," if the seminary isolates theology in a vacuum, if seminarians are not inspired to touch theology to the cultures that shape their people, the institution may get grand grades from the Association of Theological Schools, but it will be difficult to justify its existence before Christ and his Church.

Indispensable as they are, however, understanding and experience are only the prelude to actual ministry. To minister is to serve. Not necessarily to teach theology; only a relatively few of the ordained serve in that fashion. But every priest is charged to take the theological understanding that is ceaselessly seasoned by experience and communicate it, share it, make it persuasive to a culture in danger of idolizing the mighty dollar and the almighty me. And here, I submit, in communicating what we know and experience, we fail miserably. Not all priests, but all too many. Why? As I have argued in the chapter on preaching, during my half century of ministry one lack appears to outstrip all others: By and large, we do not communicate with imagination. I cannot argue with conviction that the fault lies largely with our seminaries. I do believe, however, that if professors of theology were to sprinkle a dash of imagination — John Shea or C. S. Lewis — into every thesis, if professors of Scripture were to mimic in their lectures the word pictures of the Psalmist(s) and the intestinal fire of the Hebrew prophets, tomorrow's priests might well influence our culture more profoundly than we oldsters have succeeded in doing.

A final word. Back in 1971, that remarkably perceptive historian of things Catholic John Tracy Ellis was already convinced that the rising educational level of the Catholic community had rendered our priestly vocation uncommonly difficult. "The coming generations will almost certainly be as reluctant [as], if not more reluctant than, the present one to accept in the docile manner that was characteristic of their ancestors the authority of the Church's magisterium. The role of the priest will as a consequence be a more complicated one than that of his predecessors who were able to command unquestioned obedience."[43] Ellis proceeded to put the point in words penned by the British Catholic Douglas Woodruff at the close of Vatican II: "The priesthood of tomorrow, like the episcopate of tomorrow, is likely to find itself sharing many of the experiences long painfully familiar to Protestant parsons and bishops, that they are listened to selectively, approved and commended by those who like what they say, and politely disregarded by those in the pews who withhold their assent on that point."[44]

Prophetic words indeed. To this problem, as to several others I have raised, I have no assured solution. I do submit, however, that tomorrow's priest, today's seminarian, will speak increasingly to skeptical and selective ears if he does not leave the seminary with an enthusiasm for an intellectual apostolate that speaks to the cultures he is addressing. I do not mean a 4.0. I mean an agonizing thirst for understanding: understanding of our exciting gospel and our equally exciting God; an understanding sensitively touched to men and women not only as they ought to be but as they actually are; an understanding shared so imaginatively that Christians and non-Christians alike, people of contrasting cultures, are captured by the mystery and the magic that have captivated us.

NINE

From the Samaritan Woman to the Catholic Tomorrow

Apostolate of the Laity

In 1867 Msgr. George Talbot, adviser to Pope Pius X on English affairs, wrote a letter to the archbishop of Westminster, Henry Manning. That letter contained an important question and provided a provocative answer. "What," he asked, "is the province of the laity?" His answer: "To hunt, to shoot, to entertain. These matters they understand, but to meddle with ecclesiastical affairs they have no right at all."[1]

Almost a century later, in 1965, the bishops of the Catholic Church in solemn council proclaimed: "Let the laity not imagine that their pastors are always such experts that to every problem which arises, however complicated, they can readily give a concrete solution, or even that such is their mission. Rather, enlightened by Christian wisdom and paying close attention to the teaching authority of the Church, let the laity take on their own distinctive roles."[2]

The effort to shape a theology of the laity, to discern their "distinctive roles," is in large measure a twentieth-century development. The basic lay charter is a pregnant paragraph in Vatican II's Decree on the Apostolate of the Laity:

> The redemptive work of Christ, while of itself directed toward the salvation of men and women, involves as well the renewal of the whole temporal order. Consequently, the mission of the Church is not only to bring to men and women the message of Christ and his grace, but also to penetrate and perfect the temporal sphere with the spirit of the gospel. In carrying out this mission of the Church, the laity therefore exercise their apostolate in the temporal order as well as the spiritual. These areas, though distinct, are so intimately linked in the single plan of God that God Himself intends, in Christ, to take up

265

the whole world again and make of it a new creation, initially here on earth, consummately on the last day. In both areas the layperson, at once believer and citizen, should be guided ceaselessly by one and the same Christian conscience.[3]

It is not my intention to detail the complex history that has resulted in today's theology of the laity.[4] As in previous chapters, I prefer to focus on my own involvement in the process, my growth in understanding, my increasing appreciation of Cardinal John Henry Newman's reported response to a disparaging question about "all this nonsense" over laity in the Church: "All I can say is, the Church would look awfully strange without them."

A product of my times, I took the laity for granted — in my own lay days, in my Jesuit years with simple vows, and in the early decades of my ordained priesthood. When we said "the Church," we usually meant the so-called teaching Church, i.e., primarily the hierarchy, by delegation the rest of the clergy. We did indeed hear of a lay apostolate called Catholic Action,[5] but a cruel standing joke defined this as "the participation of the laity in the inactivity of the hierarchy." Rarely if ever did a preacher discourse on a lay vocation from the stirring words of 1 Peter 2:9: "You are a chosen race, a royal priesthood, a holy nation, God's own people, in order that you may proclaim the mighty acts of Him who called you out of darkness into His marvelous light."

In his first encyclical John Paul II had occasion to recall with gratitude the teaching of Pius XII on the Church as Christ's Mystical Body. There followed a paragraph highly significant for my purposes here:

> Membership in that body has for its source a particular call, united with the saving action of grace. Therefore, if we wish to keep in mind this community of the People of God, which is so vast and so extremely differentiated, we must see first and foremost Christ saying in a way to each member of the community: "Follow me." It is the community of the disciples, each of whom in a different way — at times very consciously and consistently, at other times not very consciously and very consistently — is following Christ. This shows also the deeply "personal" aspect and dimension of this society....[6]

Rather than abide in abstractions, I propose to suggest various ways in which I have experienced the laity answering the call to follow Christ, actually working to "exercise their apostolate in the temporal order as well as the spiritual," specifically to "penetrate and perfect the temporal sphere with the spirit of the gospel." And this through selected examples from history, especially several segments of history I have come to know and admire.

Scripture

In my search for forerunners of the laity in the Church, I came late in life to look to women of the New Testament, specifically in the Gospel of John.[7] Take the Samaritan lady at the well (Jn 4:5–42). Here is a woman with a genuine missionary function. What motivates Jesus to say that "the fields are ripe for harvesting" (v. 35)? Because so many Samaritans have left the city of Sychar "and [are] on their way to him" (v. 30), and this on the strength of what the woman has told them. "This is missionary language."[8] The harvest that is the Samaritans verifies the saying "One sows and another reaps" (v. 37). In Jesus' explanation to his disciples, "I sent [Greek verb *apostellein*] you to reap that for which you did not labor. Others have done the hard work, and you have come in for the fruit of their work" (v. 38).

> Whatever this may have meant in reference to the history of the Samaritan church, in the story itself it means that the woman has sown the seed and thus prepared for the apostolic harvest. One may argue that only the male disciples are sent to harvest, but the woman's role is an essential component in the total mission. To some extent she serves to modify the thesis that male disciples were the only important figures in church founding.[9]

The quasi-apostolic role given to a woman is even more striking in John 20. As Paul saw it, two conditions were imperative for apostleship: One had seen the risen Jesus and was sent to proclaim him. John revises the tradition that claimed Peter as the first to see the risen Jesus. In John 20:2–10 Peter and the Beloved Disciple run to the tomb, but they do *not* see Jesus. In John it is to Mary Magdalene that Jesus first appears, and she is sent by the risen Lord himself to proclaim the standard apostolic announcement of Jesus' resurrection, "I have seen the Lord" (v. 18).

> Small wonder that in some Gnostic quarters Mary Magdalene rather than Peter became the most prominent witness to the teaching of the risen Lord. And in Western Church tradition

she received the honor of being the only woman (besides the Mother of God) on whose feast the Creed was recited precisely because she was considered to be an apostle — "the apostle to the apostles" (*apostola apostolorum*).[10]

From his intensive investigations into these and other passages Raymond Brown confessed his surprise in discovering "to what extent in the Johannine community women and men were already on an equal level in the fold of the Good Shepherd. This seems to have been a community where in the things that really mattered in the following of Christ there was no difference between male and female — a Pauline dream (Gal 3:28) that was not completely realized in the Pauline communities."[11]

Patristic Age

In my reading of the evidence, the miraculous triumph of early Christianity was due in large measure to a radical sense of community.[12] Indispensable facets of this communitarian sense were a conviction and a practice: a conviction about the proper use of material possessions, and impressive practical aid to the needy. Here five themes were of paramount importance.[13]

First, Christianity had to transform the values of the Greco-Roman world it inhabited. Specifically, an attitude toward property, possessions. Listen to one early document: "Do not turn away from the needy; rather, share everything with your brother, and do not say, 'It is private property.' If you are sharers in what is imperishable, how much more so in the things that perish!"[14] The value? Sharing rather than possessing.

Second, to attain that attitude, a conversion of the human heart is indispensable. To become genuine Christians, the rich must become detached from their riches. Particularly impressive in this regard is Clement of Alexandria, who succeeded Pantaenus as head of the catechetical school in that cosmopolitan city about the year 200. His homily *The Rich Man's Salvation* is a courageous, realistic, if not always exegetically defensible effort to confront difficulties faced by the prosperous among the faithful in a narrow interpretation of such Gospel commands as "If you wish to be perfect, go, sell your possessions, and give the money to the poor" (Mt 19:21). He insists that the text cannot intend to exclude the wealthy from God's kingdom. What, then, does it mean? Simply, banish from your soul your "attachment" to wealth, your "excessive desire for it," your "diseased excitement over it." "Wealth is an instrument.... You can use it justly; then it will serve justice. If it is used unjustly, it will be the servant of injustice. So what is to be destroyed is not one's possessions but the passions of the soul, which hinder the right use of one's belongings...."[15]

What can motivate men and women to be at once affluent and poor in spirit? Love of God, love of Christ, love of one's sisters and brothers. Here a remarkably original thinker and writer, Origen, waxed passionate in his effort to liberate the rich from the acquisitiveness, the greed, that the early Church regarded as a form of idolatry:

> God ... knows that what a man loves with all his heart and soul and might — this for him is God. Let each one of us now examine himself and silently in his own heart decide which is the flame of love that chiefly and above all else is afire within him, which is the passion that he finds he cherishes more keenly than all others.... Whatever it is that weighs the heaviest in the balance of your affection, that for you is God. But I fear that with very many the love of gold will turn the scale, that down will come the weight of covetousness lying heavy in the balance.[16]

Third, basic to the fresh Christian attitude is a traditional patristic belief: God created the material universe for all humankind; the rich are essentially earth's stewards. Listen to a remarkably pastoral fourth-century bishop, Ambrose of Milan: "God has ordered all things to be produced so that there should be food in common for all, and that the earth should be the common possession of all. Nature, therefore, has produced a common right for all, but greed has made it a right for the few."[17] To Ambrose, the Old Testament tale of Ahab and Naboth (1 Kgs 21:1–29) is a human constant: "Ahab is not one person, someone born long ago; every day, alas, the world sees Ahabs reborn, never to die out.... Neither is Naboth one person, a poor man once murdered; every day some Naboth is done to death, every day the poor are murdered."[18]

Significantly, the Fathers denied not the right to private property but its greedy misuse. In John Chrysostom's words, the rich they attacked "are not the rich as such, only those who misuse their wealth."[19] Still, many of the fourth-century Church Fathers saw in private property a root of human dissension; in the struggle for possessions they found a subversion of God's original order. Listen to Chrysostom again: "When one attempts to possess himself of anything, to make it his own, then contention is introduced, as if nature herself were indignant, that when God brings us together in every way, we are eager to divide and separate ourselves by appropriating things, and by using those cold words 'mine and thine.' "[20]

Fourth, an especially powerful motive: the presence of Christ in — Christ identified with — the impoverished and disadvantaged. Here Chrysostom and Augustine wed practical theology and impassioned rhetoric. Chrysostom declares that the poor are more venerable an altar than the altar of stone on which the Sacrifice is offered, on which the body of Christ rests. "The altar [of stone] becomes holy because it receives the body of Christ; the altar [of the poor] because it is the Body of Christ. Therefore it is more awesome than the altar near which you, a layperson, are standing."[21] Little wonder that Chrysostom urged his people to cover the naked Christ before they ornamented his table, forbade them to make a golden cup for Christ while they were refusing him a cup of cold water. "Don't neglect your brother in his distress while you decorate his house. Your brother is more truly his temple than any church building."[22]

For Augustine, "love cannot be divided." Love the children of God, and you love the Son of God; love the Son of God, and you love the Father. Conversely, you dare not say, you cannot say, that you love Christ if you love not the members of Christ — all his members, without discrimination. And lest we think he is limiting our love to orthodox believers, Augustine insists that the love of Catholics must be utterly catholic — offered, that is, as the grace of God is offered, to all. Even to our enemies — "not because they are your brothers, but that they may become your brothers."[23] Some, Augustine sorrows, "would limit love to the land of Africa!" No, he protests. "Extend your love over the entire earth, if you would love Christ; for the members of Christ lie all over the earth."[24]

Fifth, the Church of Christ is a community of support and sharing. It is not only the poor, the disadvantaged, the marginalized that benefit from the generosity of the materially fortunate. The orphan and the aged and the widow, wearing what Clement of Alexandria called "the uniform of love," become "the spiritual bodyguard" of the rich — a return of love that could take many forms: nursing care, intercessory prayer, a kindly word of counsel, even a stinging word of protest.[25]

Why this excursion, this apparent digression, into the early Church as community? Because what made possible the gradual ethical, religious, and political transformation of the Roman Empire, what integrated Christian culture with the more admirable elements of Greco-Roman culture, was not simply or even primarily the Church's clergy, bishops and priests, pastors and preachers, indispensable as all of these were. It was the response of the community, the Christian people as a whole. The role the laity played can hardly be exaggerated. I mention simply four ways laypersons gave life to the early Church and helped to transform the temporal order: martyrdom, political power, monasticism, and theology. I can do little more than sketch the outlines of these complex issues as they touched especially, though not exclusively, the Christian laity.

Martyrs

Despite Rome's traditional toleration of all manner of religions, the two and a half centuries that stretched from Nero to the eve of Constantine are justifiably termed the Age of Martyrs. I mean martyrs like 13-year-old Agnes — beheaded, burned to death, strangled, we know not. I mean Perpetua and her pregnant slave Felicity, flogged and eventually beheaded, together with Perpetua's teacher Saturus and her fellow catechumens Revocatus, Saturninus, and Secundulus — "never forgotten in the African Church. The account of their act of testimony to the faith, which may well have been composed by Tertullian, was read and re-read during divine service down to the days of Augustine."[26] In the cruel, well-organized persecution under Decius (249 ff.), it is true that many Christians offered the prescribed sacrifice or through bribery and other means secured certificates attesting their sacrifice. Still, in every province of the empire there were men, women, and children who were put to death or died in prison. In Valerian's edict of 258 the leading laity in the Christian community were also included. Senators and members of the order of knights were to lose their rank and possessions; they could be executed, their wives banished, if they refused to sacrifice. Imperial officials in Rome and the provinces were threatened with forced labor and confiscation of possessions. The aim? To eliminate clergy and prominent community members, and so condemn their religion to insignificance.[27] "The proportion of laity among the victims of the persecution was not inconsiderable: it was probably quite large in Egypt and highest in North Africa."[28]

Politically Powerful

Significant, too, were Christians who held influential positions at court under Emperors Commodus and Septimius Severus. I mean the men and women of Roman senatorial families, whose commitment to Christianity was known to Septimius Severus, who vouched for their loyalty against the mob. I mean persons like the freedman Prosenes, private chamberlain under Caracalla. I mean Julia Mamaea, the gifted mother of Emperor Severus Alexander, a woman with decided leanings toward Christianity, who once sent for Origen to discuss religious questions. Her tolerance was reflected in her young son, who numbered many Christians among his closer associates and entrusted the building of the library near the Pantheon to the Christian Julius Africanus.

Monks and Ascetics

Significant, too, were hermits like Antony, generally considered the father of Christian monasticism, who spent most of his 105 years seeking a solitude his admirers and followers refused him.[29] Antony exemplifies an interesting development. Through the years of bitter persecution the most obvious witness to Christianity was the martyr. The martyr was the perfect imitator of Christ, the genuine disciple; martyrdom was the palpable proof of love. But as persecution slackened, martyrdom of blood became a specialized vocation reserved for a few. In the search for perfection, the emphasis shifted from a sacrifice of life to a life of sacrifice, a spiritual, day-to-day martyrdom where one renounced not life but the world, fought not beasts but the flesh, defied not an emperor but the devil. The Colosseum had given way to the desert, Ignatius to Antony. Each had offered God a total gift of self, a perfect act of love. Here was "the monk as martyr," often a protest against a culture that extolled having over being, possessing over sharing. In his *Life of St. Antony,* Athanasius calls him "a daily martyr to his conscience, ever fighting the battles of the faith."[30]

In my more mature patristic years I was particularly struck by dedicated Christian women in the fourth century "who had embraced...an extreme type of asceticism modelled, as far as circumstances allowed, on the ideals and practices of the famous desert fathers of Egypt."[31] Two of them, Paula and Marcella, aristocratic widows, each a group leader, became fast friends of St. Jerome, as did Paula's daughters Eustochium and Blesilla, as well as Lea, an intimate friend of Marcella's. Such women, as Jerome's letters reveal them,

> provide an illuminating glimpse of what committed Christianity had come to mean for some enthusiastic believers, mainly

women, in Rome between the sixties and eighties of the fourth century. Jerome speaks of "monastic vocation" and calls Lea "the leader of her monastery"; and while formal organization under a rule had yet to come, they were effectively nuns for most practical purposes. For them all, dwelling in their stately houses, meeting for Bible study, and stealing away unobserved to the basilicas or the martyrs' tombs for worship, the Christian ideal found expression, in degrees varying with each individual, in withdrawal from ordinary society, prolonged and rigorous fasting, the wearing of coarse, even squalid clothing, the neglect of personal appearance, and the avoidance of comforts like baths, above all in chastity — the elimination as far as possible of the sexual element.[32]

I was especially intrigued by the foundations established in Bethlehem by Jerome and Paula, made possible by her wealth. The first was a monastery for men, with Jerome in charge; then came a convent for women. (I find it fascinating that Jerome "saw the monk, *like the martyr,* undergoing a second baptism, a total immolation of self which cleansed him from all the sins committed since the first."[33]) Despite barbarian invasions, these two institutions flourished, and they were the homes of Paula, Eustochium, and Jerome until they died. When Paula died and Eustochium took charge, the convent had some 50 nuns.

Rarely mentioned in this connection is the independence implicitly declared by women such as Paula. Like other female ascetics, she determined for herself what her vocation in life was meant to be. Yes, she found in Jerome a spiritual and intellectual guide, co-operated with him in their monastic adventure, but was never subservient. Though Jerome was a priest and Paula a nun, their relationship was an early example of male-female collaboration on a level of equality.

Theologians

During most of the twentieth century, patristic theology focused all but exclusively on the *Fathers* of the Church, with some attention to important ecclesiastical writers whose orthodoxy and/or holiness have been questioned. Not generally realized is that a not insignificant number of these early authors were laymen or wrote some of their works before embracing the clerical state. Justin Martyr was an itinerant teacher/philosopher; Origen was about 45 when he was ordained, and 15 years earlier had preached in Palestine with episcopal permission; Prosper of Aquitaine, defender of Augustine, was a layman all his life.

A recent movement would love to see proper recognition given to "Mothers" of the early Church, women of Christian antiquity distinguished for the significance of their Christian writing and/or Christian living. One example is Etheria (or Egeria), originally from Galicia, "a cultivated lady who belonged to a community which resembled a beguinage more than a monastery."[34] In the form of a letter sent from Constantinople between 383 and 418, her *Itinerarium* or *Peregrinatio ad loca sancta* provided her "sisters" back home with a detailed account of her travels in Egypt, Palestine, and Mesopotamia, with valuable information on the holy places and the liturgy of Jerusalem, and on the organization of monastic life and the hierarchy.[35] It is a unique document for its time, providing data on the liturgical year and its feasts, the daily liturgy with the rhythm of the offices, the recitation of the Psalter, the discipline of fasting, and the catechesis of the catechumens.

St. Macrina the Younger, sister of Basil the Great and Gregory of Nyssa, superior of one of the earliest communities of women ascetics, played an important role in the development of communities for women. In his "life" of her, Gregory depicts her as the model of the spiritual mother in the convent on the banks of the river Iris; the biography is a precious piece of early hagiographic literature. Similarly, St. Melania the Younger, ascetic granddaughter of St. Melania the Elder, an heiress to great wealth. Not only did she encourage the spread of ascetical movements; she founded a convent for nuns on the Mount of Olives, as well as a monastery nearby.

Regrettably, the theology of the early Church did not match up to the reality. For if originally the Greek term *laikos* was simply a way of designating that segment of the Christian population which had no leadership role in the community and exercised no cultic function, it was not long before a term meant to distinguish "came to connote subordination, inequality."[36] The development affected not only authority and power but spirituality as well. For once the sacred became the realm of the clergy, the laity were linked to the temporal, the "profane." And when holiness was understood as flight from the world, from the turf of the laity, the ordinary layperson had to be content with "the way of the commandments."

Middle Ages

In contrast to the highly positive meaning of *laos* in the New Testament and *laikos* in the infant Church, i.e., a member of the people of God, clergy and laity alike, the medieval *laicus* was strongly juridical, an antonym of *clerus,* synonymous with "unconsecrated" or "one under authority."[37] "The great medieval authors had little time for the layman; when they did mention him, it was usually to stress his subordination to the clergy or to note his excesses."[38] The attitude provoked by this dualistic concept of membership in the Church was crystallized in Gratian's influential *Duo sunt genera christianorum* ("There are two kinds of Christians"). It is amusingly scandalous to read of married bankers and merchants in Arras taking the tonsure to escape secular justice against their financial misdoings.

If it is a mistake to identify lay with uneducated in the Middle Ages, it is still true that the learned layman as a prominent figure in society dates from the early twelfth century onward, when such figures flourished in the Roman law schools and universities of southern Europe.

> But lay education was directed principally to secular subjects. There was nothing in the later Middle Ages to equal lay influence in the early Church, when a large number of the Fathers began their theological work as laymen, e.g., SS. Cyprian, Basil, Gregory Nazianzus, Jerome, and Augustine. Significantly, the majority of these belonged to the Eastern Church, where the tradition of the lay theologian had never died. Institutionalism in the West led to the idea that the study of the sacred sciences belonged to the clergy, and that of the profane to the laity.[39]

The medieval approach to the laity culminated in the ecclesiology of Vatican I. A pertinent section of the first draft of the Constitution on the Church of Christ, not an official document because the council adjourned before it could be decreed, is still of high significance because it embodies points considered ripe for definition. "The Church of Christ is not a community of equals in which all the faithful have the same rights. It is a society of unequals, not only because among the faithful some are clerics and some are laymen, but particularly because there is in the Church the power from God whereby to some it is given to sanctify, teach and govern and to others not."[40]

Modern Emphases

My own more mature approach to laity within the Church began with Vatican II. There I discovered a significant shift in ecclesiology. No longer was the Church's essence identified purely and simply with its hierarchical element. Avery Dulles stressed this pointedly back in 1966. "Instead of beginning with a discussion of the structures and government of the Church — as was the tendency at Vatican I — the Constitution [on the Church] starts with the notion of the Church as a people to whom God communicates Himself in love. This provides an excellent foundation for a new and creative approach to the role of the laity in the Church." In chapters 2, 4, and 5 "the dignity and responsibilities of lay Christians are presented in an inspiring manner." Authority is "viewed in terms of service rather than domination. In many respects the Constitution strikes a 'democratic' note." "[T]he Church as a whole, including the laity, has a total task which may suitably be summarized under the three captions of witness, ministry, and fellowship," the Greek New Testament's *martyrion, diakonia,* and *koinōnia*.[41] I was particularly impressed by the council's insistence that the whole People of God "shares in Christ's prophetic office." How?

> It spreads abroad a living witness to him, especially by means of a life of faith and charity and by offering to God a sacrifice of praise.... [The Holy Spirit] distributes special graces among the faithful of every rank. By these gifts [the Spirit] makes them fit and ready to undertake the various tasks or offices advantageous for the renewal and upbuilding of the Church....[42]

Intrinsic to this approach is a twin realization: (1) The Catholic Church is not two churches, or a two-storied church: clerical and lay. There is only one church, which all without exception enter through baptism. (2) The division between cleric and lay is not primarily a question of power vs. powerlessness. Each, cleric and lay, is a servant: a servant of Christ, of the gospel, and of the community.

In harmony with Vatican II, I have insisted, with voice and pen, that penetrating our culture with the spirit of the gospel, transforming our earth into a realm of justice, peace, and love, is specifically the task of the laity. I have often made bold to declare that, if council documents fail to convince the laity, a typically perky paragraph from imaginative Jesuit William O'Malley might carry the day:

We can no longer depend on the comforting simplism of "The Church Teaching" and "The Church Taught"; there are too many Ph.D.'s out in the pews now. The magisterium and the People of God are now like Henry Higgins and Eliza Doolittle at the end of "Pygmalion." He had found a tatterdemalion flower girl and turned her into a lady. But once the metamorphosis took place, neither Higgins nor Eliza knew quite what to do about the new relationship. He was no longer the all-knowing teacher, and she no longer the biddable pupil. Not only does the official church have an obligation to listen more to the people, but the people have the intimidating obligation to speak up....[43]

And so I've urged in season and out of season: Evangelizing Elizas, speak up! You are not substitutes for a decimated priesthood, to be returned to the sidelines if and when vocations to the first team blossom again. This is your God-given turf. Take hold of it — with all due modesty if you can, aggressively if you must.

Freedom to Minister

Still, Vatican II's theology of the laity is far from endowing the laity with the freedom necessary if they are to play their role effectively. One inadequacy among several has been strongly phrased by Georgia Keightley:

[E]ven if all were agreed that the world belongs principally to the laity, there is considerable question about the degree to which the hierarchy is willing to respect the former's right to discern what in effect constitutes the Catholic way. The council clearly states that because of their familiarity and expertise the laity are best suited to mind the world and its affairs (L.G. 31, 36). Yet...several texts caution that pastors alone have the right to judge the authenticity and proper use of lay charisms (A.A. 3). Furthermore, clergy are obliged to "clearly state the principles concerning the purpose of creation and the use of temporal things" (A.A. 7). This last suggests that in the final analysis, the council fathers could not bring themselves to grant lay persons full autonomy in their dealings with the world. The council's ambiguity at this point proves to be a source of continuing tension today: the conflict between lay "expertise" and clerical "discernment" reveals itself in the disputed areas of sexuality, attitudes towards the arms race and American economic policies, and the Catholic responsibilities of elected officials.[44]

Opportunities for lay ministry have indeed opened up since the council. Men and women alike serve as readers, acolytes, extraordinary ministers of the Eucharist. With the shortage of priests, laity take primary ministerial responsibility for a number of parishes. In several dioceses laypersons are chancellors; in many, laity fill important positions on tribunals. Fear has been expressed that to the extent such *ad intra* activity increases, two disadvantages may result: a clericalization of the laity and a devaluation of critical tasks *ad extra*.[45]

In the context of my project Preaching the Just Word, my own primary problem is related to the disadvantages mentioned but is somewhat different. My experience touches the problem on two levels. First, only a small proportion of Catholics engage in activities generally recognized as forms of lay ministry. They are the men and women who proclaim (and sometimes preach) the Word, distribute Communion, visit the ill and the jailed, and those who serve in national, diocesan, and parish offices such as education, social justice, peace, marriage tribunal, catechesis, Respect Life, and so on. The thesis that each and every baptized Christian is on mission has not captured lay Catholicism. Many are content to leave "Catholic action" to representatives. It is an approach that has been amusingly assailed by lay activist Ron Krietemeier. Who, he asks, would feel no need to participate in Sunday Eucharist because a group of dedicated Catholics represented them there? And yet that is precisely what the vast majority of Catholics do where, say, social justice is at issue.

A problem: The lives of most adult Catholics are so burdened, so complicated, by two-parent employment, financial worries, and internal family struggles that regular involvement in ecclesial issues is rarely feasible. It may well be that we must focus more intently on our youth, whose capacity for imaginative ministry and desire to serve have not been exploited within Catholicism with nearly the vigor of, for example, the Mormons.

My second problem has to do with a failure to recognize the extent of the word "ministry." Here I have recently been intrigued by an apparent contradiction between canon law and actual practice. Canon 207 #1 states: "Among the Christian faithful by divine institution there exist in the Church sacred ministers, who are also called clerics in law, and other Christian faithful, who are also called laity."

And yet, all over the world, laity are said to share in the Church's ministry, are called, e.g., extraordinary ministers of the Eucharist.

Dominican theologian Thomas O'Meara has perceptively asked, "How is the ordained secretary of the chancery in the ministry while the educated, full-time Christian employed in the team ministry in the urban hospital only in the lay state?" He insists that the solution to dozens of such paradoxes "can only come from a coherent theology of the ministry which replaces the clergy-laity structure with a group of concentric circles." He quotes Yves Congar describing how this shift took place in his thinking after 1970:

> I have come to see that the pastoral reality described by the New Testament imposes a view much richer [than a clerical church and a laicized world]. It is God, it is Christ who in his Spirit does not cease building the church.... The church is not built up merely by the acts of the official ministers of the presbytery but by many kinds of services, more or less stable or occasional, more or less spontaneous or recognized, some even consecrated by sacramental ordination. These services exist... they exist even if they are not called by their real name, ministries, nor have their true place and status in ecclesiology. Eventually one sees that the decisive pair is not "priesthood-laity" as I used in my book on the laity but much more that of "ministries or services and community."[46]

Pertinent here is an August 15, 1997, Instruction from eight Vatican offices, "Some Questions regarding Collaboration of Nonordained Faithful in Priests' Sacred Ministry."[47] A quotation from John Paul II, within the Instruction, on the proper use of the word "ministry" may raise lay hackles.

> 1. For some time now, it has been customary to use the word *ministries* not only for the *officia* (offices) and *munera* (functions) exercised by pastors in virtue of the sacrament of orders, but also for those exercised by the lay faithful in virtue of their baptismal priesthood. The terminological questions become even more complex and delicate when all the faithful are recognized as having the possibility of supplying — by official deputation given by the pastors — certain functions more proper to clerics which nevertheless do not require the character of orders. It must be admitted that the language becomes doubtful, confused and hence not helpful for expressing the doctrine of the faith whenever the difference "of essence and

not merely of degree" between the baptismal priesthood and the ordained priesthood is in any way obscured.

In some cases, the extension of the term *ministry* to the *munera* belonging to the lay faithful has been permitted by the fact that the latter, to their own degree, are a participation in the one priesthood of Christ. The *officia* temporarily entrusted to them, however, are exclusively the result of a deputation by the church. Only with constant reference to the one source, the "ministry of Christ" (...) may the term *ministry* be applied to a certain extent and without ambiguity to the lay faithful, that is, without it being perceived and lived as an undue aspiration to the ordained ministry or as a progressive erosion of its specific nature.

In this original sense the term ministry (*servitium*) expresses only the work by which the church's members continue the mission and ministry of Christ within her and the whole world. However, when the term is distinguished from and compared with the various *munera* and *officia,* then it should be clearly noted that only in virtue of sacred ordination does the word obtain that full, unequivocal meaning that tradition has attributed to it.[48]

The Instruction then continues on its own:

3. The nonordained faithful may be generically designated *extraordinary ministers* when deputed by competent authority to discharge, solely by way of supply, those offices mentioned in Canon 230.3[49] and in Canons 943 and 1112. Naturally, the concrete term may be applied to those to whom functions are canonically entrusted, e.g., catechists, acolytes, lectors etc.

Temporary deputation for liturgical purposes — mentioned in Canon 230.2 — does not confer any special or permanent title on the nonordained faithful.

It is unlawful for the nonordained faithful to assume titles such as *pastor, chaplain, coordinator, moderator* or other such similar titles which can confuse their role and that of the pastor, who is always a bishop or priest.[50]

Not unexpectedly, and not without some justification, parts of the document, specifically the final paragraph, have generated confusion in the practical order and raised troubling questions. Not call a nonordained man or woman a chaplain, a co-ordinator, a moderator? I am convinced that an updated ecclesiology demands the "more coherent theology of the ministry" advocated by O'Meara and Congar.

Lay Ministries to the World

Let me concretize Congar's conviction. In chapter 12 I shall argue, at some length, that Catholic healthcare facilities — medical centers, hospitals, hospices, nursing homes, care residences for the AIDS-afflicted — are in point of fact lay apostolates. Lay because in overwhelming measure the staff is lay, including the religious sisters. Apostolates to the extent that their staffs — from CEOs to doctors and nurses to maintenance personnel — are committed to the service of ailing images of God working out their redemption at a crucially significant moment of their existence. Not always curing, but always capable of healing. Ministers? Canonically, no; in actuality, yes. But "sacred" ministers? Here I suggest that we are still struggling to uncover where the sacred ends and the secular begins.

In this chapter I shall concentrate on a profession that in recent years has been the object of intense criticism, the butt of savage jokes, but merits a more objective analysis from the standpoint of ministry.

Law as Ministry

As I see it, Christian lay ministry to the world has rich potential in the legal profession, among justices, judges, and lawyers. Justice is a word central to their profession. They see to it that just laws foster the common good, that human rights written into law are protected, that the scales of Lady Justice are not weighted in favor of the rich and powerful, that men and women remain innocent until proven guilty, that the punishment fits the proven crime. Their burden is precisely to give others what is their due, not to be swayed from justice by love or sentiment, by anything less than the law on their books or the need to correct injustice. In a sense their goddess is the Roman Justitia, the lady with scales and a sword, her eyes blindfolded or closed in token of impartiality. A proud profession indeed, for without them "America the beautiful" would be a nation in anarchy, a country uncommonly unfree. "Equal before the law" is still an ideal, but largely because of the legal profession we are moving slowly if not relentlessly toward it.

True, America's legal hands are not lily-white. We look back with shame on a Dred Scott decision that declared slaves to be property.

We blush that in this "land of the free" women have been second-class citizens, that it is taking us longer to free women than to free the slaves. We weep because justice is so slow, weep when human beings rot in jail for months before they can be tried, weep when the men and women in prison return to society more brutal than before. We get cynical when the powerful can delay or gerrymander justice. And the majority in the profession must surely agonize over colleagues for whom the law is a game whose name is victory or wealth, where the prize goes to the brilliant and the prestigious, to the crafty and the manipulator.

Last but hardly least, surely the Catholic lawyer must react with outrage at the Supreme Court's historic decisions on abortion of January 22, 1973 (*Roe* v. *Wade* and *Doe* v. *Bolton*): its misuse of the Constitution, its faulty logic, its schizoid style of judicial interpretation, its utilitarian evaluation of life, its denial of personhood to the viable fetus, its misleading use of history, its defective anthropology, and much else besides.[51]

Still, the law is a justifiably proud ministry — especially because its practitioners are servants. And service has an honorable history. It goes back to ancient Athens, where the Greek word we translate as "liturgy" meant a burdensome public office or duty which the richer citizens discharged at their own expense — a service for the polis, for the commonwealth, for the people or the state. Service goes back to an Abraham who at God's command left country and kindred, "not knowing where he was going" (Heb 11:8), knowing only that he was called to shape "a great nation" (Gen 12:2). Service goes back to a Jesus who told us he "came not to be served but to serve" — in fact, "to give his life" for others (Mt 20:28). Service goes back to the best of popes, who gloried in the title "servant of the servants of God." Service goes back to lawyers like St. Thomas More, who died merrily on the scaffold declaring himself "the king's good servant, but God's first."

Bench, bar, schools of law, yes Supreme Court, all are servants. And they serve not an abstract quality called justice; they serve their own flesh and blood. At times it must be a strange, unsettling service. For some serve by prosecuting the insider trader and the murdering mafioso, the Weavers and the Wacos; others, by defending them. Sometimes they serve by shackling a sister or brother for months or years, sometimes by lifting the shackles that imprison them. Some hassle us for the IRS (what an African-American lady called the "e-ternal revenue service"), others keep corporations from being taxed to death. Constantly our legal minds confront one another;

ceaselessly they bedazzle juries and bewilder Jesuits with their rhetoric; now they may even compete for bodies on the boob tube. And every so often they prove to 12 good folk and true that one of their own flesh and blood deserves to die, should inhale a lethal gas or suffer a fatal injection.

All this they do for one overriding purpose: the common good. Not that the individual is unimportant, a slavish subject of the state, imprisoned to the whim or will of the majority. Not that the common good is a reality easily grasped. For even if we say, in broad terms, that the common good is the sum total of those conditions of social living whereby men and women are enabled to achieve their own perfection more fully and more readily,[52] even if we say more simply that the purpose of human law is "the well-being of the people and the public welfare of the political community,"[53] the common good is not static; it grows, it changes with changes in social conditions. And that calls for ceaseless discernment within the profession. Still, rather than detour in that direction, let me suggest that the privilege and the burden of our Christian minister-at-law has been captured in characteristically distinguished rhetoric by John Courtney Murray in a discussion of "The Civilization of the Pluralist Society." The passage deals with a wider society than the law, but it strikes me as peculiarly applicable to that profession.

The distinctive bond of the civil multitude is reason, or more exactly, that exercise of reason which is argument.

Hence the climate of the City is likewise distinctive. It is not feral or familial but forensic. It is not hot and humid, like the climate of the animal kingdom. It lacks the cordial warmth of love and unreasoning loyalty that pervades the family. It is cool and dry, with the coolness and dryness that characterize good argument among informed and responsible men [and women]. Civic amity gives to this climate its vital quality. This form of friendship is a special kind of moral virtue, a thing of reason and intelligence, laboriously cultivated by the discipline of passion, prejudice, and narrow self-interest. It is the sentiment proper to the City. It has nothing to do with the cleavage of a David to a Jonathan, or with the kinship of the clan, or with the charity, *fortis ut mors,* that makes the solidarity of the Church. It is in distinct contrast with the passionate fanaticism of the Jacobin: "Be my brother or I'll kill you." Ideally, I suppose, there should be only one passion in the City — the passion for justice. But the will to justice, though it engages the heart, finds its measure as it finds its origin in intelligence, in a clear understanding of what is due to the equal citizen from the City and to the City from the citizenry according to the mode of their equality. This commonly shared will to justice is the ground of civic amity as it is also the ground of that unity which is called peace. This unity, qualified by amity, is the highest good of the civil multitude and the perfection of its civility.[54]

In a 1995 lecture celebrating the 125th anniversary of the Georgetown University Law Center, I recommended that passage to the students and faculty for a meditation "some disenchanted evening." For it stems from a master of what Murray called "civilized conversation," and it touches at a profound level the high vocation that is law: a passion for justice, rooted in a clear understanding of what is due to the City and the citizen. Shall we refuse the title "ministry" to such a service, especially when it stems from the two primary commandments of the Mosaic law and the Christian gospel?

Lay Spirituality

A rising demand since Vatican II has been the call for a distinctive lay spirituality. Many of the observations I made in the chapters on justice/injustice and Jesuit spirituality (e.g., experience of God, finding God in all things, and devotion to our Lady) have pertinence here, but the area must be specifically addressed, even if not adequately covered. It is true, Ignatius Loyola directed many laypeople in his Spiritual Exercises long before his ordination, with a spirituality not at all monastic but focused on the "contemplative in action." Still, he could hardly have conceived of a Catholic laity as numerous and culturally diverse as that of the late-twentieth century, where scientific sophistication coexists with woeful ignorance, "overpopulation" with perhaps 50 million abortions a year; where the call for unprecedented freedom clashes with institutionalized serfdom, feminism with traditional roles for women; where Ignatius' Rules for Thinking with the Church must do mortal battle with an aggressive confrontation with hierarchical authority; where insistence on a faith that does justice seems hypocritical to those who organize for rights *within* the Church. The demand for a profound and practical lay spirituality challenges the Ignatian director (and others as well) perhaps more insistently than ever in our past.

Where to begin? In chapter 6, on Jesuit Spirituality, I noted Louis J. Cameli's 12-step program to dispose a man or woman to receive ever more fully the transforming power of the Spirit. While endorsing those practical steps, I suggest three broad themes of a Catholic spirituality I have found useful for social justice[55] but regard as significant for Catholics as a whole. In brief, a spirituality for Catholic lay ministry must be biblical, ecclesial, and Eucharistic.

First, a lay spirituality should be rooted in Scripture. Not only because all Christian spirituality should be based on the privileged source of God's self-revealing to us, stemming ultimately from God's Word. Specifically because the loving activity on behalf of others that supplements our belief and worship, the justice that is our fidelity to God, to people, and to the earth, must inescapably be linked to the God whose very nature it is to be just. In a special way because the Hebrew Testament and the New Testament (1) reveal the profound meaning of justice, (2) declare God's preferential option for the poor, and (3) relate justice to God's judgment on us in this life and the next.

Much of this I discussed in chapter 5. At this point I would stress what is still depressingly lacking in the wider Catholic community: a passionate love for Scripture, affective contemplation of Scripture, living in Scripture like an atmosphere in which we are bathed. It does not demand exegetical scholarship, important as such scholarship is for any Christian community. I am still impressed by Luther's recognition of the inadequacy of sheer scholarship — and this after his study of the Psalms and Romans, Galatians and Hebrews between 1515 and 1517 had transformed his theology:

> ...No one else can understand except a mind that contemplates in silence. For anyone who could achieve this without commentary or interpretation, my commentaries and those of everyone else would not only be of no use, but merely a hindrance. Go to the Bible itself, dear Christians, and let my expositions and those of all scholars be no more than a tool with which to build aright, so that we can understand, taste and abide in the simple and pure word of God; for God dwells alone in Zion.[56]

Second, a lay spirituality must be ecclesial. Why? Because it takes place within a distinctive community, within the Church Jesus founded to continue the work of salvation he began in Bethlehem and brought to a high point on Calvary. What he said to 11 apostles the day of his resurrection, he says to each baptized Christian: "Peace be to you. As the Father has sent me, so I send you" (Jn 20:21). Send you not as rugged individualists, but as part and parcel of a people, members of a body where, as St. Paul insisted, no one, absolutely no one, can say to any other, "I have no need of you" (1 Cor 12:21). A body wherein the gifts vary (wisdom, knowledge, healing, miracles — yes, administration that tied Ignatius Loyola to a desk, personal involvement that brought Dorothy Day to live and sleep with the rat-infested), but the Giver is the same (the same Holy Spirit living within Christians and ceaselessly shaping the one body).

Negatively, this means that a lay spirituality is not properly developed in a sheer me-and-Jesus relationship. That relationship is indeed vital, indispensable. As Jesus told his disciples the night before he died, "I am the vine, you are the branches. Those who abide in me and I in them bear much fruit, because apart from me you can do nothing" (Jn 15:5). Still, ever since the Holy Spirit descended upon the infant Church at the first Pentecost, St. Paul's declaration to the Christians of Corinth is basic for Christian living: "In the one Spirit we were all baptized into one body — Jews or Greeks, slaves or free — and we were all made to drink of one Spirit" (1 Cor 12:13). Of that body Jesus is indeed the head, but he is head of a living body, and it is within this body that God's grace circulates like a blood stream. Not only are the sacraments, from the waters of baptism to the final oiling, communal experiences that bring the Church together, encounters with Christ in the context of the community. By God's gracious giving, we Christians are commissioned to be channels of grace to one another.

Third, a lay spirituality at its best is Eucharistic. This demand stems from a principle that has been central to Catholic theology and was reaffirmed by Vatican II:

> The liturgy is the summit to which the Church's activity is directed; at the same time it is the source from which all her power proceeds.... The renewal in the Eucharist of the covenant between the Lord and humans draws the faithful into the compelling love of Christ and sets them afire. From the liturgy, therefore, and especially from the Eucharist, as from a fountain, grace is channeled into us, and that sanctification of men and women in Christ and the glorification of God, to which all other activities of the Church stretch and strain as toward their goal, are most effectively achieved.[57]

Begin with that truth of Eucharistic theology, exaggerated as it may sound to untutored ears, and we begin to see how the Eucharist can transform us into eucharists for the life of our world. For what is the Eucharist? It is a presence, a presence of Christ; a real presence;

a presence of the whole Christ, body and blood, soul and divinity; a presence that stems from love, the love of a God-man; a presence that leads to love, a crucified love for every man and woman born into this world. This Eucharist can make of us, demands of us that we become, genuine eucharists. For it demands that we be present to our sisters and brothers; really present; a presence of the whole person, not only mind and money but flesh and spirit, emotions and passions; a presence that springs from our unique love, loving others as Jesus loves us; a presence that leads to love in the women and men we serve.

Once again I am reminded of Dorothy Day, Communist-turned-Catholic, with her houses of hospitality and her bread lines; walking picket lines, jailed for supporting Mexican itinerant workers, squaring off against a New York cardinal in defense of cemetery strikers; arguing passionately that the poor do *not* have the gospel preached to them; living with the criminal, the unbalanced, the drunken, the degraded; reflecting with Dostoevsky that "Hell is not to love any more"; loving the Church that was so often a scandal to her, loving it because it made Christ visible.[58] With all that, the Dorothy Day who "could not go to Communion and be insensitive to the reality that someone was hungry, could not enjoy the warmth of Eucharistic consolation and know that she had a blanket while her brothers and sisters did not, could not 'go to the altar of God' and be aware that someone was sleeping over a grate on the sidewalk."[59]

Projections

What will the parish of Christianity's third millennium look like? What pastoral outlooks should it have? What changes will it bring to lay involvement? I have been uncommonly intrigued by the predictions of one experienced pastor and effective preacher, William Bausch. Twelve statements.[60]

1. The parish of the next millennium will be lay-oriented, with shared and collaborative ministry.

2. It will be grounded not so much in ordination and office as in baptism and charism, wherein the baptismal call to discipleship binds us in a common mission, and leadership, conferred with broader input, is respectful of others' gifts.

3. It will be defined relationally rather than numerically or institutionally, with a more personal, communitarian sense to being church, moving away from divisive extremes and more to the middle, to the more urgent agenda of finding God.

4. It will complete the process of moving from pyramid to koinonia church: better balance between male and female spiritualities and influence, greater female representation in decision making, married priests — and united to one another across the earth, those gone before and those to come after.

5. It will stress the wisdom tradition rather than the intellectual, retrieve the mystical, return to a more holistic spirituality.

6. It will be less program-oriented, more spiritually oriented, with the gifts of spiritual direction more widely scattered, sensitivity to the hidden God heightened, harboring Spirit and cross, a Savior by whose wounds we are healed.

7. It will retrieve the Catholic imagination, reflected in our sacred buildings, liturgy, the communion of saints, a renaissance of art, theatre, and music.

8. It will see a new priesthood, within and among the people, a common communion in ministry.

9. In a pluralistic and multicultural society, the parish will speak from weakness rather than power, will downsize, our poverty aligning us with the poor, our minority status moving us to witness, our humility to practical ecumenism.

10. Wired, it will focus on intergenerational rather than just child education.

11. It will operate on the principles of subsidiarity and collegiality.

12. It will move closer to a male-female partnership, a real balance of male-female co-operation and ministry.

I shall not live to see this development; I envy those who shall.

TEN

From Eve to Mary to...?

Women in the Church

Quite some years ago I saw a highly intriguing banner raised aloft
at a women's protest rally:

EVE

WAS

FRAMED

The proclamation sets the stage imaginatively for serious discussion of one of the most disturbing issues in the Catholic Church
as it enters Christianity's third millennium. I mean "women in the
Church." As I put together my half century of theological/pastoral
reflection and involvement, I gather that it can best be organized
under the rubric of three women: Eve, Mary, and today's woman.

The Woman That Was Eve

The passage of the years persuades me that, in the eyes of many
Christians, Eve has gotten a negative press, not all of it justified. The
arrows of some feminists are largely, but not exclusively, targeted at
Scripture. Not only the patriarchy that pervades the Hebrew Testa-
ment. The New Covenant receives special attention in the person of
Paul; more accurately, in the Pauline letters.

In the first of the two letters to Timothy, the author declares: "Let
a woman learn in silence with full submission. I permit no woman
to teach or to have authority over a man; she is to keep silent."
Why? "Because Adam was formed first, then Eve; and Adam was
not deceived, but the woman was deceived and became a transgres-
sor" (1 Tim 2:11–14). We may with justification respond that the
author is not Paul but a later follower of Paul.[1] For "Women in
the Pauline churches held responsible positions (e.g., Phoebe [Rom
16:1–2], Prisca [Rom 16:3; 1 Cor 16:19], Junia [? Rom 16:7]) and
are depicted as preaching (1 Cor 11:5) and teaching (Acts 18:26;

see *Acts P. Thec.*)."[2] Nevertheless, the Pastoral Letters have been accepted into the canon of Scripture within the Catholic Church, and even though not every sentence in the New Testament is guaranteed to be God's own word on a subject, inclusion in the canon makes for difficulties. And the author of 1 Timothy puts his emphasis squarely on the woman who failed; "Adam was not deceived." Clearly, the author implies "a certain strength and fidelity in Adam-man faced with temptation, by contrast with Eve the weak and gullible woman."[3]

Still, not even the genuine Paul has escaped all feminist criticism. Much is made of 1 Corinthians 11:2–16, specifically verses 3 and 7–9:

> I want you to understand that Christ is the source [not "head"] of every man [or "every human being"], and the source of every woman's being is man, and the source of Christ's being is God.... A man ought not to bind up his head, for he is the image and reflection [or "glory"] of God, but woman is the reflection [or "glory"] of man. Indeed, man was not made from woman, but woman from man. Neither was man created for the sake of woman, but woman for the sake of man.

I must confess that I was a septuagenarian before I understood what Paul's concern was in 1 Corinthians 11 and how he chose to address it. I came to see that Paul's primary focus in this passage is dress at liturgical assemblies. "The way in which certain men, and possibly some women, dressed their hair suggested homosexual tendencies. Paul's response is to stress the importance of the difference between the sexes."[4] Genesis 2 tells him that the difference in their creation shows that God intended men and women to be different. But is only the male God's image? Hardly. Paul was thoroughly acquainted with Jewish tradition, wherein woman was beyond doubt God's image (Gen 1:27) and reflection or glory (*Apoc. Mos.* 20:1–2). "But Paul could not say so here. He had to find a formula that underlines the difference between the sexes, and the idea that woman gave glory to man...was justified by Gen 2:18, to which he refers in v. 9."[5] Man came from the dust of the earth, woman from man's rib. Apparently Paul is insinuating that if God had meant men and women to be indistinguishable, God would have created them in the same way. I find it fascinating that whereas Jews used verses 7–10 to prove that woman was inferior to man, Paul flatly excluded such an interpretation. In the Christian community "man is not independent of woman; man comes through woman; [and] all things are from God" (vv. 11–12).

The Genesis account of Eve found strong resonances in the age of the Fathers. In my patristic experience, perhaps the most striking treatment of Eve is the primordial insight of the Fathers with respect to the mother of Jesus: Mary is the New Eve. I recall that John Henry (later Cardinal) Newman framed the question at issue with his customary lucidity, then answered it with startling brevity, in his well-known *Letter to Pusey:* "What is the great rudimental teaching of Antiquity from its earliest date concerning her? I mean the *primâ facie* view of her person and office, the broad outline laid down of her, the aspect under which she comes to us, in the writings of the Fathers. She is the Second Eve."[6]

The earliest patristic testimonies to the Eve-Mary parallelism stem from the West: from Rome, Lyons, and Carthage. The witnesses are the three most significant figures on the Western literary horizon in the latter half of the second century and the dawning of the third: Justin, Irenaeus, and Tertullian. In this vision the pattern of human redemption, as designed by God, paralleled the fall. As Irenaeus summed it up, "The knot of Eve's disobedience was loosed by Mary's obedience. For what the virgin Eve bound fast by her refusal to believe, this the virgin Mary unbound by her belief."[7]

Among early Eastern writers it is Ephraem (ca. 306–73), the most significant author of the Syrian Church, who is incomparably sensitive to the implications of the Eve-Mary analogy. As he saw it, the parallelism lies at the root of human dignity and is the crux of our immortality. "One was cause of life, the other cause of death. Through Eve death arose, and life by means of Mary."[8] Although Ephraem's Mariology, bold and prolific as it was, exercised no perceptible influence on his contemporaries, the Eve-Mary motif is discoverable in fourth-century Jerusalem, Salamis, Nyssa, Iconium, and Antioch. A conclusion was all but inevitable: It is Mary who is "mother of the living" in its more profound meaning, because in obedience to grace she gave birth to Life itself.[9]

It was the fifth century, however, that witnessed the proliferation of the parallelism in the Greek Church. Here the significant documents are homilies, particularly on the Annunciation, the Incarnation, and the divine motherhood. The primary influences on these homilies were the primitive Marian feast and the Nestorian controversy. And in the homilies impressive segments of the Greek Church made their voices heard: Egypt through Cyril of Alexandria, Thrace through Proclus of Constantinople, Galatia through Theodotus of

Ancyra, Arabia through Antipater of Bostra, and Palestine through Hesychius and Chrysippus of Jerusalem.[10] "In place of the virgin Eve, who had ministered to death, a virgin was graced by God and chosen to minister life."[11]

Why spend so much time on Eve? Because, in a genuine sense, Eve has indeed been "framed," and woman humiliated in the process. It began with "the man" inaugurating millennia of blame-shifting: "*The woman* [not 'my wife' or 'my partner' or 'flesh of my flesh'] *you* gave to be with me [I had nothing to say about it], *she* gave me fruit from the tree, and I ate" (Gen 3:12). *She* did it! And the Eve-Mary parallelism tends by its very simplicity ("death through Eve") to place a greater theological and practical burden on Eve than she should have to bear — especially when Eve-Mary is not paralleled by Adam-Christ. If we are willing to take the Eden myth and traditional Catholic theology of original sin with utmost seriousness, then "the man" was primarily responsible. *He* did it! I mean Paul's "sin came into the world through one man" (Rom 5:12).

I have discovered, to my instruction and delight, that often a feminist perspective has shed light on difficult sections of Scripture. So here, on the subordination of Eve/woman, I find Phyllis Trible splendidly illuminating.

> The woman ate; she gave to her man and he ate (3:6). At this turning point, distinctions within one flesh became oppositions. Division followed, yielding "opposite sexes." To defend himself, the man turned against the woman and betrayed her to God (3:12). Yet, according to God, she still yearns for the original unity of male and female: "for your man is your desire." Alas, however, union is no more; one flesh is split. The man will not reciprocate the woman's desire; instead, he will rule over her. Thus she lives in unresolved tension. Where once there was mutuality, now there is a hierarchy of division. The man dominates the woman to pervert sexuality. Hence, the woman is corrupted in becoming a slave, and the man is corrupted in becoming a master. His supremacy is neither a divine right nor a male prerogative. Her subordination is neither a divine decree nor the female destiny. Both their positions result from shared disobedience. God describes this consequence but does not prescribe it as punishment.[12]

Division, domination, subordination — such is not God's design, not God's desire. "Woman's original equality with her 'correspondent,' the man, is part of the loss, suggesting that the subordinate place of woman in Israelite society was not intended by God, but is rather a result of human sin."[13] The villain is sin. Interestingly, Pope John Paul II echoes this insight. It is in the Genesis story of sin that he finds God's design for man/woman equality frustrated. It is not that sin has "destroyed" our likeness to God; still, it has "obscured" our identity, "diminished" the relationship of man and woman, their ability to reflect God each in his or her own way. One effect is declared in Genesis 3:16: "Your desire shall be for your husband [or "your man"], and he shall rule over you." Patriarchy, the structural domination of men over women, reveals vividly humanity's ruptured relationship, "the disturbance and loss of the stability of that fundamental equality which the man and the woman possess in the 'unity of the two.'"[14]

Shared disobedience, ruptured relationship, patriarchal domination — the movement has been catastrophic. And the movement leads me to the woman for whom Eve has been a historical foil.

The Woman That Was Mary

During my half century of theological involvement, scholarly Catholic reflection on the mother of Jesus focused successively on four ways of envisioning her and her significance: (1) the prerogatives of Mary, (2) Mary as type or model of the Church, (3) Mary as primary disciple, and (4) Mary and the female face of God. Each merits consideration.

Prerogatives of Mary

In the mid-'50s I was asked by a good friend, genial, cigar-smoking Franciscan Juniper B. Carol, to contribute to a multivolume project on Mariology that would contain solid, up-to-date, authoritative information on the entire field of Marian theology and cult. My task was patristic and involved two papers: one on "Mary in Western Patristic Thought," the other on "Mary in Eastern Patristic Thought."[15] In harmony with traditional emphases, I researched "five prerogatives linked inseparably to our Lady in contemporary Catholic theology": Mary as Second Eve, her perpetual virginity, her motherhood, her holiness, and her death and corporeal assumption.[16] Other papers, largely theological in orientation, dealt with Mary's immaculate conception, her immunity from actual sin, her predestination, her fulness of grace, her knowledge, her spiritual maternity, her coredemption, her role as dispensatrix of all graces, her universal queenship.

Typical of such research was the enormous scholarly production occasioned by the centenary (1954) of the definition of the Immaculate Conception. Many a Mariological congress was dedicated to this subject. My own patristic concerns were stimulated by the impressive scholarship that revealed how far the Fathers of the Church were from an explicit awareness and understanding of this prerogative. The implications of Mary's holiness were only gradually uncovered. Although the problem was *posed* with sufficient clarity among the Latins in the fifth century, the Augustinian tradition on original sin and concupiscence blocked any satisfactory solution before the twelfth century; among the Greeks the terms of the problem were not adequately posed in patristic times. A dialogue between East and West would have hastened a solution.[17]

In the 1950s a Marian prerogative that generated unexpected heat was Mary's "virginity in parturition," the belief that Mary was a virgin not only before she conceived Jesus, not only after she gave him birth, but in her actual childbearing. For various reasons this doctrine, which had enjoyed a tranquil existence within the Church since the fourth century but had in latter years degenerated into a primarily physiological mystery, found itself under attack. It was regarded as dated, outmoded, anachronistic. Spurred by Albert Mitterer,[18] many a critic of the doctrine (dogma?) discovered a desirable solution to the problem: Retain the formula *virgo in partu,* but strip it of its traditional components, bodily integrity and painless childbearing. The arguments for this position were basically two. First, it was argued, these features do not belong to the concept of virginity and they run counter to the concept of maternity. Second, on the level of positive data, the highlights were the hesitations prior to the fourth century, the apparent influence of the apocrypha, and the physiological inadequacy of patristic terminology. Mitterer was attacked and defended; doctors and theologians entered the lists; the Holy Office issued a disciplinary decree (July 20, 1960) forbidding publication of such articles on the subject as would offend against Christian delicacy and contradict traditional doctrine.

For me, perhaps the most influential name in the controversy proved to be René Laurentin. In a famous article,[19] long unpublished (save privately) for discretionary reasons, Laurentin took issue with the anatomical approach. The article is not uncommonly documented; its significance lay elsewhere. It was genuinely an essay in patristic theology — better, theology with deep roots in tradition.

Laurentin insisted that the problem is not primarily a biological issue; he refused dialogue on this level. He found it imperative to restore the meaning of the Fathers and councils, that is, to restore the question to the theological level, to recapture the discretion and delicacy exemplified by the patristic approach. Not that the corporeal element of the mystery can or should be eliminated, but that we must renounce the possibility or advisability of a clinical description of Christ's birth; for here, as with Mary's assumption into heaven, we know almost nothing of the how, we have not the requisite theological criteria. Further, Laurentin thought it needful to recall what partisans and advocates of the traditional doctrine had frequently forgotten: the importance of rediscovering in patristic tradition the authentic meaning of the Incarnation and of Christian virginity, of which the mystery of *virginitas in partu* is no more than an element.

Far more attractive to me was one of the more exciting by-products of Pius XII's definition of our Lady's assumption in 1950. The document defining the dogma, *Munificentissmus Deus* (November 1, 1950), declared that Mary was taken up body and soul into the glory of heaven "when the course of her earthly life was finished." Here two issues took hold of me and would not let me go: (1) What significance did Mary's assumption have for the average Christian? (2) Did Mary die?

First, the significance of the dogma. In my patristic research I was particularly impressed by the state of the evidence on the final lot of Jesus' mother. The significant extant literature is so scanty that some scholars speak of the silence, even the ignorance, of the first three centuries, while others counter by calling the silence relative, inevitable, and eloquent.[20]

Far more prolific than theological argumentation in those early centuries were the apocryphal accounts called *Transitus Mariae* (literally, "The Passing Over of Mary"). They apparently originated before the close of the fifth century, perhaps in Egypt or Syria, in consequence of the stimulus given Marian devotion by the definition of the divine maternity at the Council of Ephesus in 431. At least a score of such accounts are extant, in Coptic, Greek, Latin, Syriac, Arabic, Ethiopic, and Armenian. All recount the death of Mary. All postulate some kind of divine intervention: a translation of Mary's body to a presumably earthly paradise, where it is preserved incorrupt under the tree of life; or a genuine assumption, a reunion of Mary's soul and body which entails her entrance into heaven.

As historical accounts, the *Transitus* literature is valueless. Theologically, the tales are precious — for at least three reasons. (1) They reveal the reaction of early Christian piety when confronted with the apparent fact of Mary's death; they evidence the first unequivocal responses to the problem of her destiny. (2) The solution is given, incorruption is postulated, on theological lines: the divine maternity, Mary's unimpaired virginity, and her unrivaled holiness. (3) The more ancient documents exercised a perceptible influence on the establishment of the Eastern feast of the Dormition ("Falling Asleep") or of the Migration of the Mother of God.

The fairest flower of patristic thought on Mary's destiny, however, blossomed from the seventh and eighth centuries in Greek homiletic literature. Mary's glorification in soul and body is accepted as indisputable by the outstanding orators of the Dormition feast (Modestus of Jerusalem, Germanus of Constantinople, Andrew of Crete) and apparently by the main body of the faithful. More significantly, here too Mary's assumption is postulated on theological premises: her maternity, virginity, and holiness.

A paragraph in a sermon of John Damascene, the last of the Eastern Fathers of the Church, summed up the Greek homiletic tradition in a striking rhetorical flourish. He told the faithful at Gethsemane 1,200 years ago:

> There was need that this dwelling fit for God be not imprisoned in the hollows of the earth. There was need that she who had entertained God in the guestchamber of her womb be brought home to the dwelling of her Son. There was need that the body of her who in childbirth had preserved her virginity without stain be preserved incorrupt even after death. There was need that she who had carried her creator as a baby on her bosom should linger lovingly in the dwelling of her God. There was need that she who had looked on her very own Son on the cross, who there felt in her heart the sword pangs of sorrow which in bearing him she had been spared, should look upon him seated with his Father. There was need that the mother of God should enter into the possessions of her Son and, as mother of God and handmaid, be reverenced by all creation.[21]

This type of argument, from the fittingness or appropriateness of an assumption of Mary, was not uncommon in the era of the Fathers. On a different level of argumentation, I recall that around the time of the definition, when it was roundly criticized on several fronts, novelist Graham Greene wrote of its significance in *Life* magazine. In the wake of World War II, with perhaps 55 million civilian and military dead, an inevitable casualty was a sense of reverence for the human body. The papal definition is implicitly a statement that the human body shares intimately in God's purpose for the human person now and into eternity.

Second, did Mary die? Pope Pius XII was clearly refusing to take a stand on so controverted a question. On this issue theologians in the Catholic community have never been totally at peace. Assume with Catholic doctrine that Mary was conceived without original sin; then was she not exempted from the death that "came through sin" (Rom 5:12)? On the other hand, given that her Son, God-made-man, died, was it not eminently fitting that his mother follow him in death? My own research into the patristic evidence[22] resulted in the following summary conclusion:

> From the evidence of the patristic age there emerges a widespread conviction of the early Church that our Lady died a natural death. This conviction, especially between the fifth and eighth centuries, was shared by hierarchy and faithful, preached by theologians, publicly affirmed in the liturgy. There is no comparable conviction to offset it; for in dissent we find only individuals, not a tradition. However, the nature of much of the evidence — sporadic comments before Ephesus, apocrypha obscure in origin and impalpable in weight, a feast still hidden in history — is too fragile to sustain an apodictic conclusion on the theological significance of this conviction.... [23]

I have never regretted the research that went into my teaching and writing on Marian prerogatives; they furnished a rich foundation for subsequent inquiry into even richer aspects of Marian theology and devotion. Still, I was a creature of my time. And Marian theology at that time lived and died around Mary's prerogatives. Not that it was unjustified or barren of theological and spiritual fruits. But in preaching on our Lady, I had to admit that those precious privileges are beyond our imitation. What, then, did I see as their deep significance, their abiding meaning, for Christian living? She is a living lesson — God's fairest lesson next to her Son — in what holiness is all about.

> Every one of her privileges — from her immaculate conception through her virginal motherhood to her glorious assumption — is a living illustration of what holiness really is. And what is that? Holiness is simply ... union with God. Why was that spotless embryo within the womb of Ann a holy thing, in fact

the holiest thing on God's earth? Because God dwelt within it. Why was that teenage virgin of Nazareth called by an angel "blessed among women"? Because the Son of God was to rest within her. Why is Mary supremely holy at this moment? Because, soul *and* body, she is one with God for ever.[24]

In Mary, I insisted, we glimpse our destiny. Not an immaculate conception, not a virginal motherhood, not even the same glorious assumption, but "that oneness with God in every phase of your life which is God's dream for you from eternity — a oneness with God which [God] will work in you through Mary *if,* like that most courageous of women, you will but have the courage to respond, 'Let it be with me as you say.' "[25]

Mary as Type or Model of the Church

A second facet of Marian research stemmed from a smoldering dissatisfaction with a Marian theology that seemed to isolate the mother of Christ from the physical Christ and from the mystical Christ. Catholic theologians were increasingly aware of an indispensable condition for a dynamic, relevant, authentically theological Mariology — what Laurentin expressed so well in 1954 when he observed that Mariology must be kept in a fruitful tension between Christology and ecclesiology.

A close link between Mariology and Christology (including soteriology) was relatively easy to recover; it was, in large measure, a matter of reorientation, with renewed efforts to discover to what extent doctrines like Mary's role in redemption are germinal in such patristic themes as the Eve-Mary parallelism. Not so the relationship between Mariology and ecclesiology. Here a lost tradition was recaptured, with unsuspected possibilities for Mariological renewal. I mean the Mary-Church parallelism.

In this area one of the most momentous works of the 1950s was Alois Müller's detailed research in the patristic field, East and West, from the Apostolic Fathers to Cyril of Alexandria and Augustine.[26] Müller recovered, with impressive documentation, three patristic insights. (1) In the mind of many Fathers, there is a striking *similarity* between the role of Mary and the role of the Church in God's redemptive plan. They are *alike* in that each, as virgin, as virgin bride, brings Christ to birth by a voluntary yes which is man's/woman's response to God's invitation, the prelude to the union of divine and human in a single individual and in the whole Church. (2) A fair number of Fathers see in Mary a *type* of the Church, at least in the sense that in God's design she foreshadows in her own person, in her own activity, what the whole Church is to be and to do. (3) A few Fathers assert or imply that Mary *is* the Church, *identify* Mary and the Church. And one may argue with a certain suasiveness that they may well mean that our Lady not merely foreshadows the Church, but is the perfect realization of the Church's inner essence, of redeemed humanity.

The thesis that Mary is type or figure of the Church, that in Mary redemption finds its consummate realization, that in her God achieves to perfection what God has designed for the whole Church, that what the mother of Jesus is, this the Church is destined to be — this thesis breathed new life into Marian theology. For this vision of Mary preserved a gratifying balance between her humanness and her uniqueness; it clarified and unified her role in redemption; it made for authentic Marian devotion; in a singular way it cast fresh light on Mary's prerogatives. This calls for detailed explanation.[27] Here, however, I can focus on only three of Mary's prerogatives: motherhood, virginity, and assumption into heaven.

Our Lady is type of the human element in redemption; she represents the believing Church, the whole community of Christians, women and men, laity and hierarchy, insofar as it hears the word of God and welcomes it within.

This personification of the Church finds its crucial hour at the Annunciation. It was not simply that God wanted Mary's motherhood to be a voluntary thing, uncompelled, unconstrained. More profoundly still, the Son of God was about to wed human nature to Himself. Therefore, as Thomas Aquinas phrases it, "what God was asking through the Annunciation was the consent of the Virgin *in the name of all humanity.*"[28] Leo XIII expressed the same idea: "The eternal Son of God, when He wanted to take to Himself the nature of the human, and so enter a mystical marriage with the whole human race, did not do so before obtaining the perfectly free consent of His mother-to-be, *who played as it were the role of the human race itself.*"[29] Mary's murmured yes may well have been her finest hour. That instant was realized in Mary the substance of the mystery of the Church to come: the union of God and humanity in the mystical Body of Christ.

In sum, Mary has a representative function. The task of the believing Church is to continue through space and time the fiat of Mary. This community of the redeemed has for its vocation to cooperate in the work of redemption by loving faith, and so bring God to birth in the human frame. The Church, therefore, is a collective Mary, and Mary is the Church in germ.

This vision of Mary's motherhood becomes clearer still if we see it in its virginal aspect. It is no longer satisfying to see in Mary's virginity before and after Bethlehem little more than a privilege, perhaps indispensable in a girl who is mother of God's Son. Even in her virginity Mary represents the community of believers. For womanly virginity has two facets. Negatively, it denies that intimate relationship with a male which we term marital, denies male initiative with respect to woman and woman's fruitfulness. But to be Christian, this negative aspect must stem from something positive: a woman's total dedication to God, a complete openness to the divine, receptivity to God alone.

So was it with Mary. No human being took the initiative in the relationship that issued in the Son of God made flesh: "The Holy Spirit will come upon you" (Lk 1:35). But the denial of human initiative stemmed from Mary's total consecration to God, an unfailing fiat, complete and exclusive.

In this Mary represents the community of believers, realizes in her own person what God intended for redeemed humanity. On the one hand, this union of God with the human, this union we call the Church, denies to humans the initiative that links them to God. Even their co-operation is a response to grace, to God's invitation. "If we but turn to God," Augustine insisted, "that itself is a gift of God."[30] And that is the positive side of the Church's virginity. Its role is total consecration to Christ, a complete openness to the divine, a sensitiveness to the action of God's Spirit, an incredible readiness to respond, "Let it be with me as you say" (Lk 1:38).

The paradox is this. It is not simply that, as Augustine said, "virginity is no hindrance to fertility." For the Church as for Mary, it is only by reason of its virginity that it can achieve fertility. It was only by Mary's total response to God's invitation that the Son of God became flesh; it is only by prolonging this response through space and time that the Church, impregnated with the Spirit, is fruitful for the formation of Christ in individual humans.

This vision of Mary as personification of redeemed humanity finds a final clarity in her bodily assumption. For several popular misconceptions have been widespread among Christians with respect to the human body. For some, the body is nothing but an instrument, a tool of the soul. For others, the body is a necessary evil, a burden from which the soul cries for release. Some Christians have actually held that the body is a punishment, a prison for the soul. All this is an echo of third-century theologian Origen with his hypothesis of pre-existent souls that sinned and according to the degree of their fall were differentiated into angels, humans, and demons. Such an attitude, I preached in the '50s,[31] pays slender homage to God. It refuses to recognize that the body is an essential part of each human person, that without the body we are creatures incomplete, that whether in heaven or purgatory or hell a separated soul, as Jean Mouroux phrased it, "still longs for its body with a purely natural impulse of love."[32]

In somewhat the same way the visible structure of the Church is an essential part of the Church. Not merely because it is an instrument through which God's life is communicated to mortals. It is that, of course; but it is more. The Church is visible of its very nature because everything which is to absorb redemption must somehow be absorbed into the Church. As the body played its part in the first sin, as the body fell with the soul from God, so does the body yearn for redemption. In the inspired language of Paul, we "groan in our hearts while we wait for adoption, the redemption of our bodies" (Rom 8:23). In baptism it is not simply the soul that wakens to the presence of God; it is the whole person. At that instant the body ceases to be Paul's "body of death" (Rom 7:24), comes spiritually alive, because it too is quickened by the Spirit of God. "Do you not know," Paul reminds us, "that your body is a temple [or "sanctuary"] of the Holy Spirit within you?" (1 Cor 6:19). And redemption will find its completion in the glory of the life to come, when the whole person, soul and body, will confront his or her Creator in an eternity of knowledge and love.

That perfection of humanity redeemed, that consummation of the Church, finds its first purely human realization in the mother of Jesus, Mary assumed into heaven soul and body. Here, perhaps more than anywhere else, is the lesson of our Lady's assumption: What Mary is, we shall be.

Mary the Perfect Disciple

In the wake of Vatican II, Mariology was reabsorbed into Christology; the mystery of Mary was more explicitly studied as part of the total mystery of Christ and his saving work. Mariology as a distinct "science" under the umbrella of theology in general held less and less attraction for theologians. This is not to say that Mariological societies devoted to an ever-deepening understanding of our Lady are obsolete. It simply submits that any "theology of Mary" (or even devotion to Mary) that is not intimately linked to her Son is less than Catholic.

A significant instance of this was the rediscovery of Mary as disciple of Jesus. Not just *a* disciple; the first disciple, the perfect disciple, the model of disciples, the most remarkable model of what Christian disciples should be, what every Christian should be.[33]

In the New Testament, to be a disciple is to be a follower; specifically, to follow in the footsteps of one master, Jesus. Not to imitate him in externals — walk in sandals, talk Aramaic, cure a military man's son, raise a widow's only child from the dead. Essential to discipleship is to have the mind of Christ. And what was that? In his own simple, profound response, "I seek not my own will but the will of Him who sent me" (Jn 5:30). It is the mind he taught us in the Our Father: "Thy will be done on earth as it is in heaven" (Mt 6:10). It is the mind he lived through bloody sweat in Gethsemane: "My Father, if it is possible, let this cup pass from me; yet not what I want but what you want" (Mt 26:39).

Such was the mind of Mary. It is splendidly summed up in Nazareth, when God asks her if she will bring into the world, give her flesh to, "the Son of the Most High." She is puzzled, of course. What teenage girl, what woman of any age, would not be? She asks one question, a natural question: How? "How . . . since I have no husband?" Once she hears "The Holy Spirit will come upon you and the power of the Most High will overshadow you," her answer is swift, unreserved: "Let it be with me as you say" (Lk 1:32–38). Your will, O Lord, your will only and always.

If that was the hour when the Son of God took flesh, it was also the hour when the first Christian disciple was born. And yet, that hour of rapture was but a beginning. As with all other mothers, so with Mary: She did not know where her yes to God, her yes to motherhood, would take her. Dear angel Gabriel did not leave her with a script. Not a word about a sold-out motel in Bethlehem, refugee status in Egypt, three obscure decades in Nazareth, three short years for her Son in the public eye, townspeople who tried to cast him from a cliff, relatives who shouted "He's mad!," a jeer-strewn journey to Jerusalem, a traitor's kiss, disciples abandoning him, a criminal's condemnation, a crown on his head and lashes on his back, twin beams of bloody wood. I am sure no angel on Calvary promised his mother, "Not to worry, Mary. He'll be back."

Did Mary worry about her Jesus, weep and bleed for him, lie sleepless and afraid? The Gospels do not say so — or only once (Lk 2:48). But we had better believe it; she was not a robot. Still, through those three decades and more, Mary never took back that initial, radical response: Whatever you want, Lord. That is what gives rich Marian meaning to an episode in Luke that could confuse, an incident that has misled many a believer down the centuries. I mean the woman who cried to Jesus from the crowd, "Blessed is the womb that bore you, and the breasts you fed on." And Jesus' response, "Blessed rather are those who listen to the word of God and keep it" (Lk 11:27–28). Not the back of his hand to his mother; quite the contrary. Simply, Mary is even more blessed because she ceaselessly said yes to Yahweh than because she gave birth to God's Son. Of course it was a unique, glorious, ecstatic act, lending her flesh for ever to the Son of the Most High. But Mary's most admirable gift to God was not the sheer tabernacle of her body. More blessedly still, she laid at God's feet her freely uttered yes — from Nazareth, through Bethlehem, to Jerusalem and beyond.

Precisely for that reason the fathers at Vatican II enclosed our Lady within a document on the Church: "The Mother of God is a model of the Church in the areas of faith, of love, and of perfect union with Christ."[34] This very human Jewish woman stands before me, before all who claim Christ as Lord and brother, in the flesh she gave her Son, stands before us not like a lifeless statue but as a living example, God's finest example, of what it means to be a disciple, how we should live here and now if we want to follow Christ. This mother of the Church ceaselessly urges on us what she said to the servants at Cana's wedding feast, "Do whatever he tells you" (Jn 2:5). She speaks not from book learning but from living experience. For in the story of humankind no sheerly human person has listened to the word of God more intently, has said yes to the word of God more unreservedly, has done the word of God more perfectly . . . even unto crucifixion.

Mary and the Female Face of God

As the '80s were drawing to a close, I was powerfully drawn to a fresh way of envisioning the significance of our Lady, an approach that stemmed in large measure from insightful feminist theologians.[35] The fresh vision has been crystallized under the rubric "Mary and the Female Face of God."

The fresh insight has for background the way in which our Christian tradition speaks of God, the way it images and imagines God. God has been locked into one predominant image: a male person. Indeed God is revealed to us as Father, and this is highly important for the way we think about God, the way we pray to God; take, for example, the Our Father that Jesus taught us. The peril in a single predominant image, however, is that over the centuries Christians have gradually come to identify God with maleness. One unfortunate result has been what is called "patriarchy," the dominance of the male in religion and society, in our thinking and living, and the subordination of woman. Like God, the male rules, commands, makes the decisions that shape family and religion, society and state. Woman obeys, goes quietly about her role as mother, homemaker, the heart of the family.

What first-rate feminists like Elizabeth Johnson were asking is this: Can we not find, in Scripture and through theology, other language, other images, other metaphors that would reap at least two splendid benefits: (1) afford us even richer insight into the incomprehensible Mystery that is God, and (2) serve the insight, the biblical revelation, that all women have an unsurpassable dignity as human beings shaped in God's image and likeness?[36]

One obvious image is the image of God as *mother.* This is not some radical irruption of off-the-wall feminists. The Hebrew Scriptures use metaphors of maternal birthing, maternal caring, to describe God's unbreakable love for a covenanted people. A moving example is the complaint of the people that God has forsaken them, has forgotten them. The Lord's reply:

> Can a woman forget her nursing child,
>   or show no compassion for the child of her womb?
> Even these may forget,
>   yet I will not forget you.
> See, I have inscribed you on the palms of my hands.
>   (Isa 49:15–16)

How does our Lady fit into this? Here Johnson is at once touchingly lyrical and theologically insightful:

> Throughout the tradition she has been portrayed predominantly as the mother par excellence, Mother of God, Mother of Mercy, Mother of Divine Consolation, our Mother. Transferring this maternal language back to God enables us to see that God Herself has a maternal countenance. All that is creative and generative of life, all that nourishes and nurtures, all that is benign, cherishes, and sustains, all that is full of solicitude and sympathy originates in Her. Maternal fruitfulness, care and warmth, and indispensable mother love flow from

God the Mother toward all creatures. All mothering on earth has its source in Her. She exercises a maternity that does not leave us orphans. In a Sunday talk Pope John Paul I once spoke of God as our Father but even more as our Mother, who wants to love us even and especially when we are bad.[37]

This is not the popular concept of heaven: a patriarchal household, a distant and judgmental God persuaded by Jesus' mother to be more approachable and lenient. Here "maternity itself is predicated of God equally with paternity, and female images of the creativity and caring intrinsic to healthy mothering may then evoke the reality of God."[38] The female face of God.

A second way in which our Lady reveals what God is like has to do with *compassion*. In much preaching and piety Mary has been presented as more approachable than Christ. Take the classical Marian antiphon *Salve regina*, "Hail, holy queen." It is Mary we call "mother of mercy," salute as "our life, our sweetness, and our hope," to whom we "poor banished children of Eve" send up our sighs and pray, "Turn, then, most gracious advocate, thine eyes of mercy toward us." Without rejecting the prayer itself, we must return this language to God, to whom it belongs most properly.

> God is the Mother of mercy who has compassionate womb-love for all Her children. We need not be afraid to approach. She is brimming over with gentleness, lovingkindness, and forgiveness, lavishing love and pity on the whole sinful human brood.... She is a true Refuge of sinners. In addition to mercifully forgiving sin, God consoles in all troubles and, in bending with care over those who suffer, is the true Comforter of the afflicted.[39]

It is not accurate to say that God's justice has to be tempered by Mary's intercession. The height and depth of compassion rests with God; in the first instance, compassion is divine. What is the primary value of Mary's compassion? It discloses in wondrous ways what God's compassion must be like, suggests vividly how far superior even to Mary's compassion God's infinite mercy must be. The female face of God.

A third way in which our Lady reveals what God is like has to do with *power and might*. Here is a strength that seeks to protect and to save, to liberate and to heal. In our age-old Marian tradition there is a pervasive sense that Mary's power is almost unlimited, "saving whom she loves if they but turn to her."[40] But once again, this kind of power, carried in the imagery of a woman who is mighty to save, is more accurately spoken of God, should lead us to understand ever more clearly how infinitely powerful is the *God* who, in the final analysis, alone can save. I find it remarkable how young Mary recognized this in her breath-taking Magnificat (Lk 1:47–55):

> My soul magnifies the Lord,
>   and my spirit rejoices in God my Savior;...
> for the Mighty One has done great things for me,
>   and holy is His name.
> His mercy is for those who fear Him
>   from generation to generation.
> He has shown strength with His arm;
>   He has scattered the proud....
> He has brought down the powerful from their thrones,
>   and lifted up the lowly.
> He has filled the hungry with good things,
>   and sent the rich away empty....

By her words and her life Mary declares that it is God who has the power to save. The female face of God.

A fourth way in which our Lady reveals what God is like has to do with what theologians call *immanence*. I mean our God not as some far-off deity in outer space, but incredibly close to us, God present to us, in us, surrounding and pervading us. A rich Catholic experience, as John Paul II has insightfully told us, is that the eternal love of the Father manifested in history through the Son given for us "comes close to each of us through this Mother and thus takes on tokens that are of more easy understanding and access by each person."[41] Once again Gerard Manley Hopkins has given striking expression to this in "The Blessed Virgin Compared to the Air We Breathe":

> Wild Air, world-mothering air,
> Nestling me everywhere...
> Minds me in many ways
> Of her....
>   I say that we are wound
> With mercy round and round
> As if with air: the same
> Is Mary, more by name.
> She, wild web, wondrous robe,
> Mantles the guilty globe....

> And men are meant to share
> Her life as life does air....
> Be thou then, O thou dear
> Mother, my atmosphere....
> World-mothering air, air wild,
> Wound with thee, in thee isled,
> Fold home, fast fold thy child.[42]

Such imagery, for all its loveliness, should be redirected to the reality that is God. Imagining our Lady in this way should help us realize that it is the Holy Spirit who is our true atmosphere, the wild Spirit who folds us fast. It is in God that "we live and move and have our being" (Acts 17:28). This image of a woman "matrix of all that is gifted with life"[43] should evoke in us the incredible nearness, the all-pervasiveness, of our God. The female face of God.

A fifth way in which Mary reveals what God is like has to do with *re-creative energy.* "May is Mary's month," Gerard Manley Hopkins sings.[44] Why? Because May is spring, and Hopkins asks,

> What is Spring? —
> Growth in everything.[45]

In devotion to Mary down the centuries Catholics have sensed that "all that is swelling, bursting, and blooming so beautifully does so under her aegis. Marian symbols of earth and water, vines, flowers, eggs, birds, and young animals evoke her connection with fertility and the motherhood of the earth."[46]

Again, our Lady would love us to redirect this imagery directly to God; for it is God who is the source of transforming energy, who is ever new and imaginative, makes things and persons new, re-creates what is in peril of dying, brings new life out of decay and death. God *is* Fertility. The female face of God.

Maternity, compassion, liberating power, intimate presence, and re-creative energy: the point and purpose of all this? To allow this imagery, so true of Mary, to disperse beyond Mary to the holy Mystery that is God, to help us see God more clearly, love Him more dearly, follow Her more nearly. After all, this is what Mary's own life was all about, from the glad tidings brought to her by Gabriel to her leave-taking from earth in soul and body. Such is her life now and for ever: pointing in her own person not to herself but to the Lord of her life. Such too, I am convinced, should be *my* life: imaging our Lady indeed, but only that I may image her Son. It is the early and continuous prayer of Ignatius Loyola to Mary, "Place me with your Son."[47]

Have We Lost Our Lady?

In our rough-and-tumble '60s, Catholics experienced a strange turnabout: We almost lost our Lady. The reasons are complex, are disputed. Was the villain the Second Vatican Council, which refused Mary a document of her own, enclosed her in a single section of the Constitution on the Church? Was it Protestant pressure to put Mary "in her place," make sure she doesn't replace Christ? Was it a fresh Catholic emphasis on essentials — word and worship, sacraments and sacrifice? Whatever the reasons, the result was patent: Mary faded into the background of Catholic devotion. Rosaries disappeared not only from pious fingers but from religious habits. Evening novenas played second fiddle to prime-time TV. Statues of Mary were retired to the sacristy. "Lovely lady dressed in blue" became a fun line for sophisticates.

Some losses I do not regret. We did bury some long-lived superstitions: Jesus administers justice, Mary ministers mercy; if you really want to get a friend out of hell, ask Mary. We are less facile in calling our Lady "our life, our sweetness, and our hope." We may well have succeeded in subordinating rosary to liturgy, Mary to Mass, mother to Son.

In the process, however, all too many rushed all too hastily to a less than Catholic extreme. They forgot, if they ever knew, that Catholicism, for all its stress on intelligence, is not a cult of cold reason; that knowledge, even grace-full, is not identical with holiness; that a saving spirituality, oneness with God, must link heart to mind, emotion to understanding, passion to purpose. In the process of purification, too many unwittingly betrayed God's Word, the Church's theology, and a Catholic art.

God's Word. Take simply one example significant for a Catholic spirituality. Like it or not, I learn from the New Testament that Mary is not only the mother of *Jesus*. I contemplate Jesus, Mary, and John on Calvary: "When Jesus saw his mother there with the disciple whom he loved, he said to his mother, 'Woman, look! Your son.' In turn he said to the disciple, 'Look! Your mother' " (Jn 19:26–27). That John has something in mind more profound than filial care for his mother is suggested by the very word "Look!" That exclamation is a formula John uses several times when he wants to reveal the mystery of a person's mission. In the summary of Raymond Brown, not one to be pressured by pious eisegesis, "In becoming the mother of the Beloved Disciple (the Christian), Mary is symbolically evocative of Lady Zion who, after the birth pangs, brings forth a new people in joy.... Her natural son is the firstborn of the dead (Col i 18), the one who has the keys of death (Rev i 18); and those who believe in him are born anew in his image. As his brothers, they have her as mother."[48]

The Church's theology. Unless I have stopped growing, I learn from Vatican II that God's mother "is a model of the Church in the areas of faith, of love, and of perfect union with Christ."[49] It goes back to the precious tradition narrated above, Mary as type and figure of the Church, Mary living, more perfectly than any other sheerly human person, the essence of discipleship, a ceaseless "Let it happen to me as you say" (Lk 1:38), Mary laying at God's feet the yes that altered history.

A Catholic art. To thrust the Mother of God into a religious attic is to lose sight of the painting and poetry, sculpture and architecture, music, dancing, and dramatic art that have nourished the Catholic imagination for centuries, more powerfully than our philosophy and theology. It is to forget Michelangelo and Botticelli, Chaucer and Chartres, Bach and Brahms. In brief, it is to forget what power there is in the way Hopkins compared our Lady to the air we breathe.

Today's Woman

Today's woman: Madonna? Phyllis Schlafly? Gloria Steinem? Princess Diana? Mother Teresa? No one woman? Let me approach the issues from my personal involvement.

Remote Involvement

My remote involvement in the issue goes back to my days as a graduate student in patristics at the Catholic University of America, 1943–46. My doctoral thesis, under Johannes Quasten, had for title *The Image of God in Man* [sic] *according to Cyril of Alexandria*.[50] Chapter 9 dealt with "Woman," mainly in Cyril but also in his theological predecessors. With respect to woman's potentialities on a properly human level, Cyril betrays a surprising pessimism. Intellect, emotions, will — in all these, woman is decidedly inferior to man. In fact, Cyril recognizes in woman less natural aptitude for the acquisition of virtue in its broad sense, and even at times for achieving supernatural perfection. His attitude recalls inevitably a thanksgiving maxim that was current among Persians, Greeks, and Jews in the environment of the New Testament: Thank God I am "not an infidel, an ignoramus, a slave, or a woman." Frankly, Cyril's ideal of woman sheerly as a human being does not touch the heights achieved by the pre-Christian Greeks with their Niobe and Penelope, Andromache and Antigone, Cassandra and Clytemnestra, Iphigeneia and Eurykleia. He was rather a precursor of John Milton:

> Oh! why did God
> Creator wise that peopl'd highest Heav'n
> With Spirits Masculine, create at last
> This noveltie on Earth, this fair defect
> Of Nature?[51]

Where grace enters in, however, Cyril leaves the general impression that "there is no longer male and female" (Gal 3:28). He usually preaches a universality and an equality "in Christ Jesus" that leaves little room for distinctions based on sex. There is, nevertheless, in Cyril as in Paul, a certain tension between the progressive and the reactionary. Paul insists that in Christianity there is no invidious distinction between male and female; and yet he can declare that in virtue of creation woman is a step further removed from God than is man (cf. 1 Cor 11:3–16). In similar vein, Cyril finds man and woman equally images of God; and still he can maintain that woman images God indirectly, by imaging man. His stimulus is Paul; for the thesis appears only under the impact of 1 Corinthians. But it is his own psychology that prepares him for Paul and permits the conclusion, "Woman, too, is indeed in God's image and likeness, but as by means of the man, so that she differs a little in nature."[52]

I cannot leave Cyril without quoting a pertinent paragraph of pastoral advice. Obviously disturbed by a sacerdotal misogyny parading as piety, he noted that Jesus' disciples were amazed at his kindness toward the Samaritan woman.

> Unlike some who have been coarsened by an excess of piety, he does not think it well to shrink from conversation with a woman, but unfolds to all his love of humankind. By this act he shows that, since there is only one Creator, it is not to males alone that he imparts the life that comes through faith; he catches in his net the female sex as well. Let this serve as a model for the teacher in the churches, and let him not refuse to be of service to women; for it is surely not his own

inclinations that he must follow but the advantage of the gospel preaching.[53]

A decade after my dissertation was published, I decided to run a seminar for theological students at Woodstock College quite outside my ordinary scholarly interests; I called it "Towards a Theology of Woman." I am not sure what motive impelled me; it may have had some connection with my interest in the patristic understanding of woman. Also, a number of studies on womanhood had attracted my attention in the '60s: Sidney Callahan's *The Illusion of Eve: Modern Woman's Quest for Identity;* Sally Cunneen's *Sex: Female; Religion: Catholic;* Margaret Mead's *Male and Female: A Study of the Sexes in a Changing World;* and perhaps most powerfully Betty Friedan's *The Feminine Mystique,* which sparked the women's-rights movement in the United States.

At any rate, I was fortunate enough to have in the seminar theological students with different specialized competences: in psychology, cultural anthropology, history, papal encyclicals, education, literature, female religious congregations, and (believe it or not) gynecology (an M.D. before entering the Jesuits). They expanded my understanding in so many areas: human sexuality in general, with particular emphasis on female sexuality in adolescence, adulthood, and the menopause; physical, emotional, psychological, and spiritual differences in male and female; values and disvalues in complementarity along lines parallel to sexual differentiation; changes in behavior patterns and attitudes of the American woman before and after marriage; woman's evolving role in society and church over four major historical areas (Age of Chivalry, Elizabethan Age, Victorian Age and Industrial Revolution, twentieth century); patristic attitudes compared with various papal encyclicals; history of, and rationale for, distinctive education for women; woman in five contemporary American writers (J. D. Salinger, Norman Mailer, Mary McCarthy, Tennessee Williams, Edward Albee); an understanding of who and what the female religious is today (this from a questionnaire sent to 15 different groups of Sisters representing ten different congregations).

What concretely did I learn in the mid-'60s? To begin with, how impossible it was to synthesize "what woman is." The issues were far too many, the facets of the question highly complex; data was incomplete, fragmentary, and research results sometimes contradictory; and we were dealing with histories, cultures, individuals. And no woman was personally on hand at old Woodstock to challenge

us![54] The "eternal woman," woman as she ought to be, no matter
what, was beyond definition — unless I wanted to be content with
unhelpfully broad generalizations, or with rhetoric that sounds like
music but says far less. For all its importance, anatomy is not a
despot. Cultural expectations, history — these influence, often justifiably, the actual way a woman develops in a particular age and
culture. And we can never disregard the peculiar potential within an
individual psyche, that "something" within an individual woman
which transcends typologies and schemata, allows a woman to be
distinctive among women without ceasing to be a woman. Here,
I felt, Karl Barth was surely right when he highlighted the danger
in any phenomenology or typology of the sexes, when he warned
us not to change *is* into *ought,* not to transform indicatives into
imperatives. For

> Real man and real woman would then have to let themselves
> be told: Thou shalt be concerned with things (preferably ma-
> chines) and thou with persons! Thou shalt cherish the mind,
> thou the soul! Thou shalt follow thy reason and thou thy in-
> stinct! Thou shalt be objective and thou subjective! Thou shalt
> build and thou merely adorn; thou shalt conquer and thou
> cherish etc.! This is commanded thee! This is thy task! By ex-
> ercising the one or the other function, thou shalt be faithful
> to thyself as man or woman! This is quite impossible. Obvi-
> ously we cannot seriously address and bind any man or woman
> on these lines. They will justifiably refuse to be addressed in
> this way....[55]

But fresh insights did emerge from the seminar. It became clear
that, for any genuinely Christian perception of woman, God's image
and likeness is of supreme importance. From creation alone, woman
mirrors God in intelligence, in love, in stewardship over earth.
Through redemption in Christ, woman's intelligence is perfected
by faith, her love by God's love, her stewardship oriented to serve
truth, justice, love, and freedom. Such Christian affirmations involve
a fundamental inference: Woman is man's equal. Paul's theolo-
goumenon — woman images God through man — is a personal
opinion, not to be identified with divine revelation, with ecclesiastical dogma. Inferiority (intellectual, physiological, psychological,
emotional, spiritual) is an outmoded concept, untenable, to be
dismissed into history.

At the time, I was persuaded that women should continue to be
conspicuous for the qualities which, according to the available evi-

dence, characterized American women: expressive vs. instrumental; a cognitive style that refused to divide and dissect; and woman's inner space, i.e., potential productivity, sense of solidarity, purposeful renunciation, meaningful experience of pain, sensitive innerness, and profound compassion. It seemed clear, however, that these qualities might have to be modified. Not indeed lost, but supplemented and complemented by an increasing emphasis on precisely those qualities that had traditionally characterized the American male: (1) action, achievement, accomplishment, conquest of geographic space and scientific fields, dissemination of ideas; (2) analysis and dissection, division and segmentation, the discursive and the logical, and the scientific approach to reality.

Why? To shape a more fully integrated person. It would bring the complementary traits into the one same person, instead of leaving them outside her, e.g., in a husband somehow complementing her without modifying her (or himself). It appeared to allow room for a legitimate adaptation to a culture in which a woman must live. It would blend superbly with the then emerging change in the young male of the species: increasing care and concern, a more holistic vision less inclined to divide and analyze to the nth degree, a sensitive innerness. Possibly the most significant and lasting result of the seminar was the realization that before we see woman as distinctively female, we must see her as a person. Here a paragraph from Ignace Lepp in 1963 had a profound effect on me:

> Not so long ago women were very proud of their mission to be the servant of the species. Today they are conscious of themselves as *persons,* and desire for themselves all that goes along with being a person, namely, independence, freedom, the right to happiness, and the right to individual development. Men have been animated for a long time by the same desires, but from now on they will not be able to satisfy these desires except in relation to those of their feminine companions.[56]

Person — here, I saw with uncommon clarity, was the basic dignity of each woman, this her inescapable obligation. Personality, however, possesses a twin facet. On the one hand, woman's perfection is within her, not in someone else; there is within her a fundamental inviolability; she is not, by her nature or God's command, a subordinate creature, inferior as a human being. On the other hand, woman, like man, is not fully a person save to the extent that she is "for others." This includes, in a significant but not exclusive way, her relationship to man — warm, vital, natural, profound, regular. Not necessarily within marriage, but still wonderfully real, human, lifelong — a remarkable reflection of the archetype of all personality, the Blessed Trinity.

Two years later my education was broadened and deepened when I was asked to speak at a Symposium on Woman sponsored by the Conference on Religious, National Conference on Catholic Charities, in Pittsburgh, November 20, 1968. I had to prepare intensively by relating what I had learned about woman in general to the life of women religious. I came to this conclusion: On broad lines, to be a female religious means that a woman, within the context of religious life, grows gradually to the fulness of femininity and personhood, and brings the fulness of her female personality to the service of the Church and the world.

The problem in 1968 was that many of the older models of the religious life had outlived their usefulness, and unfortunately the general run of American Catholics were blind to this. In consequence, as Eugene Kennedy wrote a year before, female religious were still very much

> in the position of the Negro, who has been told by a paternalistic and prospering society that, if he remains a child, he will be cared for — but on the horrendous condition that he exist only to add a touch of minstrel charm to life and should not aspire to be a man. He can serve and he will even be regarded with affection, but he cannot grow up....
>
> So the Sister is prized by a paternalistic and prospering Catholic society as a little girl, innocent and virginal, smiling sweetly, sacrificing silently, just human enough for the mindless caricatures of a dozen motion pictures. But the subtle admonitions remain: be a child and do not aspire to be a fully grown woman; take care of our children and teach them their prayers; grow weary, grow old, but don't grow up....[57]

This, I proclaimed in Pittsburgh, must change radically, or religious life will die. To begin with, the training of a female religious must be such as to allow for growth into personhood on the same scale and in the same depth as a girl can grow into a person outside the convent. This will demand a situation where the young religious can — to apply Carl Rogers' conditions — (1) be increasingly open to new, even perilous experiences; (2) develop a trust in her own organism as an instrument of sensitive living; (3) accept the locus of evaluation as residing within herself, not within her superiors; (4) learn to live not as a fixed reality but as a participant in a fluid, ongoing process, in which she is continually discovering new aspects of herself.[58] In brief, growth in personal responsibility.

To achieve this would mean drastic changes in convent life style: e.g., the end of mass institutionalization, an awareness of everyone's need for respect and privacy, a revised conception of authority and its uses, and regard for individual differences.

Moreover, given such training, "Sisters cannot be women to the Church from afar. They must bring their womanhood, silently and full of waiting perhaps, into the world where the action is."[59] Not that the contemplative life must go; rather that the majority of female religious must realize their womanliness in close human contact with the world — and not as disembodied spirits too pure to risk the contagion of an earth where men and women curse and hate, make bombs and make love, dance and cry, bleed and die.

The Church, like much of the world, had developed on a male model. A critical danger for emancipated woman, I felt, was that she might now try to do what men do in the way men do it, if only because the male model was the standard for success. Similarly within the Church: It would be tragic if the girls were simply to join the boys! It would not be enough for female religious to be in the world; they must be allowed to *be,* to bring all their nuanced distinctiveness to active creativity in the service of the human. Precisely how female personality was to reveal itself as distinctive at that point, I was not prepared to say. But surely we would only know whether or not women had something nonmasculine to offer the world and the Church if they were given room to flower, not be burdened by either models from a dead past or male models from a living present.

Proximate Influences

These experiences, however, proved to be background for understanding the feminist movement that has staggered society and church in the past quarter century. Here too some history should serve as prelude for my own subsequent development.

I became editor-in-chief of the journal *Theological Studies (TS)* in 1967, after the death of John Courtney Murray, and remained in that post till I resigned in 1990. On the occasion of *TS*'s 50th-anniversary volume (1989), I had occasion to look back upon that half century — editors and their problems, significant articles and their authors.[60] What I designated "the feminine face of *TS*"[61] revealed some embarrassing facts.

March 1971 saw our first article by a woman (volume 32):

J. Massingberd Ford's biblical essay on "speaking in tongues." She was followed the next year by Rosemary Radford Ruether's effort to reconstruct the basic symbol system of Christian theology in the light of the crisis of our contemporary human situation. A year later we published Margaret Mary Reher's note on Leo XIII and Americanism. In 1974 two women, Margaret Farley and Irma Garcia de Mazelis, contributed to our population issue. The genuine breakthrough came in December 1975, the issue entitled "Woman: New Dimensions," with seven of the nine contributions by women. Then, ironically, a six-year hiatus, 1976–81, marked only by the first appearance of New Testament scholar Sandra Schneiders, writing on developments in our understanding of the literal sense of Scripture.

The year 1982 witnessed a rebirth: a second article by Schneiders, on an unrecognized historical positivism in contemporary exegesis, and a promising new face, Elizabeth A. Johnson, on analogy in Pannenberg. In 1983 Margaret O'Rourke Boyle intrigued us with an appeal for historical method as an alternative to the hagiographical tradition on Ignatius Loyola. In 1984 Johnson returned to analyze three approaches to the use of female imagery for God, judge the "traits" and "dimensions" approaches inadequate, and deem the "equivalent of God male and female" to hold the best promise for both the renewal of the doctrine of God and the liberation of human persons. The same year Carol Tauer, applying the tradition of probabilism, concluded to some liberty in the moral treatment of early embryos. 1985 saw another giant step. Besides Catherine LaCugna's re-examination of Aquinas on God's real relatedness to creation, we welcomed ethicist Lisa Sowle Cahill, who would grace our restructured Moral Notes for three successive years. 1986 introduced Karen Jo Torgesen, with particular interest in patristic hermeneutics and women's history. 1987 brought two new authors into *TS*'s fold: Leslie Griffin, arguing that changing understandings of the spiritual and temporal in church documents call into question traditional prohibitions of clerical participation in politics, and Susan Wood, addressing the complex theological and pastoral problem of baptized couples who request the Church to witness their marriage though they profess no religious faith. In 1988 Mary Ann Donovan lent fresh insight into second-century Irenaeus, while Griffin returned to argue that the question of participation in politics by members of Roman Catholic women's religious congregations must be distinguished from arguments about priestly participation.

Of the twenty-eight articles in the 50th-anniversary volume, seven were by women. Joining Cahill (sexual ethics), Johnson (Mary and the female face of God), and Schneiders (spirituality) were newcomers Monika Hellwig (Christology), Carolyn Osiek (Bible and social sciences), Phyllis Trible (feminist hermeneutics), and Pheme Perkins (New Testament narrative criticism).

Feminism

It was in the context of such scholarly contributions by women that I began to appreciate the feminist movement. In chapter 2 above, I wrote briefly of the influence of feminist theology and biblical studies on my personal and professional development. But, granted the importance of Scripture and theology for the development of a Christian feminism, those areas do not simply define the movement. Let me try to summarize my understanding of (1) feminism as a generic term, (2) feminism in a Christian context, (3) a new feminism gaining some strength today, and (4) feminist challenges to the mother of Jesus. Several women authors who have influenced my thinking can serve to spell out these four areas.

In a generic sense, Elizabeth Johnson declares, feminism "is a worldview or stance that affirms the dignity of women as fully human persons in their own right, critiques systems of patriarchy for their violation of this dignity, and advocates social and intellectual changes to bring about freeing relationships among human beings and between human beings and the earth."[62] Obviously a powerful movement, where women are increasingly taking their lives in their own hands, refusing to continue their age-old subservient relationships with men.

What is the driving force behind the feminist movement? Women's experience of being marginalized, accessories to men, systematically devalued, unable to make significant decisions for the whole community. The offending system? Sexism, a prejudice that views women as essentially less valuable than men on the basis of biological sex. The harmful effects in civil society? Denial of political, economic, legal, and educational rights; disparity in working hours, wealth, land, literacy, and food; bodily and sexual exploitation and abuse. Feminism brings these situations to consciousness, analyzes the situations, criticizes and resists the pattern as unjust. As with other surges toward emancipation — colonized nations, subjugated peoples, people of color, the young, the economically poor — women are rising up and claiming their human worth.

What does Christian feminism add to this? Once again I find Elizabeth Johnson illuminatingly succinct:

Christian feminism is a worldview or stance that affirms the equal human dignity of women, criticizes patriarchy for violating this dignity, and advocates change to bring about more just and mutual relationships between women and men and human beings with the earth — and does so based on the deepest truth of the gospel itself. Its assumptions, criticisms, and goals are drawn from the message and spirit of Jesus the Christ encountered from the perspective of women's experience.[63]

The basic assumption of male-female equality leads to a criterion for what is true, good, and beautiful: "Theories, attitudes, laws, and structures that promote the dignity of the female human person are salvific and according to the divine will; theories or structures that deny or violate women's dignity are contrary to God's intent."[64] Christian feminism criticizes a theological sexism that has consistently defined woman as inferior to man mentally, morally, and physically, limited her imaging of God, degraded her sexuality. Its goals are a liberating community of all men and women, and a church that is a discipleship of equals, "that is, a community shaped according to the reign of God preached by Jesus, rather than one modelled on imperial Rome or the divine right monarchies of the age of absolutism."[65]

On May 4, 1996, Mary Ann Glendon, professor of law at Harvard University Law School, delivered an address in Washington, D.C., during a conference on Women and the Culture of Life.[66] She had in mind a new feminism that would bring us closer to the prize of the feminist journey, "a better, freer, more dignified life."[67] It would replace the old feminism, "official feminism," the feminism of the '70s, which many sense has veered off course. She is convinced that feminists were right on target when they criticized our culture for asking of women all sorts of sacrifices while according little respect, reward, or security to their unpaid work. But one area where organized feminism from the '70s on took a wrong turn "was in buying right into that disrespect by denigrating marriage and motherhood as obstacles to women's advancement!"[68] Three recommendations struck me as eminently sensible.

First, begin by *listening* to women as they express their needs and aspirations, instead of telling women what they should or should not want. Second, in dealing with women's issues, be wary of rigid dichotomies and false choices. Specifically, five dogmatic extremes:

"sameness" feminism that insists there is no significant difference between men and women; "difference" feminism that treats men and women as virtually different species; "dominance" feminism that proclaims female superiority; "gender" feminism that regards "male" and "female" as mere social constructs; and the rigid biological determinism (associated with some critics of feminism) that would lock women into roles that were prevalent in the 1950's, the 1850's or the time of the Babylonian captivity.[69]

Third, be inclusive rather than polarizing; treat men and women as partners rather than antagonists in the quest for better ways to love and work. In sum, be responsive, be prudent, be inclusive.

At the same conference Margaret O'Brien Steinfels, editor of *Commonweal* magazine, offered a "reality check" on feminism.[70] She liked the old feminism: Biology was no longer destiny for women; women could do more, achieve more, contribute more to society. What she does not like in today's feminism is the image of women as victims rather than morally responsible persons, feminist spokeswomen who have lost touch with ordinary women trapped rather than liberated, and a movement with a closed mind, impervious to criticism, with a litmus test for its speakers.

Will a new feminism be credible if and when it is sponsored by the Catholic Church? Steinfels admits that "the church's theory and the theology that follows from it have not yet come to grasp fully the enormous shift in women's roles in the church or in society."[71] Here the Church lacks credibility.

> The institutional, hierarchical church remains a male preserve. It is difficult for a tight-knit, self-perpetuating group of priests and bishops — not so much as individuals but as a group and institutionally placed — to comprehend and imagine the earth-shaking, world-changing revolution going on in women's lives: by education, by fewer children, by longer life expectancy and by the expansion of women's roles into every nook and cranny of the world. The failed but valiant efforts of the U.S. bishops to write a pastoral letter on women's concerns is a poignant example of our communal confusion and inarticulateness.[72]

Steinfels finds much that is true in the Catholic worldview of gender as a central distinguishing characteristic of the human person, but is convinced that, given the status of today's women, much needs to be re-examined, rethought, restated. The notion of complementarity may remain useful for discerning gender differences for theological purposes; but "we [women] know that the psychological, spiritual, physical, intellectual lives of our sons and daughters, our husbands, friends and colleagues are not predictably understood or organized on the basis of gender."[73]

In today's confusing clashes of convictions, often marked by derision and discrediting of opponents rather than "the hard work of persuasion, argumentation and negotiation,"[74] Steinfels offers three suggestions. (1) A new feminism cannot be a single-issue movement, but must speak to all the ways that threaten life: not only abortion but euthanasia, not only warfare but capital punishment, the abandoned and the immigrant, all the vulnerable. A new feminism must distinguish between morality and moralism, challenge sexual chaos and exploitation but not the power of erotic energy. (2) A new feminism must include men, in two senses: "men as a focus for feminine analysis and men as partners in carrying out that analysis and change."[75] The old feminism has too often given up on men as beyond redemption, necessary evils. (3) A new feminism should invite people in, not shut them out — not for women only, not for Catholics only. Include, too, old feminists. "And remember that in practice... feminism, like life itself, is a fuzzy reality."[76]

To round out these issues, the mother of Jesus returns — concretely through Sidney Callahan.[77] This graced psychologist is aware that feminist-inspired critiques have recently "claimed that Marian devotion is now and always has been counterproductive for women's flourishing."[78] In its most general form, the indictment focuses on Marian doctrines whereby celibate males created an ideal of womanhood that renders every other woman inadequate and incomplete. Callahan argues convincingly from history that Marian devotion "spontaneously arose among the people, particularly among women, and cannot be dismissed as a power play of celibate males"; she was the approachable Everywoman as well as the powerful queen of heaven; constantly celebrated was Mary's "embodiment and embeddedness in human affairs"; her special concern was to champion the poor and the oppressed; she was "model of risk, trust, courage, patience, perseverance."[79] Going beyond the theological insights on Mary I have detailed, Christian feminists see Marian devotion not only preserving "a feminine presence and recognition of feminine power within an officially male-dominated structure,"[80] but suggesting links to ministries still in their infancy in Catholicism, e.g., healing, the struggle for equality and justice, movements toward nonviolence and peace. Even Mary's much-discussed virginity and the virgin birth "can be interpreted as symbols of her autonomy, signaling her direct relationship to

God, unmediated through any hierarchically placed male, spouse or no."[81] And her fiat to the Incarnation heralds a new era of human reproduction: "A redeemed woman freely consents to co-operate with God and life as a responsible, responsive moral agent. Of all women in the world, Mary is the last one of whom it can be said that 'biology is destiny.' "[82]

Before God summons me to a merciful judgment, I would like to see a round table on Christian feminism fashioned of Johnson, Glendon, Steinfels, and Callahan. There is so much on which they agree. Where might they disagree? Specifically, what does the Catholic notion of equality — men and women equally images of God and of Christ — demand in the practical order, within church life, in the sanctuary? All of which leads inexorably to the question of ordination.

Women Priests?

Quite frequently in recent decades Catholic women have expressed their dismay, even their anger, at their second-class citizenship within the Church. But it is in John Paul II's pontificate that the movement for ordination has assumed unprecedented proportions. Elsewhere[83] I have summarized and commended the present pontiff's pronouncements on woman's equality with man, their equal imaging of God, their mutual relationship, the frustration of their equality and the emergence of patriarchy in the Genesis story of sin, and the rediscovery of feminine humanity's true dignity in Mary, the New Eve. What has he to say of woman's capacity for ministerial priesthood?

In the same 1988 apostolic letter, *Mulieris dignitatem*, that spoke so eloquently of woman's dignity and equality, John Paul confirmed the 1976 teaching of the Congregation for the Doctrine of the Faith, *Inter insigniores:* The Church has no authority from Christ to ordain women. Two paragraphs in that connection I find particularly significant. The first concerns the calling of the Twelve:

> In calling only men as his apostles, Christ acted in a completely free and sovereign manner. In doing so, he exercised the same freedom with which, in all his behavior, he emphasized the dignity and the vocation of women without conforming to the prevailing customs and to the traditions sanctioned by the legislation of the time. Consequently, the assumption that he called men to be apostles in order to conform with the wide-

spread mentality of his times does not at all correspond to Christ's way of acting.

The second operative paragraph has for immediate context the institution of the Eucharist:

> Since Christ in instituting the Eucharist linked it in such an explicit way to the priestly service of the apostles, it is legitimate to conclude that he thereby wished to express the relationship between man and woman, between what is "feminine" and what is "masculine." It is a relationship willed by God both in the mystery of creation and in the mystery of redemption. It is the Eucharist above all that expresses the redemptive act of Christ, the bridegroom, toward the Church, the bride. This is clear and unambiguous when the sacramental ministry of the Eucharist, in which the priest acts *in persona Christi,* is performed by a man. This explanation confirms the teaching of the declaration *Inter insigniores.*[84]

I was not surprised that the papal statement failed to curtail controversy, research, and publication. To complicate the situation, the Anglican communion had begun to ordain women; on the other hand, the Orthodox churches made it quite clear that they could not unite with a church that ordains women. It was in this context, I am convinced, that in May 1994 John Paul II addressed an apostolic letter, *Ordinatio sacerdotalis,* to Catholic bishops on priestly ordination. He made it pellucidly clear that he was writing because in some places the reservation of priestly ordination to men was still regarded as open to debate or a matter of church discipline.

> Wherefore, in order that all debate may be removed regarding a matter of great importance, a matter which pertains to the Church's divine constitution itself, in virtue of my ministry of confirming the brethren (cf. Lk 22:32) I declare that the Church has no authority whatsoever to confer priestly ordination on women and that this judgment is to be definitively held by all the Church's faithful.[85]

It was precisely the adverb "definitively" that disturbed Jesuit theologian Francis Sullivan, long-time Gregorian University professor, progressive indeed but hardly a flaming liberal. He was convinced that "definitively held" does not demand the response required by a dogma of faith.[86] What then? Cardinal Joseph Ratzinger, prefect of the Congregation for the Doctrine of the Faith, responded: "It is an act of authentic ordinary magisterium of the Supreme Pontiff, an act, therefore, that is not a defining or solemn *ex cathedra* statement, although the objective of this act is the declaration of a doctrine taught as definitive and, therefore, not reformable."[87] Sullivan's reaction? In describing the teaching as definitive and irreformable, and the assent demanded as definitive and unconditional, "claims are being made for this most recent exercise of what is officially described as 'ordinary papal magisterium' which, to my knowledge, have never before been made about any document of ordinary papal teaching."[88]

As if in response to such an argument, on June 30, 1998, John Paul II issued an apostolic letter (dated May 18) titled *Ad tuendam fidem* ("To Protect the Faith").[89] Its express purpose? "To protect the Catholic faith against attacks arising on the part of some of the Christian faithful, in particular among those who studiously dedicate themselves to the discipline of sacred theology."[90] The letter reproduces three propositions or clauses from the profession of faith published in 1989 by the Congregation for the Doctrine of the Faith and imposed on those who assume offices ordered to deeper investigation of truths and morals, or conferring special power in church governance. The first and third clauses have their legal expression in canon law; not so the second.

The first clause, "With firm faith I believe everything contained in God's word, written or handed down in tradition and proposed by the Church — whether in solemn judgment or in the ordinary and universal magisterium — as divinely revealed and calling for faith," has its own place in canon 750.

The third clause, "I adhere with religious *obsequium* of will and intellect to the teachings which either the Roman pontiff or the college of bishops enunciate when they exercise the authentic magisterium, even if they proclaim those teachings in an act that is not definitive," has its own place in canon 752.

But the second clause, "I also firmly accept and hold each and every thing that is proposed by that same Church definitively with regard to teaching concerning faith or morals," has no corresponding canon in the Code. "Yet this second clause...is of great importance because it refers to truths necessarily connected with divine revelation.... The truths definitively stated and the truths revealed are intimately linked either for historical reasons or through logical connection."[91]

Canon 750 was revised to include the existing paragraph on divinely revealed truths and to add a paragraph on truths necessarily connected with revelation; and canon 1371 "on just penalty" was fleshed out to take cognizance of the new in canon 750.[92]

Concurrently with that papal document the Congregation for the Doctrine of the Faith issued a commentary (dated June 29) on its three concluding paragraphs by Cardinal Joseph Ratzinger and Archbishop Tarcisio Bertone, prefect and secretary respectively of the Congregation.[93] A special significance of this commentary is that these officials offer some examples of doctrines to be held definitively: illicitness of euthanasia, prostitution, and fornication, legitimacy of the election of the supreme pontiff or of the celebration of an ecumenical council, the canonization of saints, the invalidity of Anglican ordinations, and the reservation of priestly ordination to males. As for the last-named:

> The supreme pontiff, while not wishing to proceed to a dog-matic definition, intended to reaffirm that this doctrine is to be held definitively, since, founded on the written word of God, constantly preserved and applied in the tradition of the Church, it has been set forth infallibly by the ordinary and universal magisterium.... [T]his does not foreclose the possi-bility that in the future the consciousness of the Church might progress to the point where this teaching could be defined as a doctrine to be believed as divinely revealed.[94]

This is not the place to analyze what appear to be the most significant arguments against the ordination of women: (1) Jesus' own call of men alone as his apostles; (2) the constant tradition of the Church, holding the example of Jesus and the actions of the apostles as normative; (3) the thesis that only males can act *in per-sona Christi*.[95] In that context, Avery Dulles has examined, with his customary care, ten of the principal objections raised against magisterial teaching on the ordination of women, and finds them substantially inadequate. He recognizes that questions may still be legitimately raised: for example, on the biblical and historical evi-dence, the iconic argument as currently presented, the precise nature of the assent required, the thinking of the world's bishops. Never-theless, he concludes that Catholics should give the full assent to an infallible teaching Pope John Paul has requested. Those who dis-agree should "abstain from strident advocacy" and "pressures for doctrinal change"; and the pastoral leadership should exercise pa-tience and "show understanding for dissenters who exhibit good will and avoid disruptive behavior."[96] In today's theological and magisterial climate, I suspect that neither recommendation will be honored.

As a developing octogenarian, am I troubled? Profoundly. Not primarily because I am still struggling, at times agonizingly, with the arguments pro and con. Not because I object to serious, even passionate theological debate. More critically because I see positions hardening beyond possibility of change or reconciliation. This induration stems in large part from presuppositions essential to each stance, yet ignored or denied by the other party.

One example. Where Scripture, tradition, and theology are at issue, the differences between the papal and the feminist hermeneutic are clear and startling, even discouraging. While "preaching the just word" in Australia, I came across Jesuit Richard Leonard, in person and in his instructive little book *Beloved Daughters: 100 Years of Papal Teaching on Women.*[97] With incisive strokes Leonard sketches the difference between papal and feminist hermeneutics. Papal hermeneutics "works from a strongly defined sense of the archetype that tradition holds and defends it in both the words of the scriptural record and the actions of Christian history." Basing Elisabeth Schüssler Fiorenza's model is "an understanding that, at most, the tradition of the church provides a prototype which we imitate, reinterpret or change."[98] Why reinterpret or change? Because she is convinced that "the feminist critique of theology and tradition is best summarized by the statement of Simone Weil: 'History ... is nothing but a compilation of the depositions made by assassins with respect to their victims and themselves.' "[99]

In that context, and within the theological/reconstructionist school of which she is a powerful representative, Schüssler Fiorenza's procedure has for cornerstone a hermeneutic of *suspicion.* She approaches all biblical texts and theological traditions suspicious that the experience of women is not reflected or recorded therein; for both "Scripture and theology express truth in sexist language and images and participate in the myth of their patriarchal-sexist society and culture."[100] Suspicion leads to a hermeneutic of *remembrance,* an effort to reconstruct the feminist history of the first Christian centuries, to reclaim the memory of New Testament women, known and unknown.

Can the chasm separating the two approaches be bridged? I am pessimistic. Relevant here are three ecclesiologies within Roman Catholicism; for, as Raymond Brown argued a quarter century ago, "the ecclesiology that dominates may well tip the scales for or against ordaining women." Blueprint ecclesiology presupposes a

God-given blueprint in which all the basic structures were mapped out; ordination of women was not included. Erector-set ecclesiology claims that Christians are free to build the Church as utility directs; if the Church needs women priests, who is to say no? In-between ecclesiology combines the better elements of the other two: neither a blueprint nor an "anything useful" mentality; rather, a set of instructions together with the will of Christ and the guidance of the Spirit. With a typically engaging humor, Brown distinguished the three as respectively "the firm, the free, and the fickle."[101]

I am pessimistic, not because there are three ecclesiologies, but because the ecclesiologies rarely if ever engage one another. Never have we needed John Courtney Murray more, to stimulate us to civilized conversation.

Women Preachers?

In 1996 I was privileged to compose a Foreword for a book titled *Extraordinary Preaching: Twenty Homilies by Roman Catholic Women.*[102] The women all belonged to the Diocese of Rochester, New York; in each instance the women "were asked and authorized to preach."[103] The model of preaching used was the perspective of a woman, especially a laywoman. This meant "preaching from one's inner voice, preaching from experience, using imagery and story, and speaking of God in the particular. The homilies...get close to the needs of the human heart."[104]

The collection failed to surprise me, but it did delight me. It failed to surprise me because over a decade I had increasingly come to appreciate the singular gifts women bring to the art and craft of preaching. The appreciation stems not simply from my reading of published sermons but more significantly from (1) actually hearing women proclaim God's word with striking effectiveness; (2) getting to know women preachers on a more direct, personal level; and (3) listening with rare humility to feminine critiques, gracious but unfailingly frank, of my own efforts from the pulpit.

Not surprised, I was delighted. What is it that emerges from these female preachers and is all too often (not always) missing from our male clergy? (1) Concreteness coupled with imagination: in language, in stories, in use of contemporary as well as biblical symbols. (2) Ability to link rich, at times profound, understanding of Scripture with current issues, cultural and individual; reconstruction of the Bible's cultural and historical milieu so as to hear God's message addressed to us today. (3) Awareness that the word of God is addressed in the first instance to the preacher. (4) Realization that the outcome, the effect, depends not so much on the preacher's gifts as on the relationship between God and the individual listener. (5) Insights into the Gospels that ordinarily escape even the most insightful of males.

Nothing bland about these homilies. They are ceaselessly provocative, sure to exasperate the hidebound and occasionally the intelligently sophisticated, but always encouraging, uplifting, urging us to be free, graced men and women the Son of God took our flesh to shape.

I have but one regret: that "the days of our life are 70 years, or perhaps 80 if we are strong" (Ps 90:10). In that context, I shall not experience the day when women preach the gospel with the same freedom I have enjoyed for more than half a century. "Alas! poor Yorick."[105]

ELEVEN

From the Apostle Paul
to John Paul II
Crisis in the Church

For many, a crisis means an impending disaster, earth-shaking or soul-shattering. Raymond Brown, insightful and hopeful as always, pointed out that "in the biblical sense a *krisis* is a moment of judgment, and there never was a crisis so great as when Jesus of Nazareth proclaimed the inauguration of God's rule among men. The Master whose initial coming was a *krisis* may be speaking again to his people in the crises of today...."[1]

In this chapter I have set myself a mission impossible. To deal adequately with crisis in the Church, I must ask three complex questions: (1) How has American society, i.e., U.S. society, changed in recent decades? (2) How has the U.S. Catholic Church changed in the same period? (3) Given these changes, can the American Church still influence American society, and if so, how? The breadth and complexity of these questions compel me to confess once again that these pages carry the limitations of one man's experience, broadened though it is by access to a discouragingly rich treasury of scholarly literature.

Change in American Society

First question: How has U.S. society changed in recent decades? With large dependence on sociologists and historians, let me sketch a handful of areas where change in the society has implications for religion, for the Church.

First, *American society is increasingly pluralistic.* In Robert Bellah's understanding, the new pluralism means "not that life has become a 'one possibility thing' but that it has become an infinite possibility thing."[2] The implications for modern faith, for the churches, are several and significant. For one thing, "doctrinal uniformity becomes more difficult to maintain."[3] It is easier now for Christians and Hindus to "cross over" into hybrid forms. It is difficult for authority to proclaim effectively, "This you must believe and/or do, under peril of ceasing to be one of us."

Second, *American society has undergone secularization.* Here I have learned to be cautious: I may not confuse secularization with secularism. Secularism is an ideology, a view of life based on the premise that the religious dimension of human living should be ignored or excluded, and certainly has no place in the public square, in politics or law, in medicine or education. Secularization is a process — a process of increasing differentiation in society. Concretely, during my lifetime, religion, the churches, have increasingly ceased to be the primary mover and shaker in society. Other institutions, other organizations, other disciplines, with their own legitimate autonomy — law, medicine, university — have taken over responsibilities that the Church used to have, functions that the Church used to control.

Is it accurate to affirm, as many do, that American society has become secular? Almost three decades ago Andrew Greeley made an impressive effort to rebut that thesis. In his *Unsecular Man*[4] he argued that the basic human needs and the basic religious functions have not changed notably since the dawn of historical life. What is true is that now "religion has no direct influence over the large corporate structures which have emerged in the last four hundred years — big government, big business, big labor, big military, and big education."[5]

In this area, I found it startling and encouraging that Vatican II recognized a rightful autonomy in earthly affairs: "that created things and societies themselves enjoy their own laws and values which must be gradually deciphered, put to use, and regulated by men and women."[6]

Third, *American society has experienced an enormous advance in the extent and level of education.* The majority of Americans go on to college. Moreover, we have reached a point where a bachelor's degree is insufficient for the highest paying, most influential positions in society. In the legal profession alone, 35,000 new lawyers come into existence each year.

Fourth, *communication is instantaneous, universal, total.* What goes on in South Africa or Northern Ireland, in Moscow or Iraq, is our possession on the evening news. Computers dredge up in an hour information — historical, scientific, medical, industrial, whatever — that used to take scholars years to uncover. Fax machines convey in minutes from England to the United States what takes the postal service days to deliver. So-called e-mail and the Internet touch the world's strangers to one another with the flick of a finger. For good and/or ill, TV is our children's primary educator. A picture is indeed worth a thousand words. I have been haunted for decades by the Vietnamese child running down the road in flames, more recently by the Croatian mother mourning her son riddled by Serbian bullets.

Put another way, "Technology is now transforming the face of the earth, and is already trying to master outer space."[7] And technology confronts our society, our churches, with ethical dilemmas. Advances in the sciences, for example, not only expand immeasurably the range of our intellectual penetration; they open up areas of awesome decision making. Amniocentesis, revealing fetal defects to prospective parents; our capacity to provide nutrition and hydration for patients in a persistent vegetative state; medicine's hope to manipulate the origins of life, to alter our genes for an improved humanity; our ability to destroy, say, Iraq with nuclear weaponry — these and a hundred other technological marvels raise ethical questions our mothers and fathers could never have imagined.

Fifth, *a fresh character ideal has come to dominate American, in fact Western, civilization.* A distinguished sociologist, Philip Rieff, described it devastatingly almost four decades ago. Over against the ancient pagan commitment to the polis, to public life, over against the Judeo-Christian commitment to a transcendent God, over against the Enlightenment commitment to the irresistible progress of reason, the new ideal type is "anti-heroic, shrewd, carefully counting his satisfactions and dissatisfactions, studying unprofitable commitments as the sins most to be avoided." The "highest science"? Self-concern. Devotion and self-sacrifice? "Constraining ideals" that must be rejected. "Spiritual guidance" in the best Freudian sense is "to emancipate man's 'I' from the communal 'we.' "[8] Learn Freud's realism: Conflict is embedded in human living, expectations are inevitably frustrated, life can have no all-embracing meaning, death is final.

In the intervening four decades the situation Rieff described has apparently been aggravated. Frightening to me was Robert Bellah's uncovering of a widespread phenomenon in our fair land: a resurgence of late-nineteenth-century rugged individualism. American society is indeed moving away from religious man/woman, away from political man/woman, as character ideals. Those ideals were oriented to the public world, the community, the common good, the other. But when the central institution in our society is no longer religion or the political order but the economy, the ideal is now economic man/woman, man and woman in pursuit of private self-interest. One of Bellah's paragraphs imbedded itself deeply in my psyche in the early '80s:

> What is significant here is not the Moral Majority . . . but something that comes closer to being amoral and is in fact a majority. This new middle class believes in the gospel of success 1980 style. It is an ethic of how to get ahead in the corporate bureaucratic world while maximizing one's private goodies. In the world of the zero-sum society it is important to get to the well first before it dries up, to look out for number one, to take responsibility for your own life and keep it, while continuing to play the corporate game. . . . [9]

Change in the U.S. Catholic Church

When Paul wrote his first letter to the Christian community in Corinth, his pen was quivering. This community he himself had brought to birth, the church he loved so dearly, was torn within. Four factions were at odds, four Christian cliques, each with its special hero. Some were mesmerized by Apollos, eloquent expert on the Hebrew Bible. Others were pledged to Peter, "top gun" in their religion. The poor and the slaves clung pretty much to good old Paul. A proud elite fixed on Christ, but claimed an inside track to Christ not open to the "great unwashed." Bad enough, such unchristian catfights; but there was more: schism and incest, lawsuits and food from pagan sacrifices, disorderly conduct in church and abuses in the Lord's Supper. Some even denied the resurrection of the body.

It is in this context that I write about my own experience of the Catholic Church, specifically in the United States. I refer especially to the decades since Vatican II, although the seeds of the crisis were sown long before; I focus particularly on the two decades of Pope John Paul II, struggling to recapture a discipline, a uniformity, a Catholic "sense" increasingly elusive as quicksilver. Let me try to suggest how the Church of my experience has changed.

First, *American Catholicism has been polarized.* I mean, Catholics in this country give vivid appearance of being divided, roughly, into two camps, two conflicting mentalities (I shall modify this later). I refuse to call them conservative and liberal, broad and narrow, Vatican I and Vatican II Catholics. These terms are not only emotional fighting words; they fail to do justice to the realities of the situation. I would plump for a pair that is not indeed totally acceptable, yet is perhaps less annoying than any of the preceding. I call the two mentalities "strict" and "elastic" — and this in the sense I found in Webster's Second Edition Unabridged (1958). Strict "implies rigorous exactness, esp. as regards conformity to rules or standards." Elastic means "readily stretched without essential alteration."

You may remind me, as I have indicated above, that Catholicism has never existed without conflict, that there have always been rebels in the ranks, that as far back as the year 54 St. Paul told the Christians of Galatia, "There are some who trouble you and want to pervert the gospel of Christ" (Gal 1:7), and remarked to the Christians of Corinth around the same time, "It has been reported to me . . . that there is quarreling among you" (1 Cor 1:11). True, but I do detect a stunning change in the American Church since the '60s. Before that, conflict was isolated, a matter of individuals or small groups, on a handful of issues, rarely if ever out of control. Not so now. Conflict is constant, Catholics-for-this and Catholics-for-that grow each year, often unto contradiction, and it seems at times as if everything once sacred is "up for grabs." There is even group polarization within theology; witness the significant differences between the Catholic Theological Society of America and the Fellowship of Catholic Scholars.

Second, *the umbrella issue covering the conflict is papal authority.* For the strict mentality, once Rome has spoken, that is the end of it. Once a decision has been made, once Rome has spoken with "authentic" teaching authority, all Catholics are obligated to respond with what Vatican II called "religious submission of will and of mind" . . . even when the Roman pontiff is not speaking ex cathedra.[10] To dissent from it publicly is to be disloyal, less than Catholic. If there is to be dissent, the dissenter must express his or her disagreement privately, to authority itself, ready to accept whatever response authority makes.

This alone, it is claimed, is the properly Catholic attitude, for the pope and bishops have been given us by God precisely to lead us into truth. For this they have a special charism, a God-given gift not available to all the faithful. Authority does not have to explain, prove, convince, appeal to human intelligence. The Church is not a democracy or a debating society. The Church proclaims — proclaims the truth; and there it stands. This vision of authority is in harmony with the classical, traditional Catholic doctrine on the relationship between freedom and authority. Those who hold office make the decisions; the faithful in the ranks submit to the decisions, execute the orders.[11]

Such was the conception of authority under which I grew up: in the home, in the school, in the Jesuits, in the Church. Parent, teacher, rector, bishop — decision making was theirs. This was their task, their responsibility, God-given, with a corresponding grace of office: God's help to fulfil their mission. My task, my responsibility, was to act in harmony with their commands (save where sin was obviously present), eyes open if possible, eyes closed if necessary. Where authority was legitimate, the decision was presumably binding. Christian virtue lay in finding within the superior's will the will of God.

Classical indeed, says the elastic Catholic, but not good enough for our time. Vatican II recognized two signs of the times as crucial — our growing consciousness in two areas. The first is an increasing awareness of my dignity as a person. Take the programmatic sentences that open the council's Declaration on Religious Freedom:

> A sense of the dignity of the human person has been impressing itself more and more deeply on the consciousness of contemporary man and woman. And the demand is increasingly made that men and women should act on their own judgment, enjoying and making use of a responsible freedom, not driven by coercion but motivated by a sense of duty.[12]

The second sign is humankind's growing consciousness of community. Many are dissatisfied with the classical, fifth-century definition of the person, "an individual substance of a rational nature,"[13] with its emphasis on self-subsistence, incommunicability, independence. To be fully a person, to be fully human, I must be with the others and for the others. It is a vision that harmonizes splendidly with the Catholic understanding of the Trinity, where the divine Persons are constituted by their relationship one to another.

Given this twin consciousness, the classical conception of authority is seen by many as inadequate. Sheer submission to a superior's will and mere execution of his or her orders do not satisfy the demands of personal dignity. As John Courtney Murray phrased it, "They do not call into play the freedom of the person at its deepest level, where freedom appears as love."[14]

In sum, the elastic mentality insists that the traditional vertical relationship of command-obedience needs to be supplemented by the horizontal relationship of dialogue between authority and the free Christian community.

Third, *the authority-freedom conflict confronts us baldly in moral or ethical issues*. I select a handful that have impressed me particularly.

Take contraception. Andrew Greeley has long insisted that Paul VI's encyclical *Humanae vitae* is a watershed within American Catholicism. The document condemned artificial contraception as intrinsically evil; today, some surveys indicate, about 80 percent of Catholic women in the United States practice artificial birth control. Here is a doctrine which some theologians (not indeed the majority, but respectable) claim can be defined as a matter of Catholic faith, or is already taught infallibly by the ordinary magisterium (this latter I fail to see),[15] and yet four-fifths of this country's Catholic women either do not accept it as binding on them or at least do not find it feasible in practice.

Take abortion. I believe that the vast majority of American Catholics regard abortion as sinful, with perhaps exceptions for hard cases such as rape and incest. And yet we have a significant number of Catholics who are prochoice, convinced that what a woman does with her body is a private affair, not open to the intrusion of a male hierarchy. And Rome slapped Archbishop Rembert Weakland's wrist sharply for even *listening* to prochoice women and their anguish.

Take medical issues. Not many decades ago the Catholic faithful, including theologians, accepted Roman pronouncements on medicomoral problems as the last word; Catholic hospitals followed the episcopal *Directives* word for word. Not so today. Not a few theologians dispute Rome's assertion that *in vitro* fertilization is illicit even for husband and wife, challenge the declaration that sterilization is absolutely evil. And is it ever licit to withdraw nutrition and hydration from irreversibly comatose patients? Here too intractable lines have been drawn, hardened positions taken, within Catholic ethics.

Take politics. Catholic politicians are increasingly at odds with American prelates. For example, pastors have been forbidden to open their parish halls to civic officials or candidates who advocate public funds for the poor in the matter of abortion. Reasoned dialogue between bishops and politicians is a rarity. With certain exceptions, bishops condemn rather than discuss; there is no room for discussion, not after a Roman document. The result? Either the condemned disregard the condemnation, or the Catholic Church and the American public are deprived of some first-rate civil servants, are saddled not infrequently with run-of-the-mill politicos who never rock the bark of Peter.

Fourth, *the Eucharist,* which has traditionally been our supreme demonstration of oneness, *now divides us,* at times mortally. Shall we stand or kneel, sing Bach or the St. Louis Jesuits, blast heaven wide-open from an organ or strum a pop song on a guitar, greet one another with a hug or a handshake (or not at all), receive our Lord in the hand or on the tongue? For all too many, these are not liturgical accidentals, of small moment; they are at the core and heart of community worship, so much so that some Catholics refuse to worship with other Catholics save on their own narrow terms, even reject the Bread that gives life.

Fifth, *we have been broken on the issue of priesthood.* A vocation that before Vatican II was held in high regard now holds slender appeal for young America. In a single ten-year period, roughly 10,000 priests left the U.S. priesthood. Morale, I noted earlier, is low: too few priests for the work at hand; unreal expectations from an increasingly educated and critical laity; the loneliness of the celibate runner; schools and churches closing under the feet of priests who have literally given their lives for the least of Christ's brothers and sisters. Add to this the number of inactive priests who yearn to serve the Church but are prohibited by Roman regulation from contributing a wealth of competence and experience to a weakened clergy.

Sixth, a crisis of *justice.* Untold thousands of women are alienated from the Church because of what they see as patriarchy, a male-dominated clerical caste that keeps women in subjection — this illustrated most vividly, but not exclusively, in the Church's refusal to ordain women.

A nationwide Gallup survey of Catholic opinion (1992) commissioned by Catholics Speak Out and other church-reform groups included the following findings:

> Eighty-seven percent of respondents think couples should make their own decisions on birth control; 83 percent want the bishops to approve the use of condoms to prevent the spread of AIDS; 75 percent favor a married priesthood; 72 percent want bishops elected by the priests and bishops of a diocese; 70 percent believe they can, in good conscience, vote for candidates who support legal abortion; 67 percent favor the ordination of women to the priesthood (up 20 percentage points since 1985!); 52 percent believe abortion should be legal in *many* or *all* circumstances.[16]

Seventh, the impact of patriarchy on the Church's *social teaching.* Feminist scholars (as well as a number of male theologians, social scientists, and economists[17]), while recognizing that Catholic social teaching strengthens the feminist movement at several major points (equality in dignity with men, right to a just wage, preferential option for the poor), find it inadequate on several significant counts. There is (so the claim runs) an almost exclusive dependence on preceding papal statements. Even more importantly, the overriding issue is patriarchy. The challenges are no longer muted. Catholic social teaching is written by men, primarily about men; it assumes that man, Western man, is normative for the human. It validates a social order where women are subordinate to men. It condemns the sin of sexism in the world but denies structural failures in the Church. It excludes women from power, keeps their voices from having any influence on the Church's teaching. It prevents the gifts of women from shaping the culture of God's reign here and now. "All of this inequality and denial of gifts is abhorrent to another principle of Catholic social teaching — the common good."[18]

Eighth, the Church and the *labor movement*. Until the early '60s, the Catholic Church was by far the largest denomination that supported labor. Its leaders were many bishops, priests, and nuns whose origins were the working class; its members were characterized by a high degree of organizational loyalty and commitment; bishops could deliver votes.

> Much of that changed in the latter half of the 1960s — partly as a result of church reform and the education of the laity, but mostly because of the upward mobility of millions of Catholics. A church of working-class immigrants was transformed into a church of relatively affluent suburbanites. In the change, labor and U.S. Catholicism, despite the continued development of Catholic social teachings, had grown estranged.
>
> For the newest immigrants, among them Hispanics and Asian Catholics, the church's old genius at organizing and assimilating had seemingly lost its charm.[19]

Assent and Dissent

During my theological lifetime "assent" and "dissent" have become increasingly troubling terms. For many Catholics, including some theologians, there should be no problem; the problem is caused by Catholics, especially theologians, who do not accept the decisive paragraph in Vatican II's Dogmatic Constitution on the Church:

Bishops teaching in communion with the Roman pontiff are to be respected by all as witnesses to divine and Catholic truth. The faithful, for their part, are obliged to agree with the official declaration of their bishop (*in sui Episcopi sententiam ... concurrere*) issued in the name of Christ in matters of faith and morals, and adhere to it with a religiously conscientious submission of mind and will (*religioso animi obsequio*). This religiously conscientious submission of will and of mind (*religiosum voluntatis et intellectus obsequium*) must be shown in a special way to the authentic teaching authority (*authentico magisterio*) of the Roman pontiff, even when he is not speaking ex cathedra — in such a way that his supreme teaching authority is acknowledged with respect and sincere assent is given to decisions issued by him, conformably to his manifest mind and will.[20]

From this passage and the acrimonious debates it has occasioned I find that two Latin words still demand extraordinarily careful investigation: *magisterium* and *obsequium*, which I have rendered "teaching authority" and (tentatively) "submission."[21]

Magisterium

The restrictive and exclusive meaning of *magisterium* as "the teaching authority of the hierarchy" began to develop among German theologians and canonists in the eighteenth century, became widely accepted in the nineteenth, probably was first used in a papal document by Gregory XVI in 1835, found ample use in the schemata of Vatican I, and from that point on "became a household term in Catholic theology."[22] The increasing use of encyclicals on an ever larger number of issues, ranging from exercise of "supreme apostolic authority" to private theological convictions, raised a question: How determine the authority of particular papal pronouncements? The problem was complicated by ever more frequent papal reliance on theologians (e.g., Roman professors, curial officials): How far was a given pronouncement a proclamation of universally held Catholic doctrine, to what extent did it reflect the opinion of a theological school?[23] To assess the weight of such documents, a new hermeneutic was necessary.

When I was a theological student at Woodstock College from 1938 to 1941, some such hermeneutic was in place. Each thesis had its "note" or theological qualification: e.g., defined as of faith, close to definition, certain and Catholic (because contained in an official document), certain and common (because commonly taught by theologians), probable (because the arguments pro were considered stronger than the arguments con). But the task was hardly complete, if only because theologians had to grapple not only with academic theses, not only with clearly papal and conciliar documents, but with a growing number of instructions, decrees, declarations, and other communications from increasingly numerous offices and commissions of the Holy See. Here a whole set of new rules was demanded and not readily available.

To trust my own experience, I find that in recent decades few Catholic theologians have tried to build on the older effort to "qualify" an official statement "by referring its content to our ancient traditions, by examining critically the source of that pronouncement, and weighing carefully the authority behind it."[24] In what I presume to term an ultraconservative, theologically indefensible, pastorally harmful approach, all too many Catholics insist that *any* official document from Rome, whether directly from the pope or from a Roman congregation with papal approval, demands immediate submission of intellect and will. Sufficient for such a demand is a simple fact: Rome has spoken. The teaching is official, authentic, hence binding on simply every Catholic.

I shudder at such simplism when I recall the solemn declaration of Boniface VIII in 1302: "We declare, affirm, and define that for salvation it is necessary for every human creature to be subject to the Roman pontiff."[25] And, as Ladislas Orsy has pointed out, "No theologian has ever succeeded in determining the specific weight of condemnation for each individual item in the *Syllabus* of Pius IX."[26] Take, more recently, the movement within Catholicism in the area of religious freedom. May we not say that Vatican II's affirmation of religious freedom based on the dignity of the human person is discontinuous with certain explicit elements within the Catholic tradition, that Catholicism now rejects what in the nineteenth century it held as doctrine, that the limits Rome imposed on John Courtney Murray in the 1950s were ill-advised?

Pertinent to the discussion of magisterium is the meaning to be given to "ordinary" magisterium. Two meanings emerge from our sources. In the standard theology textbooks before Vatican II, ordinary magisterium meant that a point of doctrine was determined as integral to Catholic faith not by an infallible decree of a general council or by a papal definition, but through its consistent affirmation as Catholic doctrine by popes and bishops. Such is the understanding retained in the 1983 Code of Canon Law, canon 750. A relatively new use, in particular by Roman authorities, applies the term simply to "the ordinary and usual teaching and preaching activity of the hierarchy, affirming a point of doctrine which (as yet) cannot be said to be part of our Catholic faith because as yet the Church has not affirmed it with a decisive judgment."[27] Legitimate use; but problems arise when the same absolute obedience is demanded in both instances.

Obsequium

I am convinced that Ladislas Orsy has uncovered a significant truth: In the documents of Vatican II there are terms and expressions that are not precise concepts.[28] They are "seminal locutions," terms or expressions that contain the truth but do not circumscribe it precisely; they call for further development, new insights through reflection or even experience. A clear example: "The Church of Christ subsists (*subsistit*) in the Catholic Church."[29] We are still in disagreement on the meaning of that all-important Latin word. The argument is not settled by going back to the discussions and drafts, indispensable as these are; for we do not know what went on in the minds of the vast majority who officially approved the document.

Obsequium, Orsy insists, is one of these seminal words.

> The discussion whether it means precisely "respect" or "submission" works on a wrong assumption, which is that the Council indeed meant it in a specific and precise way. The Council has spoken on a different level. When it spoke of religious *obsequium,* it meant an attitude toward the Church which is rooted in the virtue of religion, the love of God and the love of His Church. This attitude in every concrete case will be in need of further specification, which could be "respect" or could be "submission," depending on the progress the Church has made in clarifying its own beliefs.
>
> *Obsequium,* like *communio,* ultimately means to be one with the Church, one in mind and heart, which means one in belief and in action. *Obsequium* is a special expression of this communion, mainly in doctrinal matters. It is ideally perfect when someone is so well united in faith with the Church as to believe all that the Church holds firmly, and search with the Church when some point in our tradition is in need of clarification. In the first case we can speak of *obsequium fidei*

(one with the believing Church, holding firm to a doctrine), in the second case, of an *obsequium religiosum* (one with the searching Church, working for clarification).[30]

All this leads quite naturally into an explosive contemporary issue in the United States: dissent. An unfortunate word, for it is totally negative, ill-defined, all too sweeping, historically loaded, charged with emotion. Not a useful rubric for intelligent, civilized, profitable Christian conversation. Still, there it is, and for the time being we must live with it. And so we ask: Is public dissent from official teaching ever legitimate, and if so, what are the limits thereof? Herewith, succinctly, my approach to these questions.

1. As a believing Catholic, I recognize, gratefully, the charism within the Church, specifically its teaching authority, to determine what is to be believed as matters of faith, God's revealed truth, from Nicaea's declaration (325) that the Son is God as truly as the Father is God, to Pius XII's definition (1950) that the mother of Jesus, upon closing her life on earth, was assumed into God's presence in soul and body. Not that further development in understanding infallible doctrine is outlawed; simply that the essence of the doctrine in question, its central affirmation, its heart is beyond Catholic challenge. Is that essence itself untouchable? Hardly, but not unto contradiction.

2. As a Catholic theologian, I recognize, gratefully, the charism within the official Church to guide me in my search for God's truth. In consequence, I may not simply see noninfallible pronouncements from Rome as "up for grabs" because they are not issued with "supreme authority." They demand a respectful reception, if only because the presumption lies in favor of their truth. But does a respectful reception allow for another opinion, and that publicly asserted? I believe so, while I am convinced that there is no single solution that can be applied to all cases, e.g., all public dissent is incompatible with Catholic fidelity, or dissent is legitimate as long as the teaching has not been defined. Particular circumstances make many, if not all, cases unique. Let me speak from my personal experience.

Theology has been my life and love for six decades. In the twilight of my existence I have two especially agonizing, intertwined concerns: one for Catholic theology, the other for the magisterium.

As for Catholic theology, I much fear that we are not sufficiently self-critical. Within three decades Catholic theology has moved from a tight, self-enclosed, rigidly controlled, easily recognizable discipline to a bewildering maze of theologies where apparently many practitioners do their "thing" according to their own lights, with scant glances at Rome. In consequence, we strike most Catholics as shadowy intellectuals who build ivory towers, sit there studying dusty tomes or contemplating uninspiring navels, and occasionally descend to earth to make abstract pronouncements unconnected with real life or to emit inflammatory noises that contradict the catechism, confuse the Christian, bait the bishops, and burn a little more of Rome. I am persuaded that it is high time we *began* to get our theological act together. Not a new *summa;* we are not ready for that, may never again be. Simply a gigantic, co-operative effort at self-reflection, to determine where we are, where we are failing, where we ought to go. To what extent are our theologies serving the Church universal, the faithful as a whole, and not simply the intellectual enterprise called "religious studies"?

As for the magisterium, will it end the twentieth century repeating ill-advised approaches that began it?[31] Injurious, I suggest, to Catholic theology is the public affirmation of a U.S. archbishop that "all public dissent is illegitimate." Theology itself is a public activity, a ceaseless interchange, published critique. Inimical to Catholic theology are the "hit lists" that abound, unofficial but influential dossiers of suspect theologians. On one of these the accusations against me ranged from allowing "dissenting" articles to appear in *Theological Studies,* through destroying Jesuit spirituality in the United States, to being photographed for the public press wearing a turtleneck sweater. Inadequate for Catholic theology is unqualified repetition of Pius XII's 1950 declaration, "It is the task of theologians to show how the doctrines taught by the living magisterium are found either explicitly or implicitly in the Sacred Books and in divine tradition,"[32] without clear recognition of theology's critical function, its obligation to put its scholarly charism to work on all efforts, even magisterial, to interpret or develop the tradition. Here I was encouraged by an address of Paul VI on October 6, 1969 (at which I was present) to the newly formed International Theological Commission, wherein he expressed his intention "to recognize the laws and exigencies that are part and parcel of your studies..., to respect the freedom of expression rightfully belonging to theological science, and the need for research inherent to its progress."[33] This charism can be effectively exercised only in a context of open collaboration among the competent.

Is there danger of confusion among the less sophisticated? Yes indeed! Is there peril of that much-abused word "scandal"? Of course!

And so, in an age of communication explosion, when theology rips its way into *Time* and the Internet, we theologians must be extraordinarily careful to link insight and discovery with pastoral prudence. But not to the destruction of the discipline itself, of the elements that make it what it is. Not to a resurgence of the mid-century mentality that kept de Lubac (an unjustifiably labeled "new theology"), Congar (including his classic *True and False Reform of the Church*), and Murray (the religious freedom that was canonized by Vatican II) from enriching Catholic understanding with the fruits of their research.

In 1968, while teaching patristic theology at Woodstock College in Maryland, I expressed my dissatisfaction with the universality of the prohibition against artificial contraception. My reluctance to accept the document in its totality stemmed in large measure from a certain complex, agonizing pastoral experience which forced me to the conclusion that in some instances, rare indeed, such action might be morally justified. I have paid dearly for that "dissent." I have been asked why I do not in good honesty leave the Church, since I have for all practical purposes abandoned it. A bishop in Owensboro, Kentucky, compelled Brescia College to rescind its invitation to me to *lecture* there, because (so his letter read) his oath of fidelity to the Holy See did not allow him to permit someone who did not share that fidelity to *preach* in his diocese. After discovering late in life what I had done in 1968, a colleague who had collaborated with me for 30 years on a patristic translation project decided that he could no longer in conscience work with me. A Midwest monsignor has listed me among "dissenting Modernist maggots."

All this despite the fact that *after* my "dissent" Paul VI appointed me to his first International Theological Commission, fashioned to advise the pope in doctrinal matters. A "dissident" on the pope's own theological commission? Gratifying to me was the reaction of Cardinal Lawrence Shehan of Baltimore (Woodstock was then in his archdiocese). He asked me only whether in the pulpit, in the confessional, and in spiritual direction I could present the doctrine of *Humanae vitae* as the official, authentic doctrine of the Church. "Of course," I replied; "I would not dream of acting otherwise." Three decades later I can say that I have never swerved from that promise. Gratifying as well is the confidence placed in me by scores of American bishops who have welcomed me into their dioceses to address their clergy, religious, and laity in areas of theology and spirituality.

Common Ground

In August 1996 Chicago's late Cardinal Joseph Bernardin conceived a project he called the Catholic Common Ground Initiative (CCGI). Its purpose was "to draw American Catholics into a new mode of confronting the controversial issues that polarize and paralyze us, an invitation to all to move beyond the labels of 'liberal' and 'conservative,' 'left' and 'right,' and to listen to each other with charity, humility, and respect."[34] The initiative's founding document, "Called To Be Catholic: The Church in a Time of Peril," was prepared by the National Pastoral Life Center located in New York City. It analyzed Catholic tensions in the United States, indicated their devastating effect on liturgical life and pastoral activity, and suggested principles for acceptable dialogue. Lending incomparable credibility to the document was the dying cardinal's yearning to begin a process of healing and reconciliation that might lead the Catholic community beyond the present atmosphere of negativity and suspicion.

For the most part, the public reactions have been encouraging. But shortly after the initiative was announced, four U.S. cardinals, Bernard Law of Boston, Adam Maida of Detroit, Anthony Bevilacqua of Philadelphia, and James Hickey of Washington, D.C., expressed reservations about the document and the wisdom of starting public initiatives for reconciliation within the Church apart from the leadership of the Vatican and the National Conference of Catholic Bishops.[35] Some Catholics criticized the initiative for not being sufficiently inclusive in its sponsoring committee or sufficiently radical in its aims. Two prominent Catholic theologians, Avery Dulles and David Schindler, criticized the initiative "for not clearly distinguishing the way of reconciliation proper to Christian believers — conversion and mutual commitment to Christ within a structured eucharistic community — from the more ideologically neutral kind of public dialogue familiar to us in a modern, liberal, democratic society."[36] In consequence, they argued, the initiative would simply contribute to the current unclarity about where genuine unity is to be found.

I am not convinced. Common Ground is not a problem-solving body, does not intend to settle issues heatedly disputed, will not negotiate grievances. "Common Ground challenges the Catholic Church in America to capture the same approach to dialogue it has been engaged in for 30 years now, with considerable success, with virtually all the other Christian churches and with most of the other major world religions."[37] I remember writing to Bernardin to encourage him with a sentence from Vatican II's Decree on Ecumenism, no. 9: "Of great value [for understanding the outlook of our separated brethren] are meetings between the two sides, especially for discussion of theological problems, where each can deal with the other on an equal footing." If with separated brethren, why not with brothers and sisters of the same household?

Another agonizing instance of our inner disunity, but this time among hierarchs as well. For me, the significant question is: How shall we respond? Wait for the Vatican or the Conference of Bishops to emit a ukase denouncing errors and demanding complete surrender? Threaten membership in dissenting organizations with excommunication? Or establish lines of communication? Why not give communication a try?

In a highly recommended volume titled *American Catholic,*[38] Charles Morris has presented what he sees as the problem confronting the American Church now. If the ecclesial right wins a complete victory, the Church could very well wither, surviving as a diminished body of true believers. But if the left wins, the Church could very well go the way of mainstream Protestantism, dissolve into the larger culture, becoming more an aura than an institution. I recognize the danger. Still, I am convinced that our possibilities as a church were more fully predicted by Jesuit Bernard Lonergan three decades ago:

> The crisis . . . that I have been attempting to depict is a crisis not of faith but of culture. . . . Classical culture cannot be jettisoned without being replaced; and what replaces it cannot but run counter to classical expectations. There is bound to be formed a solid right that is determined to live in a world that no longer exists. There is bound to be formed a scattered left, captivated by now this, now that new development, exploring now this and now that new possibility. But what will count is a perhaps not numerous center, big enough to be at home in both the old and the new, painstaking enough to work out one by one the transitions to be made, strong enough to refuse half-measures and insist on complete solutions even though it has to wait.[39]

Can the Church Still Influence Society?

These citations from Morris and Lonergan may serve to introduce the third major question I raised for this chapter: Given the changes in culture and church, can the American Church still influence American society, and if so, how?

As is obvious, in a number of areas the Church's influence has been diminished, though not necessarily destroyed. At the polls, Catholic and Democrat are no longer synonymous. On many moral issues, Catholics do not speak with one voice, do not live the same lives. For many Catholics, the Church is at best a guide to be consulted, not a teacher to be obeyed. The pulpit, once the ordinary Catholic's "ordinary magisterium" for the communication of truth, labors under two obstacles: an increasingly educated, liberated, independent body of the faithful, and a largely unimpressive communication too often devoid of substance and style. What was of old a respected priesthood has been horribly hurt by pedophilia, sexual abuse, and financial malfeasance. In a word, the Catholic image does not evidence the luster that commanded respect, if not always imitation, decades ago.

This loss of a certain luster was expressed in compelling language by Irish poet Seamus Heaney, awarded the Nobel Prize for Literature in 1996. Disillusioned with the repressive elements in his Catholic past, yet gifted with the poet's ability to breathe fresh life into enfeebled or incomprehensible spiritual categories like the sacred and the sacramental, concepts like transfiguration and transcendence, he remarked in a 1996 interview for the *Irish America Magazine*:

> Obviously, I could talk until the cows come home about the minority status of Catholics in the North of Ireland, but that ground has been gone over. I would say that the more important Catholic thing is the actual sense of eternal values and infamous vices which our education or formation gives us. There's a sense of profoundness, a sense that the universe can be ashimmer with something, and Catholicism — even if I don't like sentimentalizing it — was the backdrop to that whole thing. The world I grew up in offered me a sense that I was a citizen of the empyrean — the crystalline elsewhere of the world. But *I think that's gone from Catholicism now*.[40]

Such criticism, from the poetic stream of Catholicism, shivers me. The Church of Christ was never meant to be dull, deadening, uninspiring, just another organization obsessed with its internal problems. Christians were charged by Christ to be "the salt of the earth, the light of the world" (Mt 5:13–14). Salt, seasoning God's world, keeping it from rotting; light, the divine shimmer that keeps a sinful world from the darkness of despair.

How recapture that? Let me suggest two areas where I believe that crisis, in the biblical sense of "moment of judgment," can restore to the Catholic Church not only a certain external luster and inner pride but also a significant influence on American culture.

The Catholic Intellectual

Familiar to many educated Catholics is John Tracy Ellis' 1955 article in *Thought* titled "American Catholics and the Intellectual Life."[41] Incontrovertible in his eyes was the weakest aspect of the Church in the United States, "its failure to produce national leaders and to exercise commanding influence in intellectual circles," and this at a time when U.S. Catholics' "material resources are incomparably superior to those of any other branch of the universal church." How explain this? Ellis' reasons included (1) a profound anti-Catholic prejudice in the early seventeenth century that made for a climate distinctly unfriendly to Catholic ideas and for a preference among Catholics for apologetics rather than pure scholarship; (2) the immigrant character of U.S. Catholicism from the 1820s to the 1920s; (3) absence of an intellectual tradition among American Catholics, save for the Maryland gentry; (4) lack of serious reading habits within Catholic families; (5) attachment to material goods and the desire to make a fortune; (6) the failure of lay and clerical Catholics in leadership posts to appreciate the vocation of the intellectual.

Ellis' essay sparked several decades of intense discussion; it opened the floodgates of self-criticism as nothing had before.[42] Three decades later, interviewed by Dolores Liptak and Timothy Walch,[43] Ellis was asked whether, given the changes that had taken place in American Catholicism since 1955, there were signs of improvement in our intellectual life. Ellis acknowledged improvement "here and there, but not enough, nothing like what I think it should be." Reasons: (1) too many Catholic colleges and universities; (2) a lack of desire to excel in intellectual matters. No longer, said Ellis, can we evoke our immigrant roots, poverty, anti-Catholicism. Even if we recognize the remarkable resurgence in Catholic biblical and theological scholarship since 1955, Ellis' broad picture is difficult to dispute.

It was in this context that in the spring of 1989 I addressed a Georgetown University symposium on Catholic intellectualism.[44] My thesis was this: Practicing Catholics will make their distinctive Catholic contribution to American intellectual life not in the first instance because they accept what the Church teaches, obey church law, and share in liturgical worship, but to the extent that their Catholicism is integral to their scholarship. I offered then, and I offer now, five suggestions on how that wedding might be consummated.

First, for Catholics the intellectual life should be as authentic a vocation as priesthood or marriage. Ironically, such has been a rich tradition within the Church. It goes back to the first Christian "university" in third-century Alexandria, to Origen and his four remarkable insights: recognition of the rights of reason; a sweepingly broad acquisition of knowledge; Christian criticism, the intelligent confrontation of the old with the new; love of truth wherever it is to be found, and a profound yearning to include all the scattered fragments of discovered truth under what a later pupil of Origen called "the Holy Word, the loveliest thing there is." It runs through the Benedictine tradition of education, admirably synthesized in the title of Dom Jean Leclercq's minor classic *The Love of Learning and the Desire for God*. I believe it is implicit in the 28 Jesuit colleges and universities created at stunning sacrifice in the United States.

> It was set irrevocably in the heavens by astronomers like Clavius and Secchi; multiplied over and over by mathematicians like Kircher and Boscovich; carried to the ends of the earth by missionaries like humanist-scientist Matteo Ricci; brought into our own era by Maritain and Dawson, Teilhard and Flannery O'Connor. For these and uncounted others, Catholicism and intellectualism were not isolated compartments, two parts of the human psyche. In all they accomplished, faith was the motivating force, the energy that drove them relentlessly. To be a Catholic was to prize intelligence.[45]

Within Catholicism, scholarship, research, the life of the mind is not a game, not a hobby for such as can afford the time or have leisure for loafing, not a dispensable occupation like skink catching, not irrelevant to the gospel and to salvation. It is a response to God, to God's call to serve, to open up the wonders of created reality, to pay reverence to what creation's God saw "was very good" (Gen 1:31).

Second, given faith as motive, how integrate Catholicism and professionalism more intensely? One example, I suggested, may speak more loudly than abstractions. The science of eugenics is ushering us into a future where the New Human will reveal qualities significantly greater than any we experience at present. We are on the threshold of being able to remake ourselves according to a human image of humankind. On the other hand, our Christian calling summons us to share in the humanity of Jesus, and so in his bodiedness, sacramentally now, integrally in the final kingdom. In that context Jesuit Robert Brungs, then director of the Institute for Theological Encounter with Science and Technology, asked whether and how Christ's body is normative for our bodies, whether there are physical limits to living in God's community.

It is the task, Brungs insisted, not only of Rome but of the Catholic technologist to work out the answers to five crucial questions. (1) Does a particular biological alteration enhance the innate, internal dignity of the human — which involves the sacramental and covenantal character of the body? (2) Does a particular enhancement foster personal freedom? (3) Does the proposed bodily alteration preserve (and increase) the bodily integrity needed for conformity with the body of Christ? (4) Does the alteration promote a closer integration into the human community and a closer entry into the sacramental living and growing of the covenantal community? (5) Does the proposed enhancement tend to promote worship of God, or does it lead away from that worship?[46]

Such is the kind of involvement I saw as indispensable if the technologist is to be Catholic precisely as a technologist. It demands both a broad grasp of the Church's tradition and an intimate involvement in the ceaseless struggle to link mastery of creation with submission to creation's Master. Only such a Catholic intellectual is in a position to confront effectively a type of technological, rational mentality that in ever new ways and on a global level is producing a new atheism. Michael Buckley, then (1989) professor of systematic theology at Notre Dame (now at Boston College), phrased our problem succinctly: "The confused situation which confronts the contemporary religious mind in the intellectual culture of the U.S. is not so much argument or even hostility. It is dismissal — a cultural indifference to the entire and increasingly discredited theological enterprise itself."[47]

Third, moving out from professionalism, I am concerned for the type of intellectual life that, in Sidney Callahan's words, "arises from the broader activity of thoughtful and intelligent people reading, discussing, and responding to ideas and arguments devoted to the meaning of events and the interpretation of human experience." This level of intellectual activity makes its own call for competence. Not degrees in divinity, but surely a grasp on the Catholic tradition that oils the mind for wrestling with contrasting ideas, current controversies, and opposing world views. It calls for an individual experience contextualized by the community experience that spans ages and continents. Such a grasp is less and less in evidence in a culture where the past is a museum piece and yesterday says nothing to today.

Fourth, intellectualism dares not remain mired in the sheerly rational. The life of the mind must be fired by what Jesuit William F. Lynch saw as the Christian or Christic imagination. Not the fantastic, the grotesque, the bizarre. Simply the world of intuition and wonder, of amazement and delight, of festivity and play. It's the vision and the dream, ritual and symbol, story and the fine arts. It's the Bible with its vast array of symbols from the creation story in Genesis through the parables of Jesus to the four horsemen in the Apocalypse. It's Michelangelo's *Last Judgment* and Beethoven's *Missa solemnis;* Kazantzakis' *Report to Greco* and Hopkins' "The Blessed Virgin Compared to the Air We Breathe"; Martin Luther King's dream of freedom and today's God as mother, lover, friend of the earth.

I am not downgrading abstract thought, conceptual analysis, rational demonstration, scientific experiment. These are basic to liberal education. I do insist that, for the Catholic spirit to come alive, the clear and distinct idea is not enough. Rich indeed, but not rich enough. The image is more open-ended than the concept, more susceptible of different understandings; therein lie the risk and the joy.[48]

I do not predict that without imagination intellectuals will be unhappy or unsuccessful. I do claim that without it they may miss much of the thrill in human and Christian living, that they run a greater risk of finding existence unexciting, that x-number of the dead and despairing will not be quickened to life by them, that they may fail to touch in love a living God whose glory challenges not so much our logic as our imagining. For, as metaphysician Jacques Maritain asserted six decades ago, the culmination of knowledge is not conceptual but experiential: I "feel" God.[49]

Fifth, I am convinced that Catholics whose lives are largely consecrated to ideas are not exempt from the charge laid on the People of God by the words that open Vatican II's Pastoral Constitution on the Church in the Modern World: "The joys and the hopes, the griefs and the anxieties of the men and women of this age, especially those who are poor or in any way afflicted, these too are the joys and hopes, the griefs and anxieties of the followers of Christ." One example. Intellectuals must play a significant role in episcopal documents, as they did on peace and the economy. Pastorals are not crafted by choirs of angels; they stem from women and men —

preferably women and men whose ideas have been refined in the furnace of experience.

Alluring indeed, but is such a wild idea possible? Obstacles abound. I limit myself to three. First, most educated Catholics, including clerics, lack a sense of Catholic tradition — what I have defined as the best of our past, infused with the insights of the present, with a view to a richer, more catholic future. After 16 years at two Catholic universities, I still marvel at a paradox: the number of Catholic students who live a modest or even profound spiritual life and are utterly ignorant of their rich tradition. *Pace* prejudiced dramatist Christopher Durang, Sister Ignatius did *not* tell it all.[50]

Second, allied to ignorance of tradition is an absence of historical consciousness. Despite its absence from Vatican II's *aula,* classicism still dominates much of Roman Catholic mentality, an orthodoxy where truth exists "somewhere out there," apart from history, apart from its possession by anyone. Not only un-Catholic; anti-intellectual.

Third, for intellectual discouragement, consider our intramural, internecine hostility. The Catholic Theological Society of America and the Fellowship of Catholic Scholars mirror evangelist John's Jews and Samaritans: With rare exceptions they "have no dealings" with one another (Jn 4:9). Slogans displace discussion: There are Curran Catholics and Ratzinger Catholics, *Commonweal* Catholics and American Enterprise Institute Catholics, Catholics United for the Faith and Catholics united for women's ordination. You are prolife or prochoice, and heaven help you if you insert a caveat to either — or worse, listen to the other. There is Opus Dei, there is *Fidelity,* and there is the *Wanderer* — and so on into the night.

I do not outlaw controversy; I expect it; it's been a constant in our history. It is largely through what John Courtney Murray called "civilized conversation" that concepts are clarified, the real issues break through clouds, and truth has a chance to triumph. The interfaith dialogues, such as the Lutheran-Roman Catholic dialogue I still treasure, are splendid examples. I do fear, however, that the two extremes — isolation on the one hand and bitter invective on the other — keep the Catholic community precisely as community from bringing Christ and the Church convincingly to bear on American culture. I am afraid that the picture we intellectuals present to our fellow Americans is a huge house hopelessly divided against itself. It raises a rough question: Do we actually have a Catholic intellectual *community?*

When the picture pushes me toward pessimism, I have recourse, as often, to sociologist Andrew Greeley. In an article a decade ago in *America* magazine,[51] he asserted that the denial of a Catholic intellectual and cultural elite in the United States represents "a view of the state of the laity that is pervasive in the *ecclesiastical institution*,"[52] which keeps asserting their nonexistence because it "does not know what to do with this elite. Certainly, it is not about to listen to them, much less to read their work or learn from them."[53] Somewhat harsh perhaps, but Greeley proceeded to name over 50 prominent Catholics (several clerics, Madonna too, Richard M. Daley, and Martin Scorsese) in various fields and categories. To the argument that some on his list are at best only nominal or perfunctory Catholics, Greeley suggested leaving the state of their souls to God, pointed out that they still identified themselves as Catholic, and stated that "in many cases their work reflects a Catholic vision."[54] Statistics?

> Among [Catholics] who fall in the artist-scholar-writer-performer category, 56 percent attend church regularly... (only 5 percent of these never attend Mass)....
>
> If there are 40 million Catholic adults, there are almost one million Catholics who can make some claim to be part of the intellectual and cultural creative elites. More than half of them — perhaps half a million — regularly show up at Sunday (or Saturday evening) Mass. Not bad. Has there ever been a larger or more devout elite? Perhaps not.[55]

In 1989 Greeley projected that in the next 15 years the proportion of well-educated Catholics (then half the Catholic population) would increase more than it did in the preceding fifteen. "Under such conditions the proportions in the cultural and scholarly and artistic elites will also continue to increase dramatically."[56]

Still the neuralgic question haunts me: Are we Catholic "cultural and scholarly and artistic elites" in a genuine sense a Catholic *community?*

Generation X

A second group of Catholics that has rich potential for influencing American society comprises our young. I would begin with a concerted effort directed at the generation called the Baby Busters or Generation X, born from 1961 to 1981. The University of Notre Dame's R. Scott Appleby (born in 1956) has described this generation from close study and personal experience.

Generation X has been raised on television in a way that no prior generation has been. Not only on television, but on the Internet and the World Wide Web. They are interactive in very important ways, and this is central to their religious consciousness. This generation is one that, according to one recent interpreter, is about 70% white, 13% African American, about 12% Hispanic or Latino and smaller percentages of Asian and other ethnic groups. This is the most educated generation in history, contrary to what some conservative critics say. Even though there is a broad debate about the quality of their education, certainly this is a sophisticated group of young adults. It is a group that there is much controversy about in terms of their loyalty to the institutional church.[57]

Appleby's summary statistics about some of the social and economic circumstances faced by Generation X are sobering.

Real wages peaked in this country in 1973 and have been declining ever since, yet we work an average of one month more per year than we did two decades ago. Since the mid 1970s, poverty among young adults 18 to 34 has gone up by 50 percent, while the median income for under 30 parents fell by one third. In 1993 AIDS was the top killer of young adults in sixty-four cities and five states. Twenty-five percent of all African-American men in their twenties are either in prison, on probation, or on parole. Nearly half of the new full-time jobs created in the 1980s paid less than $250 a week or $13,000 a year — below the poverty line for a family of four. Every day over 2,500 American children witness the divorce or separation of their parents. Every day 90 children are taken from their parents' custody and committed to foster homes. Every day 13 Americans aged 15 to 24 commit suicide and another 16 are murdered. Nearly one in three college graduates between 1990 and 2005 is expected to take a job that does not require a college degree. That is up from one in ten college graduates in the 1960s. Every day the typical fourteen-year-old watches three hours of TV and does one hour of homework. Every day over 2,200 kids drop out of school, 3,610 teenagers are assaulted, 630 are robbed, 80 are raped. Every day 500 adolescents begin using illegal drugs and 1,000 begin drinking alcohol. Every day 1,000 unwed teenage girls become mothers.[58]

Increasingly evident to keen observers is a segment of Generation X who feel that the Church has changed too much too soon. They harbor no bitter memories of nuns with rulers for weapons, do not equate sexuality with guilt, listen attentively to grandparents reminiscing about a Catholic life clear and serene, with its Benediction and rosary, novenas and confession, Latin Mass. They join an absence of antagonism to the Church and its ministers to a profound ignorance of Catholic doctrine and devotions. A smaller group is not so much conservative as reactionary, resists not only vernacular liturgy and Communion in the hand or from the chalice, but even Opus Dei and Mother Angelica. Then there are those University of Chicago graduate students who are discovering Maritain and Balthasar, Gilson and Guardini, "are conservative in the sense that they want to conserve what has been good, beautiful and true in the 2,000 years since the coming of Jesus."[59]

It is in this context that on June 20, 1997, during their general meeting in Kansas City, Missouri, the U.S. bishops unanimously adopted a statement titled "Renewing the Vision: A Framework for Catholic Youth Ministry."[60] The document presents at some length (1) the growth and development of the Church's ministry with adolescents, (2) goals for ministry with adolescents, (3) themes and components for a comprehensive ministry with adolescents, and (4) a guiding image for ministry with adolescents.

How move from vision to realization? I have no overall, universal program. One approach whose potential I find impossible to overestimate is experience. I mean our Catholic youngsters actually seeing survival in the slums, hearing the cries of the poor, smelling the stench of the homeless, tasting the emptiness of hunger, touching a baby HIV-positive.

Each year during my 12 years as theologian-in-residence at Georgetown University, I watched ten or so graduates leave for a year with the poor in Nicaragua and Peru, many others for two years with the International Jesuit Volunteer Corps in Micronesia, Belize, and Nepal. None of them returned to the States the same; all had lived the hurts of the poor, experienced a conversion that changed them to the depths of their being. I remember talking to a young Georgetown student who was spending hours in downtown D.C. with drug addicts, battered women, prostitutes. College life for her had taken on a different look; even the university pub looked different—not bad, just a little sad. I remember Georgetown choir members who sang liturgy at the D.C. jail. They touched what it feels like to live without windows, wear the same old blue jumpsuits, have nothing to do that delights you, languish for months before coming to trial, give birth to your baby behind bars and have the infant torn from you. Words of the Mass that had slipped so facilely from their lips took on meaning: "May the Lord accept this sacrifice at our hands to the praise and glory of God's name, for our good, and for the good of *all God's Church.*" All God's people...yes, the prisoners they had come to know.

In our Catholic colleges "we have access to about 11 percent" of the Catholic college population.[61] Among the 11 percent a fair proportion leave the campus unaffected or disaffected. Even so, I have been powerfully moved by the thousands who have thrilled to the Catholic college experience: thrilled to infectious theology teachers like Monika Hellwig and John Haught at Georgetown; thrilled to campus liturgies, some of them exciting, others more contemplative, all of them reaching out to the openness, the generosity that is a fruit of the Spirit within the young, gifts we the graying tend to miss in the rock 'n' roll of the dominant culture. That culture, with its peer pressure, is indeed disturbingly compelling. Still, I suspect that the problem is not simply with the young themselves. It begins with parents who are rarely "there," but when there, are hardly examples of Christian spirituality, are afraid of alienating their children with "thou shalt not," or have just given up on "the young and the restless."[62] It carries on with teachers who, against all the odds, can deaden not only World War II but Bethlehem and Calvary. It hardens in parishes where liturgy is obligation rather than celebration, where community gives way to "me and Jesus," where the homily does not speak to the hurts of the people, where "kneel or stand" is more important than the presence of Christ in song and dance, in God's Word and Christ's flesh and blood.

I leave our youth with one concrete example of the kind of experience that changes lives. It is the story of Kaela Volkmer, a young college graduate with Jesuit Volunteers International, who had just begun two years of service in Arica, Chile. The specific locale? A social-service agency, Hogar de la Niña (Young Girl's Home), founded by a recently beatified Chilean Jesuit, Alberto Hurtado. Kaela was working with girls abandoned, with girls abused. Her experience has been recounted in full on pages 207–8 above.

Women

I have already said much, perhaps too much, on women in the Church. Still, it may not be amiss to state my conviction that the Church of the third millennium will not experience a rebirth, will not exercise a significant influence on American culture, unless women play a prominent part in the proclamation of the gospel and in decision making that affects not only their own lives but the whole Body of Christ.

Proclamation of the gospel. Increasingly, women are spreading the message of Christ: in retreat houses and parishes, in high schools and colleges, at various types of conferences and seminars, through books and articles, at home and in Bible groups. Still the neuralgic problem persists: Women rarely preach when the millions of faithful gather for the central expression of Catholic worship, and so their influence is significantly limited. Is there not a Catholic imagination that, in conjunction with progressive (not radical) canonists, theologians, and liturgiologists, might produce a fresh direction in legislation on the charism of preaching? After all, it is the spiritual life of our people that is at issue here, men and women (children too) whose spirits are all too often not being nourished by the Word of God as proclaimed by the word of men.

A final word. On a number of occasions over the years, in homilies and lectures, especially in circumstances of scandal or controversy or official rigor, I have had occasion to express in realistic language my love for the Body of Christ that has been my mother for more than eight decades. Originally delivered at a seminary graduation, it runs like this:

> In the course of a half century, I have seen more Christian corruption than you have read of. I have tasted it. I have been reasonably corrupt myself. And yet, I love this Church, this living, pulsing, sinning people of God with a crucifying passion. Why? For all the Christian hate, I experience here a community of love. For all the institutional idiocy, I find here a tradition of reason. For all the individual repressions, I breathe here an air of freedom. For all the fear of sex, I discover here the redemption of my body. In an age so inhuman, I touch here tears of compassion. In a world so grim and humorless, I share here rich joy and earthy laughter. In the midst of death, I hear here an incomparable stress on life. For all the apparent absence of God, I sense here the real presence of Christ.

That is why I end this chapter on a note of hope. I began it with biblical *krisis*, a moment of judgment, the risen Jesus speaking to us, at times quite severely, in the crises of today's Church. I close with biblical *kairos,* a favorable time, an opportunity, a juncture of circumstances that compels Catholic Christians not only to look critically at the Body of Christ of which we are privileged to be members, but also to envision a future richer than any we have yet experienced.

T W E L V E

From Hippocrates to Kevorkian
Catholicism and the Medical Profession

More than a quarter century ago, I was invited to address the Catholic Hospital Association (now the Catholic Health Association of the United States and Canada) at its 56th annual convention in Atlantic City, N.J. It was one of the many critical moments in my priestly and scholarly existence — critical in the sense that the invitation, my research, and the address triggered serious involvement in a (for me) fresh area of human and Christian living...and dying. The Atlantic City invitation compelled me to confront a basic question: What has sickness to do with theology? It was not abstract speculation; for in the grime and grit of everyday experience I was asking: Why are avowed Christians, vowed religious, lay ministers engaged in this particular activity? Isn't our Christian "bag" redemption, saving souls?

Since that June day in 1971, I have never been far from the art and craft of healing. Several specific examples. I have pondered why the Church is involved in healthcare; I have lobbied in hospitals and medical schools to promote the ailing from patient to person; and I have plunged, perhaps precipitously, into urgent medicomoral issues, most recently physician-assisted suicide. A section on each, with a final word on psychiatry.

Sickness, Healthcare, Church

In struggling toward a theology of healthcare, I discovered that I had to begin not with sickness but with the Church.[1] Here the magic word is "mission." Rather than simply say, as for long we did, that the Church *has* missions, it had become more nuanced to say "The Church *is* mission." For it is of the Church's essence to be God's living outreach to the world. The Church is a corporate apostle, and an apostle is by definition one who is "sent," who is on mission (the Latin *mittere, missio*). Consequent on the radical mission of

God's unique Son in the Incarnation, and consequent on the Pentecostal mission of the Spirit "in order that the Spirit might for ever sanctify the Church,"[2] is the mission of the Church. It was foreshadowed when the Lord sent his disciples out two by two to begin healing a broken world. But the definitive sending that constituted apostolate, that focused on a church, took place only after Christ's resurrection, when the apostles were filled with the Holy Spirit and went forth, a fellowship of faith, hope, and love, so that "awe came upon everyone, because many wonders and signs were being done by the apostles" (Acts 2:43).

Plumbing the New Testament, I found the implications electric. For if to be a disciple meant to follow — to follow one Master only, to be an apostle meant to serve — to serve men and women after the example of Christ and in the power of the Spirit. The Church is mission, and the mission is service. The primary thrust of the Church, and therefore of every Christian, I saw summed up in the impassioned confession of St. Paul to the Christians of Corinth, "I will most gladly spend and be spent for you" (2 Cor 12:15). Not a fresh insight; we have been proclaiming this for centuries. But the post-Vatican II world was concerned not so much with principle as with performance. We were challenged not only by history, by Jewish ghettos and Spanish Inquisitions and Holy Land Crusades. The '60s, as Avery Dulles phrased it so poignantly, were calling for

> a new ecumenism — one less committed to historical theological controversies and more in touch with contemporary secular man; one less turned in upon itself, more open to the world and its concerns. . . . A cry to all the churches rises up from the heart of modern man: "Come to us where we are. Help us to make the passage into the coming technocratic age without falling into the despair and brutality of a new paganism. . . . If the charity of the Good Samaritan burns in your hearts, show that you share our desires and aspirations. In our struggle to build the city of man, we need the support which your faith and hope alone can give. If you remain comfortably in your churches and cloisters, we are much afraid that God will become a stranger to modern life. Christianity, secluded in a world of its own, will turn into a mere relic to be cherished by a few pious souls.[3]

I suspect that in the healthcare apostolate more than anywhere else we revealed to a world skeptical of religion that as an institution we sensed the pain of their agonizing monosyllables: what it means to hate, to love, to starve, to bleed, to die; what it feels like to be poor, black, sick, slave. But such impressive performance did not resolve my puzzle: What is distinctively Catholic about service to sickness?

Here I was confronted by two contrasting convictions of what the Church is all about. The first was consecrated in an expression that dominated Catholic thinking and writing for centuries: The mission of the Church is to "save souls." And my own immediate function as an individual Catholic was to save *my* soul; no point in saving other souls if my own joined St. Paul's castaways. The Church is indeed a community of service; the service is salvation; and what is saved in the first instance is my soul.

Now this vision of salvation, at least in its raw form, reflected a popular misconception among Christians. For some, the human body was nothing but an instrument, a tool of the soul. For others, the body was a burden from which the soul cried for release. This was in large measure an echo of one of my patristic heroes, the third-century Alexandrian Origen, who theorized that the soul was imprisoned in matter because it had sinned in an earlier existence. Such an attitude paid slender homage to God. It failed to recognize that the body is an essential part of the human person, that without the body I am a creature incomplete, that whether in heaven or purgatory or hell a separated soul, as Jean Mouroux phrased it, "still longs for its body with a purely natural impulse of love."[4]

The point is, the body too yearns for redemption. In the inspired language of St. Paul, "we ourselves, who have the first fruits of the Spirit, groan inwardly while we wait for adoption, the redemption of our bodies" (Rom 8:23). When my body is absorbed into the visible structure of the Church, it ceases to be what Paul called "this body of death"; it comes spiritually alive, quickened by the Spirit of God, so that less and less does "the law in my members" war against "the law of my mind" (Rom 7). This, however, is but the beginning of redemption. Redemption will find its consummation in the glory of the life to come. Not merely in the soul's vision of God, but in the transfiguration of the body, when the whole material universe will share in the perfection of redemption, when, as Vatican II declared, "the human race as well as the entire world, which is intimately related to man and woman and achieves its purpose through them, will be perfectly re-established in Christ."[5]

All well and good. And yet, I slowly realized, this could be a deceptive theology, particularly misleading for the health apostolate. If the Church's task is not simply to save the soul, neither is its mission to save soul *and* body. What the Church is all about is the human person — and that person is an incredible oneness. Oh yes, I can think of myself as soul and body, spirit and flesh; for I am a fascinating wedding of material and immaterial, of what we can see-hear-touch-taste-smell and what escapes the most sensitive of senses and instruments. And still, the real, pulsating life a man or woman lives is never one *or* the other. Aquinas at the acme of abstraction and Avila's Teresa ravished by a rose, Saul lusting for the blood of Christians and Augustine lusting for love in semipagan Carthage, none of them was disembodied soul or spiritless flesh. And the "patient" is not a man *with* melanoma, a woman *with* a scarred uterus. The whole package is one man, one woman. *He* is sick, not his chest; *she* is sick, not her womb. Surely one of the most profound insights for my life and work: It is always and inescapably a man or a woman who is born and dies, who loves or hates, laughs or cries, dances in sheer delight or winces in unbearable pain.

That is why the medical response must be a human response, a rare welding of hand and heart, of professional skill and a warm compassion born of profound understanding. What I have in mind was expressed eloquently four decades ago in a *Life* magazine article:

> Of all human acts, few can match the quiet splendor of the moment when the pale and tremulous fingers of a sick person are grasped in the firm, reassuring hands of a compassionate physician. This simple act, mutely promising that all the powers of modern science will be unsparingly invoked to restore health, is among the finest deeds of humankind. It is more than ritual. When pain and fear make a sick person feel that all is lost, the laying-on of healing hands brings solace and hope. Its strength can even turn the tide of illness and amplify the curative effect of the strongest wonder drug. It remains today, as it has always been, man's oldest medical miracle.[6]

But there is more, a significant nuance. I dare not constrict the theology of sickness to psychology alone, to "the milk of human kindness." Sickness is an ecclesial apostolate not because Dr. Tom Dooley (heroic medical missionary to Asia) or Mother Alfonsa Lathrop (daughter of Nathaniel Hawthorne and foundress of the Servants of Relief for Incurable Cancer) was in contact with an abstract reality called "person." What the healer touches is the-human-person-in-process-of-redemption. This hyphenated phrase is heavy enough to demand explanation.

Every listing in the massive encyclopedia of sickness, from the schizophrenia that disintegrates a total personality, through the cardiac insufficiencies and the intestinal diverticula, down to the acne on an adolescent's cheek, is intimate to a person. A disease is not something objective, outside of me; it is part of me, it is I, for a time or terminally — as really and existentially part of me as is my hand or my hearing, my faith and my fears, my loves and my deepest yearnings. No matter what my explicit belief or unbelief, in illness I work out my destiny as a person: I grow or I diminish; yes, in a sense I live more fully or I die a little or a lot. And if I am a Christian, sickness (like gladness) should be my share in the life of Christ, my way of realizing a relationship of love with God and with God's human images on earth; and I simply cannot divorce this religious movement from what disease does to me as a person. If disease diminishes me, it diminishes my Christianness. If disease strengthens me, I take a giant step (or many small steps) toward my salvation.

The equation is as simple as it is profound. Sickness = I, and I am a person in process — in process of redemption. In a Catholic vision of sickness, a physician or nurse is privileged to touch, as a priest is privileged to touch, a human person, an image of God, a man or woman at a critical moment in human living: when he or she is working out his or her salvation. When Christian hope is threatened by fear; when the sufferer can feel as forsaken as Jesus felt on his cross; when life or death stands at a bedside in a white coat. When a child of God is begging mutely to be treated not as a wrist tag but as a person.

In all genuine illness I face to some extent the ultimate mystery: death — that singular and solitary event which should give meaning to all that has gone before. For a Christian, not an episode I undergo, not sheer resignation to the inevitable, but a yes, an "I do." Into your hands, O Lord, I entrust not only my spirit but this whole suffering person that is a unique I.

Patient or Person?

In 1994 I had a singular opportunity to expand and deepen the person-aspect within illness and the medical profession. For on October 15 of that year I was scheduled to address Surgical Grand Rounds at the Georgetown University Medical Center. I chose the topic "Healthcare 2000: Doctor and Patient or Doctor and Person?" After summarizing the theology I have discussed above, I turned from theologian to medicine man, detailed what I had learned in recent years about an urgent need, a fresh, developing relationship between doctor and patient. This I had learned in large measure from the poets among physicians. Not poets as accomplished rhymers; rather poets as those who see beyond the obvious, even at times see the divine hidden in human flesh. What follows is an effort to express my own growth in understanding.

I have been influenced by insightful observers of the human scene. For one, Mario Cuomo put it powerfully: "Illness does not occur in a vacuum, ... the roots of illness are usually deeply implanted in homelessness, in poverty, in other persistent social ills."[7] Governor Cuomo went on to write:

> Health, perhaps more than any other aspect of our lives, depends upon the innerconnectedness of everything else we are and do. The very word "health" has the same root as "whole." It denotes an integrity based upon the immensely complex synergy that includes the workings of the human body and all the external forces that affect it. Health is not given, nor taken away, in a vacuum.... [T]he relationship between illness... and poverty... is not just a grotesque coincidence. It is causal. It is real. It is historic.[8]

It was in this context that Kevin Cahill, senior member of the New York City Board of Health, could remind us:

> The "public" served by the public health system is increasingly the disenfranchised, the uninsured, the impoverished, the homeless, the aged, the addicted. Failing their needs is more than morally indefensible in our "new world order"; it threatens the health of all. For as surely as an untreated tuberculous lesion will cavitate the lungs of a homeless vagrant, so too will the deadly mist of his infection disseminate through every social and economic class, among innocent fellow riders in the subway, or passengers in an elevator and, inevitably, from child to child in the classrooms of our city.[9]

But if illness does not occur in a vacuum, then medical treatment of illness dare not occur in a vacuum. On March 17 of that year (1994), speaking at the same medical center on the Jesuit tradition in medicine, I recalled three significant discoveries that have profoundly influenced my life as a scholar, a Catholic, and a human person. (1) I cannot understand my country today if I do not know where America came from and where it has been. Here lies the tragedy in the ignorance of history that pervades American education. (2) I cannot understand my church today if I do not know where Catholicism came from and where it has been. Here lies the tragedy among so many Catholics who have little insight into what it means to be part and parcel of a community that calls itself the Body of Christ, a church whose story at once glories in the Spirit that is its soul and echoes the weaknesses of all that is human. (3) I cannot understand who I am if I do not know where this complex, paradoxical creature came from and where I've been. Hence the significance of first-rate psychiatry. In like manner, a fourth realization has intruded more recently into my living and my lecturing. I suggest that the healthcare leaders of the twenty-first century — administrators and surgeons, internists and nurses, radiologists and anesthesiologists — will be the men and women who are concerned to discover where their patients come from and where they've been.

Not only patients' medical history on a reception room questionnaire, indispensable as this is. I mean their integral humanity: where they hurt deep inside, what they're afraid of, what if anything they hope for, the love or lack of love that makes the world turn or stop for them. Who are they? I think, concretely, of my favorite doctor who weds the scalpel of a surgeon with the pen of a poet and the heart of a lover. Listen to this episode from the experience of Dr. Richard Selzer:

> I stand by the bed where a young woman lies, her face postoperative, her mouth twisted in palsy, clownish. A tiny twig of the facial nerve, the one to the muscles of her mouth, has been severed. She will be thus from now on. The surgeon had followed with religious fervor the curve of her flesh; I promise you that. Nevertheless, to remove the tumor in her cheek, I had cut the little nerve.
>
> Her young husband is in the room. He stands on the opposite side of the bed, and together they seem to dwell in the evening lamplight, isolated from me, private. Who are they, I ask myself, he and this wry-mouth I have made, who gaze at and touch each other so generously, greedily? The young woman speaks.
>
> "Will my mouth be always like this?" she asks.
>
> "Yes," I say, "it will. It is because the nerve was cut."
>
> She nods, and is silent. But the young man smiles.
>
> "I like it," he says. "It is kind of cute."
>
> All at once I know who he is. I understand, and I lower my gaze. One is not bold in an encounter with a god. Unmindful, he bends to kiss her crooked mouth, and I so close I can see

how he twists his own lips to accommodate to hers, to show
her that their kiss still works.... [10]

I am not trying to turn doctors into daydreamers, residents into
incurable romantics. In the operating room, compassion can never
replace the scalpel. But of this I am convinced, from the experiences of unnumbered of the ailing: Intrinsic to a doctor's capacity
to cure is his or her power to heal. In fact, even when to cure is
not in the picture, to heal is still possible; for healing is broader
than curing. Doctors heal (nurses too) when a child afflicted with
Down's syndrome leaves a hospital with infectious laughter. Doctors heal when a young man diagnosed as HIV-positive goes home
persuaded that AIDS is not incompatible with human living. Doctors heal when an African-American lady, blind and legless, looks
at her doctor from a hospital bed and with a dazzling smile says,
"How good it is to see you, Doctor!" Doctors heal when just about
the last words from a dying cardiac patient are, "Thank you, Doctor. You'll never know how much life your caring has given me."
Doctors healed when a cancerous young Jesuit dear to me returned
from chemotherapy to his community strengthened to face a medically dismal prognosis (he has died since). Doctors heal (nurses too)
whenever they share, in some genuine fashion, the lot of the men,
women, and children they serve: when they hurt with those who
hurt, weep with those who weep, feel diminished whenever a sister
or brother dies.

But what precisely is it that makes for healing, even when a
strictly medical cure is unlikely or impossible? Here I have been
significantly influenced by two strong statements from Dr. Bernie
Siegel. Profoundly Jewish, occasionally controversial, past president
of the American Holistic Medical Association, a man who labored
to make patients aware of their own healing potential, he has authored a remarkable book entitled *Love, Medicine and Miracles*.
Statement 1: "I am convinced that unconditional love is the most
powerful known stimulant of the immune system."[11] Statement 2:
"Remember I said love *heals*. I do not claim love *cures* everything
but it can heal and in the process of healing cures occur also."[12]

Siegel's primary concern is the love that should pervade his *patients*. It was dramatically exemplified when a woman with breast
cancer entered his office smoking away like a small chimney. Sara's
first words to him? "I suppose you're going to tell me to stop smoking." His reply? "No, I'm going to tell you to love yourself. Then
you'll stop."[13] But this type of love can be stimulated by a doc-

tor who, Siegel insists, "can teach [the suffering] to love themselves and others fully."[14]

I myself am preoccupied as well with the love that should pervade the *physician*, the love that can leap from the physician to pervade the patient. I am aware that the word "love" is bandied like a yo-yo, is used for everything from a half century of husband-wife self-giving, through a one-night stand after a singles' bar pickup, to TV's gross "Game of Love." The love I have in mind is a strong love, the love St. Paul commended to the Christians of Corinth in deathless rhetoric:

> If I speak in the tongues of mortals and of angels, but do not have love, I am a noisy gong or a clanging cymbal. And if I have prophetic powers, and understand all mysteries and all knowledge, and if I have faith, so as to remove mountains, but do not have love, I am nothing. If I give away all my possessions, and if I hand over my body to be burned, but do not have love, I gain nothing.
>
> Love is patient; love is kind; love is not envious or boastful or arrogant or rude. [Love] does not insist on its own way; it is not irritable or resentful; it does not rejoice in wrong-doing, but rejoices in the right. It bears all things, believes all things, hopes all things, endures all things.... Now faith, hope, and love abide, these three; and the greatest of these is love. (1 Cor 13:1–7, 13)

To bring their love down to medical reality, I have suggested to practitioners of the art that the form of love which comes closest to their vocation, takes little of their medical time, and enriches their medical lore, enriches them as persons, enriches their patients as persons, is compassion. Not pity; pity looks down from a superior posture. Rather the compassion that formed the stuff of a unique Jew named Jesus, that made him uncommonly happy when he was looking with incomparable caring into the eyes of a suffering man, woman, or child. Compassion means not a weak, embarrassed sympathy but a fellowship in feeling. To be compassionate is literally to "suffer with" another. Compassion asks physicians (nurses too) not only to go where it hurts, to enter into places of pain; they are already there. Compassion asks them to share in brokenness and confusion, in fear and anguish. More broadly, compassion challenges them to cry to heaven and to earth against societal systems that wheel into emergency rooms and hospital wards inhuman beings whom society has rejected, men, women, and — yes — children whose bones and blood, hearts and hopes are beyond repairing. Cry out indeed, for physicians' tongues as well as their hearts must echo the declaration of a justice of the New York Supreme Court, "A society that loses its sense of outrage is doomed to extinction."[15]

No need to be as aggressive, as blunt, as Bernie Siegel. After all, the verbal advice to love will hardly break through the pain and the fear if the love that is compassion does not move from physicians' lips to their eyes, to their hands.

How acquire this precious quality? Once again I discover wisdom in my poet/physician Richard Selzer:

> A surgeon does not slip from his mother's womb with compassion smeared upon him like the drippings of his birth. It is much later that it comes. No easy shaft of grace this, but the cumulative murmuring of the numberless wounds he has dressed, the incisions he has made, all the sores and ulcers and cavities he has touched in order to heal. In the beginning it is barely audible, a whisper, as from many mouths. Slowly it gathers, rising from the streaming flesh until, at last, it is a pure *calling* — an exclusive sound, like the cry of certain solitary birds — telling that out of the resonance between the sick man and the one who tends him there may spring that profound courtesy that the religious call Love.[16]

To express it more prosaically, we humans ordinarily *grow into* compassion. But not automatically, thoughtlessly — like breathing. All the experience of decades will not produce a compassionate physician if he or she is not open to the experience. Physicians are, in a genuine sense, fortunate; for they need not travel for the experience. It surrounds them, is the air they breathe. Still, the difficulties can be daunting. They struggle against time, race against the clock, rarely see me at the appointed hour, are almost as hurried, harried, and desperate as TV's "Chicago Hope" portrays them. There is so much to cure, so little time to heal. The hospital becomes the enemy of the home, the office the enemy of human living. Little wonder that the suicide rate among physicians is appallingly high.

With all that, add the peril that resides in all routine. When day after day is a ceaseless round of bone and blood, of malignancy and metastasis, of cut and stitch, how rekindle the fire that burned within a Cushing and the Curies, the Menningers and the Mayos, a Pasteur, a Harvey, and a Fleming? Perhaps, paradoxically, the solution lies in the patient as a person — unique, irreplaceable, the same flesh and blood as the physician. I am reminded of a striking experience related with characteristic simplicity by Mother Teresa of Calcutta during a commencement address at Gonzaga College High School in the District of Columbia:

> One day I was walking down the street and I saw a man sitting there looking most terrible, so I went to him and shook his hand (and my hand is always very warm), and he looked up and said, "Oh, what a long, long time since I felt the warmth of a human hand." He brightened up, he was so full of joy that there was somebody that loved him, there was somebody who cared.[17]

The warmth of a human hand. Somebody who loved him, someone who cared. From such warmth, such love, such care comes healing. The patient as person; each patient a unique person; each person with a singular story; each story a key to what hurts deep within; each hurt intimate to his or her healing, even perhaps to his or her curing.

In summary, one imperative I find all-important for the medical profession: *Listen!* Doctors do, of course; it comes with the medical turf. But it involves a fresh methodology: Learn to listen for what someone called the space between sounds. Break through the obvious, the surface, the superficial, to the reality of the person beneath and beyond. One illustration, a true story related not long ago by a Dominican Sister, a story about both listening and sacrifice:

> Five year old Johnny Quinn loved his big brother, Tommy. The doctor told Johnny that his brother was very sick and needed a blood transfusion, and the doctor asked: "Johnny, would you be willing to give some of your blood to your brother?" Johnny gulped hard, his eyes got big, but after only a moment's hesitation he said: "Sure, doctor." The doctor took the blood and Johnny was resting quietly on the table. A few minutes later, Johnny looked up at the doctor and said: "When do I die, doctor?" It was only then that the doctor fully appreciated the extent of this little boy's love.[18]

My urgent, at times anguished appeal to healers dear to my heart: Do listen to the spaces between our sounds.[19] What do you actually hear when you ask me to cough, to breathe deep, to say "ah"? Do you hear a person? Do you really hear my story? And if you do, how do you respond? Do you know what hurts *me*, this unique, unrepeatable person, this commingling of flesh and spirit in the image and likeness of God?

I relish a pertinent story from the experience of Dr. Robert Coles, while working as a volunteer fifth-grade teacher in an impoverished Boston neighborhood. A ten-year-old African-American girl in the class, Cynthia, had been with her mother to see a doctor at Children's Hospital. She was amazed at the number of "sick folks in one place." She didn't mind "all the people," only "some of them." A pause, then she specified: "The doctors, they be strutters. They need teaching." When asked by a classmate, Tom, to "explain yourself," she answered, "They're busy, they are — and they let you know it." Puzzled, Tom asked why working hard meant being a strutter. Cynthia's response: "They didn't give us credit for understanding anything. They're big on talking, on telling you this and that and something here and there, but they don't listen like they should. You go off on your own, and they'll cut you off."

Still unconvinced, Tom said, "Give them a break — they're in a rush, they've got to get their job done. You can't be polite all the time!" Cynthia: "For sure, it's a lot they have to do. But if you watch them, you'll see them being nice and relaxed with each other, and if it's one of them who comes and interrupts, they'll lend an ear, but if we try to tell them something, they hurry on." Dr. Coles "shuddered with embarrassment," suggested that the class get on with their spelling. But Cynthia was not through teaching, made sure her intended point had hit home: "If they'd listen, they'd learn more; that's how you learn — through your ears, not your mouth."[20] From the mouths of children....

Strange, isn't it? Our amazing advances in technological treatment have consigned to containers of hazardous waste a 2,400-year-old remark of Hippocrates. He used to say he would rather know what sort of person has a disease than what sort of disease a person has.[21] It fits neatly with his aphorism, "Where you find love of the human person, there you find love of the Art."[22]

The Catholic Healthcare Facility

The patient-as-person issue has long drawn me from the individual to the institution. I mean the Catholic healthcare facility. On June 4, 1985, I addressed the 70th Annual Catholic Health Assembly in Orlando, Florida. My topic was framed for me by the blunt question that confronted the assembly, "Is Being 'Catholic' Worth Saving?"[23] The invitation to address so prestigious a gathering of medical personnel on its several levels compelled rigorous research, critical consultation, and robust reflection. More than a decade later,

I am even more firmly convinced that the ideas I expressed on that occasion call for intense soul-searching.

Catholic healthcare institutions were then talking about survival. They were being pressured by finances, by non-Catholic investor-owned hospital chains that lusted for their facilities and services. I asked then, and ask today, three questions: (1) What does it mean for a health institution to be "Catholic"? (2) Is such an institution, with a distinctively Catholic vision, worth saving? (3) If it is worth saving, how can a theologian help save it? A word on each.

For a healthcare facility to be genuinely Catholic, it is important, but not sufficient, that it be recognized as such by competent ecclesiastical authority. Nor is it sufficient, though important, that it subscribe and adhere to church directives on medicomoral principles and practice. Nor is it sufficient, though important, that it have a Catholic chaplain or ministry team. It is authentically Catholic to the extent that it sees itself as on mission from the Lord of life; sees itself, individually and as a family, privileged to touch a human person, a child of God, at a specially crucial moment in his or her earthly existence — when the once-proud flesh is coming apart or the once-strong spirit has been broken, when fear clutches the heart and I am alone with my naked self. Here is Gethsemane; here is another Christ sweating blood, stumbling a tortured way to Calvary, perhaps crying to heaven as Jesus cried, "Don't let me die!" The task of the institution, as a Catholic community, is to work together, each with his or her God-given gift, to help that singular, unrepeatable person trudge with Christ to Jerusalem. When I don that dismaying hospital gown, these servants — administrator and chaplain, physician and nurse — become my Christ; they are intimately involved in my redemption; they are my life, more profoundly than they imagine.

Medically speaking, I'm a fortunate man. Including tests, I've occupied a hospital bed overnight only four times in eight decades: an appendectomy in 1932 and a deviated septum-cum-tonsillectomy in 1946, a night for tests in 1992 and four days of testing in 1995. But the next time I change my black suit for a backless day-and-night dress, it might well be quite serious. After all, blood is not getting to my heart as smoothly as before; at times a hiatal hernia simulates a coronary; my left foot has been pronating unto distortion for seven years; arthritis has afflicted my lower back and a right knee that may need a replacement. If a serious operation is my lot, I shall prefer Georgetown to Sloan Ketter-

ing. Not because it is more highly rated by accreditors; I don't
know if it is. Rather because my illness will cry for more than scientific competence. It will not be an isolated episode in my life,
divorced from who I am and what I am about and where I am going. I shall be working out my salvation . . . through suffering and,
ultimately, dying.

Precisely then I shall need for surroundings a special kind of community — so that the compassionate Christ, the healing if not the
curing Christ, may show his face to me. I realize he can show his
face to me in Bellevue as well as St. Clare's. But it will be easier for
me to see his face if I see his face in such as surround me. It will be
easier if I am not simply brought Communion by a minister making
the rounds, but am encircled by doctors and nurses, administrators
and housekeepers, most of whom share some or all of my vision. If
the people around me, the men and women whose flesh still glows
with health, whose eyes sparkle and spirits soar, are obviously alive
with the life of Christ. If to them I am not a room number, a disease, a blood type, a wrist tag, a chart at the foot of my bed. If they
see me as a person working out my salvation literally in fear and
trembling. If among my life supports there is a cross above my head
to remind me that my agony need not be a waste, that I too can
murmur "This is my body [and it is] given for you" (Lk 22:19).

More than that. Even if I succeed in integrating suffering into
my vision, I must still face the ultimate in *dis*integration. I mean . . .
death. Kübler-Ross may help, but she will not be enough. She may
help me through the stages: where I deny death's imminence, get
angry at death, bargain with God, grow depressed, before I accept
reality. But the reality I must accept is more than an unavoidable
fact. I am, I shall be, anguishing toward a death which is more than
resignation, a death I hope will be my final "I do," my last gift to
the Lord of life.

You see, there is a darkness to death which even the Son of God
cried out against. Death has a blank face; death is cruel; death breaks
the whole person; I, I, I will vanish from living reach and touch. And
so I fear that, like Dylan Thomas, I shall "not go gentle into that
good night." I am much more likely to "burn and rave at close of
day; / Rage, rage against the dying of the light."[24]

In those critical hours what I shall need above all is a fresh conversion to the risen Christ. I shall need the Holy Spirit, who never
ceases to surprise me, need the Spirit to surprise me singularly, in-
expressibly. True, the conversion, the surprise, can take place in
Massachusetts General as well as Pittsburgh Mercy. Still, it will be

easier for me to turn to Christ, easier for me to recognize his Spirit, if the atmosphere around me thrills with their presence. If the front office is as much concerned over *my* cross as over Blue Cross. If my surgeon weds compassion to competence. If a nurse may discuss life and death with me without getting hell from a supervisor. If I feel there is a family around me, a family that cares, a family that senses what I am about to experience: a movement from life to, yes, life — but through a darkness I cannot even imagine, can only fear.

Is such a facility worth saving? Put the question in that form, and my response is a resounding yes. I have only one nagging worry. The facility I've described, the facility I want to save, the facility that should help save me, is such actually the facility we call the Catholic hospital?

My "saving" suggestion? Let the Catholic healthcare become, formally and resoundingly, an apostolate of the laity. Not solely for survival; more importantly because this is the laity's right and duty. I say "formally and resoundingly" because in reality healthcare has been a lay apostolate for decades, perhaps centuries. My dear deceased friend Philip Scharper made this point to the Catholic Health Association back in 1971: "We should recall ... that nuns and religious brothers are members of the laity in the canonical sense. Even though one lives under the sweet burden of the religious vows, so long as he has not received the major orders he is a member of the laity."[25] The new Code of Canon Law confirms this: "Among the Christian faithful, by divine institution, there exist in the Church sacred ministers, who are also called clerics in law, and other Christian faithful, who are also called laity."[26]

I am not, therefore, advocating a Catholic coup: Get rid of the sisters! Quite the contrary. With their history and experience, with their commitment and compassion, *these* laity should continue to play a major role in the health apostolate. But let's face it: Healthcare sisters are an endangered species; their facilities survive because they are staffed in large part by other laity, committed indeed by baptism but not consecrated by vow. As long as they are available, doing what they are paid to do, the facility may well survive. But it will survive as a *Catholic* facility only if these "other laity," the vast majority, have caught the vision of the few. Only if all the baptized Christians so serving realize that by their very baptism they share intimately in the priesthood of Christ. And the task of a priest, ordained or not, is to be a link between God and God's people. Scharper phrased it beautifully. Their task, he told them, is to make it somehow easier *because you are there* (far more by what you are than by what you will ever say) for those with whom you deal to move toward God; making it far easier because you are there for God to move toward those with whom you deal. So the priestly tasks in a hospital or in a health care center are not reserved to the chaplains only. They become the function of every baptized Christian on the staff.[27]

On that occasion Scharper developed passionately an aspect of healthcare which is indeed Catholic, even though it is shared by many who do not share the faith of Roman Catholics.

You affirm the value of every human life in a century which has seen more people die of hunger than have perished even on its battlefields or in its blasted, burned-out cities. You proclaim the value of human life in a developing world culture which threatens man with dehumanization. Because of what you are and because of what you do, you are concerned not merely with "spiritual values," but you are concerned with the quest to discover, preserve, and expand authentic human values because you share the ancient Christian tradition rooted in the faith of the Church and Christ, its founder, that *res sacra est homo;* "man is indeed a sacred being."[28]

Such a realization transmutes a job into a vocation, changes Sunday Christians into seven-day-a-week apostles, gives profound meaning to the meanest task they are called to perform, makes the humdrum come alive — Christ come alive in them and, through them, in the fearful flesh on a hospital bed.

Worth saving? Yes indeed! But the neuralgic question in the third millennium: Is it really this that our Catholic laity want to save?

Assisted Suicide

Within recent years the issue of medical compassion has been raised to a fresh level of urgent argument. The impelling force? A growing movement insisting that each human person has an inalienable right to decide when he or she has had enough of life, and therefore is justified in terminating it at will, perhaps with the assistance of a dear one or a qualified medical practitioner, especially when life becomes psychologically or physically unendurable.

The issue rose a significant legal level in 1994. In May of that year Judge Barbara Rothstein of the Federal District Court in Seattle traced a logical line from abortion rights to suicide rights and decreed that the State of Washington's 140-year-old statute banning physician-assisted suicide was unconstitutional. Her precedents were the Supreme Court's abortion decisions. One such decision, *Planned Parenthood* v. *Casey,* reaffirmed the right to abortion on the grounds that matters "involving the most intimate and personal choices a person may make in a lifetime, choices central to personal dignity and autonomy, are central to the liberty protected by the Fourteenth Amendment." The Rothstein decision was reversed by a three-judge panel of the 9th U.S. Circuit Court of Appeals (filed March 9, 1995). In a two-to-one decision, Judge John Noonan wrote that the right to privacy may encompass freedom from unwanted medical intervention but not "the right to have a second person collaborate in your death." However, more recently the same 9th Circuit Court of Appeals, sitting en banc, struck down the earlier decision by an 8–3 majority (filed March 6, 1996), holding "that a liberty interest exists in the choice of how and when one dies, and that the provision of the Washington statute banning assisted suicide, as applied to competent terminally ill adults who wish to hasten their deaths by obtaining medication prescribed by their doctors, violates the Due Process Clause."

In November 1994, citizens in Oregon voted to legalize physician-assisted suicide. A month later Judge Michael Hogan issued an injunction against the new law with a view to studying its constitutional implications.

In December 1994, New York Federal Judge Thomas Griesa decreed that there was no constitutional right to suicide. He rejected the use of abortion and termination-of-treatment decisions to argue for a right to assisted suicide; held that the state has legitimate interests in preserving life and protecting the vulnerable; argued that it is not unreasonable for the state to differentiate between refusal of treatment by the terminally ill and a dose of medication that leads to death. In 1996, however, Judge Roger Miner, writing for the 2nd Circuit Court of Appeals, rejected that differentiation. "Physicians do not fulfill the role of 'killer' by prescribing drugs to hasten death any more than they do by disconnecting life-support systems." Remarked insightful columnist Charles Krauthammer:

> This is pernicious nonsense. There is a great difference between, say, not resuscitating a stopped heart — allowing nature to take its course — and actively killing someone. In the first case the person is dead. In the second he only wishes to be dead. And in the case of life sustained by artificial

hydration or ventilation, pulling the plug simply prevents an artificial prolongation of the dying process. Prescribing hemlock
initiates it.[29]

I am aware that the distinction in question escapes not only the
average American but many an ethicist. The myopia makes for monumental tragedy, however, when it becomes incarnate in the judicial
system, when it makes for bad but binding law.

Krauthammer's insights have been furthered more recently by another respected *Washington Post* columnist, George F. Will, in an
article pointedly titled "The Fruits of *Roe* v. *Wade*."[30] In that 1973
decision the Supreme Court

> said the privacy right is really about an individual's right to
> choose. The court made abortion a choice free from interfer-
> ence by husbands or parents. And by 1992, in another abortion
> case, the court, declaring abortion a right central to "auton-
> omy," gaseously said, "At the heart of liberty is the right
> to define one's own concept of existence, of meaning, of the
> universe, and of the mystery of human life."[31]

Will, linking that decision to the 9th Circuit's affirmation of a
constitutional right to make "decisions that are highly personal
and intimate, as well as of great importance to the individual,"
responded:

> But, then, why not also declare constitutionally sacrosanct a
> decision — personal, intimate, important — to use heroin? Or
> to practice consensual incest or polygamy? Who is to gain-
> say a person's — or a judge's — contention that such practices
> accord with his definition of existence, or meaning, or the uni-
> verse, or life's mystery? Has constitutional reasoning been so
> degraded that judges can use such words as scythes to mow
> down laws across the continent, and (regarding physician-
> assisted suicide) to overturn ethical and prudential norms more
> than two millennia old?[32]

I resonate to Will's conclusion: Let the Supreme Court simply say
this is none of the federal judiciary's business. "Today's court has a
penchant for casting every complexity in terms of individual rights
and for bandying notions of constitutionally protected 'autonomy.'
It should master that penchant lest it further strengthen, as it did
24 Januarys ago, the culture of casual killing."[33]

In harmony with Will's conclusion, a unanimous Supreme Court
decision late in June 1997 denied that terminally ill patients have

a constitutional right to end their lives with the aid of a physician, thus upholding state bans in New York and Washington. Wrote Chief Justice William Rehnquist: "The asserted 'right' to assistance in committing suicide is not a fundamental liberty interest." He suggested that the issue was best left to the state legislatures. At that time 35 states had laws explicitly criminalizing euthanasia and doctor-assisted suicide; in nine states and the District of Columbia, helping someone die was considered illegal based on precedent established in case law.

I must confess that, on the sheerly human level, the argument for the "right to die" has a prima-facie attractiveness, particularly but not exclusively for men and women who espouse no religious belief, no relationship to a living, loving God, no link to the Christ of Calvary. Why prolong intolerable agony? Why continue a living death? Why not "death with dignity"?

To my mind, the "right to die" argument hides a tacit assumption: that the individual's autonomy is paramount, to the exclusion of other significant considerations. A social being with responsibilities to society? Sheer abstractions when your flesh is being eaten away, when your spirit is hopelessly dead.

I have said it before: I am not ice-cold in the face of such situations.[34] I watched my father die of lung cancer at 53, my only brother waste away with intestinal cancer at 27, my mother live her last six years in a nursing home bereft of reason and memory. Nevertheless, I may not, I refuse to, see them in isolation, removed from the broader picture. There is no moment of our existence when we have only rights, no responsibilities. We are never utterly independent, sovereignly individual, radically autonomous, connected to others only by choice. In this context I dare not deny two distinct dangers. (1) An unrestricted right to die has potentially disastrous consequences. Very simply, it is uncontrollable. Patient autonomy can move from terminal cancer to mental suffering to terminal boredom. (2) Pressures of different sorts can impact on a patient's freedom to choose. Often there are severe psychological and financial pressures on the elderly and the fragile, dependency burdens that make for a coercive atmosphere, where the freedom of a consent is in fact questionable.[35]

How have we come to this unpretty pass? My longtime Jesuit friend and colleague Richard McCormick, ethicist extraordinaire, sees the legal initiatives as representing the convergence and culmination of five cultural trends.[36] I borrow two.

1. The absolutization of autonomy: the flowering of patient au-

tonomy over against an earlier medical paternalism. The reaction has two noxious offshoots: (*a*) The patient's views are seen as the sole right-making characteristic of the choice. But what are the features that make a choice good or bad? (*b*) Dependence is regarded as intolerable. "Assisted suicide is a flight from compassion," from the grace to be dependent on others, to lean on their strength. And "Have we forgotten that dependent old age is a call to cling to a power (God) beyond our control?"[37]

2. The secularization of medicine: divorce of the profession from those values that make healthcare a human service, an increasing preoccupation with competition, liability, government controls, finances. "For many doctors and hospitals," says Joseph Califano, "the business of medicine is more business than medicine. For me, it gets harder each year to tell the difference between sitting on the board of Chrysler or K-Mart and sitting on the board of New York Hospital or Georgetown University's medical affairs committee."[38]

I am aware of the genuinely desperate cases, but hard cases do not make for good law. The relatively small number of such cases does not justify huge societal changes. Legalization of suicide can only wreak irreparable harm on our societal structure, can only add to the cycle of violence that increasingly threatens our reverence for and commitment to life. In consequence, for all my half century of agonizing pastoral experience with all manner of dying, I am unalterably opposed to the efforts of Dr. Jack Kevorkian to add suicide to the roster of American rights. And in this context I am dismayed by the movement to turn doctors committed to life into dealers of death, whether in a loving home or in an execution chamber.

In this connection, I have been frightened by a prediction in a 1994 report on assisted suicide by the New York State Task Force on Life and the Law (bioethicists, lawyers, clergy, and state health officials):

> Assisted suicide and euthanasia will be practiced through the prism of social inequality and prejudice that characterizes the delivery of services in all segments of society, including health care. Those who will be most vulnerable to abuse, error or indifference are the poor, minorities and those who are least educated and least empowered....
>
> Many patients in large, overburdened facilities serving the urban and rural poor will not have the benefit of skilled pain management and comfort care. Indeed, a recent study found that patients treated for cancer at centers that care predomi-

nantly for minority individuals were three times more likely to receive inadequate therapy to relieve pain.[39]

The Hippocratic Oath still makes medicomoral sense: "I will give no deadly medicine to anyone if asked."

Not impertinent here is the background for the assisted-suicide movement: a widespread conviction that suffering is an unmitigated evil to be avoided at all costs. Over and above Elisabeth Kübler-Ross's stages of death and dying, "there has been at work in our society a more pervasive and portentous avoidance of the distinctly human experience of suffering. Amid cultural uncertainty about good and evil, suffering has come to be viewed as a secular equivalent of sin, from which we need to be saved."[40] Even among many of the Christian faithful, there is little appreciation of suffering as a mystery that makes sense only in the context of a God-man's cross, the Jesus who "humbled himself with an obedience that meant death, even death on a cross" (Phil 2:8), the Jesus who insisted that if we want to become his followers, we have to take up our cross each day (Lk 9:23).[41] There is little understanding of St. Paul's insightful summary of suffering's redemptive role, "I am now rejoicing in my sufferings for your sake, and in my flesh I am completing what is lacking in Christ's afflictions for the sake of his body, that is, the Church" (Col 1:24).

Precious among my possessions is a letter dated July 15, 1995, from prolific Catholic coauthors John and Denise Carmody. Several years before, John had been diagnosed as afflicted with a life-threatening malignancy. When this letter was written, the myeloma had gotten the better of the chemotherapy, doubling the amount of cancer. The letter, addressed to their many friends, voiced in profound accents their Christlike reaction:

> It's a roller-coaster life, as perhaps all lives are. The invitation has been to live fully, gratefully, while practicing the art of dying. You will remember that learning to die is one of Plato's descriptions of philosophy, the love of wisdom. You will also remember that the Johannine Jesus, our current study project, works signs and dies to offer us eternal life. Dying/living. Learning to die while loving living. Realizing that an incarnate divinity knows this bi-phased rhythm of human existence from within. Trying therefore to become, not callous about pain or death, not presumptuous, but free of their power to loom up as frightening idols and block out the far greater reality of God. Any of our lives is a small thing. Measured by

the calipers of astro-physical evolution, it does not stretch for a micro-inch. And yet each of our lives stands before God, comes directly from God, utterly clear in its specificity, for God, having no limits, is not overcome by the swarm of us creatures but in the divine patience out of time can love each of us just for ourselves. So we wait, letting our aging, sickening bodies instruct us as much as our minds, and remembering that we have not been called servants but friends.

Having shared Christ's crucifixion, John now rejoices in his resurrection. As Jesus declared to Lazarus' sister Martha, "Those who believe in me, even though they die, will live, and everyone who lives and believes in me will never die" (Jn 11:25–26).

I am aware that for some feminist theologians no symbol is more problematic than the cross.[42] It is seen as a "scapegoat syndrome" encouraging women to accept the role of passive victims, especially in the context of contemporary violence against women and children; to some, it even glorifies suffering. My own approach to suffering comes closer to that of feminist theologians like Elizabeth Johnson, for whom the cross stands in history as a "life-affirming protest against all torture and injustice, and as a pledge that the transforming power of God is with those who suffer to bring about life for others."[43] I shall continue to insist that a genuinely Christian soteriology based on the historical Jesus and the theology of Paul does not glorify suffering. It grants that sheer suffering is not a good. But it submits that suffering can be transmuted into sacrifice through love, that this took place pre-eminently in Jesus, and that such sacrifice was and continues to be redemptive, liberating. An authentically scriptural soteriology will never cease to echo Paul declaring to the Christians of Galatia, "I have been crucified with Christ; and it is no longer I who live, but it is Christ who lives in me. And the life I now live in the flesh I live by faith in the Son of God, who loved me and gave himself for me" (Gal 2:19–20).

A final word on assisted suicide. It stems, unexpectedly, from a novel by Dean Koontz, *Dark Rivers of the Heart*.[44] A loose-cannon government official, Roy Miro, shoots and kills in cold blood a couple in their 40s; the husband is in a wheelchair, uses an electric lift to get out of his Dodge van. Afterward Miro arranges them carefully side by side in the van, folds the wife's right hand around her husband's left. Then he says: "It's so sad. What quality of life could they have had — with him imprisoned in a wheelchair, and with her tied to him by bonds of love? Their lives were so limited by his infirmities, their futures tethered to that damned chair. How much better now." A little later Miro says to his companion, Eve Jammer:

> Perfection in all things. Perfect love and perfect justice. Perfect beauty. I dream of a perfect society, where everyone enjoys perfect health, perfect equality, in which the economy hums always like a perfectly tuned machine, where everyone lives in harmony with everyone else and with nature. Where no offense is ever given or taken. Where all dreams are perfectly rational and considerate. Where *all* dreams come true.

Eve marvels, "I've never seen ... such *power.*" Roy responds:

> I removed two imperfect lives from creation, inching the world closer to perfection. And at the same time, I relieved those two sad people of the burden of this cruel life, this imperfect world, where nothing could ever be as they hoped. I gave to the world, and I gave to those poor people, and there were no losers.

Roy admits that his is "a great power, the greatest of all powers." But he wants Eve to understand exactly what this power is. "Unlike other power, Eve, this doesn't flow from anger. It doesn't come from hatred, either. It's not the power of rage, envy, bitterness, greed. It's not like the power some people find in courage or honor — or that they gain from a belief in God. It transcends these powers, Eve. Do you know what it is?" Eve shakes her head. Roy explains:

> My power is the power of compassion. . . . If you try to understand other people, to feel their pain, to really *know* the anguish of their lives, to love them in spite of their faults, you're overcome by such pity, such *intense* pity, it's intolerable. It must be relieved. So you tap into the immeasurable, inexhaustible power of compassion. You *act* to relieve suffering, to ease the world a hairsbreadth closer to perfection.

The source of Roy's power? He had "tapped the power of Dr. Kevorkian," which he had recently absorbed from the television in a Learjet.

Compassion as power ... "the greatest of all powers." Actually the power to kill. For all Roy's anguish, not genuinely pity-full, ultimately pitiful.

Psychiatry

During my early years as a Jesuit, psychiatry was in bad odor among Catholics, disparaged not only by the general populace but by influential intellectuals such as Bishop Fulton Sheen. Not without reason. After all, had not Sigmund Freud mounted a frontal attack on religion as a childish neurosis, our need to invent a God as a psychological crutch for our anxieties?

My own more mature understanding developed primarily in two ways. One influence came through personal friendship with two of my Jesuit students at Woodstock College who had been board-certified in other specialties before they entered the Society of Jesus: Angelo D'Agostino in urology and Louis Padovano in obstetrics and gynecology. Both went into private psychiatric practice after ordination to priesthood; both have been striking examples to me of professional counseling at its best. Padovano, born in 1930, continues to practice in New York City; D'Agostino, born in 1926, has been setting up houses for HIV-infected little children in Nairobi. And among Jesuits I dare not omit long-time friend William W. Meissner, who not only has practiced psychiatry and taught psychoanalysis for decades, but has done so while publishing his experiences with the workings of divine grace. The second and more important influence: therapy sessions with Dr. Leo H. Bartemeier, whose research and writings through half a century contributed profoundly to almost every aspect of present-day psychiatry. This contact merits a bit of detail.

In the '60s, my mother was confined for six years to a nursing home in Catonsville, Maryland, a mere half hour's drive from Woodstock. She was suffering (I have come to believe) from what we now call Alzheimer's disease — what we called senility, with loss of memory and inability to express herself in understandable language as two characteristics. In these circumstances, to my lasting discredit, I was reluctant to visit Mother. When I did, infrequently, I was not the most engaging of visitors, often impatient, hardly the model of a devoted, grateful son. Each time I returned to Woodstock, my conscience would savage me with profound feelings of guilt.

With this as background, I flew to South Bend, Indiana, for a lecture. On the flight, chest pains assailed me. An EKG at the University of Notre Dame revealed no damage, but tests-in-depth were recommended. Four days at Mercy Hospital in Baltimore terminated with the common sense of a young cardiologist on the staff. "Organically," he said, "you don't have a heart problem, or any other serious physical problem. But the fact remains, you are still having chest pains. So, why don't you see a psychiatrist?" Me see a psychiatrist? God forbid! But Jesuit superiors prevailed, and it was decided that I would consult Leo Bartemeier, good friend of the Society, then medical director of Seton Psychiatric Institute in Baltimore.

Dr. Bartemeier saw me for four sessions. Rarely have I experienced such wisdom, touched with gentleness and caring. The one instance I shall never forget occurred during our third session. I had detailed for him my experience with my mother, my reaction to her in her senile state, my anger at myself for so acting, my inability to explain my own actions. He heard me out, looked at me with strong compassion, then said very simply, "The mother you knew is dead." Six words that explained so much, opened up a small world for reflection, eased the self-scourging within me.

After the fourth session Dr. Bartemeier dismissed me! He had concluded that in all probability the chest pains were due to my grief over the death of dear Woodstock friend and colleague Father Gus Weigel several months before, a relationship so natural, so carefree, so almost casual that I never realized how profound it was. If that were behind the pains, he reasoned, those pains would gradually lessen, disappear in time. (They did.) I returned to Woodstock that afternoon to inform the Jesuit faculty that of all 20 or so of us, I was the only one who had documentary evidence to prove I was sane.

More recently, Jesuit Edwin H. Cassem, associate professor of psychiatry at Harvard Medical School and chief of psychiatry at Massachusetts General Hospital in Boston, uncovered for Washingtonians the Jesuit romance with psychiatry. His fall 1993 lecture within the series The Jesuit Tradition and Medicine, sponsored by the Georgetown University Medical Center, presented psychiatry as science and as service. As a discipline, psychiatry has three aspects. It is a neuroscience; it studies disorders and illnesses; and it tracks thought, emotion, and behavior. One paragraph on feelings merits reproduction here.

> If one is curious and honest, one takes feelings into account. In fact, I would say that from a religious viewpoint feeling is as divine as cognition. Feelings are not the ultimate criteria of judgment, but we need the evidence they provide. Reverence for our animal heritage is extremely important to understanding why it is we function as we do. The limbic system — that primitive, yet key part of the brain near the brain stem that is

thought to support emotion and behavior — is a central focus of psychiatric study. Yet, I know some of you may be thinking that I am emphasizing feeling too much. Let's think for a moment about Jesus' feelings of being overwhelmed at Gethsemane and abandoned on Calvary; these feelings are the very features that make His mastery of those events so significant. They are the things that impress us: His feelings — raw, human, sacred feelings....[45]

On psychiatry as service, Cassem reminded his audience that from its very beginning the care of the sick was an essential part of Jesuit ministry. Basing his argument on the research of first-rate Jesuit historian John O'Malley, Cassem headlined three features in the work of the early Jesuits for the sick.

The first was that they wanted to reproduce the ministry of Jesus, the actual bodily healing of the sick that He did in His time. That very action expressed the core of their pastoral self-understanding. You want to know what ministry is? Take care of the sick. You want to be a real priest? Again, take care of the sick. That's what it means to be called by God. Secondly, the Jesuits, all of whom studied philosophy, had a form of social philosophy that said that they had an obligation to contribute to the common good of all people. Finally, Jesuit service often took on a direct physical form: Jesuits built hospitals, orphanages, and places for women who had been beaten or abandoned. They did very practical, concrete things to express what is, simultaneously, a deeply spiritual commitment.[46]

I have been profoundly moved by Cassem's observation that a psychiatrist puts his stethoscope to a person's heart, to discover what meaning some "injury" has for him or her.[47] And with that, the place of faith, of a relationship with God, in each person's life. Psychiatry has come a long way since Sigmund Freud. And Jesuits, in response to imaginative Ignatius, continue to find God everywhere, in all things, ceaselessly wed ministry to the struggle for wholeness.

THIRTEEN

From Life to Life
On Turning Eighty-Five

Increasingly pertinent to me is the reminder of the Psalmist:

> Our years come to an end like a sigh.
> The days of our life are seventy years,
>   or perhaps eighty, if we are strong...
> They are soon gone, and we fly away.
>
> (Ps 90:9b–10)

It's the issue of aging, with its attendant ailing and the ultimate closure that is dying. Aging is no longer a category for me; I fall asleep in its embrace, and I rise to its greeting. I don't like it, each year passing more swiftly than its predecessor, each day my faults and infidelities weighing more heavily because I am that much closer to a cliché now pregnant with meaning, "meeting my Maker." Consequently, over the past ten years I have, understandably, given increased attention, personal and theological, to aging — the reality in itself and my own aging.[1]

Aging in Various Religions

To broaden my outlook. I have found it instructive to mull over attitudes to aging in various religions of the world.[2] I have uncovered the insight of southern Ghana's Akans: Knowledge is power, but aging is wisdom — a wisdom that calls for reverence, for respect. I resonate to the woodland Ojibway of North America as they reflect the tradition of Native Americans in their insistence, "Honor the aged; in honoring them you have life and wisdom." I marvel that for Confucians filial piety, respect for elders, is the supreme principle of morality, for it can define the very meaning of our being in this world, is a powerful binding force that produces a stable society, is a source of world peace and order. I rejoice to see the Hindu tradition refusing to focus on the physical weakness and disabilities

383

of the elderly, stressing instead their spiritual maturity and wisdom. I relate to the Buddhist attitude toward aging as not diminishment but increase, a movement toward fuller life, neither a downward spiral toward dissolution nor a triumphal procession to glory and immortality. Even the debilitating aspects of aging are a gift, because they put us in direct contact with the truth of our existence.

I have been profoundly impressed by the biblical tradition enshrined in the Prior Testament and by rabbinic reflection thereon, for there human living is governed by a theology of Presence.[3] A mortal creature, "nothing but dust and ashes" (Gen 18:27), I am in creative partnership with God, "a little lower than God" (Ps 8:5). Living in God's presence dictates the way I act in other relationships. Relating to God's presence in awe and love — the biblical expression for religion — I am motivated to similar reverence in human interaction.

Reflecting their awe of God, the younger are to "rise up before the aged and honor the face of the old" (Lev 19:32). With reverential posture and respectful speech, they acknowledge the dignity and worth of the aged somewhat as they receive the presence of God. Such reverence stems from a realization that parents, like God, are creators. "One relates to parents by the fact of birth, to his teachers and the learned by his reception of wisdom and to the aged by their achievement of experiential knowledge."[4] The aging transmit to the younger their experience of the past — not as sheer knowledge but as a living witness to God's presence. Because life is a gift of God and all moments of life are equally sacred, the period of deterioration in aging demands special concern. Every effort must be exerted — legally, socially, medically — to preserve the life of those who are facing death, and to preserve it in dignity. Reverence before God-given life — such is Jewry's precious bequest to the nations.

Aging can mean growth, experiencing again the presence that makes us genuinely human. But for that, as Abraham Joshua Heschel insisted, the old need not only recreation but a vision, not only a memory but a dream.

Aging in the United States

Unfortunately, society in our United States stands in marked contrast to the world's religions. In chapter 5 above, I stated my conviction that what the United States glorifies is youth, strength, beauty; that the ideal of aging is not to seem to age at all; with such as these the dominant culture can identify. Most Americans, I said, do not age so gracefully, so creatively, so productively. In our culture, to be retired is to be useless; the aged rarely serve a practical purpose; they don't "do" anything. That is why, three decades ago, theater critic Walter Kerr could formulate a twentieth-century law, an article of faith by which most Americans live: "Only useful activity is valuable, meaningful, moral."[5]

Against such crass utilitarianism Christianity cries in protest. True, the New Testament, understandably preoccupied with Christ and in some measure expectant of his early return, touches but lightly on old age. Exhortations to obey parents and honor widows, lectures to the elderly on virtues of their state, hardly constitute a theology of aging. It is only with the maturing of gerontology in the nineteenth century that a rich human context has developed for the reflections of theologians.[6]

In 1989 Erik Erikson, all of 87, published two new books and was at work on a third. The second of the published works, coauthored with wife Joan, had for title *Vital Involvements in Old Age.*[7] Based on personal interviews with men and women in their 80s and 90s, it examined why some of these elderly people "live hopeful, productive lives, despite failing health and alertness and why others, though relatively robust, give in to loneliness, narcissism and despair."[8]

Erikson (with Joan) became convinced that the "identity crisis" is not a single event, because identity is a lifelong process, a continuing series of challenges. In his 80s he was revisioning the human life cycle from a new perspective: the existential I, the individual transcending the sum of his psychosocial identities at each stage in life, in old age recognizing the inevitability of death — and death's problems cannot be fathomed by theories of identity.

In harmony with this focus on the existential I, allow this octogenarian to reflect on the stage of life we traditionally have styled "old age," and touch it in a special way to suffering and dying. Jesuit that I am, I should like to link together my personal experience, the experience of others, and Catholic theology.

Suffering in a Christian Context

Suffering — pain of spirit, pain of flesh — is not limited to the aging.[9] Before he was 30, Beethoven began to experience the deafness that would induce his intense spiritual crisis. Born with multiple sclerosis, Christy Brown, author of *My Left Foot,* could use only that small member to paint and to compose. Short-story writer Flannery O'Connor, afflicted with lupus, was a young 39 when she died. John

Merrick, the horribly deformed "elephant man" of stage and screen, was 26 when he left us. In our time AIDS victims are often frighteningly young. Still, it is the aging who suffer Shakespeare's "fardel of never-ending misery" precisely because of their age.

Suffering at any age is not easy for the human mind to understand. Even for those who, like myself, have grown up with a God whose very name is Love, whose Son is Goodness in flesh, much human suffering makes little or no sense: infants afflicted with multiple sclerosis, a good woman comatose for seven years, whole families wiped out in auto accidents, six million Jews destroyed in the Holocaust, 55 million civilian and military dead in World War II — the mysteries are endless. The Jews of the Prior Testament at times traced suffering to sin — the sin of parents, the sin of the nation, one's own sin. But even here there was no "answer." The Jews still asked why the ways of the wicked "prosper at all times" (Ps 10:5), consoled themselves that "the fool and the stupid perish together and leave their wealth to others" (Ps 49:10), could not help complaining, "Has God in anger shut up His compassion?" (Ps 77:9). Job, confronted with innocent suffering, found human wisdom bankrupt, came face to face with a God who refused to enlighten his mind and simply appealed to Job's love and his trust.

Suffering, especially as we age, calls not only for faith but for a spirituality. All Christian spirituality is the response of a man or woman to God revealing divine love through Christ in the Spirit. In the concrete, it consists in knowing, loving, and serving God and God's children in the context of a community of faith, hope, and love. At its core, Christian spirituality is human love responding to divine love, to a God who "so loved the world that He gave His only Son" (Jn 3:16), not only to share our flesh but to experience our pain and die our death. It is St. Paul's passionate outburst, "I have been crucified with Christ; it is no longer I who live, but it is Christ who lives in me. And the life I now live in the flesh I live by faith in the Son of God, who loved me and gave himself for me" (Gal 2:20).

In chapter 8 on ordained priesthood, I insisted that the service of priests will be most effective if we follow the Crucified, if we die with Jesus from womb to tomb. Here I insist that following the Crucified is not a privilege and burden of the ordained alone; it is the vocation of all who claim to be disciples of Christ. All genuine Christian existence is a ceaseless following of Christ, a wondrous and fearful effort to get to be in his image, and that is a struggle that never ends this side of the grave.

Job

To envision the problem in broader perspective, I find it useful for the Christian to return to Job. His story is a fascinating human story — the experience of a man who has to wrestle with God.[10] He is comparatively young, well off, a good person of high moral standards; the very first verse of the Book of Job announces that he "was blameless and upright, one who feared God and turned away from evil" (Job 1:1). But in a brief space everything he has is destroyed — not only cattle and house and servants, but sons and daughters. He is struck with a disease that gives ceaseless pain, never lets him sleep, makes him ugly to look at. Barred from human society, he lives in a community dump. People spit when they see him; even his wife says, "Curse God and die" (2:9). It has long reminded me of a powerful film I saw in the '60s, *The Pawnbroker,* where actor Ron Steiger epitomizes despair: "Everything I loved was taken from me — and I did not die."

Now Job struggles with God. To begin with, he is bewildered, confused. He doesn't understand why this is happening to him; he hasn't done anything to deserve it. He loves God, wants only to please Him, is groping for a more intimate relationship. Then why is God suddenly acting like an enemy, hostile, oppressive? Why does the Almighty torment so unimportant a creature? Is God being sadistic? Was God jealous of Job's happiness? What kind of gift is such a life, such a living death? And so Job curses the day he was born. He begs God to just leave him alone: Go away, don't bother me, let me have a little comfort before I die.

Job's friends are no help at all. For them there is no mystery: Job must be suffering for his sins. The logic is impeccable: If Job is not a sinner, then God is unjust. So, dear friend, stop protesting your innocence; your condition is clear proof of your guilt. Repent, and all will be well with you again.

But Job cannot confess what is false; he is not a guilty man. He denies deceit, denies adultery; he has respected the God-given rights of his slaves and shared his goods with the poor; gold or any creature has never been his god; his door has swung open to every wayfarer; he has never pretended to be what he is not. No, not for sin is he being punished.

In all this wrestling there are two splendid moments. The first is Job's act of faith, of trust. God only seems to have changed; God still cares. If Job's sufferings make no earthly sense, God has His own reasons. Divine abandonment is only for a time; somehow Job will see God.

But take note: If faith dissolves Job's doubts, it does not diminish his desolation. The sharpest torment of all is still there: a dark night of the soul. For all his faith, Job cannot "get through" to God. He used to experience God's presence; now he experiences only God's absence.

The second splendid moment: At last God speaks to Job. God shows God's self to this anguished believer, this rebellious lover, who has raged against his situation, has demanded that God justify God's ways. But notice: God says nothing to Job about his guilt or innocence, nothing about suffering and its meaning; God does not explain. And Job does not say, "Ah yes, now I understand. Thank you." The real experience is simply the encounter: God lets Job see Him. And in the encounter Job is happy to disown his speculations, his complaints; he even discards his ultimate support, his cherished integrity, his innocence.

> [Job's innocence] is not a bargaining counter; it is not a token he can hold up to God, saying, "For this, you owe me happiness." He is in the right, against the friends; he is not in the right, against God. He can make no claim on him. Job has to insist on his integrity, but he cannot say "God must."[11]

The Christian

The Book of Job does not solve the problem of suffering; I read it, revel in it, and human suffering remains a mystery. Even Christian theology cannot offer a satisfying answer to every "Why?" that surges from the heart and lips of a crucified man, woman, or child. Yes, children too. I shall not easily forget a story I read in the London *Tablet* while directing a Preaching the Just Word retreat/workshop in Melbourne, Australia, in June 1995. It told of a memorial Mass celebrated in Norwich, England, for a teenage student killed in a road accident on his way to school. The bidding prayers, what in the States we call the "prayers of the faithful," came from the hearts and lips of Michael's friends. In a cry from the heart so different from the sincere but routine rhetoric of my American experience, one 13-year-old stood by the altar and began: "God, why have you taken Michael away from me? He was my friend and he made me laugh...."[12] Why, God, why?

I have long since ceased to ask why. I no longer look for an "explanation" of suffering that satisfies the mind. Suffering enmeshes us in the problem of evil, and despite all the efforts of the philosophers, evil remains very much a mystery. My search focuses on meaning. If suffering does not make sheerly human sense, what is it that reveals the mind of God in this experience?

Earlier on I insisted that the essential word here is "follow." It is not only to the original apostles, to Peter and John, to James and Judas, that Jesus the Christ says, "Follow me." The invitation — better, the command — is uttered to each and every human baptized into him. Uttered, therefore, to *me,* and not for the first time when consecrated oils anointed me to ordained priesthood; uttered when sacred waters flowed over my forehead.

But what does "Follow me" involve? It calls for a progressive movement deeper and deeper into Christ. The "mind-set" that was in Christ, the mind-set Paul commended to the Christians of Philippi (Phil 2:2, 5), "goes beyond rational reflection to include the 'mind-set' that issues in a determined pattern of behavior,"[13] the mind-set that induced God's own Son to wear our flesh, walk our earth, die our death. A Christian's movement into Christ demands as an essential ingredient not only a way of thinking like his, but a kenosis, a self-emptying akin to Christ's own. Kenosis is not a virtue requested from the Lord on one's retirement from active existence. All through life Christians have to "let go": let go of where they've been, let go of the level of life where they are now, so as to live more fully. Let go of childhood and adolescence, of good looks and youthful energy, of familiar places and beloved faces, of a high-paying job and human applause, of self-righteousness and self-sufficiency. Not simply because we must, because we have no choice. Rather because only by letting go of yesterday can we grow more fully into Christ today. We do not *forget* our yesterdays; we simply dare not *live in* them.

Kenosis, self-emptying, letting go reaches a critical stage in suffering and dying. In suffering, for two reasons: because I find pain difficult to endure, and because (at least for me, as a state-of-the-art hypochondriac) each symptom is a premonition of death. And I am not yet prepared to let go of that final hold on life.

I am constantly struggling to realize, and to live, St. Paul's profound declaration to the Christians of Colossae, "I am now rejoicing in my sufferings for your sake, and in my flesh I am completing what is lacking in Christ's afflictions for the sake of his body, the Church" (Col 1:24). My sufferings can be redemptive, can bring life, God's life, to others, if only I link my arthritic fingers to a blood-stained hand pinned to a cross outside Jerusalem. A mystery indeed, but a mystery that makes divine sense out of apparently senseless suffering.

Precisely here — in life-threatening illness and actual dying, to grasp my role in redemption — is where I need Christ to show his face to me, somewhat as God showed God's face to Job.

Death

And death itself? In chapter 12 I confessed that I am fearfully aware of death's darkness, the blank face of death. Death breaks the whole person. In death a unique "I," an irreplaceable "thou," is destroyed, a wondrous wedding of spirit and senses. I who lift my eyes to mountains and the moon; I who catch with my ears the tenderness and the thunder of Handel's *Messiah* and throb to the music of a loved one's voice; I who breathe life-giving air in the smog of Washington and whose nostrils twitch to the odor of spaghetti bolognese; I who cradle Christ on my tongue and gently caress the face of a friend; I whose mind travels over centuries and continents to share Plato's world of ideas, Augustine's vision of God's city, and Gandhi's passion for peace; I who laugh and love, worry and weep, dance and dream, sing and sin, preach and pray — this "I" will be lost to the world, this "thou" lost to those who survive me.

I say it without arrogance: This "I" God will not replace, cannot replace. I am not just *some* one; I am *this* one. Through five and eighty years, for good or ill, I have touched, been touched by, a whole little world. When I die, this warm, pulsating flame of human living and loving will die with me.

And so I fear that, like Dylan Thomas, I shall "not go gentle into that good night." I am much more likely to "burn and rave at close of day, / Rage, rage against the dying of the light."[14] At times death has so terrifying a face that even God's unique Son sweated blood before it, begged his Father to remove that cup if at all possible (Mt 26:39; Lk 22:41–44). The author of the Letter to the Hebrews speaks movingly: "In the days of his flesh, Jesus offered up prayers and supplications, with loud cries and tears, to the one who was able to save him from death" (Heb 5:7).

Death as a Remedy for Sin

In my own struggle to make peace with death, I have been intrigued by a thesis prominent in the Greek theologians of the early Church and not absent from the Latin. A prime proponent of the thesis was

Methodius, bishop of Philippi in Macedonia, a martyr in 311. He insisted that God "invented death" as a remedy for sin.[15] His point was that, as long as the body lives, before it has passed through death, sin lives within it, even in the baptized, though sin's roots are concealed, its power inhibited, its sprouts checked.[16] He returned to the thesis time and again in the first book *On the Resurrection.* Here is perhaps the most intriguing passage:

> Take, for comparison, a consummate craftsman who recasts a statue. The statue as originally fashioned, from gold or some other material, was a lovely thing, every part of the body beautifully proportioned. All of a sudden the craftsman finds it mutilated — damaged by an evil man too envious to endure its loveliness. . . . If he does not recast or refashion it but simply treats and repairs it, the fire and the forge will inevitably change it from what it was originally. . . .
>
> Such, I would say, was God's dispensation in our regard. Seeing the human person, the fairest work of His art, marred by envy's malicious treachery, God, lover of the human that He was, was not content to leave the human in this condition, lest the human, with the flaw in him/her immortal, bear the blame to eternity. He dissolved the human into his/her primeval matter, in order that, by a process of remodeling, all that was blameworthy in him/her might melt away and disappear completely. For the melting down of the statue in the example corresponds to the death and dissolution of the body, while the refashioning and restoration of the original material finds its parallel in the resurrection. . . . [17]

Among many pertinent passages in the Greek Fathers, I was especially moved by a passage from Gregory of Nyssa in his *Large Catechetical Address,* a compendium of Christian doctrine dedicated to teachers who "have need of system in their instructions" (Prologue). Splendid speculative theologian and genuine mystic, Gregory links human sin with a death which is not primarily punishment.

> Because by the movement of our free will we contracted fellowship with evil, through some sensual gratification mixing this evil with our nature, like some poison seasoned with honey, and therefore falling from that blessedness we had from impassibility, we have been transformed to wickedness. For this reason the human person, like some earthen vessel, is again re-

solved into earth, in order to part with the sordidness in which
he/she is now involved, and be refashioned through the resurrection to his/her original appearance. This is the doctrine
Moses sets before you in the manner indeed of a history, and
darkly.[18]

But Gregory's theology, profound as it often is, does not begin and
end in his mind. The funeral oration he delivered in 385 for the six-
year-old Princess Pulcheria, the only child of Theodosius the Great,
ends with a final effort at consolation; and the effort runs along the
lines I have been tracing. Death is *agathon,* "a good thing"; it is a
singular way to our original state.

> Death, for humans, is nothing else but purification from
> wickedness. For in the beginning our nature was constructed
> by the God of the universe like some vessel fit to receive what
> is good; but when the enemy of our souls through treach-
> ery poured into us what is evil, no room remained for the
> good. For this reason, in order that the inborn [implanted]
> wickedness might not be eternal in us, a surpassing providence
> opportunely dissolves the vessel by death, so that when the
> wickedness has flown forth [melted away, disappeared], the
> human being might be refashioned and might be restored, un-
> mixed with evil, to its original life. For this is the resurrection:
> dissolution and regeneration of our nature to its primordial
> state.[19]

John Chrysostom, preaching at Antioch in 388 on Genesis, spoke
in the same vein. Dealing with Genesis 3:22–23 (God exiled humans
from Paradise to keep them from eating of the tree of life and living
for ever), he declared:

> Death was a dispensation of the Master to the advantage of
> humans.... [The danger was that within Paradise human sin-
> ning might be deathless; exile was preferable.] Consequently,
> human banishment from Paradise was rather an act of solici-
> tude than of anger. This is the way our Master acts: He reveals
> His solicitude for us no less when He punishes than when He
> grants favors; He inflicts this punishment for an admonition.
> If He had known that we would not become worse by sinning
> with impunity, He would not have punished; but in checking
> in advance our continued deterioration and cutting off sin's
> onward march, His punishment is an expression of His love.[20]

One quotation from an early Latin author will have to suffice here. It stems from a Roman priest, Novatian, an extreme rigorist where apostates were concerned, fomenter of a schism centered on reconciliation of the lapsed, with high hopes of becoming bishop of Rome. About the year 240 we have an uncomfortably dense sentence from Novatian, difficult to translate, yet an early witness to the tradition in question here. For clarity's sweet sake, I break the single Latin sentence into two.

> That the human is prevented [after Adam's sin] from touching [eating of ?] the wood of the tree of life does not stem from petty envy. The purpose is to keep the human from living for ever without Christ's pardon for his/her sins and so bearing about with him/her always for punishment a deathless transgression.[21]

Novatian seems to be asserting that death is not so much punishment as grace, for it puts an end to sinning.

Death as Final Free Surrender

As always, the early Christian theologians have stimulated my thinking; I have spent many an hour on death as remedy for sin. But as death becomes more and more imminent, the head trip gives less and less comfort. Death as remedy for sin is still theologically intriguing, but not what gives peace to the whole person face to face with the stark reality.

Far more stimulating is an acute awareness of what my faith and my theology tell me about dying/rising. St. Paul ceaselessly rings in my ears: "If the dead are not raised, then Christ has not been raised. If Christ has not been raised, your faith is futile and you are still in your sins.... But in fact Christ has been raised..." (1 Cor 15:16–20). Time and again at the altar I proclaim "Christ has died, Christ is risen, Christ will come again." In a homily at a Mass of the Resurrection for a middle-aged lady lawyer with two children, a dear friend at whose wedding I had presided a quarter century ago, I said to the assembled mourners:

> Indeed there is much to mourn, as there was much to mourn on Calvary. We shall have to wait for "the resurrection at the last day" (Jn 11:24) before we see the smile light up Eileen's eyes again, before we feel the gentle pressure of her touch. And that is sad, no matter how profound our faith. But the thrilling truth

remains: Eileen is alive! Alive with the life of Christ, because even in death the Holy Spirit never left her. More alive than she ever was before, because every tear is past, every malignant growth, every infirmity of our fragile humanity. In the presence of God, there is only God, there is only love. And you know who was utterly convinced of this? Yes... Eileen.[22]

In this connection I have given much thought to what it meant for Jesus to die. The depths of his death we theologians are still struggling to plumb. For it was not only an unrepeatable man that died on Calvary; it was the God-man. What happened? As so often, so here too Karl Rahner put it powerfully:

> Jesus surrendered himself in his death unconditionally to the absolute mystery that he called his Father, into whose hands he committed his existence, when in the night of his death and Godforsakenness he was deprived of everything that is otherwise regarded as the content of a human existence.... In the concreteness of his death it becomes only too clear that everything fell away from him, and in this trackless dark there prevailed silently only the mystery that in itself and in its freedom has no name and to which he nevertheless calmly surrendered himself as to eternal love and not to the hell of futility.... He who came out of God's glory did not merely descend into our human life, but also fell into the abyss of our death, and his dying began when he began to live and came to an end on the cross when he bowed his head and died.[23]

And for all that he was God's unique Son, this man died not with experience of resurrection, not with an unassailable syllogism; he died with *faith* in his Father, with *hope* of life for ever.

But why? Because with his death, death would cease to be "the enemy." Not that with Calvary death became easy; on Calvary Jesus gave death new meaning. From his death life was born. For reasons mystery-laden, God One and Three had decided that the oneness between humans and God which had been ruptured in Paradise would be restored on Calvary, that divine love would recapture human hearts through crucifixion — not our crucifixion, but the dying/rising of God-in-flesh. That is why, for me, the most rapturous words in the Gospel were spoken by Jesus the night before he died: "Because I have life, you also will have life" (Jn 14:19).

That is why the First Letter of John opens as it does, an ecstatic affirmation of him who is Life: "that which was from the beginning, which we have heard, which we have seen with our eyes, which we have looked at and our hands have touched . . . the word of life — the life was revealed, and we have seen it and testify to it, and proclaim to you the eternal life that was with the Father and has been revealed to us" (1 Jn 1:1–2).

Jesus did die, in the Christian handbook definition of death: His "soul" left his body. But that soul, that spiritual element endowed with consciousness, was very much alive, incredibly alive because the Spirit of life, the Spirit that was his Spirit, never left it. And on the birthday of new life, the first Easter, Holy Spirit, human spirit, and risen flesh were joined together — for ever. Death was defeated. Not that death no longer existed; rather that death was deprived of its despotism — we die unto resurrection. Not because Jesus died; rather because he died out of love, for his Father and for us. A crucified love.

What, then, does it means for a Christian, for me, to die? Death does not cease to be death. An "I" is still lost to the world and a "thou" to survivors. But more importantly, death is life. Not only shall I not die altogether, totally, utterly; that is true, but frightfully negative. In consequence of Calvary, death is that unique point between time and timelessness when the Spirit of Christ, the Spirit of life, can take permanent possession of my spirit, without my earthbound resistance, until the risen Christ summons my risen flesh to the fulness of humanity. That is why the Christian can cry with St. Paul, "For me, life is Christ, and [therefore] death is gain" (Phil 1:21).

But there is more. For a Christian, for me, death should not be simply an unavoidable fact, something that inevitably happens. Dying, in a theological sense, begins when living begins; I share in Jesus' dying by sharing his cross through the whole of my life. Unless I do, I cannot be his disciple (Mt 10:38; 16:24; Mk 8:34; Lk 14:27). Whatever falls under the rubric of suffering should be part and parcel of my Christian dying. And the final cross, to be completely Christian, dare not be sheer resignation: I cannot do anything about it, and so I give in. Death should be the final, decisive act of human freedom, where I accept in love the mystery that is God, where I put the final seal on my personal history, my personal destiny.[24]

In two momentous monosyllables, dying is a Christian's final "I do." *I* die. Such was the ultimate act of an earthbound Jesus as John tells it: "Bowing his head, he handed over [his] spirit" (Jn 19:30); *he* committed his spirit, entrusted it, to his Father. He made this clear in the moving discourse on the good shepherd: "I lay down my life in order to take it up again. No one takes it [or: has taken it] from me; rather, I lay it down of my own accord. I have power to lay it down, and I have power to take it up again" (Jn 10:17–18).

A disciple of Jesus, in dying I entrust my spirit to a loving Father. It is a free act; no one takes my life from me; I surrender myself unconditionally to the mystery of God's love and mercy. Believing, hoping, loving, I now enter fully into the dying of Jesus. And in dying with him, I embrace . . . life.

Reluctance to Dying

All this I believe; all this I proclaim. To be "risen with Christ" is primarily why I exist; it alone makes sense of my 85 years, of my priesthood, of my preaching, of my poverty, chastity, and obedience. Then why am I not hastening toward it with my whole undivided self? Why do I not look forward to death with incomparable anticipation? Why do I find the days, the months, the years slipping by all too swiftly? Several reasons.

To begin with, I like life on planet Earth. Not everything I read, hear, see. Not the violence on the streets and on TV. Not the sexual abuse in homes, in the Armed Services, in government. Not the wars that pit brother against brother, Christian against Christian; not the wars that rape women and butcher children; not the wars that displace millions from their homes to walk tear-streaked roads to unknown resting places. Not the rugged individualism that fractures community; not the godlessness and the culture of death. Not the personal burdens: the ileitis, the hiatal hernia, the low hematocrit, the blockages to the heart, the diarrhea, the increasing number of friends dying week after week.

What do I love about this life? Rabbi Heschel's insight marks a significant beginning: "Just to be is a blessing, just to live is holy."[25] Not just the quality of life; simply being alive. Not easy for the Jewish people, whether devout or secularized, when they live in the memory of the Holocaust, when more than a few are convinced that God died in Auschwitz. And still the vast majority live in the graced shadow of Sinai, of a Yahweh who can never forget His children, who was there in Dachau, alive in Auschwitz. I too, like Heschel, find sheer human living rich in blessings. Simply to see, to breathe deeply, to hear the racing of my heart, to feel fiercely.

I love the intellectual life, the life of the mind. I mean my research into the Fathers of the Church, four decades living and breathing scores of "men of the Church," burrowing into fascinatingly diverse minds and spirits, mystics and martyrs, geniuses and journeymen, from Clement of Rome and Ignatius of Antioch through Cyril of Alexandria and Augustine of Hippo to Isidore of Seville and John of Damascus; reliving a pilgrim church with its ceaseless calvaries and resurrections.

I shall miss teaching, the interplay of minds, of wills, of emotions; helping young minds to open up — to God, to God's people, to God's endlessly expanding universe; struggling with men and women who often do not think the way I do, who challenge me to see reality with fresh eyes.

I shall miss the life of the senses: eyeing in awe an eagle in lordly flight; drinking in Mozart's *Eine kleine Nachtmusik;* savoring the flavor of veal marsala; breathing the odor of a sparkling Burgundy; touching with reverence spring's first African violets, the brow of a newborn infant.

I shall miss preaching: wrestling with a Lord who reveals and conceals; God's word issuing from these all too human lips; the power of language when infiltrated by God's grace; the hope in eyes long sunken in grief or despair.

I love this life because Christ has assured me that we who believe and love are tabernacles of the Trinity tented within us. I love the Eucharist for the Christ who, marvel of marvels, rests within me "body and blood, soul and divinity." I love my priesthood, the endless opportunities to play Christ the servant, particularly to his "little people," the poor and the powerless.

Oh I know the standard response: All this, for all its value, is a passing phase in salvation's story. You won't miss this because none of this is actually lost; all is subsumed into a reality far richer than the human mind can conceive. "Eye has not seen...." I do not doubt it; and still I regret that it must pass, still I mourn its dying. If heaven is, as I suspect, devoid of regrets, I shall not miss the terrestrial then; still, I don't want to lose it now. For all my preaching to others on letting go in order to grow, I find myself clinging possessively to things, to people. Ignatian indifference? More powerful is my struggle with poet Francis Thompson's *Hound of Heaven:*

> Though I knew His love who followéd,
> Yet was I sore adread
> Lest having Him I should have naught beside.

As so often, I turn to Gerard Manley Hopkins, this time his sonnet "To what serves Mortal Beauty?"[26] Especially the last three lines:

What do then? how meet beauty? Merely meet it; own,
Home at heart, heaven's sweet gift; then leave, let that alone.
Yea, wish that though, wish all, God's better beauty, grace.

"Then leave, let that alone." It's all there — the ultimate Jesuit
prayer:

> Take, O Lord, and receive all my liberty, my memory, my
> understanding, my whole will, all I have and all I possess. You
> gave them to me; to you, Lord, I return it all. It is all yours,
> dispose of it entirely as you will. Give me your love and your
> grace; this is enough for me.

Only your love and your grace — enough for me. So easy to sing;
so difficult to embrace.

To love of terrestrial life I must add a second reason why I fail
to welcome death as a friend: I am afraid of a lingering, painful
dying. To be helpless, to be clothed and fed like a baby, perhaps in-
continent, to live in my flesh Jesus' prediction to Peter, "When you
grow old, you will stretch out your hands, and someone else will
fasten a belt around you and take you where you do not wish to
go" (Jn 21:18) — I shiver and shake. Undoubtedly it goes back in
some degree to my father and only brother, both victims of cancer.
Somehow Pop knew he would not return from the hospital; he said
so when he kissed my mother good-bye at our door. But especially
Eddie, 27 years young, wasting away like a vegetable. The images
have not dulled since 1940. Besides, for six years I found it sheer
torment to visit my mother in a nursing home: memory gone, recognition a problem, hiding her false teeth from the nuns and nurses,
for weeks wrestling with restraining bonds. The old love still there,
but sadly unfocused.

For all my desire to resemble my Lord, I find myself praying
enthusiastically only the first part of Jesus' prayer in Gethsemane,
"Father, if you are willing, remove this cup from me; yet, not my
will but yours be done" (Lk 22:42). Those last seven words stick
in my throat.

A third reason for dragging my feet in this life? I suspect I prefer
the imperfect living I experience and love to a perfection of living I
find terribly abstract. There are days when I wish I had my mother's
unquestioning faith. I want to be able to say, "Father, into your
hands I entrust my spirit" (Lk 23:46; Ps 31:6), without thinking,
without arguing, without wondering — wondering how the God I
worship can possibly be Three in One or One in Three; without

trying to imagine a "communion of saints" where the only flesh in a countless community is that of Jesus and Mary; what this bodiless spirit of mine will be doing while waiting for the resurrection of all flesh corrupted — even what that "risen body" might be like. Intrigued and frustrated by St. Paul's "As all die in Adam, so all will be made alive in Christ. But each in his own order: Christ the first fruits, then at his coming those who belong to Christ" (1 Cor 15:22–23). I do believe, Lord; but you must help my ... what? Not so much remove what looks like unbelief, as relax my tortured efforts to understand what is hidden from our eyes.

To understand, to see. The selfsame desires that have sparked my life as a theologian prove counterproductive as twilight gives gradual place to darkness. The time comes when even a theologian must lay thinking aside, forgo the head trip. Not quite at that stage, let me still close with a prayer composed by Pierre Teilhard de Chardin, a prayer that, quite understandably, means more and more to me with each passing day.

> It was a joy to me, O God, in the midst of the struggle, to feel that in developing myself I was increasing the hold that you have upon me; it was a joy to me, too, under the inward thrust of life or amid the favourable play of events, to abandon myself to your providence. Now that I have found the joy of utilising all forms of growth to make you, or to let you, grow in me, grant that I may willingly consent to this last phase of communion in the course of which I shall possess you by diminishing in you.
>
> After having perceived you as he who is "a greater myself," grant, *when my hour comes,* that I may recognize you under the species of each alien or hostile force that seems bent upon destroying or uprooting me. When the signs of age begin to mark my body (and still more when they touch my mind); when the ill that is to diminish me or carry me off strikes from without or is born within me; when the painful moment comes in which I suddenly awaken to the fact that I am ill or growing old; and above all at that last moment when I feel I am losing hold of myself and am absolutely passive within the hands of the great unknown forces that have formed me; in all those dark moments, O God, grant that I may understand that it is you (provided only my faith is strong enough) who are painfully parting the fibres of my being in order to penetrate to the very marrow of my substance and bear me away within yourself.

The more deeply and incurably the evil is encrusted in my flesh, the more it will be you that I am harbouring — you as a loving, active principle of purification and detachment. The more the future opens before me like some dizzy abyss or dark tunnel, the more confident I may be — if I venture forward on the strength of your word — of losing myself and surrendering myself in you, of being assimilated by your body, Jesus.

You are the irresistible and vivifying force, O Lord, and because yours is the energy, because, of the two of us, you are infinitely the stronger, it is on you that falls the part of consuming me in the union that should weld us together. Vouchsafe, therefore, something more precious still than the grace for which all the faithful pray. It is not enough that I should die while communicating. Teach me *to treat my death as an act of communion.*[27]

FOURTEEN

Epilogue
Grateful Memories

I have already spoken freely of Gustave Weigel and John Courtney Murray. Their sudden deaths, Weigel in 1964, Murray in 1967,
have affected me as few others. Not a depression; I have never experienced a slough of despondence in their regard; more an unceasing
sense of loss. They were closer to me than my own blood brother.
To say that the kinship was at once intellectual, spiritual, and fraternal is true but dreadfully abstract. It was more like "the soul of
Jonathan knit to David's" (1 Sam 18:1). And I am keenly aware of
the rich contributions each could make today: Murray to civilized
conversation within both society and church, Weigel to the respectful love that should pervade the difficult struggle for the unity of
the churches.

I have said much already of dear Johannes Quasten, the most significant personal influence on my patristic existence. One first-rate
teacher, we are told, is enough to transform a life. I sat at his feet,
enthralled, in a classroom at the Catholic University in Washington; prayed with him, absorbed, in the war-devastated cathedral in
Cologne; walked with him, relaxed, along Oxford's roads during
the International Conference on Patristic Studies; dined with him,
delighted, in several of his favorite restaurants in the District of
Columbia.

I have spoken of two strong influences on my preaching: University of Chicago professor Joseph Sittler and pastor extraordinary
David H. C. Read. I have expressed my indebtedness to Henri de
Lubac and Jean Daniélou, like their beloved Origen "men of the
Church," and like Origen devoted sons even in adversity. This final
chapter is devoted to 27 men and women who deserved more than
passing mentions in previous chapters.

Léon-Joseph Suenens

I shall never forget Cardinal Léon-Joseph Suenens. I treasure a picture taken with him in New York City in 1972, reproduced in his memoirs.[1] Then it was that I was privileged to introduce him to a large New York audience, at a time when the fundamentalist press was portraying him as a "rebel" cardinal. I said:

> Today's speaker *does* need an introduction; he is *not* all you have heard. He is not an enemy of Pope Paul; but he has written with bold accuracy: The greatest day in the life of a pope is not his coronation but his baptism, his mission "to live the Christian life in obedience to the gospel."
>
> He is not turning the Church into a democracy; but he does insist that ministry is the task of *all* Christians, that today's Christian need is *co*responsibility.
>
> You may indeed call him a radical, but only if you realize that this man, who will tell you that "in a few years history will have relativized us all," holds lovingly to all the Christian past that genuinely links Catholicism with Christ.
>
> He is hardly indifferent to the differences between churches; but he does agonize over the sobering words of Jesus: Only by our oneness will the world know that Christ has come and that God loves.
>
> He is a cardinal, yes; but he has transformed the meaning of cardinal from "prince of the Church" to "servant of man and woman."
>
> It gives me uncommon pleasure to present "Tomorrow's Church" as envisioned by a scholar whose learning enriches us all, by a priest whose parish is the world, by a very human person whose life is love.

Much in Suenens' life and work has attracted and influenced me. I mention only several aspects for which I am particularly grateful. First, his remarkably Catholic approach and relationship to authority. Unfailingly respectful to each occupant of the papal chair, confidant of John XXIII and Paul VI, he could still write, as I said above, that the most important day in the life of a pope is his baptism. One of the four "moderators" of Vatican II (the others were Cardinals Agagianian, Doepfner, and Lercaro), he had no hesitation in asking the pope for a definition of the exact position of the moderators with respect to the Co-ordinating Commission, which he characterized (in a letter, I believe, to Paul VI) as "fundamentalist."

As for his most significant conciliar adversary, Cardinal Alfredo Ottaviani, prefect of the Holy Office, Suenens was pained to find himself so often in conflict with him, for he "admired in Ottaviani the strength of his convictions, his courage, the love he had for the poor and even, occasionally, for the victims of the Holy Office!"[2] But he had to resist Ottaviani, for whom "the Holy Office stood, in effect, above the Council, and had a monopoly on authentic theology — which he identified with his own theology" and believed the council "had no business...questioning the schemata which had been proposed according to his own instructions."[3]

I was impressed by Suenens' hopes for a "new Pentecost" within the Church and his intelligent encouragement of the nascent charismatic movement, though he "felt alien to their exuberant pentecostal style."[4] He even went so far as to intercede with Paul VI for the charismatics, asking not a "benevolent attitude from outside" but "a hierarchical or theological presence at the local level, from within."[5] Cardinal Godfried Danneels, Suenens' successor as archbishop of Malines-Brussels, captured the core of the charismatic influence on Suenens in his funeral homily in early May of 1996:

> How could a cardinal with a face that did not show many emotions, with a straight and immobile stature, with a grave and steady voice, find himself at ease in the midst of a crowd that sang, danced, clapped hands and spoke in tongues? Was it a late life conversion to fantasy and imagination in a man who had been until then too rational and responsible? No. Rather, he perceived in this revival a return to the church of the Acts of the Apostles about which he had always dreamed — with a taste for the Scriptures, spontaneous prayer, joy, a sense of community, the stirrings of the Spirit, the proliferation of charisms. The renewal gave the legitimate role of the heart and the body back to the spiritual life of Christians.[6]

Suenens lived a quotation recalled to him in his seminary days by Cardinal Désiré Joseph Mercier. Mercier delighted in a remark of Bishop Louis Pie of Poitiers: "When caution is everywhere, courage is nowhere to be found. Our ancestors were not so quiescent; we shall die of prudence yet, you'll see."[7]

Yves Congar, O.P.

Dominican theologian Yves Congar (1904–95) influenced me in several significant ways.[8] First, his breath-taking productivity. Over a

half century of publication added up to more than 2,000 items —
each an example of careful reflection, many of them striking examples of a scholarship that, while ever respectful of tradition, was
impressively progressive. Second, his Christlike endurance of suffering: e.g., his five years as prisoner of war, including a failed attempt
to escape; the early '50s, during the so-called *nouvelle théologie,*
when he suffered from Roman suspicion and scrutiny, accusations
from far lesser intelligences, and was even removed from teaching;
the years in a wheelchair, still turning out books and hundreds of
articles, replying to an amazed inquirer, "What else is one to do in a
wheelchair?" Third, his profound influence on Vatican II, still to be
assessed in its fulness. He saw the twentieth century as the century
of ecclesiology, and here to his delight was a general council with
the Church as its central theme.

Congar contributed in almost unparalleled fashion to a golden
age in European theology, with France at the center.[9] Here a basic
principle, suspect in some quarters, was a "return to the sources."
It meant the end of "manual" theology in seminary and university.
It meant scholarly series such as Sources chrétiennes, with its distinguished list of editors and translators. Efforts to select his most
important production end in frustration. Was it the early, ground-
breaking *Lay People in the Church*? Or the later, three-volume *I
Believe in the Holy Spirit*? Congar was ceaselessly breaking fresh
ground or recovering old treasures. Perhaps time will tell.

Congar's very presence had a marked influence on the meetings
of the International Theological Commission. I recall that, whenever Congar intervened, all the members, whatever their theological
bent, listened intently, with respect, with expectation; we were never
disappointed. And, for all his learning, he was always remarkably
respectful of others, touchingly humbled by his accomplishments.

Jean Jadot

In December 1995 Archbishop Jean Jadot's Christmas letter contained the following characteristically moving paragraph (I translate, clumsily, from his French original):

> The course of 86 years was crossed some weeks ago. I record,
> untroubled, the slow progression of my physical and mental
> decline. But I record as well, happily, that this decline does not
> reach "the heart's understanding." Holding sway as they do
> over rational comprehension and verbal expression, stimulat-

ing human relations are stronger still. In the haze of old age, certainties, attachments, and wonders assume, for this "understanding heart" of which the Bible speaks, a density which fills the soul beyond anything it could possibly expect. Its privileged moment is prayer.

Such is the heart of one of the four or five most admirable prelates I have been privileged to encounter — in his case, to know with some intimacy. Apostolic delegate in Thailand, apostolic pronuncio in Cameroon, and apostolic delegate in the United States (1973–80), he learned with uncommon penetration what the Catholic Church in our dear land is actually like, its strengths and its weaknesses, its oneness and its divisions. When he spoke in public, he spoke always from knowledge and love. Similarly in private. With a couple of colleagues he would walk from the Apostolic Delegation to the Woodstock residence for dinner and conversation — a conversation breath-taking for his insights and revelations, his frankness and his love. As I see it, he was instrumental in the appointment of close to a hundred bishops in our country alone, with the stress on pastoral promise. And he suffered for his contribution to American Catholicism in ways I refrain from mentioning, because he himself has preserved a public silence that stems from his love for his church.

Archbishop Jadot will never write an autobiography. Still, his book-length "Conversations with Michel Dellicour"[10] is a delightful, informative introduction to an uncommon "man of the Church and of the world." They reveal a priest/diplomat consistently concerned to "see, judge, act"; aware of the world as extraordinarily one despite its extraordinary diversity; sensitive to the demands of personal dignity in all cultures; convinced that intolerance has returned in some fashion everywhere in the world and that "religions remain in fact the most significant factor in xenophobic division"; concerned over the Latin Church's long suspicion of, hostility to, feeling, emotion, the corporeal; persuaded that our contemporaries might be less inclined to turn to the East for interiority and contemplative prayer if they knew the riches within our great mystics.

From Jean Jadot I came to appreciate (better late than never) how important an "understanding heart" is if I am to grow as a Christian, as a priest, as a Jesuit, as a human person. His 1997 Christmas letter informs me that the "understanding heart" is even more necessary now that the "reasoning mind" is gradually weakening. No longer can he drive a car; legs and feet refuse to serve him as be-

fore; balance is shaky; pastoral activities are restricted. In his relative
isolation he ponders a weighty problem of the ages ahead: "reconciling unity and diversity — how to live in a world actually solidary
while promoting legitimate personal and social differences." And
so he prays: for peace throughout the world, for faith and love in
a church on pilgrimage, for a return of all God's scattered children
to the Lord.

An understanding heart indeed.

John Tracy Ellis

Over several decades I was fortunate to have the friendship of Msgr.
John Tracy Ellis, dean of American Catholic historians, who died
at 87 on October 16, 1992. His life was church history, a living
reflection of Pope Leo XIII's words on opening the Vatican Archives:
"The first law of history is not to dare to utter falsehood; the second,
not to fear to speak the truth." Not only did he keep a sense of
history alive within American Catholicism during the dark days of
nonhistorical orthodoxy. Not only did he reveal during the '50s (to
angry ecclesiastical reactions) the failure of American Catholicism
to nurture intellectual excellence. His intellectual honesty, for which
he paid many a price within the Catholic community, was integrated
with a singularly attractive Christian manner. His dear friend of half
a century Msgr. George G. Higgins phrased it with moving accuracy:

> [Ellis] was a man of exquisite courtesy, the quintessential but
> relaxed and affable gentleman, a good listener, a delightful con-
> versationalist and *raconteur*, an ecumenist before his time, a
> strong supporter of women's rights and of lay initiative and
> leadership in the church, and, last but not least, a man of
> profound and persevering prayer.[11]

Among many legacies, Ellis left with me, by deeds as well as
words, his conviction that research rigorously pursued is a spiritual
adventure, a religious experience. History was for him a priestly
work. I delighted in his ability to sustain a classical type of periodic
sentence in his lectures (very much like his beloved Cardinal John
Henry Newman), his mastery of the honest but always courteous
critique (I still treasure his frank little book on bishops — only the
deceased, of course), his conversational use of sees rather than the
holders thereof: "Philadelphia said to Chicago." Has the Lord of
history and historians broken the mold?

George G. Higgins

Our country's leading labor priest, George Higgins has never turned down an invitation to a labor meeting if he could possibly attend.[12] But his is not a tunnel vision. John Tracy Ellis, never one to exaggerate, described him as "the best informed Catholic priest in the United States." Depending on his travel schedule, he has tried to read at least three hours a day: Catholic social teaching, labor economics, theology, general cultural matters, biographies. He reads four newspapers a day, subscribes to a score of periodicals. I was a personal recipient of his extensive knowledge when I attended the 1974 Synod of Bishops in Rome as a *peritus* ("expert") serving the U.S. delegation. I had been asked to prepare a draft on "Laity in the Church" for one of our episcopal delegates. Within an hour or two, George was in my room at the Villa Stritch with three books (two in English, one in Italian), specific chapters and pages noted for my inspection.

Here is a labor priest who attended all four sessions of Vatican II, was on the drafting commission for its document on the laity, and was a prominent figure in interpreting the council to the English-speaking world at the U.S. bishops' daily press briefings. Mediating labor struggles, opposing sweetheart contracts, criticizing the "Christian right" for its fundamentalist strain, participating in Catholic-Jewish dialogue (out of close relations with Jewish leaders in the labor movement), challenging women to take leadership roles within the Church, he may be the only human I have known who could carry on serious conversation-with-Scotch till 2 or 3 in the morning, and be at his desk five or six hours later, ready for another hectic day. I recall that when budget-cutting measures retired him as director of the Social Action Department within the U.S. Catholic Conference in 1978, the uproar across the country forced a reversal of the decision.

George Higgins' message to untold thousands of us? "I think there's something to be said for sheer presence, being there when people need help." A ministry of presence.

John J. Egan

Together with George Higgins, a name that springs swiftly to my mind on social justice is John Joseph Egan.[13] From his earliest days as a priest in Chicago, people have been Jack's life. Three broad phases. (1) Before Vatican II, a pioneer: in the marriage and family apostolate, inner-city ministry, the lay apostolate, priests' associations, community organization. For him, priestly ministry was ministry to the whole Church and to the whole of society. (2) Thirteen years at the University of Notre Dame: assistant to President Theodore Hesburgh for the university's role in all church affairs, director of a new Institute of Pastoral and Social Ministry, national leader of the Catholic Committee on Urban Ministry. (3) Since 1983, back in Chicago: railing against racism in a mayoral campaign, directing the Archdiocesan Office of Human Relations and Ecumenism, deploring Chicago's holding pattern in things ecumenical, advocate for the underclass, community organizer. Wherever things were happening or not happening, Jack has been there. In line with George Higgins, he calls it the sacrament of presence. The word around Chicago: If you want to get things done, "Go see Egan."

Close friends and fellow apostles? Hundreds — even politicians, to help solve the city's problems. Community organizer Saul Alinsky said of Jack, "Now there's a priest." The University of Chicago's Martin Marty, as intuitive a recorder of the human scene as I have experienced in six adult decades, summed Jack up incisively: "He embodies and exemplifies that *interesting* mix of gifts and circumstances, shortcomings and slight stabs of saintliness, fallibilities and occasions for eucharist, which God must enjoy in priests and other sinners, having made them so evident in the ones who get to do some changing of the world, who provide reasons for others to keep on caring."[14]

Sister Thea Bowman

I never met Thea, but this African-American nun was one of several unusual humans who taught me how to live and still tries to teach me how to die. Born in 1937, growing up in Canton, Mississippi, a convert to Catholicism at 10, a novice with the Franciscan Sisters of Perpetual Adoration at 19, high school teacher for ten years, a Ph.D. in English from Catholic University at 35, consultant for intercultural awareness in the Diocese of Jackson and professor of black theology and the arts at the Institute of Black Catholics at Xavier University in New Orleans, speaker and singer at youth rallies and workshops and services throughout the States and in Canada and Africa, diagnosed at 47 with breast cancer that had spread to the lymph nodes and bones, dead six years later, March 30, 1990 — the cold facts say little if anything about a woman who transformed whatever and whomever she touched.[15]

This lady, already advanced in her cancer, told assembled U.S. bishops in heart-rending and heart-lifting syllables what it means to be black and Catholic and American, then closed with a unique request:

> Now, bishops, I'm going to ask you-all to do something. Cross your right hand over your left hand. You've got to move together to do that. All right now, walk with me. See, in the old days, you had to tighten up so that when the bullets would come, so that when the tear gas would come, so that when the dogs would come, so that when the horses would come, so that when the tanks would come, brothers and sisters would not be separated from one another.[16]

"We shall live in love," she sang. And all the bishops swayed and sang. The U.S. bishops!

For Thea, music was the sound of black spirituality. Between songs on a recording made with a 50-voice choir she had shaped, she urged all who heard it:

> Listen! Hear us! While the world is full of hate, strife, vengeance, we sing songs of love, laughter, worship, wisdom, justice, and peace because we are free. Though our forefathers bent to bear the heat of the sun, the strike of the lash, the chain of slavery, we are free. No man can enslave us. We are too strong, too unafraid. America needs our strength, our voices to drown out her sorrows, the clatter of war.... Listen! Hear us! We are the voice of negro America.[17]

As her wheelchair drove her cancerous flesh across the country, Thea's mission in life was never more evident: healing, making whole. On a September day in 1989, six months before her death, at St. Stephen's Church in Minneapolis, she celebrated healing ministry in a concert for all races AIDS-afflicted. Several sentences from her words that day are etched in my flesh:

> I have come tonight seeking a blessing. I have come tonight seeking a healing. I don't usually talk about myself, but tonight I want to tell you a little about me. I have cancer. More importantly, I have something in common with my brothers and sisters who have AIDS — weight loss, hair loss, loss of voice, weakness, fatigue, exhaustion.
>
> I'm here tonight to say, God IS. God made me. God loves

me. God gave me life, and I want to live as fully as I can live until I die. I want to live my best; I want to love my best; I want to do my best; I want to give my best.[18]

Thanks in untold measure to Thea Bowman, I too want to live as fully as I can live until I die.

Rembert Weakland, O.S.B.

Rarely does a secular magazine allot two long articles to a Catholic archbishop. But the *New Yorker* did.[19] Probably because Rembert Weakland, though intensely devoted to the Holy See, is not a papal or episcopal clone. He had recommended simply scuttling a tepid pastoral letter on the status of women in the Church; he had himself commissioned a study in 1982 on the status of women in his Archdiocese of Milwaukee and subsequently integrated women into virtually all levels of church work there. Because he held hearings with women in the archdiocese to listen to their views on abortion, and perhaps because he had criticized rather strongly some tactics of the antiabortion movement, the Vatican persuaded the theological faculty of the University of Fribourg not to award him the honorary degree already promised.

My indebtedness to Archbishop Weakland stems from several influences, but perhaps none more than his willingness to listen. Take one of his reflections on that score:

> I need to listen, though nothing may come of it. I often think I know exactly what needs to be done, but I'm terribly wrong sometimes. I need to speak both to those who are my friends and to those who are not my friends. But in real dialogue. If you want to exercise any meaningful authority in the Church today, you have to listen not just to the most agreeable voices, and not solely to the edicts of Rome. Rather, you listen to where the Spirit is — you hear one small voice, and you say, "That's it!" Not consensus — that's no way to lead. I'm surely influenced by the third chapter of the Rule of St. Benedict. When anything important is brewing, you call the community together and listen for the Spirit. And you allow the youngest, least experienced member to speak first, so he won't be overwhelmed by all the experts.[20]

Weakland's experience in Milwaukee has also confirmed my own in another delicate area: We Catholics are rarely open to even mod-

erate criticism from our fellow believers. Two of his articles in
the archdiocesan weekly reported the adverse reactions of Catholic women at his six "listening sessions" on abortion to some
aspects of prolife activity. For example, "Many dislike the nar-
rowness of so many in the pro-life movement, their tactics...their
lack of compassion...their lack of civility." He even recommended
that politicians unwilling to call for a ban on abortions be given
"as much latitude as reason permits."[21] The reaction: thousands
of hate letters. He was called "butcher," "killer," "slaughterer,"
"murderer." A Washington-based Catholic center drew a parallel
between Weakland and a German bishop who in 1933 became a
member of the S.S. and "the apologist for Nazism among German
Catholics."[22]

Within the Body of Christ all too many often claw one another
like cats in a sack; they reject accusations of uncharity by claiming
that where truth is at issue, truth alone is charity. In defense of God's
truth, no language is too harsh. By what logic or gospel?

A second impact has been Weakland's observation when returning from El Salvador in November 1990: "Only one Church will
survive in Central America. Will it be the Church of Rivera y Damas
and Romero, or will it be the Church of Cardinal Obando y Bravo?
In the States, our Church doesn't face that kind of struggle for survival. Our struggle is more subtle, and therefore more insidious. We
face being ignored."[23]

A third impact is Weakland's personal, touchingly revealing
encounter with celibacy:

> The trick in dealing with celibacy is to understand that there is
> no true substitute for the intimacy of marriage. We were taught
> that the Divine Office, your community, your prayer life were
> substitutes, but they are not. Travel, an intellectual life, and, in
> the case of a bishop, a measure of authority, power: these are
> not substitutes, either. I'm over sixty — for me, it's not about
> sex. When it hits me hardest is not when I'm in trouble or want
> to pour my heart out because I'm depressed. It's when I have a
> great idea that I'd like to share with someone, when I've heard
> a new piece of music and want someone to sit down and listen
> with me.[24]

Though aware of the freedom celibacy confers, he is convinced that
"across-the-board celibacy works to our detriment as a Church."[25]

Joseph Bernardin

When Joseph Bernardin died early on the morning of Thursday, November 14, 1996, I was in his archdiocese (Chicago) with our project Preaching the Just Word. For the next week, the *Chicago Tribune* bulged with articles on the cardinal; the city of Chicago, believers and unbelievers, went into mourning. For several reasons: his down-to-earth friendliness, the contrast in style to his predecessor, his promotion of a consistent life ethic, his compassion under unjust accusation of sexual abuse, his courage under terminal cancer. Still, I suspect that his lasting influence on unnumbered Christians and Jews will prove to be his charism for reconciliation, his ability to bring people together, his final search for "common ground." It was stunningly shown the days of his lying in state, when hundreds of thousands, of all beliefs and none, came to Holy Name Cathedral for a final look not at a ravaged body but at a beloved person; thousands wept openly as they prayed at his casket.

A splendid example was his early welcome not only to Chicago's priests but to its Jewish people: "I am Joseph, your brother." In the afterword to *A Blessing to Each Other: Cardinal Joseph Bernardin and Jewish-Catholic Dialogue,* he wrote: "I sincerely believe this both from personal relationships and from theological truth. I have tried, as a brother, first to listen to my Jewish friends. From this I have deepened my appreciation for the Jewishness of Jesus, my Savior. And I have also been able to speak of the genuine love that the Catholic church has for the Jewish community. If any of this has helped to heal past resentment and division, I am grateful."

For all this and so much more, I too am grateful. Still, at this point in my life the predominant Bernardin influence is his decade as archbishop of Cincinnati, the years he called "the greatest blessing in my priesthood." Of this he wrote:

> The priests of Cincinnati were especially helpful for my spiritual growth. Several years ago I sensed that administrative responsibilities were eating away at my interior life. I told several young priests that I felt they were praying more and better than I. I told them I wanted and needed their help. They generously took me into their lives of prayer and helped me come closer to the Lord. Theirs was a wonderful and permanent gift.[26]

His priest friend John Hotchkin recalls that "After this Cincinnati prayer experience, the skilled and gifted ecclesiastical administrator became someone indefinably different, a person of hope, not just a person of plans and expectations, but a true person of hope, hope that because it clings to the person of Jesus cannot be derailed."[27] A priest of hope because a priest of prayer.

Horace McKenna, S.J.

Horace influenced my life before I was aware of it. Newly ordained but still at Woodstock for my fourth year of theology, I spent a weekend at his black parish in southern Maryland. He volunteered to chauffeur me back to the seminary, ordinarily a drive of two or three hours. It was two hours before we exited his parish! Horace stopped the car whenever we came near an African American. He knew each one, his or her family. Always a courteous greeting by name, always a smile, always a question about father, mother, siblings, grandchildren, work, problems. Only long afterward did I realize what should have been obvious that day: Color on a face meant no more to Horace than color on a car or house. Except that the color black down there then meant poverty, discrimination, second-class citizenship.

In the District of Columbia, Horace built low-cost housing and fed the hungry; he encouraged other Jesuits whatever their particular fields of work, intellectual (myself for one), administrative, pastoral; he attended Gonzaga High School plays when his sight was almost gone; at the end of lectures he invariably raised his head from seeming sleep to ask, "And what about the poor?"

And there's the Sunday after *Humanae vitae*. Preaching to a largely impoverished congregation at St. Aloysius, Horace apparently left the impression that despite the encyclical there was still room for the exercise of individual conscience. Outside the church afterward, a lawyer came up to him (reminds me of the Gospel story) and asked, "Do you think you can reconcile what you said with loyalty to the Holy Father?" Said Horace with his slight stutter, "Ye...s, I th...ink I ca...n." Retorted the lawyer, "I don't see how you can say that. Let me make up an example. If you were working for the President of the United States, and he gave you a bag of rose seeds, and told you to plant them in the Rose Garden of the White House, and you didn't do it, would you say you were being loyal?" A bit of a pause, then quietly from Horace: "I th...ink so.....If the Rose Garden was already full!"

Edward Bennett Williams

I was privileged to know Ed Williams, perhaps the greatest trial lawyer in American history, fewer than five years. He sent a hand-delivered note to my office at Georgetown University shortly before Christmas 1983, saying that he had recently been in a New York City hospital (Sloan Kettering I believe; I did not know then that he was suffering from cancer) and that the best thing he had done was to bring with him a copy of one of my collections of homilies. He wanted me to have dinner with him. I did. At the dinner, as chair of the board of trustees at the College of the Holy Cross, Ed asked if I would accept an honorary degree from that institution. I would, and I did.

A biography by Evan Thomas[28] recalls a note Williams wrote me in December 1984 after hearing a homily of mine at Holy Trinity: "Dear Numero Uno: You are still the only man alive who can get a jaded old fart like me to write a fan letter...."[29]

What was it in Ed Williams that attracted me, transformed his friendship into a profound grace, influenced my own life? I expressed it best, I think, in a homily at a Mass which Father Byron Collins, Father William George, and I celebrated for his family in the Jesuit community chapel at Georgetown University September 21, 1988.[30] I remembered a man for others, who cared not only for well-heeled clients but for the beggar who lay in wait for him after Mass at Holy Trinity. I remembered a man of incredible courage; few realized what it cost him with his cancerous flesh to live not for tomorrow but for today — and to live each day fully, with peace on his strong brow and humor in his eyes. I remembered a Catholic Christian who loved his church with a passion, while acutely aware of its scarred and wrinkled humanity; loved his Eucharist, where he drew ceaseless strength from the flesh and blood of his Lord.

I regretted that I came to know him so late in life, regretted that I never saw him defending the famous and the infamous and the defenseless, mesmerizing a jury or a college commencement. Above all, I regretted his passing because his death diminished all of us who knew him. Not flawless, yet (like Archbishop Jadot, but in his own unique way) he inspired me to be better than I am: a more human man, a more courageous Christian, a Jesuit more like Jesus, a more passionate priest. "Grace," I preached with sorrow, "grace has been taken from our midst."

Theodore M. Hesburgh, C.S.C.

In the '80s I was invited to a dinner in Washington, D.C., honoring the president of the University of Notre Dame. It was hosted by Hubert Humphrey, unable to attend in person due to serious illness. The dinner, by invitation only, gathered 250 of Ted Hesburgh's close friends, such as Supreme Court Justice Warren Burger, Vice President Walter Mondale, Secretary of Health and Human Services Patricia Roberts Harris, officials of the A.F.L. and C.I.O.

The dinner commemorated not simply or primarily Hesburgh's long life under the Golden Dome; rather his multifaceted civic involvement: e.g., the first 5 years of the Peace Corps, 15 years on the U.S. Commission on Civil Rights (dismissed by President Nixon), 12 years on the National Science Board, membership on the State Department's Commission on International Educational and Cultural Affairs, the International Atomic Energy Agency, Gerald Ford's Presidential Clemency Board, the Select Commission on Immigration and Refugee Policy, the UN Conference on Science and Technology for Development. I remember how each of six speakers not only lauded Hesburgh for his services to the human community but commented on his priestliness; I believe he has offered Mass every day of his priestly life save one (that day he was helping to keep a vigil over a premature baby). His Mass kit is legendary, as much part of his travel items as his passport. I cannot resist a paragraph from his memoirs:

> I have said Mass with atheistic Russian Communists standing around the altar; with readers such as Rosalynn Carter and Robert McNamara; in an Anglican church that had not seen a Catholic Mass since the middle of the sixteenth century; in a dining car aboard a lurching railroad train; on all kinds of ships; in the middle of an African jungle; in thousands of hotel rooms in more than a hundred countries; and in all five languages that I speak. I even figured out a way to lay out a portable altar and say Mass in space, if and when I am ever chosen to ride the space shuttle.[31]

Why? Because "to my mind there is nothing more important than offering Mass." His pledge upon being ordained that he would celebrate a Mass every day of his life stemmed from a conviction that "it would serve as a daily act of gratitude for my being accepted as a priest, and also that it would bring me closer each day to the Holy Spirit."[32]

Hesburgh's influence on me? The example of a man who served church and state, society and world, academic freedom and inter-racial justice with an effectiveness unparalleled in the history of American Catholicism, and *never ceased to play the priest.* Not simply because he said Mass every day, but because in each of his multifaceted activities he was responding with complete awareness to the call of the Church at that particular moment in history. The well-traveled slice of humor, that the difference between God and Hesburgh is that God is everywhere while Hesburgh is everywhere except Notre Dame, conceals a profound truth: Hesburgh is every-where God, church, and world are calling. He has been a priest for all seasons, for all places, for all persons, for all needs. A rare wedding of competence, courage, and compassion.

Anne Morrow Lindbergh

Strange, isn't it, how a moment, a poem, a sentence can affect your life? Anne Lindbergh and I have lived in completely different worlds: she a thoughtful essayist and poet, wife and widow of the American aviator who made the first solo flight across the Atlantic; I a theo-logian and editor, professor and preacher. Our paths crossed only in a book and a poem. The book: her *Gift from the Sea,* each chap-ter crafted on a particular shell. One segment centered on the need to be alone. She discovered that her response to some invitations, "This is my time to be alone," was difficult for people to understand and accept. Any other excuse, like a hairdressing engagement, was acceptable, but "time to be alone" sounded to many like a secret vice. For in our hurried and harried existence, untold millions are reluctant to be alone. Each empty space has to be filled with sound, often the louder the better. Jog with a Walkman, cook with a radio, clean house with a TV talk show in your face — anything better than that frightful s-word: silence. "Actually these are among the most important times in our lives — when one is alone. Certain springs are tapped only when we are alone. The artist knows he must be alone to create; the writer, to work out his thoughts; the musician, to compose; the saint, to pray."[33]

The poem: "Saint for Our Time," on the meaning of St. Christo-pher in our age.[34] It stems from a famous story in the thirteenth-century manual of piety titled *The Golden Legend.* The strong giant who carried a child over a raging river and felt as if he had all the world on his shoulders was told by the child, "Do not be amazed. You have borne on your shoulders not only the world but him who created the world."[35] The poem is a moving prayer for Christopher to return to our earth, because no age in history needs the "Christ-bearer" more than ours, because

> we lie
> Imprisoned in our sepulchers of stone,
> Wanting your gift, O Saint, your gift alone.
>   No one will take the burden of the whole
> Upon his shoulders; each man in his soul
> Thinks his particular grief too great to bear
> Without demanding still another's share.

After describing vividly today's rising of the waters, today's lightning and thunder in a starless sky, she concludes:

> The child is crying on the further shore:
> Christopher, come back to earth once more.

A sentence and a poem: wed together, stunning reminders to me of Ignatius Loyola's call for contemplatives in action.

Albert Outler

In my limited experience, the Protestant ecumenist with the most profound influence on me was theologian Albert Outler, several times a delegate of the Methodist Church to the World Council on Faith and Order, official observer at Vatican II, author of *The Christian Tradition and the Unity We Seek*. Others quite clearly affected me, helped shape my thinking: George Lindbeck, Warren Quanbeck, Martin Marty, Joseph Sittler, Arthur Carl Piepkorn. But none quite as much as Outler. In what ways? A wedding of several characteristics.

Perhaps before all else, an astonishingly rich knowledge not only of Protestant communities but of Roman Catholicism, not only of Scripture but of various traditions. In a 1966 address at Notre Dame's post-Vatican II international conference, Outler sketched five areas where he hoped Protestant theology would be challenged by the council: a neoclassical *theism;* a major mutation in *sola gratia* in the direction of a radically reformulated doctrine of creation and grace; a reorientation toward *ecclesiology;* recovery of the biblical and patristic sense of *liturgy* as re-creation of the sacramental community; fresh impetus toward an ecumenical historiography, the history of the Christian *community.*[36]

A delicious sense of humor, often tinged with irony. In any of his addresses one thing was predictable: One or other of the Christian communities (including his own Methodism) would experience his ecumenical needle. Some years ago I was invited by distinguished preacher William Willimon to preach at a Sunday service in the Duke University chapel. Knowing that Outler had preached there the year before, I phoned him to ask for some leads, practical advice. I shall not easily forget his remarks when he was introduced. His delightful drawl I cannot reproduce, but the gist (mostly the exact words) of his recollections I can. "I began my sermon by saying: 'As I was coming through the narthex of your lovely chapel, I couldn't help noticing those two statues of undraped ladies. One has for title [in Latin] *Religio;* the other, *Educatio.* And I couldn't help wondering which of the two looked more embarrassed!' "

An ecumenist with vision. Though a scholar with close attention to detail, Outler thought it important to think big, to embrace, critically but gratefully, the whole spectrum of what we call Christian. Seriously indeed, but with a quizzical smile.

Flannery O'Connor

The title of one of my homily collections reproduces my characterization of the Catholic novelist and short-story writer Flannery O'Connor: *Grace on Crutches.* Only 25 when her incurable lupus erythematosus was diagnosed, dead at 39 in 1964, she has been for me an enduring reminder of the human and Christian struggle to "accept with passion, possibly with joy," what cannot be changed, together with a quiet conviction that "You will have found Christ when you are concerned with other people's sufferings and not your own."[37]

One of Flannery's admirers was Thomas Merton. What did they have in common? "[A] highly developed sense of comedy, deep faith, great intelligence. The aura of aloneness surrounding each of them was not an accident. It was their métier, in which they refined and deepened their very different talents in a short space of time. They both died at the height of their powers."[38] Merton said he would not compare Flannery with Hemingway, with Porter, with Sartre, but with "someone like Sophocles.... I write her name with honor, for all the truth and all the craft with which she shows man's fall and his dishonor."[39]

Many reviewers have been baffled by Flannery's stories, mainly because they center on the operations of grace in the lives of very natural men and women. I must confess that her original humor and uncommon satire, the startling violence, the linking of salvation to bloody slaughter, all have worked small miracles of grace not only on my homilies but on my spirituality. But most effectively because this woman, who often could write no more than an hour or two a day, wrote not simply from a vivid imagination but from her experience of Southern existence and a disturbing insight into the mystery of freedom. I am beginning to see why *Commonweal*'s Michael Garvey called her "the great hillbilly Thomist."[40] I read her and I still shudder — for myself.

Richard A. McCormick, S.J.

In 1990 Richard McCormick celebrated 50 years as a Jesuit. In the homily I was privileged to preach on that occasion in Toledo, Ohio,[41] I stressed three facets of his Jesuit existence that have impacted my own life and activity in the Society of Jesus.

First, McCormick is impressively open, accessible, responsive, especially to those whose ideas change a world. He has listened respectfully but not slavishly to ethicists Catholic and Protestant, dialogued with men and women of medicine, crossed swords with successors of Peter and the apostles, learned from constitutional lawyers, overleaped language barriers into Germany and France, Italy and Spain, the Netherlands. He has, in consequence, changed the face of moral theology — by argument indeed, but just as importantly by the power of his Christian personality, by his clarity, his courage, his compassion.

Second, McCormick is a man of the Church. But for him the Church is not simply its leaders; the Church is the totality of God's people. In such a vision, conflict is inevitable. Ignatius Loyola experienced it. His spiritual son Richard's specific service has focused on that extraordinarily difficult task: the life of the Catholic scholar, the effort to fuse revelation and reason, weld tradition to progress. The effort has meant occasional clashes with authority. Not because he arrogates to himself an authority given to Peter alone; only when he sees faith and the faithful poorly served. And in his opposition he is no less respectful than was Paul when he "opposed [Peter] to his face" (Gal 2:11), no less respectful than was Catherine of Siena when she told Pope Gregory XI that if he would not use his power to correct injustice, "it would be better for you to resign what you have assumed."[42]

Third, McCormick is a man of faith that does justice. His adventures in moral theology illustrate admirably how scholarship fed on fervent faith can serve the cause of social, political, and economic justice. I believe today what I preached in 1990:

> We all know that "ideas have consequences." Only God knows fully the consequences of this man's ideas...how many fetal lives have been spared and how many of the terminally ill have died with dignity; how many good people have ceased to rape God's good earth and how many of the powerful have ceased to manipulate their brothers and sisters; how many physicians have learned not simply to cure but to care and how many lawyers have added to their love of law the law of love; how many healthcare administrators can serve their communities with a more sharply honed conscience and how many confessors now counsel more compassionately. If the powerful of this world, from the laboratories for genetics to the halls of Congress, are willing to listen to Christian reason, it is largely because Christian reason is incarnate in moralists and ethicists like [Richard McCormick].[43]

Suzanne Farrell

"Balanchine's ballerina" she has been called. I first knew about her from Richard McCormick, who officiated at her wedding; I met her perhaps three times; I watched once, entranced, as she danced. But it was a bit over a decade ago that in a *Washington Post* interview[44] Suzanne entered my life once for all with four profound insights.

First insight: "I prefer to come to a score fresh...because I feel otherwise I might be painting the choreographer into a corner." A wisdom beyond the dance: If I want to dance to God's music, I dare not paint God into a corner. I must let God write the score for my living. Not passive, simply pliant, flexible, in the hands of a creative Choreographer.

Second insight: "What I do is listen to the music, and dance to the music....I can't start a ballet thinking of the level I'm going to reach — that would rob that moment of its quality. So I'm never sure what's going to happen once I get out there. Because I haven't heard the music yet — as it's going to be played then." A wise principle for Christian living: Live each moment of the Spirit's music as and when it plays. Don't try to live tomorrow at this moment. Let the Spirit surprise you...and then dance to the Spirit's tune, for all you are worth.

Third insight: "I'm not intimidated by having to struggle. I can be embarrassed. I don't always have to look great. Nothing is born with all its plumage — you grow into your feathers. A rose can be pretty at different stages of its development." I too should be patient with my imperfections, not embarrassed to grow into my feathers, always aware that the task and the thrill of loving God and my sisters and brothers with my whole heart is a lifelong process, consummated only on my own final calvary.

Fourth insight: "I give myself as fully to [other choreographers] as I did to Mr. B.... Balanchine always gave himself completely to every ballet he worked on, always one-hundred percent. If you're given something and you keep it, it's gone when you are. If you give something away, it's forever." A profound paradox. If I want my God-given gift to endure, I may not clutch it feverishly to my hot skin; I must give it away, give it to others.

Thank you, Suzanne, for giving your gift away, for giving it to me.

Gerard Manley Hopkins, S.J.

Discerning critic John Pick has declared that in Hopkins' life (1844–89) "there is really only one date of great significance: the year 1868 when he entered the Jesuit Order. This marks the turning-point of his life and divides his youth from his maturity, his adolescence from his manhood. It also marks the division between his early verse and his great poetry."[45] Specifically, it marks the beginning of his poet-or-priest struggle,[46] for as he wrote a decade later, "What I had written I burnt before I became a Jesuit and resolved to write no more, as not belonging to my profession, unless it were by the wish of my superiors."[47]

It is a mistake, I believe, to see Hopkins' Jesuit existence as a ceaseless, agonizing, unresolved conflict between poet and priest, though some evidence can be interpreted in this vein. I am convinced that the poet-priest issue can only be understood where it was actually resolved: in the context of Hopkins' central concern. I mean his struggle for perfection in line with a fundamental principle in the Spiritual Exercises of Ignatius Loyola: Whatever I elect to do, I elect it because it helps me to the end for which I have been created — to praise, reverence, and serve God. Poetry could not be an end in itself; it had to be a servant.

There was indeed movement, questioning, soul-searching; there was change; there were peaks and valleys. From the 22-year-old's sense-denying asceticism, "Be shellèd, eyes, with double dark / And find the uncreated light," he moved in four years to a sacramental view of nature, finding the beauty of the Lord in the bluebell and the starlight — here akin to Duns Scotus and Ignatius Loyola. The great ode "The Wreck of the Deutschland" is in a sense his own story, his spiritual struggles, as he felt God's finger and the call to the cross of "*Ipse,* the only one, Christ." Parish work in London and Liverpool, in Bedford Leigh and Glasgow, left him depressed over the ugliness and hollowness of nineteenth-century civilization, over industrialism's blight on natural beauty and the human soul: "all is seared with trade; bleared, smeared with toil; / And wears man's smudge and shares man's smell." As he moved among his people, a new tenderness, a fresh concern, invaded his poems: "Life all laced in the other's, / Lóve-laced!" A final five years, a melancholy that at its worst he compared to madness.

Only when I saw Hopkins laying his life and his poetry gladly at the foot of the cross could I read without surprise his deathbed words at 45, "I am so happy, I am so happy, I am so happy."

Dorothy Day

That remarkable saint of the homeless and hopeless, long a Communist, long Godless, recognized God and his Christ slowly and painfully, at strange turns in her road. She loved the Church, but "not for itself...it was so often a scandal" to her; she loved the Church because it made Christ visible.[48] And for Dorothy, Christ was crucifyingly visible in the poor and despised, the broken-down and the brokenhearted. For them she started bread lines in Depression days and houses of hospitality across the country, to feed the hungry, clothe the naked, shelter the homeless. She walked picket lines, struggled against segregation in Georgia, was jailed for supporting Mexican itinerant workers, squared off against a New York cardinal in defense of cemetery strikers. She argued passionately that "the poor do *not* have the gospel preached to them."[49] To preach it to them, she lived with them, "with the criminal, the unbalanced, the drunken, the degraded ... with rats, with vermin, bedbugs, roaches, lice. ... Yes, the smell of sweat, blood, and tears spoken of so blithely by Mr. Churchill, so widely and bravely quoted by comfortable people."[50] Including me.

It has not been my privilege to mimic Dorothy Day, ape her actions — walk her picket lines, host her hospitality houses, bunk with the besotted, play the pacifist to the hilt. Here is where only Christ can summon with authority, call with consummate conviction. But one charge of hers I dare not disdain. It goes back to a spiritual reflection by Dorothy that has for title a declaration she derived from Dostoevsky: "Hell Is Not To Love Any More." It goes back to her autobiography, *The Long Loneliness,* and the note on which it closes: "We have all known the long loneliness and we have learned that the only solution is love and that *love comes with community.*"[51]

Dorothy Day made it agonizingly clear to me that the community Christ has in mind for me is not shaped adequately by my own kind — those who look like me, smell like me, think like me, laugh with me. My community has to be all that is human — in a special way, all that is not allowed to be human.

Jaroslav Pelikan

On my office shelves lies an uncommonly treasured book, *The Emergence of the Catholic Tradition (100–600) (1971),* the first of the five volumes in Jaroslav Pelikan's monumental series The Christian Tradition: A History of the Development of Doctrine. In the preface of that opening volume Pelikan justified his admittedly "audacious" enterprise with a conviction he shared with Crusade historian Sir Steven Runciman: "The supreme duty of the historian is to write history, that is to say, to attempt to record in one sweeping sequence the greater events and movements that have swayed the destinies of man. The writer rash enough to make the attempt should not be criticized for his ambition, however much he may deserve censure for the inadequacy of his equipment or the inanity of his results" (p. x).

Pelikan's influence on me? The broad vision; the wild idea; the horizon unlimited; the grand sweep. Pelikan does not disregard detail; his five volumes are dismayingly annotated. But not for detail's sweet sake. For the sake of the vision, whether that vision be an idea down the ages, Jesus or Mary through the centuries. Pelikan has helped me to keep thinking big — in a special way these latter years, a vision of the potential in preaching, its power in the Spirit to change minds, hearts, even worlds. Potential unlimited, potential sadly untapped, save by the rare Billy Grahams, the few Fulton Sheens.

Pelikan reminds me, in a different context, of two Jesuit missionaries: Francis Xavier, with rich if frustrating memories of India and Japan, dying eyes fixed longingly on China six miles across the water; and versatile scientist Matteo Ricci, pursuing his mind-boggling objective of a hostile China turned Christian vertically,

from the top down — the court, the nobles, the circles of the
learned — comparing the successful penetration of the Middle
Kingdom to the achievement of the apostles after Jesus' resurrection.

William F. Lynch, S.J.

Bill Lynch was largely responsible for enlarging my vision of what he
termed "the Christic imagination."[52] One example, from an insight
he explored in a book we edited, an essay where Lynch saw, as
truly as did de Lubac but more imaginatively, the interpenetration
of scandal and glory in both Christ and the Church.[53]

For Lynch, there was the Isaian Christ, "no form or majesty
that we should look at him, a man of suffering, from whom others
hide their faces, accounted by us struck by God and afflicted" (Isa
53:2–4), and at the same time the Christ of the Canticles, "My
beloved all radiant and ruddy, his appearance like Lebanon, choice
as the cedars, altogether desirable, my beloved and my friend" (Cant
5:10–16). There was the Church of the Canticles, "altogether beautiful, no flaw" (Cant 4:7), and the Church described by George
Bernard Shaw:

> In Italy churches are used in such a way that priceless pictures
> become smeared with filthy tallowsoot, and have sometimes to
> be rescued by the temporal power and placed in national gal-
> leries. But worse than these are the innumerable daily services
> which disturb the truly religious visitor. If these were decently
> and intelligently conducted by genuine mystics to whom the
> mass was no mere rite or miracle, but a real communion, the
> celebrants might reasonably claim a place in the church as their
> share of the common human right to its use. But the average
> Italian priest, personally uncleanly, and with chronic catarrh
> of the nose and throat, ... punctuating his gabbled Latin only
> by expectorative hawking, ... this unseemly wretch should be
> seized and put out, bell, book, candle, and all, until he learns
> to behave himself.

The scandal, the shock, is that, like Christ, the Church is at one
and the same time wondrously flawless (its Christ, its grace) and
dreadfully flawed (its sin-scarred faithful), holy and ever in need of
reformation. Not two Christs, not two churches. One Christ, one
Church. "The race made Christ, and Christ the race — this is indeed
a challenge to the mind and imagination."[54]

In 1996 Gerald J. Bednar, associate professor of systematic theology at Cleveland's St. Mary's Seminary, published a profound study entitled *Faith as Imagination: The Contribution of William F. Lynch, S.J.*[55] Two paragraphs among a large number continue to shape my living:

> Faith is not merely "a conceptual bundle of ideas which must beg imaginative support from literature and art." Of course, it includes that "bundle of ideas," but never apart from the intuitions — the images — that faith produces. Faith is not the child of Apollo. Lynch here agrees with Nietzsche in rejecting the life of an Apollo whose guiding light comes merely from the top of his head. Lynch uses the figure of Apollo to criticize those who allow themselves, in their visions of faith, to soar into a sort of infinite dream, to bypass the concrete stuff of this world in an attempt to reach a purely ecstatic position where they can grasp truth as it is in the act of falling from heaven. Lynch parts company with Nietzsche in his choice of gods. Nietzsche chooses Dionysus, the god of revelry. If Apollo's virtues spun from his head, imposing ethereal limits on the human, Dionysus' virtue escapes all limits. Dionysus is given to ecstatic revelry that totally escapes the rational.
>
> Lynch chooses Jesus Christ as the one who encapsulates the infinite depths of the divine by remaining faithful to the very definite, concrete contours of his existence. Jesus is the perfect revelation of God, yet he is the one who could say, "I thirst." Truly Christian concepts do not come by way of deductive reasoning unless the premise is firmly rooted in the concrete and the definite dimensions of this world. This world in its concrete fullness is the truth that has fallen from heaven. The problem is how to be faithful to it, loving it as "God's other" and thereby learning its secrets.[56]

Not generally known is the emotional breakdown Lynch began to suffer in 1956. While experiencing therapy at Seton Institute in Baltimore, he would come to Woodstock College, primarily to visit with John Courtney Murray, a dear friend and a splendid healing resource with his breadth of vision, his awareness of Bill's struggles, and his strong compassion. Important too for Bill's recovery and productivity was the unconditional welcome he received from the president of Georgetown University, Edward A. Bunn, S.J. The five years of teaching English there, while also director of the honors program (1957–62), sparked some of his most significant books.

The struggle culminated several years later in the insights from his ordeal and recovery gathered in his *Images of Hope: Imagination as Healer of the Hopeless*,[57] hailed by psychologists Rollo May and Leslie Farber as a valuable contribution on the significance of the imagination and its relation to our ability to wish.

Frederick Buechner

I first heard of Buechner in an unusual way. Reviewing my collection of homilies *Sir, We Would Like to See Jesus,* the Presbyterian pastor and preacher David H. C. Read wrote in *America* magazine: "Only in the sermons of Frederick Buechner have I found such fresh language, such poetic vision, such unexpected twists and such a deep personal witness to Christ."[58] Clearly, here was a preacher I must read! I was not disappointed. Novelist as well as preacher, Buechner is an artist with words. In a 1983 address celebrating the rededication of the library at New York's Union Theological Seminary, he remarked: "Words are our godly sharing in the work of creation, and the speaking and writing of words is at once the most human and the most holy of all the businesses we engage in." He went on to say: "The ultimate purpose of language, I suspect, is so that humanity may speak to God."[59]

The fresh language and unexpected twists, the imagination salted with humor, are part and parcel of his small but precious book *Telling the Truth: The Gospel as Tragedy, Comedy, and Fairy Tale*,[60] where the tragic is the inevitable, the comic the unforeseeable. One delightful passage I quote to preachers in every single retreat/ workshop Preaching the Just Word:

> The place to start [the gospel as comedy] is with a woman laughing. She is an old woman, and, after a lifetime in the desert, her face is cracked and rutted like a six-month drought. She hunches her shoulders around her ears and starts to shake. She squinnies her eyes shut, and her laughter is all China teeth and wheeze and tears running down as she rocks back and forth in her kitchen chair. She is laughing because she is pushing ninety-one hard and has just been told she is going to have a baby. Even though it was an angel who told her, she can't control herself, and her husband can't control himself either. He keeps a straight face a few seconds longer than she does, but he ends by cracking up, too. Even the angel is not unaffected. He hides his mouth behind his golden scapular, but

you can still see his eyes. They are larkspur blue and brimming with something of which the laughter of the old woman and her husband is at best only a rough translation.

The old woman's name is Sarah, of course, and the old man's name is Abraham, and they are laughing at the idea of a baby's being born in the geriatric ward and Medicare's picking up the tab. . . . .[61]

Denis Hurley, O.M.I.

In early spring 1974, a Telex from Vincent O'Keefe, S.J., assistant to Jesuit superior general Pedro Arrupe in Rome, advised me as editor of *Theological Studies* that the papal Secretary of State had expressed his desire that an article titled "Population Control and the Catholic Conscience: Responsibility of the Magisterium," destined for publication in the March issue, not be published, and that all the other articles in that issue on population be carefully examined for fidelity to church teaching. With a sigh of relief, I was able to respond that the March issue of *Theological Studies* had come out the preceding day.

The article in question was authored by Denis E. Hurley, Archbishop of Durban, South Africa. In it he challenged the Catholic hierarchy to approach the population problem with broad vision, in all its dimensions; otherwise, he insisted, "it will not have the right to teach" (*Theological Studies* 35 [1974] 163). The article was typical of a bishop known for his integrity and vision; a man who lived alongside the poor and dispossessed; a leader of whom Desmond Tutu, shortly after being awarded the Nobel Peace Prize, told the Catholic Bishops' Conference of South Africa that he was not worthy to tie their president's shoelaces. On March 19, 1997, he completed 50 years as bishop, an occasion celebrated throughout South Africa for his constant courageous witness in the long years when the state was oppressing the great majority of the people.

Two unforgettable experiences, Hurley asserts, marked his life: the Second Vatican Council that fired him with a fresh vision of the role the Church had to play in the modern world, and the day when, as a special guest, he saw Nelson Mandela sworn in as president of a free South Africa. Eighty-one as I write, and six years "retired," he is parish priest at the cathedral and chancellor of the University of Durban. He is not likely to know how his vision and courage over a quarter century have fired an American Jesuit's fresh dream for a justice that sees in every sister and brother, especially the powerless and dispossessed, another self, another I.[62]

Andrew M. Greeley

Surprised? I suspect Andrew Greeley himself does not know how deeply he has influenced my thinking, writing, lecturing. Yes, he provokes, he irritates; his memory for slights and criticism is elephantine; he has dispatched a bishop in a one-line footnote. In his novel on the next conclave, *White Smoke,* his dissatisfaction with the "style" (not the doctrines) of the institutional Church is basic to his theme.[63] And still, to follow Greeley, sociologist or novelist, is a ceaseless education.

I watched Greeley on TV destroying a critical public-school educator with facts and figures on the parochial school. *The Mary Myth* broadened my understanding of the rich role our Lady has played over the centuries in literature and art. His *New York Times* article "Why Do Catholics Stay in the Church? Because of the Stories" (July 10, 1994) persuaded me that indeed "it is in the poetic, the metaphorical, the experiential dimension of the personality that religion finds both its origins and raw power." He resonates to the suggestion that "the most powerful of all the objects of attachment is the metaphor of Mary the Mother of Jesus representing the mother love of God." In that context, the Mary image, research reveals, continues to be the most powerful religious image for Catholic young people. And still so many "educated" Catholics continue to apologize for Mary, as for an embarrassing old relative.

The Church needs a Greeley. Not only is he a first-rate sociologist rediscovering the face our church reflects to objective research. More than that, he never allows me to sit back in utter comfort and self-satisfaction, whether as a Christian or a priest or a Jesuit or simply a human being. He constantly compels me to dig beneath the veneer, the superficial, the meretricious. A reaction to Greeley that begins with irritation, anger, or denial not infrequently ends in honest if reluctant affirmation. And, somewhat like fourth-century St. Jerome, he is sometimes wrong but never dull.

William McNamara, O.C.D.

Quite some years ago I described Discalced Carmelite William McNamara as shaped in equal parts of Irish wit and Isaian woe. A powerful presence, with the gray-black beard of a Moses. I first encountered him at a retreat in Sedona, Arizona, the first permanent headquarters of his Spiritual Life Institute of America, a dream for a contemporary and ecumenical form of contemplative life warmly approved by John XXIII. (It has since moved to Nova Scotia and Colorado.) His was a search for God in the joy and laughter of human living, in the grime and grit of God's creation, in every facet of reality — God grasped in thoughtful human encounters. Full spiritual life demands that man and woman live fully and die stretching and reaching.[64]

It was Father William who defined for me the contemplation without which the people perish: "a long loving look at the real." Paradoxically, what alone is excluded from contemplation is abstraction, the "spaced out," where a leaf is no longer green, water no longer ripples, and God no longer smiles. He once called contemplation

> a pure intuition of being, born of love. It is experiential awareness of reality and a way of entering into immediate communion with reality. You can study things, but unless you enter into this intuitive communion with them, you can only know *about* them, you don't *know* them. To take a long loving look at something — a child, a glass of wine, a beautiful meal — this is a natural act of contemplation, of loving admiration.[65]

The problem? "All the way through school we are taught to abstract; we are not taught loving awareness."

Father William urged us to read, make friends with, remarkable men and women who have themselves looked long and lovingly at the real. Not solitaries, not neurotic escapists, but flesh-and-blood in a flesh-and-blood world — unique, however, because each smashed through boundaries and stretched human limits to the walls of infinity. For me that came to mean men and women like Abraham and Mary of Nazareth, Martin Luther King Jr. and John of the Cross, Thomas More and Dorothy Day, Mother Teresa and Nikos Kazantzakis, Abraham Joshua Heschel and Anne Morrow Lindbergh, Flannery O'Connor and Thomas Merton — scores more. And William lamented, as ironic and scandalous, that we Western Christians have betrayed our rich contemplative tradition, which goes back to Jesus, to Fathers of the Church and of the desert, to medieval mystics Eckhart and Hildegarde, to Ruysbroeck and Julian of Norwich, to Teresa of Avila and Ignatius of Loyola.

Mother/Father

In one sense, I've kept some of the best wine till the end. God blessed me with uncommon parents. Uncommon for several reasons. Both were immigrants, stemming from Galizien when it was part of the Austrian-Hungarian empire. Strangely, they never reminisced to my brother and me about their past, their own parents and grandparents, what life was like in the "old country"; I do not know who my grandparents were! They rarely spoke their native languages, German and Polish, in our presence (save for Pop occasionally calling me *Esel,* "jackass"); like most immigrants of the time, they thought it best, without saying so, that we "grow up American," unaware that children can learn two or more languages simultaneously. They were lower-income. For years Pop worked long hours (3 A.M. to 3 P.M.) on a horse-drawn milk wagon. I can still smell Sloan's Liniment, Mom rubbing Pop's shoulders and back, stiff and sore from 12 hours of carrying the old, bulky milk cans — my early experience of "heavy metal."

Their Catholicism was genuine: quiet, deep, unemotional. Pop had a strong sense of justice. He could not define it, but it meant simply that if you agreed to do something, by God you'd better do it. When Xavier High School said "homework three hours each night," there was no recourse to excuses or a higher court. Mom was the wife and mother of the prevailing culture: Her life was the home. For both, brother Eddie and I were their principal reason for living, working, and loving. They had to struggle, had to borrow, to send Eddie and me to Xavier. But we never suspected. Food, clothes, fare — always there; only after many years as a Jesuit did I realize what ceaseless self-sacrifice went into making ends meet.

When I told Pop during my senior year at Xavier that I wanted to become a Jesuit, all he said was, "If that's what you want, be a good one." He did not live to see me ordained, died of cancer during my second year of theology at old Woodstock. Two weeks later my brother died, also of cancer. Mom used to visit both hospitals each day. The day Pop was buried from St. Ignatius Loyola Church in New York, Mom stayed two hours with Eddie, who was too sick to be told of Pop's death. When we returned from Eddie's burial, the apartment house Pop managed and in which they lived was on fire! Perhaps not divinely designed, but it proved a needed distraction.

What did I inherit? Pop's sense of justice, perhaps exaggerated on occasion: a generous day's work, an honest dollar, be hard on yourself, don't live off excuses. Your word is your bond; no need of signatures and multiple copies. Moderation in drinking — this from the devastating effect on the families of two alcoholic brothers. And Mom's genes: for good health, a long life, a basic gentleness, caring, sensitivity. To neither of them can I trace this state-of-the-art hypochondriac, my extraordinary attention to every symptom, every quiver of this mortal flesh.

I've been blest.

Notes

1: From Demosthenes to Damascene

1. Gerard Manley Hopkins, "The Blessed Virgin Mary Compared to the Air We Breathe," in W. H. Gardner and N. H. MacKenzie, eds., *The Poems of Gerard Manley Hopkins* (4th ed.; New York: Oxford University, 1970) 93–97, at 95.

2. Edmond Rostand, *Cyrano de Bergerac,* tr. Brian Hooker (New York: Random House, n.d.) 304–5.

3. Ignatius of Antioch, *To the Romans* 4–5 (tr. James A. Kleist, S.J., in Ancient Christian Writers 1 [New York and Ramsey, N.J.: Newman, repr. 1978, orig. 1946] 81–82).

4. See the chapter "St. Ignatius of Antioch: Sanctity and Martyrdom," in my *Saints and Sanctity* (Englewood Cliffs, N.J.: Prentice-Hall, 1965) 1–11.

5. Robert Payne, *The Fathers of the Western Church* (New York: Viking, 1951) 30.

6. Pedro de Rivadeneira, *Vida del bienaventurado Padre Ignacio de Loyola* (2nd ed.; Barcelona: Subirana, 1885) 501–2.

7. Ignatius of Antioch, *To the Philadelphians* 5, 1 (tr. ACW 1, 86).

8. Tertullian, *Apology* 50, 13.

9. Ignatius of Antioch, *To the Romans* 7, 2 (tr. ACW 1, 83).

10. John Courtney Murray, in Murray et al., "Sources chrétiennes," *Theological Studies* 9 (1948) 250–89, at 250–51.

11. This section on Quasten I borrow from my tribute to him, "ERGON KYRIAKON: Johannes Quasten as Teacher, Scholar, and Friend," in *Kyriakon: Festschrift Johannes Quasten* 2 (Münster, Westf.: Aschendorff, 1970) 915–16.

12. W. Halliday, *The Pagan Background of Early Christianity* (Liverpool and London, 1925) 3.

13. For more detailed information, see my report "Studies in Christian Antiquity," *Theological Studies* 5 (1944) 377–83.

14. See Paul Yu-Pin, "Christian Influence in Post-War China," *America* 71 (1944) 34.

15. G. Voss, "Missionary Accommodation and Ancestral Rites in the Far East," *Theological Studies* 4 (1943) 556.

16. An eye-opening example is the acute problem of the policy to be adopted by the Church toward the ancient pagan cult of the dead; see the first dissertation published in Quasten's Studies in Christian Antiquity, Alfred C. Rush's *Death and Burial in Christian Antiquity* (Washington, D.C.: Catholic University of America, 1941).

17. See "The Man Who Lives with Wisdom," in my *Tell the Next Generation: Homilies and Near Homilies* (New York and Ramsey, N.J.: Paulist, 1980) 100–103.

18. Ulrich von Wilamowitz-Moellendorff, *Erinnerungen: 1848–1914* (2nd ed.; Leipzig, 1929) 305.

19. See my "Current Patristic Projects," *Theological Studies* 11 (1950) 259–74, at 261–64.

20. *The Martyrdom of Saint Polycarp, Bishop of Smyrna* 9, 3 (tr. James A. Kleist, S.J., in Ancient Christian Writers 6 [New York and Ramsey, N.J.: Newman, repr. 1978, orig. 1948] 94).

21. John Courtney Murray, S.J., "The Christian Idea of Education," in Edmund Fuller, ed., *The Christian Idea of Education* (New Haven: Yale University, 1957) 155–56.

22. Gregory of Neocaesarea, *Panegyric on Origen* 13–14; tr. Murray (n. 21 above) 157.

23. Ibid. 6.

24. Ibid.

25. Hans Urs von Balthasar, *The Theology of Henri de Lubac: An Overview* (San Francisco: Ignatius, 1991) 13.

26. Joseph A. Komonchak, "Recapturing the Great Tradition. In memoriam: Henri de Lubac," *Commonweal* 119, no. 2 (January 31, 1992) 14–17, at 16.

27. See my bulletin "On Early Christian Exegesis," *Theological Studies* 11 (1950) 78–116.

28. Jean Daniélou, "Traversée de la mer rouge et baptême aux premiers siècles," *Recherches de science religieuse* 33 (1946) 416.

29. See, e.g., John L. McKenzie, S.J., "A Chapter in the History of Spiritual Exegesis: De Lubac's *Histoire et esprit*," *Theological Studies* 12 (1951) 365–81, at 380: "The exegete can never feel confidence in an approach to the Bible which is so free of method and control as the spiritual exegesis." But McKenzie had justifiable praise for much of de Lubac's research into Origen.

30. Henri de Lubac, S.J., "Meditation on the Church," in John H. Miller, C.S.C., ed., *Vatican II: An Interfaith Appraisal* (Notre Dame: University of Notre Dame, 1966) 258–66, at 259. For a succinct contemporary evaluation of de Lubac's theology, see the observations of Paul Valadier, S.J., within an obituary, "Henri de Lubac," in the London *Tablet* 245, no. 7885 (September 14, 1991) 1126–27. Valadier notes that de Lubac's "emphasis on the mystery of the Church does not make it easy to accept fully its human constitution and leaves the theologian floored before the approaches of sociologists or historians even though they might be illuminating" (1127). My quotation from his Notre Dame address suggests strongly that de Lubac was keenly aware of the Church's human face.

31. Charles Kannengiesser, S.J., "Fifty Years of Patristics," *Theological Studies* 50 (1989) 633–56.

32. Ibid. 656.

33. See Karl Rahner, S.J., "Towards a Fundamental Theological Interpretation of Vatican II," *Theological Studies* 40 (1979) 716–27.

34. Ibid. 726–27.

35. Elizabeth A. Clark, "The State and Future of Historical Theology: Patristic Studies," in Clark, *Ascetic Piety and Women's Faith: Essays on Late Ancient Christianity* (Studies in Women and Religion 20; Lewiston, N.Y.: Mellen, 1986) 3–19.

36. Ibid. 3.

37. Ibid. 4.

38. Ibid. 11.

39. Ibid.

40. David G. Hunter, review of Clark's *Ascetic Piety* in *Theological Studies* 49 (1988) 380–81.

41. Ibid. 11–12.

42. New Haven: Yale University, 1993.

43. See the glowing review by John F. Baldovin, S.J., in *America* 170, no. 11 (April 2, 1994) 20–21.

2. From Seminary to University

1. Here I am indebted to a remarkable article by John E. Thiel, "Theological Responsibility: Beyond the Classical Paradigm," *Theological Studies* 47 (1986) 573–98; see my article "The Face of Theology 1986," *Philosophy and Theology* 2, no. 1 (fall 1987) 3–19.

2. Thiel, ibid. 578.

3. Ibid. 578–79.

4. Ibid. 580.

5. Ibid. 581.

6. See ibid. 583–84; for background see Walter L. Reed, *Meditations on the Hero: A Study of the Romantic Hero in Nineteenth Century Fiction* (New Haven: Yale University, 1974).

7. Thiel, "Theological Responsibility" 584.

8. Ibid. 585.

9. Ibid. 586.

10. Pius X, *Pascendi dominici gregis,* no. 40.

11. See J. J. Heaney, "Modernism," *New Catholic Encyclopedia* 9 (1967) 995; Gabriel Daly, "Faith and Theology: (2) The Ultramontane Influence," (London) *Tablet,* April 18/25, 1981, 391–92.

12. Carl Rogers, *On Becoming a Person* (Boston: Houghton Mifflin, 1961) 354–55.

13. *New Blackfriars* 46 (1965) 665–72.

14. Ibid. 665.

15. Ibid. 668.

16. Ibid.

17. See Robert Johann, "Experience and Philosophy," in *Experience, Existence, and the Good: Essays in Honor of Paul Weiss,* ed. Irwin C. Lieb (Carbondale: Southern Illinois University, 1961) 25–38.

18. Ibid. 26.

19. Ibid.

20. Ibid.

21. Gerald McCool, "The Tradition of St. Thomas since Vatican II," *Theology Digest* 40 (1993) 324–35.

22. Ibid. 324–25.

23. Ibid. 335; italics mine. Early in his presentation (324) McCool mentions an impressive number of twentieth-century Catholic scholars who were influenced by Thomas: leading philosophers like Maréchal, Maritain, Sertillanges, Pieper, De Raeymaeker, and Van Steenberghen, who were proud to be called his disciples; theologians like Rousselot, Garrigou-Lagrange, and Journet, who, for

all their disagreement among themselves, were united in their devotion to him; many of the influential theologians at Vatican II such as Congar and de Lubac, who owed their intellectual formation to the Thomist tradition; pioneer medievalists like De Wulf, Mandonnet, Grabmann, Gilson, and Chenu, who made no secret of their admiration for Aquinas. Before and during the council, prominent defenders of democracy and religious freedom such as Maritain and John Courtney Murray "linked their defense of freedom to the demands of Thomas' ethics and political philosophy," and their influence on the council fathers and postconciliar papal teaching was lasting.

24. Thomas Aquinas, *Summa theologiae* 1, q. 20, a. 1; Pseudo-Dionysius, *The Names of God (De divinis nominibus)* 4.12.

25. Aquinas, ibid. 1/2, q. 28, a. 3; Pseudo-Dionysius, ibid. 4.13. See my short article "Unity through Ecstasy: A Tribute to John Courtney Murray," *Dominicana* 53, no. 1 (spring 1968) 2–5.

26. See his Yale lectures in *The Problem of God* (New Haven: Yale University, 1964). Of this slim work Notre Dame's David Burrell wrote: "Murray achieves a wedding of theological competence and cultural urbanity that would be distinguished in any age, [but] is especially valued for its rarity in ours, and *shows* what apologists have long been arguing in an alien tongue: that theology can supply an interpretation of history startling and challenging to any contemporary student of man" (review in *Theological Studies* 25 [1964] 650–53, at 651; emphasis his).

27. Murray's influence on me in this area can be detected in my John Courtney Murray Forum lecture "From Certainty to Understanding: The Exciting Pilgrimage of Contemporary Catholicism," *Catholic Mind* 67, no. 1234 (June 1969) 13–27.

28. *Documentation catholique* 58 (1961) 1523.

29. Johann, "Experience and Philosophy" (n. 17 above) 27.

30. Ibid.

31. Ibid. 28.

32. Ibid. 29.

33. Particularly through his *Adventures of Ideas* (New York: Free Press, 1967).

34. Ibid. 225.

35. Ibid. 225–26.

36. Ibid. 226.

37. Ibid.

38. Ibid. 227.

39. Ibid. 226.

40. Ibid. 227.

41. *New International Dictionary of the English Language* (2nd ed.; Springfield, Mass.: Merriam, 1958) 2562.

42. Cf. O. Rousseau, M.B., "Théologie patristique et théologie moderne," *Vie spirituelle* 80 (1949) 70–87, esp. 72–73.

43. Pierre Benoit, in A. Robert and A. Tricot, eds., *Initiation biblique* (3rd ed.; Tournai: Desclée, 1954) 43; translation mine.

44. Karl Delehaye, *Erneuerung der Seelsorgsformen aus der Sicht der frühen Patristik* (Freiburg, 1958) 135.

45. See the informative study by Joseph C. Plumpe, *Mater ecclesia: An*

Inquiry into the Concept of the Church as Mother in Early Christianity (Washington, D.C.: Catholic University of America, 1943).

46. *Letter 251* 4 (Patrologia graeca 32, 937).

47. Walter J. Burghardt, S.J., "Vatican II and Catholic Theology in America," in *Vatican II: An Interfaith Appraisal,* ed. John H. Miller, C.S.C. (Notre Dame: University of Notre Dame, 1966) 626–41, at 633–34.

48. Peter Hebblethwaite, *Paul VI: The First Modern Pope* (New York and Mahwah, N.J.: Paulist, 1993) 635.

49. Ibid. 633.

50. Karl Rahner, *I Remember* (New York: Crossroad, 1985) 84.

51. Hebblethwaite, *Paul VI* (n. 48 above) 634.

52. Avery Dulles, S.J., *The Craft of Theology: From Symbol to System* (New York: Crossroad, 1992) 3.

53. See ibid. 5–7.

54. Ibid. 14.

55. Avery Dulles, S.J., "The Future of Seminary Theology," *Catholic International* 8, no. 1 (January 1997) 38–42.

56. Ibid. 39.

57. Denzinger-Schönmetzer, *Enchiridion symbolorum* (32nd ed.; Freiburg: Herder, 1963) 3886 (2314).

58. Robert Browning, *Sonnets from the Portuguese* 43.

59. See David Tracy, *Blessed Rage for Order* (New York: Seabury, 1975) 22–42.

60. Ibid. 24.

61. Ibid. 26.

62. Ibid. 25–26.

63. Ibid. 26.

64. Ibid. 28.

65. Ibid. 31.

66. Ibid. 32.

67. Ibid. 34.

68. Tracy's concrete methodology revealed itself primarily in two books: *Blessed Rage for Order* (n. 59 above) and *The Analogical Imagination* (New York: Crossroad, 1981).

69. See Dulles' review article "Method in Fundamental Theology: Reflections on David Tracy's *Blessed Rage for Order,*" *Theological Studies* 37 (1976) 304–16, at 305–6 n. 2.

70. See Dulles' review of *Analogical Imagination* in *America* 145, no. 5 (September 5, 1981) 97.

71. Ibid.

72. New York: Herder and Herder, 1972.

73. Avery Dulles, review in *Theological Studies* 33 (1972) 553–55, at 553. I am aware that in the same review Dulles expressed his dissatisfaction with "three unhealthy separations" under which Lonergan's system appeared to labor: (1) a tendency to harden unduly the division between positive and speculative theology; (2) "functional specializations," corresponding to the four levels of intentionality, that seemed "arbitrary and restrictive"; and (3) treatment of method without attention to theories of revelation, Christology, and church.

74. *Spirit as Inquiry: Studies in Honor of Bernard Lonergan* (= *Continuum*

2, no. 3 [autumn 1964] 306–552); my sketch, 308–10, is the source of these next five paragraphs of appreciation.

75. An ironic footnote. These articles, which when published promised to do little more than lose subscribers to *Theological Studies,* were far more in demand in the early '60s than any other contribution in the quarterly's first quarter century.

76. See F. E. Crowe, S.J., "On the Method of Theology," *Theological Studies* 23 (1962) 637–42, for a résumé of the topics handled by Lonergan at the institute.

77. See *Sciences ecclésiastiques* 9 (1957) 293.

78. *Theological Studies* 3 (1942) 573.

79. Walter J. Burghardt, S.J., "Towards an American Theology," *American Ecclesiastical Review* 159, no. 3 (September 1968) 181–87.

80. Leo J. O'Donovan, S.J., "Orthopraxis and Theological Method in Karl Rahner," *Proceedings of the Thirty-fifth Annual Convention, CTSA* (1980; Bronx, N.Y.: Manhattan College, 1981) 47–65, at 47.

81. Ibid. 49.

82. Ibid. 52.

83. Ibid. 53.

84. Ibid. 57.

85. See ibid. 61–64.

86. Gustavo Gutiérrez, *A Theology of Liberation* (Maryknoll, N.Y.: Orbis, 1973) 11.

87. Gustavo Gutiérrez, *The Power of the Poor in History* (Maryknoll, N.Y.: Orbis, 1983) 61.

88. Juan Luis Segundo, *The Liberation of Theology* (Maryknoll, N.Y.: Orbis, 1976) 75. See also his more recent *The Liberation of Dogma* (Maryknoll, N.Y.: Orbis, 1994). He challenges an understanding of dogma that refers to a sheerly conceptual, abstract formulation of beliefs. For him, dogma arises from the crises of meaning within human existence; faith "punctuates" that experience in order to give shape to Christian thinking. For a largely favorable appraisal, gently critical of Segundo's admittedly selective data, see Paul Crowley's review in *America* 170, no. 17 (May 14, 1994) 24–26.

89. Ibid. 84.

90. Joseph Kruger, "Prophetic-Critical and Practical-Strategic Tasks of Theology: Habermas and Liberation Theology," *Theological Studies* 46 (1985) 3–20, at 19–20.

91. *Theological Studies* 31 (1970) 243–61.

92. Ibid. 261.

93. Anne Carr, B.V.M., "Is a Christian Feminist Theology Possible?" *Theological Studies* 43 (1982) 279–97, at 279.

94. So Carol P. Christ, "The New Feminist Theology: A Review of the Literature," *Religious Studies Review* 3 (1977) 203–12. One of the early and strongest voices was Boston College's Mary Daly; see, e.g., her *Beyond God the Father: Toward a Philosophy of Women's Liberation* (Boston: Beacon, 1973). Both Christ and Daly were convinced that Christianity's core symbolism is essentially patriarchal and in consequence irreformable.

95. See Carr, "Is a Christian Feminist Theology Possible?" (n. 93 above) 283–85.

96. *Theological Studies* 45 (1984) 441–65.

97. New York: Crossroad, 1992.

98. Ibid. 57.

99. Here I am indebted to Phyllis Trible's informative article "Five Loaves and Two Fishes: Feminist Hermeneutics and Biblical Theology," *Theological Studies* 50 (1989) 279–95.

100. See also the summary presentation of "Feminist Theology" by Rosemary Radford Ruether in *The New Dictionary of Theology*, ed. Joseph A. Komonchak, Mary Collins, and Dermot A. Lane (Wilmington, Del.: Michael Glazier, 1987) 391–96.

101. So Robert P. Imbelli, reviewing Edward T. Oakes, *Pattern of Redemption: The Theology of Hans Urs von Balthasar* in *Commonweal* 122, no. 7 (April 7, 1995) 24–25, at 24.

102. Imbelli, ibid. 24.

3. From Luther to Paul VI

1. On this, and for the documents which follow, see Gustave Weigel, S.J., *A Catholic Primer on the Ecumenical Movement* (Woodstock Papers 1; Westminster, Md.: Newman, 1957) 34–45.

2. *Acta apostolicae sedis* 19 (1927) 278; henceforth *AAS*.

3. *AAS* 20 (1928) 5–16.

4. Weigel, *A Catholic Primer* 36.

5. *AAS* 40 (1948) 257.

6. *AAS* 42 (1950) 142–47.

7. See my fuller account of the meeting, "Jesuit Patrologists at Heythrop," *Woodstock Letters* 84, no. 4 (November 1955) 319–24.

8. *Lutherans and Catholics in Dialogue IV: Eucharist and Ministry* (Washington, D.C.: United States Catholic Conference; New York: U.S.A. National Committee of the Lutheran World Federation, 1970) 22.

9. Ibid. 31–32.

10. For this phase of Weigel's life, see Patrick W. Collins, *Gustave Weigel, S.J.: A Pioneer of Reform* (Collegeville, Minn.: Liturgical, 1992) 76–109. Actually, the whole book is worth reading — a splendid reprise of Weigel's life and influence.

11. Ibid. 95.

12. Ibid. 105.

13. Ibid. 236.

14. Ibid. 7.

15. Avery Dulles, S.J., review of Collins' biography, *Catholic Historical Review* 78 (1992) 478–79, at 478.

16. *Christianity Today* 8, no. 9 (January 31, 1964) 412.

17. See my article "The Meaning of Vatican II," *Perkins School of Theology Journal* 21, no. 3 (spring 1967) 23–33, originally a lecture in the Senior Colloquy on Vatican II at Perkins (Southern Methodist University). The other lecturers were John Deschner (on the Constitution on the Church), Albert Outler (on Vatican II as a challenge to Protestantism), and John T. Noonan (on contraception).

18. John Courtney Murray, S.J., "The Declaration on Religious Freedom," in *War, Poverty, Freedom: The Christian Response* (Concilium 15; New York: Paulist, 1966) 11.

19. Michael Novak, *The Open Church: Vatican II, Act II* (New York: Macmillan, 1964) 56.

20. Ibid. 66.

21. Ibid. 68.

22. Ibid.

23. John Courtney Murray, S.J., "The Declaration on Religious Freedom: Its Deeper Significance," *America* 14, no. 17 (April 23, 1966) 592.

24. See Constitution on the Church, no. 15, and Decree on Ecumenism, nos. 13–24.

25. Decree on Ecumenism, no. 9.

26. Ibid., no. 24.

27. For other examples see Murray (n. 18 above) 7–8.

28. Translation from Novak (n. 19 above) 84–87.

29. Ibid. 87.

30. Pastoral Constitution on the Church in the Modern World, no. 1.

31. *Monumenta Xaveriana* 1, 509; translation in James Brodrick, S.J., *The Origin of the Jesuits* (New York: Longmans, Green, 1940) 133.

32. Pietro Pavan, "Ecumenism and Vatican II's Declaration on Religious Freedom," in Walter J. Burghardt, S.J., ed., *Religious Freedom: 1965 and 1975. A Symposium on a Historic Document* (Woodstock Studies 1; New York and Ramsey, N.J.: Paulist, 1976) 7–38, at 12.

33. See Donald E. Pelotte, S.S.S., *John Courtney Murray: Theologian in Conflict* (New York and Ramsey, N.J.: Paulist, 1976) 82–83. Useful are the historical introduction and the sampling of U.S. interventions on religious freedom in Vincent A. Yzermans, ed., *American Participation in the Second Vatican Council* (New York: Sheed and Ward, 1967) 615–67. American Catholics should read especially the interventions, oral and/or written, of Alter and Cushing; of Forst, Fletcher, and Franz; of Hannan and Hallinan, Helmsing and Hodges; of Lucey and McGucken, Maloney and Mussio, Meyer and Maher; of O'Boyle, Primeau, and Ritter; of Spellman, Shehan, and Sheen; of Tracy, Whealon, and Wright.

34. Here I am indebted to the recollections of Patrick V. Ahern, then Cardinal Spellman's secretary, as reported in an op-ed piece by Gerald M. Costello, "[A Vatican Council Footnote:] The Cardinal Stepped In," *Catholic New York,* October 10, 1982, 11. Costello was then editor of that archdiocesan newspaper.

35. Ibid. Murray himself was convinced that he owed his participation to Spellman. "Between us," he wrote to Notre Dame's Leo Ward, "it was my Eminent friend of New York who pried me in. He said (and meant it, I think) that the Jesuits had got too slim a deal about *periti,* and that it was 'no more than right' that I in particular should be there. Which was nice of him" (Pelotte, *John Courtney Murray* 82).

36. Ibid.

37. This analysis appeared as an article, "The Problem of Religious Freedom," *Theological Studies* 25 (1964) 503–75, and elsewhere. It was published in Dutch, French, German, Spanish, and Portuguese.

38. Costello, "The Cardinal Stepped In" (n. 34 above).

39. Pavan, "Ecumenism" (n. 32 above) 10.

40. Bernard Häring, *My Witness for the Church,* tr. Leonard Swidler (New York and Mahwah, N.J.: Paulist, 1992) 57.

41. Declaration on Religious Liberty, no. 2.

42. See Murray's *We Hold These Truths: Catholic Reflections on the American Proposition* (New York: Sheed and Ward, 1960). See the 1990 reprint, with my Preface, highlighting an urgent question in contemporary political/social philosophy: "Will the Church contribute more responsibly and more persuasively to public and ethical discourse in America if, in Murray's steps, it formulates its positions in the categories of philosophical reason, or would it be wiser to express them in the symbols of religious belief?" (v).

43. John Courtney Murray, S.J., "Religious Freedom," in *The Documents of Vatican II,* ed. Walter M. Abbott, S.J. (New York: Herder and Herder, 1966) 672–74, at 673.

44. In *Documents* (n. 43 above) 678 n. 4.

45. Joseph A. Komonchak, "The Coldness of Clarity, the Warmth of Love: The Measure of John Courtney Murray," *Commonweal* 119, no. 14 (August 14, 1992) 16–17.

46. Ibid. 17.

47. Emmet John Hughes, "A Man for Our Season," *Priest* 25 (1969) 402.

48. See the collection of papers edited by John H. Miller, C.S.C., *Vatican II: An Interfaith Appraisal* (Notre Dame: University of Notre Dame, 1966).

49. See Marc H. Tanenbaum, "A Jewish Viewpoint," ibid. 349–67. The "Jewish declaration" is part (no. 4) of the council's brief Declaration on the Relationship of the Church to Non-Christian Religions.

50. Ibid. 362.

51. Ibid. 351.

52. Ibid. 355–56.

53. Ibid. 363.

54. Miller, ed., *Vatican II: An Interfaith Appraisal* (n. 48 above) 374.

55. The sermon, "Israel: A Light to the Gentiles?," can be read in my collection *Tell the Next Generation: Homilies and Near Homilies* (New York and Ramsey, N.J.: Paulist, 1980) 156–62.

56. Bill Wagner, "Still Working for Understanding: Christians and Jews," *St. Anthony Messenger* 100, no. 3 (August 1992) 36–41, at 40.

57. See Deborah E. Lipstadt, *Denying the Holocaust: The Growing Assault on Truth and Memory* (New York: Free, 1993), an effort to untangle the arguments of those who say there was no Holocaust.

58. Arthur A. Cohen, "Notes toward a Jewish Theology of Politics," *Commonweal* 77 (1962–63) 11.

59. Quoted by Hans Küng, *The Church* (New York: Sheed and Ward, 1968) 141.

60. See, e.g., my homily for the third Sunday of Advent in the A cycle, "Shall We Look for Another?," in my collection *Sir, We Would Like to See Jesus* (New York and Ramsey, N.J.: Paulist, 1982) 29–32.

61. Dogmatic Constitution on the Church, no. 5.

62. *Time,* December 15, 1980, 74.

63. See Prof. Ruether's text and my observations in *Auschwitz: Beginning of a New Era? Reflections on the Holocaust,* ed. Eva Fleischner (New York: KTAV, 1977) 75–95.

64. The lecture was published in expanded form in my *Preaching: The Art and the Craft* (New York and Mahwah, N.J.: Paulist, 1987) under the chapter heading "Of Their Race Is the Christ: How to Preach about the Jews" (139–58).

65. See my early bulletin "On Early Christian Exegesis," *Theological Studies* 11 (1950) 78–116.

66. Dogmatic Constitution on Divine Revelation, no. 16.

67. Ibid.

68. See John L. McKenzie, "The Values of the Old Testament," in Pierre Benoit, O.P., et al., eds., *How Does the Christian Confront the Old Testament?* (Concilium 30; New York: Paulist, 1968) 5–32.

69. Ibid. 13.

70. New York: Oxford University, 1983. See especially the first two chapters (pp. 11–34), summarizing the significant literature stimulated by the Jewish experience in World War II.

71. Ibid. 16.

72. Ibid. 17.

73. Ibid. 18.

74. Ibid.

75. Ibid. 19.

76. Ibid.

77. For example, Miriam Taylor, in an Oxford dissertation, *Anti-Judaism and Early Christian Identity* (Studia post-biblica; New York: Brill, 1995), has challenged what she sees as a "scholarly consensus" initiated by Simon's *Verus Israel*. She argues that the "theological" explanation has been allotted far too little consideration. The negative references to Jews and Judaism during the second and third centuries "make much more sense as expressions of an anti-Judaism rooted in theological ideas than as responses to contemporary Jews in the context of an on-going conflict" (127). They stem from the formation of a Christian identity "that affirmed itself through the appropriation of the Jewish tradition for the church and the denial of this tradition to the Jewish people" (140). For a critical review, see David P. Efroymson in *Theological Studies* 57 (1996) 378–79.

78. Dominic M. Crossan, "Anti-Semitism and the Gospel," *Theological Studies* 26 (1965) 189–214, at 189. In this connection I should mention that Gerald G. O'Collins, S.J., "Anti-Semitism in the Gospel," ibid. 663–66, found Crossan's article "unsatisfactory on a number of points, some of which are quite important" (663). He was convinced that, though the study of NT words and events is of great import, "we must also explore the significance which Matthew, Luke, Paul, and other New Testament writers attach to these events and their theology of the obduracy of Israel. Only then can the Gospel be shown to supply no justification for anti-Semitism" (666). In the same volume of *Theological Studies,* Joseph A. Fitzmyer, S.J., focused on a crucial text omitted by Crossan, "His blood be upon us and upon our children!" (Mt 27:25). In Fitzmyer's opinion, "Probably no other New Testament text has been so often quoted against the Jews since it was first written" ("Anti-Semitism and the Cry of 'All the People,' [Mt 27:25]," ibid. 667–71, quotation at 668). Cardinal Augustin Bea and others at Vatican II explained that the cry must be understood as the cry of a Jerusalem crowd with no right to speak for the whole Jewish people.

79. Declaration on the Relationship of the Church to Non-Christian Religions, no. 4 (tr. *The Documents of Vatican II,* ed. Walter M. Abbott, S.J. [New York: Herder and Herder, 1966] 665–66).

80. From a lecture at Georgetown University, April 26, 1984; see also Tuch-

man's *The March of Folly: From Troy to Vietnam* (New York: Knopf, 1984), especially the very first chapter.

81. See Elie Wiesel, *The Gates of the Forest* (New York: Holt, Rinehart and Winston, 1966) 194.

82. See the text "Will Not God Vindicate His Chosen Ones?" in my collection *Grace on Crutches: Homilies for Fellow Travelers* (New York and Mahwah, N.J.: Paulist, 1986) 202–8.

83. *Discourse 1 against Judaizing Christians* 3, 1–3 (tr. Paul W. Harkins, *John Chrysostom, Discourses against Judaizing Christians* [Fathers of the Church 68; Washington, D.C.: Catholic University of America, 1979] 10–11). The sermon was probably delivered in August 386.

84. Tanenbaum, "A Jewish Viewpoint" (n. 49 above) 355–56.

85. Ibid. 363.

86. Vatican translation from the French in *Origins* 15, no. 7 (July 4, 1985) 102–7.

87. See ibid. 105–6, in margins.

88. My knowledge of and reference to these reactions are drawn from *Origins* (n. 86 above) 102–4, in the margins.

89. Peter Schineller, S.J., elaborated the various possibilities in a carefully crafted article, "Christ and Church: A Spectrum of Views," *Theological Studies* 37 (1976) 545–66.

90. Karl Hruby, "The Future of Jewish-Christian Dialogue 2: A Christian View," in Hans Küng and Walter Kasper, eds., *Christians and Jews* (Concilium 98; New York: Seabury, 1974–75) 87–92, at 91.

91. Joseph A. Fitzmyer, S.J., *Romans* (Anchor Bible 33; New York: Doubleday, 1993) 539–636.

92. Ibid. 558.

93. Ibid. 559.

94. Ibid. 577.

95. Ibid. 608–9.

96. Ibid. 620.

97. See Hans Hermann Henrix, "Dialogue, Not Proselytizing: Christian Attitude towards Jews and Judaism," *Theology Digest* 40, no. 4 (winter 1993) 317–21. This is a digest of "Dialog, nicht Proselytenmacherei: Zur Frage der Judenmission," *Stimmen der Zeit* 118, no. 10 (October 1993) 679–90.

98. See Pol Castel, "Looking for the Way Together in Jewish-Christian Dialogue," *America* 171, no. 19 (December 17–24, 1994) 12–15, 18–20, at 20.

99. The details that follow I know for the greater part from my personal involvement in the unfolding of the ecumenical institute that issued from this luncheon conversation; they are summarily recorded in Theodore M. Hesburgh, C.S.C., with Jerry Reedy, *God, Country, Notre Dame* (New York: Doubleday, 1990) 252–56.

100. Ibid. 256.

4. From Prior Testament Prophet to New Testament Preacher

1. Margery Frisbie, *An Alley in Chicago: The Ministry of a City Priest* (Kansas City, Mo.: Sheed & Ward, 1991) 288. The dashes are in the text, explained by Marty in a footnote: "I use dashes instead of letters because I am a

Protestant who does not want to jar the sensitivities of Protestant readers...and to provide an excuse for this footnote, because I thought this book needed a footnote" (ibid.). I should confess that in this chapter I am borrowing liberally from material in my *Preaching: The Art and the Craft* (New York and Mahwah, N.J.: Paulist, 1987).

2. Boston: Beacon, 1986.

3. Ibid. 121.

4. Quoted in an editorial by James M. Wall, "Beyond Blandness in Preaching," *Christian Century* 105, no. 16 (May 11, 1988) 467–68, at 467.

5. Yves Congar, O.P., "Sacramental Worship and Preaching," in *The Renewal of Preaching: Theory and Practice* (Concilium 33; New York: Paulist, 1968) 51–63, at 62.

6. Decree on the Ministry and Life of Priests, no. 4; italics mine. The Latin is "primum officium"; but since Latin does not have a definite or indefinite article, it is unclear whether the council intended to say that proclamation of the gospel is *the* primary obligation of a priest or simply *a* primary obligation. But even in the latter case, a high priority is involved.

7. Bishops' Committee on Priestly Life and Ministry, National Conference of Catholic Bishops, *Fulfilled in Your Hearing: The Homily in the Sunday Assembly* (Washington, D.C.: USCC, 1982) 1.

8. *Osservatore romano,* May 14, 1964, p. 3, esp. nos. VI–X. See the commentary and English translation by Joseph A. Fitzmyer, S.J., "The Biblical Commission's Instruction on the Historical Truth of the Gospels," *Theological Studies* 25 (1964) 386–408.

9. See the defense of the historical-critical method by Joseph A. Fitzmyer, S.J., "Historical Criticism: Its Role in Biblical Interpretation and Church Life," *Theological Studies* 50 (1989) 244–59. Adversaries taken into account assail the method for overemphasizing the human elements in the Bible, for gathering a liberal consensus that means the end of Catholicism, for being overly preoccupied with the prehistory of the text and neglecting its theological meaning,

10. See Carolyn Osiek, R.S.C.J., "The New Handmaid: The Bible and the Social Sciences," ibid. 260–78.

11. See Phyllis Trible, "Five Loaves and Two Fishes: Feminist Hermeneutics and Biblical Theology," ibid. 279–95.

12. See Pheme Perkins, "Crisis in Jerusalem? Narrative Criticism in New Testament Studies," ibid. 296–313.

13. Dogmatic Constitution on Divine Revelation, no. 10.

14. Ibid., no. 21.

15. See Jared Wicks, S.J., *Man Yearning for Grace: Luther's Early Spiritual Teaching* (Washington, D.C.: Corpus, 1968).

16. I have used the translation in Gerhard Ebeling, *Luther: An Introduction to His Thought,* tr. R. A. Wilson (Philadelphia: Fortress, 1970) 45–46.

17. Joseph A. Fitzmyer, S.J., *Paul and His Theology: A Brief Sketch* (2nd ed.; Englewood Cliffs, N.J.: Prentice-Hall, 1989) 90, no. 121.

18. Yves Congar, O.P., *Challenge to the Church: The Case of Archbishop Lefebvre* (Huntington, Ind.: Our Sunday Visitor, 1976) 42.

19. Monika Hellwig, "Re-emergence of the Human, Critical, Public Jesus," *Theological Studies* 50 (1989) 466–80, at 467.

20. Ibid. 467–68.

21. For detailed discussion of these three facets, see my chapter "Do This in Memory of Me" in my *Preaching: The Art and the Craft* (n. 1 above) 108–18.

22. Constitution on the Sacred Liturgy, no. 35. See also no. 52: "part of the liturgy itself."

23. See Reginald Fuller, *What Is Liturgical Preaching?* (London: SCM, 1957) esp. 20.

24. See Norman Pittenger, *Preaching the Gospel* (Wilton, Conn.: Morehouse-Barlow, 1984) 46. The whole chapter "The Setting in Worship" (45–56) is worth pondering in our context. Pittenger observes that failure to follow these Reformers on this point "has been a tragedy" and notes that "it is only in our own time that the Reformed churches have begun to recover the centrality of the Eucharist in worship . . . " (46).

25. Josef Andreas Jungmann, "Constitution on the Sacred Liturgy," in Herbert Vorgrimler, ed., *Commentary on the Documents of Vatican II* 1 (New York: Herder and Herder, 1967) 38.

26. Constitution on the Sacred Liturgy, no. 56.

27. Yves Congar, O.P., "Sacramental Worship and Preaching" (n. 5 above) 51–63.

28. Ibid. 60.

29. John L. McKenzie, "The Word of God in the Old Testament," *Theological Studies* 21 (1960) 205.

30. Ibid. 206.

31. Václav Havel, "A Word about Words," in his *Open Letters: Selected Writings 1965–1990*, ed. Paul Wilson (New York: Vintage [Random House], 1992) 378. The speech was read in Havel's absence by Maximilian Schell. It was translated by A. G. Brain and reprinted in full in the *New York Review of Books*, January 18, 1990. The speech is worth reading in its entirety for its historical, philosophical, linguistic, and even theological insights.

32. Ibid. 383–84. See also a comment by Paul Gray reviewing A. S. Byatt's novel *Babel Tower* (Random House, 1996) in *Time* 147, no. 21 (May 20, 1996) 76: "All her various plots underscore the mixed blessings of language, its power to obscure as well as reveal, to enslave as well as liberate."

33. Ibid. 385–86.

34. Ibid. 386.

35. Ibid. 389.

36. Frank McCourt, *Angela's Ashes* (New York: Scribner, 1996) 69. One of the most prolific, most effective Catholic storytellers is William J. Bausch, a priest in the Diocese of Trenton, New Jersey. See, e.g., his *Storytelling: Imagination and Faith; More Telling Stories, Compelling Stories;* and *Storytelling the Word: Homilies and How to Write Them* (Mystic, Conn.: Twenty-third, 1984, 1993, 1996, respectively).

37. Avery Dulles, S.J., "The Symbolic Structure of Revelation," *Theological Studies* 41 (1980) 55–56.

38. Sallie M. TeSelle, cited by Urban T. Holmes III, *Ministry and Imagination* (New York: Seabury, 1976) 166, from the *Journal of the American Academy of Religion* 4 (1974) 63.

39. I have borrowed this parable from Megan McKenna, *Parables: The Arrows of God* (Maryknoll, N.Y.: Orbis, 1994) 53–54. I have presumed to alter the order of words in one of the sentences.

40. Dulles, "The Symbolic Structure of Revelation" (n. 37 above) 56.

41. See my "Preaching in American Words and in American Symbols," the Prologue in my collection *To Christ I Look: Homilies at Twilight* (New York and Mahwah, N.J.: Paulist, 1990) 5–18.

42. A. N. Whitehead, *The Aims of Education and Other Essays* (New York: Macmillan, 1929) 139.

43. Gerard Manley Hopkins, "As kingfishers catch fire...," Poem 57 in W. H. Gardner and N. H. MacKenzie, eds., *The Poems of Gerard Manley Hopkins* (New York: Oxford University, 1970) 90.

44. Amos Niven Wilder, *Theopoetic: Theology and the Religious Imagination* (Philadelphia: Fortress, 1976) 67.

45. Second Vatican Council, Constitution on the Sacred Liturgy, no. 35.

46. See the fine article by homiletician Robert P. Waznak, "The Catechism and the Sunday Homily," *America* 171, no. 12 (October 22, 1994) 18–21.

47. Sloyan, quoted by Waznak, ibid. 20.

48. Frederick E. Flynn, in *Catholic Messenger* (Davenport, Iowa), August 4, 1960, 13.

49. San Francisco: Harper & Row, 1977.

50. Ibid. 97–98.

51. Urban T. Holmes III, *Ministry and Imagination* (New York: Seabury, 1976) 221.

52. Andrew M. Greeley, "Priests Should Make Preaching Their Number One Job," *U.S. Catholic* 58, no. 12 (December 1993) 13–14, at 14.

53. Marian Wright Edelman, "Say No to This Welfare 'Reform,'" *Washington Post,* November 3, 1995, A23.

54. New York: Farrar, Straus, 1956.

55. Samuel H. Dresner, "Remembering Abraham Heschel," *America* 146, no. 21 (May 29, 1982) 414.

56. New York: Harper & Row, 1962.

57. See my chapter "Shudder, You Complacent Ones: Ancient Prophet and Modern Preacher" in my *Preaching: The Art and the Craft* (n. 1 above) 29–41.

58. Heschel, *The Prophets* (n. 56 above) 4.

59. Ibid. 5.

60. On divine pathos, which was for Heschel a unique theological category, see ibid. passim, but esp. 24, 221–31, 489–92. For a strong critique of this category, see Eliezer Berkovitz, "Dr. A. J. Heschel's Theology of Pathos," *Tradition: A Journal of Orthodox Thought* 6 (spring–summer 1964) 67–104. He argued that Heschel's affirmation of divine pathos was based on a fallacious line of deductive reasoning and on a literalist interpretation of biblical texts.

61. Heschel, ibid. 231.

62. Ibid. 226.

63. From an essay "Ignatius of Loyola Speaks to a Modern Jesuit," in Karl Rahner, S.J., *Ignatius of Loyola,* with an Historical Introduction by Paul Imhof, S.J. (London and New York: Collins, 1979) 9–38, at 11–13.

64. Heschel, *The Prophets* 224.

65. Dietrich Bonhoeffer, *The Cost of Discipleship* (rev. ed.; New York: Macmillan, 1963) 45–48.

66. For a detailed effort to exemplify the thesis from my personal experience, see my *Preaching: The Art and the Craft* (n. 1 above) 175–91.

67. See Joseph A. Fitzmyer, S.J., "The Biblical Commission's Instruction on the Historical Truth of the Gospels," *Theological Studies* 25 (1964) 386–408; for my quoted phrases, see Fitzmyer's translation of the document, ibid. 404 and 405.

68. First Vatican Council, Dogmatic Constitution "Dei Filius" on Catholic Faith, chapter 2 (Denzinger-Schönmetzer, ed. 32, no. 3006 [1787]).

69. For the actual homily, preached on the 28th Sunday of the Year in the A cycle, see my collection *Sir, We Would Like to See Jesus: Homilies from a Hilltop* (New York and Ramsey, N.J.: Paulist, 1982) 121–25.

70. Dogmatic Constitution on Divine Revelation, no. 8 (tr. *The Documents of Vatican II*, ed. Walter M. Abbott, S.J. [New York: Herder and Herder, 1966] 115–16; italics mine).

71. See C. S. Lewis, *The Chronicles of Narnia* (7 vols.; New York: Macmillan, 1950 ff.).

72. Quoted by William F. Buckley Jr. in a syndicated column I found in the *Stuart News* (Florida) of April 10, 1993, A17. The judge was Edwin Torres.

73. New York: Dell/Eleanor Friede, 1977 [4].

74. Augustine, *First Catechetical Instruction* 1.2.3 (tr. Joseph P. Christopher, in Ancient Christian Writers 2 [Westminster, Md.: Newman, 1946] 15).

75. Tim Reynolds, "Thomas, Dylan," *World Book Encyclopedia* 19 (ed. 1975) 200.

76. For much greater detail on what follows, see chapter 13 ("Lord, To Whom Shall We Go?") in my *Preaching: The Art and the Craft* (n. 1 above) 192–216.

77. My text in those early days was Daniel M. O'Connell, ed., *Favorite Newman Sermons* (Milwaukee: Bruce, 1932) 13–29.

78. See the informative volume by Thomas K. Carroll, *Preaching the Word* (Message of the Fathers of the Church 11; Wilmington, Del.: Michael Glazier, 1984) 43–62.

79. *Sermon 96,* no. 4.

80. *Treatise on the Gospel of John* 7.6.

81. I have learned much about Augustine the preacher from F. van der Meer, *Augustine the Bishop* (New York: Sheed and Ward, 1961) esp. 412–52, "The Servant of the Word."

82. New York: Seabury, 1966.

83. New York: Seabury, 1969.

84. This in a review of my *Sir, We Would Like to See Jesus* (n. 69 above) in *America,* December 25, 1982, 417. Dr. Read was graciously comparing my preaching to Buechner's. For more detailed information on Buechner, his religious background and convictions, his theological works, and the significance of his novels, see Marie-Hélène Davies, *Laughter in a Genevan Gown: The Works of Frederick Buechner (1970–1980)* (Grand Rapids: Eerdmans, 1983).

85. See especially Buechner's *Telling the Truth* (n. 49 above), chapter 3, "The Gospel as Comedy" (49–72).

86. Philadelphia: Fortress, 1966.

87. I am quoting from the text as it appeared in the *Alumni Bulletin of Bangor Theological Seminary* 43, no. 2 (April 1968) 12–14.

88. See Joseph Sittler, "A Protestant Point of View," in John H. Miller,

C.S.C., ed., *Vatican II: An Interfaith Appraisal* (Notre Dame: University of Notre Dame, 1966) 422–27, at 426.

89. David H. C. Read, *This Grace Given* (Grand Rapids: Eerdmans, 1984) 105–6. This is the first half of his autobiography.

90. See Kenneth L. Woodward, "Heard Any Good Sermons Lately?" *Newsweek,* March 4, 1996, 50–52.

5. From Cain to Antichrist

1. The exact meaning of "poor" in the Old Testament varies in different periods and with different types of literature; see, e.g., John McKenzie, "Poor, Poverty," in his *Dictionary of the Bible* (New York: Macmillan, 1965) 681–84. Here I have simplified a highly complex word.

2. I essayed a similar summary in the third of my Beecher Lectures on Preaching at Yale Divinity School in February 1994, published in an expanded form by the Yale University Press in 1996 under the title *Preaching the Just Word.* Similarly, the sections in the present chapter on biblical justice and on the Catholic tradition of justice, especially our responsibility to the earth, to nonhuman creation, were developed at much greater length in the Yale volume.

3. So the Children's Defense Fund's *The State of America's Children Yearbook* (Washington, D.C.: Children's Defense Fund, 1995) 18: "15.7 million U.S. children were poor in 1993 — the highest number in 30 years." As I reread these paragraphs (August 22, 1996), President Bill Clinton has just signed into law a welfare bill on which the *New York Times* had previously editorialized, "A bill that creates child poverty is not an acceptable way to end welfare as we know it" (August 1, 1996, A26); and the *Washington Post,* "Mr. Clinton acquiesces in legislation in which the federal government washes its hands of responsibility for welfare mothers and children, hands the problem to the states and fails to equip them with the resources to solve it" (August 1, 1996, A22). In that context I wrote to the President stating that I could not in conscience vote for his re-election. "I am not questioning your sincerity; that would be inappropriate. I am questioning your willingness to take care of the most vulnerable of your citizens. They have no lobby, they have no vote. Your staff has estimated that the provisions of the welfare bill will throw a million more children into poverty. You have indeed promised to work for reversal of some of these provisions after you have signed the bill. But will Congress allow it? I doubt it. You have said that this is your last chance to fulfil your campaign promise to 'end welfare as we know it.' Your last chance? Hardly."

4. See Mary Rose McGeady, *God's Lost Children: Letters from Covenant House* (New York: Covenant House, 1991) 31.

5. See ibid., dedication.

6. See the editorial "Children Too Ready to Die Young," *Washington Post,* November 3, 1993, A26.

7. From excerpts in *Catholic Health World* 4, no. 13 (July 1, 1988) 1 and 12, with corrections from a text graciously supplied by the editor of that journal.

8. My summary is indebted to the account in the *New York Times International,* February 3, 1994, A1 and A6.

9. Maria Riley, O.P., and Nancy Sylvester, I.H.M., *Trouble and Beauty:*

Women Encounter Catholic Social Teaching (Washington, D.C.: Center of Concern et al., 1991) 6.

10. See ibid. 13.

11. See Joan Chittister, O.S.B., *Job's Daughters: Women and Power* (New York and Mahwah, N.J.: Paulist, 1990).

12. Riley and Sylvester, *Trouble and Beauty* (n. 9 above) 13.

13. See ibid. 14.

14. From Norma Hardy, *Ecumenical Decade 1988–1998: Churches in Solidarity with Women: Prayers and Poems, Songs and Stories* (Geneva: World Council of Churches, 1988) 68.

15. I am borrowing from the text in *Sister Thea Bowman, Shooting Star: Selected Writings and Speeches,* ed. Celestine Cepress, FSPA (Winona, Minn.: Saint Mary's Press, 1993) 31, itself taken from *Origins* 6 (1989) 114–18.

16. Walter Brueggemann, "The Preacher, the Text, and the People," *Theology Today* 47, no. 3 (October 1990) 237–47, at 237. He contends that in biblical scholarship "there are important resources for taking the scandalous texts seriously without pastors necessarily committing professional or personal suicide" (238).

17. Cf. *Washington Star,* May 26, 1979, D-1 and D-2; quotation at D-2; the other quotations are taken from the same article.

18. See *King's Pawn: The Memoirs of George H. Dunne, S.J.* (Chicago: Loyola University, 1990) 67–72.

19. Lawrence S. Cunningham, *The Catholic Heritage* (New York: Crossroad, 1986) 1.

20. See Harvey Cox, *The Secular City* (New York: Macmillan, 1965); also Paul Lehmann, "Chalcedon in Technopolis," *Christianity and Crisis,* June 12, 1965, 149–51.

21. For details of this tradition, see my *Preaching the Just Word* (n. 2 above) 28–51.

22. This schema and the following unfolding of the schema are largely derived from the presentations of James L. Connor, S.J., director of the Woodstock Theological Center, with some insertions of my own.

23. Constitution on the Church in the Modern World, no. 24.

24. Ibid. 32.

25. Ibid.

26. Frederick Buechner, *The Hungering Dark* (New York: Seabury, 1969) 45–46.

27. See Raymond E. Brown, S.S., *The Gospel according to John (i–xii)* (Garden City, N.Y.: Doubleday, 1966) 469.

28. Decree on the Missionary Activity of the Church, nos. 2 and 4.

29. This was pointed out by Jesuit Philip Land in his article "Justice" in *The New Dictionary of Theology,* ed. Joseph A. Komonchak, Mary Collins, and Dermot A. Lane (Wilmington, Del.: Michael Glazier, 1987) 548–53, at 548–49. Pertinent here is Dean Brackley, "Evolución del concepto de justicia con referencia al capitalismo y al socialismo," *Revista latinoamericana de teología* 10, no. 30 (September–December 1993) 263–78.

30. John R. Donahue, S.J., "Biblical Perspectives on Justice," in John C. Haughey, S.J., ed., *The Faith That Does Justice: Examining the Christian Sources*

for Social Change (Woodstock Studies 2; New York: Paulist, 1977) 68–112, at 69; italics in text.

31. See Stevan S. Schwarzchild in *Encyclopaedia judaica* 10 (1971) 476.

32. More recently Donahue has stated that his "earlier reflections should be supplemented by the reflections of J. P. M. Walsh (*The Mighty from Their Thrones: Power in the Biblical Tradition* [Philadelphia: Fortress, 1987] 1–12). "Walsh understands the social dimension of *sedeq* by describing it as 'consensus' about what is right. People in all societies have some innate sense of this, even though it differs in concrete situations. Biblical revelation of *sedeq* involves the consensus which is to shape God's people. More carefully than I, Walsh relates *sedeq* to *mispat*, the implementation of justice (*sedeq*) by action (juridical or otherwise). Finally, he treats *naqam* (literally, 'vengeance') as the process by which 'consensus' or sense of rightness is restored. The thrust of Walsh's whole work is that the biblical tradition gives a different vision of these seminal concepts than does the modern liberal tradition. In the biblical traditions these terms define a consensus against the misuse of power and disclose a God who is on the side of the marginal" (*What Does the Lord Require? A Bibliographical Essay on the Bible and Social Justice* [Studies in the Spirituality of Jesuits 25/2: March 1993; St. Louis: Seminar on Jesuit Spirituality, 1993] 20–21).

33. Donahue, *What Does the Lord Require?* 12.

34. See Norbert Lohfink, *Option for the Poor: The Basic Principle of Liberation Theology in Light of the Bible* (Berkeley: Bible, 1986).

35. See Isa 1:11–18; 42:1–4; Hos 2:18–20; 6:6; Amos 5:18–25; Mic 6:6–8; Jer 7:5–7.

36. Luke, following the Septuagint, does not specify the subject of the following verbs: Is it Spirit or Lord? The Isaian text, however, has Yahweh for the subject of "anointed" etc.

37. Here I am using the translation and punctuation of Joseph A. Fitzmyer, S.J., *The Gospel according to Luke (I–IX)* (Garden City, N.Y.: Doubleday, 1981) 525, 532–33.

38. Edward B. Arroyo, S.J., "Solidarity: A Moral Imperative for an Interdependent World," *Blueprint for Social Justice* 42, no. 1 (September 1988) 1–7, at 5.

39. John Paul II, *Sollicitudo rei socialis,* no. 38 (tr. *John Paul II, On Social Concern* [Washington, D.C.: United States Catholic Conference, n.d.] 74).

40. See Joseph Sittler, "Ecological Commitment as Theological Responsibility," *Idoc,* September 12, 1970, 75–85; also his remarks in John H. Miller, C.S.C., ed., *Vatican II: An Interfaith Appraisal* (Notre Dame: University of Notre Dame, 1966) 426–27.

41. Rosemary Radford Ruether, *New Woman, New Earth: Sexist Ideologies and Human Liberation* (New York: Seabury, 1975) 204. See her more recent *Gaia and God: An Ecofeminist Theology of Earth Healing* (San Francisco: HarperCollins, 1992).

42. See, e.g., Thomas Berry, *The Dream of the Earth* (San Francisco: Sierra Club, 1988).

43. Anne Lonergan and Caroline Richards, eds., *Thomas Berry and the New Cosmology* (Mystic, Conn.: Twenty-third, 1990) 107, 108.

44. John F. Haught, *The Promise of Nature: Ecology and Cosmic Purpose* (New York and Mahwah, N.J.: Paulist, 1993).

45. Ibid. 38.

46. Ibid. 65.

47. Ibid. 87.

48. Ibid. 139.

49. Ibid. 137.

50. See, e.g., Vatican II's Constitution on the Church in the Modern World, no. 57. The same document, however, has a section (39) on a new earth God is preparing "where justice will have its home," when "all that creation which God fashioned for humanity's sake will be delivered from vanity's bondage."

51. English text, "Peace with All Creation," in *Origins* 19, no. 28 (December 14, 1989) 465–68.

52. Ibid., no. 8 (*Origins* 466); emphasis mine.

53. Ibid., no. 15 (*Origins* 468).

54. Leo XIII, *Mirae caritatis,* May 28, 1902 (Denzinger-Schönmetzer 3364).

55. Dawn Gibeau, "Fr. Virgil, St. John's Monks Spread Idea That Liturgy Creates Community," *National Catholic Reporter* 30, no. 7 (December 10, 1993) 13.

56. J. Bryan Hehir, Foreword to *Liturgy and Social Justice,* ed. Mark Searle (Collegeville, Minn.: Liturgical, 1980) 9. For an extended treatment of the leaders, from the seventeenth century to Vatican II, who provided the scholarly basis and prepared the groundwork for the liturgical movement of the twentieth century, see J. D. Crichton, *Lights in the Darkness: Forerunners of the Liturgical Movement* (Collegeville, Minn.: Liturgical, 1996).

57. Crichton, *Lights in the Darkness* 156.

58. Dawn Gibeau, "Liturgical Movement Central to Diekmann," *National Catholic Reporter* 30, no. 7 (n. 55 above) 13–14, at 13.

59. See the splendid biography by liturgical scholar Kathleen Hughes, R.S.C.J., *The Monk's Tale: A Biography of Godfrey Diekmann, O.S.B.* (Collegeville, Minn.: Liturgical, 1991) specifically 277–82.

60. Ibid. 282; italics in text; Greeley material from a taped interview dated November 24, 1987.

61. Kevin Seasoltz, "Justice and the Eucharist," *Worship* 58 (1984) 509.

62. Here I am borrowing ideas that first appeared in chapter 9 of my book *Preaching: The Art and the Craft* (New York and Mahwah, N.J.: Paulist, 1987) esp. 127–31.

63. Brian Wicker, "Ritual and Culture: Some Dimensions of the Problem Today," in James D. Shaughnessy, ed., *The Roots of Ritual* (Grand Rapids: Eerdmans, 1973) 17. Wicker's observations were anticipated 18 years earlier by knowledgeable social activist George G. Higgins in an address, "The Mass and Political Order" published in the *Proceedings of the Liturgical Conference,* Worcester, Mass., August 1955: "Shortly after World War II an extremely well-informed German priest told me, on what I am prepared to accept as reliable evidence, that the Nazis, far from being worried about the pre-war growth of the liturgical movement in Germany, secretly encouraged it. According to my informant, they felt that an intense preoccupation with the liturgy would serve to distract the attention of Catholics and make them less inclined to engage in political action. Whether this report is accurate or not, the record will show, I think, that some of those most actively engaged in the liturgical movement not only in Germany but in other countries as well did make the mistake of ignor-

ing political and social problems or, even worse, of at least passively favoring political programs which they should have actively opposed" (130–31).

64. Mark Searle, "Serving the Lord with Justice," in Searle, ed., *Liturgy and Social Justice* (n. 56 above) 13–35, at 16. Searle has published a highly useful "Liturgy and Social Ethics: An Annotated Bibliography," *Studia liturgica* 21 (1991) 220–35.

65. Theodore Ross, "The Personal Synthesis of Liturgy and Justice," in K. Hughes and M. Francis, eds., *Living No Longer for Ourselves: Liturgy and Justice in the Nineties* (Collegeville, Minn.: Liturgical, 1990) 27–28.

66. I owe this account to J. Leon Hooper, S.J., a fellow of the Woodstock Theological Center.

67. See Searle, "Serving the Lord with Justice" 21–28.

68. Ibid. 23–24.

6. From Manresa to El Salvador

1. Avery Dulles, S.J., in his Introduction to Denis Edwards, *Human Experience of God* (New York and Ramsey, N.J.: Paulist, 1983) xiii.

2. I developed this patristic methodology in some detail in a 1964 address to the Catholic College Teachers of Sacred Doctrine, published under the title "The Fathers of the Church: Obsolete or Relevant?" in the *Proceedings* of the Tenth Annual Convention (Weston, Mass.: Regis College, 1964) 17–35, esp. 25–29. I was much influenced by the fine article of O. Rousseau, M.B., "Théologie patristique et théologie moderne," *Vie spirituelle* 80 (1949) 70–87. See also my quotation from John Courtney Murray (in chapter 1): Patristic study "admirably serves to bridge the gap that has been created, in the opinion of many, between theology and spirituality. . . . "

3. Roger Leys, S.J., *L'Image de Dieu chez saint Grégoire de Nysse* (Brussels: Desclée de Brouwer, 1951) 139–40; translation mine.

4. For the terminology, as well as other aspects of spirituality in summary form, see Walter H. Principe, C.S.B., "Spirituality, Christian," *The New Dictionary of Catholic Spirituality,* ed. Michael Downey (Collegeville, Minn.: Liturgical, 1993) 931–38.

5. See ibid. 932.

6. This last phrase is actually the title of a remarkable little book by Benedictine Jean Leclercq, which I shall treat later in this chapter.

7. A helpful brief treatment of the often hazy word "spirituality" and of fresh approaches to spirituality is Michael Downey's "Christian Spirituality: Changing Currents, Perspectives, Challenges," *America* 170, no. 11 (April 2, 1994) 8–12.

8. See Michael H. Crosby, O.F.M.Cap., "Spirituality," *The New Dictionary of Catholic Social Thought,* ed. Judith A. Dwyer (Collegeville, Minn.: Liturgical, 1994) 917–20, at 918.

9. So M. Robert Mulholland Jr., *Invitation to a Journey: A Road Map to Spiritual Formation* (Downers Grove, Ill.: InterVarsity, 1994), quoted by Lawrence S. Cunningham in a brief review, *Commonweal* 121, no. 1 (January 14, 1994) 41.

10. Harvey D. Egan, S.J., "Ignatian Spirituality," *The New Dictionary of Catholic Spirituality* (n. 4 above) 521–29, at 522.

11. Ibid.

12. Lest I be charged with inconsistency, let it be noted that I am italicizing *Spiritual Exercises* when it clearly refers to the book, keeping it roman when it refers to the "exercises" that are the book's contents.

13. *Spiritual Exercises,* no. 1 (tr. Louis J. Puhl, S.J., *The Spiritual Exercises of St. Ignatius, Based on Studies in the Language of the Autograph* [Chicago: Loyola University, 1951] 1).

14. See the useful summary of the *Spiritual Exercises* by J. Lewis, "Spiritual Exercises," *New Catholic Encyclopedia* 13 (1967) 578–82, esp. 580–81.

15. See Hans-Georg Gadamer, *Truth and Method* (New York: Seabury, 1975) esp. 235–341.

16. See ibid. 264; also the fine article (from which I have learned and drawn so much) by Sandra M. Schneiders, I.H.M., "Faith, Hermeneutics, and the Literal Sense of Scripture," *Theological Studies* 39 (1978) 719–36.

17. Schneiders, ibid. 731. She cautions: "This does not mean, of course, that a text can have any meaning which one chooses to assign to it, but rather that every significant text has a fulness of meaning which by its very nature can never be exhausted" (ibid.). She recognizes the problem of scientific control, but insists that "in the end the techniques must be subsumed in the artistic process. This subsuming does not nullify the techniques but incorporates them into a higher synthesis. There are criteria for the adequacy of artistic renditions, but they are not quantitative criteria. Just as the score remains normative for the musician, and the rendition is always judged both by the score and by the history of interpretation of the piece, so the interpretation of the exegete remains always under the judgment of the text and of the faith tradition of the Church" (733).

18. Bernard J. F. Lonergan, *Method in Theology* (New York: Herder and Herder, 1972) 31. In this connection I have been provoked to renewed reflection by Evelyn Eaton Whitehead and James D. Whitehead, "Christians and Their Passions," *Review for Religious* 52 (1993) 702–11. Rather than the traditional Catholic approach to our passions, i.e., hold them off or hold them away or hold them still, the Whiteheads find an alternative that "begins in the image of befriending. Neither denying our emotion nor abandoning ourselves to it, we acknowledge what we are feeling. We honor the arousal, confident it is not — finally — our enemy.... Spirituality is not about avoiding the flesh and its blind demands, but about purifying and harmonizing our complex desires" (711).

19. Here I owe a large debt to *A New Introduction to the Spiritual Exercises of St. Ignatius,* ed. John E. Dister, S.J. (Collegeville, Minn.: Liturgical, 1993), for which I wrote the Foreword that summarizes some of the ten authors' insights.

20. *SE* 53 (tr. Puhl [n. 13 above] 28).

21. Quotations from Peter J. Fennessy, S.J., "Praying the Passion: The Dynamics of Dying with Christ," in *A New Introduction* (n. 19 above) 73–87, at 85.

22. So Frederick E. Crowe, S.J., "The Ignatian *Exercises* and Jesuit Spirituality," *Review for Religious* 53 (1994) 524–33, at 524. He shows how the spirituality of the *Exercises* relates to various specific spiritualities (e.g., Carthusian) to which different exercitants may be called, by applying Bernard Lonergan's notion of "horizon" and "heuristic."

23. Ibid. 525. See also historian John W. O'Malley, S.J., "Some Distinctive Characteristics of Jesuit Spirituality in the Sixteenth Century," in John W.

O'Malley, S.J., John W. Padberg, S.J., and Vincent T. O'Keefe, S.J., *Jesuit Spirituality: A Now and Future Resource* (Chicago: Loyola University, 1990) 2: "I must insist that Jesuit spirituality in the sixteenth century cannot be reduced to the *Exercises,* even though grounded in them." He mentions "seemingly limitless" Jesuit correspondence, "the Constitutions and Ignatius' so-called *Autobiography,* the many exhortations and other documents for internal consumption produced by Jerónimo Nadal, the memoranda, chronicles, and pastoral aids of Juan de Polanco, the works on piety and ministry of more obscure figures like Gaspar Loarte and Cristóforo de Madrid, the catechisms by Canisius..." (ibid.).

24. *SE* 15 (tr. Puhl 6). Here I have been richly instructed by William A. Barry's recent *Allowing the Creator to Deal with the Creature: An Approach to the Spiritual Exercises of Ignatius of Loyola* (New York and Mahwah, N.J.: Paulist, 1994).

25. It is the first section (pp. 9–38) of Karl Rahner, S.J., *Ignatius of Loyola,* with an Historical Introduction by Paul Imhof, S.J. (London and New York: Collins, 1979). The translation, by Rosaleen Ockenden, was made on the German original, *Ignatius von Loyola* (Freiburg i. B.: Herder, 1978). I have reproduced this translation in my text, with several minor changes.

26. Ibid. 11–13.

27. Herbert Vorgrimler, *Understanding Karl Rahner: An Introduction to His Life and Thought* (New York: Crossroad, 1986) 11.

28. Dulles, Introduction (n. 1 above) xiii.

29. Karl Rahner, "Theological Thinking and Religious Experience," in *Karl Rahner in Dialogue: Conversations and Interviews, 1965–1982,* ed. Paul Imhof and Hubert Biallowons (New York: Crossroad, 1986) 328. For the major influences on Rahner (e.g., transcendental method) and for his terminology of religious experience, see James A. Wiseman, O.S.B., " 'I Have Experienced God': Religious Experience in the Theology of Karl Rahner," *American Benedictine Review* 44, no. 1 (March 1993) 22–57.

30. Paul D. Molnar, "Can We Know God Directly? Rahner's Solution from Experience," *Theological Studies* 46 (1985) 228–61.

31. Ibid. 231. Consider, therefore, his conclusion: "Not only does Rahner's position that we can know God directly manifest a rupture with traditional dogmatics..., but it leaves him in a position where he cannot answer the truth question which is the aim of all theological inquiry. Rahner cannot show that his ideas of God and of Christ represent a content which is really divine, since he has grounded the reality of both in human experience, which in itself is and remains human. He assumes it is more than this. But therein lies the difficulty of all theology. Can we assume that humanity has the capacity for God without ascribing divinity directly to man? In a Christian doctrine of God and in a Christology that is in line with the tradition, the answer to this has always been a clear no..." (261).

32. See Wiseman, "Religious Experience in Rahner" (n. 29 above) 50 ff.

33. Karl Rahner, "The Immediate Experience of God in the *Spiritual Exercises* of Saint Ignatius of Loyola," in *Karl Rahner in Dialogue* (n. 29 above) 176.

34. J. B. Metz, *Theology of the World* (New York: Herder and Herder, 1969) 109.

35. David Tracy, *Dialogue with the Other: The Inter-Religious Dialogue* (Grand Rapids: Eerdmans, 1990) 118; see 95–123.

36. Karl Rahner, "The Importance of Thomas Aquinas," in *Faith in a Wintry Season: Conversations and Interviews with Karl Rahner in the Last Years of His Life,* ed. Paul Imhof and Hubert Biallowons (New York: Crossroad, 1990) 51.

37. Egan, "Ignatian Spirituality" (n. 10 above) 524.

38. Harvey D. Egan, S.J., *Ignatius Loyola the Mystic* (Wilmington, Del.: Michael Glazier, 1987) 113.

39. See *Constitutions,* nos. 80, 98, 200, 261, 342, 343, 406, 530, 531, 540, 642, 644, 697.

40. For details see Cándido de Dalmases, *Ignatius of Loyola, Founder of the Jesuits: His Life and Work* (St. Louis: Institute of Jesuit Sources, 1985) passim; also Egan, *Ignatius Loyola the Mystic* 114–18 ("A Marian Mysticism").

41. *Autobiography,* no. 10; see the fine introduction, translation, and commentary by Joseph N. Tylenda, S.J., *Ignatius: A Pilgrim's Journey. The Autobiography of Ignatius of Loyola* (Wilmington, Del.: Michael Glazier, 1985).

42. Ibid. 239.

43. *SE,* no. 147 (tr. Puhl 62).

44. Hugo Rahner, S.J., *Ignatius the Theologian* (New York: Herder and Herder, 1968) 120.

45. *SE,* no. 299; translation mine.

46. I am aware that in this contemplation Ignatius speaks explicitly of "God," not of Christ. But, as Hugo Rahner states emphatically, "In full accordance with Ignatian theology, the 'creator and Lord' of this contemplation is Christ, the incarnate Word, who in virtue of what he is and of what he does, dwells in all creatures and 'behaves as one who works'..." (*Ignatius the Theologian* 134).

47. *SE,* no. 236; translation mine. Here I am reproducing in large measure part of a homily I preached on September 30, 1990, at the opening of the Ignatian Year in Cincinnati. See the text of the whole homily in my collection *When Christ Meets Christ: Homilies on the Just Word* (New York and Mahwah, N.J.: Paulist, 1993) 158–63, at 159–60.

48. Ronald Modras, "The Spiritual Humanism of the Jesuits," *America* 172, no. 3 (February 4, 1995) 10, 12, 14, 16, 29–32, at 16 and 29. For Modras, "It is precisely their spirituality, rooted in the Ignatian Exercises, and their humanism, rooted in the Renaissance, that made and continue to make Jesuits distinctive" (ibid. 30).

49. Robert F. Drinan, "Salvadoran Martyrs Live On to Transform U.S. Policy," *National Catholic Reporter* 26, no. 45 (October 19, 1990) 16.

50. New York: New American Library, 1961.

51. See ibid. 213–14.

52. The complete text can be found in *Review for Religious* 51 (1992) 166–81.

53. Vatican II, Pastoral Constitution on the Church in the Modern World, no. 59.

54. Walter J. Burghardt, S.J., "The Spiritual Exercises as a Foundation for Educational Ministry," *Review for Religious* 51 (1992) 166–81, at 168.

55. Andrew M. Greeley, *The Catholic Myth: The Behavior and Beliefs of American Catholics* (New York: Scribner's, 1990) 44.

56. Ibid. 45.

57. See ibid. 55.

58. Ibid. 45. Note Greeley's warning that the word "tend" is "used advisedly. Zero-sum relationships do not exist in the world of the preconscious" (ibid.).

59. Ibid. 253. For a detailed presentation of the origins and function of the Mary symbol, see Greeley's *The Mary Myth* (New York: Seabury, 1977).

60. Quoted from Hugo Rahner, S.J., *Ignatius the Theologian* (n. 44 above) 193.

61. *Documents of the Thirty-first and Thirty-second General Congregations of the Society of Jesus,* GC 32, I.4.48 (St. Louis: Institute of Jesuit Sources, 1977) 411.

62. Ibid. I.4.109, p. 432.

63. See Thomas E. Clarke, S.J., "Ignatian Spirituality and Societal Consciousness," *Studies in the Spirituality of Jesuits* 7, no. 4 (September 1975) 127–50, at 128–29, for the advantages of the adjective "societal" over "social" in reference to apostolate and ministry. "Social" efforts "seek immediately and personally to alleviate the misery of those individuals who are deprived." "Societal" activity "concerns itself immediately with the healing and transformation of those human structures, institutions, processes, and environments which draw persons into misery or make it difficult for them to emerge from it."

64. See Matthew Lamb, "The Social and Political Dimensions of Lonergan's Theology," in Vernon Gregson, ed., *The Desires of the Human Heart* (New York and Mahwah, N.J.: Paulist, 1988) 270.

65. I owe this paragraph to notes of James L. Connor, S.J., director of the Woodstock Theological Center, Washington, D.C., prepared for the inaugural retreat of my project Preaching the Just Word (1991).

66. O'Malley, "Some Distinctive Characteristics" (n. 23 above) 16–18.

67. Vatican II, Decree on the Appropriate Renewal of the Religious Life, no. 2 (tr. *The Documents of Vatican II,* ed. Walter M. Abbott, S.J. [New York: Herder and Herder, 1966] 468).

68. Vincent T. O'Keefe, S.J., a close associate of Father Arrupe during his term as general, has provided an informative and moving account of Arrupe's influence on contemporary Ignatian spirituality in "Jesuit Spirituality: A Resource Now and in the Future," in O'Malley, Padberg, and O'Keefe, *Jesuit Spirituality* (n. 23 above) 45–66.

69. *Acta romana* 18 (1980) 319–21.

70. *Documents* (n. 61 above), GC 32, I.2.31, p. 408.

71. From a homily delivered by Father Arrupe at the Ateneo de Manila, Quezon City, Philippines, on the feast of St. Ignatius, July 31, 1983, commemorating the fourth centenary of the arrival of the Jesuits in the Philippines; text in *Recollections and Reflections of Pedro Arrupe, S.J.,* tr. Yolanda T. De Mola, S.C. (Wilmington, Del.: Michael Glazier, 1986) 128.

72. From the address of John Paul II opening the deliberations of the Third Assembly of Latin American Bishops, Puebla, January 28, 1979, III, 2. A complete English version is available in *Origins* 8, no. 34 (February 8, 1979) 530–38, though it translates the Spanish *indispensable* as "essential," apparently unaware of a lively dispute on whether the struggle for justice is best denominated "essential" or "integral" to evangelization.

73. See Francis de Sales, *Introduction to the Devout Life* (New York: Doubleday, 1982) 216–17.

74. Louis J. Cameli, "Ecclesial Asceticism: Disciplines for the Family of Faith," *America* 175, no. 20 (December 28, 1996) 21–23.

75. Andrew Greeley, "A Post-Vatican II New Breed?" *America* 142, no. 25 (June 29, 1980) 537.

76. See James J. DiGiacomo, "Teaching the Next New Breed," *America* 144, no. 25 (June 27, 1981) 518–22.

77. Kaela Volkmer, in *Accompaniment* (A Newsletter for the Family and Friends of Jesuit Volunteers: International) 12, no. 2 (spring 1997).

78. Quoted in Robert Coles, *The Spiritual Life of Children* (Boston: Houghton Mifflin, 1990) xiv.

7. From Genesis to Bonhoeffer

1. Second Vatican Council, Constitution on the Church in the Modern World, no. 17.

2. Though a "springboard" for most of the reflection to come, Genesis 1:26–27 may itself have been stimulated by other creation stories. See, e.g., the Mesopotamian *Gilgamesh Epic*, where Enkidu is created as the likeness of the god Anu. Genesis 1 reconstructs existing myth.

3. Cf. G. von Rad, s.v. *eikōn*, in G. Kittel, *Theological Dictionary of the New Testament* 2 (Grand Rapids: Eerdmans, 1964) 391.

4. See, e.g., D. T. Asselin, "The Notion of Dominion in Genesis 1–3," *Catholic Biblical Quarterly* 16 (1954) 293–94: "Man is God's image not because of what he is, but because of what he is given: a share in the divine sovereignty over creation. He is lord of the world, yet Yahweh's vassal.... [The relation of resemblance between God and humans] is thought of as based upon a conferred dynamism." See, more recently, Richard J. Clifford, S.J., "Genesis," *The New Jerome Biblical Commentary*, ed. Raymond E. Brown, S.S., Joseph A. Fitzmyer, S.J., and Roland E. Murphy, O.Carm. (Englewood Cliffs, N.J.: Prentice-Hall, 1990) 2:4, p. 11: "The human is a statue of the deity, not by static being but by action, who will rule over all things previously created (v 26). In the ancient Near East, the king was often called the image of the deity and was vested with God's authority...."

5. E. Osterloh, *Die Gottebenbildlichkeit des Menschen* (Munich, 1939) 32.

6. Karl Barth, *Church Dogmatics* 3: *The Doctrine of Creation* 1 (Edinburgh: Clark, 1958) 186.

7. Von Rad, *Theological Dictionary of the New Testament* (n. 3 above) 391.

8. James Barr, "The Image of God in the Book of Genesis — A Study of Terminology," *Bulletin of the John Rylands Library* 51 (1968–69) 12.

9. Ibid. 13.

10. Bruce Vawter, *On Genesis: A New Reading* (Garden City, N.Y.: Doubleday, 1977) 59.

11. G. Ernest Wright, "The Faith of Israel," *The Interpreter's Bible* 1 (New York: Abingdon, 1952) 368.

12. Ibid.

13. Ibid.

14. See n. 3 above.

15. For completeness, one should recognize the indebtedness of the Alexandrian Fathers to Hellenic wisdom. On the image theme, five pertinent ideas were highly influential, though sometimes baptized and often deepened by their contact with Christian theology. I mean (1) an *intermediary image* through which a transcendent God touches this material world; (2) a natural kinship between the human and the divine, an *image* of God which confers on the human person a potency for perfection; (3) the actualization of this potency in a gradual process of assimilation whereby the human reaches genuine *likeness* to the divine; (4) the *imitation* of God by moral and virtuous living, an imitation that marks the passage from potency to realization, from image to likeness; (5) the category of *participation,* which underlies all the preceding, explains human divinization, reconciles unity and multiplicity. Put another way, Platonism and Stoicism, in their various phases, were tributary streams to the image theology of early Christianity. But I have found no stress on freedom as a significant facet in Hellenism's understanding of human likeness to the divine. For a more detailed investigation of the likeness-to-God motif in Plato, the Stoa, and Neoplatonism, see Hubert Merki, O.S.B., *Homoiosis Theo: Von der platonischen Angleichung an Gott zur Gottähnlichkeit bei Gregor von Nyssa* (Fribourg: Paulusverlag, 1952) 1–34.

16. The character of Philo's Logos doctrine is as varied as are his sources. At times, the Logos is God's creative Word, or the revealer of God, symbolized in Scripture by the angel of Yahweh. At times, after a Platonist conception, the Logos is the sum total of "ideas" and the intelligible world. At times, in harmony with Stoic theory, the Logos is the power that upholds the world, the bond that assures its cohesion, the law that determines its development. But through all these differing concepts runs a recognizable thread. The Logos is an intermediary between God and the world; through the Logos, God created the world and governs it; through the Logos, men and women know God and pray to God. Is the Logos God? In three passages Philo calls the Logos God; but in one of these texts he explains that it is an improper title; he is led to use it by the sacred text on which he is commenting. Is the Logos a person? Not really; more accurately, an "idea," a "power." See J. Lebreton, "The Logos," *Catholic Encyclopedia* 9 (1910) 328–31; also D. M. Crossan, "Logos 1: In the Bible," *New Catholic Encyclopedia* 8 (1967) 967–68.

17. See Philo, *De opificio mundi* 69–71 [23] (Cohn-Wendland, editio minor 1.19).

18. Philo, *Quod Deus sit immutablis* 47–48 [10] (Cohn-Wendland 2.64–65; translation, with modifications for clarity's sake, from Loeb Classical Library, *Philo* 3.33–35).

19. See much of the chapter on "Free Will" in Harry Austryn Wolfson, *Philo: Foundations of Religious Philosophy in Judaism, Christianity, and Islam* 1 (rev. ed.; Cambridge, Mass.: Harvard University, 1948) 424–62. On this thorough two-volume study, highly important but not without flaws, note Jean Daniélou's observation that Wolfson "tends too much to present Christian theology as though it were a mere development of the theology of Philo, thus placing it on the same plane with the theologies of Judaism and Islam. It would be better to have portrayed it as a distinct *revision* of this theology in function of a new Revelation which completes the first" (*Theological Studies* 9 [1948] 578). On

freedom, see the critique of David S. Winston, "Freedom and Determinism in Philo of Alexandria," *Studia Philonica* 3 (1974–75) 47–70.

20. See Winston, "Freedom and Determinism" 56–57; Philo, *De Cherubim* 77.

21. See Philo, *De Cherubim,* 128.

22. See *Legum allegoriae* 3.336.

23. See *De somniis* 2.253.

24. See some references in Winston, "Freedom and Determinism" 68 n. 32.

25. Ibid. 57.

26. See Rudolf Pesch, "Jesus, a Free Man," in *Jesus Christ and Human Freedom,* ed. E. Schillebeeckx and B. van Iersel (Concilium 94; New York: Herder and Herder, 1974) 56–70; also Leander Keck, "The Son Who Creates Freedom," ibid. 71–82.

27. For the development of image doctrine, I find it regrettable that in 1 Corinthians 11:7 Paul twists the sense of Genesis 1:27, understands it only of the husband, and concludes from the chronological sequence in Genesis 2 that the male is a direct reflection of the divine majesty, the female an image of that reflection.

28. The NT understanding of image is far more complex than my summary of Paul indicates, and the literature is enormous — in fact, has outstripped my own ability to stay abreast of it.

29. See Joseph A. Fitzmyer, S.J., "Reconciliation in Pauline Theology," in *No Famine in the Land: Studies in Honor of John L. McKenzie,* ed. James W. Flanagan and Anita Weisbrod Robinson (Missoula, Mont.: Scholars, 1975) 155–56.

30. Joseph A. Fitzmyer, S.J., *Paul and His Theology: A Brief Sketch* (2nd ed.; Englewood Cliffs, N.J.: Prentice-Hall, 1989) 77. See ibid. 78–82 for Paul's different explanations in Galatians and Romans for the anomalous situation that the law introduced for the human person.

31. Ibid. 83.

32. Ibid. 82.

33. Cf. H. Schlier, "*eleutheros* C: The Concept of Freedom in the NT," in G. Kittel, *Theological Dictionary of the New Testament* 2 (n. 3 above) 496–98.

34. Much of the extensive literature on NT freedom in recent decades has been generated by an increasing awareness of, and reaction against, the manifold enslavements of our time — political, economic, social, even ecclesiastical. Thus, the history of the Church in Germany was the backdrop for Ernst Käsemann's *Jesus Means Freedom* (Philadelphia: Fortress, 1970), which traces the contexts and development of freedom through the books of the NT.

35. Only two works of Irenaeus are extant: (1) *Against Heresies* [*AH*] (actual title *Detection and Overthrow of the Pretended but False Gnosis*), preserved complete only in a Latin translation differently dated by critics between 200 and 420, highly important for our understanding of Gnostic systems and the theology of the early Church; (2) *Proof of the Apostolic Preaching,* extant only in a sixth-century Armenian version discovered in 1904, a kind of compendium of theology differing from *AH* not in doctrinal content but in manner of presentation, brevity, and coherence.

36. See *AH* 5.1.3 (Harvey 2, 317); 5.6.1 (Harvey 2, 333); *Proof* 5, in Ancient Christian Writers 16, 50–51); *Proof* 55 (ACW 16, 83).

37. Henri Rondet, S.J., *Original Sin: The Patristic and Theological Background* (Staten Island, N.Y.: Alba, 1972) 37–38. See, e.g., the all-important text in *AH* 4.38.3 (Sources chrétiennes 100/2, 954–57) on "the sequence, the rhythm, the movement by which the man who was created and fashioned comes to be according to the image and likeness of the uncreated God."

38. See, e.g., *AH* 5.6.1 (Harvey 2, 333–34); *Proof* 11 (ACW 16,54), a strong passage on Adam's bodily resemblance to Christ his model, "that also what would be seen should be deiform" (J. P. Smith's literal version of the Armenian [ACW 16, 148–49]).

39. See, e.g., *AH* 5.16.1 (Harvey 2, 367–68).

40. Here Irenaeus' usage is not consistent; sometimes the terms are used interchangeably. But the distinction is there, in some of the more significant passages: e.g., *AH* 5.6.1 (Harvey 2, 333–35).

41. *AH* 3.19.1 (Harvey 2, 95).

42. See *AH* 1.1.11 (Harvey 1, 52).

43. See *AH* 2.47.2 (Harvey 1, 367–68).

44. See *AH* 1.1.9 (Harvey 1, 45–46).

45. *Proof* 11 (tr. ACW 16, 54). See also *AH* 4.60.2 (Harvey 2, 289).

46. See *AH* 4.59 (Harvey 2, 285–86).

47. See *AH* 4.59–60 (Harvey 2, 285–91).

48. See *AH* 4.60.2 (Harvey 2, 289).

49. Antonio Orbe, S.I., *Antropología de San Ireneo* (Madrid: Biblioteca de Autores Cristianos, 1969) 194–95.

50. In what follows, I have profited from the careful study of Réal Tremblay, C.SS.R., "La liberté selon saint Irénée de Lyon," in *In libertatem vocati estis: Miscellanea Bernhard Häring*, ed. H. Boelaars and R. Tremblay (Studia moralia 13; Rome: Academia Alfonsiana, 1977) 421–44.

51. Ibid. 442–44; translation mine. I have no room here to treat the second (degradation) and third (restoration) stages of Irenaeus' image theology. That he does not see the "image" (rationality and freedom) destroyed or even mutilated by Adam's sin has led to the charge, by Emil Brunner and others, that Irenaeus is the inventor of the Catholic "two-story universe," the division of the human person into natural and supernatural, the former unaffected by original sin.

52. Origen, *De principiis* 1, Preface 5 (Griechische christliche Schriftsteller [GCS] 22, 12–13; tr. G. W. Butterworth, *Origen on First Principles* [London: SPCK, 1936] 4).

53. *In Gen. hom.* 1.13 (GCS 29, 16–18). For the notion of participation in Origen, see Henri Crouzel's insightful study *Théologie de l'image de Dieu chez Origène* (Paris: Aubier, 1956) esp. 160–65; actually, much of the book is involved with this concept, so basic to Origen's theology.

54. See *In Ioannem* 1.17[19] (GCS 10, 22); *In Gen. hom.* 13.4 (GCS 29, 119); 1.13 (GCS 29, 16–18).

55. See *Fragmenta in Ioannem* 18 (GCS 10, 497).

56. See *De oratione* 22.4 (GCS 3, 348–49); *Frag. in Eph.* 3 [on Eph 1:5] (*Journal of Theological Studies* 3 [1901–2] 237).

57. *In Ioannem* 2.16 (GCS 10, 73).

58. See ibid. 20.22 (GCS 10, 355).

59. *De principiis* 1.1.7 (GCS 22, 24).

60. Ibid. 4.4.9 (GCS 22, 362); and the witness of Jerome, *Epist.* 124.14 (Corpus scriptorum ecclesiasticorum latinorum [CSEL] 56, 116–17).

61. See *In Ioannem* 20.22 (GCS 10, 354–55).

62. See *De principiis* 1.8.4 (GCS 22, 103–4).

63. See *In Gen. hom.* 13.4 (GCS 29, 119).

64. See *De principiis* 4.4.9 (GCS 22, 363).

65. So Crouzel, *Théologie de l'image* (n. 53 above) 209–10; see Origen, *Exhortatio ad mart.* 47 (GCS 2, 43).

66. See *In Gen. hom.* 1.13 (GCS 29, 16–18).

67. See *De principiis* 3.6.1 (GCS 22, 280); Origen argues from the absence of "likeness" in v. 27.

68. See *Scholia in Lucam* 14 (Patrologia graeca [PG] 17, 357–60); *Frag. in Eph.* 21 [on Eph 4:30] (*Journal of Theological Studies* 3 [1901–2] 556).

69. See *Contra Celsum* 4.30 (GCS 2, 299); *In Rom.* 5.9 (PG 14, 1044).

70. See *Scholia in Lucam* 14 (PG 17, 364–65).

71. See *Contra Celsum* 8.72 (GCS 3, 288–89).

72. See *In Rom.* 1.1 (PG 14, 839 f.).

73. *In Matt.* 13.11 (GCS 10, 209). See *In Gen. hom.* 16 and *In Exod. hom.* 8 (GCS 6.136 f., 217 f.): The captivity in Egypt symbolizes bondage to sin and vice; the exodus therefrom represents the redemption and the acquisition of freedom. See José Antonio Alcain, *Cautiverio y redención del hombre en Orígenes* (Bilbao: Universidad de Deusto, 1973).

74. My earliest introduction to Gregory's image doctrine was the careful study of Roger Leys, *L'Image de Dieu chez saint Grégoire de Nysse: Esquisse d'une doctrine* (Paris: Desclée de Brouwer, 1951).

75. See Leys, ibid. 139–40, quoted at length in the early section of chapter 6 on spirituality.

76. Gregory of Nyssa, *Oratio catechetica magna* 5 (PG 45, 24).

77. Actually, Gregory does not have a special treatise on freedom; one must work through his extensive writings, as Jérôme Gaïth has done in his *La conception de la liberté chez Grégoire de Nysse* (Paris: Vrin, 1953), a work that stimulated my own early research into Gregory and to which these pages are largely indebted. Note that Gaïth used PG 44–46 as his working text; with the exception of the first edition of *Contra Eunomium* and the letters, Werner Jaeger's critical *Gregorii Nysseni opera* was not ready when he wrote in 1953.

78. *Contra Eunomium* 3.1.125 (Jaeger 2, 45–46; PG 45, 609).

79. See Gaïth, *La conception de la liberté* (n. 77 above) 31–32. See his development of these three revelations of divine transcendence, ibid. 32–39.

80. *De anima et resurrectione* (PG 46, 101). Whether "image" and "likeness" are synonymous or not in Gregory has vexed scholars for decades. For useful observations see Hans von Balthasar, *Présence et pensée: Essai sur la philosophie religieuse de Grégoire de Nysse* (Paris: Beauchesne, 1942) 89; Jean Daniélou, *Platonisme et théologie mystique: Essai sur la doctrine spirituelle de saint Grégoire de Nysse* (Paris: Aubier, 1944) 52. I resonate to Leys (n. 74 above), who finds a distinction at times, "not as two different things but as two aspects of one same reality." Likeness is image in process of realization (116–19).

81. See *De virginitate* 12 (Jaeger 8/1, 298); *In Canticum canticorum* orat. 2 (Jaeger 6, 55; PG 44, 796); *Oratio catechetica magna* 5 (PG 45, 24).

82. *De infantibus qui praemature abripiuntur* (PG 46, 173).

83. See the detailed exposition in Gaïth (n. 77 above) 135–74.

84. Ibid. 205. For a more detailed exposition of Origen and Gregory, together with a summary of Cyril of Alexandria, see my article "Free Like God: Recovering an Ancient Anthropology," *Theology Digest* 26, no. 4 (winter 1978) 343–64. See also the full-length study of Cyril in my published doctoral dissertation, *The Image of God in Man according to Cyril of Alexandria* (Washington, D.C.: Catholic University of America, 1957). In Cyril I have isolated six facets of his image doctrine: reason, freedom, dominion, holiness, incorruptibility, and sonship. For Cyril, what copies the divine more accurately than sheer power to choose is our ability to freely elect the good. Despite sin, man and woman remained essentially good, but did not preserve the original unreserved response to grace. In the Incarnation Christ restored the unshackled power to do what is good. This is Christian liberty, proper Godlikeness, where the human person, dynamized by the indwelling Spirit, responds without constraint, images God's innate goodness, does freely only what God wants—in a word, acts like Christ.

85. For a useful array of texts and interpretation, see John E. Sullivan, *The Image of God: The Doctrine of St. Augustine and Its Influence* (Dubuque, Iowa: Priory, 1963).

86. Thomas Aquinas, *Sum. theol.* 2/2, q. 182, a. 1, ad 2.

87. *Sum. theol.* 1, q. 93, a. 4. See also Jaroslav Pelikan, "*Imago Dei:* An Explication of *Summa theologiae,* Part 1, Question 93," in *Calgary Aquinas Studies,* ed. Anthony Parel (Toronto: Pontifical Institute of Mediaeval Studies, 1978) 27–48.

88. Charles Trinkaus, *In Our Image and Likeness* (Chicago: University of Chicago, 1970).

89. Ibid. xiv.

90. Ibid. xxii.

91. Ibid. 774.

92. See, e.g., David Cairns, *The Image of God in Man* (rev. ed.; London: Collins, 1973) 127–51.

93. John Calvin, *Sermon on Job* 2.1 f.

94. See, e.g., Martin Luther's *Von der Freiheit eines Christenmenschen* (1520).

95. So John Dourley, "Carl Jung and Contemporary Theology," *Ecumenist* 12, no. 6 (September–October 1974) 90–95, at 92.

96. See his article "The *Imago Dei* as Man's Historicity," *Journal of Religion* 36 (1956) 157–68.

97. Dietrich Bonhoeffer, *Gesammelte Schriften* 1 (ed. Eberhard Bethge; Munich: Kaiser, 1958) 320.

98. Dietrich Bonhoeffer, *Ethics* (ed. Eberhard Bethge; New York: Macmillan, 1962) 49.

99. Ibid. 208–9.

100. Dietrich Bonhoeffer, *Letters and Papers from Prison* (enlarged ed. by Eberhard Bethge; London: SCM, 1971) 370.

101. Ibid. 35.

102. See Dietrich Bonhoeffer, *The Cost of Discipleship* (2nd ed.; New York: Macmillan, 1963).

103. *Letters and Papers from Prison* 370.

104. I have profited much from the biography *Dietrich Bonhoeffer: Man of Vision, Man of Courage* by his intimate friend, colleague, and editor Eberhard Bethge (ed. Edwin Robertson; New York: Harper & Row, 1970).

105. William Kuhns, *In Pursuit of Dietrich Bonhoeffer* (Dayton: Pflaum, 1967) 270–71.

106. Dietrich Bonhoeffer, *Creation and Fall: A Theological Interpretation of Genesis 1–3* (London: SCM, 1959).

107. Ibid. 33–34.

108. Ibid. 35.

109. Ibid. 36. Bonhoeffer claims that the image and likeness is not *analogia entis,* in which the human images God's being (for him, there is no such analogy between God and the human person), but *analogia relationis* (see ibid. 37).

110. Ibid. 37.

111. Ibid. 38.

112. Ibid.

113. Dietrich Bonhoeffer, *The Communion of Saints: A Dogmatic Inquiry into the Sociology of the Church* (New York: Harper & Row, 1963) 173–75.

114. Ibid. 174.

115. Dietrich Bonhoeffer, *No Rusty Swords* 1 (ed. Edwin H. Robertson; New York: Harper & Row, 1965) 43.

116. Ibid. 44–45.

117. Dietrich Bonhoeffer, *Act and Being* (New York: Harper, 1961) 90.

118. Ibid. 90–91.

119. Ibid. 175.

120. Ibid. 184.

121. See Bonhoeffer, *Ethics* (n. 98 above) 216–22.

122. Ibid. 217.

123. Ibid. 218.

124. Ibid. 219.

125. Ibid. 220–21.

126. Bonhoeffer, *The Cost of Discipleship* (n. 102 above) 269–75. Although the work was first published in 1937, the first drafts go back to 1931–32.

127. Ibid. 272.

128. Ibid.

129. Ibid. What Bonhoeffer wrote is indeed revelatory of freedom, but it can be a bloodless anthology if divorced from who he was and what he did. Eberhard Bethge has uncovered the kind of freedom exhibited by Bonhoeffer's milieu, personal growth, theology, ecclesiastical partisanship, and political action. This involved an effort to grasp the idea and reality of freedom as disclosed on five levels of his free activity: social, psychological, theological, ecclesiastical, and ethical. See Eberhard Bethge, "Freiheit und Gehorsam bei Bonhoeffer," first published in *Schöpferische Nachfolge: Festschrift für Heinz Eduard Tödt,* ed. Chr. Frey and W. Huber (Heidelberg: Ev. Studiengemeinschaft, 1978) 331–61; then in Bethge's *Am gegebenen Ort: Aufsätze und Reden 1970–1979* (Munich: Christian Kaiser, 1979) 63–82. The latter text was graciously supplied to me by Bethge in October 1981; I treasure it.

130. Bonhoeffer, *Letters and Papers from Prison* (n. 100 above) 370–71. See the revealing commentary on each of these stages in Edwin H. Robertson, ed., *The Way to Freedom: Letters, Lectures and Notes 1935–1939 from the Collected*

Works of Dietrich Bonhoeffer 2 (New York: Harper & Row, 1966) 11–21. It was intriguing for me to learn from Eberhard Bethge that the first stanza, on the need for discipline and obedience, is omitted by many publishers and by many who quote the poem "because they cannot stand it."

8. From Jesus Christ to Vatican II

1. *Summa contra gentiles* 4, chap. 74–75.
2. See Vatican II, Constitution on the Sacred Liturgy, no. 7: "It is he himself who speaks when the holy Scriptures are read in the church."
3. Constitution on the Church in the Modern World, no. 43.
4. *The Priest and Sacred Scripture*, ed. Eugene Maly (Washington, D.C.: National Conference of Catholic Bishops, 1971) 4–6.
5. Here I am summarizing Raymond E. Brown, S.S., *Priest and Bishop: Biblical Reflections* (New York: Paulist, 1970) 21–43.
6. Gregory Dix, *The Shape of the Liturgy* (Westminster, England: Dacre, 1945) 744.
7. Decree on the Ministry and Life of Priests, no. 6.
8. Dogmatic Constitution on the Church, no. 28.
9. Decree on the Ministry and Life of Priests, no. 6.
10. The text, "Crisis, Cross, Confidence: A Priest for *This* Season," can be found in *Emmanuel* 97 (1991) 66–73, 110–11.
11. Karl Rahner, "Following the Crucified," *Theological Investigations* 18: *God and Revelation* (New York: Crossroad, 1983) 157–70, at 165–66. To this article I am deeply indebted for much of what follows; it has affected my priestly life perhaps more than any other single piece of modern spiritual writing.
12. See ibid. 158.
13. See ibid. 160–61.
14. Karl Rahner, "The Spirituality of the Priest in the Light of His Office," *Theological Investigations* 19: *Faith and Ministry* (New York: Crossroad, 1983) 117–38, at 133–34.
15. Ibid. 134.
16. My account, including quotations, is taken from *Time* 135, no. 9 (February 26, 1990) 70.
17. See John W. O'Malley, S.J., "Priesthood, Ministry, and Religious Life: Some Historical and Historiograhical Considerations," *Theological Studies* 49 (1988) 223–57.
18. See ibid. 250–51.
19. Ibid. 251. O'Malley recalls that Pope John Paul II, in his allocution opening the 33rd General Congregation of the Society of Jesus, September 2, 1982, especially commended to the Jesuits ministries like "ecumenism, the deeper study of relations with non-Catholic religions, and the dialogue of the Church with cultures," and "the evangelizing action of the Church to promote justice, connected with world peace" (ibid.). See *Documents of the 33rd General Congregation of the Society of Jesus* (St. Louis: Institute of Jesuit Sources, 1984) 77–84, esp. 81–82.
20. Ibid. 253.
21. Ibid. See *Christus dominus*, no. 35, where the council asserts that the privilege of some religious of exemption from the jurisdiction of bishops "re-

lates primarily to the internal organization of the institutes...[so that] the perfection of religious life [is] promoted." But from the thirteenth century on, O'Malley declares, "the most impressive privileges of the orders related directly to ministry" (253).

22. See ibid. 254–57.

23. Ibid. 256.

24. Ibid. 256–57.

25. Ibid. 257.

26. Thomas P. Rausch, S.J., *Priesthood Today: An Appraisal* (New York and Mahwah, N.J.: Paulist, 1992).

27. Ibid. 15.

28. Ibid. 18.

29. Ibid. 22.

30. Avery Dulles, S.J., *Models of the Church* (Garden City, N.Y.: Doubleday, 1974) 158–59. See also Dulles' more recent *The Priestly Office: A Theological Reflection* (New York and Mahwah, N.J.: Paulist, 1997). Three chapters treat priestly service in and for the community: ministry of the word, ministry of worship, and pastoral care. A final chapter, "The Priest as Disciple," outlines a priestly spirituality that serves and signifies best when it is celibate.

31. See Rausch, *Priesthood Today* 49–57.

32. Rembert G. Weakland, "The Church in Worldly Affairs: Tensions between Laity and Clergy," *America* 156, no. 10 (October 18, 1986) 201–5, 215–16, at 201.

33. See John Tracy Ellis, "The Formation of the American Priest: An Historical Perspective," in Ellis, ed., *The Catholic Priest in the United States: Historical Investigations* (Collegeville, Minn.: St. John's University, 1971) 3–110, esp. 3–56; also Michael V. Gannon, "Before and after Modernism: The Intellectual Isolation of the American Priest," ibid. 293–383, esp. 293–326. See, e.g., Gannon 294: "The finding of this researcher is that, with the exception of the period 1890–1908 and the very recent years, there have been precious few...instances" of interrelationship and influence between the clergy and the American intellectual community.

34. Gannon, "Before and after Modernism" 306.

35. Sermon, "The Church and the Age," in *John Ireland, The Church and Modern Society* (Chicago: McBride, 1897) 97; quoted in Gannon, "Before and after Modernism" 324.

36. Gannon, "Before and after Modernism" 341.

37. From Greeley's *Confessions of a Parish Priest: An Autobiography* (New York: Simon and Schuster, 1986); quoted in a review by Joseph Blotner in *America* 155, no. 8 (October 4, 1986) 170.

38. John Courtney Murray, S.J., "Reversing the Secularist Drift," *Thought* 24 (1949) 37, 41.

39. Egidio Vagnozzi, "Thoughts on the Catholic Intellectual," *American Ecclesiastical Review* 145, no. 2 (August 1961) 73–79, at 78.

40. I specify "diocesan" because it is in large measure the diocesan clergy that staffs our parishes, with the consequent enviable (unenviable?) responsibility of mustering the charisms (intellectual included) of the Catholic community with a view to influencing and perhaps transforming the dominant culture. Not indeed alone; schools and other institutions have significant roles to play.

41. Félicité de Lamennais, *Des progrès de la révolution et de la guerre contre l'église* (2nd ed.; De Berlin-Mandar et Devaux, 1829) 276–77; translation from Ellis, "Formation of the American Priest" 4.

42. Decree on the Ministry and Life of Priests, no. 3; emphasis mine.

43. Ellis, "Formation of the American Priest" 92.

44. Ibid. 93; quotation from Douglas Woodruff, "The Fathers Disperse and Reflect on Whence They Came," (London) *Tablet* 219 (December 10, 1965) 1377.

9. From the Samaritan Woman to the Catholic Tomorrow

1. I have this item at second hand, from Wilfrid Ward's *The Life of John Henry Cardinal Newman* 2 (New York: Longmans, Green, 1912) 147.

2. Pastoral Constitution on the Church in the Modern World, no. 43.

3. Decree on the Apostolate of the Laity, no. 5.

4. See the wealth of historical and theological development in Yves M. J. Congar, O.P., *Lay People in the Church: A Study for a Theology of Laity* (rev. ed.; London: Chapman, 1965) esp. 400–451, on being in the world and not of it — actually a chapter on lay spirituality.

5. For a definition of the term, its origins and development, organizational forms of Catholic Action, and its theological significance, see D. J. Geaney, "Catholic Action," *New Catholic Encyclopedia* 3 (1967) 262–63.

6. John Paul II, *Redemptor hominis*, March 4, 1979 (Washington, D.C.: United States Catholic Conference, 1979) no. 21, pp. 89–90.

7. I have profited over the years from the remarkably insightful article by Raymond E. Brown, S.S., "Roles of Women in the Fourth Gospel," *Theological Studies* 36 (1975) 688–99.

8. Ibid. 691.

9. Ibid. 692.

10. Ibid. 692–93. For the tradition see, e.g., the famous ninth-century life of Magdalene by Rabanus Maurus (esp. Patrologia latina [PL] 112, 1474B, 1475A, 1475B, 1479C).

11. Ibid. 699.

12. See J. G. Gager, *Kingdom and Community: The Social World of Early Christianity* (Englewood Cliffs, N.J.: Prentice-Hall, 1976) specifically 84–88, 140. A fine summary of this communitarian aspect, with pertinent documentation, has been provided by William J. Walsh, S.J., and John P. Langan, S.J., "Patristic Social Consciousness: The Church and the Poor," in *The Faith That Does Justice,* ed. John C. Haughey, S.J. (Woodstock Studies 2; New York: Paulist, 1977) 113–51.

13. I am borrowing these themes from Walsh and Langan, "Patristic Social Consciousness," though my own long "life with the Fathers of the Church" has seen them concretized over and over again. See my *Preaching the Just Word,* a much-expanded version of my Beecher Lectures on Preaching at the Yale Divinity School in 1994 (New Haven: Yale University, 1996) 29–32. For a good introduction to the social message of the Fathers, as well as a useful selection of texts in English translation, see Peter C. Phan, *Social Thought* (Message of the Fathers of the Church 20; Wilmington, Del.: Michael Glazier, 1984).

14. *Didache* 4.8 (tr. James A. Kleist, S.J., in Ancient Christian Writers [ACW] 6 [New York and Ramsey, N.J.: Newman, repro. 1978, orig. 1946] 17). The date of this document has been highly controversial. I tend to favor the conclusion of J. P. Audet that it "does not seem to be much later than the letters of Paul. It may be considered as contemporary with the canonical Gospels. Its most likely place of origin remains the Church of Antioch, in Syria" ("Didache," *New Catholic Encyclopedia* 4 [1967] 859).

15. Clement of Alexandria, *The Rich Man's Salvation* 11–17 (Griechische christliche Schriftsteller 17, 166–70; tr. and ed. Maurice Wiles and Mark Santer, *Documents in Early Christian Thought* [Cambridge, Mass.: Cambridge University, 1975] 203–6).

16. Origen, *Homily on the Book of Judges* 2.3.

17. Ambrose, *Duties of the Clergy* 1.132.

18. Ambrose, *Naboth* 1.

19. John Chrysostom, *The Fall of Eutropius* 2.3.

20. John Chrysostom, *Homily 12 on 1 Timothy* 4 (Patrologia graeca [PG] 62, 563–64; tr. Nicene and Post-Nicene Fathers 12).

21. John Chrysostom, *Homily 20 on 1 Corinthians* 3 (PG 61, 540).

22. John Chrysostom, *Homily 50 on Matthew* 4.

23. Augustine, *Treatises on the First Letter of John* 10.7 (PL 35, 2059).

24. Ibid. 10.8 (PL 35, 2060).

25. See Clement's homily on Mark 10:17–31, *The Rich Man's Salvation*. As shown above, Clement argues that it is not necessary to rid oneself of all one owns to be saved. Were this not true, no one could support the poor.

26. Karl Baus, *From the Apostolic Community to Constantine* (Handbook of Church History 1, ed. Hubert Jedin and John Dolan; New York: Herder and Herder, 1965) 219. The reference is to the *Passio ss. Perpetuae et Felicitatis,* one of the most precious martyrdom accounts surviving from the third century.

27. See Baus, ibid. 227.

28. Ibid. 227–28.

29. For details see St. Athanasius, *The Life of Saint Antony,* as translated by Robert T. Meyer in ACW 10. "The crowning achievement of Athanasius," writes Meyer, "is that he combined the ancient literary forms of biography with the Christian element, and produced a type that was to influence all subsequent Greek and Latin hagiography" (ibid. 13).

30. Ibid. 47 (ACW 10, 60). See also Edward E. Malone, O.S.B., *The Monk and the Martyr* (Washington, D.C.: Catholic University of America, 1950).

31. J. N. D. Kelly, *Jerome: His Life, Writings, and Controversies* (New York: Harper & Row, 1975) 91. Kelly is richly informative on such ascetic women, their practices and their influence.

32. Ibid. 93.

33. Ibid. 138; emphasis mine.

34. Adalbert Hamman, "Writers of Gaul," in *Patrology* 4, ed. Angelo Di Berardino (Westminster, Md.: Christian Classics, 1985) 504–63, at 558.

35. See *Egeria: Diary of a Pilgrimage,* translated and annotated by George E. Gingras (ACW 38; New York and Ramsey, N.J.: Newman, 1970).

36. Georgia M. Keightley, "Laity," *The New Dictionary of Theology,* ed. Joseph A. Komonchak, Mary Collins, and Dermot A. Lane (Wilmington, Del.: Michael Glazier, 1987) 558–64, at 558.

37. In this section I have profited from the summary article by John T. Gilchrist, "Laity in the Middle Ages," *New Catholic Encyclopedia* 8 (1967) 331–35.

38. Ibid. 331.

39. Ibid. 333–34.

40. English translation from *The Teaching of the Catholic Church As Contained in Her Documents,* originally prepared by Joseph Neuner, S.J., and Heinrich Roos, S.J., ed. Karl Rahner, S.J. (Staten Island, N.Y.: Alba, 1967) 219–20.

41. Avery Dulles, S.J., "The Church," Introduction to the English translation of the Dogmatic Constitution on the Church in *The Documents of Vatican II,* ed. Walter M. Abbott, S.J. (New York: Herder and Herder, 1966) 9–13, at 12–13.

42. Vatican II, Dogmatic Constitution on the Church, no. 12 (tr. *Documents* 29–30).

43. William J. O'Malley, "The Goldilocks Method," *America* 165, no. 14 (November 9, 1991) 334–39, at 336.

44. Keightley, "Laity" (n. 36 above) 563.

45. See ibid. 562.

46. Thomas F. O'Meara, O.P., "Ministry," *The New Dictionary of Theology* (n. 36 above) 657–61, at 660–61. Quotation from Congar's *Power and Poverty in the Church* (London, 1964).

47. The Vatican's English text can be found in *Origins* 27, no. 24 (November 27, 1997) 397, 399–409, followed by "An Explanatory Note" in French sent from the Vatican to bishops' conferences (409–10).

48. From a speech of John Paul II to the April 1994 symposium on lay participation in priestly ministry, no. 3.

49. Here the Instruction refers in a footnote to a Response of the Pontifical Commission for the Authentic Interpretation of the Code of Canon Law, *Acta apostolicae sedis* 80 (1988) 1373.

50. Instruction, Article 1 (*Origins* 402–3). The final paragraph above has the following footnote: "Such examples should include all those linguistic expressions which in the languages of the various countries are similar or equal and indicate a directive role of leadership or such vicarious activity" (n. 58, *Origins* 408). The prohibition of the title "chaplain" has caused understandable consternation in the United States.

51. For details see Richard A. McCormick's superb "The Abortion Dossier," *Theological Studies* 35 (1974) 312–59.

52. See Pope John XXIII, *Mater et magistra,* no. 65.

53. C. H. Wu, "Law," *New Catholic Encyclopedia* 8 (1967) 545–46, at 545.

54. John Courtney Murray, S.J., *We Hold These Truths: Catholic Reflections on the American Proposition* (New York: Sheed and Ward, 1960) 7–8 (in a chapter headed "The Civilization of the Pluralist Society").

55. See my "Characteristics of Social Justice Spirituality," *Origins* 24, no. 9 (July 21, 1994) 157, 159–64.

56. I have used the translation in Gerhard Ebeling, *Luther: An Introduction to His Thought,* tr. R. A. Wilson (Philadelphia: Fortress, 1970) 45–46.

57. Vatican II, Constitution on the Sacred Liturgy, no. 10.

58. See *The Long Loneliness: The Autobiography of Dorothy Day* (New

York: Harper & Brothers, 1952) 149–50; William D. Miller, *Dorothy Day: A Biography* (San Francisco: Harper & Row, 1982) 341, 343–44.

59. Theodore Ross, "The Personal Synthesis of Liturgy and Justice," in K. Hughes and M. Francis, eds., *Living No Longer for Ourselves: Liturgy and Justice in the Nineties* (Collegeville, Minn.: Liturgical, 1990) 27.

60. See William J. Bausch, *The Parish of the Next Millennium* (Mystic, Conn.: Twenty-third, 1997) 275–79. In the paragraphs that follow I have most often used Bausch's own rhetoric without the customary quotation marks.

10. From Eve to Mary to...?

1. See Robert A. Wild, S.J., "The Pastoral Epistles," *The New Jerome Biblical Commentary,* ed. Raymond E. Brown, S.S., Joseph A. Fitzmyer, S.J., and Roland E. Murphy, O.Carm. (Englewood Cliffs, N.J.: Prentice-Hall, 1990) 56:6, p. 892.

2. Ibid. 56:33, p. 897.

3. Donal Flanagan, "An Apology to Eve," *Doctrine and Life* (Dublin and Kildare) 44, no. 1 (January 1993) 9–18, at 15. Flanagan compares the Timothy text with 2 Cor 11:3 ("the serpent deceived Eve by its cunning"), but shows that in the latter text (written a half century before 1 Timothy) "The figure of Eve is an inclusive symbol for the Church at Corinth — it stands for both women and men. It does not refer to the women of the Church of Corinth apart from the men. Paul is not suggesting that women are inherently untrustworthy or gullible or more at risk than men because Eve, the common mother of all, was misled by the serpent. The intention of his statement is not to comment on the problems of femininity as such but to talk to the Christian community of Corinth as a whole, men and women, about their common weakness in the face of temptation" (ibid.).

4. Jerome Murphy-O'Connor, O.P., "The First Letter to the Corinthians," *The New Jerome Biblical Commentary* (n. 1 above) 49:52, p. 808.

5. Ibid. 49:54, p. 809.

6. John Henry Newman, *A Letter to the Rev. E. B. Pusey, D.D., on His Recent Eirenicon* (3rd ed.; London, 1866) 33–34.

7. Irenaeus, *Against Heresies* 3.32.1 (Harvey 2, 124).

8. Ephraem, *Hymns on Blessed Mary* 2.8 (ed. Lamy 2, 525).

9. See, e.g., Epiphanius, bishop of Salamis, *Medicine Chest,* haer. 78.18 (Griechische christliche Schriftsteller 37, 468–69).

10. For details on the Western and Eastern traditions, and the theological significance which Fathers and early ecclesiastical writers attached to the parallelism, see Walter J. Burghardt, S.J., "Mary in Western Patristic Thought," in Juniper B. Carol, O.F.M., ed., *Mariology* 1 (Milwaukee: Bruce, 1955) 109–55, at 110–17, and "Mary in Eastern Patristic Thought," in Carol, *Mariology* 2 (Milwaukee: Bruce, 1957) 88–153, at 88–100.

11. Theodotus of Ancyra, *On Holy Mary Mother of God and On the Holy Birth of Christ* 11 (Patrologia orientalis 19, 329).

12. Phyllis Trible, *God and the Rhetoric of Sexuality* (Philadelphia: Fortress, 1978) 128.

13. Richard J. Clifford, S.J., "Genesis," *The New Jerome Biblical Commentary* (n. 1 above) 2:5, p. 12.

14. John Paul II, apostolic letter (1988) *Mulieris dignitatem* IV, 9–10 (tr. *Origins* 18 [1988] 268–69).

15. See n. 10 above.

16. *Mariology* 1:110.

17. See Georges Jouassard, "The Fathers of the Church and the Immaculate Conception," in *The Dogma of the Immaculate Conception: History and Significance* (Notre Dame: University of Notre Dame, 1958) 51–86.

18. See Albert Mitterer, *Dogma und Biologie der Heiligen Familie nach dem Weltbild des hl. Thomas von Aquin und dem der Gegenwart* (Vienna: Herder, 1952) 82–132.

19. René Laurentin, "Le mystère de la naissance virginale: A propos d'un livre récent," *Ephemerides mariologicae* 10 (1960) 345–74.

20. For a swift summary of the evidence, see my "Assumption of Mary," *Encyclopedia of Early Christianity* (2nd ed.; New York: Garland, 1997) 134–36. Some scholars have found the relative silence understandable, for several more fundamental facets of Christian belief had to be confronted before Mariology could claim attention. Others have called the silence normal, for it goes back to Mary's role in the early Church: not to command but to love and pray. Otto Faller and others have found Mary's assumption there in germ: in the patristic idea of recapitulation, the Eve-Mary parallelism, the analogy associating the New Eve with the New Adam in a total triumph over Satan, and the twin privileges of divine maternity and deathless virginity.

21. John Damascene, *Homily 2 on the Falling Asleep of Mary* 14 (Patrologia graeca 96, 740–41).

22. See my brochure *The Testimony of the Patristic Age concerning Mary's Death* (Woodstock Papers 2; Westminster, Md.: Newman, 1957); this is a slightly revised version of the article that appeared under the same title in *Marian Studies* 8 (1957) 58–99.

23. Ibid. 41.

24. From my homily "The Abiding Meaning of Mary," in *All Lost in Wonder: Sermons on Theology and Life* (Westminster, Md.: Newman, 1960) 149–53, at 151.

25. Ibid. 153.

26. Alois Müller, *Die Einheit Marias und der Kirche* (2nd ed.; Fribourg: University Press, 1955).

27. See my essay *"Theotokos:* The Mother of God," in Edward D. O'Connor, C.S.C., ed., *The Mystery of the Woman* (Notre Dame: University of Notre Dame, 1956) 3–33.

28. Thomas Aquinas, *Summa theologiae* 3, q. 30, a. 1 c.

29. Leo XIII, encyclical *Octobri mense,* September 22, 1981 (*ASS* 24 [1891–92] 195).

30. Augustine, *On Grace and Free Will* 5.10 (Patrologia latina 44, 888).

31. See my homily "Our Lady's Assumption," in my collection *All Lost in Wonder* (n. 24 above) 163–67.

32. Jean Mouroux, *The Meaning of Man* (New York: Sheed & Ward, 1948) 108.

33. For an insightful treatment of this issue, see Patrick J. Bearsley, S.M., "Mary the Perfect Disciple: A Paradigm for Mariology," *Theological Studies* 41 (1980) 461–504. Bearsley begins with the proposition that a paradigm in

a science provides a unity of understanding for that science. Using an analogous notion, he seeks to unite various facets of the mystery of Mary by means of the paradigm of discipleship as found in the Gospels. In the light of this paradigm, he discusses her maternity, relationship to the Church, and virginity.

34. Dogmatic Constitution on the Church, no. 63.

35. In this section, as in my ongoing reflections, I have been particularly inspired and instructed by a remarkable article of Elizabeth A. Johnson, C.S.J., "Mary and the Female Face of God," which as editor I was privileged to publish in *Theological Studies* 50 (1989) 500–526.

36. The five facets that follow stem directly from Johnson's article (n. 35 above), though in summary fashion.

37. Ibid. 520.

38. Ibid. 521.

39. Ibid. 521–22.

40. Ibid. 522.

41. John Paul II, *Redemptor hominis* (Washington, D.C.: United States Catholic Conference, 1979) no. 22.

42. Gerard Manley Hopkins, "The Blessed Virgin Compared to the Air We Breathe," ed. W. H. Gardner and N. H. MacKenzie (4th ed.; London: Oxford University, 1970) 93–97.

43. Johnson, "Mary and the Female Face of God" (n. 35 above) 524.

44. Gerard Manley Hopkins, "The May Magnificat," ed. Gardner and MacKenzie (n. 42 above) 76–78, at 76.

45. Ibid. 77.

46. Johnson, "Mary and the Female Face of God" (n. 35 above) 524.

47. At the edge of this discussion of the female face of God, I think it pertinent to mention a strong article by Elizabeth Achtemeier, "Why God Is Not Mother," *Christianity Today* 37, no. 9 (August 16, 1993) 16–20. This fine biblical scholar, while recognizing centuries-long discrimination against women, while maintaining that all women and men are called equally to discipleship in service to Christ, while finding it only fair for feminists "to ask that the church's language about *human beings* be changed to include them, so that males no longer define humanity," nevertheless insists that there is "a great difference between feminism as fairness and feminism as ideology," that "it is in relation to language *about God* that some feminists are most radically ideological. By attempting to change the biblical language used of the deity, these feminists have in reality exchanged the true God for those deities which are 'no gods,' as Jeremiah put it (2:11)."

48. Raymond E. Brown, S.S., *The Gospel according to John (xiii–xxi)* (Garden City, N.Y.: Doubleday, 1970) 925–26.

49. Vatican II, Dogmatic Constitution on the Church, no. 63.

50. Published simultaneously by the Catholic University Press and the Woodstock College Press in 1957. The extensive documentation for the material that follows can be found in that work, pp. 126–40; no need to clutter these pages therewith.

51. *Paradise Lost* 10, 888 ff.

52. Cyril of Alexandria, *On the First Letter to the Corinthians* 4.4 (Pusey, *In Ioannem* 3, 283).

53. Cyril of Alexandria, *Commentary on John* 2.5 (Pusey, *In Ioannem* 1, 287).

54. This defect was somewhat remedied in 1972 when I tried to convey these insights to a class composed of students of Woodstock College and Union Theological Seminary (some female) in New York City.

55. Karl Barth, *Church Dogmatics: A Selection* (New York: Harper and Row, 1962) 201.

56. Ignace Lepp, *The Psychology of Loving* (Baltimore: Helicon, 1963) 138.

57. Eugene Kennedy, in *Critic*, December 1966–January 1967, 33.

58. See Carl R. Rogers, *On Becoming a Person* (Boston: Houghton Mifflin, 1961) 115–22.

59. Kennedy, *Critic* 34.

60. See Walter J. Burghardt, S.J., "A Half Century of *Theological Studies*: Retrospect and Prospect," *Theological Studies* 50 (1989) 761–85.

61. Ibid. 781–82.

62. Elizabeth A. Johnson, C.S.J., "Feminism and Sharing the Faith: A Catholic Dilemma," Warren Lecture Series in Catholic Studies 29 (Tulsa, Oklahoma: University of Tulsa, 1994) 2. Much of what I say in the following several paragraphs is based on this provocative lecture.

63. Ibid. 4.

64. Ibid. 5.

65. Ibid. 6.

66. Mary Ann Glendon, "A Glimpse of the New Feminism," *America* 175, no. 1 (July 6–13, 1996) 10–15.

67. Ibid. 10.

68. Ibid. 14.

69. Ibid.

70. Margaret O'Brien Steinfels, "Obstacles to the New Feminism: Look before You Leap," *America* 175, no. 1 (July 6–13, 1996) 16–21.

71. Ibid. 19.

72. Ibid.

73. Ibid.

74. Ibid. 20.

75. Ibid.

76. Ibid. 21.

77. See Sidney Callahan, "Mary and the Challenges of the Feminist Movement," *America* 169, no. 20 (December 18–25, 1993) 6–11, 14.

78. Ibid. 6.

79. Ibid. 8.

80. Ibid. 10.

81. Ibid. 11.

82. Ibid. 14.

83. Specifically in my *Preaching the Just Word* (New Haven: Yale University, 1996) 96–98.

84. John Paul II, *Mulieris dignitatem* VII, 26 (tr. *Origins* 18 [1988] 278–79).

85. John Paul II, *Ordinatio sacerdotalis*, no. 4 (tr. from [London] *Tablet*, June 4, 1994, 720–21, at 721).

86. See Francis Sullivan, S.J., "New Claims for the Pope," (London) *Tablet*, June 19, 1994, 767–69. Worth noting here is that in the spring of 1997 a committee appointed by the Catholic Theological Society of America presented a position paper on "Tradition and the Ordination of Women" for consideration

by the CTSA at its June convention in Minneapolis. This eight-page document, arguing from canon 749 #3 of the Code of Canon Law (no doctrine is to be understood as infallibly defined unless this is manifestly established), claimed that church law justifies Catholic theologians in raising the question whether the reasons offered by the Congregation for the Doctrine of the Faith against the ordination of women clearly justify the assertion that the Church has no authority whatsoever to confer priestly ordination on women. After questioning the use of Scripture, tradition, and *Lumen gentium* 25, the committee concluded: Clearly, further study, discussion, and prayer on the part of all the Church's members are necessary if the Church is to be guided by the Spirit in remaining faithful to the authentic tradition of the gospel in our day.

87. Quoted ibid. 768.

88. Ibid. 769.

89. Issued in Latin and Italian; I use the English translation from the Latin by Ladislas Orsy in *Origins* 28, no. 8 (July 16, 1998) 113, 115–16.

90. Ibid., Introduction (*Origins* 113).

91. Ibid., nos. 2–3 (*Origins* 115).

92. Ibid., no. 4 (*Origins* 115).

93. English text in *Origins,* ibid. 116–19.

94. Ibid., no. 11 (*Origins* 118).

95. For a summary see my *Preaching the Just Word* (n. 83 above) 100–106.

96. Avery Dulles, S.J., "Gender and Priesthood: Examining the Teaching," *Origins* 25, no. 45 (May 2, 1996) 778–84.

97. Richard Leonard, *Beloved Daughters: 100 Years of Papal Teaching on Women* (Melbourne: David Lowell, 1991).

98. Ibid. 84.

99. Elisabeth Schüssler Fiorenza, "Feminist Theology as a Critical Theology of Liberation," *Theological Studies* 36 (1975) 605–26, at 611, quoting from Weil's *The Need for Roots* (New York, 1971) 225.

100. Ibid. 611.

101. Raymond E. Brown, S.S., *Biblical Reflections on Crises Facing the Church* (New York: Paulist, 1975) 50–61.

102. *Extraordinary Preaching: Twenty Homilies by Roman Catholic Women,* ed. Roslyn A. Karaban and Deni Mack (San Jose, Calif.: Resource Publications, 1996). The next several paragraphs draw on my Foreword, ibid. ix–xi, and the editors' Preface, ibid. xii–xiv.

103. Ibid., Preface xiii.

104. Ibid.

105. William Shakespeare, *Hamlet,* Act 5, Scene 1, lines 201 ff.: Hamlet's reaction when holding the skull of the king's jester, "a fellow of infinite jest, of most excellent fancy."

11. From the Apostle Paul to John Paul II

1. *Biblical Reflections on Crises Facing the Church* (New York and Paramus, N.J.: Paulist, 1975) ix.

2. Robert Bellah, *Beyond Belief* (New York: Harper & Row, 1970) 40.

3. John A. Coleman, S.J., "The Situation for Modern Faith," *Theological Studies* 39 (1978) 601–32, at 628.

4. New York: Schocken, 1972.

5. Coleman, "Situation" 622.

6. Pastoral Constitution on the Church in the Modern World, no. 36. In this connection the council specifically deplored "certain habits of mind, sometimes found too among Christians, which do not sufficiently attend to the rightful independence of science" (ibid.). The official annotation here suggests strongly that the conciliar text intended to warn against another Galileo scandal.

7. Second Vatican Council, ibid., no. 5.

8. Philip Rieff, *Freud: The Mind of the Moralist* (Garden City, N.Y.: Doubleday Anchor Books, 1961) 391, 390, 65, 361–62.

9. Robert N. Bellah, "Religion and Power in America Today," *Commonweal* 109, no. 21 (December 3, 1982) 650–55, at 652. Given the focus of this chapter, I have not found it feasible to include Bellah's remarks on the ideal of psychological man/woman, who "pushes the logic of economic man one stage further" (651).

10. Dogmatic Constitution on the Church, no. 25.

11. For details of the tradition, see my article "The Authority Crisis in Catholicism: Analysis and Prognosis," in *Hope: Psychiatry's Commitment*, Papers Presented to Leo H. Bartemeier, M.D., on the Occasion of His 75th Birthday, ed. A. W. R. Sipe (New York: Brunner/Mazel, 1970) 203–14, esp. 203–5. See also the insightful article by John Courtney Murray, "Freedom, Authority, Community," *America* 115 (1966) 734–41, a powerful influence on my development in this area.

12. Declaration on Religious Freedom, no. 1.

13. Boethius, *De persona et duabus naturis* 3 (Patrologia Latina [PL] 64, 1345); cf. Thomas Aquinas, *Summa theologiae* 3, q. 16, a. 12, ad 2.

14. Murray, "Freedom" 736.

15. See, e.g., John C. Ford, S.J., "Contraception and the Infallibility of the Ordinary Magisterium," *Theological Studies* 39 (1978) 258–312; and Joseph A. Komonchak, "*Humanae vitae* and Its Reception: Ecclesiological Reflections," ibid. 221–57.

16. Maureen Fiedler, S.L., coordinator of Catholics Speak Out, in a letter to the editors of *Commonweal* 119, no. 19 (November 6, 1992) 45.

17. I am thinking especially of the late revered Philip S. Land, S.J., who died on January 20, 1994, while his volume *Catholic Social Teaching: As I Have Lived, Loathed, and Loved It* (Chicago: Loyola University, 1995) was being prepared for publication. For the feminist strictures on Catholic social teaching in the following paragraphs, see pp. 176–81. Land used "teaching" rather than "thought" in his title because he was "persuaded that *thought* is too fixed, too determined, too eternal. It suggests 'fixed in cement.' It is already there, already thought out, the Church's possession, its doctrine, firmly set and binding, only needing to be taught.... Catholic social teaching, I now believe, consists largely of truths for social action fabricated through reading signs of the times. Alternatively, Catholic social teaching may very well evolve from a people who, suffering some particular situation, work out their social and political truth by allowing their suffering to guide their analysis and their theologizing" (xvii).

18. Ibid. 181.

19. Thomas C. Fox, in a review of *Fighter with a Heart: Writings of Charles Owen Rice*, ed. Charles J. McCollester (Pittsburgh: University of Pittsburgh,

1997) in *National Catholic Reporter* 33, no. 34 (July 18, 1997) 14. Msgr. Rice, 88 as I write, immersed himself for two generations in the struggles of working people not only in Western Pennsylvania but through much of the United States.

20. Vatican II, Dogmatic Constitution on the Church, no. 25.

21. Here I have been significantly helped by canonist Ladislas Orsy, S.J., especially his article "Magisterium: Assent and Dissent," *Theological Studies* 48 (1987) 473–97. In context, Orsy is troubled by the official Church's reluctance (or struggle) to accept evolution as a fact of life, in doctrine and elsewhere. One of many reasons is the instinct to preserve ancient traditions, with change seen as a step toward infidelity. Even in the 1983 Code of Canon Law there are no provisions for a peaceful and ordered development of ecclesiastical laws and structures. See ibid. 473 n. 1.

22. Ibid. 477.

23. Important in this regard is a footnote by Orsy (ibid. 478 n. 11): "This excessive use of theologians marked the preparatory phase of both Vatican Councils. Vatican I: The preparatory commission was composed of five cardinals, four Italians from the Curia and one Bavarian. They were helped by 96 other members and consultors, 61 of them domiciled in Rome. The first schema on Catholic faith was prepared by Johannes Franzelin, S.J., professor at the Gregorian; it was often described as a no doubt well-meant attempt by a teacher to have his textbook canonized by the Council. It underwent radical revision by Joseph Kleutgen, S.J., the theologian of the Bishop of Paderborn. Vatican II: Although the membership of the preparatory commissions was more international, the Roman schools of thought marked strongly the 73 documents prepared for approval, except the one on liturgy.... The point of all this is that the excessive influence of Roman theologians has been resisted by the councils; but when there was no council, their influence was often unhindered."

24. Ibid. 480.

25. Boniface VIII, bull *Unam sanctam* (Denzinger-Schönmetzer, *Enchiridion symbolorum,* 32nd ed. [New York: Herder, 1963] no. 875).

26. Orsy, "Magisterium" 479.

27. Ibid. 482.

28. See ibid. 487–90.

29. Vatican II, Dogmatic Constitution on the Church, no. 8.

30. Orsy, "Magisterium" 490.

31. For details see the section in chapter 2 on the aftermath of Modernism's condemnation.

32. Pius XII, *Humani generis* (Denzinger-Schönmetzer, no. 3886).

33. *Acta apostolicae sedis* 61 (1969) 715; Eng. tr. from *The Pope Speaks* 14 (1969) 202.

34. Brian Daley, S.J., "As I See It: In Quest of Common Ground," *Company* (A Magazine of the American Jesuits) 14, no. 4 (summer 1997) 28–29, at 28. Daley, a respected theologian, was a member of the sponsoring committee.

35. In an article "How Bishops Talk," *America* 175, no. 11 (October 19, 1996) 9–15, Bishop Kenneth E. Untener of Saginaw, Michigan, admired the respectful "tone" of the cardinals' objections, but found that their "quality left much to be desired." His own response to their arguments is incisive, well worth reading. Also insightful, and to me theologically provocative, is Dennis O'Brien's "The Uncommon Ground of Dialogue," *America* 176, no. 12 (April 12, 1997)

12–15; e.g., his conviction that "the dialogue should not aim for doctrinaire closure; rather it should aim to foster and maintain a creative tension that is our best human response to the mystery of Jesus as Lord. Tensions that appear polemic and destructive should be reformulated as *creative,* mutually enforcing, balancing" (15; italics in text).

36. Daley, "As I See It" 28.

37. Ibid. 29. A lengthy response to the critiques (not intended as a detailed refutation) has been offered by Bernardin's successor as head of CCGI, Archbishop Oscar Lipscomb of Mobile, Alabama; text in *Catholic International* 8, no. 8 (August 1997) 367–73. He responds to critiques based on perceptions, as well as alleged implications of the original CCGI document; addresses what some charge the statement failed to say; and discusses at some length Schindler's criticism, with quotations from ecclesial documents on the nature of dialogue in the Church's life.

38. Charles R. Morris, *American Catholic: The Story of the People, Passion and Politics behind America's Largest and Most Influential Church* (New York: Random House, 1997). In an essay adapted from his book, Morris tells "A Tale of Two Dioceses: From Lincoln to Saginaw," *Commonweal* 124, no. 11 (June 6, 1997) 11–18. It is particularly interesting and provocative because it stems from personal visits to both dioceses; and though Morris does "place the conservative and liberal models" of the Church in sharp relief (14), does discover "profound differences between a Saginaw and a Lincoln" (16), his treatment of both is quite nuanced.

39. *Collection: Papers by Bernard Lonergan, S.J.,* ed. F. E. Crowe, S.J. (New York: Herder and Herder, 1967) 266–67. The quotation is taken from chapter 16, "Dimensions of Meaning."

40. "Seamus Heaney: An Interview," *Irish America Magazine,* May/June 1996, 24–30, at 28; emphasis added. I have been inspired by John Evans' article "Strong Enough to Help: Spirituality in Séamus Heaney's Poetry," *New Blackfriars* 78, no. 917/918 (July/August 1997) 327–35; see, e.g., p. 334, Heaney's recent work as "almost a celebration of his new-found confidence in the power of poetry and the arts 'to make space . . . for imagining the marvellous' "; "poetry as imitating 'a possible order beyond itself.' "

41. *Thought* 30 (1955) 351–88.

42. See Philip Gleason, "A Look Back at the Catholic Intellectualism Issue," *U.S. Catholic Historian* 13, no. 1 (winter 1995) 19–37. Gleason's first section is a "schematic outline on how the discussion of Catholic intellectualism has developed over the past four decades" (20).

43. See *U.S. Catholic Historian* 4 (1985).

44. For the complete text, see Walter J. Burghardt, S.J., "Intellectual and Catholic? Or Catholic Intellectual?" *America* 160, no. 17 (May 6, 1989) 420–25.

45. Ibid. 421–22.

46. See Robert A. Brungs, S.J., "Biology and the Future: A Doctrinal Agenda," *Theological Studies* 50 (1989) 698–717, esp. 710–13.

47. Michael J. Buckley, S.J., "Experience and Culture: A Point of Departure for American Atheism," ibid. 443–65, at 459.

48. See chapter 4 above, on the importance of the imagination for the art and craft of preaching.

49. See Jacques Maritain, *The Degrees of Knowledge* (2nd ed.; New York: Scribner, 1938).

50. A reference to Durang's play *Sister Ignatius Tells It All*, a one-sided satire on Catholic parochial-school education.

51. Andrew M. Greeley, "Is There an American Catholic Elite?" *America* 160, no. 17 (May 6, 1989) 426, 428–29.

52. Ibid. 426.

53. Ibid. 429.

54. Ibid. 428.

55. Ibid.

56. Ibid. 429.

57. R. Scott Appleby, "American Culture and Catholicism: Maintaining Faith Identity amidst the Pluralism of Our Times," in *Formation in Faith: A Discussion on Religious Education and Spiritual Growth within a New Generation of Believers,* ed. Francis J. Butler (Washington, D.C.: Foundations and Donors Interested in Catholic Activities, Inc., 1997) 5–10, at 5.

58. Ibid. 6.

59. For details and the quotation, see the informative short article "Young and Conservative" by Willard F. Jabusch, director of the Catholic student center at the University of Chicago, in *America* 177, no. 10 (October 11, 1997) 5–6.

60. Complete text in *Origins* 27, no. 9 (July 31, 1997) 133–48.

61. So Monika K. Hellwig, executive director of the Association of Catholic Colleges and Universities, in an address "Are Catholic Colleges and Universities Addressing Effectively the Religious Formation of Their Students?" *Formation in Faith* (n. 57 above) 19–25, at 21.

62. Title of a popular TV "soap."

12. From Hippocrates to Kevorkian

1. See my article "Towards a Theology of the Health Apostolate," *Hospital Progress,* September 1971, 66–71.

2. Vatican II, Dogmatic Constitution on the Church, no. 4.

3. In *Catholic Mind,* May 1966, 31–32.

4. Jean Mouroux, *The Meaning of Man* (New York, 1948) 108.

5. Vatican II, Dogmatic Constitution on the Church, no. 48.

6. "RX: For Modern Medicine: Some Sympathy Added to Science," *Life,* October 12, 1959.

7. Mario M. Cuomo, "Public Health: Old Truth, New Realities," in Kevin M. Cahill, M.D., ed., *Imminent Peril: Public Health in a Declining Economy* (New York: Twentieth Century Fund, 1991) 123–36, at 126.

8. Ibid. 127–28.

9. Kevin Cahill, M.D., "Introduction," *Imminent Peril* (n. 7 above) 3.

10. Richard Selzer, *Mortal Lessons: Notes on the Art of Surgery* (New York: Simon and Schuster, 1976) 19.

11. Bernie S. Siegel, M.D., *Love, Medicine and Miracles* (New York: Harper & Row, 1988) 66.

12. Ibid. xii; italics mine.

13. Ibid. 66.

14. Ibid. 181.

15. Quoted by William F. Buckley Jr. in a syndicated column I found in the *Stuart News* (Florida) of April 10, 1993, A17. The judge was Edwin Torres.

16. Selzer, *Mortal Lessons* (n. 10 above) 46, 48.

17. See Gonzaga's *News from Nineteen Eye Street,* June 1988, 7.

18. Joan Delaplane, O.P., "That Two Lettered Word," *The Living Pulpit* 1, no. 3 (July–September 1992) 12. The two-lettered word is the "as" in Jesus' "As the Father has loved me, so I have loved you" (Jn 15:9).

19. For examples of "the poor" who cry out for healing, see my "Biblical Justice and 'The Cry of the Poor': Jesuit Medicine and the Third Millennium," in *Caring for the Body, the Mind, and the Soul: The Jesuit Tradition and Medicine,* ed. Mark C. Huey (Washington, D.C.: Georgetown University Medical Center, 1995) 44–54.

20. Robert Coles, "Secular Days, Sacred Moments," *America* 176, no. 1 (January 4–11, 1997) 8.

21. I have this from Siegel, *Love, Medicine and Miracles* (n. 11 above) 2.

22. Quoted by Alain K. Laing, "Hippocrates," *World Book Encyclopedia* 9 (1975) 227.

23. See my "Is Being 'Catholic' Worth Saving?" *Health Progress* 66, no. 7 (September 1985) 107–14; reprinted, with stylistic modifications, in *Georgetown Magazine,* spring 1986, 5–9.

24. *The Collected Poems of Dylan Thomas* (New Directions, 1971) 128.

25. Philip Scharper, "The Health Apostolate: Some Spiritual Dimensions," *Hospital Progress* 52, no. 9 (September 1971) 72–75, at 73–74.

26. *Codex iuris canonici,* can. 207 #1. See the informative discussion of the distinction in *The Code of Canon Law: A Text and Commentary,* ed. James A. Coriden, Thomas J. Green, Donald E. Heintschel (New York and Mahwah, N.J.: Paulist, 1985) 130–34. In the context of Scharper's remarks, see 131: "...the canon adopts the conciliar [i.e., Vatican II] approach to the question of the place of religious in the structure of the Church. Considered in terms of its hierarchical element, those who make a special consecration of their lives do not form a third state between clergy and laity (*LG* 43). Viewed from the nature of the Church as a community of holiness and mission, however, they do have a distinct place (*LG* 44)." In the light of the material from *Lumen gentium,* therefore, Scharper's valid distinction might call for nuancing.

27. Scharper, "The Health Apostolate" 74.

28. Ibid.

29. Charles Krauthammer, "First and Last, Do No Harm," *Time* 147, no. 16 (April 15, 1996) 83. To the 2nd Circuit's assurance that "there should be" no psychological pressure on the elderly and infirm to take drugs to hasten death, Krauthammer responds that "legalization of physician-assisted suicide in Holland has resulted in so much abuse — not just psychological pressure but a shocking number of cases of out-and-out *involuntary* euthanasia, inconvenient and defenseless patients simply put to death without their consent — that last year the Dutch government was forced to change its euthanasia laws" (ibid.). Will America be different?

30. *Washington Post,* January 5, 1997, C7.

31. Ibid.

32. Ibid.

33. Ibid.

34. See my *Preaching the Just Word* (New Haven: Yale University, 1996) chapter 4.

35. One widely publicized case in point was Myrna Lebov, age 52, with multiple sclerosis, pressured by her husband to accept a fatal dose of antidepressants; see the Op-Ed piece by Lucette Lagnado, "Assisted Suicide and Rational Choice," *New York Times,* August 4, 1995, A27.

36. See Richard A. McCormick, "The Consistent Ethic of Life under Challenge: Can Catholic Health Care Offer Leadership?" *Theology Digest* 42, no. 4 (winter 1995) 323–34, specifically 325–29. Useful too is his "Physician-Assisted Suicide: Flight from Compassion," *Christian Century* 108, no. 35 (December 4, 1991) 1133.

37. McCormick, "Consistent Ethic of Life" 326.

38. Joseph A. Califano Jr., *Radical Surgery* (New York Times Books, 1994) 58, quoted by McCormick, "Consistent Ethic of Life" 327.

39. Quoted by Nat Hentoff in an article insightfully titled "Judge-Assisted Suicide," *Washington Post,* April 20, 1996, A23.

40. Peter J. Bernardi, S.J., "The Hidden Engines of the Suicide Rights Movement," *America* 172, no. 16 (May 6, 1995) 14–17, at 16.

41. For a more detailed presentation of a Christian perspective on suffering and dying, see my *Preaching the Just Word* (n. 34 above) 87–93.

42. See Mary Catherine Hilkert, O.P., "Key Religious Symbols: Christ and God," *Theological Studies* 56 (1995) 341–52, at 344 ff.

43. Elizabeth A. Johnson, "Jesus and Salvation," *Proceedings of the Catholic Theological Society of America* 49 (1994) 1–18, at 15.

44. New York: Ballantine Books, 1994; see especially pp. 274–80.

45. Edwin H. Cassem, S.J., M.D., "Stethoscope for Divine Murmurs: Modern Psychiatry and the Jesuits," in *Caring for the Body, the Mind, and the Soul* (n. 19 above) 34–42, at 38–39.

46. Ibid. 39. See John W. O'Malley, *The First Jesuits* (Cambridge, Mass.: Harvard University, 1993), e.g., chapter 5, "Works of Mercy," 165 ff.

47. See Cassem, "Stethoscope for Divine Murmurs" 40.

13. From Life to Life

1. See, e.g., my "Reflections on Aging: Personal and Theological," *New Theology Review* 4, no. 1 (February 1991) 6–16, from which I borrow for some of the following material.

2. See useful articles in Francis V. Tiso, ed., *Aging: Spiritual Perspectives* (Lake Worth, Fla.: Sunday Publications, 1982).

3. See Asher Finkel, "Aging: The Jewish Perspective," ibid. 111–34.

4. Ibid. 124.

5. Walter Kerr, *The Decline of Pleasure* (New York: Simon and Schuster, 1962) 148.

6. See Jose Pereira, "A Christian Theology of Aging," in Tiso, *Aging* (n. 2 above) 135–62.

7. New York: W. W. Norton, 1989. I was first introduced to this book through an insightful article by *Newsweek*'s Kenneth L. Woodward, "Erik Erikson: Teaching Others How to See," *America* 171, no. 4 (August 13–20, 1994) 6–8. Erikson had died three months before, at the age of 92.

8. Woodward, "Erik Erikson" 7.

9. In this section I am borrowing extensively from my article "Aging, Suffering and Dying: A Christian Perspective," *Concilium* 1991/3, 65–71. I am aware that I have dealt with suffering to some extent in chapter 12, when responding to the growing call for assisted suicide; here my treatment is significantly fuller, more broadly conceived.

10. See my homily "In God We Trust," in my collection *Tell the Next Generation: Homilies and Near Homilies* (New York and Ramsey, N.J.: Paulist, 1980) 39–43.

11. R. A. F. MacKenzie, S.J., and Roland E. Murphy, O.Carm., "Job," *The New Jerome Biblical Commentary,* ed. Raymond E. Brown, S.S., Joseph A. Fitzmyer, S.J., and Roland E. Murphy, O.Carm. (Englewood Cliffs, N.J.: Prentice-Hall, 1990) 30:6, p. 467. The *New Jerome Biblical Commentary* article is a revision by Murphy of the *Jerome Biblical Commentary* article on Job by MacKenzie.

12. Quoted from Clare Richards, "The Clash in the Classroom," (London) *Tablet* 248, no. 8076 (May 27, 1995) 668–69, at 668.

13. Brendan Byrne, S.J., "The Letter to the Philippians," *The New Jerome Biblical Commentary* (n. 11 above) 48:17, p. 794.

14. *The Collected Poems of Dylan Thomas* (New Directions, 1971) 128.

15. Methodius, *On the Resurrection* 1.42.3 (Griechische christliche Schriftsteller [GCS] 27, 289).

16. See ibid. 1.41.2–4 (GCS 27, 286–87).

17. Ibid. 1.43.2—1.44.4 (GCS 27, 289–94). See also Methodius' *Symposium* 9.2 (Sources chrétiennes [SC] 95, 270): "God put an end to sin by man's death, lest man become a sinner for all eternity, and, since sin would be living in him, be under eternal condemnation" (tr. Herbert Musurillo, S.J., in Ancient Christian Writers 27, 134–35). I found background for Methodius in the first Christian theologian, Bishop Irenaeus of Lyons, late in the second century, in his masterpiece *Against Heresies* 3.23.6 (SC 34, 392).

18. Gregory of Nyssa, *Large Catechetical Address* 8 (Patrologia graeca [PG] 45, 33).

19. Gregory of Nyssa, *Funeral Oration for Pulcheria* (PG 46, 676–77).

20. John Chrysostom, *Homily 18 on Genesis* 3 (PG 53, 151–52). It is worth recalling that Chrysostom belonged to the Antiochene school of exegesis, exponent of the literal sense of Scripture.

21. Novatian, *On the Trinity* 1.7 (ed. Hans Weyer, *Novatianus De trinitate* [Düsseldorf: Patmos, 1962]) 40.

22. See "Alive, Now and for Ever," in my collection *Let Justice Roll Down Like Waters: Biblical Justice Homilies throughout the Year* (New York and Mahwah, N.J.: Paulist, 1998) 235–37, at 237.

23. Karl Rahner, S.J., *Theological Investigations* 18: *God and Revelation* (New York: Crossroad, 1983) 165–66.

24. See Robert L. Kinast, "Death and Dying," *The New Dictionary of*

Catholic Spirituality, ed. Michael Downey (Collegeville, Minn.: Liturgical, 1993) 252–56.

25. Quoted by Asher Finkel, "Aging: The Jewish Perspective" (n. 3 above) 133.

26. Text in *The Poems of Gerard Manley Hopkins,* 4th ed. by W. H. Gardner and N. H. MacKenzie (New York: Oxford University, 1967/1970) 98.

27. Pierre Teilhard de Chardin, *The Divine Milieu: An Essay on the Interior Life* (Harper Torchbooks; New York: Harper & Row, 1965) 89–90. I have retained the italics and British spellings of the printed version.

14. Epilogue: Grateful Memories

1. See Leon-Joseph Cardinal Suenens, *Memories and Hopes* (Dublin: Veritas, 1972), between pp. 192 and 193.

2. Ibid. 75.

3. Ibid. 76.

4. Ibid. 268.

5. Ibid. 270.

6. I have this from San Francisco Archbishop William Levada's "The Charism of Cardinal Suenens," *Origins* 26, no. 5 (June 20, 1996) 65, 67–73, at 71, a keynote address (May 31, 1996) at a symposium titled "Retrieving Charisms for the 21st Century," sponsored by John Carroll University in Cleveland. The symposium was held in honor of the cardinal; he was expected to attend, but death intervened on May 6. Levada's own tribute contains a number of insights into Suenens' significance.

7. In Peter Hebblethwaite, *Paul VI: The First Modern Pope* (New York: Paulist, 1993) 21.

8. For details see William Henn, O.F.M.Cap., "Yves Congar, O.P. (1904–95)," *America* 173, no. 4 (August 12–19, 1995) 23–25.

9. See Michael O'Carroll, C.S.Sp., "Yves Congar at Ninety," *Doctrine and Life* 44, no. 6 (July/August 1994) 371–72.

10. *Jean Jadot, un prêtre diplomate: 50 ans au service de l'église* (Paris: Duculot, 1992).

11. George G. Higgins, "John Tracy Ellis, R.I.P.: A Well-Ordered Life," *Commonweal* 119, no. 19 (November 6, 1992) 5–7, at 7. I have presumed to use some of Higgins' rhetoric to express my own appreciation of Ellis.

12. Besides my personal acquaintance with Msgr. Higgins, I have profited from an informative article by Jerry Filteau, "U.S. Labor Priest Calls His Life Work a 'Ministry of Presence,' " *Catholic Standard* (Archdiocese of Washington) 44, no. 35 (September 1, 1994) 19.

13. See the exciting biography by Margery Frisbie, *An Alley in Chicago: The Ministry of a City Priest* (Kansas City, Mo.: Sheed & Ward, 1991).

14. Ibid. 290; emphasis in text. On Egan and Alinsky, see Lawrence J. Engel, "The Influence of Saul Alinsky on the Campaign for Human Development," *Theological Studies* 59 (1998) 636–61, at 646 ff.

15. See *Sister Thea Bowman, Shooting Star: Selected Writings and Speeches,* ed. Celestine Cepress, FSPA (Winona, Minn.: Saint Mary's Press, 1993).

16. Ibid. 37.

17. Ibid. 44.

18. Ibid. 117.

19. See Paul Wilkes, "The Education of an Archbishop," *New Yorker,* July 15, 1991, 38–59, and July 22, 1991, 46–65.

20. Quoted in Wilkes' first article, p. 44. "Spirit" is not capitalized in the quotation, but it is surely the Holy Spirit who is meant.

21. Ibid. 53.

22. Ibid.

23. Quoted in Wilkes' second article, p. 64.

24. Ibid. 53.

25. Ibid.

26. Joseph Bernardin, *It Is Christ We Preach* (Boston: St. Paul Editions, 1982) 13.

27. John Hotchkin, "Cardinal Bernardin: A True Person of Hope," *Origins* 26, no. 25 (December 5, 1996) 409–11, at 410–11. This was a homily preached on November 20, 1996, during a memorial Mass for Cardinal Bernardin celebrated at the U.S. bishops' conference headquarters in Washington, D.C. Hotchkin, a priest of the Archdiocese of Chicago, is executive director of the bishops' Secretariat for Ecumenical and Interreligious Affairs. I had the pleasure of doing some preliminary drafting for Bernardin"s interventions at the Roman Synod of 1974.

28. Evan Thomas, *The Man to See: Edward Bennett Williams: Ultimate Insider; Legendary Trial Lawyer* (New York: Simon and Schuster, 1991). Thomas was then the Washington Bureau Chief at *Newsweek.* Worth reading, too, is the sensitive summary, based on Thomas' biography, by George W. Hunt, S.J., in his column "Of Many Things" in *America* 165, no. 17 (November 30, 1991) 402.

29. *The Man to See* 480–81.

30. See "My Body, Given for You," in *To Christ I Look: Homilies at Twilight* (New York and Mahwah, N.J.: Paulist, 1989) 139–41.

31. Theodore M. Hesburgh, C.S.C., with Jerry Reedy, *God, Country, Notre Dame* (New York: Doubleday, 1990) 155.

32. Ibid. 154.

33. Anne Morrow Lindbergh, *Gift from the Sea* (New York: Pantheon, 1955) 50.

34. See Anne Morrow Lindbergh, *The Unicorn and Other Poems* (New York: Pantheon, 1956) 45–47.

35. See Alban Butler, *The Lives of the Saints* 7, rev. Herbert Thurston, S.J., and Donald Attwater (London: Burns, Oates & Washbourne, 1932) 358–64.

36. See Albert Outler, "Vatican II and Protestant Theology in America," in *Vatican II: An Interfaith Appraisal,* ed. John H. Miller, C.S.C. (Notre Dame: University of Notre Dame, 1966) 619–25.

37. *Flannery O'Connor: The Habit of Being,* Letters edited by Sally Fitzgerald (New York: Farrar, Straus and Giroux, 1979) 453.

38. Robert Giroux, in *Flannery O'Connor, The Complete Stories* (New York: Farrar, Straus and Giroux, 1972) xiii.

39. Quoted by Giroux, ibid. xv.

40. Michael O. Garvey, "Back to the Future," *Commonweal* 124, no. 5 (March 14, 1997) 21–23, at 21.

41. See "Teach and Admonish in All Wisdom," in my collection *When Christ*

Meets Christ: Homilies on the Just Word (New York and Mahwah, N.J.: Paulist, 1993) 135–40.

42. Letter from Catherine Benencasa to Pope Gregory XI, tr. in Colman J. Barry, O.S.B., *Readings in Church History* 1: *From Pentecost to the Protestant Revolt* (Westminster, Md.: Newman, 1960) 473.

43. "Teach and Admonish" 139.

44. Alan M. Kriegsman, "Balanchine's Ballerina," *Washington Post,* September 29, 1985, G1, G5, G6. See also my homily "Grow into Your Feathers," in *Lovely in Eyes Not His: Homilies for an Imaging of Christ* (New York and Mahwah, N.J.: Paulist, 1988) 116–21.

45. John Pick, ed., *A Hopkins Reader* (New York: Oxford University, 1953) xii.

46. For details see my *Seasons That Laugh or Weep: Musings on the Human Journey* (New York and Ramsey, N.J.: Paulist, 1983) 53–61.

47. *The Correspondence of Gerard Manley Hopkins and Richard Watson Dixon,* ed. Claude Colleer Abbott (2nd [rev.] impression; New York: Oxford University, 1955) 14.

48. *The Long Loneliness: The Autobiography of Dorothy Day* (New York: Harper, 1952) 149–50.

49. Quoted in William D. Miller, *Dorothy Day: A Biography* (San Francisco: Harper & Row, 1982) 341; emphasis mine.

50. Ibid. 343–44.

51. *The Long Loneliness* 286; emphasis mine.

52. See his mind-opening *Christ and Apollo: The Dimensions of the Literary Imagination* (New York: Sheed and Ward, 1960).

53. See especially Lynch's powerful chapter, "The Catholic Idea," in *The Idea of Catholicism: An Introduction to the Thought and Worship of the Church,* ed. Walter J. Burghardt, S.J., and William F. Lynch, S.J. (Expanded edition; Cleveland: World, 1964) 57–64.

54. Ibid. 62.

55. Kansas City: Sheed & Ward, 1996.

56. Ibid. 142–43.

57. Notre Dame: University of Notre Dame, 1965. See also Nathan A. Scott, Jr., "Theology, Poetics, Psychotherapy — The Field of the Imagination: Some Reflections on the Legacy of William F. Lynch, S.J.," *Logos* 1, no. 1 (1997) 60–77. "Lynch conceived the essence of mental illness to be hopelessness, a sense of entrapment within the impossible.... But, then, what Lynch wants most principally to lay down is that hopelessness is merely a symptom of a deep failure of imagination... 'the gift that envisions what cannot yet be seen, the gift that constantly proposes to itself that the boundaries of the possible are wider than they seem' " (ibid. 73–74; quotation from Lynch, *Images of Hope* 35).

58. *America,* December 25, 1982, 417.

59. For more detailed information on Buechner, his religious background and convictions, his theological works, and the significance of his novels, see Marie-Hélène Davies, *Laughter in a Genevan Gown: The Works of Frederick Buechner 1970–1980* (Grand Rapids: Eerdmans, 1983).

60. New York: Harper & Row, 1977.

61. Ibid. 49–50.

62. For several details on Archbishop Hurley, I have profited from a short

but moving tribute by the bishop of Middlesbrough, John Crowley, "A Long-Distance Runner," (London) *Tablet,* March 15, 1997, 342.

63. Andrew M. Greeley, *White Smoke: A Novel about the Next Papal Conclave* (New York: Tom Doherty Associates, 1996).

64. For a more detailed picture of the Spiritual Life Institute, see the article I published after my initial retreat at Nada Ranch, "Without Contemplation the People Perish," *America* 127, no. 2 (July 22, 1972) 29–32.

65. See my article "Contemplation: A Long Loving Look at the Real," *Church* 5, no. 4 (winter 1989) 14–18.

APPENDIX

Publications of
Walter J. Burghardt, S.J.

Books (Author of)

1. *The Image of God in Man according to Cyril of Alexandria.* Washington, D.C.: Catholic University of America; Woodstock, Md.: Woodstock College, 1957. Pp. xvi + 194.

2. *The Testimony of the Patristic Age concerning Mary's Death.* Woodstock Papers 2. Westminster, Md.: Newman, 1957. Pp. viii + 59.

3. *All Lost in Wonder: Sermons on Theology and Life.* Westminster, Md.: Newman, 1960. Pp. xi + 220.

4. *Saints and Sanctity.* Englewood Cliffs, N.J.: Prentice-Hall, 1965. Pp. xiv + 239.

5. *Tell the Next Generation: Homilies and Near Homilies.* New York: Paulist, 1980. Pp. 225.

6. *Sir, We Would Like to See Jesus: Homilies from a Hilltop.* New York: Paulist, 1982. Pp. 220.

7. *Seasons That Laugh or Weep: Musings on the Human Journey.* New York: Paulist, 1983. Pp. 132. Paperback edition: New York: Paulist, 1984. Pp. 132.

8. *Still Proclaiming Your Wonders: Homilies for the Eighties.* New York: Paulist, 1984. Pp. 246.

9. *Grace on Crutches: Homilies for Fellow Travelers.* New York and Mahwah, N.J.: Paulist, 1986. Pp. 221.

10. *Preaching: The Art and the Craft.* New York and Mahwah, N.J.: Paulist, 1987. Pp. 250.

11. *Lovely in Eyes Not His: Homilies for an Imaging of Christ.* New York and Mahwah, N.J.: Paulist, 1988. Pp. 218.

12. *To Christ I Look: Homilies at Twilight.* New York and Mahwah, N.J.: Paulist, 1989. Pp. 220.

13. *Dare to Be Christ: Homilies for the Nineties.* New York and Mahwah, N.J.: Paulist, 1991. Pp. 214.

14. *When Christ Meets Christ: Homilies on the Just Word.* New York and Mahwah, N.J.: Paulist, 1993. Pp. 241.

15. *Speak the Word with Boldness: Homilies for Risen Christians.* New York and Mahwah, N.J.: Paulist, 1994. Pp. 230.

16. *Love Is a Flame of the Lord: More Homilies on the Just Word.* New York and Mahwah, N.J.: Paulist, 1995. Pp. 176.

17. *Preaching the Just Word.* New Haven: Yale University, 1996. Pp. x + 149.

18. *Let Justice Roll Down Like Waters: Biblical Justice Homilies throughout the Year.* New York and Mahwah, N.J.: Paulist, 1998. Pp. 277.

19. *Christ in Ten Thousand Places: Homilies toward a New Millennium.* New York and Mahwah, N.J.: Paulist, 1999.

20. *Hear the Just Word and Live It.* New York and Mahwah, N.J.: Paulist, 2000.

21. *Long Have I Loved You: A Theologian Reflects on His Church.* Maryknoll, N.Y.: Orbis, 2000.

Books (Editor of)

1. *The Idea of Catholicism: An Introduction to the Thought and Worship of the Church.* Edited with William F. Lynch, S.J. New York: Meridian, 1960. Pp. 479. Expanded edition, paperback: Cleveland and New York: World, 1964. Pp. 518.

2. *Woman: New Dimensions.* New York: Paulist, 1977. Pp. viii + 189.

3. *Religious Freedom: 1965 and 1975: A Symposium on a Historic Document.* Woodstock Studies 1. New York: Paulist, 1977.

4. *Why the Church?* Edited with William G. Thompson, S.J. New York: Paulist, 1977. Pp. ix + 138.

Booklets

1. *Towards Reconciliation.* Washington, D.C.: United States Catholic Conference, 1974.

2. *Seven Hungers of the Human Family.* Washington, D.C.: United States Catholic Conference, 1976.

3. *The Charter of Maryland: 1632, 1965, 1983.* Annapolis, Md.: Maryland Hall of Records, 1983.

4. *The Mass at Georgetown.* Washington, D.C.: Georgetown University, 1988.

5. *Redeemed by the Cross: Lenten Meditations from the Homilies of Walter J. Burghardt, S.J.,* ed. James E. Adams (St. Louis, Mo.: Creative Communications for the Parish, 1992).

Editorships

1946–90

Theological Studies (quarterly, edited from Woodstock, Md., 1940–70; from New York, 1970–74; from Washington, D.C., 1974–91): managing editor, 1946–67; editor in chief, 1967–90.

1957–70

Woodstock Papers (series of brochures written by Woodstock College faculty, published by Newman Press [now Paulist/Newman]): coeditor, 1957–70.

1958–

Ancient Christian Writers (series of translations, formerly coedited with Thomas Comerford Lawler, published by Newman Press [now Paulist/ Newman]): coeditor, 1958–.

1992–

The Living Pulpit (ecumenical quarterly, founded in 1992, theme issues, to help preachers in the preparation of sermons), cofounder and coeditor, 1992–.

Articles

1939

1. "Homer on Park Avenue," *Woodstock Letters* 68 (1939) 114–37.

1940

2. "Did Saint Ignatius of Antioch Know the Fourth Gospel?" *Theological Studies* 1 (1940) 1–26, 130–56.

1944

3. "Cyril of Alexandria on 'Wool and Linen,'" *Traditio* 2 (1944) 484–86.
4. "Studies in Christian Antiquity," *Theological Studies* 5 (1944) 377–83.

1947

5. "Catholic Youth in Oklahoma," *America* 77 (1947) 431–33.

1948

6. "Sources chrétiennes," *Theological Studies* 9 (1948) 250–89.
7. "Reverence and Cultivate God ... Eve ... Earth," *Sons of Xavier Alumnews* (Xavier High School, New York) April 1948; also in *Alumnae* (St. Ignatius Loyola Alumni Association, Cleveland [3, no. 2] First Quarter 1949) 9, 13–14.

1949

8. "Every Christian Mother Is Another Mary," *Jesuit* (Maryland Province) 7 (1948–49) 29–30.
9. "I Have Compassion on the Crowd," *Jesuit* (Maryland Province) 8 (1949–50) 13–14.

1950

10. "Thy Will Be Done," *Jesuit* (Maryland Province) 8, no. 3 (January 1950) 6–7.

11. "On Early Christian Exegesis," *Theological Studies* 11 (1950) 78–116.

12. "Current Patristic Projects," *Theological Studies* 11 (1950) 259–74.

1951

13. "The Catholic Concept of Tradition in the Light of Modern Theological Thought," *Proceedings of the Sixth Annual Convention* (1951), *Catholic Theological Society of America* (New York, 1952) 42–77.

14. "We Had Hoped...," *Jesuit Seminary News* (New York Province) 26 (1951) 3.

1953

15. "The Catholic Concept of Tradition," *Theology Digest* 1 (1953) 81–87. Digest of no. 13 above.

1955

16. "Jesuit Patrologists at Heythrop," *Woodstock Letters* 84 (1955) 319–24.

17. "The Vatican Encyclopedia," *Theological Studies* 16 (1955) 109–19 [with Edmond F. X. Ivers, S.J.].

18. "Mary in Western Patristic Thought," in *Mariology* 1, ed. Juniper B. Carol, O.F.M. (Milwaukee: Bruce, 1955) 109–55.

1956

19. "The Literature of Christian Antiquity: Current Projects," *Theological Studies* 17 (1956) 67–92.

20. "*Theotokos:* The Mother of God," in *The Mystery of the Woman,* ed. Edward D. O'Connor, C.S.C. (Notre Dame: University of Notre Dame, 1956) 3–33.

21. "The Faculty of Christian Judgment," privately printed for Loyola College, Baltimore, Md., 1956; 12 pp.

1957

22. "Mary in Eastern Patristic Thought," in *Mariology* 2, ed. Juniper B. Carol, O.F.M. (Milwaukee: Bruce, 1957) 88–153.

23. "The Testimony of the Patristic Age concerning Mary's Death," *Marian Studies* 8 (1957) 58–99.

24. "The Vision of Peter Canisius," *Catholic Mind* 55 (1957) 49–55.

1958

25. "The Second Edition of the *Lexikon für Theologie und Kirche,*" *Theological Studies* 19 (1958) 572–85.

26. "The Christian Vision of Reality," privately printed by Mercy College, Detroit, Mich., 1958; 8 pp.

1960

27. "The Beloved Physician," *Georgetown Medical Bulletin* 13, no. 3 (February 1960) 174–76.

28. "Evolution, Science and Religion: A Television Symposium on the Theories of Pierre Teilhard de Chardin," *Jubilee,* May 1960, 48.

29. "The Literature of Christian Antiquity: 1955–1959," *Theological Studies* 21 (1960) 62–91.

30. "Jesuit Patrologists at Heythrop," *Woodstock Letters* 89 (1960) 99–107.

31. "Intelligent Christian Womanhood," privately printed by Mercy College, Detroit, Mich., 1960; 14 pp.

1961

32. "Vision for a New Decade," *Marian Studies* 12 (1961) 8–14.

33. "From Classroom to Pulpit: How Preach Dogma?" *Proceedings of the Catholic Homiletic Society, Fourth Annual Convention* (1961) 23–35.

1962

34. "The Image of God in Man: Alexandrian Orientations," *Proceedings of the Sixteenth Annual Convention* (1961), *Catholic Theological Society of America* (New York, 1962) 147–60.

35. "The Mariologist as Ecumenist," *Marian Studies* 13 (1962) 5–12.

36. "Mary and Reunion," *Catholic Mind* 60, no. 1164 (June 1962) 13–18.

37. "The Return of Orthodox Christians: The Council of Florence," in *The General Council: Special Studies in Doctrinal and Historical Background,* ed. William J. McDonald (Washington, D.C.: Catholic University of America, 1962) 69–87.

38. "Catholic Education and Christian Unity," *Bulletin* (Department of Education, Archdiocese of Baltimore) 3, no. 2 (October 1962) 2–6.

39. "Adventure of the Intellect," privately printed by College of New Rochelle, New Rochelle, N.Y., 1962; 12 pp.

40. "Sanctity and Intelligence," *Catholic Mind* 60, no. 1167 (November 1962) 19–22.

41. "X Is for Excellence," privately printed by Xavier High School, New York, 1962; 5 pp.

1963

42. "A Holy Church," *The Way* (London), January 1963, 22–31.

43. "The Literature of Christian Antiquity," *Theological Studies* 24 (1963) 437–63.

44. "The Body of Christ: Patristic Insights," in *The Church as the Body of Christ* (Notre Dame: University of Notre Dame, 1963) 69–101.

1964

45. "The Fathers of the Church: Obsolete or Relevant?" *Proceedings of the Society of Catholic College Teachers of Sacred Doctrine* 10 (1964) 17–35.

46. "Bernard Lonergan: In Appreciation, from a Theologian," *Continuum* 2 (1964) 308–10. In book form in *Spirit as Inquiry: Studies in Honor of Bernard Lonergan, S.J.* (Chicago: Saint Xavier College, 1964) 8–10.

47. "The Intellectual Formation of the Future Priest," *National Catholic Educational Association Bulletin* 1 (August 1964) 58–68. Reprinted: "Today's Seminary for Tomorrow's Priest," *Catholic Mind* 62 (1964) 36–47.

48. "Catholic Education: Quest for Intelligence and Love," privately printed by the Superintendent of Schools, Archdiocese of New York; 4 pp.

49. "Catechetics in the Early Church: Program and Psychology," *Living Light* 1, no. 3 (fall 1964) 100–118.

50. "Mary: Obstacle to Reunion?" in *Ecumenism and Vatican II,* ed. Charles O'Neill, S.J. (Milwaukee: Bruce, 1964) 63–73.

1965

51. "Christian Encounter," *Catholic Mind* 63, no. 1191 (March 1965) 15–22.

52. "Screen and Altar: An Essay in Education," *The Call Board* 34, no. 3 (June 1965) 61–64.

53. "Patristic Studies," in *Theology in Transition: A Bibliographical Evaluation of the Decisive Decade, 1954–1964,* ed. Elmer O'Brien, S.J. (New York: Herder and Herder, 1965) 120–73.

54. "Patristic Thought in an Ecumenical Age," in *The Ancient World and the Modern Mind* (booklet): Cardinal Mooney Lecture Series 1964–65 (Detroit: Sacred Heart Seminary, 1965) 33–50.

1966

55. "Israel: A Light to the Gentiles?" *The Pulpit* 37, no. 2 (February 1966) 52–54.

56. "Make Room for Mary," *Sign* 45, no. 10 (May 1966) 9–12.

57. "Vatican II and Catholic Theology in America," in *Vatican II: An Interfaith Appraisal,* ed. John H. Miller, C.S.C. (Notre Dame: University of Notre Dame, 1966) 626–41.

58. "Patristic Theology in an Ecumenical Age," *Theology Digest* 14, no. 4 (winter 1966) 271–83.

1967

59. Comments on "Implications for Theological Education in Seminaries of the Study of Religion in the University," by E. Thomas Lawson, consultation held in New York City, January 26–27, 1967, *The Study of Religion in College and University and Its Implications for Church and Society* (Department of Higher Education, National Council of Churches, 1967) 87–89.

60. "George of Laodicea," *Encyclopaedia Britannica* 10 (1967 ed.) 217.

61. "George of Cappadocia," *Encyclopaedia Britannica* 10 (1967 ed.) 217.

62. "Jerome, Saint," *Encyclopaedia Britannica* 12 (1967 ed.) 1003–4.

63. "The Meaning of Vatican II," *Perkins School of Theology Journal* (Southern Methodist University, Dallas) 21, no. 3 (spring 1967) 23–33.

64. "Cyril of Alexandria, St.," *New Catholic Encyclopedia* 4 (1967) 571–76.

65. "Fathers of the Church," *New Catholic Encyclopedia* 5 (1967) 853–55.

66. "Najran, Martyrs of," *New Catholic Encyclopedia* 10 (1967) 200.

67. "Patrology," *New Catholic Encyclopedia* 10 (1967) 1112.

68. "Weigel, Gustave," *New Catholic Encyclopedia* 14 (1967) 843–44.

69. "He Lived with Wisdom: Tribute to John Courtney Murray," *America* 117, no. 11 (September 9, 1967) 248–49. Reprinted: *Jesuit Bulletin* (Chicago Province) 32, no. 2 (December 1967) 13–15; *The Jesuits: Year Book of the Society of Jesus, 1968–1969,* 104–6; *Congressional Record,* September 21, 1967, S13395–S13396; *Catholic Review* (Baltimore), August 25, 1967; *Jesuit* (Maryland Province) 33, no. 8 (October 1967) 3–7; *Woodstock Letters* 96, no. 4 (1967) 416–20. Also in *Convergence* (Gustave Weigel Society), Supplement to Vol. 2, no. 3 (August 1967); *Catholic Action Studies* (University of Dayton) no. 234 (September 1967).

70. "The Future of Theology," *Guide* (Paulist Institute for Religious Research) no. 220 (August–September 1967) 3–6.

71. "The Import of Ecumenical Developments for Theological Education–A Roman Catholic View," *Theological Education* 3, no. 2 (winter 1967) 298–307.

1968

72. "The Place of Mary in Today's Church," *Catholic Mind* 66, no. 1220 (February 1968) 27–31. Also in (Baltimore) *Catholic Review,* December 8, 1967, A-11.

73. "Constitution on Divine Revelation: Chapter II," *The Bible Today,* no. 35 (March 1968) 2426–32.

74. "A Jesuit Valentine to Films," *Variety,* March 13, 1968, 21. Reprinted: "To Films, with Love" [= original title] in *Catholic Mind* 66, no. 1223 (May 1968) 6–7; *Films 1967* (National Catholic Office for Motion Pictures), 1968, 91–92.

75. "Unity through Ecstasy: A Tribute to John Courtney Murray," *Dominicana* 53, no. 1 (spring 1968) 2–5. Reprinted: *Catholic Mind* 66, no. 1224 (June 1968) 29–31.

76. "Towards a Theology of Secularity: Greek Patristic Intimations of a World-Come-of-Age," *Alumni Bulletin of Bangor Theological Seminary* 43, no. 2 (April 1968) 1–11.

77. "The Trace of Man: 1634–1968" and "To Live the Truth in Love," privately printed by Loyola College, Baltimore, Md., 1968. Reprint of "To Live . . . ": *Koinonia Magazine* (Baltimore) 10, no. 1 (fall 1969) 2–4.

78. "Mary's Meaning Today," *Marriage* 50, no. 8 (August 1968) 33–35.

79. "Towards an American Theology," *American Ecclesiastical Review* 159 (1968) 181–87. Also in *Proceedings of the Twenty-third Annual Convention, Catholic Theological Society of America* (Yonkers, N.Y.: St. Joseph's Seminary, 1969) 20–27.

80. "Freedom and Authority in Jesuit Education," *Jesuit Educational Quarterly* 31, no. 1 (June 1968) 3–11. Reprinted: "Freedom and Authority in Education," *Theology Digest* 16, no. 4 (winter 1968) 310–16.

81. "Man for Others: Reflections on Gustave Weigel," *Woodstock Letters* 97 (1968) 604–7.

1969

82. "The Authority-Freedom Issue: Destructive or Creative?" *Spiritual Life* 15 (1969) 228–40.

83. "From Certainty to Understanding: The Exciting Pilgrimage of Contemporary Catholicism," *Catholic Mind* 67, no. 1234 (June 1969) 13–27.

84. "To Live the Truth in Love," privately printed by Mount Saint Agnes College, Baltimore, Md., 1969; 11 pp.

1970

85. "What Is Woman?" in *The Evolving Role of Women in the Modern World of Work,* ed. Francis X. Quinn, S.J. (Philadelphia: Temple University School of Business Administration, 1970) 4–29.

86. "The Church and Community Responsibility," in *Developing Community Responsibility,* ed. Francis X. Quinn, S.J. (Philadelphia: Temple University School of Business Administration, 1970) 18–36. Discussion: 35–57.

87. "Toward a Theology of the Press," in *Resource Papers and Consensus Paper of the Bishops-Editors Conference,* Bergamo Center, Dayton, Ohio, December 3, 4, 5, 1969 (New York: Catholic Press Association, 1970) 7–14. Also in *Advocate* (Archdiocese of Newark), Topic, April 1970, 2–3.

88. "Do We Deserve Peace?" *Catholic Mind* 68, no. 1241 (March 1970) 28–31.

89. "Christ Our Unity," *Theology Digest* 18, no. 4 (winter 1970) 354–64.

90. "Jewish-Christian Dialogue: Early Church versus Contemporary Christianity," in *The Dynamic in Christian Thought* (Villanova University Symposium 1; Villanova, Pa.: Villanova University, 1970) 186–207.

91. "The Authority Crisis in Catholicism: Analysis and Prognosis," in *Hope: Psychiatry's Commitment* [Papers presented to Leo H. Bartemeier, M.D., for his 75th birthday], ed. A. W. R. Sipe (New York: Brunner/Mazel, 1970) 203–14.

92. "ERGON KYRIAKON: Johannes Quasten as Teacher, Scholar, and Friend," in *Kyriakon: Festschrift Johannes Quasten* 2, ed. Patrick Granfield and Josef A. Jungmann (Münster: Aschendorff, 1970) 915–16.

93. "Apostolic Succession: Notes on the Early Patristic Era," in *Lutherans and Catholics in Dialogue* 4: *Eucharist and Ministry* (Washington, D.C., and New York: U.S. Catholic Conference and U.S.A. National Committee of the Lutheran World Federation, 1970) 173–77.

1971

94. "Towards a Theology of the Health Apostolate," *Hospital Progress* 52, no. 9 (September 1971) 66–71. Reprinted in *The Mission of Healing,* ed. Kevin D. O'Rourke, O.P. (St. Louis, Mo.: Catholic Hospital Association, 1974) 11–21.

95. "The Risk and the Joy," privately printed for Woodstock College, New York, 1971; 13 pp.

96. "Church Structure: A Theologian Reflects on History," *Proceedings of the Twenty-third Annual Convention, Canon Law Society of America,* Atlanta, Ga., October 11–14, 1971 (Canon Law Society of America, 1971) 11–22.

1972

97. "Religion of the Seventies," *Desert Call* (Spiritual Life Institute of America) 7, no. 1 (winter 1972) 3–7.

98. "Joy: New Testament and New Christian," *Catholic Mind* 70, no. 1260 (February 1972) 28–33. Reprinted: *Marriage* 54, no. 6 (June 1972) 64–69, under title "Shout at the Stars, Make Faces at the Moon!"

99. "Literature of Christian Antiquity: 1967–1971," *Theological Studies* 33 (1972) 253–84.

100. Introduction and response to Cardinal Leo Jozef Suenens' address "Toward Tomorrow's Church," John Courtney Murray Forum, New York City, *Catholic Mind* 70, no. 1264 (June 1972) 11–12, 24.

101. "Without Contemplation the People Perish," *America* 127, no. 2 (July 22, 1972) 29–32.

102. "Reconstructing the Social Order: Truth, Justice, Love–and Freedom," *Review of Social Economy* 30, no. 2, Special Issue (August 1972) 200–206.

103. "The Church and Community Responsibility," *Review of Social Economy* 30, no. 2, Special Issue (August 1972) 220–31.

104. "The Risk and the Joy," *Catholic Mind* 70, no. 1265 (September 1972) 37–42. [Cf. private printing, 1971.] Reprinted in part: "The Risk of Joy," *Emmanuel* 78, no. 11 (November 1972) 473–75.

105. "The X-Factor," privately printed by Xavier High School, New York, 1972.

1973

106. "They Recognized Him . . . ," *Emmanuel* 79, no. 1 (January 1973) 12–15.

107. "Theology: The Search for God and Man," *Theological Education* 9, no. 2 (winter 1973) 83–88.

108. "The Life and Death Question," *America* 128, no. 15 (April 21, 1973) 366–67. Reprinted as " 'I Do': A Christian Approach to Death," in *Preaching about Death,* ed. Alton M. Motter (Philadelphia: Fortress, 1975) 12–15.

109. "Crossing the Credibility Gap," *Origins* (NC Documentary Service) 3, no. 6 (July 5, 1973) 89–95.

110. "Christian Unity Today," *Christian Community* 2, no. 3 (November–December 1973) 4–6, 18–19.

111. "Is Anyone Listening, Does Anyone Care?" *Hospital Progress* 54, no. 9 (September 1973) 74–79, 92. Reprinted: *Origins* (NC Documentary Service) 3, no. 6 (July 5, 1973) 89–95; *Compassion* (Province of St. Paul of the Cross Social Concerns Bulletin) 2, no. 6 (December 1973) 2–8; *The Mission of Healing,* ed. Kevin D. O'Rourke, O.P. (St. Louis, Mo.: Catholic Hospital Association, 1974) 107–18.

112. "American Church and American Theology: Response to an Identity Crisis," *Proceedings of the Twenty-eighth Annual Convention, Catho-*

lic Theological Society of America (Bronx, N.Y.: Manhattan College, 1973) 1–14.

1974

113. "Eschaton and Resurrection: Patristic Insights," in *The Eschaton: A Community of Love* (Villanova University Symposium 5; Villanova, Pa.: Villanova University, 1974) 203–29.

114. "Jerome, Saint," *New Encyclopaedia Britannica: Micropaedia* 10 (15th ed.) (1974) 137–38.

115. "What Is a Priest?" *The Way* (London), Supplement 23 (fall 1974) 55–67.

116. "A Changing Church?" *Jesuit* (New York Province edition) 49, no. 4 (winter 1974) 6–8. Also in Wisconsin, New England, Maryland, and California editions. Reprinted: *Catholic Trustee* (Willowdale, Ont.) 15, no. 4 (December 1975) 11–14.

117. "Come, Lord Jesus!" *Marriage and Family Living* 56, no. 12 (December 1974) 3–5.

118. "A Theologian's Challenge to Liturgy," *Theological Studies* 35 (1974) 233–48.

119. "Towards a Theology of Pastoral Care," in *Pastoral Care of the Sick: A Practical Guide for the Catholic Chaplain in Health Care Facilities*, ed. National Association of Catholic Chaplains (Washington, D.C.: United States Catholic Conference, 1974) 1–8.

1975

120. "Church Structures in Historical Development: Early Patristic Era," in *Evangelium–Welt–Kirche:* Schluss-Bericht und Referate der römisch-katholisch/evangelisch-lutherischen Studienkommission "Das Evangelium und die Kirche," 1967–1971, ed. Harding Meyer (Frankfurt am Main: Lembeck, 1975) 213–61.

121. "Roman Catholic Church," *World Book Encyclopedia* 16 (1975) 375–79.

122. "Look, Love, Laugh," *Georgetown Today,* July 1975, 4–5.

123. "An Interview with Fr. Walter Burghardt, SJ," *Desert Call* 10, no. 3 (late summer 1975) 12–16.

124. "Why I Am a Jesuit," *Jesuit* (New York Province edition) 50, no. 3 (autumn 1975) 1–3. Also in Wisconsin, New England, Maryland, and California editions.

125. "Ministry as Reconciliation," *Origins* 5, no. 15 (October 2, 1975) 235–40. Reprinted: *Catholic Trustee* (Willowdale, Ont.) 15, no. 4 (December 1975) 11–14.

1976

126. "Lift Up Your Hearts," *Catholic Mind* 74, no. 1301 (March 1976) 19–25.

127. "Contemplation: A Long Loving Look at the Real," in *Contemplation: Selections from the 1975 Conference of the National Federation of Spiritual Directors* (Camarillo, Calif.: NFSD, 1976) 7–12.

128. "To Look, to Love, to Laugh," *Alive* (Family Magazine of the Diocese of Phoenix) 5, no. 8 (July 1976) 4–5.

129. "Literature of Christian Antiquity: 1971–1975," *Theological Studies* 37 (1976) 425–55.

130. "Critical Reflections," in *Religious Freedom: 1965 and 1975. A Symposium on a Historic Document,* ed. Walter J. Burghardt, S.J. (Woodstock Studies 1; New York: Paulist, 1976) 69–72.

131. "Freedom 1976: Through Love Be Servants of One Another," *Catholic Mind* 74, no. 1308 (December 1976) 4–8.

1977

132. "Look, Love, Laugh," Commencement Address, St. Joseph's College, Philadelphia, May 14, 1977, *Congressional Record,* May 26, 1977, H5173–H5174.

133. "Alive at 125," Convocation Address, 125th Anniversary, Loyola College, Baltimore, September 15, 1977, privately printed by Waverly Press, Baltimore.

134. "Stone the Theologian! The Role of Theology in Today's Church," *Catholic Mind* 75, no. 1315 (September 1977) 42–50.

135. "*Corpus christianorum:* The Greek Series," *Theological Studies* 38 (1977) 763–67.

136. English translation, "Human Development and Christian Salvation" (International Theological Commission), *Origins* 7, no. 20 (November 3, 1977) 305–13.

137. "Response to Rosemary Ruether," in *Auschwitz: Beginning of a New Era? Reflections on the Holocaust,* ed. Eva Fleischner (New York: KTAV, 1977) 93–95.

1978

138. "The Word Made Flesh Today," *New Catholic World* 221, no. 1323 (May/June 1978) 116–25.

139. "Look, Love, Laugh" (Baccalaureate Homily, Saint Mary's College, Notre Dame), *Courier* (publication of Alumnae Association of Saint Mary's College), autumn 1978, 9–12.

140. "Free Like God: Recapturing an Ancient Anthropology," *Theology Digest* 26, no. 4 (winter 1978) 343–64. (This paper was the Annual William Rossner Lecture delivered on September 26, 1978, at Rockhurst College, Kansas City, Mo.)

1979

141. "How Absurd of God," *Catholic Mind* 77, no. 1330 (February 1979) 4–6.

142. "Historical Theology," *New Catholic Encyclopedia* 17 (1979) 262–63.

143. "Academe and Arena: The Tension between Theology and Ministry" (published privately in booklet form by the Athenaeum of Ohio, Norwood, Ohio, 1979; 25 pp.). Reprinted: *Catholic Mind* 78, no. 1344 (June 1980) 10–22.

144. "Primitive Montanism: Why Condemned?" in *From Faith to Faith: Essays in Honor of Donald G. Miller on His Seventieth Birthday,* ed. Dikran Y. Hadidian (Pittsburgh Theological Monograph Series 31; Pittsburgh: Pickwick, 1979) 339–56.

145. "Pope John XXIII," in Umberto Romano, *Great Men* (New York: Dial, 1979) 60.

1980

146. "Who Cares? The Christian Mission to the Sick," *Linacre Quarterly* (A Journal of the Philosophy and Ethics of Medical Practice) 47, no. 2 (May 1980) 133–41.

147. "Literature of Christian Antiquity: 1975–1979," *Theological Studies* 41 (1980) 151–80.

148. "Preaching the Just Word," in *Liturgy and Social Justice,* ed. Mark Searle (Collegeville, Minn.: Liturgical, 1980) 36–52, 91–94.

1981

149. "This World Desperately Needs Theologians," *Catholic Mind* 79, no. 1351 (March 1981) 33–41.

150. "What Is a Priest?" in *The Sacraments: Readings in Contemporary Sacramental Theology,* ed. Michael J. Taylor, S.J. (New York: Alba, 1981) 157–70. Cf. no. 115 above.

151. "Let Go of Yesterday: The Puzzle of Passion Sunday," *Denver Catholic Register* 57, no. 24 (April 8, 1981). Reprinted from *Tell the Next Generation: Homilies and Near Homilies* (see Books above, no. 5).

152. "For Your Lenten Penance, Listen," *Congressional Record* 127, no. 62 (April 28, 1981) E1878–E1879.

153. "Models of Church, Models of Health Apostolate," *Hospital Progress* 62, no. 5 (May 1981) 35–42.

154. "Do We Deserve Peace?" in *The Twentieth Century Pulpit* 2, ed. James W. Cox (Nashville: Abingdon, 1981) 20–25. Cf. no. 88 above.

155. "Life or Death? Knowledge, Justice and Faith," *Vital Speeches of the Day* 47, no. 19 (July 15, 1981) 578–80.

156. "Blessed Are the Peacemakers," Memorial Mass for His Excellency Mohamed Anwar el-Sadat 1918–1981, *Catholic Standard* (Archdiocese of Washington) 31, no. 42 (October 22, 1981) 11.

1982

157. "Preaching for Everyday Justice," *National Catholic Reporter* 18, no. 11 (January 15, 1982) 9, 11 [most of chapter "Preaching the Just Word" in *Liturgy and Social Justice,* no. 148 above].

158. Evaluation of four books in "Religious Book Week: Critics' Choices," *Commonweal* 109, no. 4 (February 26, 1982) 122.

1983

159. "The Health Apostolate: Service, Understanding, Wonder," *Hospital Progress* 64, no. 2 (February 1983) 30–36.

160. "On Service, Understanding, and Wonder," *Catholic Digest,* July 1983, 18–26. Condensed from *Hospital Progress* article, no. 159 above.

161. "From Study to Proclamation," in *A New Look at Preaching,* ed. John Burke, O.P. (Good News Studies 7; Wilmington, Del.: Michael Glazier, 1983) 25–42.

162. "On Leaving the Asylum," *Georgetown Magazine* 15, no. 3 (July–August 1983) 7–10 [Baccalaureate Homily, Georgetown University, May 29, 1983].

163. "The Word: Forming the Preacher," *Proceedings of the National Federation of Priests' Councils* (Chicago: NFPC, 1983) 12 Pp. [no consecutive pagination in the volume].

1984

164. "He Can Deal Gently....The Catholic Priest '23 to '83," *The Serran,* March 1984, 3–4, 12. Also printed privately: Baltimore: Serra Club, 1983; 7 pp.

165. "Speaking of Good Friday and Good Samaritans," IMA-GROUP 3, no. 15 (n.d. [1984]) 6–14.

166. "Literature of Christian Antiquity: 1979–1983," *Theological Studies* 45 (1984) 275–306.

1985

167. "Is Being 'Catholic' Worth Saving?" *Health Progress* 66, no. 7 (September 1985) 107–14. Reprinted, with stylistic modifications: *Georgetown Magazine,* spring 1986, 5–9.

168. "Grazie, Signore!" *Chronicle* (Georgetown University) 1, Special Issue 2 (August 1985) 1–4 [Baccalaureate Homily, Main Campus Commencement, Georgetown University, May 29, 1985].

169. Interview, "Burghardt's 'Musings on the Human Journey,'" *Our Sunday Visitor* 74, no. 6 (June 9, 1985) 8–9.

170. Preface to reissue (1985) of John Courtney Murray, S.J., *We Hold These Truths: Catholic Reflections on the American Proposition* (Kansas City, Mo.: Sheed and Ward [1985] iii–vi).

171. "The Fine Art of Homiletics: An Interview with Father Walter Burghardt, S.J.," by Mitch Finley, *Priest* 41, no. 7–8 (July–August 1985) 31–32.

172. "The American Culture: Contemporary Climate for Preparing Future Ministers," *Journal* [of the National Federation of Spiritual Directors] 13, no. 1 (October 1985).

173. "Love Never Ends?" Homily reproduced in *Marriage Homilies,* ed. Liam Swords (New York and Mahwah, N.J.: Paulist, 1985) 16–19, from *Grace on Crutches* (see Books above) 175–78.

174. "Who Chilled the Beaujolais?" [on John Courtney Murray, S.J.] *America* 153, no. 16 (November 30, 1985) 360–63.

1986

175. "Is Being 'Catholic' Worth Saving?" *Georgetown Magazine,* spring 1986, 5–9 [adaptation of no. 167 above].

176. "The Cost of Discipleship: The Chaplain as Suffering Servant," *Special Publications, National Association of Catholic Chaplains* 2, no. 1 (May 1986) 1–16.

177. "Jesuit Education: Fact or Fancy?" *Ye Domesday Booke* [Georgetown University Graduating Class Annual] 72 (1986) 164–65.

178. "Love of Learning, Desire for God," *Portsmouth Newsletter,* summer 1986, 2–3 (Commencement Address, Portsmouth Abbey School).

179. "If Your Faith Is Alive," *Sooner Catholic* [newspaper of Archdiocese of Oklahoma City], July 27, 1986 [reprinted from *Grace on Crutches* (see Books above) 73–78].

180. Reflection on "A Jesuit Valentine to Films" (no. 74 above) by Clifford Stevens, "Exegesis of a Rare Piece of Theological Artistry," *Pastoral Life* 35, no. 7 (July–August 1986) 12–15.

181. Interview with Walter J. Burghardt, S.J., by John Burke, O.P., "Theologians Relate Theology to Preaching; Urge Reflecting on God and Life," *Good News Letter,* no. 52 (Michaelmas 1986) 1–2, at 2.

182. "From Study to Proclamation," *Military Chaplains' Review* [Preaching] 15, no. 1 (winter 1986) 76–88.

1987

183. "Roman Catholic Church," *World Book Encyclopedia* 16 (1987 ed.) 374–81 [update of no. 121 above].

184. "Godhead Here in Hiding: Eucharist and University," *Georgetown Magazine,* spring 1987, 2–19.

185. "Homily: Middleman for Christ," *Proceedings of the Forty-Second Annual Convention, The Catholic Theological Society of America* 42 (1987) 206–9 [delivered at Old St. Joseph's Church, Philadelphia, June 11, 1987].

186. "The Face of Theology 1986," *Philosophy and Theology* (Marquette University) 2, no. 1 (fall 1987) 3–19.

187. "Warning: God's Been Known to Speak through a Jackass," *U.S. Catholic* 52, no. 9 (September 1987) 13–15 [reprinted from *Preaching: The Art and the Craft* (see Books above) 45–48].

188. "The Catholic Pulpit: One Preacher's Experience," *The Christian Ministry* 18, no. 5 (September–October 1987) 10–13.

189. "How Prayer Can Strengthen Your Love for God" (Interview), *U.S. Catholic* 52, no. 12 (December 1987) 6–13. Reprinted: *The Best of* U.S. Catholic *Interviews* (Chicago: Claretian Publications, 1994) 4–8.

1988

190. "The State of Preaching in Our Catholic Parishes" (Interview by Mitch Finley), *Our Sunday Visitor* 76, no. 44 (February 28, 1988) 7, 15.

191. "Praying Better: A Theologian Talks about His Own Spiritual Life," *Catholic Digest,* March 1988, 52–57 [digest of no. 189 above].

192. "A Rising Tide of Materialism?" *Hoya* (Georgetown University), March 25, 1988, 4.

193. "How to Get the Most Out of a So-So Sermon" (Interview), *U.S. Catholic* 53, no. 6 (June 1988) 33–38.

194. "Fat Cats or Suffering Servants? Georgetown University and the Faith That Does Justice," in *Splendor and Wonder: Jesuit Character, Georgetown Spirit, and Liberal Education,* ed. William J. O'Brien (Washington, D.C.: Georgetown University, 1988) 39–58.

195. "Preaching: Blood, Sweat and Fears" (Interview by Kenneth Guentert), *Modern Liturgy* 15, no. 7 (October 1988) 10–13.

1989

196. "Intellectual and Catholic? Or Catholic Intellectual?" *America* 160, no. 17 (May 6, 1989) 420–25.

197. "Marrying Catholicism to Scholarship: 5 Suggestions, 3 Obstacles and Several Tidy Turns of Phrase," *In Trust* 1, no. 2 (autumn 1989) 24–25 [reprint of section of no. 196 above].

198. "Contemplation: A Long Loving Look at the Real," *Church* 5, no. 4 (winter 1989) 14–18.

199. "Saturday Night Live, Sunday Morning Deadly?" *Homiletic* 14, no. 2 (winter 1989) 1–4.

200. "A Half Century of *Theological Studies:* Retrospect and Prospect," *Theological Studies* 50 (1989) 761–85.

1990

201. "Contemplation: A Long Loving Look at What's Real," *Praying,* no. 35 (March–April 1990) 10–11, 24–26 [reprint of no. 198 above].

202. "The Role of the Scholar in the Catholic Church," in *Moral Theology: Challenges for the Future. Essays in Honor of Richard A. McCormick,* ed. Charles E. Curran (New York and Mahwah, N.J.: Paulist, 1990) 15–31.

203. "Theology and the Pulpit: A Priestly Problem for the Nineties," in *Priesthood: Approaching the Third Millennium. Essays Celebrating the Fiftieth Anniversary of Mary Immaculate Seminary* (Northampton, Pa.: Mary Immaculate Seminary, 1990) 23–36.

204. "Sing to the Lord a New Song," *GIA Quarterly* 2, no. 1 (fall 1990) 16–17, 44.

205. "Isaiah 60:1–7: From Gloom to Glory," *Interpretation* 44, no. 4 (October 1990) 396–400.

206. "A Rising Tide of Materialism or a Surging Wave of Service?" *Presence* [Magazine of Loyola College, Baltimore, Md.] 1990, 20–22.

207. "Preaching as Art and Craft," in *The New Dictionary of Sacramental Worship,* ed. Peter E. Fink, S.J. (Collegeville, Minn.: Liturgical, 1990) 967–75.

1991

208. "Reflections on Aging: Personal and Theological," *New Theology Review* 4, no. 1 (February 1991) 6–16.

209. "Preaching the Just Word: Problem, Preacher, Project," *Modern Liturgy* 13, no. 2 (March 1991) 8–10.

210. "Crisis, Cross, Confidence: A Priest for *This* Season," *Emmanuel* 97, no. 2 (March 1991) 66–73, 110–11.

211. "Wedding Three Facets of Justice," *Origins* 20, no. 41 (March 21, 1991) 678–80.

212. "Aging, Suffering and Dying: A Christian Perspective," *Concilium* 1991/3, 65–71.

213. "The Richness of a Resource," in *A Spirituality for Contemporary Life: The Jesuit Heritage Today,* ed. David L. Fleming, S.J. (St. Louis: Review for Religious, 1991) 1–20.

214. "The Call of the Prophet: Scripture, the Church's Tradition, and the Signs of the Times," *Proceedings, 23rd Annual Convention, National Federation of Priests' Councils* (Chicago: NFPC, 1991) 9–19. Reprinted: *Horizon: Journal of the National Religious Vocation Conference* 17, no. 1 (fall 1991) 1–9.

215. "Commencement 1991" (excerpts from commencement address at St. Peter's College, Jersey City, N.J.), *Saint Peter's: The College Magazine* 11, no. 1 (fall 1991) 5–6.

216. "Ignatius of Loyola and the Mother of Jesus" (Homily for 500th anniversary of birth of Ignatius), *Marian Library Newsletter* (University of Dayton) new series no. 23 (winter 1991–92) 1–2, 6–7.

217. "The Journalist as Proclaimer of Social Justice," *Origins* 21, no. 23 (November 14, 1991) 370–72.

218. "A Kind of Loving, for Me: Baccalaureate Sermon for a Public High School," in *Best Sermons,* ed. James W. Cox (San Francisco: Harper, 1991) 140–46 [reprinted from *When Christ Meets Christ* (see Books above) 219–24].

219. Foreword to Patrick W. Collins, *Gustave Weigel, S.J.: A Pioneer of Reform* (Collegeville, Minn.: Liturgical, 1991) 5–6.

220. "A Faith That Does Justice: Challenge of the Nineties to the Christian Community," *Warren Lecture Series in Catholic Studies* 18 (Tulsa: University of Tulsa, 1991); 11 pp.

1992

221. "Threats to Hope/Gospel of Hope," *Living Pulpit* 1, no. 1 (January–March 1992) 6–7.

222. "The Homilies You Hear Could Change the World" (Interview by Tamar Mehuron), *Salt* 12, no. 1 (January 1992) 6–12.

223. "The Spiritual Exercises as a Foundation for Educational Ministry," *Review for Religious* 51, no. 2 (March–April 1992) 166–81.

224. "Physician, Heal Your Nation!" (Commencement Homily, Georgetown University School of Medicine), *Georgetown Medical Bulletin* 44, no. 2 (summer/autumn 1992) 10–11, 49.

225. "Jesuit Education and the Faith That Does Justice," in *Faith, Discovery, Service: Perspectives on Jesuit Education,* ed. Francis M. Lazarus (Milwaukee: Marquette University, 1992) 1–22.

226. "Vatican II's *Declaration on Religious Freedom:* The Contribution of the Church in the United States," in *The American Catholic Heritage: Reflections on the Growth and Influence of the Catholic Church in the United States* (Rome: Pontifical North American College, 1992) 7–26. (Hard cover and paperback.)

1993

227. Preface to *In the Company of Preachers,* by the Faculty of Aquinas Institute of Theology (Collegeville, Minn.: Liturgical, 1993) vii–ix.

228. "Spirituality," in *The Church in the Nineties: Its Legacy, Its Future,* ed. Pierre M. Hegy (Collegeville, Minn.: Liturgical, 1993) 267–68.

229. Foreword to *A New Introduction to the* Spiritual Exercises *of St. Ignatius* (Collegeville, Minn.: Liturgical, 1993) v–vii.

230. "Aloysius Gonzaga: Role Model for Today's Young?" in *Aloysius,* ed. Clifford Stevens and William Hart McNichols (Huntington, Ind.: Our Sunday Visitor, 1993) 23–35.

231. "To Marry Is to Laugh" (Interview by Mitch Finley), *Catholic Twin Circle* 29, no. 26 (June 27, 1993) 4–5.

1994

232. "Alive! In Lent?" *Modern Liturgy* 21, no. 1 (February 1994) 12–14.

233. "A Brother Whom I Have Pardoned," *Living Pulpit* 3, no. 2 (April–June 1994) 10–11.

234. "Because *We* Are Catholic," *U.S. Catholic* 59, no. 5 (May 1994) 37–39.

235. "Conflict: Lessons from Paul and Matthew," *Living Pulpit* 3, no. 3 (July–September 1994) 7–9.

236. "Characteristics of Social Justice Spirituality," *Origins* 24, no. 9 (July 21, 1994) 157, 159–64.

237. "Love Heals," *Georgetown Medical Bulletin* 46, no. 1 (summer 1994) 19–20.

238. "Do We Deserve Peace?," in *A Chorus of Witnesses: Model Sermons for Today's Preacher,* ed. Thomas G. Long and Cornelius Plantinga Jr. (Grand Rapids: Eerdmans, 1994) 212–17 [reprinted from *Tell the Next Generation* (see Books above) 181–85].

239. "Without Contemplation the People Perish," in *A Guide to Retreat for All God's Shepherds,* ed. Reuben P. Job (Nashville: Abingdon, 1994) 107–10.

240. "A Single Community: God, Humans, Earth," *Living Pulpit* 3, no. 4 (October–December 1994) 4–5.

241. "The Priest as Prophet," *Priest* 50, no. 11 (November 1994) 10–13.

1995

242. "On Turning Eighty: Autobiography in Search of Meaning," *Origins* 24, no. 29 (January 5, 1995) 486–93.

243. "Advice from the Pulpit," *Company* 12, no. 3 (spring 1995) 7–8.

244. "Suffering: Aging and Dying," *Living Pulpit* 4, no. 2 (April–June 1995) 6–7.

245. "Homily," in *Concise Encyclopedia of Preaching,* ed. William H. Willimon and Richard Lischer (Louisville, Ky.: Westminster John Knox, 1995) 257–59.

246. "Spirituality for Urban Ministry," published privately as Patron's Day Lecture (February 1, 1995) by Allentown College of Saint Francis de Sales, Allentown, Pa.

247. "Life–and More Than Enough," *Living Pulpit* 4, no. 3 (July–September 1995) 4–5.

248. "The Christmas Paradox," *Living Pulpit* 4, no. 4 (October–December 1995) 4–5.

249. "Biblical Justice and 'The Cry of the Poor': Jesuit Medicine and the Third Millennium," in *Caring for the Body, the Mind, and the Soul: The Jesuit Tradition and Medicine,* ed. Mark C. Huey (Washington, D.C.: Georgetown University Medical Center, 1995) 44–54.

1996

250. "The Spirit Is Dynamite," *Living Pulpit* 5, no. 1 (January–March 1996) 5.

251. "What Does the Lord Require of You? Do Justice," *Bread* [Bread for the World Newsletter] 8, no. 2 (March 1996) 6.

252. "Preach Politics?" *Living Pulpit* 5, no. 2 (April–June 1996) 4–5.

253. "The Preacher Incites People to Imagine," *Theology Digest* 43, no. 1 (spring 1996) 29–36.

254. "Preaching Christian Hope," *Church* 12, no. 3 (fall 1996) 5–10.

255. Foreword to Mary K. Himens, SSCM, *Images: Sights and Insights* (Champaign, Ill.: Golden Apple, 1996).

256. "Preaching the Just Word: An Interview with Walter J. Burghardt" [by George M. Anderson, S.J.], *America* 175, no. 9 (October 5, 1996) 10–14.

257. "Gospel Joy, Christian Joy," *Living Pulpit* 5, no. 4 (October–December 1996) 38–40.

258. "Preaching: Twenty-five Tips," *Church* 12, no. 4 (winter 1996) 20–23.

259. Foreword to *Extraordinary Preaching: Twenty Homilies by Roman Catholic Women,* ed. Roslyn A. Karaban and Deni Mack (San Jose, Calif.: Resource Publications, 1996) ix–xi.

1997

260. "Aging: A Long Loving Look at the Real," in *Graying Gracefully: Preaching to Older Adults,* ed. William J. Carl, Jr. (Louisville, Ky.: Westminster John Knox, 1997) 19–27.

261. "Aging, Changing, Giving" [sermon], ibid. 27–31.

262. "Assumption of Mary," *Encyclopedia of Early Christianity* (2nd ed.) 1 (1997) 134–36.

263. "Love Heals," *Living Pulpit* 6, no. 2 (April–June 1997) 26.

264. "Will Individualism or Common Good Drive America?" *Post-Standard* (Syracuse), May 31, 1997, A-9 [Extensive excerpts from commencement address, Le Moyne College, Syracuse, N.Y.].

265. " 'Mine and Thine' in the Early Church," *Living Pulpit* 6, no. 3 (July–September 1997) 8–9.

266. "A Health Care Spirituality Rooted in Biblical Justice," *Review: Catholic Health Association of Canada* 25, no. 2 (July 1997) 3–10. French translation: "Une spiritualité des soins de santé enracinée dans la justice biblique," *Revue: Association catholique canadienne de la santé* 25, no. 2 (Juillet 1997) 3–11.

267. "Justice: Secular or Biblical?" *Florida Catholic* 58, no. 40 (September 25, 1997) C1, C4.

268. "Fire in the Belly: From Experience through Imagination to Passion," *Origins* 27, no. 18 (October 16, 1997) 311–16.

269. "Advent: Remember, Repent, Rehearse," *Living Pulpit* 6, no. 4 (October–December 1997) 4–5.

270. "Jesus, the Poor, and the Rest of Us," *Florida Catholic* 58, no. 43 (October 16, 1997) B1, B4.

271. "To Us a Child Is Born," *America* 177, no. 20 (December 20, 1997) 3. Reprinted in *Far East,* December 1998, 16.

1998

272. "Easter Reality, Easter Hope," *Living Pulpit* 7, no. 1 (January–March 1998) 4–6.

273. "*Eloquentia perfecta:* Yesterday and Today," *AJCU* [Association of Jesuit Colleges and Universities] *Higher Education Report* 21, no. 6 (February 1998) 1–2.

274. "Sabbath and Sunday Belong Together," *Living Pulpit* 7, no. 2 (April–June 1998) 8–9.

275. "Noted Jesuit Speaks on Social Justice" (Interview by Rick Sherman), *Mount Angel Seminary Bulletin* (St. Benedict, Ore.) spring 1998, 6, 8.

276. " 'I Do': Death as Final Free Surrender," *Living Pulpit* 7, no. 3 (July–September 1998) 4–5.

277. "Soul Man: Putting Fire in the Belly Is Walter Burghardt's Calling" (Interview by Ken Adelman), *Washingtonian* 33, no. 11 (August 1998) 41–44.

278. "Peace Is a Work of Justice," *Living Pulpit* 7, no. 4 (October–December 1998) 6–7.

279. "Walter J. Burghardt, S.J.," in *Extraordinary Lives: Thirty-four Priests Tell Their Stories,* ed. Francis P. Friedel and Rex Reynolds (Notre Dame: Ave Maria, 1998) 24–29.

1999

280. "Toy for Theologians or Joy for Believers?" *Living Pulpit* 8, no. 2 (April–June 1999) 8–9.

281. "Hands Cut Off?" Homily in *Wonderfully Made: Preparing Children to Learn and Succeed* (Washington, D.C.: Children's Defense Fund, 1999).

282. "Alive!...in Lent?" in *The Lent Book,* ed. Lonni Collins Pratt (San Jose, Calif.: Resource Publications, 1999) 3–5. Reprint of no. 232 above.

283. "Just Word and Just Worship: Biblical Justice and Christian Liturgy," *Worship* 73 (1999) 386–98.

Index of Personal Names

Achtemeier, Elizabeth, 471n.47
Alinsky, Saul, 408
Ambrose of Milan, St., 269
Antony, St., hermit, 272
Appleby, R. Scott, 351–52
Aquinas, Thomas, St., 30–32, 60, 225
Arrupe, Pedro, 192, 202–4
Asselin, D. T., 457n.4
Augustine of Hippo, St., vi, 139, 141–42, 224–25, 270, 300

Bach, Richard, 138
Balthasar, Hans Urs von, 64–65
Barcus, William, 151–52
Barr, James, 211
Bartemeier, Leo H., 380–81
Barth, Karl, 210–11, 226, 312
Basil of Caesarea, St., 41
Baum, Gregory, 98
Bausch, William J., 287–88
Bearsley, Patrick J., 470–71n.33
Beauduin, Lambert, 173–74
Bednar, Gerald J., 425
Bellah, Robert, 162, 328–29, 330–31
Benedict XV, Pope, 66
Benoit, Pierre, 39–40
Berkovitz, Eliezer, 446n.60
Bernardin, Joseph, Cardinal, 343, 412–13
Berry, Thomas, 171–72
Bethge, Eberhard, 463–64nn.129, 130
Bonhoeffer, Dietrich, 134–35, 227–33
Boniface VIII, Pope, 338
Bowman, Thea, Sister, 154–55, 408–10
Brown, Raymond E., 71, 242–44, 267–68, 308–9, 325–26
Brueggemann, Walter, 157
Brungs, Robert, 348
Brunner, Emil, 226
Buber, Martin, 35
Buckley, Michael, 348
Buechner, Frederick, 125, 143, 162–63, 426–27
Burrell, David, 436n.26

Cahill, Kevin, 362
Califano, Joseph, 376
Callahan, Sidney, 320–21
Calvin, John, 226
Cameli, Louis J., 205–6
Cardenal, Ernesto, 191
Carmody, John and Denise, 377–78
Carr, Anne, 63
Cassem, Edwin H., 381–82

Clark, Elizabeth A., 20–21
Clarke, William Norris, 32
Clement of Alexandria, 268–69
Clifford, Richard J., 457n.4
Clinton, Bill, 448n.3
Cohen, Arthur A., 94
Coles, Robert, 178, 208, 368
Collins, Patrick, 75
Congar, Yves, 17, 106, 114, 117, 279, 403–4
Connor, James, 155
Cox, Harvey, 160
Cross, F. L., 67, 68
Cunningham, Lawrence, 160
Cuomo, Mario, 362
Cyril of Alexandria, St., 309–11

D'Agostino, Angelo, 380
Daniélou, Jean, 17–18
Danneels, Godfried, Cardinal, 403
Day, Dorothy, 95, 178, 182, 287, 422–23
Delaplane, Joan, 367
Delehaye, Karl, 40
Deye, Walter C., 192
Diekmann, Godfrey, 174–75
DiGiacomo, James, 207
Dix, Gregory, 244
Dölger, Franz Josef, 10
Donahue, John R., 166
Drey, Johann Sebastian, 24–25
Drinan, Robert F., 195–96, 245
Dulles, Avery, 53–55, 58, 180, 189, 240–41, 256–57, 276, 324, 343, 358
Dunne, George H., 159

Edelman, Marian Wright, 128
Egan, Harvey, 189
Egan, John Joseph, 407–8
Ellis, John Tracy, 264, 346, 406–7
Empie, Paul, 72
Erikson, Erik and Joan, 385
Etheria (Egeria), 274

Farrell, Suzanne, 420–21
Fitzmyer, Joseph A., 71, 102–3
Fleming, Alexander, 198
Francis de Sales, St., 204–5
Francis of Assisi, St., 173

Gadamer, Hans-Georg, 185
Gager, John G., 97
Gaïth, Jérôme, 461n.77
Gannon, Michael, 261
Ghellinck, Joseph de, 8

Glendon, Mary Ann, 318–19
Graham, Martha, 123
Greeley, Andrew, 126, 175, 198–99, 206–7, 261, 329, 334, 351, 428
Greene, Graham, 296–97
Gregory of Neocaesarea, St., 15–16
Gregory of Nyssa, St., 13, 180–81, 190, 222–24, 391–92
Gregory the Great, Pope, 142–43
Griesa, Thomas, 373
Gumpel, Peter, 192
Gutiérrez, Gustavo, 62–63

Häring, Bernard, 86–87
Harnack, Adolf, 10
Haught, John F., 172
Havel, Václav, 119–20
Heaney, Seamus, 345
Hebblethwaite, Peter, 50–51
Hehir, J. Bryan, 174
Hellwig, Monika, 115–16
Henry, Carl, 75–76
Hesburgh, Theodore M., 71, 104–5, 415–16
Heschel, Abraham Joshua, 89, 92, 129–31, 384, 396
Higgins, George G., 406, 407, 451–52n.63
Hildegarde of Bingen, 190
Holmes, Urban, 126
Hopkins, Gerard Manley, 122, 306–7, 397–98, 421–22
Hotchkin, John, 412–13
Hughes, Emmet John, 89
Hunter, David G ., 21
Hurley, Denis E., Archbishop, 427–28

Ignatius of Antioch, St., 4–7
Ignatius of Loyola, St., 6–7, 110, 133, 181, 183–202
Imbelli, Robert P., 65
Ireland, John, 260–61
Irenaeus of Lyons, St., 112–13, 217–18
Isaac, Jules, 97–98

Jadot, Jean, Archbishop, 404–6
Jaeger, Werner, 13
Jane Frances de Chantal, St., 205
Jerome, St., 272–73
Johann, Robert, 30, 35
John Chrysostom, St., 91, 100, 142, 269–70, 392
John Damascene, St., 296
John Paul II, Pope, 32, 170–71, 172–73, 203–4, 266, 279–80, 293, 306, 321–24
Johnson, Elizabeth A., 63–64, 304–7, 317–18
Julian of Norwich, 182, 190
Jung, Carl, 226–27

Kannengiesser, Charles, 19–20,
Kaufman, Gordon, 227
Kazantzakis, Nikos, 113

Keightley, Georgia, 277–78
Kennedy, Eugene, 314
Kerr, Fergus, 28–29
Kevorkian, Jack, 376, 379
Kierkegaard, Søren Aabye, 35
King Jr., Martin Luther, 128, 175
Knox, Ronald, 125
Komonchak, Joseph, 17, 88–89
Koontz, Dean, 378–79
Krauthammer, Charles, 373–74

Lamennais, Félicité, 262–63
Land, Philip S., 474n.17
Langan, John P., 466n.13
Laurentin, René, 294–95
Leclercq, Jean, 196
Leo the Great, Pope, 141
Leo XIII, Pope, 173–74
Leonard, Richard, 325
Lepp, Ignace, 313
Lewis, C. S., 137–38
Leys, Roger, 180–81
Lindbergh, Anne Morrow, 416–17
Lohfink, Norbert, 168
Lonergan, Bernard J. F., 32, 58–60, 186, 344
Lubac, Henri de, 14, 16–18
Luther, Martin, 110–11, 225–26, 285
Lynch, William F., 94, 424–25

MacIntyre, Alasdair, 32
Macrina the Younger, St., 274
Maher, Zacheus, 159
Marcel, Gabriel, 35
Maritain, Jacques, 198
Marmion, Columba, 173
Marty, Martin, 408
McCool, Gerald, 31–32
McCormick, Richard A., 375–76, 419–20
McCourt, Frank, 120
McGeady, Rose, Sister, 149
McKenna, Horace, 413
McKenna, Megan, 121
McKenzie, John L., 96–97, 118
McNamara, William, 129, 198, 428–29
Melania the Younger, St., 274
Merton, Thomas, 182, 418
Methodius of Olympus, St., 391
Metz, Johann Baptist, 90, 191
Michel, Virgil, 174
Michelangelo, 198
Miner, Roger, 373
Mitterer, Albert, 294
Modras, Ronald, 195,
Molnar, Paul, 189–90
Moody, Dale, 126
Morris, Charles, 344
Müller, Alois, 298–99
Murnion, Philip, 156

Murray, John Courtney, 8–10, 14–15, 32–34, 72, 74, 75, 76–77, 83–89, 261, 283–84, 333, 401, 425

Newman, John Henry, Cardinal, 140–41, 291
Noonan, John, 373
Novatian, 393

O'Brien, George Dennis, 106
O'Connor, Flannery, 418–19
O'Donovan, Leo J., 61
O'Malley, John W., 201–2, 253–55, 453–54n.23
O'Malley, Sean, Bishop, 158
O'Malley, William J., 276–77
O'Meara, Thomas, 279
Origen, 14–16, 141, 219–21, 269, 359
Orsy, Ladislas, 337–40, 475n.23
Ottaviani, Alfredo, Cardinal, 85, 86–87, 403
Outler, Albert, 417–18

Padovano, Louis, 380
Paul VI, Pope, 44, 82–83, 84, 104
Paul, Apostle, 215–17
Paula, ascetic, 272–73
Pavan, Pietro, 84–85, 86
Pelikan, Jaroslav, 21–22, 423–24
Philips, Gérard, 46
Philo, 213–15
Pick, John, 421
Pie, Louis, Bishop, 403
Piepkorn, Arthur Carl, 71
Pittenger, Norman, 445n.24
Pius X, Pope, 25–26
Pius XI, Pope, 66–67
Polycarp of Smyrna, St., 14

Quanbeck, Warren, 71
Quasten, Johannes, 10–12, 141, 209

Rahner, Karl, 20, 32, 43–44, 46–48, 50–51, 60–61, 133, 188–91, 248–49, 394
Ratzinger, Joseph, Cardinal, 322–24
Rausch, Thomas, 255–57
Read, David H. C., 144–45, 426
Rehnquist, William, 375
Reumann, John, 71
Rieff, Philip, 330,
Rogers, Carl, 28, 314–15
Rostropovich, Mstislav, 252
Rothstein, Barbara, 372–73
Rousseau, Dom O., 39
Ruether, Rosemary Radford, 95, 98
Runciman, Steven, 423

Scharper, Philip, 371–72
Schindler, David, 343
Schleiermacher, Friedrich, 24–25

Schlier, H., 217
Schneiders, Sandra, 204
Schüssler Fiorenza, Elisabeth, 325
Scott Jr., Nathan A., 483n.57
Searle, Mark, 177–79
Seasoltz, Kevin, 175–76
Segundo, Juan Luis, 62
Selzer, Richard, 363–64, 366
Sheen, Fulton, 380
Shehan, Lawrence, Cardinal, 342
Siegel, Bernie, 364–65
Simon, Marcel, 98
Sittler, Joseph, 71–72, 143–44, 171
Sloyan, Gerard, 124
Spellman, Francis, Cardinal, 85
Steiger, Ron, 387
Steinfels, Margaret O'Brien, 319–20
Suenens, Léon-Joseph, Cardinal, 402–3
Sullivan, Francis, 322

Talbot, George, 265
Tanenbaum, Marc H., 91–92,
Taylor, Miriam, 442n.77
Teilhard de Chardin, Pierre, 35, 399–400
Teresa of Avila, St., 182
Teresa of Calcutta, Mother, 198, 367
Thérèse of Lisieux, St., 182
Thiel, John, 23–26
Thomas, Dylan, 140, 370, 390
Thompson, Francis, 397
Tracy, David, 55–57, 190
Tremblay, Réal, 218–19
Trible, Phyllis, 292
Trinkaus, Charles, 225
Tuchman, Barbara, 99

Vagnozzi, Egidio, 261–62
Vawter, Bruce, 211–12
Volkmer, Kaela, 207–8

Walsh, J. P. M., 450n.32
Walsh, William J., 466n.13
Weakland, Rembert G., 259–60, 410–11
Weigel, Gustave, 43–44, 73–76, 401,
Whitehead, Alfred North, 35–36, 122
Whitehead, Evelyn Eaton and James D., 453n.18
Wicker, Brian, 176–77
Wiesel, Elie, 93
Wilamowitz-Moellendorff, Ulrich von, 13, 142
Will, George F., 374
Williams, Edward Bennett, 414
Wiseman, James, 190–91
Wolfson, Harry Austryn, 458n.19
Woodruff, Douglas, 264
Woodward, Kenneth, 147
Wright, G. Ernest, 212–13

Yu-Pin, Paul, Bishop, 11